Fifth Edition

MULTICULTURAL LAW ENFORCEMENT

STRATEGIES FOR PEACEKEEPING IN A DIVERSE SOCIETY

Robert M. Shusta

Deena R. Levine

Herbert Z. Wong

Aaron T. Olson

Philip R. Harris

Prentice Hall

Boston   Columbus   Indianapolis   New York   San Francisco   Upper Saddle River
Amsterdam   Cape Town   Dubai   London   Madrid   Milan   Munich   Paris   Montreal   Toronto
Delhi   Mexico City   Sao Paulo   Sydney   Hong Kong   Seoul   Singapore   Taipei   Tokyo

Library of Congress Cataloging-in-Publication Data

Multicultural law enforcement : strategies for peacekeeping in a diverse
  society / Robert M. Shusta . . . [et al.]. —5th ed.
    p. cm.
  Includes bibliographical references and index.
  ISBN-13: 978-0-13-505088-0
  ISBN-10: 0-13-505088-X
    1. Police-community relations—United States.   2. Discrimination in law enforcement—United States.
    3. Multiculturalism—United States.   4. Intercultural communication—United States.   I. Shusta, Robert M.
  HV7936.P8M85 2011
  363.2'3—dc22

                                                                          2009043550

Editor in Chief: Vern Anthony
Acquisitions Editor: Tim Peyton
Editorial Assistant: Lynda Cramer
Director of Marketing: David Gesell
Marketing Manager: Adam Kloza
Senior Marketing Coordinator: Alicia Wozniak
Marketing Assistant: Les Roberts
Production Manager: Fran Russello
Creative Director: Jayne Conte
Cover Design: Bruce Kenselaar
Full-Service Project Management/Composition: Hemalatha/Integra
Printer/Binder: Bind-Rite

Credits and acknowledgments borrowed from other sources and reproduced, with permission, in this textbook appear
on appropriate page within text.

Pearson Education LTD.
Pearson Education Australia PTY, Limited
Pearson Education Singapore, Pte. Ltd
Pearson Education North Asia Ltd

Pearson Education, Canada, Ltd
Pearson Educación de Mexico, S.A. de C.V.
Pearson Education–Japan.
Pearson Education Malaysia, Pte. Ltd

10 9 8 7 6 5 4 3 2 1

Prentice Hall
is an imprint of

www.pearsonhighered.com

ISBN-10:   0-13-505088-X
ISBN-13:   978-0-13-505088-0

In grateful remembrance of those police officers who sacrificed their lives in the pursuit of equal justice and protection for all citizens in our country's diverse communities

CONTENTS

FOREWORD

Communities and police agencies across America have struggled for many years with the issues of race, ethnicity, culture, and gender. In the past 30 years, these struggles have become even more complex and challenging as large numbers of non-English-speaking immigrants, documented and undocumented, have come to America seeking economic, religious, or political freedom. In addition to the communication problems one experiences in a heterogeneous society, law enforcement professionals frequently encounter cultural and racial tensions among new immigrants and between majority and minority communities as neighborhoods change constantly. Clearly, effective policing of multicultural communities remains an enormous challenge. However, there is good reason for optimism as police agencies become more diverse, enhance training, and seek to build strong partnerships with diverse communities representing people from all walks of life.

By embracing the philosophy of community partnerships and community-policing strategies, law enforcement agencies, together with citizens, have created some safer towns and cities. To be effective, police officers cannot operate alone; they require the active support and assistance of citizens in their jurisdictions. Central to maintaining that support is the recognition that law enforcement agencies must reflect the diversity of the communities they serve. Every day, our officers come into contact with individuals from different cultural backgrounds, socioeconomic classes, religions, sexual orientations, and physical and mental abilities. Each of these groups brings a different perspective to police–community relations and, as a result, our officers must be prepared to respond appropriately to each group. Failure to recognize and adjust to community diversity can foster confusion and resentment among citizens and quickly lead to a breakdown in the critical bond of trust between a law enforcement agency and its community. Human relations and multicultural awareness training of peace officers provides them with the skills required to build police–community relationships.

In addition, law enforcement organizations such as the National Organization of Black Law Enforcement Executives (NOBLE), the Hispanic American Police Command Officers Association (HAPCOA), the National Asian Peace Officers' Association (NAPOA), the National Native American Law Enforcement Association (NNALEA), and other law enforcement agencies have made it a part of their mission to provide support and guidance to law enforcement agencies nationwide. Their mission stresses the importance of community policing and multicultural awareness within the departments. Many communities are experiencing divides between law enforcement and residents, which are exacerbated by underlying racial and cultural tensions. These organizations reach out to diverse communities, encouraging open dialogues around recruitment and hiring practices as well as the challenges involved in community policing.

The publication of this fifth edition of *Multicultural Law Enforcement: Strategies for Peacekeeping in a Diverse Society* is significant considering that over 95 percent of published books never enter into their second edition. Clearly, the authors have filled a gap in the law enforcement literature, and the global sales of this volume confirm that its authors have produced a highly relevant text, and one that is rich with instruction. Thus, readers are fortunate now to have access to this fifth edition. Since its first publication in 1995, this work has established itself as a classic in the criminal justice field. Its adoption by police and corrections academies, as well as for criminal justice courses at universities and colleges, is testimony to its far-reaching acceptance.

Multicultural Law Enforcement's major sections effectively address the key cultural needs of law enforcement as practitioners in increasing numbers have discovered for themselves. The practical contents of the book provide critical information and insight that will improve police performance and professionalism. The subject matter herein, especially the cultural-specific information, continues to be on the leading edge. Instructors and trainers will welcome this current edition of *Multicultural Law Enforcement* as a complete learning system that offers the following supplements to the main text: an Instructor's Manual, chapter quizzes, and PowerPoint presentations for each chapter.

Finally, this fifth edition of *Multicultural Law Enforcement* enables agencies and departments to prepare officers to form partnerships for successful community-policing practices within our multicultural communities. It touches on other related topics too, such as gangs, the homeless, the mentally ill, global terrorism, and international politics and their impact on policing in America.

I am impressed by both the diversity and the competencies of the professionals who have written *Multicultural Law Enforcement*. In addition to the vast and cumulative experience of the five coauthors, now consisting of a combined 55 years of active state and local law enforcement experience along with years of training, teaching criminal justice college classes and consulting expertise. Each author has sought additional cultural information and input from criminal justice professionals from the diverse backgrounds about which they write. I feel confident in recommending this text, and I encourage all who use it to put into action the strategies and tools of this exceptional work for the betterment of your agencies, communities, and the larger society.

Jessie Lee

Executive Director National Organization
of Black Law Enforcement Executives

PREFACE

This fifth edition of *Multicultural Law Enforcement: Strategies for Peacekeeping in a Diverse Society* is a continuing tribute to all our readers who enthusiastically received the first four editions. It is a textbook for police departments and academies as well as college and university criminal justice programs. Our text, with accompanying instructional tools, is a complete learning package designed to assist all levels of criminal justice representatives in understanding the pervasive influences of culture, race, ethnicity, and sexual orientation in the workplace and in multicultural communities. The text focuses on the contact that police officers and civilian employees have with coworkers, victims, suspects, and citizens from a wide variety of backgrounds.

NEW TO THIS EDITION:

The authors' objective for this edition has been to provide updated and expanded information for officers, managers, supervisors, and instructors. This new information is based on research of current issues facing law enforcement professionals and the communities they serve. For some new sections, authors have conducted interviews with criminal justice professionals from diverse backgrounds. The content revision includes new material on:

- Additional dimensions of diversity, including gangs, the homeless, and the mentally ill
- Community policing
- Documented and undocumented immigrants
- Recruitment and retention problems associated with women and minorities
- Relationship between tribal and civilian police
- Expanded information on immigrant women and violence
- Legislation related to the reporting of crimes and undocumented immigrants
- Multicultural issues related to terrorism, homeland security, and disaster preparedness
- Additional in-depth information on communication styles across cultures

For this fifth edition, as per reviewers' suggestions, we have combined the two chapters dealing with Homeland Security from the fourth edition. At their request, we also restored a section in Chapter 15 from our third edition entitled "Police Leadership in Professionalism and Synergy." In addition, we have included Learning Objectives at the beginning of each chapter and corresponding Summary points at the end of the chapters. We have introduced and defined new terminology in selected sections.

Throughout the text we stress the need for awareness and understanding of cultural differences and respect toward those of different backgrounds. We encourage all representatives of law enforcement to examine preconceived notions they might hold of particular groups. We outline for police executives why they should build awareness and promote cultural understanding and tolerance within their agencies.

An increasing number of leaders in law enforcement agencies and their employees have accepted the premise that greater cross-cultural competency and improved cross-racial/ethnic relations must be a key objective of all management and professional development. Demographic changes have had a tremendous impact not only on the types of crimes committed, but also on the composition of the law enforcement workforce and the people with whom officers make contact. To be effective, police executives must understand and be responsive to the diversity in their workforces and in their changing communities. Professionalism today includes the need for greater consideration across cultures and improved communication with members of diverse groups.

In an era when news is processed and accessed immediately, the public is exposed almost daily to instances of cross-cultural and interracial contact between law enforcement agents and citizens. So, too, have community members become increasingly sophisticated and critical with regard to how members of diverse cultural and racial groups are treated by public servants. Employees of police departments and other agencies entrusted with law enforcement find that they are now serving communities that carefully observe them and hold them accountable for their actions.

With cross-cultural knowledge, sensitivity, and tolerance, those who are charged with the responsibility of peacekeeping will improve their image while demonstrating greater professionalism within the changing multicultural workforce and community. Our focus has primarily been on peace officers—in addition to policing issues, this text also applies to issues and challenges faced by correctional officers, border patrol agents, marshals, federal agents, and campus and military police.

We offer our readers a complete learning package to supplement the main text, which includes an Instructor's Manual, Student Study Guide, PowerPoint presentations, and chapter quizzes. We hope our readers will find our revised and updated text, along with the learning tools, an enhancement to their criminal justice and law enforcement programs.

Robert M. Shusta, MPA
Deena R. Levine, MA
Herbert Z. Wong, PhD
Aaron T. Olson, M.Ed
Philip R. Harris, PhD

ACKNOWLEDGMENTS

This fifth edition has benefited from expert content contributions by the following people and organizations: David Barlow, PhD, Associate Professor, Fayetteville State University, North Carolina; Danilo Begonia, JD, Professor, Asian American Studies, San Francisco State University, San Francisco, California; Mohammed Berro, Corporal, Dearborn Police Department, Michigan; Ondra Berry, retired Assistant Police Chief, Reno Police Department, Reno, Nevada; Peggy Bowen, PhD, Assistant Professor of Criminal Justice, Alvernia College, Reading, Pennsylvania; John Brothers, Executive Director, Quincy Asian Resources, Inc., Quincy, Massachusetts; Patricia DeRosa, President, ChangeWorks Consulting, Randolph, Massachusetts; Ronald Griffin, Pastor and Community Leader, Detroit, Michigan; Mitchell Grobeson, retired Sergeant, Los Angeles Police Department, Los Angeles, California; Ronald Haddad, Senior Deputy Chief, Detroit Police Department, Detroit, Michigan; Sari Karet, Executive Director, Cambodian American Foundation, San Francisco, California; Marilyn Loden, Organizational Diversity Consultant with Loden Associates, Inc., Tiburon, California; Darryl, McAllister, Captain, Hayward Police Department, Hayward, California; A.L. "Skipper" Osborne, CEO of TAJFA (Truth and Justice for All), Portland, Oregon; Paula Parnagian, World View Services, Revere, Massachusetts; Oscar Ramirez, PhD, Police and Court Expert Consultant, San Antonio, Texas; Jose Rivera, retired Peace Officer, Education Director—Native American Museum, Sausalito, California; Greg Patton, Supervisor, Parole and Probation, Clackamas County Community Corrections, Clackamas, Oregon; Lourdes Rodriguez-Nogues, EdD, President, Rasi Associates, Boston, Massachusetts; Helen Samhan, Executive Director, Arab American Institute Foundation, Washington, D.C.; Margaret D. Shorter, Sgt., Royal Canadian Mounted Police and officer of the International Association of Women and Policing; Victoria Santos, President, Santos & Associates, Newark, California; Michael Stoops, Executive Director of the National Coalition for the Homeless, Washington D.C.; Reverend Onasai Veevau, Pastor and Pacific Islander Community Leader, San Mateo, California; Norita Jones Vlach, PhD, Professor, School of Social Work, San Jose State University, San Jose, California; James Zogby, PhD, Director, Arab American Institute Foundation, Washington, D.C.; John Zogby, PhD, President, Zogby International, New York, New York.

We owe special thanks to the following individuals for their helpful insights: Kim Ah-Low, Georgia; Chung H. Chuong, California; Jim Cox, Retired Police Chief, Midwest City Police Department, Oklahoma; Captain S. Rob Hardman, USCG (retired), Virginia; Bob Harrison, Police Chief of Vacaville, California (retired); Wilbur Herrington, Massachusetts; Jim Kahue, Hawaii; Lubna Ismail, President, Connecting Cultures, Washington, D.C.; James Johnson, PhD., Criminal Justice specialist on minority issues, Washington D.C.; Chief Susan Jones, California; Kara Lipsett, University of British Colombia, Canada; Charles Marquez, Colorado; Christopher Martinez, Program Director for Refugee & Immigrant Services, Catholic Charities CYO, San Francisco, California; Sarah Miyahira, PhD, Hawaii; Margaret Moore, Washington, D.C.; Jason O'Neal, Police Chief Chickasaw Nation Lighthorse Police, Ada, Oklahoma; Jim Parks, J.D., Criminal Justice Department Chair, Portland Community College, Portland, Oregon; JoAnne Pina, PhD, Washington, D.C.; Eduardo Rodela, PhD, Washington, D.C.; Jose Rivera, California State Peace Officer (retired); Chief Darrel Stephens, North Carolina; George Thompson, Founder of Verbal Judo Institute, Inc.

We would also like to thank the following reviewers: Donna Gaughan, Prince George's Community College; Kelly Gould, Sacramento City College; Darrell Mills, Pima Community College, East Campus; Ernest Uwazie, California State University, Sacramento; and Tamara Wilkins, Minnesota State University, Mankato.

ABOUT THE AUTHORS

Robert M. Shusta, Captain (retired), MPA, served over 27 years in law enforcement, and retired as a Captain at the Concord, California, Police Department. He has been a part-time instructor at numerous colleges and universities in northern California and at police academies. He is a graduate of the 158th FBI National Academy and the fourth California Command College conducted by POST. He has served on state commissions responsible for developing POST guidelines and state policy recommendations. (Retired) Captain Shusta has conducted extensive training on cultural awareness and hate crimes as well as Train the Trainer programs on combatting domestic violence.

Deena R. Levine, MA, has been providing consulting and training to organizations in both the public and the private sectors since 1983. She is the principal of Deena Levine & Associates LLC, a firm specializing in cross-cultural communication and workplace training as well as global business consulting. She and her associates, together with representatives from community organizations, have provided programs to police departments, focusing on cross-cultural and human relations. She began her career in cross-cultural training at the Intercultural Relations Institute, formerly at Stanford University, developing multicultural workforce understanding for managers and supervisors. She has written an additional widely used text on the cultural aspects of communication, entitled *Beyond Language: Cross-Cultural Communication* (Regents/Prentice Hall).

Herbert Z. Wong, PhD, a clinical and organizational psychologist, provides cultural awareness and diversity training to law enforcement officers on local, state, and federal levels nationwide. He is a professor of psychology and research director at the Graduate School of Professional Psychology, John F. Kennedy University. He is the president of Herbert Z. Wong & Associates, a management consulting firm to over 350 businesses, universities, government agencies, and corporations, specializing in multicultural management and workforce diversity. In 1990, Dr. Wong cofounded and was president of the National Diversity Conference, which became the Society for Human Resource Management's Workplace Diversity Conference. He developed and provided the national Training-of-Trainers programs for the seven-part "Valuing Diversity" videotape series used in over 4,000 organizations worldwide. Dr. Wong specializes in diversity assessments and open systems analysis for cultural competency in human services programs.

Aaron T. Olson, M.Ed., is a criminal justice instructor at Portland Community College, Portland, Oregon, where he teaches police, criminal evidence, criminal investigations, and cultural diversity courses. He designed the first cultural diversity course and curriculum for the college's criminal justice program in 2001. Outside of academia he is an organization and training consultant, specializing in staff development for businesses and government agencies, and conducting multicultural training workshops for law enforcement, corrections, telecommunications, fire services, and medical professionals. He is a retired Oregon State Police patrol sergeant and shift supervisor with 26 years of police experience in communications, recruiting, and patrol assignments. He has also instructed at Oregon's Department of Public Safety Standards and Training, teaching recruit, supervision, mid-management, and executive management courses. He established and still delivers public safety workshops to immigrants and refugees at the Immigrant Refugee Community Organization (IRCO) and is coauthor of *Multicultural and Diversity Strategies for the Fire Services.*

Philip R. Harris, PhD, is a management psychologist with extensive experience in both criminal justice system and cross-cultural studies. President of Harris International, Ltd., in La Jolla, California, he is author/editor of approximately 48 volumes, including *Managing Cultural Differences* (7th ed., Butterworth-Heinemann), *Managing the Knowledge Culture* (HRD Press), and *The New Work Culture* (2nd ed., HRD Press). A global consultant to over 200 systems, he has had as law enforcement clients: the California POST Command College, the Office of Naval Research/USMC Corrections Officers, the U.S. Customs Service, the District of Columbia Police Department, and the Philadelphia Police Department.

Impact of Cultural Diversity on Law Enforcement

Part One of *Multicultural Law Enforcement* introduces readers to the implications of a multicultural society for law enforcement, both within and outside the police agency. Chapter 1 discusses aspects of the changing population and presents views on diversity. The case studies in Chapter 1 exemplify how the presence of different cultures can affect the very nature and perception of crime itself. We present the subject of prejudice and its effect on police work, providing specific examples of its consequences in law enforcement. The chapter ends with suggestions for improving law enforcement in multicultural communities.

Chapter 2 discusses demographic changes taking place within law enforcement agencies, as well as reactions to diversity in the law enforcement workplace and responses to it. In addition to data on ethnic and racial groups, this chapter provides information on women and on gay men and lesbians in law enforcement across the country. We include a discussion of how law enforcement agencies and the community must be proactive about the elimination of discrimination and racism. In addition, we illustrate the realities of the new workforce and the corresponding need for flexibility in leadership styles.

Chapter 3 discusses challenges in the recruitment, retention, and promotion of police personnel from multiple perspectives, including those associated with race, ethnicity, and sexual orientation. We emphasize that the pool of qualified applicants for law enforcement jobs has significantly reduced not only because of the economy, but also because of societal changes and trends. We present strategies for recruitment, emphasizing the commitment required by law enforcement chief executives and the need to look inward—that is, to assess the level of comfort and inclusion that all employees experience in a given agency. If the levels are not high, hiring, retention, and promotion will be difficult. Chapter 3 describes the pressing need facing all agencies to build a workforce of highly qualified individuals of diverse backgrounds and in which all people have equal access to the hiring, retention, and promotion processes. It also presents a creative model for recruitment using community policing.

Chapter 4 provides practical information highlighting the dynamics of cross-cultural communication in law enforcement. The chapter includes a discussion of the specific problems involved when officers communicate with speakers of other languages. We present typical styles of communication that people may display when they are uncomfortable with cross-cultural contact. The chapter includes a section on the need for communication sensitivity post-9/11. In addition, it covers differences in nonverbal communication across cultures and addresses some of the communication issues that arise between men and women in law enforcement agencies. Finally, we present skills and techniques for officers to apply in situations of cross-cultural contact.

Each chapter ends with discussion questions and a list of references, including websites. The following appendices correspond to the chapter content in Part One:

   A. Multicultural Community and Workforce: Attitude Assessment
   B. Cultural Diversity Survey: Needs Assessment
   C. Listing of Consultants and Resources
   D. Self-Assessment of Communication Skills in Law Enforcement: Communications Inventory

CHAPTER 1

Multicultural Communities: Challenges for Law Enforcement

LEARNING OBJECTIVES

After reading this chapter you should be able to:

- Discuss the impact of diversity on law enforcement.
- Understand the references "melting pot" and "mosaic" society and provide a historical overview of the context in which these terms have evolved.
- Summarize key demographic trends in the United States related to the growth of minority populations.
- Provide an overview of key issues associated with immigration directly affecting law enforcement.
- Define "culture" and "ethnocentrism" and discuss the contexts in which they are relevant to law enforcement.
- List the primary and secondary dimensions of diversity.
- Apply the concepts of prejudice and stereotyping to everyday police work.

OUTLINE

- Introduction
- The Interface of Diversity and Law Enforcement
- Culture and Its Relevance to Law Enforcement
- Dimensions of Diversity
- Prejudice in Law Enforcement
- Summary
- Discussion Questions and Issues
- Website Resources

INTRODUCTION

> The 21st century will be the century in which we redefine ourselves as the first country in world history that is literally made up of every part of the world.
>
> —*Kenneth Prewitt, Former Director of the U.S. Census Bureau, 2001*

> I am the son of a black man from Kenya and a white woman from Kansas . . . I am married to a black American who carries within her the blood of slaves and slaveowners . . . I have brothers, sisters, nieces, nephews, uncles and cousins, of every race and every hue, scattered across three continents, and for as long as I live, I will never forget that in no other country on earth is my story even possible.
>
> —*Barak Obama, from "A More Perfect Union" March 18, 2008*

Multiculturalism and diversity are at the very heart of America and describe accurately the demographics of our nation. The word *multiculturalism* does not refer to a movement or political force, nor is it an anti-American term. The United States is an amalgam of races, cultures, and ethnic groups, evolving from successive waves of immigration. President Obama's family is, in part, a microcosm of the larger society. His extended family members are "black and white and Asian, Christian, Muslim and Jewish. They speak English; Indonesian; French; Cantonese; German; Hebrew; African languages . . ." ("Nation's Many Faces in Extended First Family," 2009). The United States, compared to virtually all other nations, has experienced unparalleled growth in its multicultural population. Reactions to these changes range from appreciation and even celebration of diversity to an absolute intolerance of differences. In its extreme form, intolerance resulting in crimes of hate is a major law enforcement and criminal justice concern. While the country as a whole celebrated the historical significance of the nation's first African American president, law enforcement was acutely aware of the other side of this celebration. President Obama received more threats following his election than did any other president in history; in addition, law enforcement saw an increase in hate graffiti, beatings, and threats toward other African American citizens in this same period ("The Year in Hate," 2009).

THE INTERFACE OF DIVERSITY AND LAW ENFORCEMENT

Those whose professional ideal is to protect and serve people equally from all backgrounds must face the challenges and complexities of a diverse society. A lack of communication effectiveness, coupled with little understanding of individuals' backgrounds, can result in inadvertent violation of individuals' rights as well as officer safety and risk issues. Officers, even more than others, must ensure that their prejudices remain in check and that they refrain from acting on any biased thought.

In an interview Ondra Berry, Retired Assistant Police Chief, Reno, Nevada, states:

> Law enforcement is under a powerful microscope in terms of how citizens are treated. Minority and ethnic communities have become increasingly competent in understanding the role of law enforcement, and expectations of law enforcement for professionalism have been elevated from previous years. In an age when information about what happens in a police department on the East Coast speeds across to the West Coast in seconds, law enforcement officials must be aware. They must be vigilant. They must do the right thing. (Berry, 2009)

Although our nation has been enriched by diversity, many police procedures and interactions with citizens can be more complex because of diversity. Racial tensions and communication challenges with immigrants, for example, are bound to complicate some police encounters. It would be naive to preach to law enforcement officers, agents, and managers about the value of diversity when day-to-day activities can be complicated by diversity. At a minimum, a basic acceptance of diversity on the part of all criminal justice representatives is required as a precursor to improving interpersonal relations and contact across cultural, ethnic, and racial lines.

The United States has always been a magnet for people from nearly every corner of the earth, and, consequently, U.S. demographics continue to undergo constant change. In their efforts to be both proactive and responsive to diverse communities, police officers and groups from many backgrounds around the country are working to become more closely connected in direct relationships promoted in community-based policing models. Leaders from both law enforcement agencies and the community have realized that both groups benefit when each group seeks mutual assistance and understanding. The job of law enforcement requires a certain level of comfort and professionalism in interacting with people from all backgrounds whether one is working with community members to build trust or dealing with suspects, victims, and coworkers.

Through increased awareness, cultural knowledge, and skills, law enforcement as a profession can increase its cultural competence. Acquiring cultural competence is not an instantaneous process; it is multilayered and complex, and includes:

- Exploration of officers' belief systems and biases
- Awareness of an officer's perspectives and perceptions, especially as they may differ from those associated with minority viewpoints
- Acquisition of cultural information relevant to the concerns of law enforcement, and the capacity to apply that knowledge in ethnic, racial, and other diverse communities
- Increased communication skills leading to effective rapport building and communication with all community members
- Development of a set of principles, attitudes, policies, and structures that will enable all individuals in an organization to work effectively and equitably across all cultures and ethnicities.

The strategies an individual uses to approach and build rapport with his or her own cultural group may result in unexpected difficulties with another group. The acts of approaching, communicating, questioning, assisting, and establishing trust with members of culturally diverse groups require special knowledge and skills that have nothing to do with the fact that "the law is the law" and must be enforced equally. Acquiring knowledge and skills that lead to sensitivity does not imply preferential treatment of any one group; rather it contributes to improved communication with members of all groups.

Individuals must seek a balance between downplaying and even denying the differences of others, and, on the other hand, distorting the role of culture, race, and ethnicity. In an effort to simply "respect all humans equally," we may inadvertently diminish the influence of culture or ethnicity, including the role it has played historically in our society.

The Melting Pot Myth and the Mosaic

Multiculturalism, also called cultural pluralism, violates what some consider to be the "American way of life." However, from the time the United States was founded, Americans were never a homogeneous people. The indigenous peoples of America (the ancestors of the American Indians) were here long before Christopher Columbus "discovered" them. There is even strong evidence that the first Africans who set foot in this country came as free people, 200 years before the slave trade from Africa began (Rawlins, 1992). Furthermore, the majority of people in America can claim to be the children, grandchildren, or great-grandchildren of people who have migrated here. Americans did not originate from a common stock. Until fairly recently, America has been referred to as a melting pot, a term depicting an image of people coming together and forming a unified culture. One of the earliest uses of the term was in the early 1900s, when a famous American playwright, Israel Zangwill, referring to the mass migration from Europe said, "America is God's crucible, the great Melting-Pot where all the races of Europe are melting and re-forming. . . . Germans and Frenchmen, Irishmen and Englishmen, Jews and Russians—into the Crucible with you all! God is making the American!" (Zangwill, 1908).

This first use of the term *melting pot* was not designed to incorporate anyone except Europeans. Did the melting pot ever exist, then, in the United States? No, it never did. Yet people still refer to the belief, which is not much more than a romantic myth about the "good old days." African Americans, brought forcibly to this country between 1619 and 1850, were never part of the early descriptions of the melting pot. Likewise, Native American peoples were not considered for the melting pot. It is not coincidental that these groups were nonwhite and were therefore not "meltable." Furthermore, throughout our past, great efforts have been made to prevent any additional diversity. Most notable in this regard was the Chinese Exclusion Act in 1882, which denied Chinese laborers the right to enter America. Early in the twentieth century, organized labor formed the Japanese and Korean Exclusion League "to protest the influx of 'Coolie' labor and in fear of threat to the living standards of American workingmen" (Kennedy, 1986, p. 72). Immigration was discouraged or prevented if it did not add strength to what already existed as the European-descended majority of the population (Handlin, 1975).

Even at the peak of immigration in the late 1800s, New York City exemplified how different immigrant groups stayed separate from each other, with little of the "blending" that people often imagine taking place (Miller, 2008). Three-fourths of New York City's population consisted of first- or second-generation immigrants, including Europeans and Asians. Eighty percent did not speak English, and there were 100 foreign-language newspapers in circulation. The new arrivals were not accepted by those who had already settled, and newcomers found comfort in an alien society by choosing to remain in ethnic enclaves with people who shared their culture and life experiences.

The first generation of every immigrant and refugee group, who saw the United States as the land of hope and opportunity, had always experienced obstacles in acculturation and integration into the new society. In many cases, people resisted Americanization and kept to themselves. Italians, Irish, Eastern European Jews, Portuguese, Germans, and virtually all other groups tended to remain apart when they first came. Most previously settled immigrants were distrustful and disdainful of each newcomer group. "Mainstreaming" began to occur only with children of the immigrants, although some people within certain immigrant groups tried to assimilate quickly. For the most part, however, society did not permit a quick shedding of previous cultural identity. History has never supported the metaphor of the melting pot, especially with regard to the first and second generations of most groups of newcomers. Despite the reality of past multicultural disharmony and tension in the United States, however, the notion of the melting pot prevailed.

The terms *mosaic* or *tapestry* more accurately portray diversity in America. They describe a society in which all colors and backgrounds contribute their parts to form society as a whole, but one in which groups are not required to lose their characteristics in order to "melt" together. The idea of a mosaic portrays a society in which all races and ethnic groups are seen as separate and distinct in contributing their own color, shape, and design to the whole, resulting in an enriched society.

Reactions to Multiculturalism: Past and Present

Accepting multiculturalism and diversity has always been a difficult proposition for most Americans (Miller, 2008). Typical criticisms of immigrants, now and historically, include "They hold on to their cultures," "They don't learn our language," "Their customs and behavior are strange," and "They form cliques." Many newcomers, in fact, have historically resisted Americanization, keeping themselves to ethnic enclaves. They were not usually accepted by mainstream society.

Are the reactions to newcomers today so different from people's reactions to earlier waves of immigrants? Let us look at the reactions to the Irish, who, by the middle of the nineteenth century, constituted the largest group of immigrants in the United States, making up almost 45 percent of the foreign-born population. Approximately 4.25 million people left Ireland, mainly because of the potato famine. Many of these immigrants had come from rural areas, but ended up in cities on the East Coast. Most were illiterate; some spoke only Gaelic (Kennedy, 1986). Their reception in America was anything but welcoming, exemplified by the plethora of signs saying, "Jobs available, no Irish need apply."

> The Irish . . . endure[d] the scorn and discrimination later to be inflicted, to some degree at least, on each successive wave of immigrants by already settled "Americans." In speech and in dress, they seemed foreign; they were poor and unskilled and they were arriving in overwhelming numbers. . . . The Irish found many doors closed to them, both socially and economically. When their earnings were not enough . . . their wives and daughters obtained employment as servants. (Kennedy, 1986)

If this account were written without specific references to time and cultural group, it would be reasonable to assume that it describes contemporary reactions to newcomers. We could have taken this passage and substituted Jew, Italian, or Polish at various points in history. Today it could be used in reference to Cubans, Somalis, Afghans, Mexicans, Haitians, Serbs, or Ethiopians. If we compare immigration today with that during earlier periods in U.S. history, we find similarities as well as significant differences. In the past few decades we have received people from cultures more dramatically different than those from Western Europe. For example, many of our "new Americans" from parts of Asia or Africa bring values and languages not commonly associated with or related to mainstream American values and language. Middle Easterners bring customs unknown to many U.S.-born Americans. (For cultural specifics, refer to Chapters 5–9.) Many refugees bring scars of political persecution or war trauma, the nature of which the majority of Americans cannot even fathom. The relatively mild experiences of those who came as voluntary migrants do not compare with the tragedies of many of the more recent refugees. True, desperate economic conditions compelled many early European immigrants to leave their countries and thus their leaving was not entirely voluntary. However, their experiences do not parallel those, for example, of war-torn Eastern European refugees who came to the United States in the 1990s or Afghan and Iraqi refugees who came after 2000.

Disparaging comments were once made toward the very people whose descendants would, in later years, constitute much of mainstream America. Many fourth- and fifth-generation immigrants have forgotten their history (Miller, 2008) and are intolerant of the "foreign ways" of emerging immigrant groups. Every new group seems to be met with some suspicion and, in many cases, hostility. Adjustment to a new society is and has always been a long and painful process, and the first-generation immigrant group suffers, whether Irish, Jewish, Polish, Afghani, Laotian, Filipino, or Russian. It must also be remembered that many groups did not come to the United States of their own free will but rather were victims of a political or an economic system that forced them to abruptly cut their roots and escape their homelands. Although grateful for their welcome to this country, such newcomers did not want to be uprooted. Many new Americans did not have any part in the creation of events that led to their flight from their countries.

Changing Population

Demographic estimates and projections in the twenty-first century are likely to fall short of counting the true mix of people in the United States. In the culture-specific chapters of this book, we discuss Asian and Pacific Americans, African Americans, Latino and Hispanic Americans, Arab Americans and other Middle Eastern groups, and Native Americans. These categorizations are merely for the sake of convenience; an individual may belong to two or more groups. For example, a black Latino, such as a person from the Dominican Republic or Brazil, may identify himself or herself as both black and Latino. Race and ethnic background (e.g., in the case of a black Latino) are not necessarily mutually exclusive. Hispanic is considered an ethnicity, not a race. Therefore, people of Latino descent can count themselves as part of any race. Biracial individuals, who in the 1990 census counted themselves as black, could, beginning with the 2000 census, choose both black and white and be considered as one person with two races ("Multiracial Data in Census," 2000). The U.S. Census information released in 2008 projected that, by 2050, the number of people who "identify themselves as being of two or more races" will more than triple, from 5.2 million to 16.2 million ("An Older and More Diverse Nation by Midcentury," U.S. Census Bureau, 2008).

Law enforcement officials need to be aware of the overlap between race and ethnicity and that many individuals consider themselves to be multiracial. "Every day, in every corner of America, we are redrawing the color lines and are redefining what race really means. It's not just a matter of black and white anymore; the nuances of brown and yellow and red mean more—and less—than ever" ("The Changing Face of Race in America," 2000).

Heterogeneous   Dissimilar, or composed of unrelated or unlike elements. A **heterogeneous society** is one that is diverse, and frequently refers to racial and ethnic composition.

The face of America has been changing for some time. In 1860 there were only three census categories: black, white, and "quadroon" (i.e., a person who has one black grandparent, or the child of a mulatto and a white). In the 2000 census, there were 63 possible options for marking racial identity, or twice that if people responded in the affirmative to whether or not they were of Hispanic ethnicity. As the 2000 census director, Kenneth Prewitt, wrote, the concept of classification by race is human-made and endlessly complex.

What is extraordinary is that the nation moved suddenly, and with only minimal public understanding of the consequences, from a limited and relatively closed racial taxonomy to one that has no limits. In the future, racial categories will no doubt become more numerous. And why not? What grounds does the government have to declare "enough is enough?" When there were only three or even four or five categories, maybe "enough is enough" was plausible. But how can we decide, as a nation, that what we allow for on the census form of today—63 racial groups or 126 racial/ethnic ones—is the "right" number? It can't be, nor can any other number be "right." There is no political or scientifically defensible limit. (Prewitt, 2001)

Minority Populations

Documented changes in population characteristics between 1990 and 2000 had been dramatic, and they have continued through the next decade. Consider the following data released in 2008 (U.S. Census Bureau News, 2008a):

- Minorities constitute one-third of the U.S. population, and are expected to become the majority by 2042. By 2050, minorities are expected to reach 54 percent of the population.
- The tripling of the Hispanic population is expected between 2008 and 2050. This increase means that the Hispanic population would double from 15 to 30 percent of the total population.
- The non-Hispanic, single-race white population (those self-identified as white, and not of Hispanic/Latino ethnicity) is projected to be only slightly larger in 2050 (203.3 million) than in 2008 (199.8 million).
- Projections indicate that the above-noted white population will decrease in numbers in the 2030s and 2040s, constituting 46 percent of the total population in 2050. (The United States is expected to reach a population of 439 million by 2050.)
- By 2050, Asians will comprise 9.2 percent of the population, representing an increase of 15.5 million people from that in 2008.
- The Black population is expected to increase from 14 percent of the population in 2008 to 15 percent in 2050.

Minority group   A group that is the smaller in number of two groups that constitute a whole; part of the population that, because of certain characteristics, differs from the majority population and may be subjected to differential treatment.

Exhibit 1.1 shows projected rates of growth of nonwhite groups through 2050 and the corresponding decline in the white (non-Hispanic ethnicity) population.

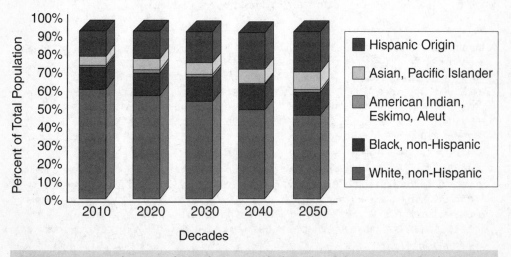

EXHIBIT 1.1   Resident population by race and Hispanic origin status—Projections: 2010 to 2050

Source: U.S. Census Bureau, Statistical Abstract of the United States, 2002.

Bronx, N.Y.	Kings (Brooklyn), N.Y.
Miami-Dade, Fla.	Harris (Houston), Texas
Los Angeles, Calif.	Santa Clara (San Jose) and Riverside, Calif.
Queens, N.Y.	Cook (Chicago), Ill
Bexar (San Antonio) and Dallas, Texas	Orange, Calif.
San Bernardino, Calif.	

EXHIBIT 1.2 "Majority-Minority" counties with a population of 1 million or more (U.S. Censes, 2008)

Source: U.S. Census Bureau, 2008.

Some of these population shifts give rise to nuances and controversies associated with the word "minority." U.S. Census information released in 2008 indicated that approximately 1 in every 10 counties across the United States was already a "majority-minority" county (see Exhibit 1.2); this meant that the percentage of minority residents in these counties had exceeded 50 percent (U.S. Census Bureau, 2008). This change has had a huge impact on many institutions in society, including the law enforcement workforce.

Immigrants

Immigration is not a new phenomenon in the United States. Virtually every citizen, except for indigenous peoples of America, can claim to be a descendent of someone who migrated, whether voluntarily or not, from another country. Immigration levels per decade reached their highest absolute numbers ever at the end of the last century, when the number of immigrants surpassed 9 million from 1991 to 2000 (see Exhibit 1.3). The U.S. Census Bureau reported that in 2007 there were 38.1 million foreign-born living in the United States. This was an increase of 5.6 million people from the corresponding figure for 2002, just five years earlier.

Immigrant or "**Permanent Resident Alien**"   "An [individual] admitted to the United States as a lawful permanent resident. Permanent residents are also commonly referred to as immigrants; however, the Immigration and Nationality Act (INA) broadly defines an immigrant as any alien in the United States, except one legally admitted under specific nonimmigrant categories [e.g., temporary workers] . . . Lawful permanent residents are legally accorded the privilege of residing permanently in the United States. They may be issued immigrant visas by the Department of State overseas or adjusted to permanent resident status by the Department of Homeland Security (DHS) in the United States." (Department of Homeland Security, 2008)

Refugee   "Any person who is outside his or her country of nationality who is unable or unwilling to return to that country because of persecution or a well-founded fear of persecution. Persecution or the fear thereof must be based on . . . race, religion, nationality, membership in a particular social group, or political opinion. People with no nationality must generally be outside their country of last habitual residence to qualify as a refugee." (Department of Homeland Security, 2008)

In addition, immigrants from 1980 to the present have come from many more parts of the world than from where they arrived at the turn of the twentieth century. From U.S. Census data

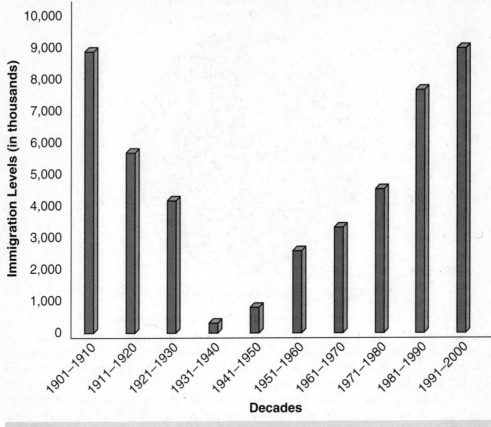

EXHIBIT 1.3   **Immigration to America in the twentieth century**

Source: U.S. Census Bureau, Statistical Abstract of the United States, 2002.

released in 2007, the top seven countries of birth for foreign-born populations were, in descending order, Mexico, China, the Philippines, India, El Salvador and Vietnam, and Korea (Exhibit 1.4). Each of the following five states had 1.7 million or more immigrants: California, Texas, Florida, New York, Illinois (U.S. Census Bureau, 2007).

Between 1990 and 2007, the fastest growth in foreign population took place in North Carolina where the population increased from 115,000 to 630,000 or by 448 percent (U.S. Census Bureau, 2007). After North Carolina, the following four states ranked (in descending order) with 200 percent or higher growth in their immigrant populations from 1990 to 2007: Georgia, Arkansas, Nevada, and Tennessee (U.S. Census Bureau, 2007).

> The **foreign-born population** includes naturalized U.S. citizens, lawful permanent residents, temporary migrants (e.g., foreign students), humanitarian migrants (refugees), and unauthorized migrants. (U.S. Census Bureau, State and Country Quick Facts: Foreign-Born Persons, 2000)

Even though most Americans, with the exception of the indigenous peoples, have been immigrants at some time in their lineage, anti-immigrant sentiment is common. Especially in times

Foreign Born Populations (Millions) in the U.S.
Top Seven Countries of Origin (2007)

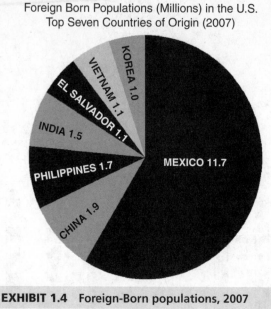

KOREA 1.0

VIETNAM 1.1

EL SALVADOR 1.1

INDIA 1.5

PHILIPPINES 1.7

CHINA 1.9

MEXICO 11.7

EXHIBIT 1.4   Foreign-Born populations, 2007

Source: U.S. Census Bureau, American Community Survey, 2007.

of recession, immigrants are often blamed for society's woes. However, the issues surrounding immigration are not as clear-cut as they may at first appear to be. Despite the problems that are inevitably created when large groups of people have to be absorbed into a society, some immigrant groups stimulate the economy, revitalize neighborhoods, and eventually become fully participatory and loyal American citizens. Nevertheless, if an officer has an anti-immigrant bias, negative attitudes may surface when that officer interacts with immigrants, especially under stressful circumstances. When officers are under pressure, negative attitudes become apparent and their communication may become unprofessional. Indeed some citizens have claimed that officers with whom they have been in contact had not attempted to understand them or that they demonstrated little patience in communicating or finding a translator. (See Chapter 4 for a discussion of communication issues and law enforcement.)

In addition, officers must be aware of "racial flash points" that are created when immigrants move into economically depressed areas with large and diverse populations. Some people feel that immigrants' moving into certain urban areas displaces economically disadvantaged groups or deprives them of access to work. (This topic is discussed further in Chapter 11.) Thus law enforcement representatives may see hostility between, for example, blacks and Korean or Arab immigrants in such cities as Los Angeles, New York, and Detroit. Although officers cannot be expected to solve these deep-seated problems, they may find themselves in situations in which they can serve as cultural mediators, helping each group to increase understanding and toleration of the other. For example, police can point out that the absence of a Korean grocer's smile or greeting of a customer is not necessarily a sign of hostility or an expression of distrust, but possibly a cultural trait. When a person complains that an Arab liquor store owner does not hire outside his or her community, officers can explain that it is usually because the business is a small, family-run operation in which employees are family members. It would be too simplistic to attribute all or even the majority of problems as cultural, but with an understanding of immigrants' backgrounds, officers can help explain points of tension to members of other ethnic groups.

Furthermore, some behaviors may be common to more than one immigrant population, yet unfamiliar to officers working with these groups. As part of his community policing outreach, one of the authors (AO) established an ongoing police outreach to Portland area immigrants and refugees in 2002. The organization, called IRCO (Immigrant Refugee Community Organization), sponsors classes in which new immigrants and refugees are oriented on interaction with American police and on how to use 911. What is learned from the immigrant community is shared with police officers in various police departments. For example:

- In the United States, most police departments do not allow the driver or the passengers to exit their car and walk back to the police car.
- In other countries like Cuba, Japan, Mexico, and Russia, it is expected that motorists exit their car and walk back to the police officer.
- Translators, court interpreters, and new immigrants are excellent sources of information on customs of their country.
- Men from Eastern Europe and South America find it difficult to believe that a man can be arrested for touching a woman and find it silly that the U.S. police do prostitution sting decoy operations.
- The police in such regions as Eastern Europe and South America expect bribes when they stop a motorist.
- Domestic violence laws are basically nonexistent in Eastern European countries because their governments view family matters as personal and private.

The more direct contact officers have with ethnic and immigrant communities, the more cultural knowledge they will gain that may have an impact on law enforcement (see Exhibit 1.5 on workshops provided to immigrants and refugees).

To better serve new immigrants and refugees coming to the United States from all countries in the world, Organization and Training Services offers public-safety and basic-law workshops through IRCO (Immigrant Refugee Community Organization, http://www.irco.org). The workshops consist of an orientation on America's police, laws, and emergency services.

    The immigrant and refugee participants typically would have been in the United States for one month and would have had no previous orientation on the American police, laws, or emergency services. The two-hour sessions are offered in the morning and afternoon, and are part of a 16-week training and employment services program for new immigrants and refugees. The classes are held at the local IRCO office.

    Interpreters translate during the presentation, which includes basic information on the following:

- State Police
- Sheriff's departments and city police departments
- Traffic and criminal laws
- Domestic violence
- What to do if stopped by a police officer
- How to use 911 for emergencies and other alternatives for nonemergencies

A question-and-answer session follows the presentation.

EXHIBIT 1.5   Workshops for immigrants and refugees on U.S. Police, laws, and emergency Services

Source: Olson, Aaron T., 2009. Used with Permission.

EUROPEAN AMERICANS   In learning about diversity in U.S. society, focus is often centered on the diversity among immigrants from cultures very different from "mainstream" U.S. culture. However, there is also a great deal of diversity among European Americans. One of the myths about European Americans is that they are all alike. The majority of people in the United States are of European descent, but most Europeans are not of the same ethnicity or nationality, nor do they even have the same physical characteristics. Europe is a continent that is divided into four regions, east, west, north, and south, and has a population of 730 million people (Population Reference Bureau, 2005). Europe has 45 different countries, each with a unique national character, government, and, for the most part, language. To illustrate Europe's diversity and hetero-geneity, the European Union has 23 different official languages for its European Parliament compared to the United Nations (which has six official languages). The European Union holds the world's largest translation operation and has 60 interpreters in use when its 25–member state Parliament is in session (Owen, 2005). The countries listed in Exhibit 1.6 represent the continent of Europe.

Undocumented Immigrants: Demographic Information

The census bureau does not ask about legal migrant status of respondents as there is no legislative mandate to do so. (U.S. Citizenship and Immigration Services [USCIS], 2009). In its 2003 report on undocumented immigrants, the former INS, now the USCIS, placed the growth of this popu-lation at 350,000 annually. This figure was 75,000 per year higher than was estimated before the 2000 census, primarily because of improved means of counting a hard-to-track population. Exact figures are difficult to obtain. In May 2006, it was estimated that 12 million undocumented people were living in the United States (Ferraro, 2006). It is difficult to obtain completely accurate information on the number of undocumented immigrants in the United States, and, as of the

1. Albania	16. Greece	31. Norway
2. Andorra	17. Holy City (Vatican City)	32. Poland
3. Austria	18. Hungary	33. Portugal
4. Belarus	19. Iceland	34. Romania
5. Belgium	20. Ireland	35. Russia
6. Bosnia and Herzegovina	21. Italy	36. San Marino
	22. Latvia	37. Serbia and Montenegro
7. Bulgaria	23. Liechtenstein	38. Slovakia
8. Croatia	24. Lithuania	39. Slovenia
9. Cyprus	25. Luxembourg	40. Spain
10. Czech Republic	26. Macedonia, the former Yugoslav Republic	41. Sweden
11. Denmark		42. Switzerland
12. Estonia	27. Malta	43. Turkey
13. Finland	28. Moldova	44. Ukraine
14. France	29. Monaco	45. United Kingdom
15. Germany	30. Netherlands	

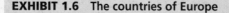

EXHIBIT 1.6   The countries of Europe

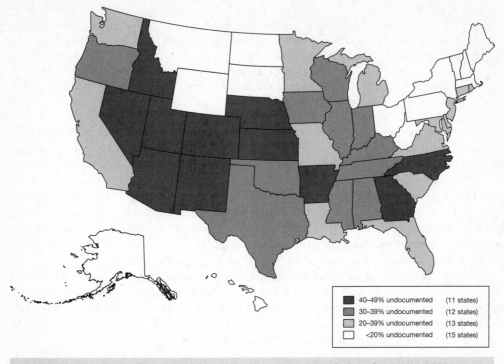

	40–49% undocumented	(11 states)
	30–39% undocumented	(12 states)
	20–39% undocumented	(13 states)
	<20% undocumented	(15 states)

EXHIBIT 1.7   **Share of Undocumented Foreign-Born Population, by State, 2000**

Source: Urban Institute, Estimates Based on Census, 2000, Reprinted with Permission.

writing of this text, 2010 data was not available. Exhibit 1.7 shows the percentage of undocumented immigrants residing in various states in 2000 (Urban Institute, 2002).

Undocumented Immigrants: Background Information

The terms *"illegal immigrant," "illegal alien,"* and *"undocumented immigrant"* are sometimes used interchangeably, but there is controversy around the use of these terms (which is beyond the scope of this chapter). There are two major groups of undocumented immigrants: those who cross the U.S. borders without having been "inspected" and those who enter the country with legal documents as temporary residents but have violated their legal admission status by extending their stay. Initially, Mexicans and other Latin Americans come to most people's minds when they hear the terms *illegal alien* and *undocumented worker.* In addition, however, there are people from the Dominican Republic who enter through Puerto Rico; since Puerto Ricans are U.S. citizens, they are considered legal. Therefore, officers may come in contact with "Puerto Ricans" who are actually from the Dominican Republic and have come to the United States under an illegal pretext. Asians are also smuggled into the United States, including women brought in for sex trade. People from other parts of the world may come to the United States on a tourist visa and then decide to remain permanently (e.g., Canadians).

Some come to the United States with the hope that they can remain legally by proving that they had escaped from the political repression in their homeland. Those who seek asylum face persecution or death if they were to return to their native countries.

Asylee   A foreign-born individual in the United States or at a port of entry who is found to be unable or unwilling to return to his or her country of nationality, or to seek the protection of that country, because of persecution or a well-founded fear of persecution. Persecution or the fear thereof must be based on the indivudal's race, religion, nationality, membership in a particular social group, or political opinion (Department of Homeland Security, 2008).

People who are often deported as undocumented arrivals are those who come as "economic refugees" (i.e., their economic status in their home country may be desperate). They generally have few occupational skills and are willing to take menial jobs that many American citizens will not accept. They fill economic gaps in various regions where low-wage labor is needed.

Outer appearances are not an accurate guide to who has legal status and who does not. Both the illegal and the legal immigrants may live in the same neighborhoods. In addition, the U.S. government has occasionally legalized significant numbers of some populations of formerly illegal immigrants, usually in recognition of special circumstances in those persons' home countries, such as large-scale natural disasters or serious political instability.

Undocumented immigrants lack the papers necessary to obtain legal residence in the United States. The societal consequences are far-reaching. Law enforcement officials, politicians, and social service providers, among others, have had to deal with many concerns related to housing, education, safety, employment, spousal violence, and health care. The undocumented segment of the immigrant population poses some difficult challenges for law enforcement officials.

Undocumented Immigrants: Fear of Deportation

The principal barrier to establishing trust with undocumented immigrants revolves around fears of being reported to the U.S. Immigration and Customs Enforcement (USICE), the largest investigative arm of the DHS. Entire communities may resist reporting crimes because of the fear of deportation. These immigrants are often already located in high-crime areas, and become even more vulnerable because of their fears of deportation.

An argument exists that supports leaving undocumented immigrants alone, unless they have committed a criminal act or are creating a disturbance. It is based on the perspective that tracking down and deporting immigrants has technically been the job of the USICE and not that of the state or local police. Sometimes the trust of the entire community, including both the illegal and the legal immigrants, is at stake. If immigrant communities know that police officers will not turn over illegal immigrants to the USICE, then there is less fear of the police when it comes to reporting crimes.

Although law enforcement agencies in Prince William and Frederick counties [Virginia] have agreed to help federal authorities enforce immigration laws, officials in many other parts of the country remain reluctant to do so, saying they fear losing the trust of the immigrant communities and worry about being accused of racial profiling . . . While recognizing that illegal immigration is a crime, . . . [El Paso's Mayor, John Cook] is also worried about a growing public perception that immigrants are criminals.

"There is a danger", he said. "Once people don't trust a police officer in immigrant communities, they become communities that foster crime, where people won't report domestic violence or [even] the theft of a TV. If people feel that they are under threat of being deported, they become silent. There has to be a delicate balance." ("Many Officials Reluctant to Help Arrest Immigrants," 2008)

Law enforcement's involvement with undocumented immigrants had been the focus of controversy for years prior to the publication of this text. "The ICE 287(g) Program: A Law Enforcement Partnership" actively began in 2006 with 29 participating law enforcement agencies. As of May 2009, the number had increased to 67 agencies in 23 states (USICE, 2009).

This partnership gave the authority to the Secretary of Homeland Security to enter into agreements with state and local law enforcement agencies, allowing officers to perform immigration law enforcement functions. Under 287(g), ICE provides state and local law enforcement with the training and delegated authority to enforce immigration law (U.S. Immigration and Customs Enforcement, 2008).

Under the new administration in 2009, the ICE 287(g) program began to undergo tremendous scrutiny. Many immigrant groups claimed that 287(g) had become a vehicle for the racial profiling of Hispanic immigrants, and that deportation by police officers for minor crimes had begun to occur with alarming frequency. Congressional hearings in early 2009 called for the monitoring, improved assessment, and closer supervision of the 287(g) program, and many local law enforcement agencies recognized 287(g) as a problem. In March of 2009, the Government Accountability Office reported the following:

> . . . the government has failed to determine how many of the thousands of people deported under the program were the kind of violent felons it was devised to root out. Some law enforcement agencies had used the program to deport immigrants "who have committed minor crimes, such as carrying an open container of alcohol," the report said, and at least four agencies referred minor traffic offenders for deportation. ("Report Questions Immigration Program," 2009)

Undocumented Immigrants: The "U" Visa and the Safe Reporting of Crimes

With the passage of the Victims of Trafficking and Violence Protection Act of 2000 (in which VAWA [Violence Against Women Act] is included), Congress also created the "U" visa, a relatively unknown piece of legislation that can affect communities and law enforcement. When undocumented immigrants call the police, chances are that they are victims of or witnesses to a crime. If they actively cooperate with law enforcement in providing information about the crime, they are entitled to a "U" visa or a nonimmigrant visa, which can eventually be used in the application for a legal work permit and a social security number. While there are many hurdles associated with obtaining the "U" visa, undocumented immigrants who are granted it may eventually apply for residency. Application for the "U" visa is an extremely challenging process, and needs to include a "certification of helplessness" from a certifying agency. This means that the individual petitioning for the "U" visa must "provide a Nonimmigrant Status Certification from a federal, state or local law enforcement official that demonstrates the petitioner 'has been helpful, is being helpful or is likely to be helpful' in the investigation or prosecution of the criminal activity." As of 2007, the United States Citizenship and Immigration Services has been able to grant up to 10,000 "U" nonimmigrant visas in any one fiscal year (U.S. Citizenship and Immigration Services, 2007).

According to Christopher Martinez, Program Director for refugee and immigrant services of the Catholic charities CYO in San Francisco, since the law passed, and in the last few years, only approximately 13,000 (as of March 2009) people across the country have applied for the "U" visa. Of these, only 65 have received the visa. Nonprofits such as the Catholic Charities have forged relationships with police departments to maximize cooperation, and have been in a position to educate officers about this provision in the Act. In Martinez's experience in San Francisco, the city has had the support of the police department and the District Attorney's Office for these nonimmigrant visa applications.

If more of the community knew about this law, more undocumented immigrants would likely come forward and out of the shadows to cooperate with law enforcement. In doing so, they could work with the police to create safer communities. It is not an easy road to obtain this kind of visa, but it can be an incentive to speak out and to help avoid becoming victimized again. About 10 years ago, a woman and her child living on the East Coast witnessed a heinous crime involving the husband. While at the time of the crime the law did not exist, this woman came forward cooperating fully with the authorities. Ultimately, the perpetrator was caught and convicted. The woman is now eligible for a "U" visa, and has the full backing of the District Attorney's office in the city in which she and her child live (Martinez, 2009).

Immigrant Women: Victims of Domestic Violence

In a 2003 report to a congressional subcommittee on immigration, Leslye E. Orloff, director of the Immigrant Women's Program (National Organization of Women's Legal Defense and Education Fund), presented a full account of problems that continue to beset battered immigrant women. Even though the frequency of domestic violence is consistent across socioeconomic classes, racial groups, and geographic areas, according to Orloff, immigrant women still face additional challenges in seeking help from their communities.

> [The] Violence Against Women Act (VAWA), passed by Congress in 1994 and improved in 2000, set out to reform the manner in which officers responded to domestic violence calls for help. Although significant improvement following the passage of VAWA has been noted, the response continues to be lacking. Some police officers' personal attitudes regarding domestic violence (i.e., it is a private problem) and how it should be handled (through mediation rather than arrest or formal charges), in essence, marginalizes victims of domestic violence. In extreme cases, victims' requests for help are disregarded. The lack of appropriate response to domestic violence from the police is further compounded when the battered woman is an immigrant. The police often do not have the capacity to communicate effectively with the immigrant victim in her own language. The police may use her abuser or her children to translate for her, and/or police may credit the statements of her citizen spouse or boyfriend over her statements to the police due to gender, race or cultural bias. (Orloff, 2003)

VAWA was reauthorized by the Congress first in 2000, after its passage in 1994, and then in December 2005. On January 5, 2006, the bill was signed into law by President George W. Bush. VAWA will be up for reauthorization in 2010.

Domestic violence is a phenomenon that exists among people from all socioeconomic classes, races, and backgrounds. Nevertheless, there are particular factors contributing to the high rate of domestic violence that some immigrant women experienced in their native countries.

Women subjected to domestic violence in their home countries confront societal, familial, and legal systems that refuse to acknowledge the seriousness of the problem or to protect the victim. In many countries, the voices of the victims go unheard, drowned out by age-old traditions that perpetuate the idea that women should serve their husbands no matter how they are treated. Often victims' own families do nothing to help the victim of spousal abuse and force her to "endure"—as generations of women have done. Outside the family network, women find little assistance in the legal system. Many countries do not codify domestic violence as a separate crime, and some countries regard domestic violence as strictly a family issue to be dealt with in a private manner. In many countries, the law fails to recognize rape by a spouse . . . Few countries have enacted protections for domestic violence victims. And, measures that have been enacted all too often fall short due to little or no enforcement. Calling the police in many countries does not ensure any real protection for the victim (Tiede, 2001).

When women who have been battered come to the United States, they carry with them the traumas they experienced earlier owing to their culture and traditions. There are multiple problems facing battered immigrant women in the United States. The following summarizes some of these, and should help law enforcement representatives understand the larger context in which an immigrant may fail to report a crime (Tiede, 2001):

- Some battered immigrant women are completely isolated in the United States. They may live secret lives, never having established a legal identity in the United States.
- Batterers frequently add to victims' fears by threatening to call ICE about deportation.
- Women fear losing their families and being deported to a hostile society upon their return. (In certain places in Latin America, for example, a woman returning to her own village without her husband and children is often ostracized.)
- Victims are often not aware that protection is available, nor do they know how to find it.
- Many victims do not speak English and have no understanding of U.S. criminal and immigration laws and systems.

In addition, a battered immigrant woman may not understand that she can personally tell her story in court, or that a judge will believe her. Based on her experience in her native country, she may believe that only those who are wealthy or have ties to the government will prevail in court. Batterers often manipulate these beliefs by convincing the victim that he will prevail in court because he is a male, is a citizen, or has more money (Orloff, 2003, p. 313).

Police can assist by being ready with resources to provide to victims. In the case of immigrant women, both documented and undocumented, officers need to be aware of community assistance programs specifically created to address their needs. In some jurisdictions, management may even encourage or mandate that officers make an initial call for help, while still with the victim, to a community organization, for example. The Women's Justice Center in Santa Rosa, California, is one such example of a community resource. Exhibit 1.8 lists advice from the Center and lets immigrant women know that their issues and fears are shared:

Immigrants must learn a great deal about U.S. laws, the law enforcement system in general, and the role of police officers. Many fear the police because police in their native countries engaged in arbitrary acts of brutality in support of repressive governments (e.g., in Central America). In some other countries, citizens disrespect police because the officers are poorly educated, inefficient, corrupt, and have a very low occupational status (e.g., in Iran). The barriers immigrants bring to the relationship with police suggest that American officers have to double their efforts to communicate and to educate. A further challenge for law enforcement is that, for the reasons mentioned above, new immigrants often become victims of violent crimes. In part, the acculturation and success of immigrants in this society depend on how they are treated while they are still ignorant of the social norms and laws. Law enforcement officials who have contact with new Americans will need extraordinary patience at times. Adaptation to a new country can be a long and arduous process. Without the knowledge of citizens' cultural and national backgrounds, law enforcement officers may observe citizens' reactions that they do not fully understand.

Women's Justice Center
HELP
Special for Immigrant Women

1. You deserve help, and as a crime victim, you have a right to all the same crime victim services as any crime victim born in the United States.

   —Do not be shy about calling police, using women's shelters, calling rape crisis centers . . . or going to restraining order clinics.

2. What if the person abusing you says that he will call ICE and get you deported if you call the police or try to get help?

   —It is very, very common for violent men to make this threat to immigrant women who are their victims. But it is virtually impossible for these men to carry out the threat.

3. If you are still afraid to seek help, ask someone to make the phone calls for you, and to be with you when you deal with police and other crisis workers.

   —It's a very good idea when you get help for domestic violence and rape to have someone at your side . . .

4. Insist on good translations.

   —The U.S. Constitution says that all persons must be given equal protection of the laws. The courts have repeatedly ruled that this means everyone from native born citizens to newly arrived immigrants, whether or not they have the proper documentation. Every human being has a right to equal protection under the laws.

EXHIBIT 1.8   Advice to Immigrant Women from the Women's Justice Center

Source: De Santis, Women's Justice Center, 2000, www.justicewomen.com, Extracted with permission.

Some immigrants carry with them memories of police from their native countries and have deep-seated fears about relating to police officers even in the United States. A Central American refugee who had received asylum in the United States recalled a police act of "handcuffing" that took place in the 1980s. He explained that such actions, and worse, were common practice for police.

I was about 14 years old. My father and I were in the car driving home late in the afternoon. It was very common to have to go through checkpoints, and we were unfortunately pulled aside at one of them. My father was asked to produce paperwork, including a license. Unfortunately, he had forgotten his wallet that day. Even though my father had also worked for the government, the police did not believe him. They took my father out of the car, put his arms behind his back, and with a string tightly tied his thumbs together as they had no handcuffs. Right away, I could see his thumbs start becoming purple. The police demanded that I go home and get his wallet. It took me about one hour to run home and back. Thankfully, I got the wallet. But, when I returned to see my father, his thumbs had turned completely black from the tight string around them. There was no way we could complain about this—things would have gotten much worse for us if we had. There was too much fear at that time in our history. We could not even look an officer in the eye without getting into some kind of trouble. . . . (Central American asylee, personal communication, 2009)

To illustrate this fear even further, the Central American interviewee added, after he shared the above story: "Please do not ever identify me by name or associate me with this anecdote. There could still be consequences for my family back home if they knew that I was speaking about the authorities like this" (Central American asylee, personal communication, 2009).

CULTURE AND ITS RELEVANCE TO LAW ENFORCEMENT

An understanding of accepted social practices and cultural traditions in citizens' countries of origin can provide officers with insight into predicting some of the reactions and difficulties new immigrants will have in America. However, some customs are simply unacceptable in the United States, and arrests must be made in spite of the cultural background. Regardless of the circumstances, immigrant suspects need to be treated with respect; officers and all others in the criminal justice system must understand the innocent state of mind the citizen was in when committing the "crime." For example, female circumcision is illegal under all circumstances in the United States but is still practiced in certain African countries. The Hmong, mountain people of Southeast Asia, and particularly Laos, have a tradition considered to be an acceptable form of eloping. This Hmong tradition allows a male to capture and take away a female for marriage; even if she resists, he is allowed to take her to his home, and it is mandated that he consummate the union. However, "Marriage by capture" translates into kidnap and rape in the United States. Perpetrators of such crimes in the United States must be arrested.

In interviews with a deputy public defender and a deputy district attorney, a legal journal posed the following question: Should our legal system recognize a "cultural" defense when it comes to crimes? The deputy district attorney's response was, "No. You're treading on shaky ground when you decide something based on culture, because our society is made up of so many different cultures. It is very hard to draw the line somewhere, but [diverse cultural groups] are living in our country, and people have to abide by [one set of] laws or else you have anarchy." The deputy public defender's response to the question was: "Yes. I'm not asking that the [various cultural groups] be judged differently, just that their actions be understood according to their own history and culture" (Sherman, 1986).

If law enforcement's function is to protect and serve citizens from all cultural backgrounds, it becomes vital to understand the cultural dimensions of crimes. Obviously, behaviors or actions that may be excused in another culture must not go unpunished if they are considered crimes in this country (e.g., spouse abuse). Nevertheless, there are circumstances in which law enforcement officials at all levels of the criminal justice system would benefit by understanding the cultural context in which a crime or other incident occurred. Law enforcement professionals must use standard operating procedures in response to specific situations, and the majority of these procedures cannot be altered for different groups based on ethnicity. In a multicultural society, however, an officer can modify the way he or she treats a suspect, witness, or victim, given the knowledge of what is considered "normal" in that person's culture. When officers suspect that an aspect of cultural background is a factor in a particular incident, they may earn the respect of—and therefore cooperation from—ethnic communities if they are willing to evaluate their arrests in lesser crimes.

Many officers say that their job is to uphold the law, but it is not up to them to make judgments. Yet discretion when deciding whether to take a citizen into custody for a lesser crime may be appropriate. When officers understand the cultural context for a crime, the crime will and should be perceived somewhat differently. Consider the Sikh religion (a strict religious tradition followed by a minority of people from northern India), which requires that its followers wear a ceremonial dagger, a sacred symbol, at all times, even during sleep. Consider Pacific Islanders having barbecues in their garages, where they roast whole pigs. And consider a Vietnamese family that eats dog meat. When officers understand the cultural context within which a "crime" takes place, then it is much easier to understand a citizen's intent. Understanding the cultural dimensions of a crime may result, for example, in not taking a citizen into custody. With lesser crimes, this may be the appropriate course of action and can result in the preservation of good police–community relations. Before looking at specific case studies of incidents and crimes involving cultural components, we present the concept of culture and its tremendous impact on the individual.

All people (except for very young children) carry cultural do's and don'ts, which some might also refer to as cultural baggage. The degree of this "baggage" is determined by their own conscious and unconscious identification with their group and their relative attachment to their cultural group's traditional values. Being influenced by cultural baggage is a natural human phenomenon. Much of who we are is sanctioned and reinforced by the society in which we have been raised. According to some experts, culture has a far greater influence on people's behavior than does any other variable such as age, gender, race, and socioeconomic status (Hall, 1959), and often this influence is unconscious. It is virtually impossible to lose one's culture completely when interacting in a new environment, yet change will inevitably take place.

The Definition of Culture

Although there are many definitions of culture, we are using the term to mean beliefs, habits, attitudes, values, patterns of thinking, behavior, and everyday customs that have been passed on from generation to generation. Culture is learned rather than inherited and is manifested largely in unconscious and subtle behavior. With this definition in mind, consider that most children have acquired a general cultural orientation by the time they are five or six years old. For this reason, it is difficult to change behavior immediately to accommodate a new culture. Many layers of cultural behavior and beliefs are subconscious. In addition, many people assume that what they take for granted is taken for granted by all people ("all human beings are the same"), and they do not even recognize their own culturally influenced behavior. Anthropologist Edward T. Hall (1959) said, "Culture hides much more than it reveals and, strangely enough, what it hides, it hides most effectively from its own participants." In other words, people are blind to their own deeply embedded cultural behavior.

To further understand the hidden nature of culture, picture an iceberg (Ruhly, 1976). The only visible part of the iceberg is the tip, which typically constitutes about 10 percent of the mass. Like most of culture's influences, the remainder of the iceberg is submerged beneath the surface. What this means for law enforcement is that there is a natural tendency to interpret behavior, motivations, and criminal activity from the officer's cultural point of view. This tendency is due largely to an inability to understand behavior from alternative perspectives and because of the inclination toward ethnocentrism.

Ethnocentrism   An attitude of seeing and judging other cultures from the perspective of one's own culture; using the culture of one's own group as a standard for the judgment of others, or thinking of it as superior to other cultures that are merely different; an ethnocentric person would say there is only one way of being "normal" and that is the way of his or her own culture.

When it comes to law enforcement, there is only one set of laws to which all citizens, whether native-born or not, must adhere. However, the following case studies illustrate that culture does affect interpretations, meaning, and intention.

Mini Case Studies: Culture and Crime

The following mini case studies involve descriptions of crimes or offenses with a cultural component. If the crime is a murder or something similarly heinous, most people will not be particularly sympathetic, even with an understanding of the cultural factors involved. However, consider that understanding other cultural patterns gives one the ability to see and react in a different way. The ability to withhold judgment and to interpret a person's intention from a different cultural perspective is a skill that will ultimately enable a person to identify his or her own cultural blinders. Each case study describes an increasingly serious crime—from driving under the influence to child abuse to murder.

Mini Case Study 1: Driving under the Influence?

The following case, among others, was the subject of discussion in an officers' course in ethnic understanding in a San Francisco Bay Area police department:

> A Tongan man living in [the Bay Area] was arrested on Highway 101 on the Peninsula for driving under the influence of kava, a relaxing elixir popular with Pacific Islanders. But a hung jury effectively acquitted [this man] in October. The jury determined, in part, that police didn't fully understand the effect and the importance of the drink. Tongans, Samoans, and Fijians say the kava ritual is an integral part of life, a way to share information and reinforce traditions. And they say it doesn't affect their ability to drive any more than soda pop. ("Officers Being Trained in Ethnic Understanding," 2000)

Mini Case Study 2: A Tragic Case of Cross-Cultural Misinterpretation

In parts of Asia, there are medical practices unfamiliar to many law enforcement officials (as well as medical practitioners) in the West. A number of these practices result in marks on the skin that can easily be misinterpreted as abuse by people who have no knowledge of these culturally based medical treatments. The practices include rubbing the skin with a coin ("coining," "coin rubbing," or "wind rubbing"), pinching the skin, touching the skin with burning incense, or applying a heated cup to the skin ("cupping"). Each practice leaves highly visible marks, such as bruises and even burns. The following is an account of a serious misreading of some very common Southeast Asian methods of traditional folk healing on the part of U.S. school authorities and law enforcement officials.

A young Vietnamese boy had been absent from school for a few days with a serious respiratory infection. His father, believing that coining would help cure him, rubbed heated coins on specific sections of his back and neck. The boy's condition seemed to improve and he was able to return to school. Upon noticing heavy bruising on the boy's neck, the teacher immediately informed the school principal, who promptly reported the "abuse" to the police (who then notified Child Protective Services). When the police were notified, they went to the child's home to investigate. The father was very cooperative when questioned by the police and admitted, in broken English, that he had caused the bruising on his son's neck. The man was arrested and incarcerated. While the father was in jail, his son, who was under someone else's custody, apparently relapsed and died of his original illness. On hearing the news, the father committed suicide in his jail cell. Of course, it is not known whether the father would have committed suicide as a response to his son's death alone. The tragic misinterpretation on the part of the authorities involved, including the teacher, the principal, and the arresting police officers, provides an

(continued)

extreme case of what can happen when people attribute meaning from their own cultural perspective.

Cultural understanding would not have cured the young boy, but informed interaction with the father could have prevented the second tragedy. All of the authorities were interpreting what they saw with "cultural filters" based on their own belief systems. Ironically, the interpretation of the bruises (i.e., child abuse) was almost the opposite of the intended meaning of the act (i.e., healing). Even after some of the parties involved learned about this very common Southeast Asian practice, they still did not accept that it existed as an established practice, and they could not fathom how others could believe that coining might actually cure illness. Their own conception of medical healing did not encompass what they perceived as such "primitive treatment."

Ethnocentrism is a barrier to accepting that there is another way, another belief, another communication style, another custom, or another value that can lead to culturally different behavior. Ethnocentrism often causes a person to assign a potentially incorrect meaning or attribute an incorrect motivation to a given act. Consider how the outcome could have differed if only one person in the chain of authorities had viewed the bruises as something other than abuse. The tragic outcome of serious cultural misunderstandings might have been averted. (Personal communication with social worker who wishes to remain anonymous)

Mini Case Study 3: Latino Values as a Factor in Sentencing

In a court of law, a cultural explanation or rationalization (i.e., a cultural defense) rarely affects a guilty or not-guilty verdict. Nevertheless, culture may affect sentencing. Consider the following case, in which, according to retired Judge Lawrence Katz, cultural considerations lessened the severity of the sentence:

A Mexican woman living in the United States became involved in an extramarital affair. Her husband became outraged when the wife bragged about her extramarital activities at a picnic at which many extended family members were present. At the same time, the wife also made comments about her husband's lack of ability to satisfy her and how, in comparison, her lover was far superior. On hearing his wife gloat about her affair, the husband left the picnic and drove five miles to purchase a gun. Two hours later, he shot and killed his wife. In a case such as this, the minimum charge required in California would be second-degree murder. However, because the jury took into consideration the cultural background of this couple, the husband received a mitigated sentence and was found guilty of manslaughter. It was argued that his wife's boasting about her lover and her explicit comments made specifically to emasculate him created a passion and emotion that completely undermined his machismo, masculine pride and honor. To understand the severity of the wife's offense, the law enforcement officer and the prosecutor had to understand what it means to be humiliated in such a manner in front of one's family, in the context of Latino culture. (Katz, 2009)

The purpose of these three mini case studies is not to discuss the "rightness" or "wrongness" of any group's values, customs, or beliefs but to illustrate that the point of contact between law enforcement and citizens' backgrounds must not be ignored. Officers must be encouraged to consider culture when investigating and presenting evidence regarding an alleged crime or incident involving people from diverse backgrounds. This consideration does not mean that standard operating procedures should be changed, nor does it imply that heinous crimes such as murder or rape should be excused on cultural grounds. However, as a matter of course, officers need to include cultural competence as a variable in understanding, assessing, and reporting certain kinds of incidents and crimes.

Law enforcement representatives have the ultimate authority to arrest or admonish someone suspected of a crime. According to retired Judge Katz, "Discretion based on cultural competence at the police level is much more significant than what happens at the next level in the criminal justice system (i.e., the courts)." Individual police officers have the opportunity to create positive public relations if they demonstrate cultural sensitivity and respect toward members of an ethnic community. Katz cited the example of police contact with the San Francisco Bay Area Samoan community, in which barbecues and parties can include a fair amount of drinking, resulting in fights. In Katz's opinion, the police, responding to neighbors' complaints, could come in with a show of force and the fighting would cool down quickly. However, word would spread that the police officers had no cultural understanding or respect for the people involved. This would widen the gap that already exists between police and many Pacific Islander and other Asian groups and would not be a way to foster trust in the Samoan community. Alternatively, the police could locate the leader, or the "chief," of this group and let that person deal with the problem in the way that he would have handled the conflict in Samoa. There is no question about the chief's ability to handle the problem. He has a prominent role to play and can serve as a bridge between the police and the community. The *matai* is also a resource; he is an elder who has earned the respect of the community.

The heads of Samoan communities are traditionally in full control of members' behavior, although this is changing somewhat in the United States. Furthermore, according to traditional Samoan values, if a family member assaults a member of another family, the head of the family is required to ensure punishment. Given the power entrusted to the chiefs, it is reasonable to encourage officers first to go through the community and elicit assistance in solving enforcement problems. This recommendation does not imply, in any way, that groups should be left to police themselves; instead, understanding and working with the leadership of a community represents a spirit of partnership.

The awareness of and sensitivity to such issues can have a significant impact on the criminal justice system, in which police have the power to either inflame or calm the people involved in a particular incident. According to Katz, "Many cases, especially those involving lesser offenses, can stay out of court." He asks, "Do you always need a show of force? Or can you counsel and admonish instead?" In certain situations, such as the one described earlier, officers can rethink traditional police methods in order to be as effective as possible. Doing so involves knowledge of ethnic communities and a desire to establish a positive and trustworthy image in those communities (Katz, 2009).

DIMENSIONS OF DIVERSITY

To make sense of the different groups in our workplace and society, we need to have functional categories and terms. Marilyn Loden, organizational diversity consultant, describes and outlines the primary and secondary dimensions of diversity (Loden, 2009). The specific categories within the dimensions of diversity are not new but rather provide a functional construction of individual and group characteristics for understanding the people in the workforce and our society. This awareness and the ability to view differences as sources of strength often results in improved interpersonal relationships and improved citizen contacts.

Primary Dimensions of Diversity

A primary dimension is a core characteristic with which a person is born that remains with the individual in all stages of his or her life. According to Loden, people have a minimum of six primary dimensions (Loden, 2009):

1. Age
2. Ethnicity

3. Gender
4. Mental/physical abilities and characteristics
5. Race
6. Sexual orientation

Most people are aware of the meaning of these categories. For the sake of clarity, the following terms are included in the category "sexual orientation": heterosexual, homosexual, lesbian, gay, bisexual, and transgender. All of the six primary dimensions are characteristics that contribute to being advantaged or disadvantaged in the workforce and in society. Victims of hate bias crimes have been targeted because of these six dimensions of diversity—age, ethnicity, gender, disability status, race, and sexual orientation. The primary dimension associated with age also includes generational differences. In the law enforcement agency workforce, values may collide among the generations; leaders and managers need to be cognizant of this dimension of diversity. Recruiting someone from "Generation Y," for example, could involve an understanding of some of the unique characteristics associated with this age group. Generation Y members (born between 1977 and 1994, and compromising 20 percent of the population) have been characterized by one global human resource and recruitment firm as a tolerant group (NAS Insights, 2006). "With the ever growing diverse population, the word 'minority' may no longer have meaning to this and future generations . . . Working and interacting with people outside of their own ethnic group is the norm, and acceptable" (NAS Insights, 2006).

Secondary Dimensions of Diversity

A secondary dimension is a characteristic a person acquires as the result of a choice he or she made or a choice someone else made for him or her (Loden, 2009). Nearly all of the secondary dimensions' characteristics contribute to the micro level demographic data. The secondary dimensions of diversity include, but are not limited to,

1. Communication style
2. Education
3. Family status
4. Military experience
5. Organizational role and level
6. Religion
7. First language
8. Geographic location
9. Income
10. Work experience
11. Work style
12. Others

Both primary and secondary dimensions of diversity influence the personal and professional lives of law enforcement personnel. Police officers need to be cognizant of these dimensions with their coworkers, and leaders with their subordinates. Tensions between supervisors and coworkers are often caused by the differences in secondary dimensions. Similarly, a police officer's ability to establish rapport with citizens can also be related to either the actual or the perceived degree to which dimensions are shared.

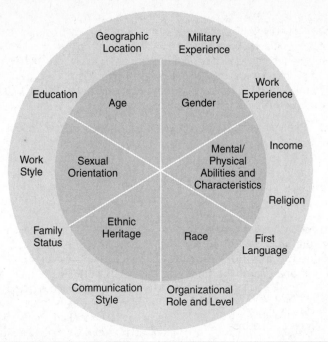

EXHIBIT 1.9   Dimensions of Diversity

Models such as the diversity wheel, designed by Loden Associates, facilitate understanding of a broad range of primary and secondary dimensions of diversity.

Source: Loden, 1996, *Implementing Diversity*, p. 16. Reproduced with Permission of Marilyn Loden.

Exhibit 1.9 shows how the primary and secondary dimensions of diversity influence people in the workforce and society. "While each dimension adds a layer of complexity, it is the dynamic interaction among all the dimensions of diversity that influences one's self-image, values, opportunities, and expectations. Together, the primary and secondary dimensions give definition and meaning to our lives by contributing to a synergistic, integrated whole—the diverse person" (Loden, 2009).

PREJUDICE IN LAW ENFORCEMENT

The following questions were asked of police officers participating in a cultural diversity program:

> "Raise your hand if you are a racist." Not a single officer raised a hand.
>
> "Raise your hand if you think that prejudice and racism exist outside this agency." Most officers raised their hands.
>
> The instructor then asked with humor: "From where were you recruited?" (Berry, 2009).

When discussing the implications of multicultural diversity for police officers, it is not enough simply to present the need to understand cultural background. Whenever two groups are from entirely different ethnic or racial backgrounds, there is the possibility that prejudice exists because of fear, lack of contact, ignorance, and stereotypes. To deny the existence of prejudice or racism in any given law enforcement agency would be to deny that it exists outside the agency.

To stereotype   To believe or feel that people conform to a pattern or manner with all other individual members of that group, lacking any individuality. People who are prone to stereotyping often categorize the behavior of an entire group based on limited experience with a very small number of people in that group. Negative stereotyping classifies many people in a group by the use of slurs, innuendoes, names, or slang expressions that depreciate the group as a whole as well as individuals in it.

To scapegoat   To blame one's failures and shortcomings on innocent people or those only partly responsible.

The movie *Crash* is an action-packed drama on film illustrating racial prejudice and discrimination. Read the following questions, and then the description and analysis of the film.

a. If you have seen the film *Crash* or have the opportunity to do so, discuss the following with your fellow officers or students:

   Which character(s), if any, surprised you? If applicable, what about the characters misled you?

   Discuss the two police officers involved—the one who appeared very open and accepting of diversity, and John. To be effective officers, what do they need to understand about themselves?

b. What interracial or interethnic dynamics, if any, have you observed or heard about in your jurisdiction or in the city in which you reside?

c. How is it of value to police officers to understand the phenomena of scapegoating and stereotyping in their line of duty?

d. What real-life examples, if any, are you aware of in your department or the city in which you reside that involve inaccurate perceptions and stereotypes leading to mistaken judgment? This question also extends to answers that relate to citizens' misperceptions of police officers.

Crash—Stereotypes and Scapegoating

Crash, winner of the Oscar for Best Picture in 2006, powerfully depicts a contemporary, metropolitan racial environment. Through a complex interweaving of storylines, *Crash* illustrates the tragic effects of racial prejudice and discrimination. The diverse cast of characters portrays the multifaceted relations between and within various races; some are victims, others are blatant perpetrators, and others seemingly champion racial equality, while harboring hidden racist attitudes themselves. This film cleverly examines and explores the interplay of perceptions of the "other" and the tendency to scapegoat as a means of displacing one's own anger. These two tendencies underlie racial prejudice, *the* dominant theme of *Crash*.

Jean Cabot is the rich, white wife of a Los Angeles Deputy Attorney, whose racial prejudices deepen after she is carjacked at gunpoint by two young black men. Shortly thereafter, she reveals racial stereotypes toward a Mexican locksmith, and takes out her frustration from the carjacking incident on her Hispanic maid. John Ryan, a white police officer with the LAPD, unabashedly displays racial prejudice. After unjustly pulling over the vehicle of a black couple, he verbally belittles them and molests the wife. On another occasion, the film reveals a frustrated, helpless side to John's character when he deals with his ailing father, whose career was ruined because of the implementation of affirmative action policies.

John's anger over his father's unemployment and his powerlessness in dealing with his father's medical condition prompt him to spout racial epithets at a black HMO employee who had nothing to do with his father's situation. In his diatribe directed at Shaniqua Johnson, the HMO employee, he declares that he cannot look at her

". . . without thinking about the five or six more qualified white men who didn't get [her] job" and that someone like her who "may have been given a helping hand might have a little compassion for someone in a similar situation." Without knowing Shaniqua's educational background or vocational experience, John instantaneously labels her as uneducated and dependent. He is judging the "other"—a member of a group to which he does not belong—based on stereotypes. He also scapegoats her (i.e., blames her, takes out his anger on her) as a means of displacing his own frustration.

After being carjacked at gunpoint, Jean Cabot displaces her anger and fear on Daniel Ruiz, the Mexican locksmith. She refers to him as "the guy in there with the shaved head, the pants around his ass, the prison tattoos," who will sell the keys to his fellow gang members. In the immediate period following the carjacking, Jean demonstrates increased racial prejudice. Even though the carjackers were black, she takes out her frustration by insulting Mexicans, and in doing so, reduces minority groups as lower status and dangerous. Daniel, the Mexican locksmith, proceeds to go home to his family and comfort his frightened daughter, completely disproving the stereotype with which he was associated. Jean lacks the knowledge of who he is as an individual, and thus oversimplifies what it means to be Mexican. The following morning, after criticizing her Hispanic maid for not putting the dishes away in a timely fashion, she realizes that her anger "had nothing to do with [her] car being stolen . . . I wake up like this every morning"; she realizes her frustration stems from the unsatisfying life she leads.

Jean's tendency to stereotype and scapegoat the "other" is the basis of her racially prejudiced behavior. Throughout the film, we see individuals making split-second judgments about other people, based not on *who* the people are, but rather on oversimplified and inaccurate views. In reality, this happens on a daily basis, often including mutually inaccurate characterizations of both police officers and minority group members.

Source: Lipsett, 2009, Adapted with Permission.

What Is Prejudice?

Prejudice is a judgment or opinion formed before facts are known, usually involving negative or unfavorable thoughts about groups of people. Discrimination is action based on prejudiced thought. It is not possible to force people to abandon their own prejudices in the law enforcement workplace or when working in the community. Because prejudice is thought, it is private and does not violate any law. However, because it is private, a person may not be aware when his or her judgments and decisions are based on prejudice. In law enforcement, the expression of prejudice as bias, discrimination, and racism is illegal and can have tragic consequences. All police must consider the implications of prejudice in their day-to-day work as it relates to equal enforcement and professionalism.

It is not uncommon in diversity or cross-cultural workshops for officers to hear sentiments such as the following: "We've already had this training on prejudice. Why do we need to go over it again and again?"

As with other training areas in law enforcement, such as self-defense tactics, the area of prejudice needs to be reviewed on a regular basis. (It's like working out at the gym; doing it once is not enough to keep a person in shape.) A person has only to read the headlines periodically to see that the problem of prejudice and racism in law enforcement is not yet solved. Although police chiefs cannot mandate that their officers banish prejudicial thoughts, this subject should be dealt with seriously. While some police officers say they have every right to believe what they want, the chiefs of all departments must be able to guarantee, with as much certainty as possible, that no officer will ever act on his or her prejudices. All officers must understand where the line is between prejudice and discrimination, whether in the law enforcement agency with coworkers or with citizens. It becomes eminently clear that prejudice in the law enforcement agency must be addressed before it turns into racism and discrimination. Indeed, an agency cannot be expected to treat its multicultural population fairly if people within the agency are likely to act on their prejudiced thoughts.

How Prejudice Influences People

Prejudice is encouraged by stereotyping, which is a shorthand way of thinking about people who are different. The stereotypes that form the basis of a person's prejudice can be so fixed that he or she easily justifies his or her racism, sexism, or other bias and even makes such claims as "I'm not prejudiced, but let me tell you about those————I had to deal with today." Coffey, Eldefonson, and Hartinger (1982) discuss the relationship between selective memory and prejudice:

> A prejudiced person will almost certainly claim to have sufficient cause for his or her views, telling of bitter experiences with refugees, Koreans, Catholics, Jews, Blacks, Mexicans and Puerto Ricans, or Indians. But in most cases, it is evident that these "facts" are both scanty and strained. Such a person typically resorts to a selective sorting of his or her own memories, mixes them up with hearsay, and then overgeneralizes. No one can possibly know all refugees, Koreans, Catholics, and so on. (Coffey et al., 1982)

Indeed, individuals may be so convinced of the truths of their stereotypes that they claim to be experts on "those people." One of the most dangerous types of prejudice can be subconscious. Subconscious prejudice (sometimes called "character-conditioned prejudice") usually runs deep; the person with this character deficiency may hold hostile attitudes toward many ethnic groups, not just one or two. People who tend to mistreat or oppress others because of their prejudices often were mistreated themselves, and this experience can leave them extremely distrustful of all others. In addition, people who have strong prejudices can be insecure and frustrated because of their own failures. Consequently, they blame or scapegoat others. They have a great deal of stored-up anger that often began to build in childhood because of dysfunctional relationships with their parents. Quite often people in racial supremacist organizations fit the description of the extremely prejudiced person for whom mistrust and hate of all others is a way of life.

Another type of prejudice is acquired during "normal" socialization. This type of prejudice results when a person belongs to a group that holds negative views of other specific groups (e.g., southern whites and blacks, Arabs and Jews, Chinese and Japanese, Puerto Ricans and Mexicans). When there is a pattern of prejudice within a particular group, the "normal" person is the one who conforms to the prejudice. From childhood, parents pass on stereotypes of the out-group into the child's mind because of their "normal" prejudices. By adulthood, the person who has learned prejudice against a particular group can justify the prejudice with rationalizations (Coffey et al., 1982).

However, not everyone in a given group holds prejudices common among the rest of the members of the group. According to Coffey and his colleagues, some people are more susceptible than others to learned (or culture-conditioned) prejudice. Those more likely to be prejudiced include (1) older people, (2) less educated people, (3) farmers and unskilled or semiskilled workers, (4) residents of rural areas or small towns, (5) people uninterested in civic affairs, and (6) people of low socioeconomic status.

Police Prejudice

Ondra Berry's diversity training for law enforcement repeatedly conveyed this message to officers: if you are normal, you have cultural blind spots that will give you an unbalanced view of people who are different from you. Officers must look at themselves first before getting into situations in which they act upon their biases (Berry, 2009).

Police prejudice received a great deal of attention in the latter half of the 1990s—so much so that it was addressed as a topic of concern in the President's Initiative on Race ("One America," 1998):

> Racial disparities and prejudices affect the way in which minorities are treated by the criminal system. Examples of this phenomenon can be found in the use of racial profiling in law enforcement and in the differences in the rates of arrest, conviction, and sentencing between whites and minorities and people of color. Law enforcement professionals have recognized, especially as they enter the twenty-first century, that prejudices unchecked and not acted on can result in not only citizen humiliation, lawsuits, loss of jobs, and long-term damage to police–community relations but in personal tragedy as well.

Sometimes, training can be successful in changing behavior and possibly attitudes. Consider the example of firing warning shots. Most officers have retrained themselves to refrain from this action because they have been mandated to do so. They have gone through a process of "unfreezing" normative behavior (i.e., what is customary) and have incorporated desired behavior. Thus explicit instruction and clear directives from the top can result in profound changes of police actions. Clear policies that, in no uncertain terms, condemn racist acts or forms of speech will prevent most outward demonstrations of prejudice. It is not acceptable to ask a citizen, "What are you doing here?" just because he or she is of a different background than those of a particular neighborhood. Officers pay attention to these specific and unambivalent directives coming from the top. It may be difficult to impossible to rid an officer of stereotypes, but eliminating acts of prejudice becomes the mandate of the department.

Peer Relationships and Prejudice

Expressions of prejudice in police departments may go unchallenged because of the need to conform or to fit into the group. Police officers do not make themselves popular by questioning peers or challenging their attitudes. It takes a leader to voice an objection or to avoid going along with group norms. Some studies have shown that peer behavior in groups reinforces acts of racial bias. For example, when someone in a group makes ethnic slurs, others in the group may begin to express the same hostile attitudes more freely. This behavior is particularly relevant in law enforcement agencies given the nature of the police subculture and the strong influence of peer pressure. Thus law enforcement leaders must not be ambiguous when directing their subordinates to control their expressions of prejudice, even among peers. Furthermore, according to some social scientists, the strong condemnation of any manifestations of prejudice can at times affect a person's feelings. Authorities or peers who keep prejudiced people from acting on their biases can, in the long run, weaken the prejudice itself, especially if the prejudice is not virulent. People conform and can behave differently, even if they hold the same prejudicial thoughts. Even if they are still prejudiced, they will be reticent to show it. National authorities have become much more vocal about dealing directly with racism and prejudice in law enforcement as an institution, especially in light of the quantity of allegations of racial profiling in police departments across the country.

A process of socialization takes place when top management has mandated change and a person is forced to adopt a new standard of behavior. When a mistake is made and the expression of prejudice occurs, a police department will pay the price in adverse media attention, lawsuits, citizen complaints, human relations commission's involvement, or dismissal of the chief or other management. What may have been acceptable at one time is now definitely not and may result in discipline and monetary sanctions.

When police officers are not in control of their prejudices, either in speech or in behavior, the associated negative publicity affects the reputation of all police officers. It reinforces the popular stereotype that police are racists or bigots. Yet, because of publicized instances of discrimination, officers become increasingly aware of correct and incorrect behavior toward ethnic minorities. One example of this was a police department that was besieged by the press and outraged citizens for over two years. Several police officers had exchanged racist messages on their patrol car computers, using the word *nigger* and making references to the Ku Klux Klan. The citizens of the town in which the incident took place ended up conducting an investigation of the department to assess the degree of racism in the institution. In their report, the committee members wrote that the disclosure of the racial slurs was "an embarrassment and a crushing blow" to the image and credibility of the city and the police department. In addition, citizens demanded the chief's resignation. In a cultural diversity workshop, some of the officers said they believed that the entire incident was overblown and that there was no "victim." These officers failed to understand that the use of derogatory terms alone is offensive to citizens. Officers who do not grasp the seriousness of the matter may not realize that citizens feel unprotected knowing that those entrusted with their safety and protection are capable of using such hateful language. While the language is offensive, the problem is more with the attitudes it conveys. Such incidents are extremely costly from all points of view; it may take years for a department to recover from one incident connected to an officer's prejudice or racism.

Officers need to be aware that anything they say or do with citizens of different backgrounds that even hints at prejudice automatically creates the potential for an explosive reaction. Here the experience of the minority and the non-minority do not even begin to approach each other. An officer can make an unguarded casual remark and not realize it is offensive. For example, an officer can offend a group member by saying "You people" (accentuating a we–they division) or by implying that if a member of a minority group does not fit a stereotype, he or she is exceptional (e.g., "She's Hispanic, but she works hard" or "He's African American, but very responsible").

Members of culturally diverse groups are up against the weight of history and tradition in law enforcement. Ethnic groups have not traditionally been represented in police work (especially in top management), nor have citizens of some ethnic groups had reasons to trust the police. The prejudice that might linger among officers must be battled constantly if they are to increase trust with ethnic communities. The perception of many ethnic group members is that police will treat them more roughly, question them unnecessarily, and arrest them more often than they arrest whites. Awareness of this perception is not enough, though. The next step is to try harder with ethnic groups to overcome these barriers. Officers should go out of their way to show extra respect to those citizens who least expect it. It is important to create nondefensiveness in citizens who have traditionally been the object of police prejudice and who expect rude or uncivil behavior from the officers.

Beyond eliminating the prejudice manifested in speech, police management can teach officers how to reduce or eliminate acts of bias and discrimination. A large metropolitan police department hired several human relations consultants to help assess community–police problems. The chief insisted that they ride in a police car for four weekends so that they would "appreciate the problems of law officers working in the black ghetto." Every Friday through Sunday night, the consultants rode along with the highway patrol, a unit other officers designated as the "Gestapo police." When the month ended and the chief asked what the consultants had learned, they replied, "If we were black, we would hate the police." The chief, somewhat bewildered, asked why. "Because we have personally witnessed black citizens experiencing a series of unjust, unwarranted intimidations, searches, and series of harassments by unprofessional police." Fortunately, that chief, to his credit, accepted the feedback and introduced a successful course in human relations skills. After this training, the officers demonstrated greater professionalism in their interactions with members of the black community.

When it comes to expressions of prejudice, people are not powerless. No one has to accept sweeping stereotypes (e.g., "You can't trust an Indian," "All whites are racists," "Chinese are shifty," and so on). To eliminate manifestations of prejudice, people have to begin to interrupt biased and discriminatory behavior at all levels. Officers have to be willing to remind their peers that ethnic slurs and offensive language, as well as differential treatment of certain groups of people, is neither ethical nor professional. Officers need to change the aspect of police culture that discourages speaking out against acts or speech motivated by prejudice. An officer or a civilian employee who does nothing in the presence of racist or other discriminatory behavior by his or her peers becomes a silent accomplice.

Eight Tips for Improving Law Enforcement in Multicultural Communities*

- Make positive contact with community group members from diverse backgrounds. Don't let them see you only when something negative has happened. Allow the public to see you as much as possible in a nonenforcement role,
- Make a conscious effort in your mind, en route to every situation, to treat all people objectively and fairly.
- Remember that all groups have some bad, some average, and some good people within them.
- Go out of your way to be personable and friendly with minority group members. Remember, many don't expect it.
- Don't appear uncomfortable with or avoid discussing racial and ethnic issues with other officers and citizens.

- Take responsibility for patiently educating citizens and the public about the role of the officer and about standard operating procedures in law enforcement. Remember that citizens often do not understand "police culture."
- Don't be afraid to be a change agent in your organization when it comes to improving cross-cultural and interracial relations within your department and between police and community. It may not be a popular thing to do, but it is the right thing to do.
- Remember the history of law enforcement with all groups and ask yourself the question, "Am I part of the past, or a part of the future?"

---

*Tips and quotes are from Ondra Berry, retired Assistant Chief of Reno Police Department, 2009.

Summary

- A diverse society contributes to the challenges of a law enforcement officer's job. Although our nation has been enriched by diversity, many police procedures and interactions with citizens can become more complex because of it. Racial tensions and communication challenges with immigrants are bound to complicate some police encounters. Officers have to work harder at building trust with certain communities. As individuals, officers need to increase their own cultural competence; as a profession, law enforcement needs to ensure that agencies promote the ideal of officer effectiveness across all backgrounds and equitable principals, policies, and structure throughout police organizations.

• Multiculturalism has been a way of life in this country since its founding; U.S. society has never been homogeneous. Until fairly recently, America has been referred to as a melting pot, a term depicting an image of people coming together and forming a unified culture. However, the melting pot did not really ever exist. The first generation of every immigrant and refugee group in the United States has always experienced obstacles to acculturation into the new society. History does not support the metaphor of the melting pot, especially with regard to the first and second generations of most groups of newcomers. The terms *mosaic* and *tapestry* more accurately portray diversity in America. They describe a society in which people of all colors and backgrounds contribute to form society as a whole—and one in which groups are not required to lose their characteristics in order to "melt" together. The idea of a mosaic portrays a society in which each group is seen as separate and distinct in contributing its own color, shape, and design to the whole, resulting in an enriched society.

• The face of America has been changing for some time. Minorities constitute one-third of the U.S. population, and are expected to become the majority by 2042. By 2050, minorities are expected to reach 54 percent of the population. U.S. Census information released in 2008 indicated that approximately 1 in every 10 counties across the United States was already a "majority-minority" county; this meant that the percentage of minority residents in these counties had exceeded 50 percent.

• New immigrants can present challenges for law enforcement officers. Immigrants must learn a great deal about U.S. laws, the law enforcement system in general, and the role of police officers. Many immigrants fear law enforcement because police in their native countries engaged in arbitrary acts of brutality in support of repressive governments. In some other countries, citizens disrespect police officers because officers are poorly educated, inefficient, and corrupt, and have a very low occupational status. The barriers immigrants bring to the relationship with police suggest that American officers have to double their efforts to communicate with and to educate new immigrants. A further challenge for law enforcement is that, for a variety of reasons, new immigrants often become victims of violent crimes. Law enforcement faces additional challenges with respect to undocumented immigrants and its own enforcement role. With the debate on immigration into the United States and transitional relationships between ICE and some law enforcement agencies going on, issues await resolution regarding the enforcement role of the police officer.

• "Culture" is defined as beliefs, values, patterns of thinking, behavior, and everyday customs that have been passed on from generation to generation. Culture is learned rather than inherited and is manifested largely in unconscious and subtle behavior. If law enforcement's function is to protect and serve citizens from all cultural backgrounds, it becomes vital to understand the cultural dimensions of crimes. Obviously, behaviors or actions that may be excused in another culture must not go unpunished if they are considered crimes in this country. Nevertheless, there are circumstances in which law enforcement officials at all levels of the criminal justice system would benefit by understanding the cultural context in which a crime or other incident occurred. Law enforcement professionals must use standard operating procedures in response to specific situations; the majority of these procedures cannot be altered for different groups based on ethnicity. In a multicultural society, however, an officer can modify the way he or she treats a suspect, witness, or victim given the knowledge of what is considered "normal" in that person's culture. It is important for an officer to understand where "ethnocentrism" comes into play. "Ethnocentrism" is defined as an attitude of seeing and judging other cultures from the perspective of one's own culture. An ethnocentric person would say there is only one way of being "normal" and that is the way of his or her own culture. When officers suspect that an aspect of cultural background is a factor in a particular incident, they may earn the respect of—and therefore cooperation from— ethnic communities if they are willing to evaluate their arrests in lesser crimes.

• A "primary dimension of diversity" is a core characteristic with which a person is born and which remains with the individual in all stages of his or her life. People have a minimum of six primary dimensions: age, ethnicity, gender, mental/physical abilities and characteristics, race, and sexual orientation. A "secondary dimension of diversity" is a characteristic that a person acquires as the result of a choice he or she made or a choice someone else made for him or her. The secondary dimensions of diversity include, but are not limited to, communication style, education, family status, military experience, organizational role and level, religion, income, first language, geographic location, income, work experience, and work style.

• When discussing the implications of multicultural diversity for police officers, it is not enough simply to present the need to understand cultural background. Whenever two groups are from entirely different ethnic or racial backgrounds, there is the possibility that prejudice exists because of fear, lack of contact, ignorance, and stereotypes. To deny the existence of prejudice or racism in any given law enforcement agency would be to deny that it exists outside the agency. Members of the law enforcement profession have to examine their words, behaviors, and actions to evaluate whether they are conveying professionalism and respect to all people within the workplace and on the streets, regardless of their race, culture, religion, or ethnic background. All officers and civilian employees must be free of all expressions of prejudice and must recognize when stereotypes are contributing to biased judgments and potentially differential treatment of citizens.

Discussion Questions and Issues

1. *Views on the Multicultural Society.* The following viewpoints regarding our increasingly multicultural population reflect varying levels of tolerance, understanding, and acceptance. Discuss these points of view and their implications for law enforcement:
   • Diversity is acceptable if there is not too much of it, but the way things are going today, it is hard to absorb and it just may result in our destruction.
   • They are here now, and they need to do things our way.
   • To advance in our diverse society, we need to accept and respect our differences rather than maintain the myth of the melting pot.

2. *Police Work and Multiculturalism.* Describe three reasons why police officers need to show multicultural respect to their coworkers and citizens in their community. Also list three ways to demonstrate this respect and the benefits that will result.

3. *Dealing with Illegal Immigrants.* Does the police department in which you work (or in the city in which you reside) have a policy regarding

undocumented immigrants? Are officers instructed not to inquire into their status unless a crime has been committed? How do you think police officers should deal with undocumented immigrants?

4. *Mini Case Study 1.* Reread, then discuss.

   Driving under the Influence?

   a. Has this issue (kava drink and its use among Pacific Islanders) been identified as an issue or problem in your jurisdiction? If so, what has the prosecuting attorney said about dealing with these cases?

   b. What would the officer's and the police department's liability be if he released the driver and the erratic driving continued?

5. *Mini Case Study 2.* Reread, then discuss.

   A Tragic Case of Cross-Cultural Misinterpretation

   a. Do you think this case would have proceeded differently if all the authorities involved understood the cultural tradition of the medical practice ("coin rubbing") that caused the bruising? Explain your answer.

b. Discuss whether you think Southeast Asian refugees should give up this medical practice because it can be misinterpreted.

6. *Mini Case Study 3.* Reread, then discuss.

Latino Values as a Factor in Sentencing

a. Discuss whether culture should play any part in influencing the sentencing of a criminal convicted of violent crimes such as murder and rape. Was the lighter verdict in this case justified? Explain your answer.

b. According to retired Superior Court Judge Katz, culture influenced the sentencing in this case. In your opinion, if the husband involved were not Latino, would the sentence have been the same?

7. *Prejudice and Discrimination in Police Work.* In your own words, define prejudice and discrimination. Give examples of (a) discrimination in society in general, (b) discrimination against police officers, and (c) discrimination toward minorities by police officers. Discuss two strategies for each one to help eradicate the discrimination and the benefits that will result.

Website Resources

Visit these websites for additional information related to the content of Chapter 1.

The Population Reference Bureau: http://www.prb.org

The website informs people around the world about population, health, and the environment, and empowers them to use that information to advance the well-being of current and future generations. PRB analyzes complex demographic data and research to provide the most objective, accurate, and up-to-date population information in a format that is easily understood by advocates, journalists, and decision makers alike.

Vera Institute of Justice: http://www.vera.org

The Vera Institute of Justice works closely with leaders in government and civil society to improve the services people rely on for safety and justice. It creates innovative programs, studies social problems, and provides practical advice and assistance to government officials around the world. The Vera Institute has publications on many topics of interest to law enforcement.

The International Association of Chiefs of Police: http://www.theiacp.org

This comprehensive website provides a wide variety of information on police-related topics. It includes research, publications, and such topics as leadership and training. It also contains selected publications on community policing from the viewpoints of Chiefs of Police.

Urban Institute: http://www.urban.org

Urban institute conducts nonpartisan economic and social policy research. Their website includes a wide variety of information on immigration, race, ethnicity, and US cities demographics.

U.S. Census Bureau: http://www.census.gov

This website provides comprehensive information about changing demographics in the United States.

The U.S. Government's Official Web Portal: http://firstgov.gov

The official U.S. Government website connects to millions of web pages from federal government; state, local, and tribal governments; and foreign nations around the world. Most of these pages are not available on commercial websites. FirstGov offers the most comprehensive search of government data anywhere on the Internet.

References

Berry, Ondra. (2009, March). Retired Assistant Police Chief, Reno, Nevada, Police Department, personal communication.

Coffey, Alan, Edward Eldefonson, and Walter Hartinger. (1982). *Human Relations: Law Enforcement in a Changing Community*, 3rd ed. Englewood Cliffs, N.J.: Prentice-Hall.

Department of Homeland Security. (2008). Definition of Terms, http://www.dhs.gov/ximgtn/statistics/stdfdef.shtm#8.

De Santis, Marie. (2000). "Help: Special for Immigrant Women." Women's Justice Center. Retrieved April 15, 2009, from www.justicewomen.com.

Ferraro, Thomas. (2006, May 1). "Immigrants set for massive rallies." *ABC News*. Retrieved June 24, 2006, from http://abcnews.go.com/US/wireStory? id=1908521

Hall, Edward T. (1959). *The Silent Language*. Greenwich, Conn.: Fawcett.

Handlin, Oscar. (1975). *Out of Many: A Study Guide to Cultural Pluralism in the United States*. Anti-Defamation League of B'nai B'rith. Louisville, KY: Brown & Williamson Tobacco Corporation.

Katz, Lawrence. (2009, January). Retired Presiding Judge, Juvenile Court of Contra Costa (California) County, personal communication.

Kennedy, John F. (1986). *A Nation of Immigrants*. New York, NY: Harper & Row, p. 14.

NAS Insights. (2006). "Generation Y: The Millenials. Ready or Not, Here They Come." NAS Recruitment Communications. Retrieved February 14, 2009, from http://www.nasrecruitment.com/talenttips/NASinsights/GenerationY.pdf

"Nation's Many Faces in Extended First Family." (2009, January 20). *New York Times*. Retrieved January 30, 2009, from http://www.nytimes.com/2009/01/21/us/politics/21family.html.

Lipsett, Kara. (2009, April). Crash: A Social-Psychological Analysis of Racial Prejudice. University of British Columbia. Adapted with permission.

Loden, Marilyn. (1996). *Implementing Diversity*. New York, NY: McGraw-Hill.

Loden, Marilyn. (2009, May). Organizational Diversity Consultant with Loden Associates, Inc., personal communication.

"Many Officials Reluctant to Help Arrest Immigrants." (2008, August 23). *The Washington Post*, p. B01.

Martinez, Christopher. (2009, March). Program Director for Refugee & Immigrant Services, Catholic Charities CYO, San Francisco, Calif., personal communication.

Miller, Char. (2008, February). (Former) Professor of history, Trinity College, San Antonio, Tex, personal communication.

"Multiracial Data in Census Adds Categories and Controversies." (2000, December 10). *San Francisco Chronicle*, p. A-14.

Obama, Barak. (2008, March 18). A More Perfect Union—"The Race Speech," Philadelphia, Pa.

"Officers Being Trained in Ethnic Understanding." (2000, November 29). *San Jose Mercury News*, p. A3.

Olson, Aaron T. (2009). Workshops for Immigrants and Refugees on USA Police, Laws, and Emergency Services. Organization and Training Services. Retrieved June 23, 2006, from http://www.pcc.edu/staff/index.cfm/174,2200,30.html

"One America in the 21st Century: Forging a New Future," Executive Summary, Advisory Board to the President's Initiative on Race, September 1998.

Orloff, Leslye. (2003, February 27). Testifying as the director of the Immigrant Women Program, NOW Legal Defense and Education Fund, before the Subcommittee on Immigration, Border Security, and Claims House Judiciary Committee.

Owen, James. (2005). "With 20 Official Languages, Is EU Lost in Translation?" *National Geographic News*, February 22, 2005. Retrieved June 23, 2006, from http://news.nationalgeographic.com/news/2005/02/0222_050222_translation.html.

Population Reference Bureau. (2005). 2005 World Population Data Sheet. Retrieved June 23, 2006, from http://www.prb.org/pdf05/05WorldDataSheet_Eng.pdf

Prewitt, Kenneth. (2001, Fall). "Beyond Census 2000: As a Nation, We Are the World." *The Carnegie Reporter*, 1(3), 1.

Rawlins, Gary H. (1992, October 8). "Africans Came 200 Years Earlier." *USA Today*, p. 2a.

"The Changing Face of Race in America." (2000, September 18). *Newsweek*, p. 38.

"Report Questions Immigration Program." (2009, March). *New York Times*, U.S. Section. Retrieved May 27, 2009, from http://www.nytimes.com/2009/03/04/us/04immigrants.html?_r=1

Ruhly, Sharon. (1976). *Orientations to Intercultural Communication: Modules in Speech Communication*. Chicago, Ill.: Science Research Associates.

Sherman, Spencer. (1986). "When Cultures Collide." *California Lawyer*, 6(1), 33.

Tiede, Lydia Brashear. (2001). "Battered Immigrant Women and Immigration Remedies: Are the Standards too high?" *Human Rights Magazine*. Section Individual Rights and Responsibilities, American Bar Association, Winter 2001; Vol. 28, No. 1. (Excerpted with permission June, 2009)

Urban Institute. (2002). Share of Undocumented Foreign-Born Population, by State, 2000. Retrieved March 17, 2009, from http://www.urban.org/publications/1000587.html.

U.S. Census Bureau, State and Country Quick Facts: Foreign-Born Persons. (2000). Retrieved February 15, 2009, from http://quickfacts.census.gov/qfd/meta/.S. Census Bureau. (2006, February). Population Division.

U.S. Census Bureau. (2007). Percent of People Who Are Foreign Born, American Community Survey.

U.S. Census Bureau. (2008). "2008 National Population Projections."

U.S. Census Bureau News. (2008a, August 14). "An Older and More Diverse Nation by Midcentury."

U.S. Census Bureau News. (2008b, August 7). "La Paz, Ariz., Population Is Nation's Oldest County." Retrieved May 3, 2009, from http://www.census.gov/Press-Release/www/releases/archives/population/012463.html.

U.S. Citizenship and Immigration Services. (2007, September 5). Fact Sheet; USCIS Publishes Rule for Nonimmigrant Victims of Criminal Activity, Office of Communications.

U.S. Citizenship and Immigration Services. (2009). Information Resources and Immigration Services, Data Integration Division, U.S. Census Bureau, http://www.uscis.gov/portal/site/uscis.

U.S. Immigration and Customs Enforcement. (2008). The ICE 287(g) Program: A Law Enforcement Partnership.

U.S. Immigration and Customs Enforcement. (2009, May). State Local Coordination. Retrieved May 27, 2009, from http://www.ice.gov/pi/news/factsheets/section287_g.htm.

"The Year in Hate." (2009, spring). Special Issue of *Intelligence Report*, Issue 133. Southern Poverty Law Center, Montgomery, Ala.

Zangwill, Israel. (1908). *The Melting Pot: Drama in Four Acts*. New York, NY: Macmillan.

CHAPTER 2

The Changing Law Enforcement Agency: A Microcosm of Society

LEARNING OBJECTIVES

After reading this chapter you should be able to:

- Identify how the ethnic, racial, and gender composition of law enforcement agencies is changing in the United States.

- Define racism and understand the steps organizational managers and supervisors can take to identify and control prejudicial conduct by employees.

- Describe methods for defusing conflicts within the organization and community related to issues of gender, sexual orientation, race, and ethnicity.

- Explain the history of women in law enforcement, the issues confronting them, and how support and mentoring programs help them make transitions into the workplace.

- Define the terms lesbian, gay, bisexual, and transgender and the meaning of the acronym or initials LGBT.

- Relate how chief executives of law enforcement agencies must establish clear policies stating that discrimination or harassment of LGBT or any other individual is unacceptable and will result in corrective action, if not severe disciplinary action.

- Explain the role of the chief executive in providing a workplace environment that is comfortable for all employees, especially for women and the individuals from diverse backgrounds.

OUTLINE

- Introduction
- Changing Workforce
- Racism within the Law Enforcement Workforce
- Women in Law Enforcement
- Gay Men and Lesbians in Law Enforcement
- The Chief Executive
- Summary

- **Discussion Questions and Issues**
- **Website Resources**

INTRODUCTION

In Chapter 1, we reviewed the evolution of multicultural communities and the demographic changes that the United States has experienced in recent decades. The most notable demographic changes mentioned involve the increases in racial, ethnic, and immigrant populations in our country. Diversity is becoming so commonplace in communities that terms such as *majority group* and *minority group* have been questioned for some time. There is often a negative reaction to the term *minority*, which critics find not just outmoded but offensive. The word carries overtones of inferiority and inequity. The word, technically, is used to describe numerical designations, but over the years it has come to have much larger implications. While in this book we continue to use the term in some contexts, we also want to remind the reader of the controversy around the term.

The range of reactions to these changes in society as a whole is no different from the reactions within law enforcement agencies. Members of police communities across the country have demonstrated both tolerance of and resistance to the changing society and workforce. Some officers dislike the multicultural workforce and the involvement of women in policing, although the latter is becoming a nonissue. They may resent diversity because of their own prejudices or biases. This resentment is due in part to perceived or actual advantages others receive when competing for law enforcement positions, either entry level or promotional. In addition, because of inept affirmative action hiring in the past (i.e., management rushed to fill quotas but did not focus on competence), some officers perceive that affirmative action (where still being used) means lowering standards. Indeed, where standards have been lowered, everyone suffers, especially the less-qualified employees hired because of affirmative action. (This issue is discussed further in Chapter 3.)

Leading positively and valuing the diversity within an agency are the keys to meeting the challenge of policing multicultural communities. As discussed in Chapter 1, racial and ethnic tensions still exist in the law enforcement community. Agency personnel must address the conflicts in their own organizations before dealing with racial, ethnic, or sexual orientation issues in the community. For example, if there are allegations of harassment, a hostile work environment, or differential treatment within the agency, these allegations must be addressed on a timely basis, or they fester and result in lawsuits, court injunctions, and unhappy employees who do not remain with the organization.

Law enforcement agencies themselves determine, by their action or inaction, whether social problems that manifest within the agencies are resolved. Across the United States, the national press has reported numerous cases in which law enforcement agencies did nothing or took the wrong action. Whether they like it or not, police officers are primary role models for citizens and are judged by a higher standard of behavior than are others. While supervision of police officers is important to ensure that this higher standard of behavior is maintained, no amount of supervision of officers working with the public, no matter how thorough and conscientious, will prevent some officers from violating policies; there simply are too many police officers and too few supervisors. Thus, it is important that police officers demonstrate integrity and a stable set of core virtues. These virtues must include the ability to remain professional in protecting and serving a diverse public.

As stated in Chapter 1, those concerned with peacekeeping and enforcement must accept the realities of a diverse society as well as the heterogeneity within their workforce. The irony is that the peacekeepers sworn to uphold laws pertaining to acts of bias sometimes themselves become perpetrators, even against their peers. If police departments are to be representative of the populations served, police executives must effect changes. These changes have to do with the treatment of peers as well as recruitment, selection, and promotion of employees who have traditionally been underrepresented in law enforcement. The argument (Chapter 1) that the United States has never really been a melting pot applies also to the law enforcement community. In some cases, relationships within the law enforcement workplace, especially as diversity increases, are characterized by disrespect and tension. Although many in the police subculture would argue that membership implies brotherhood or familial relationship (and therefore belonging), this membership has traditionally excluded certain groups in both subtle and obvious ways.

CHANGING WORKFORCE

As microcosms of their communities, law enforcement agencies increasingly include among their personnel more women, members of ethnic and racial minorities, and gay males and lesbians. Although such groups are far from achieving parity in most law enforcement agencies in the United States, advances have been made. Exhibit 2.1 shows the percentages of women and minorities in the U.S. labor force for 1995 and 2005, and makes predictions for the year 2020.

This profound shift in demographics has resulted in notable changes in law enforcement. In many regions of the country, today's law enforcement workforce differs greatly from the workforce of the past. For one example, the Hispanic population is growing at such a rate that it is difficult for public sector agencies, especially law enforcement, to achieve parity. It is also difficult to keep up with the organizational change required not only to provide police services, but also to recruit and retain personnel from this subset of the population. For a law enforcement agency to maintain the support and trust of any community, it is essential that the organization reflect the diversity of the area it serves. In communities across the nation, officers come into contact with persons from different cultural or ethnic backgrounds, socioeconomic classes, religions, and sexual orientations on a daily basis. Each of these groups brings a different perspective to police–community relations. As a result, sworn and nonsworn law enforcement personnel must be prepared to respond to each group in the appropriate fashion. Frustration and resentment often result among citizens when their law enforcement agency fails to recognize and adjust to the diversity in the community. Such a failure can lead to the breakdown of the important, and often critical, bond of trust between them.

Law Enforcement Diversity: A Microcosm of Society

As of September 2004, state and local law enforcement agencies across the country employed more than 1 million full-time sworn personnel. "From 1987 to 2003 minority representation among local police officers increased from 14.6 percent to 23.6 percent. In sheriffs' offices,

EXHIBIT 2.1 Percentage of Women and Minorities in U.S. Labor Force, 1995, 2005, 2020

	1995	2005	2020
Whites, Non-Hispanic	76%	73%	68%
Women	46%	48%	50%
Hispanic	9%	11%	14%
African American	11%	11%	11%
Asian American	4%	5%	6%

Source: "Workforce 2020," Hudson Institute, 2005.

minorities accounted for 18.8 percent of sworn personnel in 2003 compared to 13.4 percent in 1987" ("Local Police Departments and Sheriffs' Offices 2003," 2006).

As of 2004, federal agencies employed about 106,354 full-time personnel authorized to make arrests and carry firearms (excluding officers in foreign countries). "Of all federal officers, 16.1 percent were women and 33.2 percent a racial or ethnic minority. This included 17.7 percent who were Hispanic or Latino, and 11.4 percent who were black or African American" ("Federal Law Enforcement Officers, 2004," 2006).

With increases in minorities came a corresponding reduction in the number of white officers and deputies in law enforcement workforces. Exhibits 2.2 and 2.3 provide more details on the percentages of women and ethnic and racial groups in local police and sheriffs' departments between 1987 and 2003.

Some major law enforcement agencies have achieved parity in terms of the percentage of diverse groups in their workforce compared to the percentage in the community; most have not, but the numbers are improving. In local police departments and sheriffs' offices, from 2000 to 2003, the proportion of

- Black or African American police officers increased by 3 percent; black or African American deputies increased by 13 percent.
- Hispanic or Latino police officers increased by 13 percent; Hispanic or Latino deputies increased by 20 percent.
- Officers and deputies from other minority groups increased by 7 percent.
- Women police officers and deputies increased from 10.6 percent to 11.3 percent.

When looking at minority female representation in U.S. law enforcement, the percentages were much lower with

- 2.7 percent African American female officers; 2.6 percent deputies.
- 1.3 percent Latina female police officers; 0.9 percent deputies.
- 0.3 percent "other" (Asian, Native Hawaiian, American Indian, and Alaska Natives) women officers in local police departments; 0.2 percent deputies.

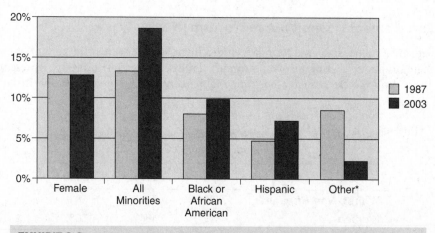

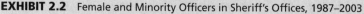

EXHIBIT 2.2 Female and Minority Officers in Sheriff's Offices, 1987–2003

Source: "Sheriffs' Offices 2003," U.S. Department of Justice, May 2006, BJS 211361.

*Includes Asians, Native Hawaiians and other Pacific Islanders, American Indians, Alaska Natives, and any other racial or ethnic minority.

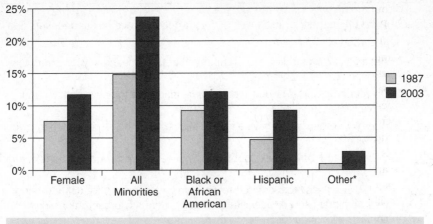

EXHIBIT 2.3 Female and Minority Local Police Officers, 1987–2003

Source: Local Police Departments 2003, U.S. Department of Justice, May 2006, BJS 210118.

*Includes Asians, Native Hawaiians and other Pacific Islanders, American Indians, Alaska Natives, and any other racial or ethnic minority.

Measuring Responsiveness to Diversity

A manual produced by the Canadian Association of Chiefs of Police includes a 10-question checklist and scoring method for law enforcement organizations to determine how responsive they are in adapting to diversity. It is reproduced here (Exhibit 2.4) for use in rating your own agency.

RACISM WITHIN THE LAW ENFORCEMENT WORKFORCE

There are three major types of racism: personally mediated, institutional, and internalized. Personally mediated racism is what most people think of when they hear the word *racism* (Feagin, 2006). It includes specific attitudes, beliefs, practices, and behaviors involved in acts of prejudice, discrimination, bias, and stereotyping by individuals directed toward others. It is beyond the scope of this text to delve into internalized racism.

Racism   Total rejection of others by reason of race, color, or, sometimes more broadly, culture.

Institutional Racism   The failure of an organization (public or private) to provide goods, services, or opportunities to people because of their color, culture, ethnic origin.

Discrimination   Treatment or consideration based on class or category rather than on individual merit; differential and/or unfair treatment of individuals on the basis of race.

Prejudice   A judgment or opinion formed before facts are known, usually involving negative or unfavorable thoughts about groups of people.

Bias   Preference or an inclination to make certain choices that may be positive (bias toward excellence) or negative (bias against people), often resulting in unfairness. "Bias" encompasses what most people think of as "stereotypes" and "prejudice."

Circle and count the number of initiatives that your police service has undertaken. See how you rate.

_____ 1. Are members of ethnic/cultural communities participating in your community and crimeprevention programs?

_____ 2. Do your programs provide for community input into the development and implementation of local policing programs?

_____ 3. Does your organization have a race relations policy that is integrated into your overall mission?

_____ 4. Do your patrol officers use foot patrols in areas of high concentrations of ethnic minorities?

_____ 5. Do you use translators or interpreters from within your police department or from local immigrant service agencies or ethnic community organizations in your contacts with linguistic minorities?

_____ 6. Are your ads and brochures multilingual, and do they depict a multicultural community?

_____ 7. Do you have a recruitment campaign that actively targets ethnic and visible minorities?

_____ 8. Have your hiring and promotional practices been evaluated to see if they recognize and value knowledge and skills related to community policing, especially with ethnic/cultural communities?

_____ 9. Have your in-service training programs dealt with the issue of diversity?

_____ 10. Have your officers participated in multicultural or race relations training programs for trainers?

Scoring

0–3   Don't panic. The fact that you did the checklist shows that you are interested. Start small, but start today!

4–6   Good start. You are part of a community-based policing movement. You are beginning to tackle some of the issues that face police services in a multicultural environment.

7–9   Well done. It is obvious that you understand and value the benefits of ethnoculturally sensitive and community-based policing. You're on the right track; keep up the good work!

10   Congratulations. Your challenge is to maintain the momentum and evaluate the effectiveness of your initiatives.

EXHIBIT 2.4   How Responsive Is Your Organization?

Source: "Police Race Relations: Raising Your Effectiveness in Today's Diverse Neighborhoods through Community Policing," Canadian Association of Chiefs of Police, 1992.

Racism involves the underlying assumption that one race, almost always the white race, is superior to all others. _Racist_ is the term applied to those who subscribe to this belief. Examples of racism are found not only in the words and actions of white supremacist groups, however, but also, unfortunately, in the words and actions of members of society who are not part of hate groups. However, often the definition of "racism" is too simplistic— a guy in a white sheet burning crosses and using the "n-word." Racism takes many forms, is often unconscious, and affects all kinds of people.

Institutional racism, or the appearance of same, can be devastating to those impacted by the practice, whether it is intentional, unintentional, or covert. One example of institutional racism could be the use of pre-employment standardized tests. There are claims that this kind of assessment can be significantly biased toward people of a certain cultural and social background, so that in much of the Western world, racial minorities tend to score lower. Unpaved roads in predominantly black neighborhoods could be seen as another example of institutionalized racism, as could the presence of older-edition, used textbooks in predominantly black schools.

Racism within law enforcement agencies, which can be personally mediated or institutional, has been documented for decades. An African American history display at the New York Police Academy, observed by one of the authors, contains the following written account of the experiences of one of the first black officers in the New York Police Department:

> Seven years before the adoption of the charter creating New York City, Brooklyn, then an independent city, hired the first black policeman. Wiley G. Overton was sworn in on March 6, 1891. . . . His first tour of duty was spent in civilian clothing because fellow officers breaking with tradition refused to furnish him with a temporary uniform. . . . Officers in his section refused to sleep in the same room with him. . . . The officers in the precinct ignored him and spoke only if it was necessary in the line of duty.

The New York Police Department is not alone. Racism can occur in police departments regardless of size or region. Unfortunately, racism has been an issue for decades.

The authors, over the years of producing this textbook, have spoken with officers from different states about racism in their departments. Those interviewed requested that their names not be included, because they felt they might face repercussions. One African American officer recalled almost coming to blows with a white officer who used a racial slur against him; the use of such slurs was commonplace for the white officer and his friends. A Cuban American officer recounted the story of a nonresistant Latino suspect who was caught in the commission of a minor crime and beaten by the white arresting officers, who used racial epithets. One major city in Massachusetts suspended a deputy superintendent of police for using the word "nigger" directed toward one of his own officers. An African American officer in a large city in Florida was fired after using racial epithets against other blacks in violation of a strict citywide policy. In this particular case, the African American officer's conduct was reported by another officer at the scene. In yet another city, an African American officer was overheard telling a white prisoner, "Wait until you get to central booking and the niggers get hold of you."

Institutional or personally mediated racism and discrimination is combated by using federal law. Under Title VII of the Civil Rights Act of 1964, the Americans with Disabilities Act, and the Age Discrimination in Employment Act, it is illegal to discriminate in any aspect of the hiring process or in employment. The three Acts applied to state and local governments the provisions of federal laws concerning discriminatory practices. These practices include harassment on the basis of race, color, religion, sex, national origin, disability, or age (called "protected classes"). Note that sexual orientation is not included as of 2009. A U.S. government agency, the Equal Employment Opportunity Commission (EEOC), investigates, litigates, and resolves complaints and allegations of discrimination, including charges of retaliation. Retaliation refers to measures taken by an employer against an employee or former employee for participation in some type of protected conduct (usually opposing perceived discriminatory practices or filing a discrimination charge). The U.S. Supreme Court ruled recently that workers who cooperate with their employers' internal investigations of discrimination may not be fired in retaliation for implicating colleagues or superiors ("Court rules on worker retaliation," 2009, p. A13).

Title VII also prohibits employment decisions based on stereotypes and assumptions about abilities, traits, or the performance of individuals of certain racial and ethnic groups. Also prohibited are both intentional discrimination and neutral job policies that disproportionately exclude minorities and that are not job-related. The EEOC receives complaints from both the private and the public sector. In fiscal year 2008, the number of charges, number resolved, and monetary benefits received by charging parties and other aggrieved individuals were:

- *Race discrimination:* 33,937 charges; resolved 28,321; $79.3 million
- *Religion-based discrimination:* 3,273 charges; resolved 2,727; $7.5 million
- *National origin–based discrimination:* 9,396 charges; resolved 8,498; $25.4 million

The numbers in almost all categories represent an increase over previous years ("EEOC Enforcement Statistics and Litigation," 2009). Chief executives, managers, supervisors, and employees should recognize from these figures the importance of defusing and controlling institutional or personally mediated racism and discrimination in the workplace.

Defusing Racially and Culturally Rooted Conflicts

To defuse racist attitudes, behaviors, and/or practices in any organization (public or private) or school, the organization must be upfront and proactive about racism. It is essential that employers and parents (or elders) get involved in any concerted effort to defeat this problem. A good place to start is to recognize that all cultures, races, ethnic groupings, and nations are susceptible to racist (or exclusionary) attitudes, practices, and behaviors. It should be understood that white people are no more—or less—inclined toward racism than are people of other races or ethnicities. This must be established before any useful dialogue, experience, or insight can take place.

Racism exists within our law enforcement organizations; police are not immune to social ills.

One of the greatest challenges for police officers is dealing with their own conscious or unconscious negative bias, stereotypes, and prejudices. No one can be forced to simply abandon long-held prejudices. However, police must recognize that in law enforcement, acting in discriminatory or racist ways is not only unprofessional, but can lead to tragic consequences.

The first step in addressing the problem is for police department personnel, on all levels, to admit, rather than deny, that racism exists. Police researcher David Shipler, after two years of interviews across the country, maintained that he encountered very few black officers who had not been "hassled by white cops." He was quick to point out, however, that not every white police officer is a bigot and not every police force a bastion of racism; in fact, some agencies have made great strides in improving race relations within their organization and the community they serve.

Shipler recommends that law enforcement should combat and defuse racism by using the U.S. Army model developed during a time of extreme racial tension in the military in the early 1970s ("Report Recommends Using Military Model," 1992). Obviously, no model of training will bring guaranteed success and alleviate all acts of prejudice and racism. However, professional groups can build on each other's attempts, especially when these efforts have been proven to be fairly successful. Shipler recognizes that police officers are not identical to soldiers, because the former have constant contact with the public (where they see the worst) and must use personal judgment in dangerous and ambiguous situations. Nevertheless, he suggests that some military approaches are adaptable to law enforcement. According to Shipler, the basic framework for combating and defusing racism in the military has been:

- *Command commitment:*   The person at the top sets the tone all the way down to the bottom. Performance reports document any bigoted or discriminatory behavior. A record of racial slurs and discriminatory acts can derail a military career.
- *Training of advisers:*   Military personnel are trained at the Defense Equal Opportunity Management Institute in Florida as equal opportunity advisers. The advisers are assigned to military units with direct access to commanders. They conduct courses locally to train all members of the unit on race relations.
- *Complaints and monitoring:*   The advisers provide one channel for specific complaints of racial and gender discrimination, but they also drop in on units unannounced and sound out the troops on their attitudes. Surveys are conducted and informal discussions are held to lessen racial tensions. ("Report Recommends Using Military Model," 1992)

Sondra Thiederman (1991) provides nine tips that will help organizational managers or leaders identify and resolve conflicts that arise because of cultural (not only racial) differences in the workplace. She states that the following guidelines are applicable no matter what cultures, races, religions, or lifestyles are involved:

1. Give each party the opportunity to voice his or her concerns without interruption.
2. Attempt to obtain agreement on what the problem is by asking questions of each party to find out specifically what is upsetting each person.
3. During this process, stay in control and keep employees on the subject of the central issue.
4. Establish whether the issue is indeed rooted in cultural differences by determining:
   a. If the parties are from different cultures or subcultures.
   b. If the key issue represents an important value in each person's culture.
   c. How each person is expected to behave in his or her culture as it pertains to this issue.
   d. If the issue is emotionally charged for one or both of the parties.
   e. If similar conflicts arise repeatedly and in different contexts.
5. Summarize the cultural (racial, religious, or lifestyle) differences that you uncover.
6. State the negative outcomes that will result if the situation is not resolved (be specific).
7. State the positive outcomes that will result if the situation is resolved (be specific).
8. Negotiate terms by allowing those involved to come up with the solutions.
9. Provide positive reinforcement as soon as the situation improves.

Thiederman's approach is based on conflict resolution and crisis intervention techniques training that many police and correctional officers receive in either their academy or in-service training. Civilians working in the criminal justice system should receive similar training. Police department command must encourage the use of conflict resolution techniques by officers of all backgrounds as a way of handling issues prior to their becoming flash points. With professionalism and patience, the use of conflict resolution techniques to reduce racial and ethnic problems will work within both the workforce and the neighborhoods.

As a result of allegations of racism against it, the Alameda, California, Police Department developed a series of general orders as one approach to remedy the problem. Violation of the department general orders (DGOs) carries progressive disciplinary ramifications up to and including termination. The general orders deal with control of prejudicial conduct based on race, religion, ethnicity, disability, sex, age, or sexual orientation and are as follows:

1. *Code of ethics:*   Commits to personal suppression of prejudice, animosities, malice, and ill will, as well as respect for the constitutional rights of all persons.
2. *DGO 80-1:*   Specifically addresses discrimination and racial remarks and requires courtesy and respect for all persons. It states: "Discrimination or racism in any form shall never be tolerated."
3. *DGO 80-2:*   Requires impartiality toward all persons and guarantees equal protection under the law. Prohibits exhibition of partiality due to race, creed, or influence.
4. *DGO 90-3:*   Deals with harassment in the workplace based on race, religion, color, national origin, ancestry, disability, marital status, sex, age, or sexual preference.

The Alameda Police Department also produced an in-service training guide listing "mortal sins" or actions not condoned, which include:

1. Racism, racial slurs, racial discrimination.
2. Sexism, offensive sexual remarks, sexual harassment, sexual discrimination.
3. Discrimination or harassment for sexual orientation.
4. Religious discrimination.

This department sent a clear message to its employees that its leaders will not tolerate discriminatory behavior. The same department adapted a San Diego Police Department attitude assessment survey instrument on perceptions regarding contact with the multicultural community and workforce. The survey instrument is reproduced in Appendix A.

Police Fraternal Organizations

Police fraternal religious and ethnic organizations offer their members social activities, fellowship, counseling, career development, resources, and networking opportunities with persons of common heritage, background, or experience. The New York Police Department, for example, has many clubs, societies, and associations to address the needs of its pluralistic organization. The Irish are represented by the Emerald Society, African Americans by the Guardians Association, Christian officers by Police Officers for Christ, those of Asian or Pacific Islander heritage (which includes Chinese, Japanese, Korean, Filipino, and Asian Indian officers) by the Asian Jade Society, Italian officers by the Columbia Association, and so on. The police subculture can be a stressful environment, so it is only natural that persons different from the majority workforce members seek emotional comfort zones with those of similar background. Membership in these groups provides emotional sanctuary from the stereotyping, hostility, indifference, ignorance, or naïveté that members encounter within their organizations and communities.

Occasionally we hear of criticism within a department or by the public that such organizations actually highlight the differences between groups of people. At a National Organization of Black Law Enforcement Executives (NOBLE) conference, a white female (nonparticipating attendee) asked the meaning of the acronym NOBLE. When given the answer, she asked: "Is it ethical for blacks to have their own organization? Could whites have an organization called the 'National Organization of White Law Enforcement Executives' without being referred to as racists? Why can't the multicultural, social, and professional organizations that already exist satisfy the needs of everyone?"

The woman's concern was brought up directly with one of the conference participants, Sergeant Thomas Hall, an African American who at the time was a Virginia state trooper. Sergeant Hall explained:

> In America, we need independent black institutions . . . to foster cultural pride, and have a place where we can go and feel comfortable. We cannot express ourselves in society. We cannot assimilate in society. We cannot even assimilate like some Hispanic groups can because of their complexions. I can't assimilate on a bus. As soon as I step on the bus, you are going to realize there is a black guy on the bus. I can't assimilate in a police organization . . . so without these black institutions, I cannot survive. We all have survival mechanisms. I have cultural needs and I have to be around people that share my needs and frustrations. I cannot do that in organizations that are predominantly white. The whites don't suffer from the racial pressures and tensions that I suffer from. So how can they [mostly white organizations] meet my interests and needs? It is impossible. (Hall, 1992)

Hall stressed that African American law enforcement organizations provide him with a network of persons with similar interests, concerns, and backgrounds.

Another nonprofit organization is the Hispanic National Law Enforcement Association (HNLEA), which was formed in 1988. According to its website, HNLEA is "involved in the administration of justice and dedicated to the advancement of Hispanic (Latino) and minority interests within the law enforcement profession." The organization is trying to increase the representation of Hispanics and other minorities in the law enforcement field, and acts as a liaison to various communities, minority officers, and law enforcement agencies.

The racial, ethnic, religious, and sexual orientation organizations within law enforcement are not meant to divide but rather to give support to groups that traditionally were not accepted in law enforcement fully and had no power within the organization. Yet the sentiment expressed by the white female who inquired into the meaning of NOBLE is not uncommon among police officers. Police command officers and supervisors must not ignore this debate (whether expressed or not). They must address the issues underlying the need for the support groups within the department. They must also foster dialogue and shared activities between all formalized groups within the organization. All officers must hear an explanation of the benefit they receive from membership in the groups of different ethnic, racial, and sexual orientation perspectives. Officers must be willing to discuss ways to guard against divisiveness, either real or perceived, within their agencies.

Assignments Based on Diversity

There has been limited research on the assumption that an increase in the proportion of any underrepresented group in a police agency would have a positive effect in the community. Some believe that an increase in Hispanic, African American, or Asian officers in a neighborhood of the same race or ethnicity would improve police–community relations. The same argument could be made regarding gay and lesbian officers. We might speculate that there would be a more sensitive response of "like folks," who are aware of needs and issues of "their kind." In fact, historically, immigrants (Irish, Italians, and Germans) were hired by police departments because they could communicate and operate more effectively than could nonimmigrant officers in neighborhoods with large concentrations of immigrants.

Although citizens appreciate having officers of their own color or national origin work their area, this deployment strategy may result in unfairness. Studies have concluded that this practice can result in a career path for minorities that may be very different from that of white officers in agencies that follow this practice (Benson, 1992). For example, instead of receiving specialized assignments in traffic, investigations, special weapons and tactics (SWAT) team, and so on, the minority officer who is working effectively in the minority community may have an extended tour of duty in that function. In addition, the area to which this officer is assigned is often a tougher, high-crime area, which means that he or she is exposed more frequently to violence.

Officers of the same background as the predominant ethnicity or race in the neighborhood do not necessarily make the best crime fighters or problem solvers there. Not all racially or ethnically diverse officers may have the skills or desire to work with their own cultural or racial group. Assignments based on diversity alone, therefore, are generally unfair and may be a disservice to both the officer and the neighborhood. Officers should not be restricted to working in specific areas based on the notion that police–community relations will improve automatically. In addition, it cannot be assumed that an officer of the same background as the citizens will always show sensitivity to their particular needs.

Ronald Hampton, a retired Washington, D.C., Metropolitan police officer and executive director of the National Black Police Officers Association since 1989, illustrated this point at a NOBLE conference when he discussed the reasons why a new African American recruit wanted to work the black areas of Washington, D.C. The recruit said that he could tell people of his own race what to do and could not always do so in predominantly white neighborhoods. Hampton noted, however, that the young recruit "called people from his neighborhood 'maggots.'" Hampton made the point that supervisors must hold subordinates accountable for their conduct, and the chief executive must make it known that inappropriate behavior will be disciplined no matter what the neighborhood (Hampton, 2009). We present this example to illustrate that some officers may have internalized the hatred society has directed toward them and consequently are not automatically the most effective officers in certain neighborhoods.

When Chief Robert Burgreen was the top executive of the San Diego Police Department, he, like many other law enforcement managers, did not deploy officers according to color, sexual orientation, or ethnicity. Deployment was based on the best fit for the neighborhood and was related to an officer's competence and capabilities. However, Chief Burgreen had four community relations sergeants, each acting as a liaison for one major group in the city: Hispanic, African American, Asian, and gays and lesbians. He described these sergeants as his "eyes and ears" for what was going on in the various communities. Some cities use cultural affairs committees to perform a similar function, made up of people from diverse groups in the community and the officers who provide them service.

WOMEN IN LAW ENFORCEMENT

Women have always been part of the general workforce in American society, although for many years in primarily traditional female employment roles, such as nurses, secretaries, schoolteachers, waitresses, and flight attendants. The first major movement of women into the general workforce occurred during World War II. With men off to war, women entered the workforce in large numbers and successfully occupied many nontraditional employment roles. A nontraditional occupation for women is defined as one in which women comprise 25 percent or less of total employment. After the War, 30 percent of all women continued working outside the home ("History of Woman in Workforce," 1991). By 2003, almost 60 percent of women in the United States worked outside the home, a 5 percent increase from 1990 ("Women in the Labor Force," 2005). Women continue to make inroads into nontraditional occupations (i.e., traditionally male-dominated occupations) such as detectives, architects, chefs, clergy, truck drivers, firefighters, aircraft pilots, and construction occupations, to name a few ("Quick Facts on Nontraditional Occupations for Women," 2006). According to the Bureau of Labor Statistics, between 1983 and 2002, in the male-dominated occupations of police detectives and supervisors, the number of female workers increased 360 percent ("Many U.S. Jobs," 2005).

Women hired as police officers during the early years were given duties that did not allow or require them to work street patrol. Assignments and roles were limited to positions such as juvenile delinquency and truancy prevention, child abuse, crimes against women, and custodial functions (Bell, 1982). In 1845, New York City hired its first police "matron." In 1888, Massachusetts and New York passed legislation requiring communities with a population over 20,000 to hire police matrons to care for female prisoners. According to More (1992), during the first half of the nineteenth century, a number of police practices were challenged, thus allowing for the initial entry of women into the police field. In 1905, the Portland, Oregon, Police Department boasted of its first woman sworn to uphold duties of a police officer; however, she did not work patrol. In 1922, the International Association of Chiefs of Police passed a resolution supporting the use of policewomen; no women worked patrol or as detectives at the time. Historically, it has been a predominant belief that women were not capable of performing the law enforcement functions of exercising authority and using force.

It was not until 1968 that the Indianapolis Police Department made history by assigning the first two female officers to patrol on an equal basis with their male colleagues (Schulz, 1995), finally overcoming this perception. Other landmarks for women in law enforcement occurred in 1985, with the appointment of the first woman chief of police in a major city (Portland, Oregon), and in 1994, with the appointment of the first African American woman chief of police in Atlanta.

Title VII of the Civil Rights Act of 1964 was discussed earlier in this chapter. This law played an important role in opening up police departments to women. Adoption of affirmative action policies, now illegal in many states, along with court orders and injunctions, also played a role in bringing more women into law enforcement. Although more women were entering law enforcement, they still encountered blatant and open skepticism, resentment, and hostility from male officers.

Historically, law enforcement agencies' requirements or standards pertaining to minimum height and weight, strength, and agility posed one of the many barriers to female entry into the police field (Polisar & Milgram, 1998). Most civil service tests modified these requirements in order to comply with court-ordered legal mandates and injunctions by the early 1980s (Balkin, 1988). However, a study published by the National Center for Women and Policing (NCWP) in 2003 concluded that there is still an adverse impact on women due to entry-level physical agility testing that eliminates a large number of women. NCWP suggests that there are other options that will yield the benefits of qualified women entering the profession and eliminate this obstacle to their being hired ("Tearing Down the Wall," 2003). This study is discussed more fully in Chapter 3.

The number of women in law enforcement remains small and is increasing very slowly (see earlier discussion and Exhibits 2.1, 2.2 and 2.3). Recall that as of 2004, the latest year for which statistics are available, women represented only 11.3 percent of local police departments, 12.9 percent of sheriffs' offices, and 16.1 percent of federal law enforcement officers nationwide. Researchers in the late 1980s had made various predictions of the numbers of women expected to be in law enforcement professions by the turn of the twenty-first century, ranging from 47 to 55 percent of the workforce, but those predictions never materialized.

Women were gaining in numbers at approximately half a percentage point per year in their representation within large police agencies from 1972 to 1999, but the trend halted or even reversed in 2000 and 2001 and has continued to decline since then. Researchers studying this phenomenon believe that the decline of women in law enforcement can be attributed to the decrease in the number of consent decrees still in effect among the agencies surveyed: eight consent decrees, involving the agencies studied, mandating the hiring or promotion of women or minorities had expired. A review of the statistics makes it clear that women are underrepresented in law enforcement. It should be noted that according to the Bureau of Labor Statistics records for 2005, the participation of women in the whole of the labor force in 2004 was 46.4 percent.

However, law enforcement does not constitute the only field that saw a numbers reduction in women workforce, as the following statement from an article based on a study by the Federal Reserve of Dallas, Texas, indicates: ". . . since the start of this decade, the workforce participation of women in prime working years—between 25 and 54—has experienced its largest sustained decline since World War II" ("More Women Leaving Labor Market," 2005). This particular research found that mostly the women who were dropping out have been educated, married, with children, and with higher incomes, and that many were leaving to go back to school or to have families. The study did not focus on women in law enforcement, so further research is needed to verify if retention problems are occurring in this occupation for the same reasons.

The integration of women into policing and the problems with their retention have led many law enforcement chief executives, managers, and supervisors to grapple with workplace issues within their departments.

Workplace Issues

Women still face some unique challenges, including overcoming the attitudes of society and of some of their male coworkers and bosses. Workplace issues confronting law enforcement agencies, and especially women in law enforcement, involve sexual harassment, gender discrimination, role barriers, the "brotherhood," a double standard, differential treatment, and career-versus-family issues.

SEXUAL HARASSMENT   The following are considered sexual harassment in the workplace:

- *Hostile Environment,* which consists of unwelcome sexual behavior, such as "jokes," cartoons, posters, banter, repeated requests for dates, requests for sexual favors, references to body parts, or physical touching, that has the purpose or effect of unreasonably interfering with an individual's work performance or creating an intimidating, hostile, or offensive working environment.
- *Quid pro quo sexual harassment,* which means one is asked to perform sexual acts in return for a job benefit. For example, you are told you will pass probation, get a promotion, get a good performance evaluation, or not be written up for doing something wrong if you will engage in some type of sexual behavior.
- *Gender harassment,* which is behavior that is not based on sexual behavior but is based on gender. It is also known as sex-based harassment. Examples include comments such as "women are not brave enough to be police officers," and "women should stay home and have babies and leave policing to real men." ("Workplace Issues," 2005).

Sexual harassment can occur in a variety of circumstances including, but not limited to, the following:

1. The victim, as well as the harasser, may be a woman or a man. The victim need not be of the opposite sex.
2. The harasser can be the victim's supervisor, an agent of the employer, a supervisor in another area, a coworker, or a nonemployee.
3. The victim need not be the person harassed, but could be anyone affected by the offensive conduct.
4. Unlawful sexual harassment may occur without economic injury to or discharge of the victim.
5. The harasser's conduct must be unwelcome.

Employers are encouraged to take steps necessary to prevent sexual harassment from occurring, because prevention is the best tool to eliminate sexual harassment in the workplace. They should clearly communicate to employees that sexual harassment will not be tolerated. They can only do so by establishing an effective complaint or grievance process and taking immediate and appropriate action when an employee complains ("Facts about Sexual Harassment," 2008). Although sexual harassment exists in both private and public sectors, we believe it is particularly problematic in law enforcement—an occupation that is still mostly male-dominated.

The majority of women officers interviewed for each edition of this book (who requested that their names not be used) said they had been sexually harassed in the workplace. Most of the women indicated that when they were exposed to offensive behavior by male officers, they remained quiet for fear of negative male backlash. This lack of reporting can also be directly attributed to the code of silence in law enforcement agencies and the severe retaliation that occurs when women report misconduct. Those interviewed revealed that sexual harassment occurs at all levels of an organization and is not limited to male harassment of women. In 2003, Seklecki and Allen (2004) of the University of Minot, North Dakota, administered a survey to 2,000 female police officers, selected at random, in departments across the United States. The survey contained questions designed to collect information about employment motivations, experiences, and attitudes of women who became law enforcement officers. The response rate was approximately 27 percent (531 female police officers and deputies). The summary of their findings is:

> When examining sexual harassment, it appears as though the situations most frequently encountered by female officers were: putting women down, being insulted and called homosexual by citizens, someone trying to have a sexual relationship with an officer despite her objections, someone making sexually suggestive remarks at or about the officer, and hearing dirty jokes and/or stories being told. What is most amazing is, there was not one situation presented which no female officer had never encountered. This becomes extremely interesting given that 377 officers reported that they had never been sexually harassed (72.8%). That is, this sample of female officers reported frequencies for experiencing every sexual harassment situation, yet the majority of officers reported that they had never been sexually harassed. (Seklecki & Allen, 2004, p. 38)

Department executives must institute a zero-tolerance sexual harassment policy and send that message throughout the department. Policy-specific training must also be provided on sexual harassment and its prevention. Some departments have revised their promotional exam to include questions on the department's sexual harassment policies and procedures. The Albuquerque, New Mexico, Police Department went so far as to move the investigation of sexual harassment complaints from within the department to an external city agency with expert Equal Employment Opportunity investigators on staff. According to the Albuquerque PD, this approach tends to speed up the process, ensure impartiality, and increase confidence in the procedures. Officers who make a complaint do not have to go through the chain of command. An eight-hour police-specific training course for sworn supervisors on preventing sexual harassment, developed by the Institute for Women in Trades, Technology and Science (IWITTS), is also of value. It is presented in a case-study format that analyzes police legal cases, and it has been highly rated by those who have attended. Information on IWITTS can be found on its website, listed in the Website Resources section of this chapter. The IWITTS course provides those who attend with a "Law Enforcement Asessment Tools" kit, which enables law enforcement agencies to conduct a self-assessment and develop a strategic plan to recruit women, prevent sexual harassment, and ensure fair promotion.

When harassment takes place, the results can be devastating in terms of the involved employees' careers, the internal environment of the organization, and the department's public image. The importance of training all law enforcement employees (sworn and nonsworn) on the issues of sexual harassment cannot be stressed enough. The once male-dominated occupation of law enforcement is in a process of transition to a multicultural work environment, with increased representation of both men and women with differing cultural identities in race, ethnicity, and sexual orientation. As judicious policies and directives are put in place in this new environment, and training and procedures are developed and presented, sexual harassment can be expected to decrease. Training on discrimination and sexual harassment should deal not only with legal and liability issues but also with deep-seated attitudes about differences.

GENDER DISCRIMINATION   Gender discrimination occurs when a person is subjected to unequal treatment in the workplace on the basis of sex. A few examples of what might constitute workplace gender discrimination are:

- Assignments to jobs or programs that are considered "traditionally women's" instead of the nontraditional positions such as SWAT teams, K9, gang units, and narcotics.
- Tests for promotions or other job opportunities that are not job-related or represent a small part of the job duties, which result in women not getting promoted at the same rate that men are promoted.
- Women are held to a higher or different level on performance evaluations.
- Women are not given equal consideration for specialized training, conferences, specialty job assignments, and the like.
- Pregnant women are not given light duty, but men who are injured off-duty are given such assignments. ("Workplace Issues," 2005)

Some agencies have unlawfully discriminated against pregnant employees. One of the biggest complaints from pregnant female sworn officers is that when they notify their department that they are pregnant, they are removed from their position and there is little or no effort to find a light-duty position ("Workplace Issues," 2005). Discrimination on the basis of pregnancy, childbirth, or a related medical condition is discrimination on the basis of gender.

The U.S. Equal Employment Opportunity Commission (EEOC) receives private- and public-sector complaints alleging sex-based (gender) discrimination, sexual harassment, and pregnancy discrimination. In 2008, the number of charges, number resolved, and monetary benefits received by charging parties and other aggrieved individuals were as follows:

- *Sex-based (gender) discrimination:*   28,372 charges; resolved 24,018; collecting $109.3 million
- *Sexual harassment (15.9 percent male):*   13,867 charges; resolved 11,731; collecting $47.4 million
- *Pregnancy discrimination:*   6,285 charges; resolved 5,292; collecting $12.2 million ("EEOC Enforcement Statistics and Litigation," 2008).

City, county, state, and federal employers must know the laws pertaining to such workplace issues and train their employees accordingly to avoid costly lawsuits. The National Center for Women and Policing (NCWP) has produced a document titled "Model Pregnancy Policy Guidelines," which should be referred to for more information (see Website Resources at the end of this Chapter).

ROLE BARRIERS   Barriers and hostility toward women in the workplace based on gender have diminished, both in the general population and within law enforcement. For example, ideas about protection differ by gender—who protects whom? In American society, women may protect children, but it has been more socially acceptable and traditional for men to protect women. In the act of protecting, the protectors become dominant and the protected become subordinate. Although this gender-role perception has not completely broken down, especially in the law enforcement and corrections workforce, it is subsiding because of the number of women and young male officers in those professions today. There are now fewer veteran male officers who have never worked with women. Many veteran police and correctional officers initially had difficulty with the transition as women came into the dangerous, male-dominated, nontraditional occupations that men felt required "male" strength and abilities. The result has been described as a clash between cultures—the once male-dominated workforce versus the new one in which women are integral parts of the organizational environment. The veteran male police or correctional officers, socially conditioned to protect women, often feel that in addition to working with inmates or violent persons on the streets, they have the added responsibility of protecting the women officers with whom they work.

These feelings, attitudes, and perceptions can make men and women in law enforcement positions uncomfortable with each other. Women sometimes feel patronized, overprotected, or merely tolerated rather than appreciated and respected for their work. Again, these attitudes and perceptions are diminishing as many in the new generation of male officers are more willing to accept women in law enforcement. In our numerous interviews with veteran officers, we found that, with few exceptions, women were generally accepted by men, but the acceptance was related to how well a specific woman performed her duties. The National Survey of Female Police Officers 2003 study, previously cited, questioned those participating about how they were treated, and:

> the majority of respondents felt they were treated equally and were made to feel as welcomed as their male counterparts upon entering the field of law enforcement. However, 39 percent of respondents indicated they were made to feel less welcomed than males, and almost 32 percent indicated they were treated worse than male officers when they first began their careers in law enforcement. Thus, there are a large number of respondents who feel they were treated less favorably than male officers upon beginning their careers in policing. (Seklecki & Allen, 2004, p. 31)

THE BROTHERHOOD   Women who are accepted into the "brotherhood" of police or correctional officers have generally had to become "one of the guys." (Refer to Chapter 4 for more information on how language used in the brotherhood excludes women.) According to Susan Jones, Chief of Police of the Healdsburg, California, Police Department, and other women interviewed, the term *brotherhood* still exists today along with the associated behaviors. Chief Jones hopes that one day there will be just the "family of law enforcement" (Jones, 2009). The term "brotherhood" is outdated in today's co-ed law enforcement environment, and those who still use it demonstrate a lack of cultural competency.

Often a woman who tries to act like one of the guys (be part of the brotherhood) on the street or in a jail or prison is considered too hard, too coldhearted, or too unemotional and may be criticized by peers and supervisors. Although perhaps this is a little exaggerated, some women have been described as "Jane Waynes" because they swagger, swear, spit, and are highly aggressive. Yet if a female officer is too feminine or not sufficiently aggressive, men will not take her seriously and she will not do well either in police or in correctional work. So women are confronted with a dilemma: they must be aggressive enough to do the job but feminine enough to be acceptable to male peers, and they must also be able to take different approaches to problems.

When women feel compelled to behave like men in the workplace, the results can be counterproductive and can even result in disciplinary action. Women may feel that to succeed they have to stay within the narrow bands of acceptable behavior and exhibit only certain traditionally masculine or feminine qualities. Walking this fine line is difficult. This phenomenon is not unique to law enforcement, as women in construction trades, historically male-dominated turf, have asserted. One example is a woman ironworker who reported that she and her coworkers feel that no matter how skilled they are, they still have to prove themselves over and over again.

Most women police officers have a different style of policing—"service-oriented style"—and they see their roles as peace restorers (Skolnick & Bayley, 1986). Male officers typically view their roles as crime fighters also involved in maintaining the brotherhood. The following is a summary of research related to policing styles and gender, conducted both in the United States and internationally:

> [W]omen police officers rely on a style of policing that uses less physical force. They are better at defusing and de-escalating potentially violent confrontations with citizens and less likely to become involved in problems with use of excessive force. Additionally, women officers often possess better communication skills than their male counterparts and are better able to facilitate the cooperation and trust required to implement a community-policing model. In an era of costly litigation, hiring and retaining more women in law enforcement is likely to be an effective means of addressing the problems of excessive force and citizen complaints. As an additional benefit, female officers often respond more effectively to incidents of violence against women—crimes that represent one of the largest categories of calls to police departments. Increasing the representation of women on the force is also likely to address another costly problem for police administrators—the pervasive problem of sex discrimination and sexual harassment—by changing the climate of modern law enforcement agencies. Because women frequently have different life experiences than men, they approach policing with a different perspective, and the very presence of women in the field will often bring about changes in policies and procedures that benefit both male and female officers. All of these factors can work to the advantage of those in the police profession and the communities they serve. (NCWP, 2002a)

Another study by the same organization in 2002 had similar findings. The executive summary provides a concise overview:

> Research from seven major U.S. police agencies has documented what many police and community leaders have known for a long time: women officers are substantially less likely than their male counterparts to be involved in problems of excessive force. Whether citizen complaints, sustained allegations, or civil liability payouts are used as the measure, women officers are dramatically underrepresented in excessive force incidents. (NCWP, 2002b, p. 2)

The same report also reflected the following:

> Given that women currently comprise 12.7% [2001] of sworn personnel in big city police agencies, we would expect that female officers in these agencies should be involved in approximately 12.7% of the citizen complaints, sustained allegations, or payouts for excessive force. Yet the data indicate that only 5% of the citizen complaints for excessive force and 2% of the sustained allegations of excessive force in large agencies involve female officers. Women also account for only 6% of the dollars that are paid out in court judgments and settlements for excessive force among these large agencies. (NCWP, 2002b)

Captain Foster, a veteran of the Fresno, California, Police Department, researched this issue, and his findings suggest that the differences in officers' willingness to use force to resolve conflict may be explained by men being, in most cases, inherently stronger than women.

> Some might suggest that male officers are more concerned with improving their physical characteristics [i.e., strength training and tactical skills] rather than their intellectual capacities [i.e., persuasion and negotiation skills]. This notion may be due to the belief that strength counts when persuasion and negotiation fail. Generally speaking, female police officers often rely on negotiation, persuasion, and effective communication to resolve conflict. ("Gender and Excessive Force Complaints," 2006, p. 8)

Foster's study suggests that most women who come into law enforcement with limited upper body strength or knowledge of arrest and control techniques develop physical strength and become proficient in the tactics of arrest over time. He asserts, however, that "female police officers never forget how to use their most valuable tool in law enforcement—their ability to prevent and/or defuse conflict rather than provoking it and/or responding to it" ("Gender and Excessive Force Complaints," 2006, pp. 8–9).

One woman sergeant, who recently retired from a large police department in Florida, told one of the authors, "Usually men are physically stronger than women. But even so, women can use this to their advantage when arresting a male subject. Because it's a given that a male is stronger, he usually does not feel the need to prove his masculinity by fighting with a female officer. However, in a confrontation with a male officer, the male subject might feel the need to prove 'he's a man,' and fight back with the male officer" (Bierstedt, 2009). Sgt. Bierstedt told the author that on many occasions she had told an aggressive male that he was stronger and would probably win if he resisted arrest, but that he could let her handcuff him and go quietly with dignity. If not, she could have other officers respond to subdue him, at which time, he would likely receive injuries as well as additional charges for resisting arrest and the battery of the officers. That seldom failed to ensure compliance. Verbal skills are a must not only for the female officers, but for all officers.

A DOUBLE STANDARD   Interviews with women officers for each of the editions of this book showed clearly that the majority felt they had to perform better than male officers just to be considered equal—a double standard. These women spoke of how they imposed pressures on themselves to perform up to or exceed the expectations of their male peers. (Note that minority, gay, and lesbian employees often express the same sentiment.) One woman officer explained that many women were using a community policing philosophy long before it became the practice of their agency. She mentioned that when she tried to do problem solving, she was criticized in her evaluations. Her supervisor rated her negatively for "trying too hard to find solutions to complainants' problems" and said she "spends too much time on calls explaining procedures" and "gets too involved" (Jones, 2009). Today, however, women police officers report that the double standard is less common because of the emphasis that law enforcement places on Community-Oriented Policing. Now this approach is seen as the norm and is expected of all officers (Jones, 2009).

DIFFERENTIAL TREATMENT   Many women in law enforcement, when interviewed for prior editions of this text, indicated that they were treated differently from men by staff members. They said that they were frequently held back from promotions or special assignments in areas like special weapons and tactics, homicide investigations, and motorcycle units because of the perception that these are "male" jobs. They reported feeling that they were also held back from training for these assignments and were not promoted at the same rate as men. Over the years, some change has occurred: more women officers are now serving in special assignment and showing no special problems with performance. Women are also being promoted to executive, managerial, and supervisory positions; however, their numbers in these positions are still low. Recall that the U.S. Department of Labor indicated that women in the workforce held half of all management, professional, and related occupations in 2004 ("Women in the Labor Force," 2005). This is far from the case in U.S. law enforcement.

Police executives must determine if their female officers are receiving equal opportunities for assignments and training that will provide the groundwork and preparation for their eventual promotion. They need to determine if female officers are applying for promotions in numbers proportionate to their representation in the department. If not, perhaps women officers need encouragement from their supervisors, mentors, and informal network associates. It is also possible that the promotion process disproportionately screens out female officers. Research shows that the more subjective the process is, the less likely women are to be promoted. The use of assessment center and "hands-on" testing is said to offer some safeguards against the potential for the perception of bias against women. Utilizing structured interviews and selecting interview board members who represent different races and both sexes can also minimize this risk. Many departments are now training interview board members on interviewing techniques. The IWITTS has developed a well-received half-day training session for supervisors, "Creating a Supportive Work Environment," to address issues of integration and retention of women. See the Website Resources at the end of this chapter.

CAREER VERSUS FAMILY   Women in law enforcement are faced with another dilemma— trying to raise a family and have a successful career, two goals that are often difficult to combine. Women, especially single parents, who had children when they entered law enforcement frequently find that they have difficulty balancing their commitments to family and work. If they had children after entering the occupation, they may be confronted with inadequate pregnancy policies and maternity-leave policies (see earlier discussion). In both cases, women often feel a sense of guilt, stress, and frustration in trying to both do well in a job and maintain a family. Progressive criminal law enforcement organizations offer innovative work schedules, modified duty assignments during pregnancy, child care programs, mentoring and support groups, and a positive work atmosphere for women. Such programs benefit all employees within the organization. Today, men are taking a more active role in parenting and family; therefore, child care, creative work schedules, and even maternity leave should be of importance to them as well.

Sgt. Bierstedt, mentioned earlier, also told the author that during the hiring process, officers sign a document that informs them they are required to work various shifts and sites, including graveyard. The form also notifies them that assignments are based upon seniority. However, based upon extenuating circumstances, such as a severely ill family member, they can submit a "hardship" request. If granted, it is a one-time exception and only for a period of one shift change, approximately four months. This is to allow time to make arrangements as necessary. This "hardship" is usually requested for officers in Uniform Patrol, as specialized units make adjustments as their staffing needs allow. Also, having children does not constitute a "hardship." She also said that women with children in a two-parent home are reminded that their spouse should also care for their child or children in the event this was needed (Bierstedt, 2009).

Mentor and Informal Networking Programs for Women

Women's performance and attitudes can be enhanced if they have access to a **mentor** and to **informal network** programs. The mentor provides information, advice, support, and encouragement to someone who is less experienced. Mentoring involves leading, developing, and guiding by example to facilitate the protégé's personal development, for the benefit of both the individual and the organization. There is a great deal of research on the topic of mentoring and networking for women as well as for minorities. Law enforcement management is well advised to consult these studies, the information from which will contribute to the successful creation of such programs.

Mentor   A trusted counselor or guide.

Informal networks   A system of influential colleagues who can, because of their position or power within an organization, connect the employee with information, resources, or other contacts helpful to the employee's promotion or special-assignment prospects.

Usually mentoring occurs in a one-on-one coaching context over a period of time through suggestions, advice, and support on the job. There are many reasons for law enforcement agencies to provide for or encourage the use of mentor and support programs. Studies over the years have found that women who had one or more mentors reported greater job success and job satisfaction than reported by women who did not have a mentor. Conferences are held in some states to provide women the opportunity to learn about networking and leadership in a nonthreatening environment. In 2006, the first Women Leaders in Law Enforcement (http://www.wlle.net) conference was held in California. This annual conference is sponsored by the California Police Chiefs' Association, State Sheriffs' Association, the Highway Patrol, and the State Peace Officers' Association.

A 2001 *Catalyst* (the newsletter of a nonprofit group by the same name that studies women's issues and business trends) reported on a study wherein women and men were

EXHIBIT 2.5   Barriers to Women's Advancement

	WOMEN	MEN
Lack of mentoring opportunities	70%	38%
Commitment to personal and family responsibilities	69%	53%
Exclusion from informal networks of communication	67%	25%
Lack of women role models	65%	35%
Failure of senior leadership to assume accountability for women's advancement	62%	22%
Stereotyping and preconceptions of women's roles and abilities	61%	27%
Lack of opportunities to take on visible and/or challenging assignments	54%	12%
Lack of significant general management or line experience	51%	47%

Source: *Catalyst* Newsletter, July 2001.

surveyed on what they perceived as barriers to their advancement. Exhibit 2.5 shows that 70 percent of the women responding to the survey (compared to 38 percent of men) believed the lack of mentoring opportunities was a barrier to their advancement. A report ("Advancing Asian Women in the Workplace") released in 2003 by *Catalyst* stated that Asian American women also face difficult challenges in the workplace. "Many have trouble finding mentors or feel their managers don't understand their culture" ("Obstacles Hinder Minority Women," 2003, p. C1). The report mirrors one released earlier in 2003 about Latinas in business. Latinas and Asian American women are among the fastest-growing groups in the U.S. labor force.

The *Catalyst* Barriers series focuses on women's perception that lack of access to networks of influential colleagues is a key barrier to promotions and special assignments to women in the workforce. The report states:

> This issue is particularly pronounced for women of color who face "double exclusion" in the workplace, based on both their gender and race/ethnicity. In fact, lack of access to networks of influential colleagues underlies all major barriers identified by women of color, including lack of influential mentors or sponsors (as one needs connections with others to obtain mentors and sponsors); lack of company role models of the same racial/ethnic group (reflecting a shortage of similar others who might form part of an influential network); and lack of high-visibility assignments (which are often facilitated by personal relationships with those wielding influence). ("Connections that Count," 2006, p. 1)

Exhibit 2.5 shows that 67 percent of women identified exclusion from informal networks of communication (compared to 25 percent of men) as a barrier to advancement.

Several associations provide an organized voice for the interests of women in policing: the International Association of Women Police (IAWP), the National Association of Women Law Enforcement Executives (NAWLEE), and the National Center for Women and Policing (NCWP). The NAWLEE focuses on helping women to strengthen their leadership roles in policing, while the NCWP focuses on growth and leadership. However, while these organizations provide excellent resources, they cannot take the place of departmental, in-house mentoring programs or informal networks for women.

In both *Catalyst* Barriers surveys, Latinas and Asian American women said they encounter stereotypes in the workplace. Asian women said they often feel overlooked by their companies' diversity programs, in part, because they are labeled "overachievers" who don't require specific diversity efforts. Both reports suggest that managers should encourage more experienced Asian American women and Latinas to serve as mentors for younger women, as well as make more of an attempt to understand the cultural background of their diverse workforce. It is stressed, however, that those in need of a mentor should be able to "choose from a wide range of networking opportunities. Women of color should not be limited to networking only with people of their own race or ethnicity, nor should they feel compelled to network exclusively with others in the work environment who do not share their cultural background" ("Connections that Count," 2006, p. 6).

The Transition of Women into Law Enforcement

The survey administered by Seklecki and Allen (2004), mentioned earlier, reports interesting findings pertaining to the transition of women into law enforcement:

> Our research indicates that female law enforcement officers have made a promising transition from their professional status some thirty years ago. While still a minority, they view themselves quite often as equally, if not more capable than their male peers, and upon completion of training, the overwhelming majority of women officers are intent to stay on their present career path. In addition, we must note the perception of working conditions has clearly improved as agencies have become more harassment conscious, while remaining undeniably male influenced. The study respondents confirm the continued presence of the traditional "male behaviors"; however, most female officers, surprisingly, do not take great exception to them. This suggests the female officers entered the profession expecting to encounter these behaviors and consider such behavior normal to the work setting. (Seklecki & Allen, 2004, p. 39)

GAY MEN AND LESBIANS IN LAW ENFORCEMENT

The terms **homosexual, lesbian, gay, bisexual**, and **transgender** are used in our discussion of sexual orientation.

Homosexual   Characterized by sexual attraction to those of the same sex as oneself.

Gay   A male homosexual.

Lesbian   A homosexual woman.

Bisexual   The ability to be sexually attracted to both men and women.

Transgender   Covers a range of people, including heterosexual cross-dressers, homosexual drag queens, and transsexuals who believe they were born in the wrong body.

There are also those who consider themselves to be both male and female, or intersexed, and those who take hormones and believe that is enough to complete their gender identity without a sex change. The acronym or initials LGBT is used throughout this section, which stands for lesbian, gay, bisexual, and transgender.

Most authors and police administrators group "gay" and "lesbian" together as if the experiences of the two groups are identical. However, nowhere is the dichotomy more visible than within law enforcement. Many officers still assume that "macho" women are lesbians and that stereotypically "feminine" women are heterosexual—an assumption stemming from persistent sexism—although such mapping of gender roles onto sexual orientation is frequently erroneous. This topic is discussed later in this chapter.

Policy versus Practice

According to Mitchell Grobeson (2009), a retired Los Angeles Police Department sergeant who is gay, the past two decades have seen the removal of the explicit ban on employing gay men and lesbians by most law enforcement agencies. Some agencies did so out of fear of litigation and negative publicity, and some because research indicated gay men and lesbians should not be excluded from law enforcement professions. Despite this apparently dramatic paradigm shift, the reality remains that the vast majority of law enforcement agencies, including many of those within urban areas with large, openly gay populations, find ways to surreptitiously avoid hiring or retaining openly gay men. To a lesser extent, this includes openly lesbian individuals. The rejection of homosexuals in law enforcement by some agencies continues, despite studies that have shown that the presence of openly LGBT personnel enhanced service and did not negatively impact morale or unit cohesion in integrated police departments; the San Diego Police Department provides one example of this (Belkin & McNichol, 2002). There are similar examples in the armed forces of Israel, Britain, and Australia (Belkin & McNichol, 2002). However, a study by Amnesty International USA published in 2005 found:

> Anecdotal evidence suggests there are relatively few LGBT officers who are in a position to be open about their sexual orientation or gender identity, although LGBT police officer associations exist in some larger cities; for example, GOAL in New York. However, Amnesty International is only aware of a fairly small number of LGBT officers who serve on police forces in the U.S. . . . . Only four of 29 responding departments in Los Angeles; New York, New York; Fargo, North Dakota; and Salt Lake City, Utah, reported any kind of affirmative action hiring practice for LGBT individuals. ("Stonewalled," 2005, p. 81)

A deputy chief of a large department, one of the highest-ranking openly gay officers, told *Frontiers* that in terms of how gay and lesbian officers are treated currently, "The discrimination is much more sophisticated than discrimination in the past . . ." (Brooke, 2005, p. 18).

Recruitment

Grobeson indicates that many urban law enforcement agencies engage in public relations campaigns as substitutes for actual recruitment efforts. His observation is that many city or county personnel departments place recruitment advertisements in the gay and lesbian media or assign officers to attend gay and lesbian events such as gay pride festivals. However, he believes that these agencies are only providing "lip service," while avoiding actual recruitment. Law enforcement administrators seeking to have a workforce on parity with their community need to be cognizant of artificial barriers. To ensure equal opportunity, it is important to conduct applicant tracking, in which applicant information is taken at an event and contact with the applicant is maintained to determine if the applicant is hired or at which point in the process he or she is disqualified. If a disproportionate number of these applicants are failing during a specific part of the hiring process, such as oral interviews, background investigations, or polygraph exams, then administrators must be able to capture this information starting from the original point of contact. Further, this approach can help determine if committing resources for LGBT events or advertisements is an effective use of public funds. Another area to monitor to determine if a department provides equal opportunity is the number of openly gay and lesbian officers who voluntarily participate in events with the LGBT communities and the number of those who are willing to be named when interviewed by the mainstream media.

Department personnel who cite numbers of gays and lesbians on a police force are usually viewed skeptically by LGBT officers and by LGBT community organizations. While the trend over the past decade has been for many gay and lesbian officers to become more comfortable being open to select coworkers, for most gay male police officers, it is still clear that choosing to be open about their sexual orientation places both their career and their lives in jeopardy (Brooke, 2005). Even though there has been a steady increase in the hiring of openly gay and lesbian officers in cities and counties outside of those historically known to accept such applicants, their numbers remain low (Brooke, 2005). This is true despite the growing acceptance of gay and lesbian characters in the media.

MILITARY VETERANS' RECRUITMENT   Some law enforcement agencies commit time and resources to recruiting veterans who discharge, separate, or retire from military service. Veterans often make excellent law enforcement employees because of their experience within a military organizational structure. An emerging trend in the late 2000s decade is the increase in the number of LGBT military veterans who apply for law enforcement or corrections occupations. The availability of LGBT military veterans for employment is an issue of major importance to executives and managers within the criminal justice system. First, is the chief executive willing to hire an LGBT military veteran? And second, is the chief executive willing to hire an LGBT veteran whose military service was satisfactory, but who received a less than "honorable" discharge because of his or her sexual orientation?

In order for criminal justice executives to make informed decisions, they must know the difference between *discharge* and *separation* from military service, and whether the discharge/separation was voluntary or involuntary. The vast majority of those leaving the service after completing an initial enlistment obligation are *separated* (voluntary) rather than discharged. This may mean there is an additional military service obligation to be carried out in the Individual Ready Reserve. The key difference is that a *discharge* completely relieves the veteran of any unfulfilled service obligation. A separation may also be involuntary when the service member is released for punitive reasons based upon specifically identified conduct. It is important to know the type or *basis* of the discharge or separation and the *characterization of service*. Basis is the reason for which the person is being administratively separated (e.g., a pattern of misconduct, convenience of the government for parenthood, weight control failure). Characterization of service refers to the quality of the individual's military service, for example, honorable, general (under honorable conditions), other than honorable, bad conduct, or dishonorable (Uniform Code of Military Justice [UCMJ], 1950).

As the wars in Afghanistan and Iraq have continued, many LGBT service personnel have been allowed to retain their positions within the military under the "Don't Ask, Don't Tell" policy even if their sexual orientation had become known. There have, however, been some LGBT veterans discharged under the characterization "general." The "general" characterization means:

> If a member's service has been honest and faithful, it is appropriate to characterize that service under honorable conditions. Characterization of service as general (under honorable conditions) is warranted when significant negative aspects of the member's conduct or performance of duty outweigh positive aspects of the member's military conduct or performance of duty.("Military Justice 101 – Part 3, Enlisted Administrative Separations," 1998)

Thus, a general discharge is given to a service member whose performance is satisfactory but is marked by a departure from duty performance and conduct expected of military members. The reasons for such a characterization of service vary, but discharge is always preceded by some form of nonjudicial punishment (i.e., no court-martial). The non-judicial punishment is typically utilized by the service member's unit commander to correct unacceptable behavior prior to initiating discharge action. If the reason is homosexual conduct or drug abuse, discharge is mandatory. Punitive discharges are punishments authorized by a court-martial and result in either a dishonorable discharge or bad conduct discharge. A court-martial is generally held for the most serious violation(s) of the Uniform Code of Military Justice (UCMJ).

Recently, there has been an increasing number of dishonorable discharges solely based upon discovered or believed homosexuality. This becomes an employment issue when the person applies for a criminal justice career. In the past, the armed forces had agreed to release "homosexual" personnel under the category of general discharge. ("The Military Discharged about 12,340 People between 1994 and 2007 under 'Don't Ask, Don't Tell,'" 2008). Virtually all law enforcement and correctional agencies mandate disqualification of persons who have been discharged from military service with anything less than "honorable." Major cities, particularly those with large LGBT communities, recently altered this practice to accept applicants who have a general discharge, when the sole issue was sexual orientation, with no "related misconduct."

Within the past decade, those agencies progressive enough to hire an LGBT military veteran who has been discharged solely for being "homosexual" (where there was no misconduct) have found that these individuals have been some of the most outstanding and well-respected members of their organizations. This has been especially noted within the San Diego Police Department, which employed a large number of active and former military personnel. In late 2008 and early 2009, more than 100 senior military commanders, many of whom commanded troops in combat, testified before Congress and addressed both President Bush and President Obama. They asked for the recall of "Don't Ask, Don't Tell," which has been military policy since 1993. They claimed that the arbitrary nature of the policy has not only caused hardships for individuals, but has unnecessarily hampered military efforts, readiness, and mission ("Admirals, Generals: Repeal 'Don't Ask, Don't Tell,'" 2008).

The Controversy

Some police officers view openly gay and lesbian individuals as extremist militant types who publicly display their sexuality in offensive or socially unacceptable ways. This is a stereotype; most heterosexuals do not draw attention to their sexual preference, and neither do most homosexuals. Concerns about homosexuals in the military or in law enforcement include beliefs that gay soldiers or police officers will walk hand in hand, dance together at clubs, make passes at non-gay colleagues, and display aspects of their private lives. These arguments for bans are not based in reality, however, since most gays in the military and the criminal justice system are as work-oriented as their heterosexual colleagues. They do not wish to provoke anyone in the system; rather, like most other officers, homosexual officers want to accomplish their missions, work special assignments, be promoted, and avoid confrontation. In fact, gay and lesbian officers and military personnel are much less likely than their heterosexual counterparts to engage in even such mundane acts as putting a picture of their partner on their desk or posted inside their locker. Gay and lesbian officers are no different from others in wanting to support the disciplinary processes, and they believe that any inappropriate conduct should be handled with proper discipline. Research at the beginning of the twenty-first century on the subject of homosexuals in the military and in law enforcement concluded that the presence of gays and lesbians has not caused morale to drop in either setting. The research also determined that there were no negative consequences within urban police departments that adopt nondiscrimination statutes and actively recruit and hire homosexual officers. One comprehensive study, still valid today, of gays and lesbians in a large police agency had been designed to discover whether the integration of self-disclosed gay and lesbian officers has undermined the organizational effectiveness of the San Diego Police Department (SDPD).

> Based on an analysis of prior research and a 3-day site visit, our findings are that a quiet process of normalization has reduced much of the emotional charge that heterosexual officers originally anticipated. Although integration has proceeded largely uneventfully, subtle forms of discrimination do persist, and gay officers who do not already enjoy respect may face challenges. Despite these uneven effects, integration has enhanced cohesion as well as the SDPD's standing with the communities it serves. (Belkin & McNichol, 2002, p. 63)

The report indicates that the integration of gay men and lesbians into law enforcement has been similar to the earlier experiences of women and minorities. Initial reactions among officers within the organization and some prominent community members were often negative, and longstanding work cultures were slow to change. Research on police culture through the early 1990s depicts a work environment that was seeking to reinforce traditional notions of masculinity and describes casual remarks ridiculing or stereotyping homosexuals as being commonplace in formal and informal settings (Belkin & McNichol, 2002, p. 64). The report's key finding is that:

> the increasing participation of self-disclosed homosexuals in the SDPD has not led to any overall negative consequences for performance, effectiveness, recruiting, morale, or other measures of well-being. Even though incidents of harassment and discrimination continue and new internal tensions have arisen concerning the integration of homosexuals, self-disclosed gay personnel, their peers and commanders, and outside observers all agree that disruptive incidents continue to decline in frequency and are usually handled effectively through both informal and formal channels. (Belkin & McNichol, 2002, p. 65)

The researchers noted that complaints by gay and lesbian officers at the San Diego Police Department about harassment or discrimination are extremely low, resulting in underestimates of the actual number of occurrences. They hypothesize that the low number is related to the fact that closeted personnel fear being identified as gay and are reluctant to complain. The study also suggests, however, that another reason might be that, as in most departments, the work culture of the San Diego Police Department strongly emphasizes the informal and discreet resolution of problems at the unit level. The report concludes that:

> concern over working with openly gay men and lesbians has subsided as day-to-day interactions with gay colleagues become more commonplace. In many divisions, for straight and gay people alike, sexual orientation issues are relatively unimportant vis-à-vis the daily challenges of being a cop. Although isolated comments and misconduct may occur, the professional working environment and strong support for equal treatment from headquarters tend to diffuse their frequency and significance. . . . Virtually all respondents believe that the increasing taken-for-grantedness [sic] of gay cops reflects in part the more tolerant values of new recruits coming into the department. Younger cohorts of recruits have brought with them more diverse views and greater comfort levels with gay issues than in years past, and EEO policies and training programs are allowing for more candid give-and-take as recruits wrestle with uncertainties over how to work with gay people. (Belkin & McNichol, 2002, p. 76)

Differences in Treatment of Gay versus Lesbian Officers

Many law enforcement professionals have voiced opinions that because of the "macho" requirements of police work, a double standard exists with respect to the way gay and lesbian officers are viewed. The traditional male dominance of the profession has made it difficult for many male officers to accept that women or gay men are equally able to perform the same tasks they do. They view their work as an occupation for only the "strongest and the toughest." Male officers' self-esteem can be threatened by the ability of women and gay men to do "their" job. (This issue has already been discussed in this chapter under the section "Women in Law Enforcement.")

According to Grobeson, there has been a trend of acceptance of "macho" lesbians into law enforcement. Many male officers are more accepting of lesbian officers, particularly those who are not openly homosexual, than they are of heterosexual women. It appears that male officers are more fearful that "feminine" women will not provide them with sufficient backup where physicality is required. They are more willing to rely on lesbian officers, whom they stereotype as being macho and athletic. Grobeson believes that there is still a great deal of discrimination directed toward women who break the cultural mores and choose to be open or apparent about their sexual orientation.

In addition, the pervasive stereotype of gay men as effeminate remains a factor in most officers' bias against the hiring of and working with gay men. Allowing openly gay men to serve as officers is perceived by many as threatening to the macho image of police work: if a gay man can successfully complete the necessary tasks, then their job is less macho. Further, those officers whose self-image is based on their job, perceiving themselves as "John Wayne," are generally the most uncomfortable with the concept of working with gay officers.

Grobeson asserts that gay men are relegated to the least desirable status of any minority group in terms of acceptance in police culture. Homophobic jokes and nicknames, for example, are still prevalent locker room banter, whereas racial epithets have mostly been eliminated. One stereotype characterizes effeminate men as unworthy of trust as partners, despite that many gay officers are military combat veterans with awards and accolades for bravery, heroism, and service under fire. There are also many homosexual officers in agencies of all sizes who have received medals or citations for their valor. Officers suspected of being homosexual are often teased, belittled, or openly harassed with little or no intervention from supervisors or managers. Some newly hired homosexual officers have reported that they believe it is important to stay "in the closet" until they have proven to their peers and supervisors that they are effective officers.

Gay and lesbian officers often identify more readily with their fellow officers than they do with members of the LGBT community. Many gay and lesbian individuals still view law enforcement as society's arm of social control. With many law enforcement officers still hostile toward gay men and lesbians, LGBT officers feel forced to choose a side, particularly when it comes to the issue of vice enforcement. Therefore, gay and lesbian officers are often accepted by neither the gay community nor their peers.

Gay male officers also assert that management in some law enforcement agencies serving large LGBT populations gives preferential treatment to lesbian officers. Law enforcement managers who were willing to be honest about the subject have admitted that lesbian officers are chosen for specific specialized assignments over both their heterosexual counterparts (male and female) and gay male officers. These assignments have included recruitment, background investigation, internal affairs/management control, community relations, and liaisons from the chief's office. There have been two reasons cited for this reverse discrimination: first, managers get a "3-for" in which their selection is approved by personnel departments and policymakers because it fulfills affirmative action obligations in as many as three protected categories: gender, sexual orientation, and, often, ethnicity or race. Second, law enforcement managers believe that by involving lesbian officers in both the disqualification of gay male applicants and in disciplinary actions against gay officers, they have decreased their liability with regard to claims of bias based upon sexual orientation. In short, lesbian officers are used against gay men, as well as against their fellow lesbian officers, to avoid claims of sexual orientation discrimination or harassment (Grobeson, 2009).

The Transition of LGBT Individuals into Law Enforcement

Problems will inevitably surface within law enforcement agencies as gay and lesbian officers "come out of the closet." Many organizations and employees will be hesitant to welcome such a major change and may resist it unless measures are taken to allay their fears. Officers thought to be or are openly gay or lesbian may encounter discriminatory treatment and/or hostility because of other employees' negative stereotypes and attitudes. People without proper education on acquired immune deficiency syndrome (AIDS), for example, may be afraid of AIDS transmission. This and other fears may mean that gay men will have an even more difficult time assimilating into departments than ethnic or racial minorities, heterosexual women, or lesbians.

As more officers who are openly gay or lesbian are recruited and hired or "come out of the closet," the law enforcement organizational atmosphere will undoubtedly become more tolerant. Individual and group prejudices and assumptions about LGBT employees, for example, will be challenged. Because of the small number of openly gay and lesbian officers in law enforcement today, there are currently few policies dealing specifically with inappropriate displays of sexuality; obviously, discipline would have to be applied equally to both the homosexual and the heterosexual officers who behave unprofessionally. Among gay and lesbian law enforcement officers, however, there is a strong desire to conform to the norms of the organization and to prove their worth as members of that organization. They seldom engage in behaviors that would challenge those norms, or shock or offend fellow officers. Law enforcement agencies should have written-policies to assist gay and lesbian officers' transition into the department as well as operational plans to promote employee acceptance of these officers.

With notable exceptions such as the San Francisco Sheriff's Department, the police departments of San Francisco, San Diego, and New York, the presence of openly gay and lesbian officers within law enforcement departments is relatively new. As such, it is still critically important that agency officials establish openly gay and lesbian liaisons to the LGBT community. This assignment provides role models to qualified LGBT persons who may desire a career in law enforcement. Critically, with the increasing prevalence of hate crimes, it also gives an agency the ability to provide victims with the expertise and compassion of LGBT officers, which will likely elicit both cooperation and information that could impact the outcome of the investigation. Police officials realized years ago that it is an invaluable service to provide women rape victims the comfort of being interviewed by female officers. That need is duplicated when it comes to LGBT hate crime victims (see Chapter 11). Moreover, given the reticence of LGBT crime victims to come forward due to the real or perceived bias of law enforcement personnel, the availability of an LGBT officer helps negate the fear of "double victimization." In the end, the community as a whole, as well as the law enforcement agency, benefit from the presence of such forthright and honest personnel.

Policies against Discrimination and Harassment

Even though there have been gains in the reduction of discrimination and harassment of LGBT employees after decades of complaints and lawsuits, the practice still takes place. Some of these high-profile cases have resulted in millions of dollars of jury awards and settlements by city, county, and state employers (police, fire, corrections) nationwide. A few of those include:

- California: The city of Huntington Beach settled a case in which an officer alleged that peers repeatedly harassed him ("City to Pay Gay Officer up to $2.15 Million," 2008).
- New Jersey: The town of Dover settled an employment discrimination suit brought by a lesbian police sergeant in the town of Dover in 2008 for $750,000. She claimed she was harassed and discriminated against because of her gender and sexual orientation ("Dover to Pay Ex-Sergeant $750,00 to Settle Suit," 2008).
- New York: The city of New York, based on a jury verdict in 2007, paid an NYPD sergeant $500,000 for employment discrimination based on the perception that he was gay. A lieutenant and captain sued for retaliation for speaking out against it. Each recovered approximately $500,000 in a jury verdict ("N.Y. Jury Charges $1.5M to City," 2007).

Some court cases that seek to protect LGBT personnel are filed as class action lawsuits because state and local ordinances prohibiting harassment and discrimination are seldom used. Even where there are policies in place, often there is neither enforcement nor means of forcing compliance by the law enforcement agency. Municipalities often choose to settle lawsuits rather than risk a court trial; a settlement gag order is sometimes required (Grobeson, 2009). The elimination of discrimination and harassment of LGBT employees should remain an area of concern to agency leadership, whose success in preventing the development of a hostile workplace environment will have the added benefit of fewer lawsuits.

The chief executive must establish departmental policies and regulations regarding LGBT officers. These policies must clearly state that discrimination, harassment, and failure to assist fellow LGBT officers are unacceptable and will result in severe disciplinary action. The chief executive must obtain the support of his or her supervisors and managers to ensure that the intent of these rules, policies, and procedures is clear and that all employees adhere to these regulations. All employees must be held accountable, and those who do not support these antidiscrimination policies should not be promoted or awarded special assignments. Department executives must be aware that gay and lesbian officers might not report victimization by other employees. For example, one independent investigation determined that 64 percent of gay and lesbian employees would fear retaliation if they made a complaint against another officer for discrimination or harassment. A gay law enforcement officer told Amnesty International:

> If someone were to use words like "n——r" or "spic," they would be immediately disciplined. However, if they use the word "faggot," generally nothing happens to them. Discipline only happens if someone steps forward, complains, and says they are offended. Jokes and innuendoes in the locker room are still tolerated. This still happens rampantly across law enforcement. Racial jokes and slurs are immediately dealt with, regardless if there is a "complaining party" or not, but with gay jokes, if no one complains, no one is disciplined ("Stonewalled," 2005, p. 96).

If the state does not have one, the city, county, or law enforcement agency should adopt an antidiscrimination policy with regard to sexual orientation or gender identity in the workplace. As of 2007 and 2008, the following statistics pertaining to laws banning discrimination based on sexual orientation or gender identity were in place: seven states have laws banning discrimination based solely on sexual orientation ("State Non-Discrimination Laws in the US," 2008) and 13 states, 90 cities and counties, and the District of Columbia currently ban discrimination based on sexual orientation as well as gender identity/expression ("Scope of Explicitly Transgender-Inclusive Non-Discrimination Laws," 2007). There are an additional 200 municipalities with some form of ordinance banning antigay workplace discrimination, including protections in nongovernmental (private sector) employment ("Workplace Discrimination: Sexual Orientation," 2008).

City or county officials must support and possibly even champion such legislation. The policy should establish that:

- Sexual orientation is not a hindrance in hiring, retention, or promotion.
- Hiring is based solely on merit and all individuals meet objective standards of employment.
- Hiring is done on the basis of identical job-related standards and criteria for all individuals.

Law enforcement managers and supervisors must routinely check to ensure that this policy is being carried out as intended.

Training on Gay, Lesbian, and Transgender Issues

Cultural awareness programs that train department personnel on diversity within communities and in the workforce must also educate employees on LGBT issues. The training should address and demonstrate the falsehood of stereotypes and myths. It must also cover legal rights, including a discussion of statutes and departmental policies on nondiscrimination and the penalties for violating them. These penalties include liability for acts of harassment and discrimination. Often, involving openly gay or lesbian officers (from other agencies, if necessary) in these training programs provides the best outcome. Ideally, this training will enable employees to know the gay or lesbian officers they work with as human beings, reduce personal prejudices, and dispel false assumptions, and thus change behavior. This type of training furthers the ideal of respect for all people. A secondary benefit of this training is the decreased likelihood of personnel complaints and lawsuits by gay or lesbian employees or community members against a city, county, or individual officer.

For a nondiscrimination policy to be implemented effectively, managers must provide regular and ongoing training at all levels of their department (see curricula in Instructor's Manual). The

RAND National Defense Research Institute conducted a study on the compatibility of homosexuality within the U.S. military, which was published in 1993 and is still the best resource on this subject today. The RAND study addressed the efficacy of types of training on LGBT issues relative to both military and paramilitary (law enforcement) organizations. The finding was one that had been supported by many law enforcement trainers, including those in the San Francisco Police Department, and was contrary to the positions maintained by LGBT community and professional groups. The report stated that because homophobic attitudes are present among the rank and file, and because sensitivity training and similar programs usually provoke resentment rather than tolerance, the emphasis on training is most successful when it focuses on strict standards of professional conduct and behavior. According to Grobeson (2009), this is the strategic difference between "diversity" training (which is marked by role playing and command officer disciplinary statements) versus "sensitivity" training (which is what is usually presented by LGBT groups within the business and professional community). Grobeson also points out that localized surveys have shown that due to the media, tolerance toward gay men and lesbians is increasing among the younger generations. The increasing tolerance may improve the ability to host effective recruit academy training on many LGBT issues, especially as young gay or lesbian recruit officers are gradually becoming more willing to be open about their sexual orientation. Grobeson is quick to point out that such may still not be the case for in-service training for officers, with tenured veterans tending to be the most vocal opinion leaders. In time, Grobeson states, this tendency will even prove true for military veterans, who often comprise the primary hiring pool for law enforcement agencies.

Cultural diversity training, which is much more confrontational than sensitivity training but is not abrasive, challenges officers' current attitudes without being condescending. In measuring officers' attitudes, beliefs, feelings, and knowledge, this type of training has been shown to have a positive impact. The training uses simulated situations in which officers deal with partners who are gay. Managers and supervisors are required to handle situations in which a fellow officer is being harassed for perceived homosexuality. Such presentations are most successful when conducted by gay or lesbian officers who are experienced diversity trainers, but this is not to suggest that trainers will be qualified or successful merely because of their sexual orientation.

It is recommended that the training include discussion panels made up of local LGBT community members, business owners, service providers, and community groups, as well as gay youth and gay youth services providers. For supervisors and managers, additional panels comprising attorneys, including municipal attorneys who prosecute hate crimes and who specialize in defense work dealing with homosexual arrestees, HIV issues, and sexual orientation employment discrimination, should be provided. Another new critical area for law enforcement training pertaining to the LGBT community involves the issue of domestic violence.

DOMESTIC VIOLENCE IN LGBT RELATIONSHIPS   Just as in heterosexual relationships, domestic violence occurs among gay and lesbian couples, and in all cases, it is very problematic. There have been attempts to document, both by the government and by LGBT advocacy organizations, how many incidents of gay and lesbian domestic violence and homicide occur in the United States each year. One such organization, The National Coalition of Anti-Violence Programs (NCAVP), compiles domestic violence data submitted by regions across the country in an annual report. After review, they have observed a major discrepancy between the number of LGBT domestic violence reports to community-based LGBT organizations and the number of incidents documented by law enforcement agencies. NCAVP reports: "we know that the numbers are drastically under-reported and that we have seen a sharp spike in domestic violence-related calls at

NY[New York]C AVP in October 2008 as the economy worsens" ("2007 NCAVP Report on LGBT Domestic Violence," 2008). According to LGBT advocates, there are many reasons for the discrepancy between the two sets of figures. The reasons include:

- the police not identifying incidents between intimate or married same-sex partners as domestic violence on crime reports
- victims not reporting the crime (especially if it involves sexual abuse) due to the stigma and shame experienced
- victims not reporting the crime for fear of the police (especially among LGBT immigrants from countries where they were mistreated or persecuted by the police, community, or courts because of their sexual orientation or gender identity)
- victims' belief that the police will not take the action necessary to protect them
- victims' concern that the police will be rude and hostile toward them or be indifferent
- language barriers for non-English-speaking victims trying to access domestic violence services and organizations, the courts, or law enforcement
- a cutback on staff members within law enforcement and LGBT organizations owing to a poor economy, so that statistics are not collected or analyzed

It should be noted that a similar spike has been seen across U.S. society by the National Domestic Violence Hotline, which "reported calls were up 21 percent in the third quarter of 2008 compared with a year earlier." ("Signs of Growing Home Violence amid Downturn," 2009).

Domestic violence in the LGBT community is also known as "intimate partner violence." For police officers, domestic violence calls are often the most difficult and the most dangerous part of their job. The added problem for police officers in communities today is how to recognize and handle cases involving intimate-partner or same-sex marriage violence. One reason that domestic violence between LGBT persons might be especially challenging for officers is the lack of training by their agencies and appropriate resources and referrals within the immediate community. According to Grobeson, for some law enforcement officers, it may be difficult to recognize such incidents, determine who the victim is, and respond effectively with appropriate action and referrals. The fact that batterers are often skilled at presenting themselves as victims presents another problem. "Additionally, intimate partner violence can be difficult for LGBT communities to publicly acknowledge and address at a time when there is a struggle for legal recognition of LGBT relationships. Traditional domestic violence programs do not always offer services specific to LGBT victims of domestic violence, which may prevent some LGBT victims from seeking services" (Grobeson, 2009).

Another issue is that few officers are aware of "domestic partnership" laws when they are responding to incidents of LGBT domestic violence. The same problem exists in states that recently established same-sex marriage laws. Similarly, court personnel are less likely to be knowledgeable about issues of custody, adoptions, and visitation within LGBT relationships. They also may hesitate to assist because the cases are seen as being too complicated or there are no policies or procedures on how to handle them.

The recommendation for the criminal justice system regarding LGBT domestic violence is to:

1. prepare policies, procedures, and protocol regarding victims and abusers;
2. determine what resources and referrals are available in the community for the victims and abusers;
3. develop appropriate referral and resources forms.

TRANSGENDER POLICIES, PROTOCOL, AND TRAINING   According to Grobeson (2009), in communities where there are transgender persons, the relationship between law enforcement and those members continues to be one that demands attention. Agencies must develop policy ("Transgender Protocol") to provide guidelines to assist sworn and nonsworn employees on the arrest and search of transgender individuals. This recommendation followed the 2005 publication of a 150-plus page report by Amnesty International. The Amnesty International investigation determined that 72 percent of police departments responding to their survey had no specific policy regarding interaction with transgender people, and only 31 percent instruct their officers on how to strip search a transgender individual ("Stonewalled," 2005). Departments should also have programs or designated liaison officers to work with transgender organizations or transgender individuals in the community. Departments that have policies, liaison, and employee training improve rapport and relations with the transgender community, which also reduces exposure to complaints and lawsuits.

Police officers are the protectors of individuals in a diverse society that includes LGBT people. Although we recognize that police officers are human and entitled to their own personal beliefs, they cannot display biased behavior or engage in discriminatory actions. Police officers who are prejudiced against LGBT people must still uphold their rights. When prejudice or bias by an officer results in an overt discriminatory act, he or she must be appropriately punished. Officers also cannot remain silent if they witness a harassing or discriminatory act or crime of any kind committed by fellow employees. These same officers must maintain a good working relationship with peers who may be different from themselves. Police officers represent the entire community. Any discriminatory act they commit while on duty (or off duty) can bring dishonor not only to them but also to their agency, the community they serve, and the entire profession of law enforcement.[1]

Support Groups for Lesbian, Gay, Bisexual, and Transgender Officers

LGBT officers benefit from support groups and peer counselors in their own or neighboring police agencies. In the early 1980s, openly gay and lesbian officers formed networks of support within the San Francisco Sheriff's Department. In the late 1980s, the San Francisco and New York City police departments, along with other agencies, assisted gay and lesbian officers in forming support groups. In the early 1990s, chapters of the Golden State Peace Officers Association (founded in San Francisco) and the Gay Officers Action League (founded in New York) were established in southern California to assist officers there. In addition to networking opportunities, mentoring and support are provided by these groups for their members. Heterosexual employees who support the rights of LGBT personnel have also joined as members and associate members of these organizations. It is important that agency executives and managers provide opportunities for LGBT individuals to not only enter into law enforcement careers but also assimilate comfortably into the organization.

THE CHIEF EXECUTIVE

The chief law enforcement executive should follow specific guidelines to meet the challenge of policing a pluralistic community. As emphasized previously, he or she must first effectively manage the diversity within his or her own organization. Progressive law enforcement executives are aware that before employees can be asked to value diversity in the community, it must be made

---

[1] For more information on conducting diversity training, refer to the Instructor's Manual for this textbook, which offers suggestions for a cultural diversity training program that includes LGBT awareness.

clear that diversity is valued within the organizations. Managing differences in the law enforcement workplace is therefore of high priority.

> Perhaps the biggest challenge facing police executives of the 21st century will be to develop police organizations that can effectively recognize, relate and assimilate the global shifts in culture, technology and information. Changing community expectations, workforce values, technological power, governmental arrangements, policing philosophies, and ethical standards are but a sample of the forces that must be understood and constructively managed by the current and incoming generation of chief executives. ("Police Leadership in the 21st Century," 1999)

Executive leadership and team building are crucial to managing a pluralistic workforce and establishing good minority–community relations. The chief executive must take the lead in this endeavor by:

- Demonstrating commitment.
- Developing strategic, implementation, and transition management plans.
- Managing organizational change.
- Developing police–community partnerships (community-based policing).
- Providing new leadership models.

Demonstrate Commitment

The organization must adopt and implement policies that demonstrate a commitment to policing a diverse society. These policies must be developed with input from all levels of the organization and community. The chief executive must reflect the imperative to value diversity and treat all persons with respect. His or her personal leadership and commitment are the keystones to implementing policies and awareness training within the organization and to successfully building bridges to the community. One of the first steps is the development of a "macro" mission statement for the organization; it should elaborate the philosophy, values, vision, and goals of the department to foster good relationships within a diverse workforce and community. All existing and new policies and practices of the department must be evaluated to determine how they may affect women, members of diverse ethnic and racial groups, gay men, lesbians, bisexuals, and transgender employees on the force. Recruitment, hiring, and promotional practices must be reviewed to ensure that there are no institutional barriers to particular groups in an agency. The chief executive must stress, via mission and values statements, that the agency will not tolerate discrimination, abuse, or crimes motivated by hate against protected classes within the community or within the agency itself. The policy statements should also include references to discrimination or bias based on physical disability or age.

The executive must use every opportunity to speak out publicly on the value of diversity and to make certain that people both inside and outside the organization know that upholding those ideals is a high priority. He or she must actively promote policies and programs designed to improve community relations and use marketing techniques to sell these programs, both internally and externally. Internal marketing is accomplished by involving senior management and the police association in the development of the policies and action plans. The chief or sheriff can use this opportunity to gain support for these policies by demonstrating the value of community support to increasing both the department's and the officers' effectiveness. External marketing is accomplished by involving representatives of community-based organizations in the process.

Police leaders must institute policies that develop positive attitudes toward a pluralistic workplace and community even as early as the selection process (see discussion in Chapter 3). Using background interviews, polygraphs, and psychological exams, candidates for law enforcement employment must be carefully screened. The questions and processes can help determine candidates' attitudes and beliefs and, at the same time, make them aware of the agency's strong commitment to a diverse workforce.

Develop Strategic, Implementation, and Transition Management Plans

Textbooks and courses that teach strategic, implementation, and transition management planning are available to law enforcement leaders. The techniques, although not difficult, are quite involved and are not the focus of this book. Such techniques and methodologies are planning tools, providing the road map that the organization uses to implement programs and to guide the agency through change. Action plans that identify specific goals and objectives form an essential component. These plans include budgets and timetables and establish accountability—who is to accomplish what by when. Multiple action plans involving the improvement of police–community relations in a diverse society would be necessary to cover such varied components as policy and procedural changes; affirmative action recruitment, hiring, and promotions (where legal); cultural awareness training; and community involvement (i.e., community-based policing).

Manage Organizational Change

The department leadership is responsible for managing change processes and action plans. This is an integral part of implementation and transition management, as discussed previously. The chief executive must ensure that any new policies, procedures, and training result in increased employee responsiveness and awareness of the diversity in the community and within the organization's workforce. He or she must require that management staff continually monitor progress on all programs and strategies to improve police–community relations. In addition, the chief must ensure that all employees are committed to those ideals. Managers and supervisors need to ensure application of these established philosophies and policies of the department, and they must lead by example. When intentional deviation from the system is discovered, retraining and discipline should be quick and effective. Employees (especially patrol officers) must be rewarded and recognized for their ability to work with and within a pluralistic community. The reward systems for employees, especially first- and second-line supervisors, would recognize those who foster positive relations with individuals of different gender, ethnicity, race, or sexual orientation both within and outside the organization. As we have illustrated, the chief executive, management staff, and supervisors are role models and must set the tone for the sort of behavior and actions they expect of employees.

Develop Police–Community Partnerships

Progressive police organizations have adopted community-based policing as one response strategy to meet the needs and challenges of a pluralistic workforce and society. The establishment of community partnerships is a very important aspect of meeting today's challenges. For example, a cultural awareness training component will not be as effective if police–community partnerships are not developed, utilized, and maintained. The chief executive must establish and maintain ongoing communication with all segments of the community. These lines of communication are best established by community-based policing (discussed in detail in Chapter 14).

Provide New Leadership Models

Leadership is exercised when one takes initiative, guides or influences others in a particular direction, and demonstrates how a process or procedure is performed. Leaders should possess a good balance of conceptual, technical, and professional competence and demonstrate good judgment and excellent people skills. Good leaders are not only creative change agents but also practical futurists, exercising foresight and the capacity to see the "big picture" and the "long view." Today, as we transition into a new information age and multicultural work environment, leaders need to be both transformational and culturally sensitive. That is, such high performers innovate by:

- Transforming workplaces from the status quo to appropriate environments.
- Renewing organizations and becoming role models by transmitting intellectual excitement and vision about their work.
- Helping personnel to manage change by restructuring their mindsets and values.

Leaders help to improve their organizations by preparing the next generation of supervisors and professionals. They do this primarily through the human resource development program that they initiate and/or supervise (Harris, 2005). At a more personal level, they become mentors and coaches to high-performing personnel with potential to rise within the organization.

In terms of the intercultural aspect, such leaders deal with all persons fairly, regardless of gender, race, color, religion, sexual orientation, or cultural differences. A leader seeks to empower a more diverse workforce in law enforcement to be reflective of the communities served. Furthermore, culturally sensitive leaders cut across cultural barriers while combating prejudice, bigotry, and racism wherever found in the organization and the community. Police supervisors, for example, exercise this leadership through anticipatory thinking, strategic planning, creative decision making, and effective communication (Harris, 2005). In the past, all methods or models of management and organizational behavior were based on implicit assumptions of a homogeneous, white male workforce. Even bestsellers such as *The One-Minute Manager* (Blanchard & Johnson, 1983) and *In Search of Excellence* (Waterman & Peters, 1984) that continue to be useful management tools are based on that traditional assumption.

Managers must learn to value diversity and overcome personal and organizational barriers to effective leadership, such as stereotypes, myths, and unwritten rules and codes (one of those being that the organizational role model is a white male). New models of leadership must be incorporated into law enforcement organizations to manage the diverse workforce.

Good leaders not only acknowledge their own ethnocentrism, but also understand the cultural values and biases of the people with whom they work. Consequently, such leaders can empower, value, and communicate more effectively with all employees. Developing others involves acquiring or developing mentoring and coaching skills, important tools for modern managers. To communicate responsibly, leaders must understand the diverse workforce from a social and cultural context and be able to use a variety of verbal and nonverbal communication strategies with employees. Modern leaders are also familiar with conflict mediation in cross-cultural disputes.

To be leaders in the new workforce, most managers will have to unlearn practices rooted in old mindsets, change the way their organization operates, shift organizational culture, revamp policies, create new structures, and redesign human resource systems. The vocabulary of the future managers involves leading employees rather than simply managing them. People want to be led, not managed, and the more diverse the working population becomes, the more leadership is needed. This approach to leadership was echoed in the introduction to *Transcultural Leadership—Empowering the Diverse Workforce.* Transcultural leadership addresses a new global reality: today productivity must come from the collaboration of culturally diverse women and men. It insists that leaders change organizational culture to empower and develop people. It demands that employees be selected, evaluated, and promoted on the basis of *performance and competency*, regardless of sex, race, sexual orientation, religion, or place of origin. Beyond that, leaders must learn the skills to enable men and women of all backgrounds to work together effectively (Simons, Vazquez, & Harris, 1993).

Management, to build positive relationships and show respect for a pluralistic workforce, must be aware of differences, treat all employees fairly (and not necessarily in identical ways), and lead. The differing needs and values of a diverse workforce require flexibility by organizations and their leaders. Modern leaders of organizations recognize not only that different employees have different needs but also that these needs change over time. To bridge cultural and racial gaps within their organizations must be a goal of law enforcement leaders.

Summary

- In the United States, there has been a profound shift in demographics, which has resulted in notable changes in the composition of the workforce in law enforcement agencies. Every agency has more women, ethnic and racial minorities, and gay and lesbian members.
- Racism exists within our law enforcement organizations; police are not immune to social ills. The basic framework for combating and defusing racism in law enforcement agencies is to use the military model involving command commitment, training of advisers, and the investigation of complaints and monitoring of results. Officers must have knowledge of conflict resolution techniques to reduce racial and ethnic problems.
- In 1972, the passage of the Equal Employment Opportunity (EEO) Act applied to state and local governments the provisions of Title VII of the Civil Rights Act of 1964. The EEO Act prohibited employment discrimination on the basis of race, color, religion, sex, or national origin. The law played an important role in opening up police departments to women.

- The past two decades have seen the removal of the explicit ban against employing gay men and lesbians by most law enforcement agencies. The rejection of homosexuals in law enforcement by some agencies continues despite studies that have shown that the presence of openly LGBT personnel enhanced service and did not negatively impact morale or unit cohesion in integrated police departments. The chief executive must establish departmental policies and regulations regarding LGBT officers. These policies must clearly state that discrimination, harassment, and failure to assist fellow LGBT officers are unacceptable and will result in corrective, including disciplinary, action.
- Law enforcement leaders must be committed to setting an organizational tone that does not permit racism or discriminatory acts and must act swiftly against those who violate these policies. They must monitor and quickly deal with complaints both from within their workforce and from the public they serve.

Discussion Questions and Issues

1. *Measuring Responsiveness to Diversity.* Using the check-off and scoring sheet (Exhibit 2.4), determine how responsive your police department has been to the diversity of the jurisdiction it serves. If you are not affiliated with an agency, choose a city or county police department and interview a command officer to determine the answers and arrive at a score. Discuss with the command officer what

initiatives his or her department intends to undertake to address the issues of community diversity.

2. *Defusing Racially and Culturally Rooted Conflicts.* What training does the police academy in your region provide on defusing racially and culturally rooted conflicts? What training of this type does your local city or county law enforcement agency provide to officers? What community (public and private) agencies are available as referrals or for mediation of such conflicts? Discuss what training should be provided to police officers to defuse, mediate, and resolve racially and culturally rooted conflicts. Discuss what approaches a law enforcement agency should utilize.

3. *Women in Law Enforcement.* How many women officers are there in your local city or county law enforcement agency? How many of those women are in supervisory or management positions? Are any of the women assigned to nontraditional roles such as special weapons and tactics teams, motorcycle enforcement, bomb units, hostage negotiations, or community relations? Have there been incidents of sexual harassment or gender discrimination against women employees? If so, how were the cases resolved? Has the agency you are examining implemented any programs to increase the employment of women, such as flextime, child care, mentoring, awareness training, or career development? Has the agency been innovative in the recruitment efforts for women applicants? Discuss your findings in a group setting.

4. *Diversity in Law Enforcement.* Comment on the diversity in your local city or county law enforcement agency. What is the breakdown in your agency's hierarchy? For example, who holds supervisory or management positions? Have there been reported acts of discrimination against people of diverse backgrounds? Has the agency you are examining implemented any programs to increase the employment of minorities? Discuss your findings in a group setting.

Website Resources

Visit these websites for additional information related to the content of Chapter 2.

Catalyst: http://www.catalyst.org

A research and advisory, nonprofit membership organization working with businesses and the professions to build inclusive environments and expand opportunities for women at work. Catalyst conducts research on all aspects of women's career advancement and provides strategic and web-based consulting services globally.

Hispanic National Law Enforcement Association (HNLEA): http://www.angelfire.com

The website has information about this nonprofit organization—its history and purpose, community events, job opportunities, and lobbying and related activities.

International Association of Chiefs of Police: http://www.theiacp.org

An online resource for law enforcement issues publications including "Recruitment/Retention of Qualified Police Personnel: A Best Practices Guide," December 7, 2001.

International Association of Women Police (IAWP): http://www.iawp.org

A website for information about training conferences, careers, jobs, publications, and research pertinent to women in law enforcement.

Institute for Women in Trades, Technology and Science (IWITTS): http://www.womenpolice.com

This website features fact sheets, news articles, and publications for departments on women and policing, including a free "Women in Policing" e-newsletter, which provides best practice information.

Minorities in Law Enforcement (MILE): http://www.mile4kids.com

The Minorities in Law Enforcement organization is a culturally diverse, nonprofit coalition of law enforcement professionals working in concert with elected officials and the private sector to give at-risk urban youth better alternatives to crime, violence, gangs and drugs. Membership is not limited to law enforcement officers.

National Center for Women and Policing (NCWP): http://www.feminist.org

This website provides information concerning regional training seminars on recruiting and retaining women. It also is a resource for the latest research about women in policing and other critical issues. The organization has consultants to help agencies identify and remove obstacles to recruiting and retaining women.

National Association of Women Law Enforcement Executives (NAWLEE): http://www.nawlee.com

The website contains resources, news, member directory, conference and training information, seminars, and an information exchange forum for women executives in law enforcement.

National Organization of Black Law Enforcement Executives (NOBLE): http://www.noblenational.org

The website contains information and publications pertaining to the following purposes: to unify black law enforcement officers at executive and command levels; to conduct research in relevant areas of law enforcement; to establish linkages and liaisons with organizations of similar concern; to evaluate and recommend legislation relating to the criminal justice process; to

establish effective means and strategies for dealing with racism in the field of criminal justice; to develop communication techniques for sensitizing police executives, police officers, institutions and agencies in the criminal justice system to the problems of the black community; to develop mechanisms that will facilitate the exchange of information among black police executives; to articulate the concerns of black executives in law enforcement.

Vera Institute of Justice: http://www.vera.org

The Vera Institute of Justice works closely with leaders in government and civil society to improve the services people rely on for safety and justice. Vera develops innovative, affordable programs that often grow into self-sustaining organizations, studies social problems and current responses, and provides practical advice and assistance to government officials around the world. They have publications on many law enforcement subjects.

References

"Admirals, Generals: Repeal 'Don't Ask, Don't Tell.'" (2008, November 18). Servicemembers Legal Defense Network. Retrieved March 4, 2009, available: www.sldn.org.

Balkin, J. (1988). "Why Policemen Don't Like Policewomen." *Journal of Police Science and Administration,* 16(1), 29–38.

Barriers to Women's Advancement. (2001, July). *Catalyst Newsletter,* pp. 1–7.

Belkin, Aaron, and Jason McNichol. (2002, March). "Pink and Blue: Outcomes Associated with the Integration of Open Gay and Lesbian Personnel in the San Diego Police Department." *Police Quarterly,* 5(1), 63–96.

Bell, Daniel. (1982). "Policewomen: Myths and Reality." *Journal of Police Science and Administration,* 10(1), 112.

Bierstedt, Kathy. (2009, March). Sergeant retired, Florida police department, personal communication.

Benson, Katy. (1992, August). "Black and White on Blue." *Police,* p. 167.

Blanchard, Kenneth H., and Spencer Johnson. (1983). *The One-Minute Manager.* New York, NY: Berkley.

Brooke, Aslan (2005). *Frontiers,* p. 18.

"City to pay gay officer $2.5 million." (2008, June 30). *The Orange County Register,* p. 1.

"Connections That Count: The Informal Networks of Women of Color in the United States." (2006). *Catalyst,* pp. 1–40.

"Court Rules on Worker Retaliation." (2009, January 27). *Contra Costa Times,* p. A13.

"Dover to Pay Ex-Sergeant $750,000 to Settle Suit." (2008, August 1). By Leslie Kwoh, *The Star-Ledger* (Newark, NJ), p. 1.

Equal Employment Opportunity Commission. "Enforcement Statistics and Litigation Charge Statistics FY 1997–FY 2008." Retrieved March 3, 2009, available: www.eeoc.gov/stats/enforcement.html.

Equal Employment Opportunity Commission, "Facts About Sexual Harassment 2008." Retrieved March 3, 2009, available: www.eeoc.gov/types/sexual_harassment.html.

"Federal Law Enforcement Officers 2004." (2006, August). Bureau of Justice Statistics. NCJ 212750.

Feagin, Joe R. (2006). *Systemic Racism: A Theory of Oppression.* New York, NY: Routledge.

Foster, Keith. (2006, August). "Gender and Excessive Force Complaints." *Law and Order,* 54(8), 95–99.

Grobeson, Mitchell. (2009). Sergeant-retired, Los Angeles, CA, Police Department, personal communication.

Hall, Thomas. (1992, October). Sergeant, Virginia State Troopers, personal communication.

Hammond, Teresa, and Brian Kleiner. (1992). "Managing Multicultural Work Environments." *Equal Opportunities International,* 11(2), pp. 6–9.

Hampton, Ron. (2009). "Unfinished Business: Racial and Ethnic Issues Facing Law Enforcement II." Paper presented at a conference sponsored by the National Organization of Black Law Enforcement Executives and the Police Executive Research Forum, Reno, Nevada.

Harris, Philip. (2005). *High Performance Leadership.* Amherst, MA: HRD Press.

"History of Woman in the Workforce." (1991, September 19). *Business Week,* p. 112.

Human Rights Campaign Fund. (2006). Available: http://www.hrc.org.

Jones, Susan. (2009). Chief of Police, Healdsburg, CA, Police Department, personal communication.

"Local Police Departments and Sheriffs' Offices 2003." (2006). Bureau of Justice Statistics. Retrieved April 20, 2009, available: www.ojp.usdog.gov/bjs.

"Many U.S. Jobs Have Become Less Male-Dominated." (2005, April). Department of Labor, Bureau of Labor Statistics.

"The Military Discharged about 12,340 People between 1994 and 2007 under 'Don't Ask, Don't Tell.'" (2008, November 18). *Servicemembers Legal Defense Network.* Retrieved March 4, 2009, available: www.sldn.org.

"Military Justice 101—Part 3, Enlisted Administrative Separations." (1998). Retrieved March 1, 2009, available: www.usmilitary.about.com/od/justicelawlegislation/a/miljustice.htm.

More, Harry. (1992). *Male-Dominated Police Culture: Reducing the Gender Gap.* Cincinnati, OH: Anderson Publishing, pp. 113–137.

"More Women Leaving the Labor Market." (2005, December 21). *Dallas Morning News,* p. C5.

National Center for Women and Policing. (2002a). *Equality Denied: The Status of Women in Policing.* Los Angeles, CA: Feminist Majority Foundation, pp. 1–17.

National Center for Women and Policing. (2002b). *Men, Women, and Police Excessive Force: A Tale of Two Genders.*

National Center for Women and Policing. (2002c). Survey on the Status of Women in Policing, 1997, 2000, 2001.

"2007 NCAVP Report on LGBT Domestic Violence." (2008, October 20). National Coalition of Anti-Violence Programs press release by Sharon Stapel, Executive Director of the New York City Anti-Violence Project. Retrieved March 1, 2009, available: www.ncavp.org.

"N.Y. Jury Charges $1.5M to City." (2007, February 1). LRP Publications. Employment Practice Liability Verdicts and Settlement Publications No.126981-2002 (N.Y. Sup. Ct.), Vol. 8, No.11.

"Obstacles Hinder Minority Women." (2003, August 7). *Contra Costa Times,* p. C1.

Police Leadership in the 21st Century: Achieving and Sustaining Executive Success. (1999). Bobby D. Moody, President IACP.

Polisar, J., and Milgram, D. (1998, October). "Recruiting, Integrating and Retaining Women Police Officers: Strategies That Work." *Police Chief,* pp. 46–60.

"Quick Facts on Nontraditional Occupations for Women". (2006, May 30). U.S. Department of Labor, Women's Bureau, p. 1. Retrieved April 19, 2009, available: www.dol.gov/wb.

Report recommends using military model to defuse racism in police departments. (1992, May 26). *New York Times,* p. A17.

Schulz, Dorothy M. (1995). *From Social Worker to Crime Fighter: Women in United States Municipal Policing.* Westport, CT: Praeger, p. 5.

"Scope of Explicitly Transgender-Inclusive Non-Discrimination Laws." (2007, October). *Transgender Law and Policy Institute and National Gay and Lesbian Task Force.* Retrieved March 1, 2009, available: www.thetaskforce.org/issues/transgender.

"Signs of Growing Home Violence amid Downturn." (2009, April 11). *Contra Costa Times,* p. A8.

Seklecki, Richard, and Rebecca Allen. (2004, March). "A National Survey of Female Police Officers: An Overview of Findings." Paper presented at the Academy of Criminal Justice Sciences Conference in Las Vegas, Nevada.

Simons, George, Carmen Vazquez, and Philip Harris. (1993). *Transcultural Leadership—Empowering the Diverse Workforce.* Houston, TX: Gulf Publishing.

Skolnick, J., and Bayley, D. (1986). "The New Blue Line." *Police Innovation.* New York, NY: Free Press.

"State Non-Discrimination Laws in the US." (2008, July 31). *National Gay and Lesbian Task Force.* Retrieved March 20, 2009, available: www.thetaskforce.org.

"Stonewalled: Police Abuse and Misconduct against Lesbian, Gay, Bisexual and Transgender People in the U.S." (2005). Amnesty International.

"Tearing Down the Wall: Problems with Consistency, Validity, and Adverse Impact of Physical 'Agility Testing in Police Selection.'" (2003, Spring). *National Center for Women & Policing*, pp. 1–10.

Thiederman, Sondra. (1991). *Bridging Cultural Barriers for Corporate Success.* San Francisco, CA: Jossey-Bass.

Toosi, Mitra. (2004, February). "Labor Force Projections to 2012: The Graying of the U.S. Workforce." *Monthly Labor Review,* pp. 1–4.

Uniform Code of Military Justice. (**UCMJ**, 64 Stat. 109, 10 U.S.C. ch. 47, 1950). Retrieved May 5, 2009, available: www.au.af.mil/au/awc/awcgate/ucmj.htm.

Waterman, Robert H., and Tom Peters. (1984). *In Search of Excellence.* New York, NY: Harper & Row Publishers, Inc.

"Women in the Labor Force: A Databook." (2005, May 13). U.S. Department of Labor, Bureau of Labor Statistics. Retrieved April 19, 2009, available: www.dol.gov/wb.

"Workplace Discrimination: Sexual Orientation." (2008, July 21). *Consumer Health Interactive*, Bruce Mirken. Retrieved April 19, 2009, available: www.consumerhi.com.

"Workplace Issues." (2005). National Center for Women and Policing. Available: www.womenandpolicing.org.

CHAPTER 3

Multicultural Representation in Law Enforcement: Recruitment, Retention, and Promotion

LEARNING OBJECTIVES

After reading this chapter you should be able to:

- Recognize the historical perspectives of women and minorities in law enforcement.
- Discuss the ongoing challenges of recruitment trends with respect to women and minorities in law enforcement agencies.
- Explain recruitment difficulties, and strategies for success.
- Describe the importance of retention and promotion of minorities and women in law enforcement careers.
- Identify promotional policies and practices in law enforcement agencies that would demonstrate the valuing of differences in our workplaces and communities.

OUTLINE

- Introduction
- Recruitment of a Diverse Workforce
- Selection Process
- Retention and Promotion of a Diverse Workforce
- Discussion Questions and Issues
- Website Resources

INTRODUCTION

Our increasingly diverse society has created a demand for law enforcement officers and agents who can work effectively with many different types of people. For this reason, hiring and retaining qualified employees, especially women, blacks, Asians, Hispanics, and members of other nontraditional groups, continues to be a concern and a priority of law enforcement agencies nationwide. Many agencies have had difficulty finding qualified applicants, however, which has lead to a recruitment crisis. This crisis, although influenced by economic circumstances, appears to be primarily the result of changing societal and demographic trends.

RECRUITMENT OF A DIVERSE WORKFORCE

The recruitment of women and members of **diverse groups** is not a new issue in the history of U.S. law enforcement. In 1967, for example, a President's Crime Commission Report recommended that more minorities be hired, and that they receive opportunities for advancement. Soon after the Watts riots in Los Angeles, the 1968 Kerner Commission Report identified the underrepresentation of blacks in law enforcement as a serious problem. The report recommended improved hiring and promotion policies and procedures for minorities. The Warren Christopher Commission report on the Los Angeles Police Department, released soon after the 1992 riots following the first Rodney King trial, cited the problems of racism and bias within the LAPD. The Commission recommended, among other things, improved hiring and promotion processes that would benefit all groups.

> **Diverse Groups**   Diverse or diverse groups, in this textbook, will refer to persons of a different race or ethnicity than the majority population. The term also includes those persons who are gay, lesbian, bisexual, or transgender.

Recruitment Crisis and Trends

The past two decades have seen major shifts in employment trends in law enforcement agencies nationwide. Among these changes is the difficulty in recruiting qualified candidates for law enforcement positions. This reduction in the pool of qualified applicants can be attributed not only to the economy, but also to significant societal changes during this period.

GOOD ECONOMY   In the late 1990s and into 2000, the United States experienced the lowest unemployment rate in 30 years (approximately 4 percent) because of a robust economy. Although there were plenty of jobs in law enforcement, the number of applicants was substantially lower than in the past. Due to the employees' market, those seeking jobs could be very selective. Many jobs in private industry, especially high-tech jobs, came with high salaries, stock options, signing and year-end bonuses, company cars, and broader opportunities for advancement. Public sector employers had difficulty competing with such incentives and opportunities; thus, public safety occupations seemed less attractive. Court decisions (and pretrial settlements) against such companies as Coke, Texaco, and Wall Street's Smith Barney in race bias lawsuits also factored into recruitment difficulties during this time. Many large companies, aware that the populations within their recruitment areas were diversifying, knew that their employee demographics had to match those of the world outside or they, too, would be subject to lawsuits and/or criticism. As a result, they scrambled to recruit and promote talented women and minorities. This was particularly true of companies that sell products or services to the public. The wide-open market also made for transitory employees, especially those with experience, causing retention problems for employers. During this period, smaller law enforcement agencies lost staff as larger agencies lured experienced officers away with promises of better benefits. The recruitment effort, in which everyone was competing for the same pool of qualified candidates, has been compared to the National Football League draft.

At the same time, police departments experienced a reduction in staff because many officers who had been hired in the police expansion wave of the 1960s and 1970s (known as the baby boomers) began to retire. The fact that there were fewer births in the United States after 1960 (Shrestha, 2006) and that our population is aging represents a significant trend (p. 1). "In 1996 the first wave of 'baby boomers' turned 50, marking the start of a 'senior boom' in the United States. By 2010, one in every four Americans will be 55 or older" (Manning & Proctor, 1989). Most law enforcement officers retire before age 55, earlier than is typical in other civilian occupations. As the baby-boom-era officers began retiring at an accelerated rate, due in part to improved retirement benefits that became an industry standard during the early 2000s, the result was a shortage of employees. The problem was particularly acute because a large number of those baby boomers were members of minority groups.

A further strain on law enforcement agencies and their ability to recruit occurred as a result of the September 11, 2001, terrorist attacks on our country. Police departments were now asked to assume new homeland security and intelligence duties in addition to their normal, ongoing public safety responsibilities. As demand for police services expanded, agencies, with limited resources, still tried to recruit qualified personnel.

Another consequence of "September 11" was that law enforcement agencies began to face competition for recruits from an expanding number of federal and private security jobs created by the two-front war in Afghanistan and Iraq. In addition, the national military response to terrorism also affects the ability of existing police officers to meet traditional and new police missions, particularly in small and rural police departments where the call-up of even one or two officers who serve in the National Guard or Reserves can have a noticeable impact.

BAD ECONOMY   Beginning in late 2007, the United States experienced the worst economic downturn since the Great Depression (according to some economists), seriously impacting local, state, and federal governments. By June 2009, unemployment was at 9.5 percent, according to the Bureau of Labor Statistics (Bureau of Labor Statistics, 2009). Cities and counties were forced to reduce personnel through layoffs and attrition, as well as by freezing department size and limiting the number of trainees in academies. Unfortunately, layoffs disproportionately affect employees who were hired most recently, so that women and people of diverse ethnic and racial groups are often the first to lose their jobs, canceling any gains made in achieving a multicultural and multiracial workforce.

Agencies also responded to the downturn by reducing salaries and benefits. In some cases, seasoned officers moved to other agencies or occupations that better met their financial needs. Police forces in many cities and counties, their numbers diminished, had to cut back on services or use extensive amounts of overtime just to cover shifts. The tremendous downturn in the economy (in 2009) is expected to set the stage for an upsurge in crime, which will also create pressure on the whole criminal justice system.

One of the causes of the economic woes of city and county agencies was that tax revenues were shrinking while costs for police and firefighters' wages and benefits were escalating. Some municipalities had been saddled with labor contracts they could no longer afford to maintain. For example, some government agencies entered into contracts with their law enforcement and firefighters' unions that called for enhanced retirement benefits known as "3-at-50." This benefit allows employees to retire at age 50 with retirement pay of 3 percent of their highest annual salary multiplied by the number of years they served. If any agency in a given region offers this benefit, others must follow suit in order to stay competitive and retain personnel. As more and more eligible employees reached the age of 50, a major exodus of workers took place, severely impacting the budgets of many public agencies and creating vacancies that could not be filled owing to the poor economy.

In short, there were conflicting trends. Cost-cutting throughout local, state, and federal government forced layoffs, cutbacks in service, and unfillable vacancies. At the same time, there was public pressure for more effective services and protection from terrorist threats. Many of the new jobs in law enforcement require higher skill levels than in the past, yet the pool of qualified young workers is shrinking. Finally, beyond the issues of an aging workforce and the national response to terrorism, additional factors relating to education, drug use, criminal history, and physical fitness among youth have contributed to the decrease in the size of the applicant pool.

Recruitment Difficulties

Shifting economic forces, as described above, combined with social and demographic changes, have led to challenges for agencies in recruiting qualified workers. These challenges are intensified by recruitment standards set by local, state, and federal law enforcement agencies, which have historically eliminated many candidates seeking employment. For example, in California, according to Peace Officer Standards and Training (POST) spokesman Bob Stresak, "out of every 1,500 new law enforcement applicants, only 100 make it through the intensive hiring process that includes a thorough background and credit check, physical, psychological, and polygraph test. Of those 100 who make the initial cut, 10 percent drop out of the training academy and another 10 percent that graduate leave before completing field training" ("Law Enforcement Agencies Statewide Compete to Find Enough Qualified Candidates to Serve Their Communities," 2007).

Law enforcement agencies screen job applicants using standards that address age, height, weight, education, drug use, criminal history, and physical and mental fitness. As mentioned, many of those interested in a career in law enforcement cannot meet these rigorous standards, so some standards have had to change over the past few decades in response to social forces.

AGE, HEIGHT, AND WEIGHT   As the population has aged, some agencies have raised their upper age limit for new hires: for example, Boston (from 32 to 40), Indiana State Police (from 35 to 40), and Houston (from 36 to 44). There are even agencies that have no upper age limit, usually out of fear of age-discrimination lawsuits. However, the older job candidates are still required to meet the same physical fitness requirements during the testing processes and in the academy as their younger colleagues are required to meet. Most agencies have eliminated height requirements, requiring only that the candidate's weight be proportional to height and that they pass the training academy. In the past decade, the national obesity epidemic has also had an impact on law enforcement and military recruitment. In response, some agencies, such as the Juneau Police in Alaska, changed their weight standard and relaxed their fitness requirements.

DRUG USE AND CRIMINAL HISTORY   For many years, most law enforcement organizations were not considering job candidates who had a history of drug use of any sort. However, agencies have found it increasingly difficult to locate suitable applicants unaffected by the drug culture and have therefore eased their standards. The trend is that agencies will not disqualify candidates for minor drug use or even drug convictions that occurred well prior to their application.

According to a National Survey on Drug Use and Health study (NSDUH Report, 2005), teenaged girls are as likely as their male counterparts to use illegal drugs. The result is that women, too, have difficulty passing strict public agency background investigations. In addition, more women are being incarcerated for offenses that make them ineligible for law enforcement careers. A report by the New York–based Women's Prison Association documents the huge nationwide increase in incarceration of women over the past 30 years. The report indicates that the number of female state inmates serving sentences of more than a year grew by 757 percent between 1977 and 2004, nearly twice the 388 percent increase for men during the same period of time ("States Vary on Imprisoning Women," 2006). These trends pose a challenge to law enforcement agencies desiring to increase the number of women in their departments. For all these reasons, many criminal justice agencies no longer require that candidates for jobs have a perfectly clean criminal record.

EDUCATION   A high school education is usually required of applicants for most police departments. Some departments require 1 or 2 years of college coursework, and a few expect a 4-year college degree. Many law enforcement agencies had raised their educational standards for entry-level employees from high school to 2 years of college or more. However, almost one-third of high school students nationwide now drop out before graduating, according to a report in *Education Week* ("High School Dropout Rates," 2006), which also highlights the disparity between graduation rates among different ethnic groups. Approximately 55 percent of Latino and 50 percent of black students do not earn a high school diploma. Thus, even though the population is becoming more racially and ethnically diverse, many members of underrepresented groups are not eligible for law enforcement occupations.

Because of these concerns about the eligibility of minority officers, especially in diverse, urban areas from which an agency may be trying to recruit, only a small fraction of agencies now require that candidates hold a 4-year college degree. Typically, those recruits who do possess such a degree can expect a higher salary than their peers with fewer years of education. Most potential applicants do not have a college degree, however, and those who do are attracted to careers other than law enforcement for many reasons, including salary and benefits.

To increase their applicant pools, therefore, agencies such as St. Petersburg and Tampa, Florida, have eliminated the requirement of 2 years of college if the candidate has military or law enforcement experience. The relaxation of standards has been prompted in large part by a dire need to fill vacancies. At the same time, agencies are attempting to recruit candidates who are wiser, more worldly, and cooler-headed in a crisis.

ADDITIONAL FACTORS   There are other reasons why many individuals have been deterred from seeking a career in law enforcement. Highly publicized scandals involving police departments in some major cities have had a negative effect on recruitment. In addition, because of a history of acrimonious relationships between members of the minority community and the police, members of those communities—the very people law enforcement seeks to attract—may shy away, fearing disapproval from their peers for joining with the perceived enemy.

Another reason that has been suggested for the reluctance of young people to apply for careers in law enforcement is the paramilitary structure of most agencies, a rigid hierarchy that is unappealing to today's youth. In addition, most young people do not like to be micromanaged. For these reasons, policing has become a less attractive profession.

RECRUITMENT OF NON-SWORN PERSONNEL   The same factors impeding the recruitment of sworn personnel apply to nonsworn law enforcement staff as well. For example, most agencies today have a shortage of civilian dispatchers. This is a highly stressful job for which sound judgment and coolness under pressure are crucial. Candidates for dispatcher typically must pass a written and an oral test, a criminal background check, a polygraph, and a psychological exam. The job is so stressful that retention of good dispatchers is difficult. The long hours and night, weekend, and holiday shifts contribute to the high turnover rate for this position. Competition among agencies for seasoned dispatchers is fierce, and openings are frequent.

Cultural Diversity at Work, a newsletter addressing multicultural issues, presented a list of 10 most frequent causes of the failure to attract and retain high-level minority and female employees. The following is a brief synopsis, still valid today, of those most pertinent to law enforcement (Micari, 1993):

1. *Senior management is not sending the "diversity message" down the line.*   Senior management does not always demonstrate commitment in the form of value statements and policies emphasizing the importance of a diverse workforce.
2. *Informal networking channels are closed to outsiders.*   Women and minorities often experience discomfort within the traditional all-white, all-male informal career networks, including extracurricular activities. For example, some women police officers are uncomfortable participating in police association activities that involve recreational gambling, fishing, sports activities, or the roughhousing that can take place at meetings.
3. *In-house recruiters are looking in the wrong places.*   Recruiters must use different methods and resources to find diverse candidates than those they have traditionally used.
4. *Differences in life experience are not taken into account.*   Some applicants, both women and minorities, will have had life experiences that differ from those of the traditional job candidate. For example, the latter has typically had some college experience, with a high grade point average, and is often single (and thus does not have the many responsibilities associated with marriage and children). On the other hand, many minority job candidates have had to work through school and are married, and may have children. Therefore, their grade point averages may have suffered.
5. *Negative judgments are made based on personality or communications differences.*   Although not everybody's style reflects cultural, racial, or gender characteristics, there are distinct differences in communication style and personality between women/minorities and the traditional white, male job applicants. Communication style differences are especially apparent when English is the applicant's second language. Generally speaking, women are not as assertive as men in communication. Sometimes these factors can affect the outcome of a preemployment interview and become barriers to a job offer.
6. *The candidate is not introduced to people who are like him or her.*   It is important that the candidate or new hire meet people of the same gender, race, or ethnicity within the agency. A mentor or support group may be crucial to a successful transition into the organization.
7. *Organizations are not able or willing to take the time to do a thorough search.*   Recruitment specialists indicate that searches for qualified minority and women candidates take 4–6 weeks longer than others. These searches take commitment, resources, and time.
8. *Early identification is missing from the recruitment program.*   Programs that move students into the proper fields of study early on and that provide the education required for the job are essential. Examples of such programs include internships, scholarships, and police programs (e.g., Police Athletic League) that bring future job candidates into contact with the organization.

Recruitment Strategies

Recruitment strategies to attract diverse candidates involve:

1. *Commitment:*   The chief executive and the department must demonstrate a genuine commitment.
2. *Planning:*   A strategic marketing plan must be developed which includes the action steps, objectives, goals, budget, accountability, and timetables.
3. *Resources:*   Adequate resources, including money, personnel, and equipment, must be made available to the recruitment effort.
4. *Selection and training of recruiters:*   Recruiters are ambassadors for the department and must be selected carefully, be trained to reflect the diversity within the community, and include women.
5. *Recruiting incentives:*   Police executives should consider using financial and other incentives to recruit women and minorities.
6. *Community involvement:*   The community should be involved in recruiting and hiring women and minorities for sworn and nonsworn positions.
7. *Military involvement:*   Efforts should be made to network with the various military branches to recruit discharged veterans.
8. *Internship, cadet, reserve, explorer scout, and high school police academy programs:*   High school and college students are potential future recruits, so programs should be available that address these groups.

To build a diverse workforce, recruitment strategies used in the past will no longer be sufficient and will not provide agencies with high-quality applicants. Agencies with maximum success in recruiting women and minorities have had specific goals, objectives, and timetables in place; these policies must be established at the top level of the organization.

COMMITMENT   Recruiting minority and women applicants, especially in highly competitive labor markets, requires commitment and effort. Police executives must communicate that commitment to their recruiting staff and devote the resources necessary to achieve recruitment goals. This genuine commitment must be demonstrated both inside and outside the organization. Internally, chief executives should develop policies and procedures that emphasize the importance of a diverse workforce. Affirmative action and/or programs that target certain applicants (where legal) will not work in a vacuum. Chief executives must integrate the values that promote diversity and affirmative action into every aspect of the agency, from its mission statement to its roll-call training. Externally, police executives should publicly delineate the specific hiring and promotion goals of the department to the community through both formal (e.g., media) and informal (e.g., community-based policing, networking with organizations representing the diverse groups) methods. While chief executives promote the philosophy, policies, and procedures, committed staff members, who are sensitive to the needs for affirmative hiring and promotions, carry them out. Executives should also build partnerships with personnel officials so that decisions clearly reflect the hiring goals of the department. It is recommended that police executives audit the personnel selection process to ensure that neither the sequencing of the testing stages nor the length of the selection process is hindering the objective of hiring women and minorities.

Although chiefs may be genuine in their efforts to champion diversity and affirmative action hiring, care must be taken that their policies and procedures do not violate Title VII of the Civil Rights Act of 1964. Also, agencies in states that have enacted laws prohibiting affirmative action hiring programs and the targeting of "protected classes" (e.g., California's Proposition 209, passed in 1996, which is discussed later in this chapter) must adhere to these regulations. A knowledgeable personnel department or legal staff should review policies and procedures prior to implementation.

PLANNING   A still-valid study by the NCWP, published in 2001 by the Bureau of Justice Assistance of the Department of Justice, offers recommendations for greatly increasing the pool of qualified female applicants. Among other suggestions, the study stresses the importance of making an assessment of your department's current recruitment practices and developing a strategic marketing plan. A strategic marketing plan would include the action steps that commit the objectives, goals, budget, accountability, and timetables for the recruitment campaign to paper. Demographic data should form one of the foundations for the plan, which must also take into account the current political, social, and economic conditions of the department and the community. To avoid losing qualified applicants to other agencies or private industry, the plan should provide for fast-tracking the best candidates through the testing and screening processes. Fast-tracking is an aggressive recruitment process wherein a preliminary, qualifying check quickly takes place concerning the driving, credit, and criminal history of the applicant before any other screening process occurs. Applicants who do not meet established standards are immediately notified. The remaining applicants are then interviewed by a trained, ranking officer or civilian holding the position for which the candidate is applying. Applicants earning a passing score on the personal interview immediately receive a letter advising them that they passed, thereby giving them tangible evidence that the agency is seriously considering hiring them. The letter also informs them that they must pass additional qualifying steps, including a background investigation, which must commence immediately. The applicant must complete the final testing within 10 days, or the agency may withdraw the offer. To streamline the process, background investigators have established blocks of time for other testing such as polygraphs and psychological and medical evaluations. Streamlining is important because in today's labor market, the best-qualified applicants will not wait for months while the testing proceeds at a slow pace; they will get hired elsewhere.

The strategic recruitment plan should include an advertising campaign that targets:

- Colleges and universities, including ROTC and sports departments
- Military bases and reserve units
- Churches, temples, synagogues, and other places of worship
- Minority community centers in minority neighborhoods; Associations for Hispanics, Native Americans, Asians, and African Americans
- Gymnasiums, fitness and martial arts studios, athletic clubs, and the like

Participation of women and minority officers within the department is crucial in recruitment efforts (see "Recruiting Incentives"), as is the involvement of groups and organizations that represent the target groups. If within the community there are high-profile minorities and women, such as athletes and business executives, they should be enlisted to promote police work as a career through media releases and endorsements on flyers and brochures.

The Fulton, New York, Police Department offers one example of how such planning can be accomplished. For them, newspaper advertising proved the most significant medium through which candidates learned about their department's police test, followed closely by television advertising. The department went a step further, however. They learned that 45 percent of candidates obtained police test packages from the police station, and 33 percent from the personnel office, so they made test packages available 24 hours a day, 7 days a week at the station because the personnel office is only open 8:00 a.m. to 5:00 p.m. Monday through Friday (Spawn, 2003).

RESOURCES Adequate resources, including money, personnel, and equipment, must be made available to the recruitment effort. Financial constraints challenge almost every organization's recruitment campaign. The size or financial circumstances of an agency may necessitate less expensive—and perhaps more innovative—approaches. For example, many small law enforcement jurisdictions can combine to implement regional testing. One large county on the West Coast successfully formed a consortium of agencies and implemented regional testing three times per month for law enforcement candidates. To participate, each agency pays into an account based on the population of its jurisdiction. Alternatively, each agency can pay according to how many applicants it hired from the list. The pooled money is then used for recruitment advertising (e.g., billboards, radio, television, newspapers) and the initial testing processes (e.g., reading, writing, and agility tests, including proctors). The eligibility list is then provided to each of the participating agencies, which continue the screening process for applicants in whom they have an interest. Police agencies should not see other agencies as competitors with respect to recruiting. By combining their efforts, they may be able to:

- Save money (consolidate resources)
- Develop a larger pool of applicants
- Become more competitive with private industry and other public agencies
- Test more often
- Reduce the time it takes from application to hire

In terms of recruiting a diverse workforce, the second benefit listed above—developing a larger pool of applicants—is central to reaching beyond the traditional applicant pool. Law enforcement agencies, taking advantage of the Internet's global coverage, can post position openings on their websites in an effort to recruit individuals with a wide variety of backgrounds and skills. Agencies now commonly maintain their own websites describing their departments and offering information on jobs available, testing dates, and how to obtain applications. Department websites have been found to be valuable recruiting tools when used to highlight the work of women and minorities within an agency.

Law enforcement career fairs, usually lasting no more than 2 or 3 hours, should be held on a weekend or an evening, so that people who are already employed will have the opportunity to attend. A media and publicity campaign should be used to attract women and minorities to the event. At the career fair, a role-model panel of women and minority officers from a variety of assignments within the law enforcement agency can describe their jobs and answer questions. A high-ranking minority or female officer should also address those in attendance to persuade them to consider becoming employees. Information about the application and selection process, the physical agility test, and the academy should also be available.

As mentioned, progressive agencies advertise openings and career fairs on free websites such as YouTube and Craigslist, as well as continuing to utilize more traditional venues. This technology is an inexpensive way to reach thousands of potential candidates for both sworn and nonsworn positions. It provides an opportunity for the agency to give job-hunters in-depth information about the department, and also about the recruitment and selection process. One agency on the West Coast discovered that in the year they created a women's section on the recruitment website, the percentage of females in the academy jumped from 8 percent to 50 percent. The website featured biographies and photos of the department's diverse workforce. The Internet has become the number one way that candidates for law enforcement careers learn of job openings and about agencies across the country.

SELECTION AND TRAINING OF RECRUITERS   A recruiter is an ambassador for the department and must be selected carefully. Police recruiters should reflect the diversity within the community and include women. Full-time recruiters are a luxury most often found only in large agencies. The benefit of a full-time recruiter program is that frequently the employees in this assignment have received some training in marketing techniques. They have no other responsibilities or assignments and can therefore focus on what they do, and do it well. They develop the contacts, resources, and skills to be effective. Whether recruiters are full time, part time, or assigned on an as-needed basis, however, the following criteria should be considered when selecting them:

- Commitment to the goal of recruiting
- Belief in a philosophy that values diversity
- Ability to work well in a community policing environment
- Belief in and ability to market a product: law enforcement as a career
- Comfort with people of all backgrounds and ability to communicate this comfort
- Ability to discuss the importance of entire community representation in police work and its advantages to the department without sounding patronizing

Recruiters must be given resources (e.g., budget and equipment) and must have established guidelines. They must be highly trained with respect to their role, market research methods, public relations, and cultural awareness. They must also understand, appreciate, and be dedicated to organizational values and ethics. They must be aware and in control of any biases they might have toward individuals, or groups of people, who might be different from themselves.

Almost every state's Commission on Peace Officer Standards and Training (POST) has developed a course on the techniques and methods of recruitment. Large, progressive agencies (or a consortium of agencies) could develop an in-house program patterned after these model courses. The Institute for Women in Trades, Technology and Science (IWITTS) can provide resources and training programs on recruiting and retaining women. The organization conducts national workshops, and also provides technical assistance to departments via personal contact or via the Internet. Their materials include a law enforcement environmental assessment tool (LEEAT) involving institutional checklists and data collection methods to help determine the best recruiting strategies for a particular law enforcement agency.

RECRUITING INCENTIVES   It is recommended that police executives consider using financial and other incentives to recruit women and minorities where such programs are lawful (monetary incentive programs may be adversely affected by Fair Labor Standards Act considerations). Financial and other incentive programs are especially useful to agencies that cannot afford full-time recruiters. They are used to encourage officers to recruit bilingual whites, women, and ethnically and racially diverse candidates, informally, while on or off duty. One possible program would give officers overtime credit for each person they recruit in those categories who makes the eligibility list, additional credit if the same applicant is hired, and additional credit for each stage the new officer passes until the probation period ends. Some departments offer officers (not assigned to recruiting) up to 20 hours compensatory time for recruiting a lateral police officer. Department members can also receive an additional 40 hours of compensatory time for recruiting a lateral who is bilingual or from a protected class.

An East Coast agency awards $250 to employees who recruit applicants (of any racial or ethnic group) who are hired, complete all phases of the background process, and start the academy. The same department awards $250 to employees who recruit lateral police officer candidates once they complete all phases of the background process, are hired, and report for duty. When these recruits make it through probation, the employee who recruited them receives $250 as an additional incentive. Encouraging all department members to be involved in the recruitment effort, including the promotion of law enforcement as a career, is usually effective. To be competitive in recruiting employees, especially minorities and women, agencies must offer incentives just as corporations do.

The loss of employees through retirement or transfer, or the pressure of the high cost of living in some communities makes offering incentives necessary and appropriate to attract qualified replacements to the organization. Some cities and counties offer signing bonuses to experienced officers from other agencies. For example, in 2008, the city of Oakland, California, offered experienced officers from the city of Vallejo a $25,000 signing bonus to join their department ("Vallejo Police Recruiting a Tough Go," 2008, p. A32). Some departments offer academy-trained applicants a $3,000 signing bonus. The amounts vary, but the practice of offering these bonuses has been used in other cities and counties across the nation by agencies that can afford it. Some jurisdictions also offer law enforcement officers help with down payments and interest-free loans on their first home. Such offers are used not only to encourage current police officers to stay with the department, but also to recruit new hires who might not be able to live in a high-cost community ("San Francisco Housing Aid for Teachers, Police," 2007, p. A36). Watching personnel leave for greener pastures can be frustrating for the department that invested time and money in the employee. It takes about a year to hire a new officer, at a cost of approximately $4,000 for the screening processes, and thousands more for academy training. Thus the use of incentives to attract and retain personnel with experience ultimately saves the agency money.

COMMUNITY INVOLVEMENT   Successful law enforcement agencies involve the community in recruiting and hiring women and minorities. The community must have some involvement early in the effort to recruit candidates for police work. Representatives from different ethnic and racial backgrounds should be involved in initial meetings to plan a recruitment campaign. They can assist in determining the best marketing methods for the groups they represent, and can help by personally contacting potential candidates. They should be provided with recruitment information (e.g., brochures and posters) they can disseminate at religious institutions, civic and social organizations, schools, and cultural events. Community-based policing also offers the best opportunity for officers to put messages out regarding agency recruiting.

Community leaders representing the diversity of the community should also be involved in the selection process, including sitting on oral boards for applicants. The San Francisco Police Department utilizes community leaders in all the processes mentioned. Many progressive agencies have encouraged their officers to join community-based organizations, in which they interact with community members and are able to involve the group in recruitment efforts for the department.

MILITARY VETERANS   Some law enforcement agencies commit time and resources to recruiting veterans who discharge, separate, or retire from military service. Veterans often make excellent law enforcement employees because of their experience within a military organizational structure. (See Chapter 2 for a further discussion of the recruitment of military veterans who are gay or lesbian.)

INTERNSHIP, CADET, RESERVE, EXPLORER SCOUT AND HIGH SCHOOL POLICE ACADEMY PROGRAMS   Law enforcement agencies should have various programs available to high school students, as they are potential future recruits. These are often referred to as "grow your own cops" programs. One such innovative recruitment tool was launched in San Jose, California, in 2002. Called the "Santa Teresa High School Police and Fire Academy," it is a year-long academy program that helps students prepare for careers in fire services or law enforcement. The Academy provides recruiters with a pool of candidates. The program is offered to about 60 students at a time from six school districts in Santa Clara County, California. The students spend half of each day at the academy and the other half at their own schools. Students, who wear uniforms, learn police and fire job skills, which help prepare them for those vocations. Another purpose of the Academy is to instill a sense of community service and spirit in the youth who attend, and to provide positive mentor/role-model guidance from professional law officers, firefighters, graduate students, and community members. Cadets collectively perform 6,000 to 8,000 hours a year of community service ("High School Police Academy," 2003).

As a part of a high school police academy, or of other programs geared toward this age group, role model and mentoring components should be incorporated. Mentoring would involve police officers associating with youth in positive ways before the young people have made the decision to use drugs, commit crimes, or drop out of school. Such programs would include an emphasis on the importance of developing good speaking and writing skills; weaknesses in these areas disqualify many candidates from careers in law enforcement. Police Athletic Leagues, which have operated in many agencies across the nation for decades, have also traditionally filled this mentorship role.

Young people are clearly a very important part of any recruitment effort, so law enforcement agencies should develop and use surveys of the demographics and attitudes of this age group. Such surveys could help gauge the level of interest in law enforcement careers, and help determine what changes police might need to make to attract the best candidates. The survey can also provide an opportunity to promote such programs as police intern, cadet, explorer, and high school academy.

Mini Case Study: Richmond, California, Police Department

[Police Chief Chris Magnus of the Richmond, California, Police Department] has repeatedly stressed his intention to hire more locals to help fill a deficit in staffing that, in 2004, left vacant a quarter of Richmond's authorized contingent of officers. That new emphasis on finding local recruits, and those who reflect the region's diversity, has noticeably increased the flow of applicants through Richmond's recruitment office this year [2006] for its two dozen officer vacancies. "We are looking at a greater pool of people, and we are tapping pools of talent where we did not previously recruit," said Sgt. Lori Curran, the department's recruitment supervisor. Richmond is using not just traditional police recruitment tactics, which include visiting undeclared regional academy cadets, college students enrolled in criminal justice courses, and recently discharged military veterans, but also new venues, which include churches and temples of various faiths across the region, private-sector job fairs, and the city's extensive network of neighborhood councils. They are also seeking applicants from the private sector within the community—store clerks, office workers, and the like. ("Department Finds Recruits," 2006, p. A27)

SELECTION PROCESSES

Prior to initiating any selection process, law enforcement agencies must assess the satisfaction level of current employees and the workplace environment of the department.

Satisfaction Level of Employees

The first step before outreach recruitment can take place is for the department to look inward. Are any members, sworn or nonsworn, experiencing emotional pain or suffering because of their race, ethnicity, nationality, gender, or sexual orientation? A department seeking to hire applicants from these groups cannot have internal problems, either real or perceived, related to racism, discrimination, or hostility toward female, gay male, or lesbian officers. A department with a high turnover rate or a reputation for not promoting women, minorities, or gays and lesbians will also deter good people from applying. The department must resolve any internal problems before meaningful recruitment can occur. To determine the nature and extent of any such problems, law enforcement agencies can perform an assessment of all their employees through anonymous surveys about their work environment. There should be a review of policies and procedures (especially those related to sexual harassment and gender discrimination) and an examination of statistical information such as the number of officers leaving the department and their reasons for doing so, as well as which employees are promoted. The goal is not only to evaluate the workplace environment for women and minorities, but also to determine what steps need to be taken to dissolve barriers confronting them. See Appendix A for a sample survey that can be used for this purpose.

Supervisors and managers must talk with all members of their workforce on a regular basis to find out if any issues are disturbing them. They must then demonstrate that they are taking steps to alleviate the sources of discomfort, whether this involves modifying practices or simply discussing behavior with other employees.

The field-training program for new recruits should also be reviewed and evaluated to ensure that new officers are not being arbitrarily eliminated or subjected to prejudice or discrimination. By the time a recruit has reached this stage of training, much has been invested in the new officer; every effort should be made to see that he or she completes the program successfully. Negligent retention, however, is a liability to an organization. When it is well documented that a trainee is not suitable for retention, release from employment is usually the best recourse regardless of race, ethnicity, sexual orientation, or gender.

Role models and networking and mentoring programs should be established to give recruits and junior officers the opportunity to receive support and important information from senior officers of the same race, ethnicity, gender, or sexual orientation. Many successful programs, however, include role models of different backgrounds than the recruits.

Applicant Screening (Employment Standards)

A bad hire, in any occupation, can be very costly to an organization. Law enforcement agencies, therefore, must create a complete plan to recruit, screen, and hire solid candidates to fill openings. The hiring agency must have an accurate, up-to-date job description and an understanding of current standards for the position(s) for which they are hiring. An applicant should know exactly what the standards for employment are and what the job requires so there are no surprises. Those agencies needing assistance in establishing effective and defensible standards for the employment and training of peace officers should contact the International Association of Directors of Law Enforcement Standards and Training (IADLEST). (See Website Resources at the end of this chapter.)

Law enforcement agencies must assess applicants along a range of dimensions (employment standards) that include, but are not limited to:

- Basic qualifications such as education, requisite licenses, and citizenship
- Intelligence and problem-solving capacity
- Psychological fitness
- Physical fitness and agility
- Current and past illegal drug use
- Character as revealed by criminal record, driving record, work history, military record, credit history, reputation, and polygraph examination
- Aptitude and ability to serve others (see "Innovations in Police Recruitment and Hiring: Hiring in the Spirit of Service," 2001)
- Racial, ethnic, gender, sexual orientation, and cultural biases

The last dimension, testing for biases, deserves particular attention. An agency whose hiring procedures screen for unacceptable biases demonstrates to the community that it seeks police officers who will carry out their duties with fairness, integrity, diligence, and impartiality—officers who will respect the civil rights and dignity of the people they serve and with whom they work. Such screening should include not only the use of psychometric testing instruments developed to measure attitudes and bias, but also careful background investigation of the candidate by personnel staff. The investigation should consider the applicant's own statements about racial issues, as well as interviews with references who provide clues about how the applicant feels about and treats members of other racial, ethnic, gender, and sexual-orientation groups. These interviews would include questions on:

- How the applicant has interacted with other groups
- What people of diverse groups say about the applicant
- Whether the applicant has ever experienced conflict or tension with members of diverse groups or individuals, and how he or she handled the experience

Because of the emphasis on community-oriented policing, law enforcement recruiters must also seek applicants who demonstrate the mentality and ability to serve others (not just fight crime). Recruiters therefore are looking for candidates who are adaptable, analytical, communicative, compassionate, courageous (both physically and morally), culturally sensitive, decisive, disciplined, ethical, goal-oriented, incorruptible, mature, responsible, and self-motivated. Agencies also expect officers to have good interpersonal and communication skills, as well as sales and marketing abilities, so applicants should be screened for these attributes, and for their desire for continued learning and ability to work in a rapidly evolving environment. Officers more and more are encountering the challenges of different language(s), cultural and generational differences, and the diverse opinions of members of the communities they serve. Agencies must develop means of generating trust among the diverse groups. The importance of bilingual officers and officers with cultural understanding is paramount in today's communities.

The search for recruits should focus on those who demonstrate an ability to take ownership of problems and work with others toward solutions. These potential officers must remain open to people who disagree with them or have opinions that differ from their own. Law enforcement agencies should make their goals and expectations clear to candidates for employment, recognizing that some candidates will not match the department's vision, mission, and values, and therefore should be screened out at the beginning of the process.

Robert Jones, professor of psychology at Southwest Missouri State University, says that recruiters can get a clear appraisal of applicants in service-related jobs, such as law enforcement, by applying the five basic traits of human behavior: (1) emotional stability, (2) extroversion versus introversion, (3) openness to experience, (4) agreeableness versus toughness, and (5) conscientiousness. Today, effective law enforcement agents work closely with neighborhood groups, social welfare agencies, housing code officials, and a host of others in partnerships to control crime and improve quality of life. Law enforcement agents must be eager to understand a task, draw up a plan, and follow it through to completion in concert with others. Without an agreeable nature, officers and deputies faced with today's changing attitude toward crime fighting would not have a chance.

It is in the best interest of law enforcement agencies to complete a job analysis before implementing tests. Although it is a time-consuming process, the final result is a clear description of the job for which applicants are applying and being screened. Utilizing the job analysis data, tests and job performance criteria can be developed and made part of the screening process. Applicants when provided with a copy of the job analysis can decide in advance if they fit the criteria.

Aptitude for a law enforcement career can also be determined from structured oral interviews. The oral interview panel should be gender and racially diverse, and include members of the local community to reduce the possibility of bias. The panel should also include both sworn and civilian law enforcement employees. It is important that all raters are supportive of women and minorities in policing, and thoroughly trained in the rules of the interview process. Questions should be developed in advance for the oral interview, and should test for the skills and abilities needed for community policing, including the ability to work with all types of people, to de-escalate violence, to mediate disputes, and to solve problems. The same questions should be asked of each candidate, regardless of whether the candidate is male or female.

The authors believe that one of the most useful new tools for law enforcement recruitment (a paradigm shift in recruitment philosophy) comes from the findings of the federally funded project Hiring in the Spirit of Service (HSS). The project's recommendations represent a major change in recruitment strategy, as agencies using HSS are seeking and hiring service-oriented law enforcement personnel.

HIRING IN THE SPIRIT OF SERVICE   The HSS program, developed in the late 1990s, suggests ways of recruiting applicants who are not drawn to a law enforcement career because of the spirit of adventure ("crime fighter") associated with the profession, but are attracted because they are service-minded. Recruitment should not just be for those who are educated, but for those who will work well within COP (community-oriented policing) and POP (problem-oriented policing) philosophies. These philosophies require intelligent individuals who can solve problems. The individuals' size (a move away from recruiting "big tough cops") should not matter if they have interpersonal and service-oriented skills. Those recruited must be able to accept diversity not only within the community they work, but also within their own workforce.

The HSS program targets persons whose qualifications are consistent with other service-oriented professions, like teaching, nursing, and counseling, as long as they are able to meet strict physical training and fitness demands. Historically, candidates who did not fit the "crime fighter" mentality were discouraged from applying or disqualified at some point in the testing process. Those departments using the HSS selection process reach out to service-minded candidates, attracting them to law enforcement professions they might not have considered. The HSS project involved a cooperative agreement awarded to the Community Policing Consortium (CPC) by the U.S. Department of Justice Office of Community-Oriented Police Services (the COPS Office). The CPC examined the components of traditional screening procedures in order to find creative ways to revise traditional practices to make them consistent with the principles of community (service-oriented) policing.

> The CPC was particularly interested in a strong emphasis on community engagement—the core of community policing—which enables the building of trust, the development of collaborative problem-solving partnerships, and greater accountability to the community. These emphases set community policing apart from the professional model of policing and have been instrumental in introducing change to the police culture. ("Innovations in Police Recruitment," 2001, p. 1)

Through a competitive process, five law enforcement agencies were selected to serve as demonstration sites for the study. The five agencies were selected because they represent the gamut of law enforcement challenges in the United States. The sites were Burlington, Vermont, a small department with a growing multicultural community; Sacramento, California; Detroit, Michigan; Hillsborough County, Florida; and King County, Washington (both of the latter are full-service sheriffs' offices).

The HSS project report noted the great lengths to which the agencies went to involve citizens in substantive ways in the processes, and how the communities influenced strategies and outcomes. The report also stressed that the complicated processes of HSS are neither easy nor quick, especially the involvement of community members. Each agency encountered many challenges during the study. The study findings and recommendations resulted in revisions to each agency's recruitment and hiring practices, which are now based on the identified personal characteristics and required competencies necessary to perform the community policing function.

A study by the NCWP produced a self-assessment guide to assist agencies seeking to recruit and retain more women in sworn law enforcement positions. The resulting publication, *Recruiting and Retaining Women: A Self-Assessment Guide for Law Enforcement*, provides assistance to federal, state, and local law enforcement agencies in examining their policies and procedures to identify and remove obstacles to hiring and retaining women at all levels of the organization. The guide also provides a list of resources for agencies to use when they plan or implement changes to their current policies and procedures. The guide promotes increasing the number of women at all ranks of law enforcement as a strategy to strengthen community policing, reduce police use of force, enhance police response to domestic violence, and provide balance to the workforce. It is also recommended that chiefs of police, police recruiters, and city and county personnel department employees review *Recruitment and Retention of Qualified Police Personnel—A Best Practices Guide*, published by the International Association of Chiefs of Police. The National Institute of Justice (NIJ) has published *Hiring and Keeping Police Officers*, the findings of a study that examined recent experiences of police agencies nationwide in hiring and retaining sworn officers (Koper, 2004). This report is available online at www.ojp.usdoj.gov or by calling the Criminal Justice Reference Service. Another study, *Tearing down the Wall*, by NCWP also provides insights on physical agility testing (National Center for Women and Policing, 2003).

Examples of Successful Recruiting Programs

Successful recruitment programs vary by community. If recruitment efforts result in a large enough pool of qualified applicants, the pool will contain individuals of all backgrounds. The following agencies have had success in recruiting female and minority applicants, and might be contacted to determine the strategies they used: Portland, Oregon; Madison, Wisconsin; Pittsburgh,

Pennsylvania; Albuquerque, New Mexico; Tucson, Arizona; Burlington, Vermont; Sacramento, California; Detroit, Michigan; Hillsborough County, Florida; and King County, Washington.

To assist law enforcement agencies that wish to increase the number of women employees in their workforce, the NCWP offers the following services:

- A regional training seminar on recruiting and retaining women. This 2-day seminar helps law enforcement agencies develop effective recruiting programs to increase the number of female employees.
- Online updates to the self-assessment guide. New programs in law enforcement agencies across the country are described on the website, where readers can access the latest research about women in policing and other critical issues.
- Onsite consulting by a team of professional law enforcement experts to help agencies identify and remove obstacles to recruiting and retaining women.

For additional information on these services, contact the NCWP; see their website address at the end of this chapter.

Legal Issues and Affirmative Action

The authors acknowledge that there may be some controversial and even legal aspects in some states or jurisdictions to recruitment efforts that target women and diverse candidates for law enforcement jobs. Federal law prohibits programs that require meeting specific hiring goals for any particular group except when necessary to remedy discrimination.

In California, Proposition 209, which outlawed governmental discrimination and preferences based on race, sex, color, ethnicity, or national origin, was passed in 1996. The law provides that any government agency that offers preferential treatment in hiring or promoting employees could be penalized by having the state cut off its tax dollars. In September 2000, justices of the California Supreme Court affirmed that the proposition was legal. The justices, in their decision, placed strict limits on employers regarding the types of outreach programs they can legally use to recruit employees; any outreach program that gives minorities and women a competitive advantage is a violation of Proposition 209. Many other states followed California's example by enacting similar legislation, but not all. In 2008, Colorado voters became the first in the nation to reject a ballot proposition that would have banned affirmative action programs allowing the consideration of race or gender in state hiring, contracting, and college admissions. Agencies need to research what strategies are legal and appropriate within their state and jurisdiction.

Affirmative action and consent decrees have enjoyed only moderate success in attempts toward achieving parity in the hiring of women and individuals from ethnically and racially diverse backgrounds. There has been even less success with promotions of members of these groups to command ranks. In fact, studies have found that affirmative action has produced uneven results by race, gender, and occupation across the nation.

An unfortunate problem that can be associated with the promotion of women and nonwhites is that doubts are raised about their qualifications: Are they qualified for the job, or are they products of affirmative action? Peers may subtly or even explicitly express to each other that the promotion was not the result of competence, and the promoted candidate may feel that his or her success is not based entirely on qualifications. Consequently, employees may experience strained relationships and lowered morale. There is no denying the potential for a strong negative internal reaction in an organization when court orders have mandated promotions. Some white employees feel anger or frustration with consent decrees or affirmative action–based promotions. Clearly, preventive work must be done to avoid such problems.

The National Organization of Black Law Enforcement Executives (NOBLE) has consistently endorsed affirmative action to increase the numbers of minorities in the profession. NOBLE has met with recruiters and other representatives of law enforcement across the nation to discuss potentially successful minority recruitment strategies. One such strategy involves the creation of a pilot project with 10 historically black colleges to increase the number of graduates pursuing law enforcement careers. The project includes workshops, lectures, and miniconferences, as well as internships in law enforcement. NOBLE has also sponsored job fairs that attract prospective candidates for employment, who then meet with representatives from participating agencies (details available at www.noblenational.org, 2008).

Mini Case Study: What Would You Do?

You are the new personnel sergeant responsible for a department with 50 sworn officers. The department has one African American man, two Hispanic men, and two women officers. There has never been a large number of minority or women candidates applying for sworn positions in the department, and your agency does not reflect the demographics of the city. Your city has an affirmative action program, but to date, no outreach programs have been initiated to recruit women and minorities. Your chief has asked that you provide a proposal on what strategies you would suggest to recruit women and minorities. Develop a list of what you would propose. Make a list of what other departmental processes should take place prior to applicant testing.

RETENTION AND PROMOTION OF A DIVERSE WORKFORCE

Recruiting officers who reflect the gender, racial, ethnic, and sexual orientation demographics of the community is one important challenge for law enforcement agencies. Retention and promotion of them are equally important. Retention of any employee is usually the result of good work on the part of the employee and a positive environment wherein all employees are treated with dignity and respect. A high rate of retention is most likely in organizations that meet the basic needs of employees, offer reasonable opportunities for career development, and have mentoring and networking programs. In fact, once an agency earns a reputation for fairness, talented men and women of all ethnicities and races will seek out that agency and will remain longer. In addition, "some law enforcement agencies find that an ongoing professional development program increases job satisfaction. To be successful in a constantly changing occupation, employees must increase their skills. If they work for an organization that does not provide such benefits, they will go elsewhere to find them" ("Increasing Officer Retention through Educational Incentives," 2009, p.12). Training for officers of all ranks should continue throughout their careers. Such training should not only address the necessary, practical skills involving search and seizure, firearms, defensive tactics, arrest procedures, and so on, but also "include current issues, especially pertaining to interaction in a diverse community and communications skills" ("Increasing Officer Retention through Educational Incentives," 2009). Also, departments with programs that help their employees obtain advanced degrees find that such a practice often results in happy and productive members who stay with that agency.

The lack of promotions of protected classes and women to supervisor and command ranks has been cited as a severe problem in policing for over three decades by scholars and police researchers alike. Authors and advocates for the promotion of women have used the term *glass ceiling* to describe an unacknowledged barrier that inhibits those officers from reaching ranks above entry level. Whether there is a glass ceiling or not, women still constitute only a small proportion of police supervisors and managers. Within organizations, women and others of diverse backgrounds are frustrated when promotional opportunities seem more readily available to white males than to them. The disenchantment that often accompanies frustration frequently leads to low productivity and morale, early burnout, and resignation; to those individuals, opportunities appear better elsewhere. Lack of attention to equal opportunity promoting practices at some law enforcement agencies has resulted in court-ordered promotions. These have a negative impact on a department's operations and relationships, both internally and externally, and often lead to distrust and dissatisfaction.

> In a healthy job market, an unhappy employee will leave for a 5 percent salary increase, but it will take a 20 percent increase for a happy employee to leave. Some situations occur where employees would not leave for anything less than 30 percent because their present position fulfills them. Exit surveys have identified several reasons why individuals choose to leave employment. The most common was a perceived limited potential for professional growth, characterized as a lack of hope in the present position. Others included a lack of respect or support from supervisors; compensation-related issues pertaining to the individual's value or worth; the perception that supervisors lack leadership skills; and issues related to the employee's work hours (e.g., inflexible schedule, not enough overtime, or an undesirable shift). ("Increasing Officer Retention through Educational Incentives," 2009, pp. 11–12)

Exit interviews should be utilized to determine the reason why any employee is leaving. "Many employees state during exit interviews that they are leaving for a better-paying position. Leaders should personally meet with them and ask questions to clarify whether that is the real reason" ("Executive Coaching for Law Enforcement," 2008, p. 18).

Police executives and city or county managers cannot afford to minimize the consequences of poor retention and inadequate promotional opportunities for women and diverse members of their organizations. Some departments have done very well in recruiting and hiring women, but, for reasons that are yet to be studied, women have left departments more quickly than men. A 1998 study by the IACP found that about 60 percent of the women who leave law enforcement occupations do so between their 2nd and 5th year on the job. The reasons vary, but family pressures are the most frequently cited cause. The report recommended fairer screening procedures, tougher sexual harassment policies, and sustained drives designed to attract women and keep them on the job. A more recent study (2004) by *Catalyst* (see Website Resources) determined the top three reasons for which senior-level women would leave their current organization: 42 percent cited increased compensation; 35 percent, the opportunity to develop new skills or competencies, and 33 percent, greater advancement opportunities ("Women and Men in U.S. Corporate Leadership," 2004).

Chief executives need to determine if female officers are applying for promotions in numbers that are proportional to their numbers in the department. If not, perhaps female officers need encouragement from their supervisors, mentors, or informal network associates. It is also possible that the promotion process disproportionately screens out female officers. Research shows that the more subjective the process is, the less likely women are to pass it. Some safeguards against bias include weighting the process toward "hands-on" tasks (e.g., assessment center testing), conducting structured interviews, selecting board members who represent different races and both sexes, and training the board members on interviewing techniques.

Failure to promote qualified candidates representative of the diverse populations agencies serve, including women, can result in continued distrust of the police by the communities. Underrepresentation within police departments also aggravates tensions between the police and the community. Some scholars and criminal justice experts argue that underrepresentation at all levels within law enforcement agencies hurts the image of the department in the eyes of the community.

GENERATION Y   In Chapter 1, the authors introduced the subject of "Generation Y" based on a study published in 2006. The study uses the terms *Generation Y* or *Millennials* to refer to those persons born between 1977 and 1994, a group that includes over 70 million people in the United States, or 20 percent of the population as of 2006. The study suggests that employers, managers, and supervisors wishing to recruit and retain members of this generation will need to understand their unique characteristics, learning styles, and work attitudes (NAS Insights, 2006). One particular characteristic that sets members of this generation apart is their technological proficiency, especially when compared to preceding generations.

Mini Case Study: How Would You Handle It?

You are a male lieutenant in charge of the special weapons and tactics unit. The first female officer will be assigned to your specialized unit shortly. The special weapons and tactics team members are voicing negative opinions about a female officer being assigned to the unit. They are complaining that standards will be lowered in the unit because women are not as physically fit as men for this assignment. When you have overheard these conversations, or when they have been addressed to you directly, you have refuted them by pointing to the women in the department who are in outstanding physical shape. This strategy has not been effective, as the squad members continue to complain that women officers can't do the job and that their personal safety might be in jeopardy. What would you do?

Summary

- Population changes, particularly those that result in greater diversity, create a demand for law enforcement personnel who have the ability to work with different types of people. The nature of policing has also broadened, requiring officers to master a complex set of skills. The adoption of the community-policing model requires departments to be more representative of and responsive to the communities served.
- Recruiting, hiring, retaining, and promoting a diverse workforce will remain a challenge in law enforcement for a long time. The number of people available and qualified for entry-level jobs will continue to decrease; more employers, both public and private, will be vying for the best candidates. Hiring and promoting women and minorities for law enforcement careers are achievable goals.
- Successful recruiting involves *commitment* by the chief executive; *planning*, including an assessment of current recruitment practices; adequate *resources*; properly selected and trained *recruiters*; the use of *incentives*; and *community involvement*. Law enforcement will have to use

innovative and sophisticated marketing techniques and advertising campaigns to reach the desired population of potential applicants, and it must develop fast-track hiring processes.

- The Hiring in the Spirit of Service (HSS) program suggests that to recruit applicants who historically would not be targeted by law enforcement agencies, departments must seek service-minded individuals having qualifications consistent with professions such as teaching, nursing, and counseling. In the past, candidates who did not fit the "crime fighter" image were discouraged from applying or disqualified during the testing process.

- Law enforcement is still in transition away from the aggressive, male-dominated (and predominantly white) culture of the past, so must now overcome the common perception that policing is a profession that requires only physical strength. With the shift to community policing, women can thrive. Departments are looking for people with good interpersonal skills who are community and service-oriented, and they are finding that women meet these qualifications. Law enforcement

executives should seek minority employees for the same reasons.

- Prior to initiating any recruitment effort, every agency must assess the satisfaction level of the current employees and evaluate the workplace environment. A department seeking to hire applicants from women and minority groups must first resolve internal problems, either real or perceived, related to racism, discrimination, or hostility toward female, gay male, or lesbian officers. A high turnover rate or a reputation for not promoting women, minorities, or gays and lesbians will also deter potential applicants.

- Retention of employees is crucial and requires a positive environment wherein all employees are treated with dignity and respect. A high rate of retention is most likely to occur in organizations that meet the basic needs of employees, offer reasonable opportunities for ongoing professional career development, and have mentoring and networking programs. Once an agency earns a reputation for fairness, talented men and women of all ethnicities and races will seek out that agency and will remain longer.

Discussion Questions and Issues

1. *Institutional Racism in Law Enforcement.* Law enforcement agencies typically operate under the pretense that all their members are one color, and that the uniform or job makes everyone brothers or sisters. Many members of diverse ethnic and racial groups, particularly African Americans, do not agree that they are consistently treated with respect, and believe that there is institutional racism in law enforcement. Caucasians clearly dominate the command ranks of law enforcement agencies. Discuss with other students in your class whether you believe this disparity is the result of subtle forms of institutional racism, or actual conscious efforts on the part of the persons empowered to make decisions. Consider whether tests and promotional processes give unfair

advantage to white applicants, and whether they discriminate against department employees of other races and ethnicities. Do officers from diverse groups discriminate against members of other, different cultures?

2. *Employment of a Diverse Workforce and Police Practices.* How has the employment of a diverse workforce affected police practices in your city or county? Is there evidence that significant changes in the ethnic or racial composition of the department alter official police policy? Can the same be said of gay male and lesbian employment? Does employment of protected classes have any significant effect on the informal police subculture and, in turn, on police performance? Provide examples to support your conclusions.

Website Resources

Visit these websites for additional information about recruitment and related issues.

Bureau of Justice Statistics (BJS): http://www.ojp.us.doj.bjs

BJS is a resource of crime statistics collected and analyzed by the Federal Bureau of Investigation.

Catalyst: http://www.catalyst.org

Catalyst is a research and advisory nonprofit membership organization working with businesses and professions to build inclusive environments and expand opportunities for women at work. Catalyst conducts research on all aspects of women's career advancement and provides strategic and web-based consulting services globally.

Community Policing Consortium (CPC): http://www.cops.usdoj.gov

The Community Policing Consortium, also known as COPS, is a partnership of five police organizations: International Association of Chiefs of Police (IACP); National Organization of Black Law Enforcement Executives (NOBLE); National Sheriffs' Association (NSA); Police Executive Research Forum (PERF); and Police Foundation. Community Policing Consortium is administered and funded by the U.S. Department of Justice, Office of Community Oriented Policing Services (COPS).

International Association of Chiefs of Police (IACP): http://www.theiacp.org

The website is an online resource for law enforcement issues and publications, including *Recruitment and Retention of Qualified Police Personnel: A Best Practices Guide.*

International Association of Directors of Law Enforcement Standards and Training (IADLEST). http://www.iadlest.org

The website contains information about this international organization of training managers and executives dedicated to the improvement of public safety personnel. The Association serves as the national forum of Peace Officer Standards and Training agencies, boards and commissions, as well as statewide training academies throughout the United States, except Rhode Island and Hawaii. IADLEST does research and shares ideas and innovations that assist states in establishing effective and defensible standards for employment and training of peace officers.

International Association of Women Police (IAWP): http://www.iawp.org

It is a website for information about training conferences, careers, jobs, publications, and research pertinent to women in law enforcement.

Institute for Women in Trades, Technology and Science (IWITTS): http://www.womenpolice.com

This website features fact sheets, news articles, and publications for departments on women and policing, including a free women-in-policing e-newsletter, which provides best-practice information.

National Association of Women Law Enforcement Executives (NAWLEE): http://www.nawlee.com

The website contains resources, news, member directory, conference and training information, seminars, and an information exchange forum for women executives in law enforcement.

National Career Academy Coalition (NCAC): http://www.ncacinc.org

The website offers information concerning career academies.

National Center for Women and Policing (NCWP): http://www.feminist.org

This website provides information concerning regional training seminars on recruiting and retaining women. It also is a resource for the latest research about women in policing and other critical issues. The organization has consultants to help agencies identify and remove obstacles to recruiting and retaining women.

National Organization of Black Law Enforcement Executives (NOBLE): http://www.noblenatl.org

This website is a good source of information on many subjects, including recommended police policy and procedure, NOBLE publications, press releases and training material, resources, and classes.

References

Bureau of Labor Statistics, U.S. Department of Labor. *Occupational Outlook Handbook, 2008–09 Edition, Police and Detectives.* Retrieved June 5, 2009, available at www.bls.gov/oco/ocos160.htm.

"Department Finds Recruits from Community." (2006, April 16). *Contra Costa Times,* p. A27.

"Executive Coaching for Law Enforcement." (2008, February). *FBI Law Enforcement Bulletin,* pp. 18–23.

"High School Dropout Rates on the Rise." (2006, June 21). *Contra Costa Times,* p. A1.

"High School Police Academy." (2003, January 5). *Contra Costa Times,* p. A37.

"Increasing Officer Retention through Educational Incentives." (2009, February). *FBI Law Enforcement Bulletin,* pp. 11–15.

"Innovations in Police Recruitment and Hiring: Hiring in the Spirit of Service." (2001). U.S. Department of Justice, Office of Community Oriented Policing Service. Project #2001-CK-WX-K094, p. 1.

Koper, Christopher. (2004). *Hiring and Keeping Police Officers.* U.S. Department of Justice, Office of Justice Programs. Available at www.ojp.usdoj.gov/nij.

"Law Enforcement Agencies Statewide Compete to Find Enough Qualified Candidates to Serve Their Communities." (2007, February 6). *Contra Costa Times,* pp. 1, 19.

Manning, Anita and Proctor, David. (1989). "Senior Boom: The Future's New Wrinkles." *USA Today,* p. 1D

Micari, Marina. (1993, September). "Recruiters of Minorities and Women Speak Out: Why Companies Lose Candidates," *Cultural Diversity at Work,* 6(1), 1.

NAS Insights. (2006). "Generation Y: The Millennials, Ready or Not, Here they Come." Available at www.nas-recruitment.com/talenttips/NASinsights/generationY.pdf.

National Center for Women and Policing. (2003, Spring). *Tearing Down the Wall: Problems with Consistency, Validity, and Adverse Impact of Physical Agility Testing in Police Selection,* pp. 1–10.

NSDUH Report. (2005, September 16). Available at www.oas.samhsa.gov.

"Police Agencies Find It Hard to Require Degrees." (2006, September 18). *USA Today,* p. 3A.

"San Francisco Housing Aid for Teachers, Police." (2007, October 21). *Contra Costa Times,* p. A36.

Shrestha, Laura. "The Changing Demographic Profile for the United States." (2006, May). *Congressional Research Service for the Library of Congress.* Order code RL 32701.

Spawn, Mark. (2003, March). "Recruitment Strategies—A Case Study in Police Recruitment." *FBI Law Enforcement Bulletin,* p. 2.

"States Vary on Imprisoning Women." (2006, May 21). *Contra Costa Times,* p. A17.

"The Military Discharged about 12,340 People between 1994 and 2007 under 'Don't Ask, Don't Tell.'" (2008, November 18). *Servicemembers Legal Defense Network.* Retrieved March 4, 2009, available at www.sldn.org.

"Vallejo Police Recruiting a Tough Go." (2008, March 30). *Contra Costa Times,* p. A 32.

"Women and Men in U.S. Corporate Leadership: Same Workplace, Different Realities?" (2004). *Catalyst.*

CHAPTER 4

Cross-Cultural Communication for Law Enforcement

LEARNING OBJECTIVES

After reading this chapter you should be able to:

- Identify the impact of language barriers in everyday law enforcement situations.
- Develop skills that demonstrate sensitivity toward speakers of English as a second language.
- Describe cultural frameworks, including hierarchy and "context," that influence communication.
- Explain typical communication dynamics in cross-cultural, cross-racial, and cross-ethnic encounters.
- List key interviewing and data-gathering skills that contribute to an officer's effectiveness.
- Identify verbal and nonverbal communication style differences across cultures.
- Describe appropriate male–female communication in law enforcement.

OUTLINE

- Introduction
- Language Barriers and Law Enforcement
- Attitudes toward Limited-English Speakers
- Cross-Cultural Communication in the Law Enforcement Context
- Cross-Cultural Communication Dynamics
- Interviewing and Data-Gathering Skills
- Nonverbal Communication
- Male–Female Communication in Law Enforcement
- Summary
- Discussion Questions and Issues
- Website Resources

INTRODUCTION

In multicultural training sessions for officers, we sometimes hear that there are too many groups about which to learn, and that it is impossible to modify behavior accordingly. Indeed, officers do not have to remember every microdetail about culturally influenced communication, and this is especially true when officers respond to emergencies. Officers *are* correct when they point out that the key to effective communication with citizens is respect. They are also correct when they say that, no matter what the background of the citizen is, they have to enforce the law and be consistent with everyone. That said, there are generalities related to cross-cultural communication and a recognition of these will enhance an officer's overall understanding of certain communication components that they experience or observe. We can reassure officers that there are not hundreds of cultural details to learn despite the myriad cultural, national, and racial groups that officers encounter.

After years of working with citizens from nearly every background, Dr. George Thompson, former police officer and Founder of the Verbal Judo Institute, believes that there are some communication essentials that contribute to effectiveness regardless of background. Exhibit 4.1 introduces and outlines these.

To paraphrase Thompson, the default is always respectful communication. Thompson takes the key concept of respect one step further: "Talking about respecting people [from all cultural backgrounds] is vague. But treating people with respect is an act that is highly specific" (Thompson, 2009). Ultimately, an officer needs to display respect in the "highly specific" ways that officers would, themselves, like to have respect demonstrated.

Even though we emphasize the universality of basic respectful communication, officers increase their cultural competence when they learn about cultural nuances that can result in communication obstacles or misunderstanding. For example, on the topic of respect, there is a cross-cultural framework to keep in mind especially when dealing with newcomers. In Exhibit 4.1, Thompson's second point is "In all cultures, everyone likes to be asked rather than told what to do." Newcomers from extremely hierarchical cultures are quite used to being told what to do, and at first may be a bit surprised that an authority figure would communicate to them in any other way. In fact, their fear of authority may be so deep that, initially, the respect and an absence of a direct command may even be perplexing. But this does not suggest that individuals want to be fearful of authority, but rather that they have been culturally conditioned in this manner over the course of their lives.

Understanding cultural differences and how they impact communication is critical. But there's a huge caveat. Let's also understand how we are similar, and what kinds of communication works with people of all backgrounds:

1. Remember that everyone, in all cultures, wants to be respected.
2. In all cultures, everyone likes to be asked rather than told what to do.
3. For all cultural, racial, or ethnic groups, it is better to provide options rather than make threats.
4. All people would like a second chance. Ask: "Is there anything I (we) can say or do to get your cooperation? I (we) would like to think there is."

EXHIBIT 4.1   Effective Communication across All Backgrounds.

Source: George Thompson, Founder of Verbal Judo Institute, Personal Communication, 2009.

Eye contact is another area related to respect where there are variations across cultures. In many parts of Asia, Africa, and the Middle East, people often show respect by not making eye contact. Some officers think of this behavior as defiant, but first-generation refugees or immigrants from these parts of the world are, in fact, communicating respect in the default way that they have learned. In addition, if the citizen has a certain tone of speech or is talking loudly, an officer may assume him to be out of control or aggressive. Because of their inborn ethnocentrism, all officers can fall into the trap of making judgments about citizens just by the way they talk.

In dealing with an individual who is not a native speaker of English, it is of key importance to keep these three points in mind:

- A listener can easily misinterpret speech patterns; intonation, in particular, carries emotion and intentionality; what one hears is not always what is intended.
- A listener can easily misunderstand spoken words when a speaker is not fluent in English.
- A listener should use several indicators for interpreting correctly what a citizen is attempting to say.

LANGUAGE BARRIERS AND LAW ENFORCEMENT

It is not only police officers who experience frustration in an encounter with someone who is not fluent in English. The following is a personal account of a Vietnamese police officer's struggles with English when he first came to the United States.

For the first few months of being here, I was always tired from speaking the language. I had to strain my ears all day long and all my nerves were bothered. It was hard work to make people understand my broken English and to listen to them. Sometimes, I just could not anymore and I just stopped speaking English. Sometimes I had to pretend I understood what they said and why they were laughing. But inside I felt very depressed. I am an adult and my language sounded worse than a child's. Sometimes it was better not to say anything at all. (Personal communication, 2009)

Nationwide, changing demographics have resulted in the need for law enforcement to deal increasingly with a multicultural population that includes speakers of other languages who do not have equivalent skills with English. From citizens who report crimes using limited English to crime suspects and victims, there is no absolute assurance that officers will understand them. Officers are justifiably frustrated by language barriers and find it difficult to do their jobs the way they have been trained. On a "good day" some officers make it a point to modify their English so that they will be better understood; on a stressful day, many officers are frustrated at having to slow down and listen more patiently. Some law enforcement officers are noticeably impatient when they deal with nonnative English speakers. Citizens who do not speak English know when police are not listening to their side of the story. As a result, citizens who are facing language barriers are not successful at communicating even the minimum amount of necessary information. Perhaps most difficult is the situation in which a person with limited English skills is traumatized, further affecting the victim's ability to speak English. Officers need to be aware of the potential for inadvertent discrimination based on a citizen's language background, which could fall under "language and national origin discrimination" (Fernandez, 2000).

Clearly, the higher the number of bilingual officers a department has, the more efficient and effective the contact is with non-English-speaking citizens. Many agencies subsidize foreign-language training for their personnel or seek recruits with multiple-language skills. When the resources are not available for such programs, however, there can be serious and sometimes tragic consequences. Non-English-speaking citizens may not understand why they are being arrested or searched. They may not know their rights if they are unfamiliar with the legal system, as is the case with many recently arrived immigrants and refugees. Using the wrong translator can mislead officers, so much so that a victim and his or her translator may give two completely different versions of a story—for example, using the friend of a suspected child abuser to translate the allegations of the child who has been abused.

Language barriers can lead to serious problems for non–English speakers. In some cases there is no sensitivity when it comes to language obstacles. For example, in a largely Spanish-speaking area in Los Angeles, a deputy, according to witnesses, asked a Hispanic male to get out of his car. The man answered in Spanish, "I'm handicapped," and he reached down to pull his left leg out of the car. The deputy apparently believed that the man was reaching for a weapon and con-sequently "struck him on the head with the butt of his gun" ("The Troubled LA County Sheriff's Department," 1992). This incident, while dated, is a lesson for all existing and future generations of police officers not to overreact on a motorist traffic stop.

Another Spanish language example has to do with the word "molestar," which means "to bother" or "to annoy." In the extreme, a Spanish-speaking individual could answer "yes" to an officer's question "Did you molest your niece?" The answer could be "yes" if the non-English speaking individual thought there was something about his own behavior that irritated or annoyed his niece. Certainly, the more the number of bilingual officers there are, the better. However, even without learning another language, officers can learn about features of other languages that may confuse an interaction when a limited-English speaker communicates with a police officer. For example, some languages do not have verb tenses (e.g., Chinese and certain languages of India), and thus you will hear, "I eat today, I eat tomorrow, and I eat yesterday." When recounting a crime observed, individuals not fluent in English might make verb-tense errors, potentially leading officers to think that they are not reliable witnesses or that they are not telling the truth. Similarly, in some languages such as Tagalog (one of the main languages spoken in the Philippines), there are no terms for gender in the he/she form. In English, some Filipinos mix up gender, again potentially giving an impression that they may be confused about the facts.

Intolerance of language differences and difficulties is sometimes voiced by police officers in cultural diversity in-service training workshops; similarly, recruit police officers attending cul-tural diversity classes in police academies echo this sentiment. It is not uncommon to hear "Why do I have to learn about their language and their customs?" In response to such questions, students need to be challenged and asked "Who benefits in citizen–police contacts when the police officer has effective communication skills?" The response clearly would be that both the police officer and the non- or limited-English speaking individual benefit.

Communication across cultures and with people for whom English is a second language can be frustrating and exacts a great deal of patience from officers. Exhibit 4.2 lists basic guidelines for communicating with others for whom English is only their second language. Sensitivity to the diffi-culties of those who do not speak English is in order, but that is only a partial solution to the prob-lem. In attempting to cope with the problem of dealing with non-English-speaking citizens, suspects, and criminals, many departments not only have increased the number of bilingual officers

1. Speak slowly and enunciate clearly.
2. Face the person and speak directly even when using a translator.
3. Avoid concentrated eye contact if the other speaker is not making direct eye contact.
4. Do not use jargon, slang, idioms, or reduced forms (e.g., "gonna," "gotta," "wanna," "couldja").
5. Avoid complex verb tenses (e.g., "If I would have known, I might have been able to provide assistance").
6. Repeat key issues and questions in different ways.
7. Avoid asking questions that can be answered by yes or no; rather, ask questions in such a way that the answer can show understanding.
8. Use short, simple sentences; pause between sentences.
9. Use visual cues such as gestures, demonstrations, and brief written phrases.
10. Use active rather than passive verbs (e.g., "I expect your attention" [active] rather than "Your attention is expected" [passive]).
11. Have written materials duplicated in bilingual format.
12. Pause frequently and give breaks. Monitor your speed when you speak.
13. Limit to only one idea per sentence.
14. Respect the silence that nonnative English speakers need to formulate their sentences and translate them in their minds.
15. Check comprehension by having the listener repeat material or instructions, and summarize frequently.
16. Encourage and provide positive feedback on the person's ability to communicate.
17. Listen even more attentively than you do when communicating with a native speaker of English.
18. Be patient. Every first-generation immigrant struggles with the acquisition of English.
19. Do not speak louder than you usually do. It will not help.

EXHIBIT 4.2   Basic Guidelines for Communicating with People for Whom English Is Only Their Second Language.

in their forces but have also begun to utilize translation services, some of which provide translation in over 170 languages, 24 hours a day. Some 911 emergency centers have interpreters available 24 hours a day for many languages.

Government agencies that serve the public are required by the Executive Order 13166 (see Exhibit 4.3) to provide "meaningful access" to all of its services. Commercial language lines have made it possible to support 911 call centers, extend victim support, issue Miranda rights, and even assist officers with routine traffic stops. Having access to multilingual interpretation services as well as community referrals is a first step in addressing the challenge of communication with those who speak no or limited English, but it is not a long-term solution. Having bilingual officers or bilingual nonsworn personnel, however, constitutes a more direct method of addressing the problem. Many departments across the country encourage on the job language classes with tuition reimbursement for classes and extra pay for second-language proficiency. Police department training personnel are encouraged to look for classes specially designed for law enforcement. If they do not exist, a few selected officers and language educators should form a partnership so that officers can guide language teachers in the development of police-specific second-language curricula (i.e., to meet the specialized needs of officers on the street).

> **Executive Order 13166**
> **Improving Access for Persons with Limited English Proficiency (LEP)**
>
> On August 11, 2000, President Bill Clinton signed Executive Order 13166. "Each Federal agency shall examine the services it provides and develop and implement a system by which LEP persons can meaningfully access those services"

EXHIBIT 4.3 **Executive Order Mandating Access to Services for LEP.**

Source: U.S. Department of Justice, Civil Rights Division, 2000.

A certain amount of distrust among cross-cultural and racial groups undoubtedly originates with language and communication problems. There is a strong and positive message to the community when departments provide some type of language teaching as well as match the appropriate language skills to a community's particular demographics.

Increasing bilingual hires is one of the most practical directions in which to go; as an additional advantage, bilingual officers often have a better understanding of the communities they serve. Some community-based police programs use trained community volunteers to assist them in situations in which English is not the language spoken. When translation is not available, officers have no choice but to rely on English. In such situations, the tips listed in Exhibit 4.2 on modifying one's language will be helpful.

ATTITUDES TOWARD LIMITED-ENGLISH SPEAKERS

It is important not to stereotype someone with little knowledge of English or an accent. An individual might have immigrated to the United States after the age at which people lose their accents (e.g., usually in their teens). Many immigrants have broken English, and may give all appearances of being "foreign" because their English is not perfect. The key is to not make inferences about individuals based on their accent or level of fluency; this includes the assumption as to whether they are documented or undocumented immigrants as well.

Citizens' use of a second language and the accompanying frustrations for officers can be overwhelming. In general, whether the society at large (or police as a microcosm of society) is concerned about a particular group's use of their native language seems to be directly related to the population size of that group. For example, when large groups of Cubans or Puerto Ricans speak Spanish there is often a higher level of anxiety among the dominant white population than when a few Armenians speak their native language. Virtually every immigrant group is said to resist learning English, yet the pattern of language acquisition among the generations of immigrants follows a predictable course. Members of the second and third generations of an immigrant family almost always become fluent in English, while many of the first-generation immigrants (the grandparents and the parents) struggle, sometimes partly learning English and sometimes not learning it at all. Many immigrants, however, are extremely motivated to learn English and become productive members of society. In urban areas, access to English classes is often limited (e.g., there have been known to be 4- and 5-year waiting lists for English programs at Los Angeles community colleges). Newcomers are fully aware that without English they will never be able to integrate into the society.

Nevertheless, some people, including established immigrants, have a tendency to overgeneralize their observations about newcomers. It is true that some people do not want to learn English and that even some middle-class U.S.-born Americans do not make efforts to improve their language abilities. How often do we hear that high school graduates who are native English speakers have not learned to write or speak well? In such cases, laziness or lack of high-quality education or both may have contributed to this aspect of illiteracy. In fairness, all groups have a percentage of lazy people, but sometimes people tend to stereotype others. Although not all first-generation immigrants learn English, there is a great deal of mythology around the "masses" of immigrants who hold on to their native language.

The native language for an immigrant family is the language of communication for that family. It is not uncommon to hear comments such as "They'll never learn English if they insist on speaking their native tongue at home." When one is away from one's family all day, it is not reasonable to expect that an individual could comfortably express affection, resolve conflicts, show anger, and simply relax in another language? Language is an integral part of a person's identity. During the initial months, and even years, of communicating in a second language, a person does not truly feel like himself or herself. Initially, an individual often has a feeling of play acting or taking on another identity when communicating in a second language.

From a physiological perspective, communicating in a foreign language can be exhausting. In speaking any given language, a person uses a set of muscles to articulate the sounds of that language. Changing to another language, particularly as an adult, requires the use of an entirely new set of muscles. Doing so causes mental strain and facial tension, which can lead to a person's "shutting down"—the result being an inability to communicate in the new language. It is no wonder that in the multicultural workforce, clusters of people from different ethnic groups can be seen having lunch together, taking breaks together, and so on. Simply put, it is more relaxing to be able to speak one's own language than to struggle with a new one all day.

Sometimes police officers say, "I know they speak English because they speak it among themselves" (i.e., when the group is culturally mixed). "The minute I'm on the scene, it's 'No speak English.' Why do they have to play dumb? What do they think I am—stupid?" It would be naïve to say that this situation does not occur. There will always be some people who try to deceive others and use or not use English to their own advantage. However, there may be other reasons that people "feign" not knowing English. Several factors affect an immigrant's ability to use English at any given moment. A few of these are of particular significance to law enforcement officers. Generally speaking, an immigrant's ability to express himself or herself in English is at its best when that person is comfortable with the officer. So, the more intimidating an officer is, the higher the likelihood that anxiety will affect the speaker's ability in English. Language breakdown is one of the first signs that a person is ill at ease and stressed to the point of not being able to cooperate and communicate. It is in the officer's best interest to increase the comfort level of the citizen, whether a victim, a suspect, or simply a person requiring help. However, language breakdown in a person, who is otherwise fairly conversationally competent in English, can also occur as a result of illness, intoxication, fatigue, and trauma.

Finally, officers' attitudes about immigrants and nonnative English speakers, whether positive or negative, are likely to affect their interaction with them. This is especially true when an officer is under pressure and negative attitudes are more likely to surface in communication.

CROSS-CULTURAL COMMUNICATION IN THE LAW ENFORCEMENT CONTEXT

To understand the need for skillful communication with members of culturally and ethnically diverse groups, including women, officers should recognize some of the special characteristics of cross-cultural communication in the law enforcement context (Exhibit 4.4). To best protect and serve communities made up of individuals from many different racial and cultural backgrounds, officers

- Officers have traditionally used styles of communication and language that at one time were considered acceptable. Now, because of diverse groups within the police agency and within our cities, the unspoken rules about appropriate and inappropriate communication are changing.
- For officers, communication can be tense in crises and in culturally unfamiliar environments.
- Officers' perceptions of a cultural group may be skewed by the populations they encounter.
- Officers' communication will be enhanced when they are aware of
  1. Perceptions
  2. Cultural filters
  3. High- and low-context communication (see explanation in text)
  4. Possible biases and stereotypes
- Through communication, officers have tremendous power to influence the behavior and responses of the citizens they contact. A lack of knowledge of the dynamics of cross-cultural communication will diminish this power.
- Improved communication with all citizens will also result in safer interactions for officers.

EXHIBIT 4.4   Key Cross-Cultural Areas in Communication for Officers to Consider.

as peacekeepers, crime fighters, and law enforcement representatives need to look beyond the "mechanics" of policing and examine what takes place in the process of cross-cultural communication. Communication, in general, is a challenge because "although the words are the same the meaning can be completely different. The same expression can easily have a different connotation or emotional emphasis. Misinterpretation is so common and consistent that eventually we develop limiting perspectives of each other" (Gray, 2002, p. 23). Does communication pose this much of a challenge? Talking to others, making one's points, and giving explanations should not be so difficult.

Every communication act involves a message, a sender, and a receiver. Given that any two human beings are fundamentally different, there will always be a psychological distance between the two involved (even if they have the same cultural background). Professional police officers have learned ways of bridging the gap, or psychological distance, between the two very different worlds of sender and receiver. In instances of cross-cultural communication, including crossracial and cross-ethnic interactions, in which the sender and receiver are from different cultures, officers have an even greater gap to try to bridge. Exhibit 4.4 summarizes key factors that can potentially contribute to cross-cultural and cross-racial communication challenges. Psychological distance exists between any two human beings because every individual is "wired" differently from the next. Styles of communication that differ across cultures can contribute to perceptions or misperceptions and incorrect filtering of communication "data."

The Influence of Hierarchy and Power on Communication

Hierarchy   A deeply embedded system of societal structure whereby people are organized according to how much status and power they have. Hierarchical societies have specific and defined ways in which people must behave toward those lower and higher on the hierarchy. Communication is restricted in hierarchical societies, and people are always aware of where they stand in terms of status and power vis-à-vis another individual.

Why is hierarchy important as a potential communication obstacle with some non–U.S. born citizens? First, when people come from hierarchical cultures, relationship building, at least in the initial stages, may be challenging. Law enforcement would have to recognize that "opening up" can take longer, and that the need to gain trust, a critical step with all citizens, may take more effort. (The reader can review the section on undocumented immigrants in Chapter 1 to understand other elements of the fear factor and communication with law enforcement.)

There is a strong link among the elements of hierarchy, power and communication. This has implications for law enforcement workforce interaction not only because agencies are hierarchical, but also because of workforce cultural diversity within an agency and attitudes that may be brought to work by first-generation immigrants and refugees. Beginning in the early 1980s and continuing through at least 2001, social psychologist Geert Hofstede researched and wrote about the effects of national culture on workplace behavior, including communication. One of the key areas that Hofstede discusses is directly related to hierarchy. It is the notion of "power distance," which was measured by "the degree to which the less powerful members of organizations, institutions and national cultures accept and expect that power is distributed unequally." In cultures where the power distance is high (e.g., India, China, the Philippines, Mexico, Venezuela, Egypt), there is more of an acceptance that this inequality is "normal," this belief being shared by both leaders and subordinates.

In a study entitled "Culture in the Cockpit: Do Hofstede's Dimensions Replicate?" researcher Ashleigh Merritt used Hofstede's concept of power distance (as one measurement) and applied it to communication in the cockpit between captains and first officers. Her findings revealed that in cultures where the power distance is high (i.e., a strong sense of hierarchy), there was a significantly higher incidence of plane crashes (other factors were studied as well). The data, compiled from 9,417 pilots in 26 airlines and 19 countries, meshed with Hofstede's earlier work on power distance: the countries in which there was a higher rate of plane crashes also happened to be countries with high power distance (Merrit, 2000). Where the pilot respondents (First Officers) indicated that their aviation companies had more of an autocratic or directive leadership style, they also responded that "subordinates [more frequently] are afraid to express disagreement in this case with the Captains" (Merrit, 2000).

While accounting for other factors contributing to plane crashes, the researchers of the study concluded that "effects of national culture can be seen over and above the professional pilot culture, and that a one-size –fits-all training is not appropriate . . ." (Merrit, 2000). What Hofstede's original work and this study show is that cultural influences have consequences, and that this has implications for the communication that takes place among different levels of hierarchy in culturally diverse law enforcement agencies.

High- and Low-Context Communication

Edward Hall is the author of three dated but still seminal books in the field of cross-cultural communication: *The Silent Language, Beyond Culture*, and *The Hidden Dimension* (Hall, 1959, 1966, 1976). He coined the terms *high-context* and *low-context* communication to describe very different frameworks of communication across cultures and individual styles. (Exhibit 4.5 depicts a view of the high- to low-context communication continuum across regions.) An understanding of the continuum of high- to low-context communication—which is related to hierarchy—will contribute to officers' understanding of direct and indirect communication, and explicit and implicit communication. In communication, people or cultural groups who tend toward the high-context end of this communication continuum exhibit the following characteristics, to varying degrees:

- Tendency to avoid saying no
- Tendency to avoid conflict
- Difficulty answering yes/no and either/or type questions; usually not either/or thinkers or communicators; awareness of shades of gray and broad context or scope

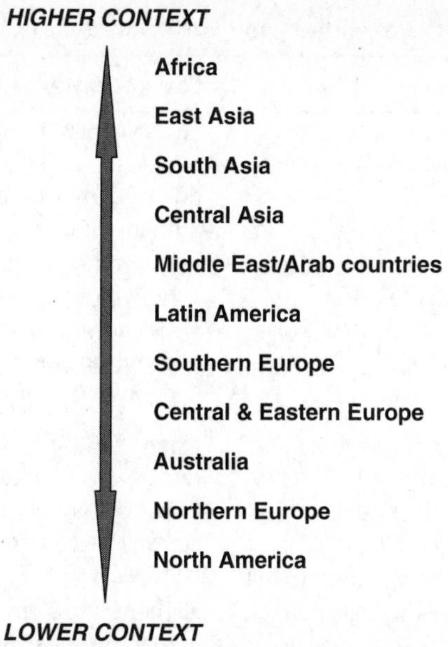

HIGHER CONTEXT

Africa

East Asia

South Asia

Central Asia

Middle East/Arab countries

Latin America

Southern Europe

Central & Eastern Europe

Australia

Northern Europe

North America

LOWER CONTEXT

EXHIBIT 4.5   High- and Low-Context Continuum across Regions.

Source: Adapted from Edward Hall—Beyond Culture (1976), Hofstede Geerte (2001).

- Concerned about saving face (theirs and others)
- Preference for harmonious communication; avoidance of disagreement
- Focus on "wide context" of interaction—past events, tone, nonverbal communication, relationship, and status of speakers; good readers of implicit communication
- Preference for getting to the point slowly and/or indirectly
- Appearance of "beating around the bush" (i.e., this is a low-context communicator's perception and filter of the higher-context style); in high-context communication, beating around the bush is seen as a polite style of communication and the "right" way to communicate

Lower-context communication tendencies include the following:

- "Yes" equals "yes" and "no" equals "no"
- Ease with direct communication and responding directly to conflict
- Saving face, one's own and others', not as important as saying the "truth"
- Focus more on words and what is verbalized—less focus on tone, nonverbal, relationship, status, past events, implicit communication
- Preference for getting right to the point; "beating around the bush" seen as negative

Exhibit 4.6 expands on these tendencies and provides a list of other cultural behaviors associated with them.

As officers know, rapport-building with all citizens is essential for building trust, and this is often preliminary to people's willingness to communicate freely with the officers. This is especially true when communicating with people who have higher-context communication styles. Typically, these styles are more characteristic of Asian and Latin American cultures. Within a lower-context culture, there are gender differences as well (i.e., women tend to have a higher-context style than do men). The style of communication in law enforcement is essentially a lower-context communication

EXHIBIT 4.6   Characteristics of Higher- and Lower-Context Cultures.

Higher-Context Cultures	Lower-Context Cultures
The relationship between two people determines, in large part, how communication should take place.	The style of communication is similar between people regardless of their relationship. People do not generally speak more formally to an authority figure.
• There is greater deference to authority. • There is more of a distance between people in authority and those who are not. • This distance often manifests itself in more formal and polite communication and more restraint.	• There is less deference to authority than in higher-context cultures. • It is acceptable for casual and informal communication to take place between people at all levels of the hierarchy.
Individuals who perceive themselves to be "lower" on the hierarchy tend to refrain from asking questions or offering their opinion in the presence of the authority figure.	Open and transparent communication can more easily take place in lower-context cultures, in general. (Organizations, however, can still be hierarchical even in lower-context cultures.)
• In a high-context culture, people tend to tell authority figures what they think authority wants to hear.	• There is less emphasis on pleasing authority than on speaking one's mind.
There is a greater focus on the importance of relationship rather than on task.	There is greater focus on task than on relationship.
• Accordingly, time allows for more interruptions, and attention to people (vs. tasks).	• Accordingly, there is a high value placed on task achievement and getting things done.
To a lower-context, task-oriented person, constant interruptions may appear unfocused, and the communication style may seem digressive.	• To a higher-context individual, task orientation may appear "cold" and can interfere with rapport building.

Source: Adapted from Edward Hall—Beyond Culture (1976).

style, but police officers should at least be able to identify when individuals are using a higher-context communication style. Chapter 5 provides several examples of higher-context communication in the law enforcement context and makes recommendations for responding effectively to this style. (See Section "Communication Styles of Asian/Pacific Americans"in Chapter 5).

One of the key tools for building rapport in law enforcement is neurolinguistic programming (NLP), a communication model and a set of techniques for establishing rapport. Officers have successfully used this communication tool to build rapport in interviews with witnesses and victims of crimes. The techniques involved have to do with a fundamental principle in interpersonal relationships, which is the need to create harmony with others in order to establish rapport. As such, the type of communication used with NLP is that of "matching" nonverbal and verbal behavior with a witness, victim, or interviewee. Doing so may prove to be especially challenging, with people from different cultural backgrounds, but is useful as a way to minimize the cultural gap between the officer's style and that of the citizen with whom he or she is interacting. It is beyond the scope of this chapter to detail the theory behind and steps involved in NLP. However, we have included in the Website Resources a link to an informative FBI publication entitled "Subtle Skills for Building Rapport."

CROSS-CULTURAL COMMUNICATION DYNAMICS

It is naturally less challenging to interact with people from one's own background than with those from a different group. Communication can be strained and unnatural when there is no apparent common ground. The "people are people everywhere" argument and "just treat everyone with respect" advice both fall short when we understand that there can be basic differences in the areas of behavior and communication across cultures. Some police officers feel that understanding of cross-cultural communication is unnecessary if respect is shown to every person. Yet, if officers have had limited contact with people from diverse backgrounds, they may inadvertently communicate their lack of familiarity. In the next few sections, we exemplify typical ways people attempt to accommodate for or react to cultural or racial differences and how they may cover up their discomfort in communication across cultures.

Using Language or Language Style to Become Just Like One of "Them"

Black officer to a white officer: "Hey, what kind of arrest did you have?"
White officer: "Brotha-man was trying to front me. . . ."

Captain Darryl McAllister from the Hayward, California, Police Department uses the preceding example to illustrate how obviously uncomfortable some non–African Americans are when communicating cross-racially. One of his pet peeves is hearing other officers trying to imitate him in speech and trying to act like a "brother." He explained that this type of imitative language is insincere and phony. The artificiality makes him feel as if people are going overboard to show just how comfortable they are when, in fact, they may not be. He explained that he does not feel that this style of imitation is necessarily racist but that it conveys others' discomfort with his "blackness" (McAllister, 2009).

Similarly, officers attempting to establish rapport with citizens should not pretend to have too much familiarity with the language and culture or use words selectively to demonstrate how "cool" they are (e.g., using "señor" with Spanish-speaking people, calling an African American "my man," or referring to a Native American as "chief"). People of one cultural background may find themselves in situations in which an entire crowd or family is using a particular dialect or slang. If the officer lapses into the manner of speaking of the group, he or she will likely appear to be mocking that style. Ultimately, the officer should be sincere and natural. "Faking" another style of communication can have extremely negative results.

Walking on Eggshells

When in the presence of people from different cultural backgrounds, some people have a tendency to work hard not to offend. Consequently, they are not able to be themselves or do what they would normally do. In a cultural diversity session for city government employees, one white participant explained that he normally has no problem being direct when solicitors come to the door trying to sell something or ask for a donation to a cause. His normal response would be to say "I'm not interested," and then he would promptly shut the door. He explained, however, that when a black solicitor comes to the door, he almost never rudely cuts him or her off, and most of the time he ends up making a donation to whatever cause is being promoted. His inability to be himself and communicate directly stems from his concern about appearing to be racist. It is not within the scope of this subsection to analyze this behavior in depth, but simply to bring into

- Self-awareness about one's early life experiences that helped to shape perceptions, filters, and assumptions about people
- Self-awareness about how one feels toward someone who is "different"
- Management of assumptions and discomfort in dealing with people who are different (e.g., do I try to deny that differences exist and laugh differences away, or imitate "them" in order to appear comfortable?)
- Ability to be authentic in communication with others by modifying communication style when necessary

EXHIBIT 4.7   Key Areas for Officers to Consider: Self-Awareness.

awareness some typical patterns of reactions in cross-cultural and cross-racial encounters. A person must attempt to recognize his or her tendencies to reach the goal of communicating in a sincere and authentic manner with people of all backgrounds (Exhibit 4.7).

"Some of My Best Friends Are . . ."

In an attempt to show how tolerant and experienced they are with members of minority groups, many people often feel the need to demonstrate their tolerance strongly by saying things such as "I'm not prejudiced" or "I have friends who are members of your group" or "I know . . . people," or, worse, "I once knew someone who was also [for example] Jewish/Asian/African American." Although the intention may be to break down barriers and establish rapport, these types of statements often sound patronizing. To a member of a culturally or racially different group, this type of comment comes across as extremely naïve. In fact, many people would understand such a comment as signifying that the speaker actually does have prejudices toward a particular group. Minority-group members would question a nonmember's need to make a reference to others of the same background when there is no context for doing so. These types of remarks indicate that the speaker is probably isolated from members of the particular group. Yet the person making a statement such as "I know someone who is Asian" is trying to establish something in common with the other person and may even go into detail about the other person he or she knows. As one Jewish woman reported in a cross-cultural awareness session, "Just because a person I meet is uncomfortable meeting Jews or has very little experience with Jews doesn't mean that I want to hear about the one Jewish person he met 10 years ago while traveling on a plane to New York!"

"You People" or the We–They Distinction

Some may say "I'd like to get to know you people better" or "You people have made some amazing contributions." The use of "you people" may be another signal of prejudice or divisiveness in a person's mind. When someone decides that a particular group is unlike his or her own group (i.e., not part of "my people"), that person makes a simplistic division of all people into two groups: "we" and "they." Often, accompanying this division is the attribution of positive traits to "us" and negative traits to "them." Members of the "other group" (the out-group) are described in negative and stereotypical terms (e.g., "They are lazy," "They are criminals," "They are aggressive") rather than neutral terms that describe cultural or ethnic generalities (e.g., "They have a tradition of valuing education" or "Their communication style is more formal than that of most Americans"). The phenomenon of stereotyping makes it very difficult for people to communicate with each other effectively because they do not perceive others accurately. By attributing negative qualities to another group, a person creates myths about the superiority of his or her own group. Cultural and racial put-downs are often attempts to make people feel better about themselves.

"You Stopped Me Because I'm . . ." or Accusations of Racial Profiling

There are three recurring situations in which an officer may hear the accusation: "You stopped me because I'm [black, Arab, etc.]." The first situation is when citizens from a neighborhood with people predominantly from one culture are suspicious of any person in their neighborhood from another background. Thus they may call 911 reporting a "suspicious character" and may even add such statements as "I think he has a gun" when there is no basis for such an accusation. In this situation, the police officer must understand the extreme humiliation and anger citizens feel when they are the object of racist perceptions. Once the officer determines that there is no reason to arrest the citizen, it is most appropriate for the officer to apologize for having made the stop and to explain that department policy requires that officers are obliged to investigate all calls.

Indeed, many incidents occur all over the country in which citizens call a police department to report a "suspicious character" just because he or she does not happen to fit the description of the majority of the residents in that area. Since there is a history of stopping minorities for reasons that are less than legitimate, the officer must go out of his or her way to show respect to the innocent citizen who does not know why he or she has been stopped and is caught totally off guard. Many people reported to be "suspicious" for merely being of a different race would appreciate an officer's making a final comment such as "I hope this kind of racism ends soon within our community" or "It's too bad there are still people in our community who are so ignorant." Comments such as these, said with sincerity, may very well get back to the community and contribute to improved future interactions with members of the police department. Of course, some people who are stopped will not appreciate any attempt that the officer makes to explain why the stop was made. Nevertheless, many citizens will react favorably to an officer's understanding of their feelings.

A second situation in which an officer may hear, "You stopped me because I'm . . ." may occur not because of any racist intentions of the officer but rather as a "reflex response" of the citizen (in other words, it has no bearing on reality). Many people have been stopped without reason in the past or know people who have; they carry this baggage into each encounter with an officer. One police officer explained: "I don't consider myself prejudiced. I consider myself a fair person, but let me tell you what happens almost every time I stop a black in city X. The first words I hear from them are 'You stopped me because I'm black.' That's bugging the hell out of me because that's not why I stopped them. I stopped them because they violated the traffic code. It's really bothering me and I'm about to explode."

Officers accused of racially or ethnically motivated stops truly need to remain professional and not escalate a potential conflict or create a confrontation. Law enforcement officials should not only try to communicate their professionalism, both verbally and nonverbally, but also try to strengthen their self-control. The best way to deal with these types of remarks from citizens is to work on your own reactions and stress level. One could potentially receive such remarks on a daily basis. People react to officers as symbols and are using the officer to vent their frustration.

This response assumes no racial profiling has taken place.

Let's assume that the officer did not stop a person because of his or her ethnicity or race and that the officer is therefore not abusing his or her power. George Thompson, founder and president of the Verbal Judo Institute, believes that in these situations, people bring up race and ethnicity to throw the officer off guard. According to Thompson (who is white and a former

English professor and police officer), the more professional an officer is, the less likely he or she is to let this type of statement become a problem. Newer officers, especially, can be thrown off guard by such allegations of racism when, in fact, they are simply upholding the law and keeping the peace as they have been trained to do. Thompson advocates using "verbal deflectors" when citizens make such remarks as "You stopped me because I'm. . . ." He recommends responses such as "I appreciate that, but you were going 55 miles in a 25-mile zone," or "I hear what you're saying, but you just broke the law." Verbal deflectors (1) are readily available to the lips, (2) are nonjudgmental, and (3) can be said quickly. Thompson believes that statements from citizens should not be ignored. Silence or no response can make people even more furious than they already were because they were stopped (Thompson, 2009).

> Pay attention to what citizens say, but deflect their anger. You are not paid to argue with citizens. You are paid to keep the peace. If you use tactical language and focus every word you say so that it relates to your purpose, then you will sound more professional. The minute you start using words as defensive weapons, you lose power and endanger your safety. If you "springboard" over their arguments and remain calm, controlled, and nonjudgmental, you will gain voluntary compliance most of the time. The results of this professional communication are that (1) you feel good, (2) you disarm the citizen, and (3) you control them in the streets (and in courts and in the media). Never take anything personally. Always treat people with respect and explain the "why" in your communication with them. (Thompson, 2009)

The third and final situation in which an officer may hear "You stopped me because I'm . . ." is when the citizen is correct and, indeed, racial profiling is taking place. Police department personnel are not immune from the racism that still exists in our society. Reflecting biased attitudes outside the law enforcement agency, some officers use their positions of power to assert authority in ways that cannot be tolerated. We are referring not only to the white officer who subjugates citizens from different backgrounds but also, for example, to an African American officer who has internalized the racism of the dominant society and may actually treat fellow group members unjustly. Alternatively, this abuse of power could take place between, for example, a black or Latino officer and a white citizen. (See Chapter 13 for a detailed description of racial profiling.)

Officers must consider the reasons a citizen may say "You stopped me because I'm . . ." and respond accordingly. The situations described above (i.e., citizens call in because of racist perceptions and the "suspicious character" is innocent; the citizen stopped is simply "hassling" the officer, and may or may not have been unjustly stopped in the past; and the citizen making the accusation toward the officer is correct) call for different responses on the part of the officer. The officer would do well, in all three situations, to remember the quote included in the final section of Chapter 1: "Remember the history of law enforcement with all groups and ask yourself the question, Am I part of the past, or a part of the future?" (Berry, 2009).

Communication Considerations Post-9/11

Many Arab Americans, in particular, feel that they are automatic suspects when approached by law enforcement representatives. Since 9/11, there has been what Lobna Ismail, Arab American cross-cultural specialist, characterizes as collateral damage to the entire Arab American community. They may hesitate to call the police when they are victims of crimes, and they fear being treated as suspects rather than victims of a crime (Ismail, 2009). While there has been progress in some jurisdictions in bridging the cultural gap with police in the years following 9/11, mutual distrust between some Arab American communities and law enforcement lingers. Some of this has come about because of 9/11, but, in addition, some immigrants bring with them a fear of law enforcement from their native countries where widespread police corruption as well as police brutality were and are facts of life (NIJ, 2008). It is therefore imperative to consider the importance of building trust, rapport, and relationships with Arab Americans and people from the Middle East. According to Dr. James Zogby, president of the Arab American Institute Foundation in Washington, D.C., the more a community-policing mindset has developed in a particular locale, the more easily do communication barriers come down between law enforcement and Arab Americans. "We have found that when FBI and police department leadership, for example, are willing to sit down and dialogue with community leaders, then it is much more likely that citizens will be willing to share information and provide tips because officers have gone out of their way to build trust" (Zogby, 2003).

Regarding communication with Arab Americans (and this applies to communication with other cultural groups as well), officers should not try too hard, and in an unnatural way, to demonstrate cultural sensitivity. An officer should understand differences in communication style where they exist, but should not act stiff or uncomfortable in an attempt to get it right. With cultural groups that may appear very different from ones own, or where sensitivities may be high, as with members of the Arab American community, law enforcement representatives need to think about approaching others in a way that will increase their comfort level. This means being natural, not beginning with the assumption that they are foreign and strange, and avoiding such thoughts as "I can't communicate with them unless I know their ways" (Zogby, 2006). In the end, the spirit of respect toward fellow human beings, with some knowledge of cultural detail, will lead to effective communication.

INTERVIEWING AND DATA-GATHERING SKILLS

Interviewing and data-gathering skills form the basic techniques for communication and intervention work with multicultural populations. For the officer, the key issues in any interviewing and data-gathering situation are as follows:

- Establishing interpersonal relationships to gain trust and rapport for continual work
- Bringing structure and control to the immediate situation
- Gaining information about the problems that require the presence of the law enforcement officer
- Giving information about the workings of the law enforcement guidelines, resources, and assistance available
- Providing action and interventions as needed
- Bolstering and supporting the different parties' abilities and skills to solve current and future problems on their own

Listed in Exhibit 4.8 are helpful guidelines for providing and receiving information in a better way in a multicultural context.

In the area of data gathering and interviewing, the officer in a multicultural law enforcement and peacekeeping situation cannot assume that his or her key motivators and values are the same as those of the other parties involved. Recognizing such differences in motivation and values will result in greater effectiveness. For example, the values of saving face and preserving one's own honor as well as the honor of one's family are extremely strong motivators for many people from Asian, Latin American, and Mediterranean cultures. An Asian gang expert from the Oakland, California, Police Department illustrated this value system with the case of a niece who

1. Be knowledgeable about who is likely to have information. Ask questions to identify the head of a family or respected community leaders.
2. Consider that some cultural groups have more of a need than others for rapport and trust building before they are willing to share information. Do not consider the time it takes to establish rapport a waste of time. For some, this may be a necessary step.
3. Provide background and context for your questions, information, and requests. Cultural minorities differ in their need for "contextual information" (i.e., background information) before getting down to the issues or business at hand. Remain patient with those who want to go into more detail than you think is necessary.
4. Expect answers to be formulated and expressed in culturally different ways. Some people tend to be linear in their answers (i.e., giving one point of information at a time in a chronological order), some present information in a zigzag fashion (i.e., they digress frequently), and others tend to present information in a circular style (i.e., they may appear to be talking in circles). And, of course, in addition to cultural differences, there are individual differences in ways of presenting information.
5. It is important to speak simply, but do not make the mistake of using simple or "pigeon" English. Remember, people's comprehension skills are usually better than their speaking skills.
6. "Yes" does not always mean "yes"; do not mistake a courteous answer for the facts or the truth.
7. Remember that maintaining a good rapport is just as important as coming to the point and getting work done quickly. Slow down!
8. Silence is a form of speech; do not interrupt it. Give people time to express themselves by respecting their silence.

EXHIBIT 4.8   Interviewing and Data Gathering in a Multicultural Context.

had been chosen by the police to translate for her aunt, who had been raped. The values of honor and face-saving prevented the aunt from telling the police all the details of the crime of which she was the victim. Her initial story, told to the police through her niece's translation, contained very few of the facts or details of the crime. Later, through a second translator who was not a family member, the rape victim gave all the necessary information. Precious time had been lost, but the victim explained that she could not have revealed the true story in front of her niece because she would have shamed her family.

Exhibit 4.9 lists key values or motivators for police officers. In any given situation, these values may be at odds with what motivates the victim, suspect, or ordinary citizen of any background. However, when the officer and the citizen are from totally different backgrounds, additional cultural or racial variables may also be in conflict.

Finally, when interviewing and data gathering in the area of hate incidents and crimes (as well as threats [phone calls, letters]) targeted at individuals of particular backgrounds, the officer's need for control and structure may have to encompass hysterical or at least highly emotional reactions from other people of the same background. In the officer's attempt to control the situation, he or she must consider that there is also a community needing reassurance. For example, an officer must be willing to respond sensitively to heightened anxiety on the part of group members and not downplay their fears. Interviewing and data gathering may therefore last much longer when the officer is required to deal with multiple community members and widespread fears.

1. Survival or injury avoidance
2. Control and structure
3. Respect and authority
4. Use of professional skills
5. Upholding laws and principles

6. Avoiding conflict and tension
7. Harmony and peacekeeping
8. Conflict resolution and problem solving
9. Self-respect and self-esteem

EXHIBIT 4.9   Key Values or Motivators in Law Enforcement.

NONVERBAL COMMUNICATION

Up until this point in the chapter, we have primarily discussed verbal communication across cultures and its relevance to the law enforcement context. Nonverbal communication, including tone of voice, plays a key role in the dynamics between any two people. Dr. Albert Mehrabian of the University of California, Los Angeles, described in the classic and highly quoted book *Silent Messages* (1971) the general impact on the interaction between two or three people when a person's verbal and nonverbal messages contradict each other. In this scenario, it is almost always tone of voice and body language, including facial expressions, that convey an individual's true feelings. Of course officers have to attend to citizens' words; however, tone of voice and body language can reveal much more. In addition, across cultures, there are other considerations that relate directly to the interpretation of meaning.

Consider the following examples of reactions to differences in nonverbal communication across cultures and their implications for day-to-day police work:

He didn't look at me once. I know he's guilty. Never trust a person who doesn't look you in the eye.

—American police officer

Americans seem cold. They seem to get upset when you stand close to them.

—Jordanian teacher

As in the first example, if an officer uses norms of eye contact as understood by most Americans, he or she could make an incorrect judgment about someone who avoids eye contact; or as in the second example, an officer's comfortable distance for safety might be violated because of a cultural standard defining acceptable conversational distance. The comments demonstrate how people can misinterpret nonverbal communication when it is culturally different from their own. Misinterpretation can happen even with two people from the same background, but it is more likely when there are cultural differences. Universal emotions such as happiness, fear, and sadness are expressed in similar nonverbal ways throughout the world; however, nonverbal variations across cultures can cause confusion.

Take the example of the way people express sadness and grief. In many cultures, such as Arab and Iranian cultures, people express grief openly and out loud. In contrast, in other parts of the world (e.g., in China and Japan), people are generally more subdued or even silent in their expressions of grief. In Asian cultures, the general belief is that it is unacceptable to show emotions openly (whether sadness, happiness, or pain). Without this cultural knowledge, in observing a person who did not openly express grief, for example, one might conclude that he or she is not in emotional distress. This would be an incorrect and ethnocentric interpretation based on one's own culture.

The expression of friendship is another example of how cultural groups differ in their nonverbal behavior. Feelings of friendship exist everywhere, but their expression varies. It is acceptable for men to embrace and kiss each other (in Saudi Arabia and Russia, for example) and for women to hold hands (in China, Korea, Egypt, and other countries). Russian gymnasts of the same sex have been seen on television kissing each other on the lips; this is apparently an acceptable gesture in their culture and does not imply that they are gay or lesbian. What is considered "normal" behavior in one culture may be viewed as "abnormal" or unusual in another.

The following areas of nonverbal communication have variations across cultures; the degree to which a person displays nonverbal differences depends, in part, on the age of the person and the degree of his or her acculturation to the United States.

1. *Gestures:*   A few American gestures are offensive in other cultures. For example, the OK gesture is obscene in Latin America, the good luck gesture is offensive in parts of Vietnam, and the "come here" gesture (beckoning people to come with the palm up) is very insulting in most of Asia and Latin America.

2. *Position of Feet:*   A police sergeant relaxing at his desk with his feet up, baring the soles of his shoes, would most likely offend a Thai or Saudi Arabian (and other groups as well) coming into the office. To show one's foot is insulting in many cultures because the foot is considered the dirtiest part of the body. (Another example of this was the intended insult toward Saddam Hussein when Iraqis hit a statue of him with their shoes.) Officers need to be mindful of this taboo with respect to the foot, and should refrain, whenever possible, from making physical contact with the foot when, for example, someone is lying on the ground.

3. *Facial expressions:*   Not all facial expressions mean the same thing across cultures. The smile is a great source of confusion for many people in law enforcement when they encounter people from Asian, especially Southeast Asian, cultures. A smile or giggle can cover up pain, humiliation, and embarrassment. Some women (e.g., Japanese, Vietnamese) cover up their mouths when they smile or giggle. Upon hearing something sad, a Vietnamese person may smile. Similarly, an officer may need to communicate something that causes a loss of face to a person, resulting in the person smiling. This smile does not mean that the person is trying to be a "smart aleck"; it is simply a culturally conditioned response.

4. *Facial expressiveness:*   People in law enforcement have to be able to "read faces" in certain situations in order to assess situations correctly. The degree to which people show emotions on their faces depends, in large part, on their cultural background. Whereas Latin Americans, African Americans and people from Mediterranean regions tend to show emotions facially, other groups, such as many of the Asian cultural groups, tend to be less facially expressive and less emotive. An officer may thus incorrectly assume that a person is not being cooperative or would not make a good witness.

5. *Eye contact:*   In many parts of the world, eye contact is avoided with authority figures. In parts of India, for example, a father would discipline his child by saying, "Don't look me in the eye when I'm speaking to you"; an American parent would say, "Look me in the eye when I'm speaking to you." To maintain direct eye contact with a police officer would be disrespectful in some cultures. Direct eye contact with some citizens can also be perceived as threatening to that citizen. A security officer in a large store in San Jose, California, offered the example of officers looking directly at Latino/Hispanic young people suspected of stealing items from the store. On a number of occasions, the officers' direct eye contact was met with a physical reaction (i.e., the young person attempting to punch the officer). He explained that the Latino/Hispanic individual mistook the eye contact as confrontation and a challenge for a fight.

6. *Physical or conversational distance:*   All people unconsciously keep a comfortable distance around them when communicating with others, resulting in invisible walls that keep people far enough away. (This subcategory of nonverbal communication is called *proxemics*.) Police officers are perhaps more aware than others of the distance they keep from people in order to remain safe. When someone violates this space, a person often feels threatened and backs away or, in the case of an officer, begins to think about protective measures. Although personality and context also determine interpersonal distance, cultural background comes into play. In general, Latin Americans and Middle Easterners are more comfortable at closer distances than are northern Europeans, Asians, and the majority of Americans. An officer should not necessarily feel threatened, for example, if approached by an Iranian or a Greek in a manner that feels uncomfortably close. While maintaining a safe distance, the officer should also consider cultural background. Consider the example of a Middle Eastern suspect who ignores an officers' command to "step back." The social distance for interacting in the Middle East (as in many other areas of the world) is much closer than it is in the United States. For officers, for whom safety is paramount, this could easily lead to misinterpretation. Generally, Americans are comfortable at a little more than an arm's distance from each other.

For the law enforcement professional, nonverbal communication constitutes a major part in all aspects of peacekeeping and enforcement. For multicultural populations, it is even more important that the officer be aware of the variety of nuances and differences that may exist from one group to another. Studies show that a large percentage of interpersonal communication is understood because of the nonverbal body language aspects of the speaker. Moreover, in many cultures, as is true for many ethnic minorities in the United States, greater weight and belief are placed on the visual and nonverbal aspects of communication (Exhibit 4.10 and 4.11).

---

1. Body language and nonverbal messages can override an officer's verbal content in high-stress and crisis situations. For example, the officer's statement that he or she is there to help may be contradicted by a body posture of discomfort and uncertainty in culturally unfamiliar households.
2. For people of different ethnic backgrounds, stress, confusion, and uncertainty can also communicate unintended messages. For example, an Asian may remain silent and look nervous and anxious at the scene of a crime. He or she may appear to be "uncooperative" when in fact this person may have every intention of helping the officer.
3. For people with limited English skills, the nonverbal aspects of communication become even more important. Correct gestures and nonverbal cues help the nonnative English speaker in understanding the verbal messages.
4. It is important for officers to learn about and avoid offensive gestures and cultural taboos. However, immigrants and international visitors are quick to forgive and to overlook gestures and actions made out of forgetfulness and ignorance. Officers should realize, too, that, in time, newcomers usually learn many of the nonverbal mannerisms with which officers are more familiar. Nevertheless, learning about offensive gestures can help officers avoid interpersonal offenses.

Note: Each of the culture-specific chapters (Chapters 5–9) contains information about nonverbal characteristics of particular groups.

EXHIBIT 4.10   Nonverbal Communication: Key Points for Law Enforcement.

- When is touch appropriate and inappropriate?
- What is the comfortable physical distance between people in interactions?
- What is considered proper eye contact? What do eye contact and lack of eye contact mean to the people involved?
- What cultural variety is there in facial expressions? For example, does nodding and smiling mean the same in all cultures? If someone appears to be expressionless, does that mean he or she is uncooperative?
- What are appropriate and inappropriate gestures for a particular cultural group?

- Is the person in transition from one culture to another and therefore lacking the knowledge of communication?

EXHIBIT 4.11   Key Questions Concerning Nonverbal Communication across Cultures.

Officers must be authentic in their communication with people from various backgrounds. When learning about both verbal and nonverbal characteristics across cultures, officers do not need to feel that they must communicate differently each time they are in contact with someone of a different background. However, understanding that there are variations in communication style will help the officer interpret people's motives and attitudes more accurately and, overall, assess situations without a cultural bias.

MALE–FEMALE COMMUNICATION IN LAW ENFORCEMENT

You have to go along with the kind of kidding and ribbing that the guys participate in; otherwise, you are not one of them. If you say that you are offended by their crass jokes and vulgar speech, then you are ostracized from the group. I have often felt that in the squad room men have purposely controlled themselves because of my presence, because I have spoken up. But what I've done to them is make them act one way because of my presence as a woman. Then they call me a prude or spread the word that I'm keeping track of all their remarks for the basis of a sexual harassment suit down the road. I have no interest in doing that. I simply want to be a competent police officer in a professional working environment. (Comments by a woman police officer [who wishes to remain anonymous] at a Women Peace Officers' Association [WPOA] Conference)

With the changing workforce, including increasing numbers of women in traditionally male professions, many new challenges in the area of male–female communication are presenting themselves. Within law enforcement, in particular, a strong camaraderie characterizes the relationships mainly among the male members of a police force, although, in some cases, women are part of this camaraderie. Women allowed into what has been termed the "brotherhood" have generally had to "become one of the guys" to gain acceptance into a historically male-dominated profession. As noted in Chapter 2, in today's co-ed law enforcement profession, the term "brotherhood" is outdated. One suggested term, inclusive of women, is "family of law enforcement."

Camaraderie results when a group is united because of a common goal or purpose; the glue cementing the camaraderie is the easy communication among its members. The extracurricular interests of the members of the group, the topics selected for conversation, and the jokes that people tell all contribute to the cohesion or tightness of police department members. In some departments, women find that they or other women are the objects of jokes about sexual topics or that there are simply numerous references to sex. Because certain departments within cities have consisted mostly of men, they have not had to consider the inclusion of women on an equal basis and have not had to examine their own communication with each other.

Young women who are new to a department feel that they must tolerate certain behaviors in order to be accepted. A female sheriff participating in a WPOA conference said that on a daily basis she confronts vulgar language and sexual references in the jail where she works. Her list was long: "I am extremely bothered about the communication of the men where I work. Without mincing words, I'll tell you—at the county jail, officers are very degrading to women. They sometimes make fun of rape victims, they are rude and lewd to female inmates, and they are constantly trying to get me to join into the 'fun.' A woman is referred to as a 'dyke,' a 'cunt,' a 'douche bag,' a 'whore,' a 'hooker,' a 'bitch,' and I'm sure I could come up with more. The guys don't call me those names, but they use them all the time referring to other women." This sheriff also noted that she did not experience the disrespectful verbal behavior in one-to-one situations with male deputies, but only when they were in a group. She wondered out loud, "What happens to men when they group with each other? Why is there the change?"

It is not only the male grouping phenomenon that produces this type of rough, vulgar, and sexist language. One study of a large urban police department conducted for California Law Enforcement Command College documented inappropriate communications from patrol cars' two-way radios and computers. The language on the official system was often unprofessional—rough, vulgar, offensive, racist, and sexist. Obviously, both discipline and training were needed in this agency.

Certainly, not all men behave and talk in offensive ways, but the phenomenon is frequent enough that women in traditionally male work environments mention this issue repeatedly. Some women join in conversations that make them uneasy, but they do not let on that their working environment is uncomfortable and actually affecting their morale and productivity. Some women seem to be comfortable with the sexual comments of their male counterparts and may not object to the use of certain terms that other women find patronizing (e.g., "honey," "doll," "babe"). However, the percentage of women who fall into this category may very well be decreasing. Through sexual harassment policies, both women and men have learned that, for some, sexual innuendoes and patronizing terms can contribute to a hostile working environment.

In male-dominated institutions, vocations, and professions, women find that speaking out against this type of talk and joking creates discomfort for them and puts them in a double bind. A female police officer at a workshop on discrimination in the workplace said she felt that women's choices regarding communication with fellow male officers were limited. She explained that when a woman objects or speaks up, she risks earning a reputation or label that is hard to shed. If she remains quiet, she must tolerate a lot of verbal abuse and compromise her professionalism. This particular police officer decided to speak up in her own department, and, indeed, she earned a reputation as a troublemaker. In fact, she had no interest in going any further than complaining to her supervisor but nevertheless was accused of preparing for a lawsuit. She explained that a lawsuit was the farthest thing from her mind and that all she wanted was professional respect.

Some women who have objected to certain mannerisms of their male counterparts' communication say that when they come into a room or office, the men stop talking. The result is that the communication that normally functions to hold a group together is strained and tense. The ultimate result is that the workplace becomes segregated by gender. When shut out from a conversation, many women feel excluded and unempowered; in turn, many men feel resentful about having to modify their style of communication.

- Use terms that are inclusive rather than exclusive. Examples: "police officer," "chairperson," "commendations" (instead of the informal "atta boys")
- Avoid using terms or words that many women feel diminish their professional status. Examples: "chick," "babe"
- Avoid using terms or words that devalue groups of women or stereotype them. Example: Referring to women officers as "dykes"
- Avoid sexist jokes, even if you think they are not offensive. (Someone is bound to be offended; the same applies to racist jokes.)
- Avoid using terms that negatively spotlight or set women apart from men. Examples: "For a woman cop, she did a good job" (implying that this is the exception rather than the rule); this also applies to references about other cultural groups: "He's Latino, but he works hard," "He's black, but he's really skilled.

EXHIBIT 4.12   Inclusive Workplace Communication.

Women in traditionally male work environments such as police and fire departments find that they are sometimes put in a position of having to trade their professional identity for their personal one. A woman officer who proudly tells her sergeant about the arrest she made may be stunned when he, totally out of context, compliments the way she has been keeping in shape and tells her how good she looks in her uniform. This is not to say that compliments are never acceptable. But in this context, the woman is relating as a professional and desires reciprocal professional treatment. Men and women often ask, "Where do I draw the line? When does a comment become harassment?" In terms of the legal definition of sexual harassment, when the perpetrators are made aware that their comments are uninvited and unwelcome, then they must be reasonable enough to stop making them. It is not within the scope of this chapter to detail sexual harassment and all its legal implications (see Chapter 2). However, it should be noted that everyone has his or her own limits. What is considered harassment to one individual may be appreciated by another. When communicating across genders, each party must be sensitive to what the other party considers acceptable or insulting (see Exhibits 4.12). It is also the responsibility of the individual who has been offended, whether male or female, to make it clear that certain types of remarks are offensive.

Summary

- Communication with people for whom English is a second language can exact a great deal of patience from officers. The language barriers can lead to serious problems for non–English speakers and law enforcement. Using the wrong translator can mislead officers, so much so that a victim and his or her translator may give two completely different versions of a story. In some cases, more sensitivity on the part of law enforcement is needed when it comes to language obstacles. Increasing bilingual hires is one of the most practical solutions if budget allows; as an additional advantage, bilingual

officers often have a better understanding of the communities they serve. At a minimum, officers should know what the basic guidelines are for communicating with speakers of other languages. In addition, officers can become sensitive to features of other languages that frequently cause confusion when limited- or non-English speakers attempt to communicate in English.
- Officers' attitudes about immigrants and nonnative English speakers, whether positive or negative, are likely to affect their interaction with them. One important guideline is

to refrain from making inferences about individuals based on their accent or level of fluency; this also includes the assumption as to whether they are documented or undocumented. From a physiological perspective, communicating in a foreign language can be exhausting and cause mental strain, potentially resulting in a person's "shutting down" or not being able to communicate in the new language. In general, limited-English-speaking individuals' ability to express themselves in the second language is at its best when they are comfortable with officers. The more intimidating an officer is, the higher the likelihood that anxiety will affect the speaker's ability in English. Language breakdown is one of the first signs that a person is ill at ease and stressed to the point of not being able to cooperate and communicate. It is in the officer's best interest to increase the comfort level of the people with whom they interact, whether victims, suspects, or simply people requiring help.

- Rapport-building with all citizens is essential for building trust, and this is often preliminary to people's willingness to communicate freely with officers. This is especially true when communicating with people who have "higher context" communication styles. Typically, these styles are more characteristic of cultural groups coming from Asian, African, and Latin American cultures. There are gender differences even in "lower context" cultures as well (i.e., women tend to have a higher-context style than do men). The style of communication in law enforcement is essentially a lower-context communication style; police officers must understand the framework of "context" when interacting with individuals who exhibit different styles than their own. Hierarchy and power are two strong elements related to "context" in communication.

- Officers' own filters and perceptions influence the responses they choose to exhibit in cross-cultural and cross-racial encounters. As with all people, officers have blind spots and emotional "hot buttons" that may negatively affect communication with individuals from races, ethnicities, and backgrounds different from their own. Officers may unknowingly communicate biases or a lack of comfort with members of certain groups. Examples of this include using an inauthentic style of language or making statements that unknowingly signal prejudice.

- Interviewing and data-gathering skills form the basic techniques for communication and intervention work with multicultural populations. For the officer, the key issues include establishing interpersonal relationships to gain trust and rapport; bringing structure and control to the immediate situation; gaining information about the problems that require the presence of the law enforcement officer; giving information about law enforcement guidelines, resources, and assistance available; providing action and interventions as needed; and bolstering and supporting the different parties' abilities and skills to solve current and future problems on their own.

- Nonverbal communication across cultures can have a direct impact on police–citizen interaction and police perception of behavior. These behaviors include gestures, eye contact, physical or conversational distance, facial expressions, and the degree to which an individual is facially expressive. Police officers may have more difficulty assessing sincerity and truthfulness if they cannot "read" facial expressions or an individual's degree of facial expressiveness. For the law enforcement professional, body language always plays a major role in communication and officers need to be attuned to nonverbal cues. With multicultural populations, it is even more important that the officer be aware of a variety of nuances and differences that may exist from one group to another.

- Officers have used styles of communication and language in the past that were considered acceptable not only within the police agency but with citizens as well. Because of cultural diversity in the population and the accompanying need to respect all individuals, the unspoken rules about what is appropriate have changed dramatically. This includes the need to use inclusive communication with women within the law enforcement profession, and to be aware of the ways in which communication within the context of the "brotherhood" excluded women. Through communication, officers have tremendous power to influence the behavior and responses of the citizens with whom they contact. This is true of all citizens, regardless of background. A lack of knowledge of the cross-cultural aspects of communication will diminish that power with people whose backgrounds differ from that of the officer.

Discussion Questions and Issues

1. *Communicate with respect.* The introduction to this chapter presents a view of what all people would like in communication, and that is respect. "Remember that everyone in all cultures wants to be respected . . . talking about respecting people [from all cultural backgrounds] is vague. But treating people with respect is an act that is highly specific" (Thompson, 2009). Describe in detail the behaviors that define, for you, "respectful communication." In your experience, do these behaviors work with all cultural groups? Explain your answer.

2. *The Origins of Stereotypes.* In this chapter, we argue that officers need to recognize how their early experiences in life and later adult experiences shape their perceptions and "filters" about people from groups different from their own. What do you remember learning about various ethnic and racial groups when you were young? Did you grow up in an environment of tolerance, or did you hear statements such as "That's the way they are," or "You've got to be careful with those people" or "They are lazy [or dishonest, etc.]"? Also discuss your experiences as an adult with different groups and how those experiences may be affecting your perceptions.

3. *Police Officer Interaction with Speakers of Other Languages.* The following dialogue illustrates a typical interaction between a police officer and a nonnative speaker of English, in this case a Vietnamese man. Judging from the English that the Vietnamese is speaking, how would you rate the officer's use of English? Analyze this interaction by being specific as to how the officer can improve.

The following dialog takes place when an officer pulls a car over, gets out of his car, and approaches the driver. The driver, who is Vietnamese, says, in poor English, "What happen? Why you stop me?"

OFFICER: I pulled you over because you ran a red light.

CITIZEN: (No response)

OFFICER: This is a traffic violation. (Receives no feedback). Do you understand?

CITIZEN: (Nodding) Yeah, I understand.

OFFICER: I'm going to have to issue you a traffic citation.

CITIZEN: (Stares at officer)

OFFICER: Where's your driver's license?

CITIZEN: License? Just a minute. (Leans over to open glove compartment, but finds nothing; gets out of car and goes to trunk)

OFFICER (IRRITATED AND SLIGHTLY NERVOUS):   *Hey!* (In a loud voice) What's going on here? I asked to see your driver's license. Are you the registered owner of this car?

CITIZEN: Yeah. I go get my license.

OFFICER (SPEAKING MUCH LOUDER):   Wait a minute. Don't you understand? Are you not the owner of this car? Do you even have a license?

CITIZEN: Wait. (Finds license in trunk and produces it for officer)

OFFICER: Okay. Would you mind getting back into the car now?

CITIZEN: (Does nothing) Yeah, I understand.

OFFICER (POINTING TO THE FRONT SEAT):   Back into the car!

CITIZEN: (Does as told)

The officer could make improvements in at least four areas: (1) choice of words, (2) manner of asking questions, (3) use of idioms (there are at least two or three that could be changed to simple English), and (4) tone and attitude.

4. *Police Officers' "Hot Buttons."* Discuss how citizens (e.g., suspects, victims, complainants) affect your reactions in communication. Specifically, what words and attitudes do they use that break down your attempts to be professional? What emotionally laden language "sets you off"?

5. *Professional Communication with Citizens.* After you have discussed what affects your communication negatively (Question 4), role-play with fellow officers situations in which you respond professionally to abuses you hear. (Refer back to the section on accusations of racial profiling if you need suggestions.)

6. *Derogatory Remarks Associated with Race and Sexual Orientation.* Marge Schott (1928–2004) was the controversial primary owner, president, and CEO of the Cincinati Reds for almost 15 years. She was the first female owner of a baseball team. Prior to being forced to sell her major interests to the team in 1999, she was suspended and fined for making racist remarks and negative comments regarding sexual orientation over a period of 7 years; she allegedly called two Reds outfielders her "million-dollar niggers" and admitted to keeping a swastika armband in her desk drawer. She also told *The New York Times* that Hitler was "good" but that he went too far. In addition, she said she did not want her players to wear earring because "only fruits wear earrings," and she did not see using the slur "Jap" as being offensive. Schott publicly told people she was not a racist. One of the issues related to her racially and culturally insensitive remarks was that her comments were made in front of other people, but no one said anything to her or objected. Some felt that she should have been confronted.

    Answer the following questions as accurately as you can. If you were with friends in a social gathering and one friend made an off-color remark similar to those of Schott, what would you do? If you think that you would say something, what would it be? If you know that you would not say anything, does this mean that you condone the behavior? Would things change if the remarks were made in the law enforcement agency or you overheard officers on the streets making such remarks? Explain your answer and include what strategies you could use to correct the inappropriate behavior.

7. *Cultural Observations.* Make a list of your observations for each of the cultural groups with which you have had a substantial amount of contact. Then try to find someone from that culture with whom you can discuss your observations.

    a. Display of emotions and expressions of feelings
    b. Communication style: loud, soft, direct, indirect
    c. Expressions of appreciation; conventions of courtesy (i.e., forms of politeness)
    d. Need (or lack thereof) for privacy
    e. Gestures, facial expressions, and body movements
    f. Eye contact
    g. Touching
    h. Interpersonal space (conversational distance)
    i. Taboo topics in conversation
    j. Response to authority

8. *Discomfort with Unfamiliar Groups.* Try to recall a situation in which you found yourself in a culturally unfamiliar environment (e.g., responding to a call in an ethnically different household or being the only minority person of your background among a group of people from another cultural or ethnic group). How much discomfort, if any, did you experience? If the situation was uncomfortable, did it affect your communication effectiveness or professionalism?

9. *Accusations of Racially or Ethnically Motivated Stops.* Have you encountered, "You stopped me because I'm [any ethnic group]?" If so, how did you handle the situation? How effectively do you think you responded?

Website Resources

Visit these websites for additional information about cross-cultural and general communication applicable to law enforcement.

Verbal Judo Institute: http://www.verbaljudo.com

    This website centers around "verbal Judo," a tactical form of communication used to generate voluntary compliance from citizens under difficult situations. It lists various types of verbal Judo courses available as well as books and articles on the subject. There is a link to law enforcement explaining the applicability of verbal Judo to police officers.

United States Department of Justice Federal Bureau of Investigation: http://www.fbi.gov/publications/leb/2001/aug01leb.htm

This FBI website makes available an excellent article on neurolinguistic programming entitled "Subtle Skills for Building Rapport" by Vincent A. Sandoval and Susan H. Adams (Sandoval & Adams, 2001).

Royal Canadian Mounted Police (RCMP): http://www.rcmp-learning.org/vietnam/module_a.htm

This is the website for the Royal Canadian Mounted Police (RCMP) and their Cross-Cultural Communications Series—"The Vietnamese" is the second in a new series of individualized instruction modules that have been developed to educate and sensitize employees of the RCMP.

International Association of Campus Law Enforcement Agencies (IACLEA): http://www.iaclea.org/

This is the website for the IACLEA, which has many publications, including, specifically, "If I Look Confused and Lost, It's Probably Because I Am." This is a video workshop on cross-cultural communications with a focus on foreign students. Created and conducted by Dr. Jennifer Lund, Director of International Student Services at Georgia State University, this 57-minute videotape is intended for use in training campus staff to deal positively with foreign students, and it comes with a discussion guide. The video covers mutual perceptions of foreign and U.S. students, behavioral and attitudinal differences, and the 12 "shoulds" to improve communication.

References

Berry, Ondra. (2009, March). Retired Assistant Police Chief, Reno, Nevada, Police Department, personal communication.

Fernandez, Donya. (2000, December). Language Rights Attorney for the Language Rights Project, Employment Law Center/Legal Aid Society, San Francisco, CA, personal communication.

Gray, John. (2002). *Mars and Venus in the Workplace.* New York: Harper Collins.

Hall, Edward. (1959). *The Silent Language.* Garden City, NY: Doubleday.

Hall Edward. (1966). *The Hidden Dimension.* Garden City, NY: Doubleday.

Hall Edward. (1976). *Beyond Culture.* Garden City, NY: Doubleday.

Hofstede, Geerte (2001). *Culture's Consequences: Comparing Values, Behaviors, Institutions, and Organizations across Nations.* Thousand Oaks, CA: Sage Publications.

Ismail, Lobna. (2009, April). President of Connecting Cultures, a training and consulting organization specializing in Arab American culture, personal communication.

McAllister, Daryl. (2009, March). Captain Hayward Police Department, (California) personal communication.

Mehrabian, Albert. (1971). *Silent Messages.* Belmont, CA: Wadsworth Publishing.

Merritt, Ashleigh. (2000, May). "Culture in the Cockpit: Do Hofstede's Dimensions Replicate?" *Journal of Cross-Cultural Psychology, 31*(3), 283–301.

National Institute of Justice (2008, July). Policing in Arab-American Communities after September 11 (By Nicole Henderson, Christopher W. Ortiz, Naomi F. Sugie and Joel Miller). Available: http://www.ncjrs.gov/pdffiles1/nij/221706.pdf. Retrieved: April 19, 2009.

Sandoval, V.A., and Susan H. Adams. (2001, August). "Subtle Skills for Building Rapport." *FBI Law Enforcement Bulletin, 70*(8), 1–9. Available: http;//www.fbi.gov/publications/leb/2001/aug01leb.htm.

"The Troubled LA County Sheriff's Department." (1992, July 21). *Los Angeles Times,* p. A18.

Thompson, George. (2009, March). Founder of Verbal Judo Institute, Inc., personal communication.

U.S. Department of Justice (2000). Civil Rights Division. Coordination and Review Section: Executive Order 13166. Available: http://www.usdoj.gov/crt/cor/Pubs/eolep.php. Retrieved: April 1, 2009.

Zogby, James. (2006). Director of the Arab American Institute Foundation, personal communication.

Cultural Specifics for Law Enforcement

Part Two presents information on Asian/Pacific, African American, Latino/Hispanic, Middle Eastern, and Native American cultural backgrounds with regard to the needs of law enforcement and criminal justice representatives. We have selected these groups, as opposed to other groups not described in this book, for one or more of the following reasons: (1) the group is a relatively large ethnic or racial group in the United States; (2) the traditional culture of the group differs widely from that of mainstream American culture; (3) typically or historically there have been problems between the particular group and law enforcement officials.

   In these culture-specific chapters, general information is presented on the following areas: historical background, demographics, and diversity within the cultural group. Following the introductory information, we present specific details relevant to law enforcement and criminal justice related to communication styles (both verbal and nonverbal), group identification terms, offensive labels, stereotypes, and family structure. Each chapter ends with key concerns for officers regarding the particular cultural group, a chapter summary, discussion questions, and resources for additional information.

Important note: Although we present the specific cultural and racial groups in this part of the book, we wish to remind the reader that individuals in our multicultural population do not always easily fall into neat categories of only one race or culture. There can be an overlap of race and ethnicity, as in the case of a black Latino. Our categorization of different groups is a convenient way of presenting information; we do not wish to imply that there can be no overlap among the group categories.

CHAPTER 5

Law Enforcement Contact with Asian/ Pacific Americans

LEARNING OBJECTIVES

After reading this chapter you will be able to:

- Describe the historical background of the Asian/Pacific American community in the United States.
- Highlight the demographic features and diversity of this population.
- Discuss the implications of group identification terms for Asian/Pacific Americans.
- Identify the myths and stereotypes applied to this group.
- Identify selected characteristics of traditional Asian/Pacific American extended family structure as it relates to law enforcement contact.
- Discuss the communication styles used by Asian/Pacific Americans.
- Highlight key law enforcement concerns and skills, resources, and practices for addressing some of these concerns.

OUTLINE

- Introduction
- Asian/Pacific American Defined
- Typology of Asian/Pacific Americans
- Historical Information
- Demographics: Diversity among Asian/Pacific Americans
- Labels and Terms
- Myths and Stereotypes
- The Asian/Pacific American Family
- Communication Styles of Asian/Pacific Americans
- Key Issues in Law Enforcement
- Summary
- Discussion Questions and Issues
- Website Resources

INTRODUCTION

The label *Asian Americans/Pacific Islanders* encompasses over 40 different ethnic and cultural groups. For ease of use, we use the shortened version Asian/Pacific Americans to refer to members of these ethnic groupings. We first define this very diverse group and then present a historical overview, focusing on the relationship between law enforcement or other criminal justice personnel and citizens. We present demographics and elements of diversity among Asian/Pacific Americans as well as issues related to ethnic and cultural identity. Aspects of the Asian/Pacific American family are discussed, including myths and stereotypes, assimilation and acculturation processes, the extended family and community, gender roles, generational differences, and adolescent and youth issues.

The Section "Communication Styles of Asian/Pacific Americans" discusses the subtle aspects of nonverbal and indirect communications that peace officers and others in emergency-related public safety roles often find troublesome. The closing section presents several key issues for law enforcement: underreporting of crimes, differential treatment, increasing Asian/Pacific American community-police services, increasing the number of Asian/Pacific peace officers, and the rise in crimes within the Asian/Pacific community. Finally, we review recommendations for improved communication and relationships between law enforcement personnel and Asian/Pacific American communities.

For the past four decades, the Asian/Pacific American population has experienced the largest proportional increases of any ethnic minority population in the United States (over 100 percent growth for the decades from 1960 to 1990 and 76 percent growth for the decade from 1990 to 2000). The population growth can be attributed to (1) higher immigration from the Pacific Rim countries, (2) greater longevity, (3) higher birth rates, (4) admission of immigrants with special skills and expertise for work in high-technology industries in the United States, and (5) addition of existing ethnic groups to this population category (including the Asian/Pacific Americans who consider themselves "multiracial"). Growth in major urban areas has been particularly striking, as is seen in New York City, Los Angeles, San Jose (CA), San Francisco, Honolulu, San Diego, Chicago, Houston, Seattle, Fremont (CA), Fairfax (VA), and Quincy (MA). Growth in the population as a whole is most dramatically reflected in terms of increased numbers of Asian/Pacific Americans in politics, community leadership, business, education, and public service areas. Law enforcement contact with Asian/Pacific people has increased because of their greater presence in communities. Asian/Pacific Americans have one of the highest citizenship rates among all foreign-born groups; in 2006, 52 percent of the immigrants from Asian/Pacific countries were naturalized citizens (U.S. Bureau of the Census, 2009).

ASIAN/PACIFIC AMERICAN DEFINED

The term *Asian/Pacific Americans* is actually a contraction of two terms: *Asian Americans* and *Pacific Islander* peoples. Although used throughout this chapter as referring to a single ethnic/cultural group, *Asian/Pacific Americans* is, in fact, a convenient summary label for a very heterogeneous group. There certainly is no universal acceptance of this labeling convention, but for practical purposes it has been adopted frequently, with occasional variations (e.g., Asian and Pacific Americans, Asian Americans/Pacific Islanders, Asians and Pacific Islanders). It represents the self-designation preferred by many Asian and Pacific peoples in the United States, particularly over the more dated (and, to some, offensive) term *Orientals*. The U.S.

government and other governmental jurisdictions usually use "Asian Americans/Pacific Islanders" to refer to members within any of the 40 or more groups comprising this category.

At least 40 distinct ethnic and cultural groups might meaningfully be listed under this designation:

1. Bangladeshi
2. Belauan (formerly Palauan)
3. Bhutanese
4. Bruneian
5. Cambodian
6. Chamorro (Guamanian)
7. Chinese
8. Fijian
9. Hawaiian (or Native Hawaiian)
10. Hmong
11. Indian (Asian, South Asian, or East Indian)
12. Indonesian
13. Japanese
14. Kiribati
15. Korean
16. Laotian
17. Malaysian
18. Maldivian
19. Marshallese (of the Marshall Islands, to include Majuro, Ebeye, and Kwajalein)
20. Micronesian (to include Kosrae, Ponape, Truk, and Yap)
21. Mongolian
22. Myanmarese (formerly Burmese)
23. Nauruan
24. Nepalese
25. Ni-Vanuatu
26. Okinawan
27. Pakistani
28. Pilipino (preferred spelling of Filipino)
29. Saipan Carolinian (or Carolinian, from the Commonwealth of the Northern Marianas)
30. Samoan
31. Singaporian
32. Solomon Islander
33. Sri Lankan (formerly Ceylonese)
34. Tahitian
35. Taiwanese
36. Tibetan
37. Tongan
38. Thai
39. Tuvaluan
40. Vietnamese

While there are marked differences among the 40 groups listed, individuals within any of the 40 groups may also differ in a vast number of ways. From the viewpoint of law enforcement, it is important to recognize some of the differing factors that may cut across or be common to all Asian/Pacific ethnic groups. For example:

1. Area of residence in the United States
2. Comfort with and competence in English
3. Generational status in the United States (first, second, third generation, and so forth)
4. Degree of acculturation and assimilation
5. Education (number of years outside and inside the United States)
6. Native and other languages spoken and/or written
7. Age (what is documented on paper and what the real age may be)
8. Degree of identification with the home country and/or region of self or parents' origin
9. Family composition and extent of family dispersion in the United States and globally
10. Extent of identification with local, national, and global Asian/Pacific sociopolitical issues
11. Participation and degree to which the individual is embedded in the ethnic community network

12. Religious beliefs as well as cultural value orientation
13. Economic status and financial standing
14. Sensitivity to ethnic and cultural experiences and perceptions as an Asian/Pacific person in the United States
15. Identification with issues, concerns, and problems shared by other ethnic/racial groups (e.g., racial profiling and other discrimination issues voiced by African American, Latino/Hispanic Americans, and Middle Eastern and Arab Americans)

It should be noted that the definition itself of the Asian/Pacific group points to and embodies an ever-emerging, ethnic mosaic of diverse constituencies. Groups are added and removed based on self-definition and needs for self-choice. In our definition, we have not added immigrants or refugees from the Central Asian nations of Kazakhstan, Kyrgyzstan, Tajikistan, Turkmenistan, and Uzbekistan (i.e., countries that were part of the former Soviet Union). We also do not include certain countries on the Asian continent even though they are specified in the "World Population Data Sheet" by the Population Reference Bureau (2008) because of the self-choice issue. As more immigrants from Central Asia settle in the United States, these groups may (or may not) be added to the definition of Asian/Pacific Americans. Clearly, the pooling of separate Asian and Pacific Islander groups under the label of Asian/Pacific Americans emerged, in part, out of the necessity to have a larger collective whole when a greater numerical count may make a difference (especially in political and community issue areas). Merging of these 40 ethnic groups into a collective entity allowed for sufficiently large numbers for meaningful representation in communities and other arenas.

Although one may focus upon nationality or nation of origin as the basis of identifying Asian/Pacific American groupings (e.g., "Korean" for those whose ancestry is from Korea, "Vietnamese" for those whose ancestry is from Vietnam), there may be other demographic variables of greater importance than that of nationality. For example, whether one is from the Central Asian nation of Uzbekistan, the Southeast Asian nation of Vietnam, or the Pacific Island nation of Micronesia, the demographic variable of ethnicity, if one were Chinese, may be a more important identifier than is national origin for some persons or groups. As another example, one's religion may be a more important group identifier than either ethnicity and/or nationality, as might be seen with Muslims (i.e., people who practice Islam). Given that the four countries with the largest Muslim populations are in South Asia, that is, Indonesia, Pakistan, India, and Bangladesh (Glasse & Smith, 2003), Asian/Pacific American people who practice Islam might see religion as a more important identifier than ethnicity and nationality.

Other Key Definitions

Since a large proportion of Asian/Pacific Americans whom law enforcement officers may encounter are born outside the United States, it is important to understand some of the key differences that relate to immigration status. One key difference is that of Asian/Pacific Americans who are considered refugees and those who are considered immigrants at the time they enter the United States. Some of the between-group hostilities (within the Asian/Pacific community and among other ethnic minority communities) have been a result of not understanding how refugee status differs from immigrant status in the United States.

Refugees are sponsored into the United States under the authority of the U.S. government. Although many ethnic groups have come in under the sponsorship of the federal government with refugee or émigré status, the largest numbers have come from Southeast Asia as a result of the past upheaval brought on by the Vietnam War. Refugees, since they are sponsored into the United States by the government, are expected to utilize public support services fully (welfare, English as a Second Language [ESL] programs, educational tuition, job training programs, and case management). Since it is part of being a "good refugee" to participate fully, case managers are often assigned to refugee families to ensure that family members are fully utilizing all of the services provided. However, such participation in public programs may also create dependency and learned helplessness that can result from having others help or interfere with what many would have done for themselves.

Immigrants enter into the United States under the direct sponsorship of individuals' families. The federal government establishes that immigrants are allowed to enter the United States only if their families can completely support or establish work for them. In fact, one criterion for being able to attain permanent residence status (a "green card") is that the immigrant will not become a burden to the government; this means that participation in any public-funded program may jeopardize that individual's chances for attaining permanent residence status. (Thus, immigrants try very hard to avoid getting involved in public or community programs and services.) In contrast to being a refugee, being a "good immigrant" means avoiding any participation in public service programs.

TYPOLOGY OF ASIAN/PACIFIC AMERICANS

Looking at Asian/Pacific American individuals, families, and communities, we have developed a seven-part typology that will be useful in understanding and summarizing some of the differences between individuals within this group (see Exhibit 5.1).

Our typology suggests that as law enforcement and public safety organizations prepare and train their personnel to work with Asian/Pacific American communities, a focus on the key differences within each of the typological groups would be most effective. We will come back to this typology in a later section to discuss how the motivational components within each of the groupings can affect the way Asian/Pacific American persons may respond in law enforcement situations.

Type I	Asian/Pacific recently arrived immigrant or refugee (less than 5 years in the United States, with major life experiences in Asia or the Pacific Islands)
Type II	Asian/Pacific immigrant or refugee (5 or more years in the United States, with major life experiences in Asia or the Pacific Islands)
Type III	Asian/Pacific American (second generation; offspring of immigrant or refugee)
Type IV	Asian/Pacific Immigrant (major life experiences in the United States)
Type V	Asian/Pacific American (third or later generations in the United States)
Type VI	Asian/Pacific national (anticipates return to Asia or to the Pacific Islands; this includes visitors and tourists)
Type VII	Asian/Pacific national (global workplace and residency)

EXHIBIT 5.1   Typology of Asian/Pacific Americans.

HISTORICAL INFORMATION

The first Asians to arrive in the United States in sizable numbers were the Chinese in the 1840s to work on the plantations in Hawaii. Then, in the 1850s, they immigrated to work in the gold mines in California and later on the transcontinental railroad. Of course, the native populations of the Pacific Island areas (e.g., Samoans, Hawaiians, Guamanians, Fijians) were there before the establishment of the 13 original colonies of the United States. The Chinese were followed in the late 1800s and early 1900s by the Japanese and the Pilipinos[*] (and in smaller numbers by the Koreans and South Asian Indians). Large numbers of Asian Indians (nearly 500,000) entered the United States as a result of Congressional action in 1946 for "persons of races indigenous to India" to have the right of naturalization. Most immigrants in those early years were men, and most worked as laborers and at other domestic and menial jobs. Until the change of the immigration laws in 1965, the number of Asian and Pacific Islander peoples immigrating into the United States was severely restricted (families often had to wait a decade or longer before members of a family could be reunited). With the change in the immigration laws, large numbers of immigrants from the Pacific Rim came to the United States from Hong Kong, Taiwan, China, Japan, Korea, South Asia (e.g., India, Ceylon, Bangladesh), the Philippines, and Southeast Asia (e.g., Vietnam, Thailand, Singapore, Cambodia, Malaysia). After the Vietnam War, large numbers of Southeast Asian refugees were admitted in the late 1970s and early 1980s. The need for engineering and scientific expertise and skills in "high-tech" and Internet companies resulted in many Asian/Pacific nationals (under special work visas) immigrating to the United States in the late 1990s and early 2000s. Highly skilled workers entering with "high tech visas" (i.e., the H-1B visa) continue to contribute to the growth of the Asian/Pacific American population in the United States (Schlafly, 2008).

Law Enforcement Interactions with Asian/Pacific Americans: Law Enforcement as Not User-Friendly

Asian/Pacific Americans have found the passage and enforcement of "anti-Asian" federal, state, and local laws to be more hostile and discriminatory than some of the racially motivated community incidents they have experienced. Early experiences of Asians and Pacific Islanders were characterized by the majority population's wanting to keep them out of the United States and putting tremendous barriers in the way of those who were already here. It was the role of law enforcement and criminal justice agencies and officers to be the vehicle to carry out these laws against Asian/Pacific American immigrants. From the beginning, the interactions of Asian/Pacific Americans with law enforcement officials were fraught with conflicts, difficulties, and mixed messages.

ANTI-ASIAN FEDERAL, STATE, AND LOCAL LAWS   Almost all of our federal immigration laws were written such that their enforcement made Asian newcomers feel neither welcomed nor wanted. Following the large influx of Chinese in the 1850s to work in the gold mines and on the railroad, many Americans were resentful of the Chinese for their willingness to work long hours for low wages. With mounting public pressure, the Chinese Exclusion Act of 1882 banned the immigration of Chinese laborers for 10 years, and subsequent amendments extended this ban indefinitely. Because of this ban and because the Chinese population in the United States was primarily male, the Chinese population in the United States dropped from 105,465 in 1880 to 61,639

---

[*] Preferred spelling for Filipino

in 1920 (Takaki, 1989a). Since the Chinese Exclusion Act applied only to the Chinese, Japanese immigration started around 1870 to Hawaii and in larger numbers to the mainland in the 1890s to work as laborers and in domestic jobs on farms on the West Coast. Similar to the case of the Chinese, public pressure to restrict Japanese immigration ensued. In the case of the Japanese, however, the Japanese government did not want a "loss of face" or loss of international prestige through having its people "banned" from immigrating to the United States. Rather, a "Gentleman's Agreement" was negotiated with President Theodore Roosevelt in 1907, which resulted in the Japanese Government voluntarily restricting the immigration of Japanese laborers to the United States. Family members of Japanese already in the United States, however, were allowed to enter. Under the Gentleman's Agreement, large numbers of "picture brides" began entering into the United States, resulting in a large increase in Japanese American population—25,000 in 1900 to 127,000 in 1940 (Daniels, 1988). Subsequent laws banned or prevented immigration from the Asiatic countries: The Immigration Act of 1917 banned immigration from all countries in the Pacific Rim except for the Philippines (a U.S. territory). The Immigration Act of 1924 restricted migration from all countries to 2 percent of the countries' national origin population living in the United States in 1890. This "2 percent" restriction was not changed until 1965. Moreover, it was not until 1952 that most Asian immigrants were eligible to become naturalized citizens of the United States and therefore have the right to vote. (African Americans and American Indians were able to become citizens long before Asian/Pacific Americans were given the same rights.)

While Pilipinos had been immigrating to the United States since the early 1900s (primarily for "practical training" as selected, sponsored, and funded by the U.S. government), large numbers of Pilipino laborers began entering in the 1920s because of the need for unskilled laborers (and due in part to the unavailability of Chinese and Japanese immigrants whose entry was restricted by law). Similar to the immigration of previous Asian groups, Pilipino immigration was soon to be limited to a quota of 50 immigrants per year with the passage of the Tydings–McDuffie Act of 1934. Moreover, Congressional resolutions in 1935 reflected clear anti-Pilipino sentiment by providing free, one-way passage for Pilipinos to return to the Philippines on the agreement that they will not return to the United States.

Anti-Asian immigration laws were finally repealed starting with the removal of the Chinese Exclusion Act in 1943. Other laws were repealed to allow immigration of Asians and Pacific Islanders, but the process was slow. It was not until 1965 that amendments to the McCarran–Walter Act opened the way for Asian immigrants to enter in larger numbers (a fixed quota of 20,000 per country, as opposed to 2 percent of the country's national origin population living in the United States in 1890). The 1965 amendment also established the "fifth preference" category, which allowed highly skilled workers needed by the United States to enter this country. Because of the preference for highly skilled workers, a second major wave of immigrants from Hong Kong, Taiwan, India, Korea, the Philippines, Japan, Singapore, and other Asiatic countries entered in the mid-1960s. The earlier wave of South Asian immigrants (from India, Pakistan, and Sri Lanka) with expertise to help with America's space race against the Soviets led to large numbers of professional and highly educated South Asians immigrating into the United States under the "fifth preference" after 1965. For example, 83 percent of the Asian Indians (about 60,000) who immigrated under the category of professional and technical workers between 1966 and 1977—as part of the second wave of immigration—were scientists with PhDs (about 20,000) and engineers (about 40,000) (Prashad, 2001).

With the upheaval in Southeast Asia and the Vietnam War, the third major wave of close to 1 million refugees and immigrants arrived in the United States from these affected Southeast Asian countries starting in the mid-1970s and lasting through the mid-1980s. The Refugee Act of 1980

(1) established the definition for "refugee," (2) reduced limits on the numbers of refugees entering the United States, (3) created the Office of Refugee Resettlement, and (4) permitted refugees to adjust their statuses after 1 year to become permanent residents, and after 4 more years, to become U.S. citizens (Povell, 2005). From the mid-1990s to the early 2000s, the need for personnel with high-tech, engineering, and Internet skills led to an additional influx of immigrants from India, Pakistan, Singapore, Korea, China (including Hong Kong), Taiwan, and other Asiatic countries.

Note that even today, in some state and local jurisdictions, anti-Asian laws need to be changed and removed, as shown by the following example:

> Asians can be barred from owning property in Florida or so it says in the state constitution. Amendment 1 on the Nov. 4 ballot would repeal a 1926 amendment that allowed the Legislature to ban "aliens ineligible for citizenship" an old code word for Asian immigrants from buying and owning real estate. Although the provision was never enforced and was invalidated by subsequent federal court rulings, backers of Amendment 1 believe the words should still be removed from the constitution. "It's just not right to have institutionalized racism remain in our constitution even if it's not enforceable," said state Sen. Steve Geller, D-Cooper City, who sponsored the ballot measure. (Madkour, 2008)

Although many immigrant groups (e.g., Italians, Jews, Poles) have been the target of discrimination, bigotry, and prejudice, Asian/Pacific Americans, like African Americans, have experienced extensive legal discrimination, hindering their ability to participate fully as Americans. This discrimination has gravely affected their well-being and quality of life. Some states had laws that prohibited intermarriage between Asians and whites. State and local laws imposed restrictive conditions and taxes specifically on Asian businesses and individuals. State courts were equally biased; for example, in the case of *People v. Hall*, heard in the California Supreme Court in 1854, Hall, a white defendant, had been convicted of murdering a Chinese man on the basis of testimony provided by one white and three Chinese witnesses. The California Supreme Court threw out Hall's conviction on the basis that state law prohibited blacks, mulattos, or Indians from testifying in favor of or against whites in court. The court's decision read:

> Indian as commonly used refers only to the North American Indian, yet in the days of Columbus all shores washed by Chinese waters were called the Indies. In the second place the word "white" necessarily excludes all other races than Caucasian; and in the third place, even if this were not so, I would decide against the testimony of Chinese on the grounds of public policy. (*People v. George W. Hall*, 4 Cal. 399 [October 1854])

This section on anti–Asian/Pacific American laws and sentiments cannot close without noting that Japanese Americans are the only immigrant group of Americans in the history of the American people who have been routed out of their homes and interned without due process. President Roosevelt's Executive Order 9066 resulted in the evacuation and incarceration of 100,000 Japanese Americans in 1942. For Asian/Pacific Americans, the internment of Japanese Americans represents how quickly anti-Asian sentiments can result in victimization of innocent people in the form of incarceration and punishment by law.

DEMOGRAPHICS: DIVERSITY AMONG ASIAN/PACIFIC AMERICANS

As we noted in the section defining Asian/Pacific Americans, this is an extremely heterogeneous population comprised of many different ethnic and cultural groups with generational differences within the United States, educational and socioeconomic diversity, and many other background and life experience differences. Asian/Pacific Americans currently number about 15.2 million and represent approximately 5 percent of the U.S. population (U.S. Bureau of the Census, 2009). As stated, the Asian/Pacific American population more than doubled with each census from 1970 to 1990 (1.5 million in 1970, 3.5 million in 1980, and 7.3 million in 1990) and increased by 76 percent from 1990 to 2000 (12.8 million in 2000). While greater longevity and higher birth rates contribute to this population increase, the major contributor to the growth of the Asian/Pacific American population is immigration from the Pacific Rim countries. Since the 1970s, Asian/Pacific American immigration has made up over 40 percent of all immigration to the United States (U.S. Bureau of the Census, 2002). As is evident in Exhibit 5.2, Chinese are the largest group, making up 23.3 percent of the total Asian/Pacific American population. Pilipinos are close behind, accounting for 20.1 percent of this population; in the next decade, Pilipinos will be the largest Asian/Pacific American group in the United States. Asian Indians are the fastest growing among the Asian and Pacific American population, making up 18.2 percent. Vietnamese comprise 10.8 percent of the Asian/Pacific American population, and Koreans are close behind comprising 10.3 percent. The Japanese American population was the third largest in 1990, but dropped to the sixth place in 2000, constituting approximately 8 percent in 2007, in part because of the lower immigration from Japan. All other Asian/Pacific American groups account for 9.3 percent of this population (U.S. Bureau of the Census, 2007a).

For law enforcement officers, the key Asian/Pacific American groups to understand are the six largest groups: Chinese, Pilipino, Asian Indian, Vietnamese, Korean, and Japanese (considering, in addition, local community trends and unique qualities of the community's populations). Knowledge of the growing trends among these Asian/Pacific American populations is also important for officer recruitment and other human resource considerations. Currently the Asian/Pacific Americans involved in professional law enforcement and criminal justice careers are largely Japanese, Chinese, and Korean Americans. To plan for the changing Asian/Pacific

---

EXHIBIT 5.2   Asian/Pacific American Population by Groups.

Asian/Pacific American Groups	Percentage of Total Asian/Pacific American population
Chinese	23.3
Pilipino	20.1
Asian Indian	18.2
Vietnamese	10.8
Korean	10.3
Japanese	8.0
All other Asian/Pacific groups	9.3
All Asian/Pacific Americans	100.0

Source: U.S. Bureau of the Census (2007a). 2007 American Community Survey.

EXHIBIT 5.3	**Distribution of Foreign-Born Asian/Pacific Americans by Country of Birth.**
Country of Birth	**Number of Foreign-Born**
China	1,391,000
Philippines	1,222,000
India	1,007,000
Vietnamese	863,000
Korean	701,000

Source: Bennett (2002). A Profile of the Nation's Foreign-Born Population from Asia (2000 Update), U.S. Bureau of the Census. P23-206.

American population base, it is critical to recruit and develop officers from the Pilipino, Vietnamese, and Asian Indian communities. Moreover, given the anticipated growth of the world population in the coming decades, it would be wise to recruit and develop officers with cultural knowledge, languages, and skills pertaining to China, India, Indonesia, and Pakistan—nations with the largest populations in the world (Population Reference Bureau, 2009).

More than half of all Asian/Pacific Americans are foreign-born (7.2 million) and comprise 26 percent of the foreign-born population in the United States (Bennett, 2002). Five countries contributed the largest numbers of foreign-born Asian/Pacific Americans, as seen in Exhibit 5.3.

As noted earlier, foreign-born Asian/Pacific Americans constitute the second highest percentage of immigrants becoming naturalized citizens at 52 percent; only those born in Europe had a higher rate (U.S. Bureau of the Census, 2009). The vast majority of all Asian/Pacific Americans were not born in the United States. Most of the Japanese, Pilipinos, Cambodians, and Indonesians reside in the western states. Chinese, Koreans, Vietnamese, Laotians, and Thais are fairly widely distributed in the large urban areas of the United States. Most of the Asian Indians and Pakistanis live in the eastern states. The state of Minnesota and the city of Fresno, California, have the largest Hmong populations in the country. Proficiency in English language varies within groups: groups that have immigrated most recently (Southeast Asians) have the largest percentage of those not able to speak English well.

Law enforcement and peace officers, depending on their jurisdictions, need to determine what additional languages and skills training might be appropriate in their work with Asian/Pacific American communities.

For many Asian/Pacific American groups, especially those who have recently immigrated into the United States, the law enforcement system is somewhat of a mystery. Thus, Asian/Pacific Americans may find it difficult to cooperate with officers and to participate fully in law enforcement.

To the Vietnamese immigrant, our law enforcement system doesn't seem to serve his community well. In Vietnam, if you are arrested, then the work of the attorney is to prove that you are innocent. You remain locked up in jail until your innocence is proven. In the United States, a suspect who is arrested is released either upon posting bail or on their own recognizance, usually within 24 hours. To the Vietnamese immigrant, it would seem that if you have the money, you can buy your way out of jail! (Vietnamese community advocate's comments at a Community Meeting about a local merchant's reluctance to cooperate with the police)

Asian/Pacific Americans' Key Motivating Perspectives

Earlier in this chapter, we provided a typology for viewing Asian/Pacific Americans. We provide in Exhibit 5.4 the same typology and have appended to it the key motivating perspectives for members in each group. By understanding some of these key motivating perspectives, law enforcement officers might be able to understand better the behaviors exhibited by citizens from these groups.

For example, the key to understanding the behavior of the most recent immigrants and refugee group (Asian/Pacific Refugee Type I; Exhibit 5.1) is to recall that members are in a survival mode (see Exhibit 5.4). (Many members from this category may remember that law enforcement and police officers in their country of origin were corrupt, aligned with a repressive government and the military, and swayed by bribes by those who were more affluent.) All their activities tend to be guided by this framework, which is to survive, to get through. This perspective also makes sense in terms of the traumatic ordeals faced by refugees in their journey to the United States. Encounters of these people with law enforcement personnel usually involve saying and doing anything to discontinue the contact because of possible fears of personal harm (e.g., not speaking English, not having any identification, "Yes, I will cooperate!").

With regard to Asian/Pacific immigrants (Type II), understanding their behaviors should focus on preserving their home culture as the motivating perspective. Since the majority of their life experiences occurred in Asia or the Pacific Islands, members are trying to preserve much of the values and traditions of their culture as it was alive and operating. Many Asian businesspersons and investors in the United States are included in this category. Much intergenerational conflict between grandparents or parents and youths occurs within this group. Members are inclined to keep to their ethnic communities (e.g., Little Saigons, Chinatowns,

EXHIBIT 5.4   Key Motivating Perspectives by Typology of Asian/Pacific American Groups.

Type	Description	Key Motivating Perspective
Type I	Asian/Pacific recently arrived immigrant or refugee (less than 5 years in the United States, with major life experiences in Asia or the Pacific Islands)	Surviving
Type II	Asian/Pacific immigrant or refugee (5 or more years in the United States, with major life experiences in Asia or the Pacific Islands)	Preserving
Type III	Asian/Pacific American (second generation; offspring of immigrant or refugee)	Adjusting
Type IV	Asian/Pacific Immigrant (major life experiences in the United States)	Changing
Type V	Asian/Pacific American (third or later generations in the United States)	Choosing
Type VI	Asian/Pacific national (anticipates return to Asia or to the Pacific Islands; this includes visitors and tourists)	Maintaining
Type VII	Asian/Pacific national (global workplace and residency)	Expanding

Koreatowns, Japantowns, Manilatowns) and have as little to do with law enforcement as possible. Many remember that the police have not served them well in the past (e.g., immigration laws, Japanese internment).

For example, various South Asian community members have been targets of hate crimes because they stay within their ethnic community enclaves, preserve their ethnic customs and dress, and are stereotyped and/or misidentified. In the Detroit area, there is a sizeable South Asian community from Bangladesh (the people are called Bengalis). These citizens are Muslim and dark-skinned, and are often mistaken for Arabs. South Asians who wear turbans (Sikhs) are often stereotyped as Arabs.

> Removing a Sikh's turban in public is the same as a strip search. Not all Arabs are Muslim. A kirpan [or a sheathed knife] is not a concealed weapon. Those lessons and others were delivered Wednesday to about 75 Pennsylvania law enforcement officers during a four-hour seminar at the Allegheny County Police Academy. Sponsored by the U.S. Department of Justice's Community Relations Service, the seminar was designed to teach local agencies about Arab, Muslim and Sikh cultures, officials said . . . Rajbir Datta, a Pittsburgh native and associate director of the Sikh American Legal Defense and Education Fund, said that although Sikhs speak a different language (Punjabi), practice a different religion (Sikhism) and generally come from a different continent (India), they often are mistaken in America for Arab Muslims. Most men wearing turbans in the United States are Sikh . . . If a police officer must search a turban, Datta urged them to explain why, to do so in a private setting, and to offer the Sikh something to cover his hair during the search. "Turbans are very religious, very personal," he said. "Many men never reveal their hair in public, so making them remove it would be like a public strip search." Datta said many Sikhs carry a kirpan, a 3- to 6-inch sheathed knife that symbolizes a Sikh's commitment to protect the weak and promote justice. An officer who has to confiscate a kirpan should explain why and handle the knife with respect, Datta said. (Togneri, 2007)

Asian/Pacific Americans (second generation, Type III) tend to be whom we picture when we hear the term Asian American. Those of the second generation work very hard at being assimilated into the mainstream, adjusting and changing to be a part of mainstream America. Often, the expectations of second-generation parents are high; parents will sacrifice so that their offspring will "make it" in their lifetime. Members may interact primarily with non-Asians and take on many of the values and norms of the mainstream society. This group may be considered "marginal" by some in that, try as each person may to become like the mainstream ("become white"), others may still consider them Asian. Many from this group try to minimize their contact with law enforcement personnel and agencies primarily because of the immigration and other experiences relayed to them by their parents' generation. Individuals of the second generation who were born in the United States before the mid-1960s may have had relatives (or parents) who entered the United States by using false papers. Fears of disclosure of such illegal entries have prevented many Asian/Pacific Americans from cooperating with peace officers and with other human and social service agencies and programs. With the emphasis on homeland security in the United States, many from this group have taken extra efforts to not be misidentified about their ethnicity (e.g., South Asians with darker skin tones being mistaken for Middle Easterners) or stereotyped because of their religion (e.g., Asian/Pacific Americans who are moderate Muslims, not fundamentalists).

The Asian/Pacific immigrant (Type IV), whose major life experience is in the United States, focuses much of the member's energies on changes (through assimilation or acculturation) that have to be made in order to succeed. Although these individuals have tended to continue to value the cultural and ethnic elements of their former homeland, most know that changes are necessary. Members of this group reflect the socioeconomic standings of the different waves on which each entered into the United States. For example, individuals who entered as part of the first wave of laborers and domestic workers (primarily Chinese and Japanese, with some Pilipinos, Koreans, and Asian Indians) represent one grouping. Others entered more as part of the second wave of immigration as foreign students and/or under the "fifth preference" as professional skilled workers. Asian/Pacific immigrants (Type IV) who are designated as entering the United States under the "fifth preference" are those who checked the fifth category on the Immigration and Nationalization Service form. This category indicates that the reason for immigration into the United States was that the person has a professional skill that is in short supply in the United States and it would be in the best interest of the United States to allow that person to enter. This group consists of educated, professional individuals (e.g., the largest numbers of foreign-trained medical doctors and psychiatrists in the United States are from India, the Philippines, Pakistan, China, and South Korea [Mullan, 2005]). Since the fall of Saigon in 1975 and the beginning of the immigration of Southeast Asians into the United States, a third wave has included over 1 million Asian/Pacific immigrants who suffered great trauma in their escape; many are young adults today. For members of this group, reactions to law enforcement officials vary depending on their time of immigration and socioeconomic experiences. For law enforcement officers, it is critical to understand the differences among the immigrant groups (i.e., do not confuse the professional Asian/Pacific immigrant with one of the other groups).

The Asian/Pacific American (third or later generation, Type V) category includes individuals who are more able to choose which aspects of the old culture to keep and which of the new culture to accept. The focus is on choosing activities, values, norms, and lifestyles that blend the best of Asian/Pacific and American cultures. Being bicultural is a unique and important aspect of this group. Many may no longer have as much skill with their native language as they have with English, and may rely on English as their primary or only language (thus an individual can be bicultural and not bilingual). Contact by members of this group with law enforcement personnel may not be any different than contact by any other Americans.

For the last two categories, Asian/Pacific nationals, we make a key distinction between those who plan to return to their own country following a work assignment in the United States (Type VI) and those whose work is truly global, in that individuals may have several residences in different parts of the world (Type VII). Those in the former category (Type VI, on a work assignment in the United States that may last 5 to 7 years) maintain their home-base cultural orientation and experiences knowing that when the work assignment is over, they will go back to their home country again. Because they mean to maintain their native cultures, some individuals of this group may be inadequately prepared to understand many of the laws and practices of the United States. For members of this group, being able to stay in the United States to complete their assignments is of key importance. Often, individuals may not be aware of the differences between "minor" violations (e.g., minor traffic violations, small claims) and "major" violations and crimes. Let's look at the following example:

> Mr. Sato is a manager assigned to oversee a technical department in a joint United States–Japan automobile plant in the Midwest. One evening, while driving home from a late night at the plant, Mr. Sato did not see a stop sign and went right through it on a nonbusy intersection. A police officer in a patrol car saw the violation and pulled Mr. Sato over. The interaction puzzled the police officer, since Mr. Sato seemed very cooperative but kept asking the officer "to forgive him and to please let him go!" After much discussion and explanation, it was discovered that Mr. Sato thought that the officer would have to confiscate his passport because of the stop-sign violation (something that is done in many Asiatic countries) and that he might be "kicked out" of the country and thus be unable to complete his work assignment. Upon clearing up this misconception, Mr. Sato accepted the traffic citation "with appreciation." (Police officer's anecdote in a cultural awareness training session)

For the second group of Asian/Pacific nationals (Type VII), the key focus is on their ability to "expand" their actions and behaviors effectively into different global environments. These individuals see themselves as being able to adapt to life in a variety of global environments; many may speak three or more languages (including English). Individuals within this group pride themselves in knowing about the different laws, norms, values, and practices of the countries they encounter. Law enforcement personnel would find this group equally able to understand and to follow the laws and practices of a given community as well.

LABELS AND TERMS

As we noted earlier, the term *Asian/Pacific Americans* is a convenient summarizing label used to refer to a heterogeneous group of people. Which particular terms are used is based on the principle of self-designation and self-preference. Asian and Pacific Islander people are sensitive about the issue because up until the 1960 census the population was relegated to the "Other" category. With the ethnic pride movement and ethnic minority studies movement in the late 1960s, people of Asian and Pacific Islands descent began to designate self-preferred terms for group reference. The terms were chosen over the previous term *Oriental*, which many Asian/Pacific Americans consider to be offensive. *Oriental* is considered offensive because it symbolizes to many the past references, injustices, and stereotypes of Asian and Pacific people. It was also a term designated by those in the West (i.e., the Occident, the Western Hemisphere) for Asian people, and reminds many Asian/Pacific Americans of the colonial mentality of foreign policies and its effects on the Pacific Rim countries.

In federal and other governmental designations (e.g., the Small Business Administration), the label used is "Asian American/Pacific Islanders." Although very few Asian/Pacific Americans refer to themselves as such, the governmental designation is used in laws and regulations and in most reports and publications. By individuals within any of the groups, often the more specific names for the groups are preferred (e.g., Chinese, Japanese, Vietnamese, Pakistani, Hawaiian). Some individuals may prefer that the term *American* be part of their designation (e.g., Korean American, Pilipino American). For law enforcement officers, the best term to refer to an individual is the term he or she prefers to be called. It is perfectly acceptable to ask an individual what ethnic or cultural group(s) he or she identifies with and what he or she prefers to be called.

The use of slurs such as "Jap," "Chink," "Gook," "Chinaman," "Flip," "Babas," and other derogatory ethnic slang terms is never acceptable in crime-fighting and peacekeeping, no matter how provoked an officer may be. The use of other stereotypic terms, including "Chinese fire drill," "DWO (Driving While Oriental)," "Fu Man Chu mustache," "Kamikaze kid," "yellow cur," "yellow peril," "Bruce Lee Kung Fu type," "slant-eyed," "Turban man," "Vietnamese bar girl," and "dragon lady," does not convey the professionalism and respect for community diversity important to law enforcement and peacekeeping and must be avoided in law enforcement work. Officers hearing these words used in their own departments (or with peers or citizens) should provide immediate helpful feedback about such terms to those who use them. Officers who may out of habit routinely use these terms may find themselves (or their superiors) in the embarrassing situation (on the evening news) of explaining to offended citizens and communities why these terms were used and that they had intended no prejudice.

MYTHS AND STEREOTYPES

Knowledge of and sensitivity to Asian/Pacific Americans' concerns, diversity, historical background, and life experiences will facilitate the crime-fighting and peacekeeping missions of peace officers. It is important to have an understanding about some of the myths, environmental messages, and stereotypes of Asian/Pacific Americans that contribute to the prejudice, discrimination, and bias they encounter. Many Americans do not have much experience with the diversity of Asian/Pacific American groups and learn about these groups only through stereotypes, often perpetuated by movies and the media. The effect of myths and stereotypes is to reduce Asian/Pacific Americans to simplistic, one-dimensional characters whom many people lump into one stereotypic group. Often, the complexities of the diverse Asian/Pacific American groups in terms of language, history, customs, cultures, religions, and life experiences become confusing and threatening, and it is easier to deal with stereotypes of these groups. Nonetheless, it is important for law enforcement officers to be aware of the different stereotypes of Asian/Pacific Americans. The key to effectiveness with any ethnic or racial group is not the complete elimination of myths and stereotypes about the group, but rather the awareness of these stereotypes and management of one's behaviors when the stereotypes are not true of the person with whom one is dealing.

Some of the stereotypes that have affected Asian/Pacific Americans in law enforcement include the following:

1. *Viewing Asian/Pacific Americans as "all alike."*   That is, because there are many similarities in names, physical features, and behaviors, many law enforcement officers may make comments about their inability to tell people apart, or they may deal with them in stereotypic group fashion (e.g., they are all "inscrutable," involved in gangs).
2. *Viewing Asian/Pacific Americans as successful "model minorities" or as a "super minority."*   Some hold the stereotype that Asian/Pacific Americans are all successful, and this stereotype is further reinforced by the media (Kawai, 2005). Such stereotypes have resulted in intergroup hostilities and hate crimes directed toward Asian/Pacific Americans and have served to mask true differences and diversity among the various Asian and Pacific

Islander groups. Some Asian/Pacific American groups have had to highlight the incorrect perceptions of the "model minority" stereotype:

> A newly released study on youth crime in Richmond shatters the so-called "model minority myth," by showing high crime rates among Southeast Asians . . . a diverse coalition of community leaders including Contra Costa County Supervisor John Gioia and Richmond Mayor Irma Anderson said the study's findings revealed that Vietnamese and Laotian families in Richmond are isolated by language barriers and little understanding of social systems. As a result, the families struggle economically and their children are performing poorly in school. They are also more likely to get involved in crime. Vietnamese and Laotian youth are arrested on a per capita basis more than any other ethnic group besides blacks, according to the study. "Before now, Southeast Asians have always been compared to Chinese and Japanese, who are usually associated with over-achievement," said Sang Saephan, 21, a member of Southeast Asian Leaders. "This study gives a better idea of how each subgroup is doing" . . . The study points to a disturbing trend that was previously unknown, presenters said. In the West Contra Costa Unified School District, about 48 percent of ninth-grade Vietnamese students scored at or above the national average, while 43 percent were well below the average. Many Laotian students, 69 percent, failed to achieve average scores. (Geluardi, 2006)

Clearly no group of people are "all successful" or "all criminals." Nonetheless, the "success" and the "model minority" stereotypes have affected Asian/Pacific Americans negatively. For example, because of their implied success, law enforcement organizations may not spend the time to recruit Asian/Pacific American individuals for law enforcement careers (assuming that they are more interested in other areas such as education and business pursuits). This stereotype also hides the existence of real discrimination for those who are successful, as seen in glass ceilings in promotional and developmental opportunities, for example. The success stereotype has resulted in violence and crimes against Asian/Pacific persons. Two examples, one older but etched in the memories of many Asian/Pacific Americans, and the other more recent, are representative of issues very salient to Asian/Pacific Americans today:

> The murder of Vincent Chin, and the subsequent inability of the court system to bring the murderers to justice, is now a well-known case among Asian/Pacific American communities. The perpetrators in this case, Ronald Ebens and Michael Nitz, were two white automobile factory workers who blamed Vincent Chin (a Chinese American) for the success of the Japanese automobile industry that was, in turn, blamed for taking away American jobs in the automobile factory. (Takaki, 1989b)

> Two Queens men have been charged with hate crimes after a confrontation that began in Douglaston with racial slurs shouted at a car full of Chinese-American students and escalated into a vicious roadside attack, then led to a fight with two police officers blocks away, the authorities said yesterday. By the time it was over early Saturday, one of the students had been struck with his own steering wheel

lock, one of his companions had been beaten in the face and body, and both officers had suffered minor injuries. All were released from hospitals after receiving treatment. The events came as a shock yesterday to many people across Flushing, Douglaston, Little Neck and other neighborhoods of northern Queens that have attracted large concentrations of immigrants from China and Korea. According to a law enforcement official, who insisted on anonymity because of the nature of the case, the epithets directed by the suspects, both white, at the four students, all of them native New Yorkers of Chinese descent, were laced with a racially derisive term rarely heard since the Korean War. " 'The defendants' alleged actions are a throwback to a dark time and place in American history and are an affront to civilized society," Richard A. Brown, the Queens district attorney, said in a statement yesterday. (Lueck, 2006)

3. *Viewing some Asian/Pacific Americans as possible "foreign" terrorists because of their religious affiliation and cultural dress.*   Many Asian/Pacific Americans immigrate from countries with very large populations that practice Islam (e.g., Indonesia, Pakistan, Bangladesh, India, and China), and the majority of these Muslims are from the more moderate wing of Sunni Islam (not from the more fundamentalist branch). However, it is highly possible for the unfamiliar to group Asian/Pacific Americans who are Muslims into a collective group associated with fundamentalism and terrorism. Moreover, for many immigrants who may stay close to their cultural traditions and cultural dress (e.g., Sikhs who wear turbans and have beards), it is easy to misidentify cultural dress and nuances and come to stereotypic conclusions about who might be a "foreign" terrorist. Two examples: (1) One of the first suspects detained for questioning on September 11, 2001 (as seen on the national television news) was a Sikh who was wearing a turban and was misidentified as an Afghanistan Taliban (who also wear a head covering that is called a turban), and (2) South Asians (e.g., Bengalis) with darker skin tones in the Midwest were often misidentified as Arabs and were detained for questioning on homeland security issues.

A Brooklyn Hospital manager says cops have stopped him 21 times since the NYPD began searching subway riders—and there's no way that's random. Jangir Sultan, who is of South Asian descent, says in a new federal suit that the odds of his being stopped randomly that many times are 1 in 165 million. "If a bomb-sniffing dog [detected something] or an alarm went off, good, fine, stop me. But to say getting stopped over and over is random—no, sorry, it's racial profiling," said the 32-year-old Sultan, who was born in Brooklyn but whose parents are from Kashmir. The law-abiding Sultan said he had no objections when the NYPD started the subway bag searches in July 2005 in response to transit bombings in London. Even after Sultan was repeatedly stopped at various stations in Manhattan and Brooklyn, he assumed all New Yorkers were bearing the same burden to prevent another terror attack. But in talks with friends and colleagues, Sultan learned most were never stopped. "Yet the number of times I was stopped kept growing. It was embarrassing. Did I look like someone who would blow something up? Getting all this attention from the NYPD was a little intimidating," he said. After he was stopped for the 13th time, Sultan started reporting the incidents to the Civilian Complaint Review

Board, which takes complaints about police misconduct. Sultan filed eight complaints with the CCRB. Six of the stops were at Brooklyn's Borough Hall Station, which is near his downtown condo. "I'm a homeowner and taxpayer. There has to be a better way than this," Sultan said. (Gendar, 2009)

From a law enforcement perspective, many hate crimes against Asian/Pacific Americans are related to the stereotyping of the group as foreigners and not as Americans.

4. ***Misunderstanding Asian/Pacific cultural differences and practices and viewing differences stereotypically as a threat to other Americans.*** The more than 40 Asian/Pacific American groups encompass great differences in life experiences, languages, backgrounds, and cultures. It is easy to make mistakes and draw incorrect conclusions because of such cultural differences. Certainly, when we lack information about any group, it is natural to draw conclusions based on our own filtering system, stereotypes, and assumptions. Most of the time, these incorrect assumptions and stereotypes are corrected by favorable contact and actual interpersonal relationships with Asian/Pacific American people. From a law enforcement perspective, the thrust of community policing, as well as cultural awareness training, is to provide the opportunities to modify stereotypes and learn about ethnic communities. Law enforcement agencies, however, have to intervene in situations in which individuals and/or groups view Asian/Pacific American cultural differences as perceived threats to themselves. Stereotypic and racially biased views of Asian/Pacific Americans as threats require the ongoing attention of law enforcement agencies.

THE ASIAN/PACIFIC AMERICAN FAMILY

Obviously, with over 40 different cultural groups under the label of Asian/Pacific Americans, we find great differences in how families operate within the various subgroups. We would like to share some common characteristics to describe Asian/Pacific American families that might be of value in crime-fighting and community peacekeeping. Asian/Pacific American families generally exhibit very strong ties among extended family members. It is not unusual for three to four generations of the same family to live under one roof. Moreover, the extended family can even have an ongoing relationship network that spans great geographic distances. For example, family members (all of whom consider themselves as one family) can be engaged in extensive communications and activities with members of the same family in the United States, Canada, Hong Kong, and Vietnam, all simultaneously. It is not uncommon for an officer to come into contact with members of the extended Asian/Pacific American family in the course of servicing these communities. One key to the success of law enforcement officers in working with an extended family network is the knowledge of how best to contact an Asian/Pacific American family and which family member to speak to for information, help, and referral.

Culture Shock and the Asian/Pacific American Family

Because the traditional cultures of Asia and the Pacific Islands are so very different from that of the United States, many Asian/Pacific American families (whether refugees, immigrants, businesspersons, students, or tourists) experience some degree of culture shock when they enter and reside in the United States. Culture shock results not only from differences in values and traditions but also from differences in urbanization, industrialization, and modernization owing to technology that may be different from that in their homeland. Peace officers need to be aware that Asian/Pacific Americans may cope with their culture shock by becoming "clannish" (e.g., Chinatowns, Koreatowns). Other survival mechanisms include avoiding contact and interaction with those who are different (including police officers).

The Role of the Man and the Woman in an Asian/Pacific American Family

In most Asian/Pacific American families, relationship and communication patterns tend to be quite hierarchical, with the father as the identified head of the household. Although many decisions and activities may appear to be determined by the father, other individuals may influence his choices. Generally, if there are grandparents in the household, the father would still act as the spokesperson for the family, but he would consult the grandparents, his wife, and others regarding any major decision. As such, it may be important in any kind of law enforcement contact that requires a decision and/or choice to allow the parties time to discuss issues in, as much as feasible, a "private" manner. Self-control and keeping things within the family are key values for Asian/Pacific Americans. An officer thus may find that there is more control in a situation by allowing the Asian/Pacific American to come to the same conclusion as the officer with respect to a situation and to exercise his or her own self-choice (which may be the same as what the officer would want the parties to do anyway). For example, the officer can explain an arrest situation to the father of a family member, and instead of saying directly to the family member to be arrested that he or she has to leave with the officer, the officer can allow the father to suggest to the family member that he or she leave with the officer. What may appear to be a minor consideration in this case can result in a higher degree of persuasion, control, and cooperation by all parties concerned.

Although there are no clear-cut rules as to whether one goes to the male head of the household or to the female head to make a law enforcement inquiry, the general rule of thumb is that one would not go too wrong by starting with the father. It should be noted that for most Asian/Pacific American families, the role of the mother in discipline and decision making is very important. While the household may appear to be "ruled" by the father, the mother's role in finances, discipline, education, operations, and decision making is major.

Children, Adolescents, and Youths

Most Asian/Pacific American families involve at least two or more individuals within the same household working outside of the home. Thus, if young children are present, there is a high reliance on either family members or others to help care for them while the parents are at work. It is not uncommon for older children to care for younger children within a household. Moreover, latchkey children within an Asian/Pacific American home are common, especially in families that cannot afford external child care. In recent immigrant and refugee families, Asian/Pacific American children have a special role in being the intermediaries between parents and the external community because of the ability of the younger individuals to learn English and the American ways of doing things. Children often serve as translators and interpreters for peace officers in their communication and relations with Asian/Pacific American families comprising recent immigrants and refugees. In such situations, it is suggested that the officer review the role expected of the youthful member of the family and determine how sensitive an area the translated content is to the different family members and the consequences if the content is incorrectly translated. (For example, asking a juvenile to translate to his or her parents who speak no English that the juvenile had been involved in a sexual abuse situation at the school may result in significant omission and/or changed content because of the embarrassment caused to the juvenile and possibly to the parents.) In all cases, when a child is acting as a translator, the officer should direct all verbal and nonverbal communication to the parents (as one would normally do without a translator). Otherwise, the parents may view the officer's lack of attention to them as an insult.

Asian/Pacific American Family Violence

Keeping family issues within the family and using self-help and personal effort strategies are part of Asian/Pacific cultural values and norms. Research studies on family violence (e.g., spousal physical abuse, child abuse, sexual abuse) by Asian/Pacific Americans show an increasing trend. It is only during the past two decades that researchers and community advocates have begun collecting such data.

> The murder-suicide in Santa Clara last week is a tragedy for this South Asian family and the entire South Asian community. According to news reports, police say family conflict could have triggered the killings. The incident comes shortly after the February beheading of a Muslim woman in New York. Her husband faces murder charges. And just last June in Atlanta, a Pakistani man confessed to killing his daughter because she wanted a divorce, which would bring shame to his family. Then there was the October murder-suicide in California's San Fernando Valley, where a jobless Indian-American man ended the lives of five family members before turning the gun on himself. These tragedies strike at the heart of our South Asian society and point to an inadequately addressed problem of silent violence in our communities. South Asians are close-knit and very private people. We keep our troubles close to our hearts. Seeking help from professionals outside our immediate families is a foreign notion, largely unacceptable and ridiculed in our culture. Many in our community have become silent sufferers, producing inner turbulence that silently bubbles away until it erupts into devastating acts of violence. (Afrid, 2009)

The few reported studies that exist seem to indicate significant and emerging problems with family violence within the Asian/Pacific American community. Tjaden and Thoennes (2000) conducted a telephone survey of a nationally representative sample of 8,000 men and 8,000 women of all ethnic backgrounds. Results showed that 12.8 percent of the Asian/Pacific American women reported having been physically assaulted by an intimate partner at least once during their lifetime (and 3.8 percent reported having been raped). Abraham (2000), in her survey of community-based women's service organizations, found that over 1,000 South Asian women sought help for abuse and family violence. The National Asian Women's Health Organization (2002) conducted telephone interviews with 336 Asian American women, aged 18 to 34, in the San Francisco and Los Angeles areas and found that 16 percent of the respondents reported having experienced "pressure to have sex without their consent by an intimate partner" and that 27 percent reported "emotional abuse" by an intimate partner. Tjaden and Thoennes (2000) also indicate that family violence within Asian/Pacific American communities has been underestimated and underreported. Song (1996) noted that most of the abused women used self-help efforts to keep the problem within the home (e.g., fought back physically and verbally, ignored the battering or did nothing, stared at the abusing person), and 70 percent of the battered women indicated that they did not know about community services that could have helped them.

The availability of bilingual outreach services is of key importance to the Asian/Pacific American community, as is illustrated in the following example:

> Shock rippled through Southern California's Asian-American community this month when three Korean-American fathers—including one in Fontana—killed their children. Financial strains may have pushed them over the edge, authorities said. As police continue to investigate the crimes, the community has been doing a bit of soul-searching. Was this just a bad string of coincidences? Or, as some community leaders have suggested, do these crimes highlight the need for more support services for the growing Asian immigrant population here? There are no service agencies serving the monolingual Asian-speaking population, said Janet Chang, a professor of social work at Cal State San Bernardino. "There's a huge service gap," Chang said. . . . Police say Bong Joo Lee shot and killed his 5-year-old daughter Iris Araa Lee on April 8 at his Fontana home with a 9 mm handgun and then killed himself. Police have said Lee had more than $200,000 in gambling debt. Court records show that Lee and his wife Gina split in 2004, the same year Lee pleaded no contest to battery on a spouse. Lee's ex-wife was awarded custody of their daughter, but Lee was granted visitation so long as he completed an anger management program. (Quan, 2006, p. B01)

The role of peace officers in detecting, assessing, and intervening in family violence situations within Asian/Pacific American communities is a critical one given this area of emerging needs and problems. The sensitivity of the peace officer to the cultural influences and patterns of communication (as noted in the next section) will be significant in the effective gathering of initial information and subsequent referral and interventions with Asian/Pacific American families involved in domestic violence and other issues of abuse.

COMMUNICATION STYLES OF ASIAN/PACIFIC AMERICANS

We do not wish to create any kind of stereotypes, but there are key features of Asian/Pacific American verbal and nonverbal communication styles that necessitate explanation. Misunderstanding resulting from style differences can lead to perceptions of poor community services from police agencies, conflicts, and safety and control issues for peace officers.

1. It is important that officers take the time to get information from witnesses, victims, and suspects even if the individuals have limitations to their English speaking abilities. The use of officers who may speak different Asian/Pacific dialects or languages, translators, and language bank resources would greatly enhance this process. Often Asian/Pacific Americans have not been helped in crime-fighting and peacekeeping situations because officers could not or did not take information from individuals who could not speak English well.

   > "We don't have a ton of stuff on Asian gangs," said Sgt. Bill Beall of the Fort Worth police gang unit. "Everything is really closemouthed. We can have a hard time getting information." . . . Several major clashes have come to police officers' attention in the past year, including the gang-related killing of a 21-year-old college student last year outside a Euless bowling alley. Police said two women

held the student down while a man shot her in the head. . . . Language barriers discourage adults who are aware of gang problems from going to police, he said. That's why he thinks cities need more storefront programs like the one Haltom City had with Vietnamese-speaking officers about five years ago. Vietnamese-Americans could go to them with information and concerns, he said. "We need more police officers who understand the Vietnamese culture," Ha said. "People feel comfortable with them." (Branch, 2006)

2. Asian/Pacific Americans tend to hold a greater "family" and/or "group" orientation. As such, the lack of the use of "I" statements and/or self-reference should not be evaluated as being evasive about oneself or one's relationships. The officer may be concerned because an Asian/Pacific American may wish to use the pronoun "we" when the situation may call for a personal observation involving an "I" statement. For example, in a traffic accident, the Asian/Pacific American may describe what he or she saw by saying "We saw. . . ." Using such group statements to convey what the individual saw is consistent with the family and group orientation of Asian/Pacific Americans.

3. The officer should be aware that for many Asian/Pacific Americans, it is considered to be rude, impolite, and to involve a "loss of face" to directly say "no" to an authority figure such as a peace officer. Peace officers must understand the following possibilities when an answer of "yes" is heard from an Asian/Pacific American. It can mean (1) "Yes, I heard what you said (but I may or may not agree with you)"; (2) "Yes, I understand what you said (but I may or may not do what I understand)"; (3) "Yes, I can see this is important for you (but I may not agree with you on this)"; or (4) "Yes, I agree (and will do what you said)." Because the context of the communication and the nonverbal aspects of the message are equally meaningful, it is vital for law enforcement officers to be sure of the "yes" answers received, as well as of other language nuances from Asian/Pacific Americans. Two examples might be illustrative: (1) If an Asian/Pacific American says that he or she will "try his or her best to attend," this generally means that he or she will not be there, especially for most voluntary events and situations such as community neighborhood safety meetings. (2) If an Asian/Pacific national says in response to a question "It is possible," this generally means, "do not wait for the event to happen." Such communications, as noted previously, may be more applicable to some Asian/Pacific Americans than others, but sensitivity on the part of law enforcement officers to these language nuances will facilitate communication. Specific rules for interacting with each Asian/Pacific American group are not necessary, but officers should have a general understanding of language and cultural styles. In a communication situation in which the response of "yes" may be ambiguous, it is suggested that law enforcement officers rephrase the question so that the requested outcome in action and understanding are demonstrated in the verbal response. For example:

Ambiguous Response:
OFFICER: "I need you to show up in court on Tuesday. Do you understand?"
ASIAN WITNESS: "Yes!"

Rephrasing the Question to Elicit a Response That Shows Understanding and Outcome:
OFFICER: "What are you going to do on Tuesday?"
ASIAN WITNESS: "I will be in court on Tuesday. I must go there."

4. Asian/Pacific Americans tend to be "high context" in communication style. This means that the officer must provide both interpersonal and situational contexts for effective communications. Context for Asian/Pacific Americans means that members of the community know the officers in the community. Community members may have had previous working relationships with the officer (e.g., crime prevention meetings, police athletic league). Moreover, other members of the community may help to provide information and context for police cooperation based on past relationships. Context also means providing explanations and education to members or groups within Asian/Pacific Americans about procedures and laws before asking them questions and/or requesting their participation in an activity. By providing background information and by establishing prior relationships with Asian/Pacific American communities, the Asian/Pacific American individual has a context for cooperating with law enforcement agencies and officers.

5. Be aware of nonverbal and other cultural nuances that may detract from the effective communication of the officer with a member of the Asian/Pacific American community. Many Asian/Pacific Americans find it uncomfortable and sometimes inappropriate to maintain eye contact with authority figures like police officers. It is considered in many Asian/Pacific American cultures to be disrespectful if there is eye contact with someone who is of higher status, position, importance, or authority. As such, many Asian/Pacific Americans may look down on the ground and/or avert their eyes from gazing at a police officer. The officer should not automatically read this nonverbal behavior as indicating a lack of trust or respect, or as a dishonest response. Likewise, for the police officer, he or she should be aware of possible nonverbal gestures and actions that may detract from his or her professional roles (e.g., gesturing with the curled index finger for a person to come forward in a manner that might be used only for servants in that person's home culture).

6. Asian/Pacific Americans may not display their emotionality in the way that the officer expects. The central thesis guiding Asian/Pacific Americans is the Confucian notion of "walking the middle road." This means that extremes, too much or too little of anything, are not good. As such, Asian/Pacific Americans tend to moderate their display of positive and/or negative emotion. Often, in crisis situations, nonverbal displays of emotions are controlled to the point that the affect of the Asian/Pacific American appears "flat." Under such circumstances, the officer needs to correctly understand and interpret such displays of emotion appropriately. For example, just because the parent of a murder victim does not appear emotionally shaken by an officer's report does not mean that the person is not experiencing a severe emotional crisis.

KEY ISSUES IN LAW ENFORCEMENT

Underreporting of Crimes

Asian/Pacific Americans, because of their past experiences with some law enforcement agencies (e.g., anti-Asian immigration laws, health and sanitation code violations in restaurants, perceived unresponsiveness by police), are reluctant to report crimes and may not seek police assistance and help. Many Asian/Pacific Americans remember how police in their home countries have brutalized and violated them and others (e.g., in Southeast Asian and other Asian countries). Crimes that occur within a family's home (e.g., home invasion, family violence) or within the confines of a small family business (e.g., robbery of a Chinese restaurant) often go unreported unless these crimes are connected to larger criminal activities, as in the example that follows:

> The modus operandi was always the same: Criminals staked out a business, sometimes calling to ask for closing times, then trailed the owners home. After parking their cars, the victims were confronted at gunpoint, forced inside and robbed of jewelry, cash, and other valuables. The scenario was repeated at least 14 times in recent months, including three times in a single day. The victim was always an Asian or Asian-American. The home invasion spree, along with three recent murders of Asian-Americans over the past few months, has left residents and community leaders here shaken. Police say the victims were targeted by criminals who believed they would be easy marks because of their ethnicity. "The bad guys that we've talked to . . . are pretty much assuming that Asian business people deal in cash and not banks, that Asian business people are docile and won't fight back, and they keep their money at home or in their business," state police Capt. David Young said. Asian-American leaders dispute the stereotype, but Young said even the perception on the part of criminals would make members of the community a target. And although Philadelphia crime statistics show a slight decrease in robberies of people of Asian descent, authorities believe many crimes may go unreported if victims are reluctant to come forward, for example, fearing trouble over their immigration status. (Todt, 2009)

Many immigrants and refugees are simply not knowledgeable about the legal system of the United States and therefore avoid any contact with law enforcement personnel. Outreach and community-policing perspectives will enhance the contact and relationship with Asian/Pacific American communities, helping to correct the underreporting of crimes.

Differential Treatment

Several areas have been highlighted for Asian/Pacific Americans who may have received different treatment in police services as a result of their culture or ethnic heritage. Incidents reported include police excessive force, misconduct, and harassment. The following case is an example:

> The family of a Vietnamese woman who was shot and killed in her kitchen by police as she brandished a vegetable peeler will receive $1.8 million in a settlement of its lawsuit against the city. The federal suit claimed that San Jose police officers were not properly trained or supervised and that the officer who shot Cau Bich Tran, 25, used excessive force. The settlement ends more than two years of litigation over the death of Tran, a Vietnamese mother of two who was shot while holding a vegetable peeler that police mistook for a cleaver. Tran, an immigrant who spoke little English, was killed July 13, 2003, after authorities were called to her home by a neighbor who reported hearing screaming and pounding. Officer Chad Marshall, 30, testified previously before a grand jury investigating criminal wrongdoing that he believed Tran was about to throw the item at him when he shot her. Marshall was ultimately cleared. The shooting outraged many in the Vietnamese American community, who pressed for an open inquiry into Tran's death. Critics wondered how Tran, who stood barely 5 feet tall and weighed less than 100 pounds, could be considered a credible threat. (Associated Press, 2005)

Positive Collaborative Asian/Pacific American Community and Law Enforcement Agencies

Increasingly we see that when there are collaborative and cooperative efforts among the law enforcement, criminal justice, and community advocacy systems, the Asian and Pacific American communities will begin to gain greater trust and confidence resulting from effective multicultural and multidisciplinary law enforcement actions taken. The following all-Cantonese Citizen Police Academy is a positive example of how police, community advocates, and citizens join together to collaborate on police services in the Asian community:

> They learned how to recognize handicapped parking spots, sit quietly when pulled over by a police officer, and obey speed limits. But before graduating yesterday from the Police Department's first all-Cantonese Citizen Police Academy, more than 50 senior Chinese residents were also encouraged to be more trusting of government officials, Western medicine, and police . . . As the Police Department prepares to hire three more Cantonese-speaking officers for its 200-member force, Quincy officials say they also are trying to help older Asians overcome their wariness of authority, a holdover of their experiences in communist China, where many police officers are corrupt. The department plans to periodically offer the Citizen Police Academy for Asian residents. . . . They focused on items such as the nuances of city ordinances, motor vehicle safety, and how to defend themselves if they are attacked. "This was very good, very important," said Duk Woo, 74, one of the few course participants who can speak English conversationally. "It's common-sense things, but not many people know, especially the old-timers, the Asian people." (Cramer, 2006b)

Asian/Pacific American officers involved in community policing in their local neighborhoods have been seen as a viable model for cities with growing Asian/Pacific American populations:

> Hwanhee Kim, who helps crime victims and witnesses for the Fairfax County police, recalled one woman of Korean background who said she had been beaten regularly by her husband since their honeymoon. For many years, she never considered reporting the abuse to the police. After police intervened, Kim recounted, the woman said that "she felt like a human for the first time." Fairfax Lt. Gun M. Lee said that in the mid-1990s, he was summoned to a fender-bender. One of the drivers, a woman of Asian descent, was practically hysterical because she spoke no English, couldn't give her side of the story and was fearful of the police, Lee said. Countless officers in Northern Virginia have similar stories, facing language and cultural differences as they try to quickly help residents. In 2004, a group of officers formed the Washington area Asian Law Enforcement Society. The group tried for the first time Saturday to reach out to Asian Americans to discuss issues such as gangs and online crime, and maybe try to persuade a few people to consider donning the uniform themselves. "There's quite a need for us to increase our diversity from a law enforcement standpoint," said Lee, who helped form the society and is its president, "Not just for Fairfax County but around the region. If we could have more officers communicate with Asian citizens, not just linguistically but culturally, that would be such effective policing for us" . . . Fairfax, with 40 Asian American officers, has one

of the biggest such contingents of area departments, but those officers are about 3 percent of the county's force. About 15 percent of Fairfax residents are of Asian background, census figures show. (Jackman, 2008)

The Los Angeles Police Department Airport Police Bureau was one of the first police departments to establish storefront outreach efforts that resulted in improved police–community relationships and better service benefits to the Asian/Pacific American neighborhood in the Korean area of Los Angeles (Chin, 1987). Storefront outreach efforts are now utilized in most urban cities with large Asian/Pacific American communities like San Francisco, New York, Oakland, Chicago, Boston, and Seattle. (See Chapter 14 for further information on community policing.) Another outreach approach is the use of Asian/Pacific American bilingual community service officers (CSOs), nonsworn officers with badges and uniforms, who serve the Southeast Asian communities in San Diego, California. The CSOs provide many of the supportive services available from the police department by using bilingual nonsworn personnel.

Increasing Asian/Pacific American Peace Officers

There is a noticeable underrepresentation of Asian/Pacific Americans in federal, state, and local law enforcement and criminal justice positions, although the number of Asian/Pacific Americans as peace officers and in law enforcement has increased in the past decade. According to a survey conducted by the Bureau of Justice Statistics in 2002, of the 93,000 full-time federal personnel authorized to make arrests and carry firearms in the 50 states and the District of Columbia, 2.5 percent are Asian/Pacific Americans. The federal agencies that employ the largest number of Asian/Pacific American peace officers are (1) Internal Revenue Service, (2) Postal Inspection Service, (3) Customs Service, and (4) the Bureau of Diplomatic Security (Reaves & Bauer, 2003). No specific local police and sheriff data were reported with respect to the percentages of Asian/Pacific American peace officers in the latest available Bureau of Justice Statistics Reports (Hickman & Reaves, 2006a, 2006b).

John H. Chen spent nearly 25 years working undercover, busting drug dealers, infiltrating Asian street gangs, conducting vice investigations and tracking violent offenders. He even got dropped by helicopter onto the deck of a Greek ship in the Gulf of Mexico to investigate the homicide of a Korean national. But with his promotion Tuesday to assistant chief of the Houston Police Department, the 52-year-old Chen said he wants to take time to mentor younger officers. "It's always been exciting, but it comes to a time when you want to share your successes and failures with younger officers, to help in their careers," he said. Chen, who was born in Seoul, South Korea, and moved to Houston as a teenager, will complete 27 years with the department in June. His last assignment was as lieutenant with the Central Patrol Division. His appointment was welcomed by Houston's growing Asian community, some of whom expressed disappointment to the City Council when Police Chief Harold Hurtt said he was not planning to replace retiring Assistant Chief Herman Wong. "This is very significant if we have an Asian officer promoted as chief, because we are really concerned about safety in the entire city," said Nine-Min Cheng, director of community outreach at the Chinese Community Center. "This is great, great news for the Asian community." (Pinkerton, 2009, p. 3)

The small numbers of Asian/Pacific American officers has hampered many departments in neighborhoods with large Asian/Pacific American populations in effectively serving those communities with appropriate role models and bicultural expertise. A variety of reasons exist for such underrepresentation, including (1) history of law enforcement relationships with Asian/Pacific American communities, (2) interest (lack of) of Asian/Pacific Americans in law enforcement careers, (3) image of law enforcement personnel in Asian/Pacific American communities, (4) lack of knowledge about the different careers and pathways in law enforcement, (5) concern with and fear of background checks, physical requirements, and the application process, and (6) limited number of role models and advocates for law enforcement careers from Asian/Pacific American communities. With the growing Asian/Pacific American populations in areas throughout the United States, law enforcement has emphasized the importance of diversity in its recruitment efforts:

> Growing up in Minnesota's Twin Cities, Bob Yang never liked law enforcement. Routine traffic stops that turned into lengthy searches left the first-generation Hmong American suspicious and distrustful of the authorities. Yang's distrust was turned on its head, however, when a white officer treated him with respect during a traffic stop and urged him to use his Hmong language skills on the force in St. Paul and Minneapolis. "It opened my eyes and got me thinking that it was something I'd like to try," said Yang, 26. "I felt the opportunity not only to show my family but to show the Hmong community that it's a good thing—law enforcement is a good thing." Now, Yang wants to change the minds of other young people about his profession when he hits the streets this month as one of the Sacramento Police Department's newest officers. Often underrepresented in the nation's police forces, ethnic minorities are helping change the face of law enforcement in the Sacramento region. Sacramento's most recent recruit classes boast more women and ethnic minorities than ever, with—for the first time—a near-even split between white men, women and ethnic minorities, said Police Chief Albert Najera. "It helps the organization to have various cultural perspectives when we're working on a crime series or problems in an area," Najera said. Among the new faces are rookies like Yang, the Police Department's second Hmong American man, and Nou Khang, its first Hmong American woman. Selina Lu, the department's first Chinese American woman, graduates in June. The department's first native Russian speaker, Yevgeniy "Eugene" Chernyavskiy, starts the six-month academy in July. The Sacramento County Sheriff's Department recently graduated its first Hmong American woman, Melissa Thao. (Jahn, 2006)

Crimes within Asian/Pacific American Communities

Many crimes committed in Asian/Pacific American communities, particularly among Asian/Pacific refugee and Asian/Pacific immigrant groups, are perpetrated by members within the same community. Law enforcement officials have often found it difficult to get cooperation from refugee and immigrant victims of human trafficking, extortion, home robbery, burglary, theft, blackmail, and other crimes against persons. In part, the lack of cooperation stems from a fear of retaliation by the criminal, who is often from within the Asian/Pacific American community. Other concerns of Asian/Pacific American victims include (1) the perceived level of responsiveness of the peacekeeping officers and agencies, (2) lack of familiarity with and trust in police services, (3) perceived level of effectiveness of law enforcement agencies, and (4) prior stereotypes and images of law enforcement agencies as discriminatory (e.g., immigration laws) and unresponsive to crimes against Asian/Pacific Americans. Recent Asian/Pacific American refugees and immigrants are often prime targets, in part because of their distrust of most institutions (e.g., banks, police departments, hospitals). As a result, they are more inclined to hide and store cash and other valuables in the home. A key challenge for police agencies is to educate this group and to work cooperatively with Asian/Pacific Americans to reduce the crimes within these communities.

Human trafficking has been highlighted as one of the crimes by Asian/Pacific Americans perpetuated on other Asian/Pacific Americans (Cramer, 2006a). Law enforcement agencies estimated that more than 1 million people worldwide (including 150,000 from South Asia and 225,000 from Southeast Asia) are trafficked annually around the world, while some researchers and experts say it could be more than twice that number (Asian Development Bank, 2003).

Human Trafficking The transportation of persons for sexual exploitation, forced labor, or other illegal or criminal activities.

Human trafficking has become a global business, with many victims from the Asian countries, and such illegal activities generate huge profits for traffickers and organized criminal groups (Office to Monitor and Combat Trafficking in Persons, 2006). Because of its secretive and hidden nature, human trafficking is likely to remain an increasingly underreported crime. As noted by the Asian Anti-Trafficking Collaborative (AATC), "Preying on the desperation and dreams of vulnerable immigrants around the world, human traffickers lure their victims to the U.S. with false promises and tales of living the American dream. Most victims are pulled to the U.S. by the hope of opportunity and pushed from their home country by the lack of the same chances of making a better life for themselves and their loved ones. But once in the U.S., the experiences of these individuals are strikingly similar: abuse, threats of violence and retaliation, elimination of personal liberty and free agency, and dehumanizing treatment that crushes the dignity, self esteem, and self worth of the victim" (API Legal Outreach, 2005). Law enforcement officers' involvement with Asian/Pacific American communities on human trafficking has emerged as one of the major areas of work as seen in the following example:

> Five Chinese citizens are in custody in the South Bay, charged with running an international smuggling ring that brought Asian women to residential neighborhoods to work as massage parlor prostitutes. The alleged half-million-dollar enterprise shuffled Taiwanese, mainland Chinese and Korean women among 10 massage parlors that men visited for sex in San Jose, Santa Clara, Sunnyvale and San Mateo, according to federal and state investigators who spent a year working undercover on the "Operation Bad Neighbor" case. The brothels operated out of homes and were called "10-day houses," because the women were moved every 10 days to avoid detection. Customers found the homes through word of mouth and Internet ads. After Wednesday's raid, officials took 31 women to safe houses, where they are being interviewed to determine if they came to California willingly or were trafficked—forced, defrauded or coerced into serving as sex slaves. The women range in age from 19 to 35. Victims of human trafficking can testify against their abusers in exchange for visas that will allow them to stay in the United States for three years plus receive monthly benefits, housing and job assistance. Those who refuse to testify or who say they came to the United States to work as prostitutes are deported. (May, 2005, p. B4)

Worldwide, police agencies in six countries (Cambodia, China, Laos, Myanmar, Thailand, and Vietnam) have agreed to collaborate on the investigation and prosecution of human traffickers, as well as working on the repatriation of and help for victims (Reuters, 2005).

Summary

- As a result of the early immigration laws and other discriminatory treatment received by Asian/Pacific Americans in the United States, the experiences of Asian/Pacific Americans with law enforcement officials have been fraught with conflicts, difficulties, and mixed messages. Some Asian/Pacific Americans still remember this history and carry with them stereotypes of police services as something to be feared and avoided. Law enforcement officials may need to go out of their way to establish trust and to win cooperation in order to accomplish their goals effectively when serving and protecting Asian/Pacific Americans.

- The label Asian Americans/Pacific Islanders encompasses over 40 very diverse ethnic and cultural groups. Significant differences exist among the 40 diverse ethnic groups (e.g., different cultural and language groups) as a result of individual life experiences as well as generational experiences of members within any one of the 40 groups. There is tremendous diversity among Asian/Pacific Americans and no one way to understand individuals within these communities. Although there are many ethnicities, cultures, and languages among the 40 or more groups within Asian/Pacific American communities, officers can learn about the various motivational determinants of individuals within different generational and immigrant groups. We provided a seven-part typology that will assist officers in understanding some of these motivational frameworks. The preferred term for referring to Asian/Pacific Americans varies with contexts, groups, and experiences of the individual. Which particular terms are used is based on the principle of self-designation and self-preference. Law enforcement officials need to be aware of terms that are unacceptable and derogatory as well as terms that are currently used. When in doubt, officers have to learn to become comfortable in asking Asian/Pacific Americans which terms they prefer. Officers are advised to provide helpful feedback to their peers when offensive terms, labels, and/or actions are used with Asian/Pacific Americans. Such feedback will help reduce the risk of misunderstanding and improve the working relationships between officers and Asian/Pacific American communities. Moreover, it will help enhance the professional image of the department for those communities.

- The complexities of the diverse Asian/Pacific American groups in terms of language, history, customs, cultures, religions, and life experiences can become confusing and threatening. Accordingly, it is sometimes easier to deal with stereotypes of these groups. A key stereotype of great concern to Asian/Pacific Americans is that they are regarded by mainstream Americans as very much alike. It is important that peace officers not make such errors in their interactions with Asian/Pacific Americans. Some hold the stereotype that Asian/Pacific Americans are all successful; this stereotype is further reinforced by the media. Such stereotypes have resulted in intergroup hostilities and hate crimes directed toward Asian/Pacific Americans. The stereotypes have served to mask true differences and diversity among the various Asian and Pacific Islander groups.

- With over 40 different cultural groups under the label of Asian/Pacific Americans, we find great differences in how families operate within the various subgroups. Asian/Pacific American families generally exhibit very strong ties among extended family members. It is not unusual for three to four generations of the same family to live under one roof.

Moreover, the extended family can even have an ongoing relationship network that spans great geographic distance. One key to the success of law enforcement officers in working with Asian/Pacific American families is the knowledge of how best to address family members for information, help, and referral. Asian/Pacific American families generally use their strong ties among extended family and community members to deal with cultural shock issues. Peace officers need to be aware that Asian/Pacific Americans may cope with their culture shock by becoming "clannish" (e.g., Chinatowns, Koreatowns).

• Many Asian/Pacific Americans are concerned with their inability to communicate clearly, and this is of particular concern among Asian/Pacific Americans who are immigrants and refugees. Peace officers must recognize that bilingual individuals and nonnative English speakers want to communicate effectively with the officers, and officers must take the time to allow them to do so. Maintaining contact, providing extra time, using translators, and being patient with speakers will allow Asian/Pacific Americans to communicate their concerns. Officers need to be aware of nonverbal aspects in the communication styles of Asian/Pacific Americans, including eye contact, touch, gestures, and affect (show of emotions). Verbal aspects such as accent, limited vocabulary, and incorrect grammar may give officers the impression that an Asian/Pacific American individual does not understand what is communicated. It is important to remember that the English listening and comprehension skills of Asian/Pacific American immigrants and refugees are usually better than their speaking skills.

• In most Asian/Pacific American families, relationship and communication patterns tend to be quite hierarchical, with the father as the identified head of the household. Generally, if there are grandparents in the household, the father would still act as the spokesperson for the family, but he would consult the grandparents, his wife, and others regarding any major decision. Although there are no clear-cut rules as to whether one goes to the male head of the household or to the female head to make a law enforcement inquiry, the general rule of thumb is that one would not error by starting with the father. In recent immigrant and refugee families, Asian/Pacific American children have a special role in being the intermediaries between parents and the external community because of the ability of the younger individuals to learn English and the American ways of doing things. Children often serve as translators and interpreters for peace officers in their communication and relations with Asian/Pacific American families involving recent immigrants and refugees.

• Asian/Pacific Americans, because of their past experiences with law enforcement agencies, along with their own concerns about privacy, self-help, and other factors, are reluctant to report crimes and may not seek police assistance and help. Law enforcement departments and officials need to build relationships and working partnerships with representative groups from the Asian/Pacific American communities. Relationship building is often helped by outreach efforts such as community storefront offices, bilingual officers, and participation of officers in community activities.

Discussion Questions and Issues

1. **Law Enforcement as Not User-Friendly**. Many anti–Asian/Pacific American laws and events may leave Asian/Pacific Americans with the view that law enforcement agencies are not user-friendly. What are the implications of this view for law enforcement? Suggest ways to improve negative points of view.

2. **Diversity among Asian/Pacific Americans.** The Asian/Pacific American category comprises over 40 diverse ethnic and cultural groups. Which groups are you most likely to encounter in crime-fighting and peacekeeping in your work? Which groups do you anticipate encountering in your future work?

3. **How Asian/Pacific American Groups Differ.** A typology for understanding motives for some of the behaviors of Asian/Pacific American people (in terms of their generational and immigration status in the United States) was provided. How might you apply this typology to better understand (a) an Asian/Pacific American refugee involved in a traffic moving violation? (b) an Asian/Pacific American immigrant involved as a victim of a house robbery? (c) an Asian/Pacific national involved as a victim of a burglary? (d) Southeast Asian youths involved in possible gang activities?

4. **Choice of Terms.** The term *Asian Americans and Pacific Islanders* is used in many publications and by many people to refer to members of the more than 40 diverse groups included in this category. How might you find out which is the best term to use in reference to an individual if ethnic and cultural information of this kind is necessary?

5. **Offensive Terms and Labels.** We strongly urge that offensive terms such as Chinks, Gooks, and Flips not be used in law enforcement work at any time. Give three practical reasons for this perspective.

6. **Effects of Myths and Stereotypes.** Myths and stereotypes about Asian/Pacific Americans have greatly affected this group. What are some of the Asian/Pacific American stereotypes that you have heard of or encountered? What effects would these stereotypes have on Asian/Pacific Americans? Suggest ways to manage these stereotypes in law enforcement. How might your awareness of Asian/Pacific American stereotypes be helpful in an interview with an Asian/Pacific American about homeland security issues?

7. **Verbal and Nonverbal Communication Style Variations among Cultures.** How do you think that the information in this chapter about verbal and nonverbal communication styles can help officers in their approach to Asian/Pacific American citizens? Does understanding the cultural components of the styles and behaviors help you to become more sensitive and objective about your reactions? Provide some examples of rephrasing questions in such a way that they elicit responses that show understanding and the intended actions on the part of Asian/Pacific Americans.

8. **Self-Monitoring and Avoidance of Law Enforcement.** Why do you think many Asian/Pacific Americans keep to their own communities and express the desire for self-monitoring and within-community resolution of their problems? When are such efforts desirable? When are they ineffective? How can police agencies be of greater service to Asian/Pacific American communities in this regard?

Website Resources

Visit these websites for additional information about law enforcement contact with Asian/Pacific Americans as well as about Asian/Pacific American community organizations.

Academy for Educational Development (AED): http://www.humantrafficking.org

This website brings government agencies in East Asia and the Pacific together to cooperate and learn from each other's experiences in anti–human trafficking efforts. The website has country-specific information such as national laws and action plans and contact information on useful governmental agencies.

American Immigration Law Foundation (AILF): http://www.ailf.org

This website provides information to increase public understanding of immigration law and policy and the value of immigration to American society; to promote public service and excellence in the practice of immigration law; and to advance fundamental fairness and due process under the law for immigrants.

Asian American Legal Defense and Education Fund (AALDEF): http://www.asianamericanalliance.com/AALDEF.html

This website provides information about civil rights issues with Asian/Pacific Americans and highlights issues of immigration, family law, government benefits, anti-Asian violence and police misconduct, employment discrimination, labor rights, and workplace issues.

Asian American Network: http://www.asianamerican.net

This website provides a national listing of many of the networks of Asian/Pacific American community-based organizations in the United States (as well as some in Asia).

Asian and Pacific Islander Institute on Domestic Violence: http://www.apiahf.org

> This website provides information on a national network of advocates and community members to serve as a forum for and a clearinghouse on information, research, resources, and critical issues about violence against women in Asian/Pacific American communities.

Asian and Pacific Islander Outreach: http://www.apilegaloutreach.org

> This website provides information about Asian/Pacific Islander Legal Outreach (API Legal Outreach), which has worked to tear down long-standing barriers that have denied Asians and Pacific Islanders equal justice and equal access to the U.S. legal system. The website's section on Asian human trafficking provides information on prevention, reporting, prosecution, and best practices.

National Asian Pacific American Legal Consortium: http://www.napalc.org

> This website provides a national network of information about legal and civil rights issues affecting Asian/Pacific Americans in terms of litigation, advocacy, public education, and public policy.

National Asian Peace Officers Association: http://www.napoaonline.org/

> This website provides information to promote the interests of Asian American peace officers on community issues, career development and opportunities, education and workshops, and awareness about the Asian culture.

National Coalition for Asian Pacific American Community Development: http://www.nationalcapacd.org/

> This website provides information on a coalition of more than 100 organizations and individuals in 17 states that serve Asian Americans, Pacific Islanders, Native Hawaiians, refugees and immigrants nationwide. National CAPACD is the first national advocacy organization dedicated to addressing the community development needs of diverse and rapidly growing AAPI communities.

References

Afrid, F. (2009, April 9). "Opinion: The Price of Silent Violence for South Asian Families." *San Jose Mercury News* (CA).

Abraham, M. (2000). *Speaking the Unspeakable: Marital Violence against South Asian Immigrant Women in the United States.* New Brunswick, NJ: Rutgers University Press.

Asian Development Bank. (2003). *Combating Trafficking of Women and Children in South Asia.* Washington, D.C.: Asian Development Bank.

Asian Pacific Islander (API) Outreach. (2005). "Asian Anti-Trafficking Collaborative (AATC)." Available: http://www.apilegaloutreach.org/trafficking.html/

Associated Press. (2005, December 1). "Family of Vietnamese Police Shooting Victim Settles Suit for $1.8M." Available: http://ncc1701.libprox.jfku.edu:2075/us/lnacademic/returnTo.do?returnToKey=20_T7405180909

Bennett, C. E. (2002). *A Profile of the Nation's Foreign-Born Population from Asia (2000 Update).* Washington, D.C.: U.S. Census Bureau.

Branch, A. (2006, January 20). "Asian Gangs Pose New Problems for Police." *Fort Worth Star-Telegram* (TX).

Chin, J. (1987). "Crime and the Asian American Community: The Los Angeles Response to Koreatown." *Journal of California Law Enforcement,* 19, 52–60.

Cramer, M. (2006a, January 28). "Police Seek to Stop Surge in Prostitution: Advocates Fearful for Women; Most Are Immigrants." *Boston Globe,* p. B12.

Cramer, M. (2006b, October 26). "Arresting Fear, Bridging Cultures Quincy Police Reach Out to Asians," *Boston Globe,* p. A1.

Daniels, R. (1988). *Asian America: Chinese and Japanese in the United States since 1850.* Seattle, WA: University of Washington Press.

Gendar, A. (2009, February 20). "Man Stopped by Cops 21 Times Sues City." *Daily News* (NY), p. 2.

Geluardi, J. (2006, March 14). "Southeast Asian Youths at Risk, Study Concludes; Data on Vietnamese, Laotian Arrests Challenges Stereotype of 'Model Minority;' Language Barrier Plays a Role." *Contra Costa Times,* p. F4.

Glasse, C., and Smith, H. (2003). *The New Encyclopedia of Islam (Revised).* Walnut Creek, CA: Alta Mira Press.

Hickman, M. J., and Reaves, B. A. (2006a, May). "Local Police Department, 2003." Bureau of Justice Statistics: Law Enforcement Management and Administrative Statistics.

Hickman, M. J., and Reaves, B. A. (2006b, May). "Sheriffs' Offices, 2003." Bureau of Justice Statistics: Law Enforcement Management and Administrative Statistics.

Jackman, T. (2008, June 22). "To Serve and Protect, with an Eye to Culture: Officers Reach out to Asian Americans." *Washington Post*, p. PW04.

Jahn, C. (2006, May 11). "New Officers Reflect Diverse Face of City: More Women, Ethnic Minorities Now Recruits." *Sacramento Bee*, p. B1.

Kawai, Y. (2005). "Stereotyping Asian Americans: The Dialectic of the Model Minority and the Yellow Peril." *Howard Journal of Communications.* 16(2), 109–130.

Lueck, T. J. (2006, August 14). "Two Men Are Accused of a Hate Attack in Queens." *New York Times*, p. B1.

Madkour, R. (2008, October 14). "Amendment 1 Targets Florida's Anti-Asian Land Laws." Associated Press.

May, M. (2005, October 28). "5 Chinese Citizens Charged with Running Prostitution Ring: Police Move Women to Safe Houses to See If They Were Coerced." *San Francisco Chronicle*, p. B4.

National Asian Women's Health Organization. (2002). *Silence, Not an Option!* San Francisco, CA: Author.

Mullan, F. (2005). The Metrics of the Physician Brain Drain. *New England Journal of Medicine*, 353, 1810–1818.

"Office to Monitor and Combat Trafficking in Persons." (2006, June 5). *Trafficking in Persons Report.* Washington, D.C.: U.S. Department of State.

Pinkerton, J. (2009, April 22). "New Roles, New Responsibilities. Area's Asian Community Hopes John Chen Makes Impact in New HPD Position," *Houston Chronicle*, p. 3.

Population Reference Bureau. (PRB). (2009). *World Population Data Sheet.* Washington, D.C.: Author.

Povell, M. (2005). *The History of Vietnamese Immigration.* Washington, D.C.: The American Immigration Law Foundation. Available: http://www.ailf.org.

Prashad, V. (2001). *The Karma of Brown Folk.* Minneapolis, MN: University of Minnesota Press.

Quan, D. (2006, April 17). "Slayings Stun Asian Community; Soul-searching: Slayings of Their Children by Three Fathers Bring Calls for More Support Services," *The Press Enterprise.* (Riverside, CA), p. B01.

Reaves, B. A., and Bauer, L. M. (2003, April). "Federal Law Enforcement Officers, 2002." Bureau of Justice Statistics Bulletin.

Reuters. (2005, March 31). "Six Asian Nations Act to Stop Human Trafficking."

Schlafly, P. (2008, June 26). "American Innovation Supremacy at Risk." *Copley News Service.*

Song, Y. I. (1996). *Battered Women in Korean Immigrant Families.* New York: Garland.

Takaki, R. (1989a). *Strangers from a Different Shore: A History of Asian Americans.* Boston, MA: Little, Brown.

Takaki, R. (1989b). "Who Killed Vincent Chin?" In G. Yun (Ed.), *A Look Beyond the Model Minority Image: Critical Issues in Asian America.* New York: Minority Rights Group, p. 23–29.

Tjaden, P., and Thoennes, N. (2000). *Extent, Nature, and Consequences of Intimate Partner Violence: Research Report.* Washington, D.C.: National Institute of Justice and the Centers for Disease Control and Prevention.

Todt, R. (2009, March 16). "PA Asian Americans Fearful after Rash of Crimes." *Associated Press.*

Togneri, C. (2007, September 27). "Law Enforcement Seminar Strips away Stereotypes." *Pittsburg Tribune Review*, para. 1.

U.S. Bureau of the Census. (2009, March 3). *Facts for Features—Asian/Pacific Heritage Month: May 2009.* Washington, D.C.: U.S. Government Printing Office.

U.S. Bureau of the Census. (2007a). *2007 American Community Survey.* Washington, D.C.: U.S. Government Printing Office.

U.S. Bureau of the Census. (2007b, February). *The American Community—Asians: 2004.* Washington, D.C.: U.S. Government Printing Office.

U.S. Bureau of the Census. (2002). *Census 2000 Brief Reports.* Washington, D.C.: U.S. Government Printing Office.

CHAPTER 6

Law Enforcement Contact with African Americans

LEARNING OBJECTIVES

After reading this chapter you should be able to:

- Describe the historical background of African Americans especially as it relates to the dynamics between citizens and police.

- Describe key aspects of African American diversity within African American communities, including those of class, culture, and religion.

- Explain the evolution of African American identity movements and self-identification terms.

- Explain the impact of African American stereotypes on law enforcement and cross-racial perceptions.

- Identify selected characteristics of African American extended families, gender roles, single mothers, and youth as they relate to law enforcement contact.

- Exemplify the potential for misperception by describing characteristics of African American verbal and nonverbal communication styles as distinguished from mainstream cultural styles.

- List and discuss key issues associated with law enforcement contact and African American communities.

OUTLINE

- Introduction
- Historical Information
- Demographics: Diversity among African Americans
- Issues of Identity and Group Identification Terms
- Stereotypes and Cross-Racial Perceptions
- The African American Family
- Language and Communication
- Key Issues in Law Enforcement

- Summary
- Discussion Questions and Issues
- Website Resources

INTRODUCTION

We must learn to live together as brothers or perish together as fools.

—Martin Luther King, 1964

There is no point in telling blacks to observe the law . . . It has almost always been used against them.

—Senator Robert Kennedy after visiting the scene of the Watts Riot, 1965

The impact of slavery, racism, and discrimination plays a significant role in black–white relations. The history of intimidation of African Americans by police continues to affect the dynamics of law enforcement in some black communities even today; however, cultural differences also play a role. Understanding both the history and culture of African Americans is especially important for law enforcement as police work toward improving relations and changing perceptions. African Americans are fourth- and fifth-generation Americans. Aspects of the black culture are heavily influenced by African culture, and those of white culture, by European culture. Cultural differences are seldom considered, even though they can cause communication problems between citizens and police officers. Failing to recognize the distinctiveness of black culture, language, and communication patterns, in addition to the history, can lead to misunderstandings, conflict, and even confrontation.

HISTORICAL INFORMATION

The majority of African Americans or blacks (terms used interchangeably) in the United States trace their roots to West Africa. They were torn from their cultures of origin between the seventeenth and the nineteenth centuries when they were brought here as slaves. Blacks represent the only migrants to have come to the Americas, North and South, against their will. Blacks from Africa were literally kidnap victims, kidnapped by Europeans or purchased as captives by Yankee traders. This experience has made African Americans, as a group, very different from immigrants who chose to come to the United States to better their lives, and different from refugees who fled their homelands to escape religious or political persecution. Slavery is the centerpiece of many of the societal dynamics we see today among blacks and whites; law enforcement bears a particular burden because of the role it has played in the treatment of African Americans.

A slave is an "inferior" being, and by definition is entirely under the domination of some influence or person.

> The criminal justice system for free and enslaved blacks in colonial and antebellum Virginia was designed to keep blacks as powerless and submissive as possible to insure the preservation of slavery and the domination of the white race over the black. A master's authority over his black human beings was total—he could beat,

maim, torture, and in many circumstances even kill the slave. Legitimized cruelty was the natural consequence of such a system. It was a system which explicitly demanded that for the slave there be no choice but total submission, and little or no remedy for the master's cruelty. (Higginbotham & Jacobs, 1992)

Slave owners inwardly understood that treating people as animals to be owned, worked, and sold was immoral, but they wanted to think of themselves as good, religious, moral people. Hence they had to convince themselves that their slaves were not really human, but a lower form of life. They focused on racial differences (skin color, hair texture, etc.) as "proof" that black people were not really people, after all. Racism began, then, as an airtight alibi for a horrifying injustice. A slave was counted as three-fifths of a person during census-taking as dictated by the Constitution, that is, the foundation of the U.S. judicial system. Many slave owners routinely and brutally raped their female slaves, often before puberty, as well as forcing their healthiest slaves to couple and breed regardless of the slaves' own attachments and preferences. (The fact that many African Americans' genetic background is part Caucasian is testimony to the slave owners' "tendencies" to violate slave girls and women.)

The notion of the slave, and by extension, any African American, as less than human has created psychological and social problems for succeeding generations of black citizens. Slavery and the system of apartheid that followed (i.e., Jim Crow laws) led to legalized discrimination—inferior housing, schools, health care, and jobs for black people—persisting to this day.

The institution of slavery formally ended in 1863, but the racist ideas born of slavery persisted. These ideas continue even now to leave deep scars on many African Americans from all socioeconomic classes. The psychological heritage of slavery, as well as current discrimination, continues to prevent equal opportunity and protection in many realms of life.

The history that has been taught in educational institutions presented a distorted, incomplete picture of black family life. This picture emphasized breakdown during the slave era, which had crippling effects on families for generations to come. This version of history never examined the moral strength of the slaves nor the community solidarity and family loyalty that arose after emancipation. There is no doubt that these strengths have positively affected the rebuilding of the African American community. Further, "it has long been hypothesized that one's racial identity attitudes relate to sense of self, comfort with one's own racial group, and comfort with persons of diverse racial groups" (Ponterotto, Utsey & Pederson, 2006).

Despite slave owners' attempts to destroy black family life, slaves did manage to form lasting families headed by a mother and a father, and many slave couples enjoyed long marriages. Although white slave masters would often do everything possible to pull families apart (including the forced "breeding" and the selling of slaves), there is evidence that slaves maintained their family connections as best as they could and produced stable units with admirable values. According to U.S. historian Char Miller, "Despite the fact that slavery tore apart many families, blacks maintained links, loves, and relationships just as anyone else would under these circumstances" (Miller, 2008). A more accurate version of history counters the impression that all slave families were so helpless that they were always torn apart and could never reestablish themselves, or that their social relationships were chaotic and amoral. The resolve of large numbers of blacks to rebuild their families and communities as soon as they were freed represents an impressive determination in a people who survived one of the most brutal forms of servitude that history has seen.

> According to almost all witnesses, the roads of the South were clogged in 1865 [after emancipation] with Black men and women searching for long-lost wives, husbands, children, brothers and sisters. The ingathering continued for several years and began in most communities with mass marriage ceremonies that legalized the slave vows. This was a voluntary process for husbands and wives who were free to renounce slave vows and search for new mates. Significantly, most freed men, some of them 80 and 90 years old, decided to remain with their old mates, thereby giving irrefutable testimony on the meaning of their love . . . (Bennett, 1989)

African American survival, and consequently, African American contributions to American society, deserve a high level of respect and testify to a people's great strength. It is not within the scope of this chapter to discuss African American contributions to society, but suffice it to say that the perceptions of some people in law enforcement are often conditioned by their exposure to the black underclass, for whom crime is a way of life.

Law Enforcement Interaction with African Americans: Historical Baggage

> Many of the police and African-American problems in our communities today go way back and stem from history. Some of the issues can be traced directly from the Civil War reconstruction era, in slavery days, when police and the military were required to return runaway slaves. (Patton, 2009)

In the United States during the late seventeenth and eighteenth centuries, prior to and following slave uprisings in a number of colonies, the colonists created strict laws to contain the slaves. Even minor offenses were punished harshly. This set the negative tone between law enforcement and blacks. American police were called on to form "slave patrols" and to enforce racially biased laws (Williams & Murphy, 1990). In many areas of the country, police were expected to continue enforcing deeply biased, highly discriminatory laws including those setting curfews for blacks and barring blacks from many facilities and activities.

Most police officers have had some exposure to the historical precedents of poor relationships between police and minority communities. The damages of the past give us no choice but to make a greater effort today with groups such as African Americans for whom contact with law enforcement has long been problematic.

DEMOGRAPHICS: DIVERSITY AMONG AFRICAN AMERICANS[*]

As of 2007, blacks comprised about 13.4 percent of the U.S. population, or approximately 40.7 million people (U.S. Census Bureau News, 2008). The First Great Migration involved the movement of 1.3 million blacks and took place between 1916 and 1930. The Second Migration occurred between 1941 and 1970, and involved 5 million blacks who migrated initially to the north and then to the west coast, largely seeking better job opportunities (Lemann, 1992). Although this was one of the primary reasons for such a mass exodus from the South, it was not the main reason. Many blacks left the South for the sole purpose of escaping racism and discrimination.

---

[*] Refer back to Chapter 1, Section "Changing Population," for information about individuals who do not "neatly" fit into one demographic category such as black.

Historically, over 50 percent of the black population has lived in urban areas. The rural black population has decreased, in large part because of the great migrations; the shifting flow has contributed to the increase in numbers in suburban areas (some rural blacks may migrate directly into the inner city while others may move to more suburban areas; the flow is not actually known). In any case, urban cores experience cycles of repopulation, mainly by blacks, Hispanics, and various new immigrant groups. One of the most vivid examples is the city of Detroit, where, approximately 82 percent of the population is black (U.S. Bureau of the Census, 2008) while most whites and immigrant groups have settled in outlying areas. Similarly, other cities, such as Washington D.C., St. Louis, Chicago, and Cleveland, are populated mainly by blacks and new immigrants, creating layers of tension where diverse groups with conflicting values and customs suddenly find themselves crowded into the same urban neighborhoods.

These population shifts have created "two Americas." One America is suburban America, which is heavily populated by whites, and the schools, recreational facilities, and community resources are of higher quality than of those in the other America. The other America is urban America, where many African Americans reside. This America has less access to educational and job opportunities, and the living conditions more resemble those of cities in ravaged developing countries than those of America's comfortable suburban environment.

Although many African Americans are among the lower socioeconomic class, they are represented in all the socioeconomic classes, from the underclass to the upper class, and have moved increasingly into the middle class. As with all racial/ethnic groups, there are significant class-related differences among blacks affecting values and behavior. However, color, more than class, determines how the larger society reacts to and treats blacks. Therefore, the racial experience of many African Americans in the United States is similar, regardless of an individual's level of prosperity or education.

> We mistakenly believe that blacks who achieve economic success in this country are shielded from racism and discrimination and that the color of their skin is somehow neutralized by money. This could not be further from the truth. Many successful blacks have reported being on the receiving end of racially motivated discriminatory behavior, and this includes treatment by law enforcement. (Johnson, 2009)

Despite the commonalities of the racial experience, there is a great deal of cultural diversity among African Americans. Over the last 400 years, black families have come from many different countries (e.g., Jamaica, Trinidad, Belize, Haiti, and Puerto Rico). By far the largest group's forefathers came directly to the United States from Africa. In addition, there are cultural differences among African Americans related to the region of the country from which they came. As with whites, there are "southern" and "northern" characteristics as well as urban and rural characteristics.

Religious backgrounds vary, but the majority of American-born blacks are Protestant, and specifically Baptist. The first black-run, black-controlled denomination in the country was the African Methodist Episcopal church. It was created because churches in the North and South either banned blacks or required them to sit apart from whites. Another percentage of blacks belong to the Black Muslim religion, including the Nation of Islam and American Muslim Mission. (The term *Black Muslim* is often used but is rejected by some members of the religion.) There are also sizable and fast-growing black populations among members of the Seventh-Day Adventists, Jehovah's Witnesses, Pentecostals (especially Spanish-speaking blacks, See Exhibit 6.1),

- **Protestant**   **78%**
  –Historically Black Churches (59%)
    e.g., Baptist (40%)
    Methodist (5%)
    Pentecostal (6%)
    Holiness (1%)
  –Evangelical Protestant Churches (15%)
  –Mainstream Protestant Churches (4%)
- **Catholic**   **5%**
- **Jehovah's Witness**   **1%**
- **Muslim**   **1%**
- **Unaffiliated**   **12%**
- **Other***   **3%**

*Mormon, Orthodox, other Christian, Jewish, Buddhist, Hindu, other world religions, other faiths, "don't know".

EXHIBIT 6.1   Religious Affiliation among African Americans.

Source: Pew Forum, 2008. Retrieved on May 30, 2009 from http://religions.pewforum.org/

and especially among those of Caribbean origin—Santeria, Candomble, Voudun, and similar sects—blending Catholic and West African (mainly Yoruba) beliefs and rituals. Rastafarianism has spread far beyond its native Jamaica to become an influential religious movement among immigrants from many other English-speaking Caribbean nations.

ISSUES OF IDENTITY AND GROUP IDENTIFICATION TERMS

In the 1960s and 1970s, the Civil Rights Movement and the Black Pride Movement marked a new direction in black identity. The Civil Rights Movement resulted in increased educational and employment opportunities and active political involvement. Some adults marched in the Civil Rights Movement knowing that they themselves might never benefit directly from civil rights' advances; they hoped that their efforts in the struggle would improve the lives of their children. The middle-class youths who attended community churches and black colleges became the leaders in the movement for equal rights (McAdoo, 1992).

Many blacks, both American-born and Caribbean-born, inspired by a growing sense of community identification and increased pride in racial identity, have also placed an emphasis on learning more about and identifying with African cultures. Despite the great differences in culture between African Americans and Africans, blacks throughout this hemisphere are discovering that they can take pride in the richness of their African heritage, including its high ethical values and community cohesiveness. Examples of African cultural values that have influenced American black culture or are held in high esteem by many African Americans are (Walker, 1992):

- Cooperative interdependence among and between peoples—contrasted with Western individualism
- Partnership with nature and with the spirit world reflected in the approach to ecology and in communication with the spirit world—closer to Native American beliefs

- Balance and harmony among all living things, reflected in the placing of human relations as a priority value—contrasted with the Western view of achievement and "doing" as taking priority over nurturing of human relations
- Joy and celebration in life itself
- Time as a spiral, focused on "now"—contrasted with the Western view of time as "money" and time running away from us
- Focus on the group and not on the individual
- Giving of self to community
- Renewed interest in respecting elders

The combination of the Black Pride Movement of the 1960s and 1970s and the more current focus on cultural roots has freed many African Americans from the "slave mentality" that continued to haunt the African American culture long after emancipation. A new pride in race and heritage has, for some, replaced the sense of inferiority fostered by white racial supremacist attitudes.

Several ethnic groups, including African Americans, in a positive evolution of their identity and pride, have initiated name changes for their group. Although it can be confusing, it represents, on the part of group members, growth and a desire to name themselves rather than be named by the dominant society. Until approximately the early 1990s, the most widely accepted term was *black,* this term having replaced *Negro* (which, in turn, replaced *colored people*). *Negro* has been out of use for several decades, although some older blacks still use the term (as do some younger African Americans among themselves). To many, the term *Negro* symbolizes what the African American became under slavery. The replacement of *Negro* with *black* came to symbolize racial pride. The exception to the use of *Negro* and *colored* is in titles such as United Negro College and National Association for the Advancement of Colored People (NAACP). *African American*, a term preferred by many, focuses on positive historical and cultural roots rather than on race or skin color.

In the 1990s, the use of the term *African American* grew in popularity. (It is the equivalent of, for example, Italian American or Polish American.) Many feel that the word *black* is no more appropriate in describing skin color than is white. Yet, some Americans who are black do not identify with African American because it does not fully represent their background, which may be Caribbean or Haitian; they may not identify with the African part at all. Since the 1980s and early 1990s, the term *people of color* has sometimes been used, but this catchall phrase has limited use for police officers because it is used to describe anyone who is not white and can include Asian/Pacific Americans, Latino/Hispanic Americans, as well as Native Americans. Indeed, there is much controversy and history associated with broad, collective terms that attempt to categorize people too quickly.

The use of racial epithets is never acceptable, especially in crime-fighting and peacekeeping, no matter how provoked an officer may be. Although it is not uncommon for some blacks to use a particular racial epithet in normal conversation, it is absolutely taboo for outsiders, especially for outsiders wearing badges. Police who do not like to be called "pigs" can likely relate to a person's feelings about being referred to in animal terms, whether "gorilla," "baboon," or "monkey." Officers must develop the professionalism to not only refrain from using derogatory terms, but also advise their peers of the prejudice that such terms convey.

STEREOTYPES AND CROSS-RACIAL PERCEPTIONS

Many of the impressions people in society, and consequently, in law enforcement, form about African Americans come from their exposure to messages and images in the media. Here the phenomenon of stereotyping is as much at work as it is when citizens see all police officers as repressive and capable of brutality. Police officers know that they will all take a beating nation-wide when there is publicity about an instance of police brutality against blacks or reports of racial profiling.

The white majority's view of blacks reflects the same problem. Those who are bent toward prejudice may feel that their racism is justified whenever a crime involving an African American makes the evening news. A suburban African American mother addressing a community forum on racism pointed out: "Every time I hear that there has been a murder or a rape, I pray that it is not a black who committed the crime. The minute the media reports that a black person is responsible for a crime, all of us suffer. When something negative happens, I am no longer seen as an individual with the same values and hopes as my white neighbors. I become a symbol, and even more so my husband and sons become feared. People treat us with caution and politeness, but inside we know that their stereotypes of the worst criminal element of blacks have become activated" (Personal communication, source wishes to remain anonymous).

Even the fact of a crime rate that is disproportionately high among young black males does not justify sweeping statements about all African Americans. Certainly, 40.7 million African Americans cannot be judged by a statistic about the criminal element. Unfortunately for the vast majority of the African American population, some whites do base their image of all blacks largely on the actions of America's criminal class. It is well known that women clutch their purse harder when they see a black man approaching. Similarly, officers have been known to stop blacks and question them simply for not "looking like they belong to a certain neighborhood."

> For many Americans, television's overpowering images of Black deviance, in terms of frequency and regularisty, are impossible to ignore. . . . These negative images have been seared into the public's collective consciousness, which contributes to most Americans' believing that Blacks are responsible for committing the majority of the nation's crime (Russell, 1999). This belief contributes to a police officer's decision to pull over Black motorists in nice cars or in affluent neighborhoods; the pedestrian's decision to cross the street or clutch her purse when approaching a Black male; the salesperson's decision to follow a Black customer throughout the store for fear of theft; and the politician's decision to use a Black face to kindle fears that crime is out of control. (Johnson, 2008)

Harboring unreasonable fears about black people is a result of the prevalence of stereotypes associated with criminality. In the chapter section entitled Children/Adolescents/Youth, an example is provided of demeaning conversation between law enforcement representatives and innocent young black people. Stereotypes indeed give way to the labels that people assign to others (Johnson, 2009). This consequence of stereotyping is a common phenomenon known in the fields of both sociology and criminology, and has clear implications for law enforcement behavior. (See Chapter 13 on Racial Profiling.)

Prejudice, lack of contact, and ignorance lend themselves to groups' developing perceptions about the "other" that are often based on biased beliefs. Unfortunately, perceptions are reality for the individuals and groups who hold them. Perceptions are seen as the truth, whether or not they *are* the truth. Exhibit 6.2 illustrates differing perceptions that some members of the dominant society have toward black and white males. In this case, the media and popular literature have contributed to the differing perceptions.

EXHIBIT 6.2	Are People Viewed in Equal Terms?
Black Male	**White Male**
Arrogant	Confident
Chip on shoulder	Self assured
Aggressive	Assertive
Dominant personality	Natural leader
Violence prone	Wayward
Naturally gifted	Smart
Sexual prowess	Sexual experimentation

How about the perceptions the African Americans have developed of police officers' actions? Because of a past history of prejudice and discrimination toward blacks, it would not take much to validate pre-existing negative perceptions among some African Americans. While many officers no longer exhibit racism, the perceptions remain. The description of perceptions listed in Exhibit 6.3 were presented to Northern California police officers in the early 1990s by the then vice president of the Alameda, California, NAACP chapter (the late Al Dewitt). When Dewitt presented these perceptions to police officers, he explained that, over time, African Americans formed perceptions about police behavior that led to a lack of trust, riots, and race problems. According to Greg Patton (an African American; former Washington State Patrol Trooper, district attorney investigator, and now a parole and probation supervisor and adjunct community college criminal justice cultural diversity instructor), the perceptions listed

EXHIBIT 6.3	Perceptions of Police Officers' Actions by Some Blacks.
Police Action	**Black Perception**
Being stopped or expelled from so-called "white neighborhoods."	Whites want blacks to "stay in their place."
Immediately suspecting and reacting to blacks without distinction between dope dealer and plainclothes police officer.	Police view black skin itself as probable cause.
Using unreasonable force, beatings, adding charges.	When stopped, blacks must be submissive or else.
Negative attitudes, jokes, body language, talking down to people.	Officers are racists.
Quick trigger, take-downs, accidental shootings.	Bad attitudes will come out under stress.
Slow response, low priority, low apprehension rate.	Black-on-black crime not important.
Techniques of enforcing local restrictions and white political interests.	Police are the strong arm for the status quo.
Police stick together, right or wrong.	Us-against-them mentality; they stick together, so we have to stick together.

in Exhibit 6.3 are still entirely valid today. Improving and preventing racial misperceptions will take time and effort on the part of the officer but will inevitably benefit him or her by way of increased cooperation and officer safety (Patton, 2009).

THE AFRICAN AMERICAN FAMILY

African American families generally enjoy very strong ties among extended family members, especially among women. Female relatives often substitute for each other in filling family roles; for example, a grandmother or an aunt may raise a child if the mother is unable to do so. Sometimes several different family groups may share one house. When there is a problem (i.e., an incident that has brought an officer to the house), extended family members are likely to be present and to want to help. An officer may observe a number of uncles, aunts, brothers, sisters, cousins, and boyfriends or girlfriends who are loosely attached to the black household. Enlisting the aid of any of these household members, no matter what the relationship, can be beneficial.

The Role of the Man and the Woman

A widespread myth holds that African American families are a matriarchy, in which women are typically the heads of the household. Historically, it is true that [black] women did play a crucial role in the [black] family, because of repeated attempts to break down "black manhood" (Bennett, 1989). However, a true matriarchy (female-ruled society) is systematic and organized, and women control property and economic activities. This is not generally true of black America; the "system" of women running the household has come about purely by default because of the absence of fathers. Police have observed that in some urban core areas, and in particular housing projects, it is not uncommon to find that a huge majority of African American women live alone with children.

> African American women are considered by mainstream America to be less threatening than their male counterparts. As a result, they are able to be more assertive in public situations and receive fewer negative consequences. This perception also holds true when it comes to contacts with law enforcement. However, unlike African American females, African American males often feel that they are at risk for arrest or some form of mistreatment if they exhibit anything other than passive behavior toward the police. (Johnson, 2009)

African American fathers usually view themselves as heads of the household; therefore, any decisions regarding the family should include the father's participation. It is insulting and disrespectful for officers to direct their questions to and their focus on the mother when both parents are present. A mother's assertiveness does not mean that the father is passive or indifferent and thus should be ignored, nor does a father's silence indicate agreement with the officer's action. It is always worthwhile to get his view of the situation first.

The Single Mother

The single mother, particularly in the inner city, does not always receive the respect that she is due; outsiders may be critical of the way she lives—or the way they think she lives. She is often stereotyped by officers who doubt their own effectiveness in the urban black community. For instance, in theory, an unmarried African American mother on welfare who has just had a fight with her boyfriend should receive the same professional courtesy that a married white suburban mother is likely to receive from an officer of the same background; however, in practice, this is not always the case. A common complaint made by African American women is that white officers in general treat them poorly. According to these complaints, officers feel comfortable using profanity and other obscenities in the presence of black women, something that is less likely to occur with white women.

Ondra Berry, retired Assistant Police Chief, Reno, Nevada, and an African American, offers advice regarding relations between the peace officer and the single African American mother. He advises officers to go out of their way to establish rapport and trust. Following are his suggestions for assisting the single mother (Berry, 2009):

- Offer extra assistance to low-income mothers such as connecting them with community resources.
- Proactively engage youth and encourage them to participate in organized social activities.
- Give your business card to the mother to show that you are available for further contact.
- Make follow-up visits when there are no problems so that the mother and the children can associate the officer with good times.
- Make sure that you have explained to the mother her rights.
- Use the same discretion you might use with another minor's first petty offense (e.g., shoplifting); consider bringing the child home and talking with the mother and child rather than sending the child immediately to juvenile hall.

All of these actions will build a perception on the part of the African American single mother and her children that you can be trusted and that you are there to help. "Since you are dealing with history, you have to knock down barriers and, at times, work harder with this group than with any other group" (Berry, 2009). That said, "Economics does not negate history. Married middle-class black women share the same history of slavery and discrimination as lower-class single black women" (Johnson, 2009). Thus, efforts need to go into relationship-building with women as a whole.

Children/Adolescents/Youth

Since there are so many black households, especially in the inner city, in which the father is absent, young boys in their middle childhood years (7 to 11) are at risk for serious behavioral problems, and school is often where these problems show up. According to Berry, many single mothers unwittingly place their young sons in the position of "father," giving them the message that they have to take care of the family. These young children can get the mistaken impression that they are the heads of the household, and in school situations, they may try to control the teacher—who is often female and often white. An officer who refers these children to agencies that can provide role models, even if on a limited-time basis, stands more of a chance of gaining the family's and community's trust and respect. Eventually, he or she will win more cooperation from community members.

Among older African American male children, especially in inner cities, statistics indicate a disproportionately high crime rate, stemming from the difficult economic conditions of their lives. Officers have to remind themselves that the majority of African American teenagers are law-abiding citizens. African American teens and young adults report being stopped on a regular basis by police officers when they are in predominantly "white neighborhoods" (including those where they happen to live). For example, a 19-year-old African American male living in an upper-middle-class suburban neighborhood in Fremont, California, reported that he was stopped and questioned four times in two weeks by different officers. On one occasion, the conversation went this way:

OFFICER: What are you doing here?

TEEN: I'm jogging, sir.

OFFICER: Why are you in this neighborhood?

TEEN: I live here, sir.

OFFICER: Where?

TEEN: Over there, in that big house on the hill.

OFFICER: Can you prove that? Show me your I.D. (Racial profiling is discussed in depth in Chapter 13.)

LANGUAGE AND COMMUNICATION

Racial conflicts between African Americans and non–African American citizens can cover up communication style differences, which until the 1990s had been largely ignored or minimized. Yet many would acknowledge that cultural differences between, for example, a white officer and a Vietnamese citizen could potentially affect their respective communication styles as well as their perceptions of each other. Similarly, language comes into play when looking at patterns of communication among many African Americans.

"Ebonics," or African American Vernacular English

"The use of [what has been called] black language does not represent any pathology in blacks . . . The beginning of racial understanding is the acceptance that difference is just what it is: different, not inferior. And equality does not mean sameness" (Weber, 1991). There are many varieties of English that are *not* "substandard," "deficient," or "impoverished" versions of the language. Instead, they often have a complete and consistent set of grammatical rules and may represent the rich cultures of the groups that use them. For example, Asian Indians speak a variety of English that is somewhat unfamiliar to Americans, while the British speak numerous dialects of British English, each of them containing distinctive grammatical structures and vocabulary not used by Americans. Similarly, some African Americans speak a version of English that historically has been labeled substandard because of a lack of understanding of its origins.

Many African Americans use, or have used at least some of the time, what has been called *Black English*, *African American Vernacular English* (AAVE), *African American English*, *Black Vernacular*, or *Black English Vernacular*. Colloquially, it is known as *Ebonics*.

African American Vernacular English   A recognized language and a dialect of English that meets all of the requirements of a language; it possesses a coherent system of signs; it has a grammar of elements and rules; and it is used for communication and social purposes (Patrick, 2006).

While some African Americans only speak this version of English, many enjoy the flexibility and expressiveness of speaking Ebonics among peers and switching to "standard English" when the situation calls for it (e.g., at work, in interviews, with white friends).

Many people cling to an unscientific and racist view of language varieties of African Americans. However, the fact that some of the same grammatical structures—spoken in a wholly different accent—are found throughout the English-speaking Caribbean, as far south as Trinidad, points to an earlier, African origin for the grammar. Ebonics has been ridiculed by people, including educators, who have no understanding of its foundation and legitimacy, and was at the heart of an extensive educational controversy in the Oakland, California, schools in the late 1990s.

> Ebonics is a full fledged language variety with distinctive features of pronunciation, grammar and vocabulary. And its deep-rooted and widespread use among African Americans affects the teaching of reading and the language arts in ways that most other American dialects do not. (Rickford, 2000)

Linguists have done years of research on the origins of Ebonics and now believe that it developed from the grammatical structures common to several West African tribal languages. For example:

Ebonics:	You lookin good.
Standard English:	You look good right now.
Ebonics:	You be looking good.
Standard English:	You usually look good.

That is, the presence of the word *be* indicates a general condition and not something related only to the present. Apparently, some West African languages have grammatical structures expressing these same concepts of time. According to Dr. John R. Rickford, Stanford University Linguistics Professor and AAVE specialist, "This example captures a distinction that was missed by many of those who tried to poke fun of Ebonics in cartoons and columns during the [late 1990s] Ebonics controversy" (Rickford, 2009).

> One [view] says that there was African influence in the development of the language and the other says that there was not. Those who reject African influence believe that the African arrived in the United States and tried to speak English. And [according to this first view], because he lacked certain intellectual and physical attributes, he failed. This hypothesis makes no attempt to examine the . . . structures of West African languages to see if there are any similarities . . . when the German said "zis" instead of "this," America understood. But, when the African said "dis" [instead of "this"], no one considered the fact that [the sound] *th* may not exist in African languages. (Weber, 1991)

Black English evolved as slaves "learned" English from their slave masters and as they communicated amongst themselves despite their many tribal language differences. They also developed a type of "code language" so that they could speak among themselves and not be understood by their slave owners.

Many people still assume that Ebonics is "bad" English, and they display their contempt either nonverbally or through an impatient tone of voice. Acceptance of another person's variety of English can go a long way toward establishing rapport. People interacting with blacks who do not use "standard" English should realize that blacks are not necessarily speaking poorly. In fact, verbal skill is a highly prized value in most African-based cultures.

Finally, when attempting to establish trust and rebuild relations with a race of people who historically have had few reasons to trust the police, white officers should not try to imitate black accents, dialects, or styles of speaking. These imitations can be viewed as very insulting and may give blacks the impression that they are being ridiculed—or that the officer is seriously uncomfortable with them. (See Chapter 4 for more information.) Officers should not try to fake a style that is culturally different from their own. Being authentic and sincere when communicating with all African Americans, while remaining aware and accepting differences, is key to beginning to build better relationships with African Americans.

Nonverbal Communication: Style and Stance

Social scientists have been studying aspects of African American nonverbal communication that have often been misunderstood by people in positions of authority. Psychologist Richard Majors at the University of Wisconsin termed a certain stance and posturing as the "cool pose," which is demonstrated by many young black men from the inner city. "While the cool pose is often misread by teachers, principals and police officers as an attitude of defiance, psychologists who have studied it say it is a way for black youths to maintain a sense of integrity and suppress rage at being blocked from usual routes to esteem and success" (Goleman, 1992).

Majors explains that while the cool pose is by no means found among the majority of black men, it is commonly seen among inner-city youth as a tactic for psychological survival to cope with everyday rejections (Goleman, 1992). The goal of the pose is to give the appearance of being in control. As Majors points out, it is a way for black youths to say, "[I'm] strong and proud, despite [my] status in American society" (Goleman, 1992). This form of nonverbal communication may include certain movements and postures (e.g., walking, standing, talking, and having aloof facial expressions) designed to emphasize the youth's masculinity. Problems, however, may occur when others, particularly police officers, misread this nonverbal communication. For example, when questioning a black male who is engaged in a cool pose, a white police officer may mistakenly interpret the cool pose as a sign of apathy or as an act of defiance. This can cause an otherwise benign situation to turn into a hostile encounter. Communication styles across cultures have the potential of being misinterpreted; the "cool pose" is generally not intended to be a threatening or rude stance.

Verbal Expressiveness and Emotionalism

> The Ebonics vernacular style of speech emphasizes emotional response—being "real" is the term. This means it is okay to express one's indignation, to be emotional, and to express to someone how you feel. Many African Americans perceive that the mainstream culture is taught to be reserved and to temper their emotions. This is a cultural difference that can be misread by law enforcement. (Patton, 2009)

Linguist and sociologist Thomas Kochman has devoted his professional life to studying differences in black and white culture that contribute to misunderstandings and misperceptions. Of historical significance, Chicago's African American mayor Harold Washington passed out copies of Kochman's book *Black and White Styles in Conflict* (1981) to the city hall press corps because he believed that he was seriously misunderstood by the whites of the city. According to Kochman, "If a person doesn't know the difference in cultures, that's ignorance. But if a person knows the difference and still says that mainstream culture is best, that 'white is right,' then you've got racism" (Kochman, 1981).

In his book, Kochman explains that blacks and whites have different perspectives and approaches to many issues, including conversation, public speaking, and power. This notion is supported in the following advice given to police officers by former Reno Assistant Police Chief Ondra Berry: "Don't get nuts when you encounter an African American who is louder and more emotional than you are. Watch the voice patterns and the tone. Blacks can sound militant [even when they are not]. Blacks have been taught (i.e., socialized) to be outwardly and openly emotional. Sometimes we are emotional first and then calm down and become more rationale" (Berry, 2009). Berry went on to say that often whites are rational at first but express more emotion as they lose control. This cultural difference has obvious implications for overall communication, including how to approach and react to angry citizens.

Kochman explains that many "whites [are] able practitioners of self-restraint [and that] this practice has an inhibiting effect on their ability to be spontaneously self-assertive." He also states that, "the level of energy and spiritual intensity that blacks generate is one that they can manage comfortably but whites can only manage with effort" (Kochman, 1981). The problems in interaction come about because neither race understands that there is a cultural difference between them. Kochman states: "Blacks do not initially see this relative mismatch, because they believe that their normal animated style is not disabling to whites . . . Whites are worried that blacks cannot sustain such intense levels of interaction without losing self-control [because that degree of 'letting go' of emotions for a white would signify a lack of control]" (Ibid., 1981). In other words, a nonblack person, unaware of the acceptability in black culture of expressing intense emotion (including anger) may not be able to imagine that he himself could express such intense emotion without losing control. He may feel threatened, convinced that the ventilation of such emotion will surely lead to a physical confrontation.

While racism may also be a factor for some in communication breakdowns, differing conventions of speech do contribute in ways that are not always apparent. In several cultural awareness training sessions, police officers have reported that white neighbors upon hearing highly emotional discussions among African Americans called to report fights. When the police arrived on the scene of the "fight," the individuals involved responded that they were not fighting, just talking. While continuing to respond to all calls, officers can still be aware of different perceptions of what constitutes a fight. The awareness of style differences should have an impact on how an officer approaches citizens: Pastor Ronald Griffin, a prominent African American leader in Detroit, and now on the Detroit Police Department Board of Commissioners, recalled a communication style that was common among friends and neighbors as they got together and played cards. He said, "If anyone was listening from the outside, they would have heard us, at times, laughing, and, at times, talking loudly and pounding the table. These were intense moments of fellowship, and if you had been there you would have understood" (Griffin, 2009).

Berry illustrated how a white police officer can let his or her own cultural interpretations of black anger and emotionalism influence judgment. He spoke of a fellow officer who made the statement: "Once they [i.e., blacks] took me on, I wanted to take control." This officer, working in a predominantly black area for a 3-month period, made 120 stops and 42 arrests (mainly petty offenses such as prowling and failure to identify). He then worked in a predominantly white area for the same period of time, made 122 stops and only 6 arrests. The officer went on to say that "one group will do what I ask; the other will ask questions and challenge me." His need to "take control" over people whom he perceived to be 'out of their place" was so extreme, it resulted in his being sued (Berry, 2009). His perception of the level of threat involved was much higher in the black community than in the white. One of the factors involved was, arguably, the officer's inability to deal with having his authority questioned or challenged. If he had used communication skills, he might have been able to work situations around to his advantage rather than creating confrontations. Listening professionally, instead of engaging in shouting matches with citizens of other backgrounds, can require a great deal of self-control, but it will usually bring better results. (Once again, George Thompson [2009] of the Verbal Judo Institute reminds officers, "You are not paid to argue." [See Chapter 4.])

Threats and Aggressive Behavior

Kochman, who has conducted cultural awareness training sessions nationwide (for police departments as well as corporations), asks the question, "When does a fight begin?" Many whites, he notes, believe that "fighting" has already begun when it is "obvious" that there will be violence ("when violence is imminent"). Therefore, to whites, a fight begins as soon as the shouting starts. According to whites, then, the fight has begun whenever a certain intensity of anger is shown, along with an exchange of insults. If, in addition, threats are also verbalized, many whites would agree that violence is surely on its way (Kochman, 1981).

Kochman (1981) explains that while verbal confrontation and threats may also be a prelude to a fight for blacks, many blacks tend to make a clear distinction between verbal jostling and physical confrontations. Kochman uses a quote to illustrate how fighting does not begin for some blacks until one person does something physically provocative:

> "If two guys are talking loudly and then one or the other starts to reduce the distance between them, that's a sign [that an act of violence is likely to occur], because it's important to get in the first blow. Or if a guy puts his hand in his pocket and that's not a movement he usually makes, then you watch for that—he might be reaching for a knife. But if they're just talking—it doesn't matter how loud it gets—then you got nothing to worry about." (Allen Harris quoted in Kochman, 1981)

Officers who are trained to think about officer safety, however, might have a problem believing that they "got nothing to worry about" when encountering two belligerent individuals of a different culture than their own. Similarly, a threat in today's society, where anyone may be carrying semiautomatic weapons, may be just that—a very real threat that will be carried out. A threat must always be taken seriously by officers. However, there can be instances when cultural differences are at work, and extreme anger can be expressed without accompanying physical violence. When this is the case, an officer can actually escalate hostilities with an approach and communication style that demonstrates no understanding of culturally/racially different modes of expression.

KEY ISSUES IN LAW ENFORCEMENT

Differential Treatment

The results of a national survey entitled "Police Attitudes toward Abuse of Authority" showed race to be a divisive issue for American police. In particular, black and nonblack officers had significantly different views about the effect of a citizen's race and socioeconomic status on the likelihood of police abuse of authority (Weisburd & Greenspan, 2000).

"I am not prejudiced. I treat all citizens fairly." This type of statement by police officers can be heard around the country. Inevitably, this statement holds true for some officers, although explicit utterance of this type of statement usually signals prejudice. In the wake of many publicized allegations of differential treatment of minority groups, officers who do hold prejudices have to face them and recognize when the prejudices result in action:

> My partner and I several years ago went to an all-white nightclub. He found cocaine on this white couple. He poured it out and didn't make an arrest. Later we were at an all-black nightclub. He found marijuana on one individual and arrested him. I was shocked, but I didn't say anything at the time because I was fairly new to the department. He had told me on two occasions that he "enjoyed" working with black officers and "has no difficulty" with the black community. (African American police officer, wishes to remain anonymous)

Dr. James Johnson, researcher on criminal justice and minority group issues, reacted to the above-noted incident: "This officer validated and legitimized his white partner's discriminatory behavior by exercising the Blue Code of Silence.* Because the black officer did not say anything, the white officer will see no need to face or recognize his racially biased behavior" (Johnson, 2009).

Some officers have encountered the allegation, "You stopped me because I am Black." The truth most likely lies between the categorical denial of some police officers and the statement, "We're always being stopped only because we're black." Undoubtedly, there are police procedures of which citizens are unaware, and they do not see all the other people whom an officer stops in a typical day. However, the citizen is not getting paid to be professional, truthful, or even reasonable with the officer. We know that some officers feel that they are doing "good policing" when they stop citizens who they feel will be guilty of a crime. However, this "feel" for who may be guilty can actually be a reflection of a bias or an assumption that substitutes for real "data." Observing and selecting "guilty-looking" motorists can be the result of unconscious biased thinking. (Refer to Chapter 13 for an explanation of the "Ladder of Inference" with respect to racial profiling.)

Racial Profiling in the African American Community

Linda Hills, Executive Director, ACLU of San Diego and Imperial Counties and Randa Trapp, President of NAACP of San Diego, writes:

> An ordinary commuter turns the key in the ignition, glances in the rear view mirror, and pulls away from the curb. Rounding the corner, his slightly worn tires slip on a fresh layer of light rain. He executes a perfect "California rolling stop" at an intersection and enters the freeway, accelerating to a comfortable 70 mph for the cruise into downtown. Our commuter just violated the traffic code at least four times, just as we all do each time we get behind the wheel. But if our commuter is a person of color, there's a good chance he won't make it to work without being pulled over for "driving while black or brown." (Hills, 2000)

---

* For further information on the Blue Code of Silence, see http://www.ethicsinstitute.com/pdf/Code%20of%20Silence%20Facts%20Revealed.pdf. For an opportunity to discuss the above example, and the commentary, see Discussion Question 3 at the end of the chapter.

Officers in cultural awareness training have said they have been surprised when suburban middle-class African Americans express as much anger and outrage about differential treatment, including racial profiling, as do poorer blacks in inner-city areas. Many middle- and upper-class parents whose children have experienced the types of stops described here are likely to be even less forgiving: stops like these are painful indications that, despite much hard-won social and economic success, race still prevails as the defining characteristic.

Reactions to and Perceptions of Authority

As a response to a series of racial events (in California) that received national and international attention in the 1990s, including the beating of black motorist Rodney King in 1991, riots in Los Angeles in 1992, and the trial of O. J. Simpson in 1995, the Public Policy Institute of California asked two social scientists to begin a study on ethnic reactions to legal authority. The researchers questioned 1,500 residents of Los Angeles and Oakland, California, and the following are three of the major findings of the study (Huo & Tyler, 2000):

- Compared to whites, African Americans report lower levels of satisfaction in their interactions with legal authorities. They also report less willingness than whites to comply with the directives of the authorities they deal with. This pattern of difference between minorities and whites was especially apparent among those who reported interactions with the police compared to those who reported interactions with authorities in court.
- Much of the difference between minorities and whites in their reactions to legal authorities can be accounted for by differences in their perceptions of how fairly or unfairly they were treated. When asked whether the legal authorities involved in their encounters used fair procedures to make decisions, African Americans (and Latinos) reported experiencing less procedural fairness than experienced by whites.
- The perception of fair treatment and positive outcomes was the most important factor in forming reactions to encounters with the police and courts. It was more important than the concerns about the outcomes people received from legal authorities. This pattern held up across different situations and ethnic groups.

African Americans (and Latinos) are still reporting more negative treatment from legal authorities than reported by whites. These perceptions, on the part of minorities, are significant in that they directly relate to compliance rates with authority among members of minority groups (Huo & Tyler, 2000). The study indicated that all groups were equally satisfied with their experiences in the court and that, as a result, there was compliance with court directives. However, African Americans (and Latinos) were less willing to comply with directives from police. The findings in this study were similar to the results of the Milwaukee Domestic Violence Experiment conducted in 1997. In that study, African Americans (and Latinos) perceived that "legal authorities treated them with less procedural fairness than they do whites" (Paternoster, Brame, & Sherman, 1997). The results of both studies suggest that "group differences in perceived procedural fairness may lead to group differences in compliance with legal directives" (Huo & Tyler, 2000).

Even as opinion polls across the country reflect the perception among both blacks and whites that race relations are improving, according to a 2003 ABC/Washington Post poll, only 28% of blacks think that they "receive equal treatment as whites from police," as opposed to 66% of whites, who believe that both groups are treated equally. The poll found that within the black population, 65% of the men surveyed reported being stopped "just because of your race," as opposed to 22% of black women; from that, 61% of the women and 79% of the men said that blacks don't get the same treatment as whites from the police in their communities. ("Despite a Chasm in Perceptions of Racism, Public Views of Race Relations Improve," 2003)

Excessive Force and Brutality

A controversial and complex issue is the use of excessive force by the police which is a problem heavily concentrated in minority communities. The International Association of Chiefs of Police defines excessive force as "the application of an amount and/or frequency of force greater than that required to complete compliance from a willing or unwilling subject" (IACP, 2001). When excessive force is used by a police officer, the conduct of the police often comes under public scrutiny and will receive attention from the media, the community, and legislators. A police officer's use of excessive force usually results in lawsuits by members of the public who feel they have been treated with unnecessary physical or deadly force (i.e., surviving family in case of deadly force). When the use of excessive force is aberrant behavior by the actions of an individual officer or is a common practice of the culture of the law enforcement agency, public opinion will erode the police department's credibility.

The case of Rodney King, in 1992, brought public attention to the fact that excessive force and brutality were serious problems in America. The existence of brutality has been a problem that blacks and other racial and ethnic groups have asserted, but until the early 1990s (i.e., with several highly publicized cases), many whites either did not believe or closed their eyes to this reality. Nearly a decade after the Rodney King event, in 1997, Americans and citizens worldwide witnessed another incident of brutality against a black American, Abner Louima, a Haitian immigrant who was arrested and sodomized with a broomstick inside a restroom in the 70th Precinct station house in Brooklyn. "The case became a national symbol of police brutality and fed perceptions that New York City police officers were harassing or abusing young black men as part of a citywide crackdown on crime" ("The Abner Louima Case, 10 years later," 2007).

Then again in 2002, the nation saw on television, an Inglewood, California, city police officer, Jeremy Morse, caught on videotape slamming 15-year-old Donovan Jackson's face onto the trunk of a police patrol vehicle. It was later revealed that the teenager suffered from a mental impairment that left him unable to respond rapidly to verbal commands (Schmalleger, 2005).

On November 25, 2006, Sean Bell, an African American, died in a "hail of 50 bullets fired by a group of five officers. The shooting shocked the city and brought back memories of the deaths in other high-profile police shootings . . . it prompted unsettling questions about the changes in police procedures adopted in recent years, and about whether black men remained unfairly singled out for aggressive police action" ("Sean Bell", 2009).

Clearly, the large majority of police officers around the nation do not use excessive force, and there have been great strides made between law enforcement and many minority communities. Nevertheless, we know from the above examples that police brutality is not yet a phenomenon of the past.

Controlling racist and prejudicial behavior must be a priority training issue in all police departments across the country (Chapter 1 deals with prejudices and biases). Police departments need to recognize that reducing an officer's buildup of stress has to be addressed as frequently and effectively as, for example, is self-defense. Finally, the individual officer must remember that even though abusive behavior from citizens constitutes one of the worst aspects of the job, it is not the citizens who have to behave like professionals.

Law Enforcement Interaction with African American Communities

Many police officers feel that they are putting their lives in danger when they go into certain African American communities where the crime rate is high. As a result, some of African Americans feel as though the police are not providing adequate protection to their communities. Increases in drug use and the availability of firearms in the black community contribute to defensive reactions among both the police and the African Americans. There is a vicious cycle that escalates and reinforces hostilities. Police are not expected to solve the social ills of society, and do not always have access to either the resources or the training to deal with problems rooted in historical, social, political, and economic factors. But they are expected to devote the same amount of time and resources to serving and protecting all communities equally.

African Americans and police officers are often frustrated with each other, and barriers seem insurmountable. While the following quote comes from a source in the early 1970s, officers have validated that the dynamic described is still operative:

> Many policemen find themselves on the alert for the slightest sign of disrespect. One author [McNamara] has shown that the police [officer] is often prepared to coerce respect and will use force if he feels his position is being challenged. Likewise, the attitudes and emotions of the black citizen may be similar when confronted with a police [officer]. Intervention by police is often seen as an infringement on the blacks' rights and as oppression by the white population. Consequently many blacks are on the alert for the slightest sign of disrespect that might be displayed by the police [officer]. (Cross & Renner, 1974; Patton, 2009)

Cross and Renner (1974) explain that fear of belittlement and fear of danger operate for both the African American citizen and the officer, and these fears cause both sides to misinterpret what might otherwise be nonthreatening behavior. The problem often arises not from the reality of the situation but as the result of mutual fears. In some parts of the country, this is as true now as it was in the mid-1970s when the article cited previously was written. Johnson adds that "black men are more concerned about being respected, rather than fearing belittlement, and treated like men and not 'boys'" (Johnson, 2009). He also points out that "the 'power distance' between an officer and an African American usually *only* leads to a verbal protest or the filing of a formal complaint if he or she senses that the officer is about to or has resorted to the use of force. In this case, the citizen is unlikely to use physical force as a response so he or she resorts to verbal means which the officer, then, interprets as belligerence" (Johnson, 2009).

Victimization: Offenders and Incarceration

The following data is from the Bureau of Justice Statistics' 2008 report on homicide trends:

- Based on the data from 1976 to 2005, blacks were disproportionately represented as both homicide victims and offenders. The victimization rates for blacks in 2005 were six times higher than those for whites. The offending rates for blacks in the same year were more than seven times higher the rates for whites (USDOJ BJS, 2008).

The following is from the Bureau of Justice Prison Statistics' from mid-year 2008:

- On June 30, 2008, there were approximately 2,311,000 prisoners in federal, state, or local jails across the United States. There were an estimated 509 prison inmates per 100,000 U.S. residents, up from 411 in 1995. There were 4,777 black males in the U.S. prisons per 100,000 black males as compared to 1,760 Hispanic male inmates and 727 white male inmates (per 100,000 Hispanic males and white males, respectively) (USDOJ BJS, 2009).

Of interest, Clinton's Council of Economic Advisors found that "Discriminatory behavior on the part of police and elsewhere in the criminal justice system may contribute to blacks' high representation in arrests, convictions, and prison admissions. . . ." (Council of Economic Advisors, 1998). At the time of the writing of this 5th edition, Clinton was the last U.S. president to conduct a study on the disproportionate representation of African Americans in the criminal justice system.

African American Women and Police

It is beyond the scope of this book to delve in depth into the specific issues and attitudes of African American women toward police and authority. However, one area is particularly worthy of attention. Historically, the sexual assault of an African American woman has not been considered as serious by law enforcement as the sexual assault of a white woman; past and current perceptions and experiences may contribute to lower reporting rates:

> Research shows white women indicated a greater likelihood to report rape or sexual assault to law enforcement than did women of other races. Although these data do not report actual rates of reporting behavior among women of different ethnic groups, they do suggest that white women are more likely to report a sexual assault to law enforcement agencies than are women of other races. Race—because of commonplace stereotypes and myths about blacks and rape—is likely to affect attitudes, perceptions, judgments, and reactions concerning rape. (Wheeler & George, 2005)

Law enforcement officials alone cannot solve social ills but should realize that African Americans in disadvantaged communities desperately need excellent police protection. The perception that whites in middle-class communities are better served by the police forces naturally reinforces existing antipolice attitudes among the lower class.

Addressing the Needs of the Inner City

"Black-on-black crime seems to be tolerated and even accepted as inevitable" ("Black on Black Crime," 1991). This statement, made by an African American chief of police in 1991, is as true today as it was then. African Americans and other racial and ethnic groups have criticized law enforcement for underpolicing their communities; however, progress has been made to improve relations between police and community members. There are increasing numbers of African American officers and police executives who are influencing and changing policy that directly affects police–black relations. Many departments have put into writing strict rules regarding the use of excessive force, discourtesy, racial slurs, racial profiling, and aggressive patrol techniques.

While, ideally, there should not be a need to put the requirements for basic human decencies in writing, the reality is different.

Efforts toward a Positive Relationship between Police and the Community

Communities and police departments differ widely in the way they build positive relationships with each other. "Consent decrees" have forced a change of inappropriate (prejudicial or unjust) behavior or actions, but are not always viewed in a positive light.

> **Consent decree** An out-of-court settlement whereby the party agrees to modify or change behavior rather than plead guilty or go through a hearing on charges brought to court (CSIS, 2003).

It is beyond the scope of this chapter to explore the controversy surrounding consent decrees; however, many inappropriate police actions within African American communities have resulted in the implementation of consent decrees. Some police leaders believe that a consent decree is not a symbol of a positive relationship; at the same time, many community leaders have supported them.

> One leader mentioned that the . . . decree had given the community greater confidence in the police. Another leader commented that the consent decree "gave people an opportunity to feel as though they had a voice." One community leader felt that some white and black officers were working better together and that they were responding more quickly to calls for service from the African-American community. "It seems they are trying to ask more questions and there is more respect for the community," she said. (Davis, Ortiz, Henderson, Miller, & Massie, 2002)

While there is controversy around consent decrees, and some officers complain that they add too much paperwork and bureaucracy to their already demanding jobs, they serve a purpose. They are an attempt, on the part of the federal government, local and state police departments, and communities, to try to improve community–police interaction in a quick and dramatic manner. Some outcomes can be influenced informally and others by consent decrees. The key to improved relationships deeply rests on all of the following:

- Leadership
- Vision
- Respect
- Goals
- Strategies
- Mutual benefits for police and community
- Effective communication and practices of both law enforcement agencies and the community

In addition to the above list, personal means—one-on-one and face-to-face interaction—as well as goodwill need to be relied upon by community members, leaders, and police officers to improve community–police relations. Pastor Ronald Griffin, a prominent leader in the Detroit African American community, echoes these sentiments:

> Face-to-face contact opens up dialogue where we have a chance to listen and to be heard. We as human beings really say we listen, but we often don't, and instead we come prepared to respond. So sometimes we put up our defenses and get into attack mode. We're already predisposed and most of us, then, are willing and ready for battle. This leads to a lot of pointless negative action even if both sides have a lot in common. We have had executive officers come to church activities to encourage the members and to help the members see officers in another light. So we're building on this and learning to trust each other. There's nothing I can't ask of the precinct, and the same from them of me. (Griffin, 2009)

Summary

- The experiences of both slavery and racism have shaped African American culture and continue to leave psychological scars on many African American communities and individuals. Law enforcement officials, in particular, represent a system that has oppressed African Americans and other minorities. The task of establishing positive rapport with African Americans is challenging because of what the officer represents in terms of past discrimination. To protect and serve in many African American communities across the nation necessarily means that officers will need to go out of their way to establish trust and win cooperation.

- African Americans are represented in all socioeconomic classes, from the underclass to the upper class, and have moved increasingly into the middle class. As with all racial and ethnic groups, there are significant class-related differences among blacks affecting values and behavior. However, color, more so than class, determines how the larger society reacts to and treats blacks. Therefore, the racial experience of many African Americans in the United States is similar, regardless of an individual's level of prosperity or education. As with whites, there are significant regional differences among African Americans as well as differences associated with rural and urban backgrounds. In addition, religious backgrounds vary, although the majority of American-born blacks are Protestant and are specifically Baptist.

- The Civil Rights and Black Pride movements, along with positive identification with African culture, have for some replaced the sense of inferiority fostered by white racist supremacist attitudes. The changing terms that African Americans have used to refer to themselves reflect stages of racial empowerment and cultural growth. The choice of terms represents on the part of group members growth and a desire to name themselves rather than be named by the dominant society.

- The single mother, particularly in the inner city, does not always receive the respect that she is due. A respectful officer, who takes the time to establish rapport and make appropriate and helpful referrals, will stand more chance of gaining the family's and community's trust, respect and cooperation.

- Many African Americans switch back and forth between language styles or use what is commonly referred to as *Ebonics* or *African American Vernacular English*. Historically, this version of English has been labeled substandard because of a lack of understanding of its origins. Acceptance of another person's variety of English can go a long way toward establishing rapport. People interacting with blacks who do not use "standard" English should realize that blacks are not necessarily speaking poorly. Regarding communication style, within African

American cultural norms, it is acceptable to be highly expressive and emotional in speech. This is in contrast to an unspoken white mainstream norm that discourages the open and free expression of emotion, especially anger. Therefore, officers from different backgrounds should not overinterpret a style, which may differ from their own, as necessarily being aggressive and leading to violence. Cultural differences in verbal communication can result in complete misinterpretation. Similarly people in positions of authority can misinterpret certain ways of walking, standing, and dressing, and perceive these styles as defiant.

- The issues of differential treatment, racial profiling, excessive force, and brutality are still

realities in policing and interaction with African Americans in the United States. When acts of bias, brutality, and injustice occur, everyone suffers, including officers and entire police departments. An additional challenge is addressing the needs of the inner city, and the need for increased police protection. Regarding perceptions, African Americans are still reporting more negative treatment from legal authorities than are whites. Bridging the gap that has hindered relationships between the police and African Americans involves radical changes in attitudes toward police–community relations. Together with changes initiated by management, greater efforts to have positive contact with African Americans must be made by individual officers.

Discussion Questions and Issues

1. *Racism: Effects on Blacks and Whites.* Under the "Historical Information" section in this chapter, the authors state that slavery has created great psychological and social problems for succeeding generations of black citizens. How does the legacy of slavery continue to impact both blacks and whites? What are the implications for law enforcement?

2. *Offensive Terms.* Officers are advised to refrain from using racial epithets at all times, even when there are no African Americans present. Give two practical reasons for this.

3. *Blue Code of Silence.* Discuss the example that is provided (p. 182) where an African American officer fairly new to a department did not speak up when it came to his partner's differential treatment of black citizens in the nightclub. What do you think held this officer back from speaking up? What might the consequences of this silence be with respect to the ongoing relationship between the black and white officers? How should this example of differential treatment have been handled? After you have answered these questions, discuss how departments, in community-policing forums with African American and other ethnic communities, can convey their commitment to police professionalism and ethics—a step that is crucial in rebuilding trust with communities that have historically not had positive relations with law enforcement.

4. *Inner Cities: Officers' and Citizens' Reactions.* Toward the end of the chapter, the authors mention the vicious cycle that is created in urban areas, especially where citizens have become increasingly armed with highly sophisticated weapons and officers, consequently, have to take more self-protective measures. Each views the other with fear and animosity and approaches the other with extreme defensiveness. Obviously, there is no simple answer to this widely occurring phenomenon, and police alone cannot solve the ills of society. Discuss your observations of the way officers cope with the stresses of these potentially life-threatening situations and how the coping or lack thereof affects relations with African Americans and other minorities. What type of support do police officers need to handle this aspect of their job? Do you think police departments are doing their job in providing the support needed?

5. *When Officers Try to Make a Difference.* Many young African American children live without a father in the household. This means that they do not have a second parental figure as a role model and are consequently deprived of an important source of adult support. No one can take the place of a missing parent, but there are small and large things a police officer can do to at least make an impression in the life of a child. Compile a list of actions officers can take to demonstrate their caring for children in these environments. Include in your first list every gesture,

no matter how small; your second list can be more realistic and include the actions that can be taken given the resources available. Select someone to compile both sets of suggestions (i.e., the realistic and ideal suggestions). Post these lists as reminders of how officers can attempt to make a difference in their communities not only with African American children but with other children as well.

Website Resources

American Civil Liberties Union (ACLU): http://www.aclu.org

This website contains multiple locations for information about many issues, including racial profiling.

National Organization of Black Law Enforcement (NOBLE): http://www.noblenatl.org

This website provides information on the public service organization itself and its involvement in issues of interest and concern to law enforcement and the black community. It is the source of information on many subjects, including recommended policy and procedure. It provides information on NOBLE activities such as community outreach and professional development. The goal of NOBLE is to be recognized as a highly competent, public service organization at the forefront of providing solutions to law enforcement issues and concerns as well as to the changing needs of communities.

Police Executive Research Forum (PERF): http://www.policeforum.org/racial.html

This website has an abundance of information about racial profiling and model programs. PERF has produced a free video and guide to facilitate police–citizen discussions on racially biased policing. They also have produced a helpful guide titled *Racially Biased Policing: A Principled Response.*

National Association of Black Criminal Justice (NABCJ): http://www.nabcj.org

This website provides information on the organization itself (e.g., member chapters and events) as well as on issues toward improving law enforcement. NABCJ seeks to focus attention on relevant legislation, law enforcement, prosecution, and defense-related needs and practices, with emphasis on the courts, corrections, and the prevention of crime. Among its chief concerns is the general welfare and increasing influence of African Americans and people of color as they relate to the administration of justice.

VERA Institue of Justice: http://www.vera.org

This website provides information on the research projects and activities of the VERA Institute of Justice. This organization works closely with leaders in government and civil society to improve the services people rely on for safety and justice. VERA develops innovative, affordable programs that often grow into self-sustaining organizations, studies social problems and current responses, and provides practical advice and assistance to government officials in New York and around the world.

African American Web Connection: http://www.aawc.com/aawc.html

This website is devoted to providing the African American community with valuable resources on the Web. It includes such topics as arts and poetry, business, churches, organizations, and topics of concern, to name a few.

References

"The Abner Louima Case, 10 Years Later." (2007, August 9). *New York Times* (New York/Region section). Retrieved: April 30, 2009, from http://cityroom.blogs.nytimes.com/2007/08/09/the-abner-louima-case-10-years-later/

Bennett, Lerone Jr. (1989, November). "The 10 Biggest Myths about the Black Family." *Ebony*. pp. 1, 2.

Berry, Ondra. (2009, May). Retired Assistant Police Chief, Reno, Nevada, Police Department, personal communication.

"Black on Black Crime." (1991, April 24). *USA Today*.

Council of Economic Advisors. (1998, September). *Changing America: Indicators of Social and Economic Well-Being by Race and Hispanic Origin.* Chapter 7,

Crime and Criminal Justice. President's Initiative on Race (National Center for Health Statistics, Bureau of Justice Statistics).

Cross, Stan, and Edward Renner. (1974). "An Interaction Analysis of Police–Black Relations." *Journal of Police Science Administration, 2*(1), 55–61.

CSIS. (2003). Consumer Services Information Systems Project—Glossary. Available: http://csisweb.aers.psu.edu

Davis, Robert C., Christopher W. Ortiz, Nicole J. Henderson, Joel Miller, and Michelle K. Massie. (2002). "Turning Necessity into Virtue: Pittsburgh's Experience with a Federal Consent Decree," Vera Institute of Justice. Available: http://www.cops.usdoj.gov/Default.asp?Item=565.

"Despite a Chasm in Perceptions of Racism, Public Views of Race Relations Improve." (2003, January 20). *ABC News*, Washing Post. Race Relations.

Goleman, Daniel. (1992, April 21). "Black Scientists Study the 'Pose' of the Inner City." *New York Times.* Retrieved on September 14, 2009 from http://www.nytimes.com/1992/04/21/science/black-scientists-study-the-pose-of-the-inner-city.html?pagewanted=1

Griffin, Ronald Pastor. (2009, April). Detroit-based Pastor and Community Leader, Vice Chair of Detroit Board of Police Commissioners, personal communication.

Higginbotham, Leon A. Jr., and Anne F. Jacobs. (1992). "The Law Only as an Enemy. The Legitilization of Racial Powerlessness through the Colonial and Antibellum Criminal Laws of Virginia," North Carolina Law Review, April 1992. 70 NCL Rev.969 (p. 64).

Hills, Linda. (2000, October 13). "Beyond the Mythology of Racial Profiling." *San Diego Union-Tribune,* Opinion Page.

Huo, Yuen J., and Tom R. Tyler. (2000). *How Different Ethnic Groups React to Legal Authority.* San Francisco, CA: Public Policy Institute of California.

International Association of Chiefs of Police. (2001). Police Use of Force in America 2001. Alexandria, VA: IACP.

Johnson, James L. (2009, April). Probation Administrator, Office of the U.S. Courts, personal communication.

Johnson, James L. (2008). "The Construction of Mass Incarceration as a Means of Marginalizing Black Americans." *Dissertation Abstract International,* 69(3), 130A. (UMI No. AAT 3305791).

Kochman, Thomas. (1981). *Black and White Styles in Conflict.* Chicago, IL: University of Chicago Press, p. 121.

Lemann, Nicholas. (1992). The Promised Land: The Great Black Migration and how it Changed America. New York, NY: Vintage Books.

McAdoo, Harriet Pipes. (1992). "Upward Mobility and Parenting in Middle Income Families," in *African American Psychology.* Newbury Park, CA: Sage.

Miller, Char. (2008, February). (Former) Professor of History, Trinity College, San Antonio, Texas, personal communication.

Paternoster, R., Bachman, R., Brame, R., and Sherman, L. W. (1997). "Do Fair Procedures Matter? The Effect of Procedural Justice on Spouse Assault." *Law and Society Review.* pp. 163–204.

Patrick, Peter L. (2006). Answers to Questions about Ebonics. University of Essex, U.K. Retrieved July 8, 2006, from http://privatewww.essex.ac.uk/~patrickp/aavesem/EbonicsQ&A.html.

Patton, Greg. (2009, May). Supervisor, Parole and Probation, Clackamas County Community Corrections, Clackamas, Oregon; Adjunct Criminal Justice Cultural Diversity Instructor at Portland Community College, personal communication.

Pew Forum. (2008). "U.S. Religious Landscape Survey." Retrieved April 28, 2009, from http://religions.pew-forum.org/pdf/report-religious-landscape-study-chapter-3.pdf

Ponterotto, Joseph G., Shawn O. Utsey, and Paul B. Pederson. (2006). *Preventing Prejudice: A Guide for Counselors, Educators, and Parents,* 2nd ed. Thousand Oaks, CA: Sage.

Rickford, John Russell. (2000). *Spoken Soul.* New York: John Wiley & Sons, Inc. p. 205.

Rickford, John Russell. (2009, June). Linguistics Professor; specialist in African American Vernacular English, personal communication.

Schmalleger, Frank. (2005). *Criminal Justice Today,* 8th ed. Upper Saddle River, N.J.: Pearson Prentice Hall.

"Sean Bell." (2009, April). *New York Times.* (Times Topics Section); Retrieved April 30, 2009, from http://topics.nytimes.com/top/reference/timestopics/people/b/sean_bell/index.html.

Thompson, George. (2009, March). Founder of Verbal Judo Institute, Inc., personal communication.

U.S. Census Bureau, American Community Survey. (2008). "2002 American Community Survey Profile." (Population and Housing profile; Detroit City, Michigan)

U.S. Census Bureau, American Community Survey. (2008). "The American Community—Blacks: 2004." Issued February, 2007.

U.S. Census Bureau News. (2008). "U.S. Hispanic Population Surpasses 45 million Now 15 Percent of Total." Retrieved May 15, 2009 from http://www.census.gov/Press-Release/www/releases/archives/population/011910.html.

U.S. Department of Justice Bureau of Justice Statistics (2008). Homicide trends in the U.S. Retrieved April 28, 2009, from http://www.ojp.usdoj.gov/bjs/homicide/race.htm.

U.S. Department of Justice Bureau of Justice Statistics. (2009, March). Prison Inmates at Mid-Year 2008. Retrieved April 28, 2009, from http://www.ojp.usdoj.gov/bjs/prisons.htm.

Walker, Samuel. (1992). *The Police in America*. New York, N.Y.: McGraw-Hill.

Weber, Shirley N. (1991). "The Need to Be: The Socio-Cultural Significance of Black Language," in *Intercultural Communication: A Reader*, 6th ed. Larry Samovar and Richard Porter (Eds.). Belmont, CA: Wadsworth Press.

Weisburd, David, and Rosann Greenspan. (2000, May). "Police Attitudes toward Abuse of Authority: Findings from a National Study." National Institute of Justice Research in Brief.

Wheeler, Jennifer, and William H. George. (2005). "Race and Sexual Offending," in *Race, Culture, Psychology, & Law*. In K. Holt and W. George (Eds.). Thousand Oaks, CA: Sage.

Williams, H., and Murphy, P. V.. (1990). *The Evolving Strategy of Police: A Minority View*. Washington D.C.: The National Institute of Justice, U.S. Department of Justice.

CHAPTER 7

Law Enforcement Contact with Latino/ Hispanic Americans

LEARNING OBJECTIVES

After reading this chapter you will be able to:

- Discuss the implications of group identification terms for Latino/Hispanic Americans.
- Describe the historical background of the Latino/Hispanic American community in the United States.
- Highlight the demographic features and diversity of the Latino/Hispanic community.
- Identify the myths and stereotypes applied to Latino/Hispanic Americans.
- Explain the importance of family structure of Latino/Hispanic Americans for law enforcement.
- Discuss the communication styles used by Latino/Hispanic Americans.
- Highlight key law enforcement concerns, and skills, resources, and practices for addressing some of those concerns.

OUTLINE

INTRODUCTION

Latino/Hispanic Americans are the fastest growing cultural group in the United States in terms of overall numbers of people. The population increased by more than 27.8 percent, from 35.6 million in 2000 to 45.5 million in 2007 (U.S. Census, 2008). The Hispanic population reached 45.5 million as of July 1, 2007, according to national estimates by the U.S. Census Bureau (2008). Growth in all urban and rural areas of the United States has been striking, with the Hispanic population having a sizeable presence in virtually all geographic areas within the United States. The population growth can be attributed primarily to higher birthrates (Cohn, 2005) and secondarily to the following three factors: (1) higher immigration from Mexico, Central and South America, and the Caribbean; (2) greater longevity, since this is a relatively young population; and (3) larger numbers of subgroups being incorporated into the Latino/Hispanic American grouping (Korzenny & Korzenny, 2005). Moreover, the U.S. Census estimates for 2007 did not include the number of undocumented immigrants or unauthorized migrants. The Pew Hispanic Institute estimated that the total number of unauthorized migrants in the United States in 2004 was 10.3 million, with 5.9 million from Mexico and another 2.5 million from the rest of Latin America (Passel, 2005). In Chapter 1, we discussed general issues related to the undocumented immigrants. Various other labels have been applied to this group of unauthorized migrants, including *illegals*, *illegal aliens*, and *undocumented immigrants*. For the Latino/Hispanic American community, we use the specific term *unauthorized migrant* to mean "a person who resides in the United States, but who is not a U.S. citizen, has not been admitted for permanent residence, and is not included within a set of specific authorized temporary statuses permitting longer-term residence and work" (Passel, Van Hook, & Bean, 2004).

The total number of unauthorized migrants from Mexico and the rest of Latin American is estimated to be 8.3 million, and if these numbers were added to the Census estimates for the documented Hispanic population in the United States, the total Hispanic presence would be 53.8 million people. A total of 53.8 million Latino/Hispanic people in the United States would make it the second-largest nation in the world for Latino/Hispanic presence, second only to Mexico, and with a population greater than the third-largest Hispanic nation, Spain, with 40 million people (Central Intelligence Agency, 2009). Although Brazil, with 188 million people, is in South America, the vast majority of the people are of Portuguese descent, and only a minority would be considered to be Latino/Hispanic (Korzenny & Korzenny, 2005). Given the current and anticipated growth of this population, all federal, regional, state, and local law enforcement agencies need to prepare to serve this growing presence in our communities.

LATINO/HISPANIC AMERICANS DEFINED

Hispanic is not a racial group; for example, a person can be white, black, or Asian and still be considered Hispanic. *Hispanic* is a generic term referring to all Spanish-surname and Spanish-speaking people who reside within the United States and Puerto Rico (a commonwealth). *Latino* is generally the preferred label on the West Coast, parts of the East Coast, and the Southeast. The term *Latino* is a Spanish word indicating a person of Latin American origin, and it reflects the gender-specific nature of its Spanish-language derivation: Latino, for men, and Latina, for women. Hispanic is generally preferred on the East Coast, specifically within the Puerto Rican, Dominican, and Cuban communities (although individual members within each of these communities may prefer the specific term referring to their country of heritage). Objections to the use of the term *Hispanic* include the following: (1) *Hispanic* is not derived from any culture or place (i.e., there is no such place as "Hispania"), and (2) the term was primarily invented for use by the U.S. Census Bureau. In the most recent decade, many Latino/Hispanic Americans, inspired by (1) a growing sense of community identification, (2) high-profile and successful role models, and (3) increased pride in ethnic and cultural identity, have embraced the use of *Hispanic* and *Latino/Latina* for self- and group reference. A new and dynamic pride, confidence, and self-esteem in the Latino/Hispanic culture and heritage have emerged for many (especially among the younger Latino/Hispanic Americans) and have replaced some of the past negative associations with the terms *Latino* and *Hispanic*, often fostered in the past by negative stereotypes, government designations, undocumented immigration statuses, migrant work roles, educational underachievement, and impoverished communities.

Sometimes, the term *Spanish-speaking or Spanish-surnamed* may be used to recognize that one may have a Spanish surname but may not speak Spanish (which is the case for a large number of Latino/Hispanic Americans). *La Raza* is another term used, primarily on the West Coast and in the Southwest, to refer to all peoples of the Western Hemisphere who share a cultural, historical, political, and social legacy of the Spanish and Portuguese colonists, and the Native Indian and African people; it has its origins within the political struggles of this region and the mixing of the races, *el mestizaje*. Like La Raza, *Chicano* is another term that grew out of the ethnic pride and ethnic studies movement in the late 1960s. Chicano refers specifically to Mexican Americans, and it is used primarily on the West Coast, in the Southwest, and in the Midwest. It is also commonly used in college communities across the United States that provide an ethnic studies curriculum.

In 1976, Congress passed Public Law 94-311, called the "Roybal Resolution," which required the inclusion of a self-identification question on Spanish origin or descent in government surveys and censuses. As such, *Hispanic* is the official term used in federal, state, and local governmental writings and for demographic references. Federal standards implemented in 2003 allow the terms *Latino* and *Hispanic* to be used interchangeably (Office of Management and Budget, 1997).

As noted earlier, the terms *Hispanic* and *Latino/Latina* have been more readily accepted and embraced in the past decade, especially by the younger generation. The definition of Latino/Hispanic is still considered by many (especially among those who have fought to be identified by the different specific Hispanic nationalities and cultures) to be associated with stereotypical perceptions caused by a "megalabel" that does not represent well all members within this group. This point of view is illustrated in the following example:

> One version of this objection argues against all existing ethnic names, and particularly "Hispanic" or "Latinos/Latinas," because these labels have bad connotations among the general population. They create a negative perception of those named and tend to perpetuate their disadvantageous situation in society. To call someone Hispanic or Latino/Latina, like calling someone negro or colored, carries with it all sorts of negative baggage, demeaning the person and harming him or her in diverse ways. (Gracia, 2000)

As the Latino/Hispanic American communities grow and develop in the United States, the preferred and specific terms to be used will evolve and change according to the preferences of those community members.

Labels and Terms

As noted earlier, the term *Latino/Hispanic* American is a convenient summarizing label to achieve some degree of agreement in referring to a very heterogeneous group of people. Similar to the case of Asian/Pacific Americans, the key to understanding which terms to use is based on the principle of self-preference. Sensitivity is warranted in the use of the term *Hispanic* with the Latino/Hispanic American community. For those who have origins in the Caribbean (e.g., Puerto Rican, Cuban, Dominican), the term *Latino* may be equally problematic for self-designation and self-identification.

Until 2003, federal and other governmental designations used only Hispanic; Latino and Hispanic are now used interchangeably. The governmental designations are used in laws, programs, and regulations and in most reports and publications. For individuals within any of the groups, often the more specific names for the groups are preferred (e.g., Mexican, Puerto Rican, Cuban, Dominican, Argentinean, Salvadorian). Some individuals may prefer that the term *American* be part of their designation (e.g., Mexican American). For law enforcement officers, the best term to use in referring to individuals is the term that they prefer to be called. It is perfectly acceptable to ask individuals what nationality they are.

The use of slurs like "wetback," "Mex," "Spic," "Greaser," or other derogatory ethnic slang terms are never acceptable for use by law enforcement officers, no matter how provoked an officer may be. Other stereotypic terms like "Illegal," "New York Rican," "Macho man," "Latin lover," "Lupe the Virgin," and "Low Rider" do not convey the kind of professionalism and respect for community diversity important to law enforcement and peacekeeping, and must be avoided in law enforcement work. Officers hearing these or similar words used in their own departments (or with peers or citizens) should provide immediate feedback about the inappropriateness of the use. Officers who may, out of habit, routinely use these terms may find themselves or their superiors in the embarrassing situation of explaining to offended citizens and communities why they used the term and how they intended no bias, stereotype, or prejudice.

HISTORICAL INFORMATION

The historical background of Latino/Hispanic Americans contains key factors that affect their interactions with and understanding of law enforcement and peacekeeping personnel. Clearly, this brief historical and sociopolitical overview can only highlight some of the commonalities and diverse cultural experiences of Latino/Hispanic Americans. Our historical review focuses primarily on the larger Latino/Hispanic communities in the United States (those with Mexican, Puerto Rican, and Cuban ethnic and historical roots).

In the 1800s, under the declaration of Manifest Destiny, the United States began the expansionist policy of annexing vast territories to the south, north, and west. As Lopez y Rivas (1973) noted, the United States viewed itself as a people chosen by "Providence" to form a larger union through conquest, purchase, and annexation. With the purchase (or annexation) of the Louisiana Territories in 1803, Florida in 1819, Texas in 1845, and the Northwest Territories (Oregon, Washington, Idaho, Wyoming, and Montana) in 1846, it seemed nearly inevitable that conflict would occur with Mexico. The resulting Mexican–American War ended in 1848 with the signing of the Treaty of Guadalupe Hidalgo, in which Mexico received $15 million from the United States for the land that is now Texas, New Mexico, Arizona, and California, with more than 100,000 Mexican people living in those areas. As is obvious from this portion of history, it makes little sense for many Mexican Americans to be stereotyped as "illegal aliens," especially since more than a million Mexican Americans (some of whom are U.S. citizens) can trace their ancestry back to families living in the southwestern United States in the mid-1800s (Fernandex, 1970). Moreover, for Latino/Hispanic Americans (especially Mexican Americans), the boundaries between the United States and Mexico are seen as artificial. "The geographic, ecological, and cultural blending of the Southwest with Mexico is perceived as a continuing unity of people whose claim to the Southwest is rooted in the land itself" (Montiel, 1978).

While one-third of Mexican Americans can trace their ancestry to families living in the United States in the mid-1800s, the majority of this group migrated into the United States after 1910 because of the economic and political changes that occurred as a result of the Mexican Revolution.

Puerto Rico, on the other hand, was under the domination of Spain until 1897, at which time it was allowed the establishment of a local government. The United States invaded Puerto Rico and annexed it as part of the Spanish–American War (along with Cuba, the Philippines, and Guam) in 1898. Although Cuba (in 1902) and the Philippines (in 1949) were given their independence, Puerto Rico remained a territory of the United States. In 1900, the U.S. Congress passed the Foraker Act, which allowed the president to appoint a governor; to provide an Executive Council consisting of 11 presidential appointees (of which only five had to be Puerto Rican); and to elect locally a 35-member Chamber of Delegates. In reality, the territory was run by the president-appointed governor and the Executive Council. The Jones Act of 1917 made Puerto Ricans citizens of the United States. It was not until 1948 that Puerto Rico elected its first governor, Luis Munoz Marin. In 1952 Puerto Rico was given Commonwealth status, and Spanish was allowed to be the language of instruction in the schools again (with English taught as the second language).

Following World War II, large numbers of Puerto Ricans began migrating into the United States. With citizenship status, Puerto Ricans could travel easily, and they settled in areas on the East Coast, primarily New York City (in part because of the availability of jobs and affordable apartments). The estimated number of Puerto Ricans in the United States is 2 million on the mainland (Therrien & Ramirez, 2002) and 3.97 million on the island (Central Intelligence Agency, 2009).

Cubans immigrated into the United States in three waves. The first wave occurred between 1959 and 1965 and consisted of primarily white, middle-class or upper-class Cubans who were relatively well educated and had business and financial resources. The federal government's Cuban Refugee Program, Cuban Student Loan Program, and Cuban Small Business Administration Loan Program were established to help this first wave of Cuban immigrants achieve a successful settlement (Bernal & Estrada, 1985). The second wave of Cuban immigrants occurred between 1965 and 1973. This wave resulted from the opening of the Port of Camarioca, allowing all who wished to leave Cuba to exit. Those who left as part of the second wave were more often of the working class and lower middle class, primarily white adult men and women. The third wave of immigrants leaving Cuba from Mariel occurred from the summer of 1980 to early 1982. This third wave was the largest (about 125,000 were boat-lifted to the United States) and consisted primarily of working-class persons, more reflective of the Cuban population as a whole than were previous waves. Most immigrated into the United States with hopes for better economic opportunities. Within this group of Marielito were many antisocial, criminal, and mentally ill persons released by Fidel Castro and included in the boat lift (Gavzer, 1993).

In addition to the three major groups that have immigrated to the United States from Mexico, Puerto Rico, and Cuba, there are immigrants from 21 countries of South and Central America, as well as the Caribbean. Arrival of these immigrants for political, economic, and social reasons began in the early 1980s and has added to the diversity of Latino/Hispanic American communities in the United States. The total numbers of some groups, such as the Dominicans (a rapidly growing group on the East Coast), are difficult to determine because of their undocumented entry status within the United States.

DEMOGRAPHICS: DIVERSITY AMONG LATINO/HISPANIC AMERICANS

The historical background illustrates the heterogeneity of Latino/Hispanic Americans. Composed of many different cultural groups, this broad label encompasses significant generational, educational, and socioeconomic differences; varying relocation experiences; and many other varieties of life experience. Although the Spanish language may provide a common thread among most Latino/Hispanic Americans; there are cultural and national differences in terms and expressions used, including nonverbal nuances. Moreover, the language of Brazil is Portuguese, not Spanish, and thus the language connection for Brazilian Latino/Hispanic Americans is unique. As noted earlier, the U.S. Census indicates that the Latino/Hispanic American population numbers about 45.5 million and represents 15.1 percent of the U.S. population making Latino/Hispanic Americans the largest minority group in the United States. (This does not include the 3.97 million people who live in Puerto Rico.) About 76.9 percent of Latino/Hispanic Americans trace their roots to Mexico, Puerto Rico, and Cuba, while the remaining 23.1 percent are from other countries of Central and South America, the Caribbean, and Spain (U.S. Census, 2007). The numerical growth of the Latino/Hispanic American population is the fastest of all American ethnic groups, with more than 10 million people added to the U.S. population between the 1990 and 2000 censuses (Therrien & Ramirez, 2002).

Latino/Hispanic Americans are concentrated in six states: California (29.1 percent), Texas (18.9 percent), Florida (8.3 percent), New York (6.9 percent), Arizona (4.2 percent), and Illinois (4.2 percent). Some of the key demographics information about this population includes the following from the 2007 U.S. Census American Community Survey (the implications of the following demographic information is presented in the "Key Issues in Law Enforcement" section):

1. *Age:*   The Latino/Hispanic American population tends to be younger than the general U.S. population. The median age is 27.6 years, in contrast to 36.4 for the rest of America.
2. *Size of household:*   The average Latino/Hispanic household consists of 3.5 people, nearly one person more for every Latino/Hispanic household than for other U.S. households, which average 2.6 persons per household.
3. *Birthrate:*   Latino/Hispanic Americans have a higher birthrate than the general U.S. population. The average Latino/Hispanic American woman has a birthrate of 2.3 children whereas the average U.S. woman has a birthrate of 1.7 children ("Hispanic Fertility Drives U.S. Population Growth," 2008).
4. *Purchasing power:*   The estimated purchasing power of Latino/Hispanic Americans in the United States will exceed $1.2 trillion by 2012 ("Hispanics Are the Largest Minorities," 2008).
5. *Urban households:*   About 88 percent of all Latino/Hispanic Americans live in metropolitan areas, making this group the most highly urbanized population in the United States. For example, Latino/Hispanic Americans constitute notable percentages of the population for the following large cities: El Paso (74 percent), Corpus Christi (57 percent), San Antonio (52 percent), Fresno (41 percent), Seattle-Tacoma (40 percent), Los Angeles (38 percent), Albuquerque (38 percent), Miami-Ft. Lauderdale (37 percent), Tucson (27 percent), San Diego (25 percent), Austin (24 percent), and San Francisco-Oakland (19 percent) (Therrien & Ramirez, 2002).

6. *Language:* Latino/Hispanic American self-identification is most strongly demonstrated in the knowledge and use of Spanish. The Spanish language is often the single most important cultural aspect retained by Latino/Hispanic Americans. The 2000 U.S. Census indicated that 80 percent of the Latino/Hispanic Americans reported that they spoke Spanish at home. However, the same Census data indicated that over 70 percent of those who spoke Spanish in the home also spoke English "well" or "very well." Latino/Hispanic Americans continue to grow and emerge as a bilingual community capable of communicating in both Spanish and English. The 2003 Yankelovich Monitor Multicultural Study reported that for Latino/Hispanic Americans who learned Spanish as their first language, 44 percent stated that they understood English "very well" and 18 percent stated "somewhat." Over 60 percent of the Latino/Hispanic Americans whose first language is Spanish indicated that they were also proficient in English. The bilingual preferences of Latino/Hispanic Americans were illustrated by the following examples (Yankelovich Monitor, 2003):

- 62 percent of the respondents indicated that "the Spanish language is more important to me now than it was 5 years ago."
- 70 percent stated that Spanish was one of the elements of the culture and traditions that was most important to preserve.
- 84 percent agreed that "all immigrants should learn English if they plan to stay in this country."

In the same 2003 Yankelovich Monitor Multicultural Study, when Latino/Hispanic Americans were asked, "What language would you prefer to use if you could only use one?" 51 percent of the respondents indicated English and another 15 percent did not have a preference for one language over the other. As might be expected, with the large number of Latino/Hispanic Americans born in the United States, English may soon be the dominant language as this population moves into successive future generations.

Typology of Latino/Hispanic Americans

Similar to our typology for Asian/Pacific American individuals, families, and communities, we have developed a seven-part typology that may be useful in understanding and summarizing some of the differences between individuals within the Latino/Hispanic American group (see Exhibit 7.1).

Type I	Latino/Hispanic recently arrived immigrant or refugee (less than 3 years in the United States with major life experiences in Mexico, the Caribbean, or South and Central America)
Type II	Latino/Hispanic immigrant and refugee (3 or more years in the United States with major life experiences in Mexico, the Caribbean, or South and Central America)
Type III	Latino/Hispanic American (second-generation offspring of immigrant or refugee)
Type IV	Latino/Hispanic immigrant (major life experiences in the United States)
Type V	Latino/Hispanic American (third generation or higher in the United States)
Type VI	Latino/Hispanic national (anticipates return to Mexico, the Caribbean, or South and Central America; to include visitors and tourists)
Type VII	Latino/Hispanic multinational (global workplace and residency)

EXHIBIT 7.1 Typology of Latino/Hispanic Americans.

Our typology suggests that as law enforcement, criminal justice, and public safety organizations prepare and train their personnel to work with Latino/Hispanic American communities, a focus on the key differences within each of the typological groups would be most effective. Please refer to Chapter 5 for examples with Asian and Pacific Americans on the use of this typology. It is a convenient framework for discussing how the motivational components within each of the group may affect the way people respond in a law enforcement situation (in this case, people of Latino/Hispanic descent).

MYTHS AND STEREOTYPES

Knowledge of and sensitivity to Latino/Hispanic Americans' concerns, diversity, historical background, and life experiences will facilitate the crime-fighting and peacekeeping mission of law enforcement officers. It is important to have an understanding about some of the myths and stereotypes of Latino/Hispanic Americans that contribute to the prejudice, discrimination, and bias this population encounters. Many law enforcement officers do not have much experience with the diversity of Latino/Hispanic American groups and learn about these groups only through stereotypes (often perpetuated by movies) and through the very limited contact involved in their law enforcement duties. Stereotypic views of Latino/Hispanic Americans reduce individuals within this group to simplistic, one-dimensional characters and have led many Americans to lump members of these diverse groups into one stereotypic group: "Mexicans." It is important for law enforcement officers to be aware of the different stereotypes of Latino/Hispanic Americans. The key to effectiveness with any ethnic or racial group is not that we completely eliminate myths and stereotypes about these groups, but that we are aware of these stereotypes and can monitor our thinking and our behaviors when the stereotypes are not true of those persons with whom we are interacting.

Some of the stereotypes that have affected Latino/Hispanic Americans in law enforcement include the following:

1. *Viewing all Latino/Hispanic Americans as illegal aliens:* Although many may argue over the number of undocumented Latino/Hispanic people in the United States, most Latino/Hispanic Americans do not fall into this stereotype; the vast majority are U.S. citizens or legal residents (U.S. Census, 2008). The issues of undocumented immigrants are complex (see Chapter 1 and previous discussion), but cultural awareness and sensitivity will allow officers the knowledge to avoid an offensive situation often created by acting on the stereotype of Latino/Hispanic Americans as illegal immigrants. The following illustrates this point:

> It is peak season for Mexican migrants looking to cross the Texas border for work this spring and summer. But in this southwestern city known as "the gateway to Mexico," more than 15,000 illegal immigrants have already been thwarted. Gino Rodriguez is a good part of the reason why. While driving along Laredo's dusty western border on a quiet morning, Rodriguez, 43, told me, "I feel I am serving the country. I'm serving my country by helping protect it" . . . But the irony is that many of those who keep watch over our borders each day are, in fact, Mexican-American. Although the U.S. Border Patrol doesn't keep statistics on where its agents are born, agency spokesman Mario Martinez says at least 6,700 of the country's 12,800 Border Patrol agents identify themselves as Hispanic.

> Perhaps not surprisingly, the nation's highest-ranking Border Patrol agent, David Aguilar, also bears a Spanish surname. So, of course, does Rodriguez. He is the son of working-class Mexican immigrants, and many of his relatives still live across the border. Bucking the stereotype of the Mexican-flag-waving, non-English-speaking Latino, Rodriguez has been a proud member of the Border Patrol for 18 years. He has turned away drug smugglers, bandits, gang members and, frequently, illegal migrant workers from Mexico. (Miniter, 2007)

2. *Viewing Latino/Hispanic Americans as lazy and as poor workers:*   This is a stereotype that has been perpetuated in the workplace. Moreover, this stereotype of Latino/Hispanic Americans is often extended to include being a "party people." A workplace law enforcement example illustrates this stereotype:

> A flyer was sent out through interdepartmental mail announcing the retirement party for Sergeant Juan Gomez. The flyer showed a man (with sergeant's stripes) dressed in traditional Mexican garb (sombrero, serape, sandals) sleeping under a large shade tree. While Sergeant Gomez did not appear offended by the stereotype, a Latina nonsworn departmental employee was deeply offended by this flyer and requested that it not be used to announce a party by the organization. The people planning the event said that she was being "overly sensitive" and ignored her request. (police officer's anecdote told at a cultural awareness training session)

It is difficult to understand why some people continue to hold this stereotype or what factors continue to perpetuate it given what we know about the Latino/Hispanic American workforce in the United States and globally. Latino/Hispanic American community advocates make the argument that it is difficult to imagine anyone being labeled as "lazy" or "poor workers" when they are willing to work as laborers from dawn to dusk in the migrant farm fields, day in and day out, year after year.

3. *Perceiving Latino/Hispanic Americans as uneducated and uninterested in educational pursuits:*   Prior to 1948, many Latino/Hispanic American children were denied access to the educational system available to others and instead were relegated to "Mexican" schools. A challenge in the U.S. courts on segregated schools allowed Latino/Hispanic children access to the "regular" school system (see *Mendez v. Westminster School District*, 1946; *Delgado v. Bastrop Independent School District*, 1948). This stereotype of "uneducated" relates to how Latino/Hispanic officers may be inappropriately stereotyped and seen in terms of their ability to learn and to achieve in law enforcement and other professional peacekeeping training. Latino/Hispanic Americans who are native-born have higher educational attainments than those who are foreign-born. Of the native-born Latino/Hispanic Americans 45.9 percent have some college or a college degree, and another 31.5 percent are high school graduates (U.S. Census, 2007). In May 2009, Judge Sonia Sotomayor, a Puerto Rican, was nominated to the Supreme Court. Her education (Yale, Princeton) and her prestigious teaching positions in law (New York University and Columbia Law Schools) were a source of tremendous pride to all groups of Hispanic/Latino Americans. The Washington Post ran an article entitled, "The Latino Reaction: Disparate Group United in Pride" (May 27, 2009). "Her confirmation created widespread joy [in the Latino/Hispanic community] because her biography offers an antidote to so many cultural stereotypes" (Saslow, 2009). Sotomayor was widely held up

as role model as her background defied the possibilities of what she could achieve educationally and professionally.

> "Nobody expects you to be chosen someday for the Supreme Court when your father was a welder with a third-grade education," wrote Richard Lacayo in Time magazine. He is right—the expectations are all otherwise. You can see them on display in many of the reports about Sotomayor's background. She was raised in public housing projects. She grew up in the Bronx . . . Your mind can live anywhere. In the case of the young Sotomayor, it was between the covers of Nancy Drew novels and watching Perry Mason on television. She imagined she could become a lawyer. Now, maybe, a girl like her can imagine becoming a Supreme Court justice. (Cohen, 2009)

> The instructive and inspirational qualities of Sotomayor's life story were also put to immediate use a couple of miles north of the White House, in Columbia Heights. Laura Ramirez Drain, who leads a nonprofit Latina mentoring group, gathered half a dozen schoolgirls and turned Sotomayor's success into part of their morning lesson. "You have to study very hard, and be good, and never break the law, and follow your dreams," Drain told them. (Saslow, 2009)

Most Latino/Hispanic immigrants from Mexico and Central America are uneducated and come from poor or lower-income backgrounds. However, young people, with their access to mass media, are wiser than the older generation about how things work in the United States. On the other hand, most of the South Americans in the United States have been fairly well educated within formal schools because they are often from affluent and educated backgrounds. Because of the great geographic distance, they are usually the only ones who can afford to come to the United States, while their poorer counterparts cannot afford to make the long journey. In the United States, the estimated Latino/Hispanic American population in 2007 with origins in South America is only about 5.3 percent (U.S. Census, 2007).

4. **Seeing Latino/Hispanic American young males as gang members and drug dealers:** Some hold the stereotype, especially among young males in inner cities, that Latino/Hispanic Americans are commonly involved in gangs and the illegal drug trade. Latino/Hispanic cultures are group oriented, and people, young and old, tend to congregate and be identified as groups rather than as individuals or couples. "Hanging out" as a group tends to be the preferred mode of socialization. However, given the stereotype of Latino/Hispanic American young males as being gang members, it is easy to perceive five young Latino/Hispanic males walking together as constituting a "gang." Such stereotypes have resulted in suspicion, hostility, and prejudice toward Latino/Hispanic Americans and have served to justify improper treatment (e.g., routine traffic stops) and poor services (e.g., in restaurants and stores). Such stereotypes can lead law enforcement officers to associate Latino/Hispanic Americans with criminal activity as illustrated in the following account:

> The case of mistaken identity along a White Center street four years ago ultimately sparked an excessive-force complaint, an internal investigation and a lawsuit, but in the end it netted few results: Sandoval-Jimenez was never charged, the officers avoided discipline and the lawsuit eventually was abandoned. The case

did generate piles of paperwork, however. And buried within interview transcripts and internal reports that deconstruct the questionable arrest by Seattle Lt. Donnie Lowe is a telling detail in law enforcement's real-world application of the controversial "obstructing a public officer" offense: How it's sometimes used as leverage. Seattle narcotics officers commonly arrest people for minor offenses, such as obstructing, then offer to drop charges if the suspect provides information fingering other drug suspects, an internal investigation report says. "(Lowe) told the subject that if the subject provided him with at least two names, they would not pursue charges of obstruction and resisting arrest," internal investigations Capt. Mark Evenson wrote. "This is a fairly common practice in narcotics enforcement." But one big problem in this case was Sandoval-Jimenez wasn't a bona fide drug suspect. The then-22-year-old Latin American immigrant and undocumented worker knew nothing about Seattle's drug trade, his attorney says. Officers "kept accusing him of using drugs, but he didn't know what they were talking about," attorney Antonio Salazar said. "My client was clean. He didn't know nothing. They arrested the wrong guy and then tried to justify it." (Kamb, 2008)

5. ***Assuming that all Latino/Hispanic Americans speak Spanish:*** As noted earlier in the chapter, the 2000 U.S. Census data indicated that over 70 percent of those who spoke Spanish in the home also spoke English "well" or "very well." For many Latino/Hispanic Americans, their ancestors have been in the United States for six generations or more, and English is the only language they speak and write. George Perez is a Latino/Hispanic American cultural awareness trainer for many law enforcement, emergency service, and other public service organizations. As one of the outstanding trainers in his field, he is not surprised by the frequently heard stereotypic comment, "You speak English so well, without an accent. How did you do it?" His reply is, "It's the only language I know! I'm a fifth-generation Latino/Hispanic American. I grew up in northern California and received my bachelor's and master's degree in the field that I teach."

THE LATINO/HISPANIC AMERICAN FAMILY

Understanding the importance of family for Latino/Hispanic Americans might be of significant value in community peacekeeping and crime-fighting. Obviously, with over 25 different cultural groups that make up the Latino/Hispanic American category, many differences exist among the groups in this collective in their family experiences. We would like to address some family characteristics that many of the different cultural groups share. *La familia* is perhaps one of the most significant considerations in working and communicating with Latino/Hispanic Americans. (In places where we use the Spanish term, we have done so to indicate the additional cultural meanings encompassed in a term such as *La familia* that are not captured in the English term *family*.) The Latino/Hispanic American family is most clearly characterized by bonds of interdependence, unity, and loyalty, and includes nuclear and extended family members as well as networks of neighbors, friends, and community members. Primary importance is given to the history of the family, which is firmly rooted in the set of obligations tied to both the past and the future. In considering the different loyalty bonds, the parent–child relationship emerges as primary, with all children owing *respeto* to parents (*respeto* connotes cultural meanings beyond those in the English term *respect*). Traditionally, the role of the father has been that of the discipli-narian, decision maker, and head of the household. The father's word is the law, and he is not to be questioned. The father tends to focus his attention on the economic and well-being issues of the family and less on the social and emotional issues. The mother, on the other hand, is seen as balancing the father's role by providing for the emotional and expressive issues of the family. Extended family members such as grandmothers, aunts and uncles, and godparents (*compadrazgo*) may supplement the mother's emotional support. In the Latino/Hispanic American family, the oldest son is traditionally the secondary decision maker to the father and the principal inheritor (*primogenito*) of the family. Because of the central nature of the Latino/Hispanic American family, it is common for police officers to come into contact with members of nuclear and extended families in the course of working with the Latino/Hispanic American community. One key to the success of law enforcement officers in working with the Latino/Hispanic American extended network is the knowledge of how best to communicate within the family context and an understanding of whom to speak with for information, observa-tions, and questions.

The Role of the Man and the Woman in a Latino/Hispanic American Family

In many Latino/Hispanic American families, the relationship and communication patterns are hierarchical with the father as the identified head of the household, who is held in high respect. When it comes to family well-being, economic issues, and discipline, the father may appear to be the decision maker; however, many other individuals may come into the picture. Generally, if there are grandparents in the household, the father may consult them, and also his wife, on major decisions. In the case of law enforcement matters, it may be of great importance if officers can provide the father and the family with some privacy, as much as possible, to discuss key issues and situations. With central values like *respeto* and *machismo* in the Latino/Hispanic American culture, it is critical for the father and other family members to demonstrate control in family situations. Thus, law enforcement officers may find that there is more control in a situation by allowing the citizen to think through a decision, come to the same conclusion as that of the officer, and exercise self-control in behaving in the best interests of all parties concerned.

Within the Latino/Hispanic American family, the sex roles are clearly defined; boys and girls are taught from childhood two different codes of behavior (Comas-Diaz & Griffith, 1988). Traditional sex roles can be discussed in the context of the two codes of gender-related behaviors: *machismo* and *marianismo*. *Machismo* literally means maleness, manliness, and virility. Within the Latino/Hispanic American cultural context, *machismo* means that the male is responsible for the well-being and honor of the family and is in the provider role. Machismo is also associated with having power over women, as well as responsibility for guarding and protecting them. Boys are seen as strong by nature and do not need the protection that is required by girls, who are seen as weak by nature.

Women are socialized into the role of *marianismo*, based on the beliefs about the Virgin Mary, in which women are considered spiritually superior to men and therefore able to endure all suffering inflicted by men (Stevens, 1973). Women are expected to be self-sacrificing in favor of their husbands and children. Within the context of the Latino/Hispanic American family, the role of the woman is as homemaker and caretaker of the children. In the current U.S. context, the traditional gender roles of women and men in the Latino/Hispanic American community have undergone much change, which has resulted in key conflicts. Since women have begun to work, earn money, and have some of the financial independence men have (e.g., they can go out and socialize with others outside of the family), they have started pursuing many experiences inconsistent with the traditional Latino/Hispanic female role. Although there are no clear-cut rules as to whether officers should go to the male head of the household or to the female family member, law enforcement officers would probably be more correct if they address the father first in law enforcement inquiries. Consistent with the cultural values of *machismo* and *marianismo*, the Latino/Hispanic American household appears to be run by the father; however, in actual practice, the mother's role in discipline, education, finance, and decision making is also central.

Children, Adolescents, and Youth

Within the Latino/Hispanic American family, the ideal child is obedient and respectful of his or her parents and other elders. Adults may at times talk in front of the children as if they are not present and as if the children cannot understand the adults' conversations. Children are taught *respeto*, which dictates the appropriate behavior toward all authority figures, older people, parents, relatives, and others. If children are disrespectful, they are punished and scolded. In many traditional families, it is considered appropriate for parents (and for relatives) to physically discipline a disrespectful and misbehaving child.

In Latino/Hispanic American households, there is a high reliance on family members (older children and other adults) to help care for younger children. Both parents within a Latino/Hispanic American family often work. As such, it is not uncommon for Latino/Hispanic American families to have latchkey children or have children cared for by older children in the neighborhood. As in other communities in which English is the second language, in Latino/Hispanic American community children have a special role in being the intermediaries for their parents on external community matters because of the ability of the younger individuals to learn English and the American ways of doing things. Children often serve as translators and interpreters for peace officers in their communication and relations with Latino/Hispanic American families involved in legal matters, immigration concerns, and community resources. Although the use of children and family members as translators is viewed as professionally and culturally inappropriate, often it is the only means available to the law enforcement officer. In such situations, it is suggested that the officer review what role is expected of the youthful member of the family. The officer needs to see how sensitive a topic might be for different family members. Moreover, the consequence of an incorrect translation must be evaluated. (For example, asking a juvenile to translate to his or her parents, who speak no English, that the juvenile has been involved in drinking and riding in a stolen vehicle may result in significantly changed content.) Because of the embarrassment and fear of punishment on the part of the juvenile, and possibly a sense of shame or embarrassment to the parents, the message may be altered by the child to avoid negative ramifications. In all cases, when a child is acting as a translator for parents, the officer should direct all verbal and nonverbal communication to the parents. Otherwise, the parents may view the officer's lack of attention to them as an insult. Such sensitivity by the peace officer is particularly important for Latino/Hispanic Americans because of the cultural value of *personalismo*, which emphasizes the importance of the personal quality of any interaction. This cultural concept implies that relationships occur between particular individuals as persons, not as representatives of institutions (e.g., law enforcement), or merely as individuals performing a role (e.g., as a person who enforces the law).

Cross-National Family Issues

The typology of the Latino/Hispanic American provided in Exhibit 7.1 helps to identify the different immigration and migration patterns within Latino/Hispanic American communities. This typology can also be used to understand the family, personal, and political issues involved in the interactions of Latino/Hispanic Americans crossing several types. For example, the Latino/Hispanic American (third generation or later; Type V) category consists of individuals who desire to choose which aspects of the old culture to keep and which of the new culture to accept. The focus is on choosing activities, values, norms, and lifestyles that blend the best of that which is Latino/Hispanic and the best of that which is American. Being bicultural is a unique and important aspect of this group. However, much conflict may occur when there are family issues that involve cross-national value differences between being American and being bicultural, as was illustrated in the custody case of 9-year-old Elian Gonzalez (Lewis, 2000). In this particular case, Elian Gonzalez had escaped from Cuba with his mother, and during the hazardous trip, the mother died at sea. Elian's relatives in Miami took the boy into their home; however, Elian's father, a Cuban national, fought to regain legal custody of his son and to return him to Cuba. Local law enforcement agencies were working with the Cuban American community in Miami to maintain order while the family was trying to negotiate a workable settlement with Elian Gonzalez's father. In the meantime, U.S. Attorney General Janet Reno ordered armed U.S. immigration agents to seize the boy in a surprise predawn raid. The boy was returned to his father in Cuba, and the Cuban American community protested and clashed with the Miami police, resulting in more than 260 arrests (Bragg, 2000). As illustrated by the case, today's law enforcement personnel may often have to intervene in such family and domestic disputes as well as in cross-national political situations involved in community peacekeeping assignments.

COMMUNICATON STYLES OF LATINO/HISPANIC AMERICANS

Although we do not wish to create stereotypes of any kind, key features of Latino/Hispanic American verbal and nonverbal communication styles necessitate explanation. Misunderstanding resulting from style differences can result in perceptions of poor community services from police agencies, conflicts resulting from such misunderstandings, and safety and control issues for the peace officer.

1. Latino/Hispanic Americans' high cultural value for *la familia* results in a very strong family and group orientation. As such, officers should not view the frequently seen behavior of "eye checking" with other family members before answering and the lack of the use of "I" statements and/or self-reference as Latino/Hispanic Americans not being straightforward about themselves or their relationships. The officer may be concerned because a Latino/Hispanic American witness may wish to use the pronoun "we" when the situation may call for a personal observation involving an "I" statement. For example, a Latino/Hispanic American family member who witnessed a store robbery may first non-verbally check with other family members before describing what he or she saw. Such verbal and nonverbal behavior is consistent with the family and group orientation of Latino/Hispanic Americans.

2. Speaking Spanish to others in the presence of a law enforcement officer, even though the officer requested responses in English, should not automatically be interpreted as an insult to or an attempt to hide information from the officer. In times of stress, those who speak English as a second language automatically revert to their first and native language. In a law

enforcement situation, many individuals may find themselves under stress and may speak Spanish, which is the more accessible and comfortable language for them. Moreover, speaking Spanish gives the individual a greater range of expression (to discuss and clarify complex issues with other speakers and family members), thus yielding clearer, more useful information to law enforcement personnel about critical events.

3. It is important for officers to take the time to get information from witnesses, victims, and suspects even if the individuals have limited skills in speaking English (the use of officers who speak Spanish, translators, and language bank resources will help). Often Latino/Hispanic Americans have not been helped in crime-fighting and peacekeeping situations because officers could not or did not take information from nonnative English speakers.

> The officer was penned in by about 20 people outside a dimly lit apartment complex. That number swelled as more people streamed out of their homes, yet he remained at ease. His hands moved rapidly—punctuating each of his sentences—but they never strayed toward the firearm or radio attached to his belt. The only thing he needed this night was his voice. "That's something they don't teach you at the academy," he said as the crowd began to disperse after a lengthy chat. "Getting surrounded is the last thing you'd want, but I'm not trying to arrest anybody. I just want to talk." Ivan Pena, a 16-year Jacksonville Sheriff's Office veteran, is one of a new breed of community-oriented officers who is more ambassador than enforcer. He is a member of the International Affairs Unit, which he said was formed in 2006 to provide a pipeline to Duval County's non-English-speaking population. It's a segment that has privately voiced concerns about sometimes being profiled or ignored. The three members of the unit, who are stationed in a crowded room in the Police Memorial Building downtown, are Puerto Rican and speak fluent Spanish. Officer Leticia Freeman occasionally alternates tongues. "I can hablo Espanol muy bueno, thank you very much," she said to a caller asking for translation assistance. Freeman, a recent addition to the unit, also is a 16-year Sheriff's Office veteran. The team is rounded out by Officer Marta Crespo. They all help with translation and assist detectives with Spanish-speaking suspects and witnesses, but they each has specific functions within the unit. Pena takes to the streets and mingles in Hispanic communities. He said he provides residents with tips to avoid criminals looking to prey on targets burdened by problems with the language. Crespo goes to businesses in Spanish neighborhoods to gauge area safety. Freeman serves as the utility player, filling in the blanks between her co-workers' beats. (Coleman, 2009)

4. Although Latino/Hispanic Americans may show respect to law enforcement officers because of police authority, they do not necessarily trust the officers or the organization. *Respeto* is extended to elders and those who are in authority. This respect is denoted in the Spanish language by the use of *usted* (the formal you) rather than *tu* (the informal you). Showing respect, however, does not ensure trust. The cultural value of *confianza* (or trust) takes some time to develop. Like many from ethnic minority communities, Latino/Hispanic Americans have experienced some degree of prejudice and discrimination from the majority community, and citizens with such experiences need time to

develop trust with law enforcement officers, who are identified as being a part of the majority community.

5. The cultural value of *personalismo* emphasizes the importance of the person involved in any interaction. Latino/Hispanic Americans take into strong consideration not only the content of any communication but also the context and relationship of the communicator. This means, for effective communications, it is important for the officer to provide information about why questions are asked, who is the person asking the question (i.e., information about the officer), and how the information will be used in the context. In addition, context for Latino/Hispanic Americans means taking some time to find out, as well as to self-disclose, some background information (e.g., living in the same neighborhood, having similar concerns about crime). Additional contextual elements, such as providing explanations and information to Latino/Hispanic Americans about procedures, laws, and so forth before asking them questions or requesting their help, will ease the work of the officer. By providing background information and establishing prior relationships with community members, law enforcement agencies and officers build a context for cooperation with Latino/Hispanic American individuals.

6. Officers should recognize nonverbal and other cultural nuances that may detract from effective communication. Many Latino/Hispanic Americans, especially younger individuals, find it uncomfortable and sometimes inappropriate to maintain eye contact with authority figures such as police officers. Strong eye contact with someone who is of higher position, importance, or authority is considered a lack of *respeto* in Latin/Hispanic American cultures. As such, many citizens from this background may deflect their eyes from police officers. It is important that officers not automatically read this nonverbal behavior as indicative of a lack of trust or as a dishonest response.

7. Latino/Hispanic Americans may exhibit behaviors that appear to be evasive, such as claiming not to have any identification or saying that they do not speak English. In some of the native countries from which many Latino/Hispanic Americans have emigrated, the police and law enforcement agencies are aligned with a politically repressive government. The work of the police and of law enforcement in those countries is not one of public service. Therefore, many Latino/Hispanic Americans may have similar "fear" reactions to law enforcement officers in the United States. It is suggested that officers take the time to explain the need for identification and cooperation, and that they acknowledge the importance of comprehension on the part of the Latino/ Hispanic American individual(s) involved.

> Carlos and his family had escaped from one of the South American countries where he saw the police serving as part of the politically repressive force upon his community. He was aware of the role of some of the police as members of the "death squad." He and his family were admitted to the United States and given political asylum and lived in southern California. Although he speaks fluent English and Spanish and has been in the United States for over 5 years, he relates how on one occasion when he was pulled over by the police (for a broken taillight) he automatically had this fear reaction and had the thought of saying to the officer, "No habla English," in the hope of avoiding any further contact. (Latino/Hispanic American trainer's anecdote told in a police cultural awareness training course)

KEY ISSUES IN LAW ENFORCEMENT

Underreporting of Crimes

Latino/Hispanic Americans, because of their past experiences with some of the law enforcement agencies within their countries of origin (e.g., repressive military force in their native country as well as perceived "unresponsiveness" by police), are reluctant to report crimes and may not seek police assistance or help. Many people bring with them memories of how police within their home countries have brutalized and violated them and others (e.g., as members of the death squad). In addition, many immigrants and refugees are just not knowledgeable about the legal system of the United States and may try to avoid any contact with law enforcement personnel. Outreach and community-policing perspectives will enhance the contacts and relationships with Latino/Hispanic American communities and may help alleviate the underreporting of crimes.

Police are concerned that some Hispanic residents aren't reporting when they are victims of crime.

> Since January, 10 aggravated robberies have been reported to the Rogers Police Department, Cpl. Kelley Cradduck said. In each case, victims reported being robbed by two or more Hispanic men who stole wallets, money or personal items. In all but one of the cases, the victims have also been Hispanic. But Cradduck said the number of Hispanic victims is expected to be much higher, but they are not reporting crimes out of fear. He said it's possible that because Hispanics don't report crimes, it makes them a target. "[Hispanics] don't always report because they don't trust cops," Cradduck said Friday. "It's sad because they may have information that will solve the case." According to a recent victimization study by the U.S. Department of Justice, Hispanics are less likely to report crimes to police than non-Hispanics by at least 8 percent. (Crawford, 2005)

Victimization

The Bureau of Justice Statistics National Crime Victimization Survey (Catalano, 2005), "Criminal Victimization 2004," indicated that Hispanics were victims of overall violence and simple assault at rates lower than were non-Hispanics in 2004. Hispanics and non-Hispanics were equally likely to experience rape/sexual assault, robbery, aggravated assault, and theft. Although the Bureau of Justice Statistics' report indicated lower rates of overall violence and simple assault victimization of Latino/Hispanic Americans, advocates of Latino/Hispanic American community are concerned that such crimes may be underreported, as noted in the following example:

> You've heard the explanations of why Hispanics are targeted for robbery: They're less likely to have bank accounts and are more likely to carry cash. And they're less likely to run to the cops since the police, as well as the banks, in their homelands tend to be untrustworthy. Because of that, "they're the perfect victim," said Richmond police Lt. Michael A. Zohab, who covers a section of South Richmond with a high percentage of Hispanics. Citywide, Hispanics represent 8 percent to 10 percent of the population, based on estimates from Richmond's Hispanic Liaison Office. The 2000 census indicated that Hispanics made up about 3 percent of Richmond's population. Zohab said robbery victims "weren't even calling the police because they were scared we were going to do something to them." Police and community activists have been working hard to combat

> that perception, and it's working. Hispanics are now much more likely to report crimes than they were three years ago. In 2004, they represented 11 percent of the city's 1,300 robbery victims. In 2005, they made up 16 percent of the victims. Now, it's 25 percent. "It's going to go even higher," Zohab predicted. (Holmberg, 2006, p. B1)

As noted by Rennison (2002) in the Bureau of Justice Statistics Special Report "Hispanic Victims of Violent Crime, 1990–2000," Hispanics most vulnerable to violent crimes were males (54 victimizations per 1,000 annually), juveniles aged 12 to 17 (90 per 1,000), those with household incomes under $7,500 (64 per 1,000), and those who had never married (72 per 1,000). Violence against Hispanics, as with other victims, most often took the form of simple assault (59 percent). About equal percentages of Hispanics were robbed (20 percent) or were victims of aggravated assault (19 percent). Two percent of Hispanic victims of violence sustained a rape or sexual assault in 2000 (Rennison, 2002). The following case example illustrates the specifics of the report:

> Anthony Michael Hatcher, 18, and Dominique Vallier, 17, were wanted by the Baton Rouge Police Department on multiple warrants for violent offenses stemming from shootings that occurred in the Boulevard de Province area. The duo was also charged with other individual robbery counts and Hate Crimes charges for specifically targeting Hispanic victims due to their nationality. Baton Rouge Police Department Detectives have charged the two suspects in connection with the shootings of two Hispanic men at 1718 Boulevard de Province last month. The shootings occurred on Monday, February 23rd and Tuesday, February 24th. In the first case, a 26-year old Hispanic male was shot in the leg when he intervened in the attempted robbery of his 29-year old brother. In that incident the robber's gun was taken away from him during the struggle. In the second case, a 37-year old Hispanic male was shot in the chest at the same apartment complex in apparent retaliation for the previous day's resistance, even though this victim was not in any way involved in the earlier incident. Detectives identified Hatcher as the shooter in both cases and Vallier as an accomplice in the attempted robbery/shooting on the 23rd. Both men were also book [sic] as fugitives from the Houma, Louisiana Police Department. Houma PD Detectives have charged both men with 1st Degree Murder and Attempted 1st Degree Murder for unrelated cases there. (U.S. Department of Justice, 2009)

Differential Treatment

Many of the crimes within Latino/Hispanic American communities are perpetrated by members themselves of the same ethnic group. In addition, for this community, as noted in the Bureau of Justice Statistics Report, more than half of the violent crimes are committed by strangers (Rennison, 2002). Law enforcement officials have often found it difficult to get cooperation from Latino/Hispanic American crime victims. To some degree, this lack of cooperation relates to the fear of retaliation within the Latino/Hispanic community. Other concerns of the Latino/Hispanic American victim include (1) the perceived nonresponsiveness of the peacekeeping officers and agencies, (2) lack of familiarity with and trust in police services, (3) perceived lack of effectiveness of the law enforcement agencies, and (4) stereotypes and images of law enforcement agencies as discriminatory. A key challenge for police agencies is to educate this group and to work cooperatively with the communities to reduce crime.

Racial Profiling of Latino/Hispanic Americans

Racial profiling, as discussed in Chapter 13, is a major problem and concern for people within minority groups. This is particularly so for African Americans and Arab Americans, and also for Latino/Hispanic Americans. They believe that the determining factor in whether peace officers exercise their discretion in stopping a vehicle driven by a Latino/Hispanic American has to do with the driver's race and ethnicity. To many Latino/Hispanic Americans, racial profiling may even be "encouraged," as noted in the following example:

> U.S. Immigration and Customs Enforcement agents arrested 24 Hispanics at a convenience store in Baltimore two years ago after their supervisor told them to "bring more bodies" because they were behind their annual quota of 1,000 arrests per team, according to an ICE report released Wednesday. The immigration rights group CASA de Maryland, which has accused ICE of racial profiling in the 2007 raid, released the agency's internal investigation report and said it shows that the agents acted improperly. The report contradicts some sworn declarations made by ICE agents involved in the sweep, prompting the agency's Acting Assistant Secretary John Torres to ask for an investigation into inconsistencies, ICE spokeswoman Ernestine Fobbs said Wednesday. Meanwhile, CASA officials have called on Department of Homeland Security Secretary Janet Napolitano to review the agency's enforcement policies. "Government agents should not be in the business of judging people based on the color of their skin, clothing and employment, which is what seems to have occurred here," the Rev. Simon Bautista Betances, vice president of CASA's board of directors said Wednesday. CASA officials have charged that ICE agents ignored blacks and whites at the 7-Eleven store as they rounded up all of the Hispanics, even crossing the street to detain Hispanics waiting at a bus stop. (Gaynair, 2009)

According to Hill and Trapp (2000), "Every study of racial profiling shows that, contrary to popular belief, people of color are not more likely to carry drugs or other contraband in their vehicles than whites. In Maryland, the percentage of black and white drivers carrying contraband was statistically identical. The U.S. Customs Service's own figures show that while over 43 percent of those searched were minorities, the 'hit rates' for these searches were actually lower for people of color than for whites." In a study by the San Diego Police Department (Hill & Trapp, 2000), African Americans and Latino/Hispanic Americans were stopped more often than would be expected given their numbers in the local population; that is, 40 percent of those stopped and 60 percent of those searched were African Americans or Latino/Hispanic Americans, whereas both groups together represent only 28 percent of the driving population. The Associated Press (2005) study conducted in Illinois illustrates the racial profiling issues for Latino/Hispanic Americans (and other minorities):

> Black and Hispanic drivers in large downstate cities are pulled over by police at a rate that far exceeds their share of the local population, according to an analysis of data from more than 2 million traffic stops last year. Springfield had the biggest gap: 42 percent of its traffic stops involved minorities even though its population is only 16 percent minority. It was followed by cities such as Peoria, Rockford and Joliet. An Associated Press analysis of the traffic study also found that after being pulled over, minorities were more likely to be ticketed than white drivers. And minority drivers

were more likely to have their cars searched and to be found with drugs and weapons, the numbers show. Some police departments contend the data is flawed and doesn't paint an accurate picture of their work. But minority leaders say the results show police sometimes target minorities. "I really don't need statistics to tell me racial profiling is an issue or that it exists," said Sen. Kwame Raoul, D-Chicago. "I think the statistics serve more than the purpose of identifying whether a problem exists. It helps hopefully to target the problem." The study was approved in 2003 at the urging of minority groups and lawmakers who complained that too many people were being pulled over simply for "driving while black" or Hispanic. (Associated Press, 2005)

Law Enforcement Issues Involving Immigration and Customs Enforcement (ICE)

One of the key situations for a law enforcement agency involves decision making whereby the local public safety agencies and departments become involved in enforcing and working with the Immigration and Customs Enforcement (ICE) section, now a part of the Department of Homeland Security, as noted in Chapter 1. The ramifications for Latino/Hispanic American community relationships and network-building are significant. The decision making and strategic responses to the enforcement of ICE efforts are not clear cut, nor "givens," for any law enforcement agency. However, the general argument in support of leaving undocumented immigrants alone (unless they have committed a criminal act or are creating a disturbance) is based on the perspective that tracking down and deporting undocumented workers is technically the job of the ICE and not the police. Central to the clarity of roles required by the officer in the field is the delineation by police agencies of specific policies related to determining, reporting, and turning in such immigrants to ICE. Sometimes the trust of the entire community (undocumented and documented) is at stake with the Latino/Hispanic American community. Police departments have clearly made it known to immigrant community members the circumstances under which the decisions are made not to contact and/or to turn in undocumented immigrants to ICE. This has often been the result of Latino/Hispanic American citizen complaints.

The Balcones Heights Police Department will no longer call immigration authorities when encountering people without identification, city leaders said this week. The change in practice comes after several community activists held a protest rally against the Police Department last month, accusing officers of racially profiling Hispanics and committing other egregious acts, such as going into homes and asking residents their immigration status. While city officials deny wrongdoing by officers, they agreed to no longer use U.S. Immigration and Customs Enforcement to help identify people. "We just want the department to be consistent, so that there can't be any perception that we're treating people differently," City Attorney Frank Garza said. City officials also stress that despite the activists' claims, no one has come forward to file a formal complaint against the department for racial profiling. Victor San Miguel of the Brown Berets, which helped organize the Feb. 9 protest, lauded city administrators for being receptive to activists' concerns and agreeing to investigate any complaints that may be filed. (Zarazua, 2009)

Latino/Hispanic Americans must be able to trust that they will be treated fairly and protected as part of their involvement and association with local law enforcement and public safety. This is of particular importance when there might be some perceptions, assumptions, and/or stereotypes among community residents as to who might end up being reported to ICE and who might be questioned by ICE (with the possibility of deportation and detention because of real or suspected immigration status). The following recommendations are made for local law enforcement agencies in working with the Latino/Hispanic American community, concerning legal and undocumented immigration status:

1. ***Develop agency and departmental policies with regard to reporting and working with ICE:***   Law enforcement agencies must have clear policies and procedures to address the circumstances in reporting to ICE. The policy must include (1) the circumstances under which a person will be reported to ICE; and (2) that no person will be reported or referred to ICE where no laws have been violated.

2. ***Maintain contact with the Latino/Hispanic American community leaders:***   Law enforcement officers need to work closely with community leaders to establish a cooperative plan to inform them of the agency's policies and their implementation. Often, announcements made by Latino/Hispanic American community leaders, to inform their respective communities of any fears associated with reporting crimes and/or assistance to the police department, have been very helpful. Community leaders could, for example, work with law enforcement agencies' community relations officers to develop a communication plan for the effective dissemination of information about their policies in working with ICE.

3. ***Utilize a communication plan:***   It is essential to have a well-developed and pilot-tested communication plan to ensure that the proper messages are provided to the community when it involves a person who may or may not be reported or referred to ICE. This is particularly important when language translations and interpreting are necessary. A carefully pretested "core message" regarding the department's procedures will usually work better than on-the-spot messages subject to the momentary interpretation of those who first hear such information.

4. ***Clearly define the implications for any contact with the law enforcement agency and possible reporting to ICE:***   When it comes to the possibility that a contact with the local police department may result in a person being questioned by ICE and/or being involved in deportation procedures, members from Latino/Hispanic American communities tend to be quite cautious. The fear that they might be stereotyped as "illegal" (or having experienced prejudice by others in this regard) would naturally make any contact with law enforcement agencies and officers tenuous. It is essential to provide clearly defined procedures and information as to how any contact would normally be reported or not be reported to ICE. In addition, if there are possible consequences of such reporting, these elements should be clearly stated to ensure an ongoing relationship of trust with members of the Latino/Hispanic American community involved.

5. ***Train all sworn and nonsworn personnel with respect to the agency or departmental policy for working with ICE:***   Law enforcement agencies need to provide training and education to enable officers to effectively utilize legal enforcement tools so that they can perform their work professionally and effectively within today's multicultural communities. Clearly, most law enforcement officers know not to act based on the prejudices and stereotypes that they might hold. However, the nature of prejudice is such that some people are not aware of their prejudices or biases. Therefore, they make inferences and take actions toward certain groups based upon these biased perceptions, such as who might or might not be an unauthorized migrant and/or an undocumented immigrant. Establishing training that provides accurate

information concerning groups for which officers might have prejudices and stereotypes is one of the approaches police departments should use to ensure implementation of the department's policy in working with ICE.

6. *Utilize Latino/Hispanic American law enforcement personnel and translators/interpreters from the same or similar communities:*   To the extent that it is possible, the use of law enforcement personnel from the same or similar Latino/Hispanic American communities would add to the sustaining of relationships and trust necessary in law enforcement within these communities.

7. *Ensure Latino/Hispanic community outreach services:*   Every police and community interaction requires a strong, ongoing link to community groups and advocacy organizations. A link is established when community task forces are assembled to address issues, especially issues involving possible police interactions with undocumented immigrants and/or unauthorized migrants. These steps demonstrate respect for the Latino/Hispanic American community and create shared responsibility for whatever action is taken. The police hold primary responsibility for community outreach on every level, but the community is also responsible for becoming involved in activities that form positive relationships with the police. Policing within the community can function only in an environment of mutual engagement and respect.

8. *Provide real-time linkage and referral to Latino/Hispanic community-based advocacy services:*   Police departments may want to provide real-time linkage and referral to the resources and community-based advocacy services available to facilitate knowledge dissemination regarding any police interactions that might involve people with undocumented immigration issues. In this way, Latino/Hispanic American citizens would have a third-party opinion and support for their actions. Law enforcement's referral of Latino/Hispanic citizens to these services would facilitate and support the trust-building and relationships necessary to work effectively in the Latino/Hispanic American community.

ICE cooperation by local law enforcement agencies is of particular concern for the Latino/Hispanic American community where there has been a history of legal as well as undocumented immigration. Indeed, some Latino/Hispanic American community members will be prosecuted and deported. However, where no wrong has been committed, then law enforcement must keep a check on potential stereotyping and the prejudicial act of singling out individuals based on those stereotypes.

Exposure to Environmental Risk and Job Hazards

"Still Toxic after All These Years: Environmental Justice in the San Francisco Bay Area" (Cuff, 2007), a Report of the Center for Justice, Tolerance, and Community at the University of California, Santa Cruz, continues to echo the concerns raised by Morales and Bonilla (1993) that Latino/Hispanic Americans in the state of California lived in some of the most polluted neighborhoods and worked in many of the most hazardous jobs. For example, in Oakland, California, 24 percent of whites and 69 percent of Latino/Hispanic Americans live in communities with hazardous waste sites; in Los Angeles, the percentages are 35 for whites and 60 for Latino/Hispanic Americans. In addition to Latino/Hispanic American community members' concerns regarding crime and violence are the concerns for the environmental safety of their homes and fears over their exposures to environmental hazards and risks. Such concerns add to the role of law enforcement and peace officers within Latino/Hispanic American communities.

In addition, some job risks are related to stereotypic and oppressive actions of coworkers in creating a hostile work environment:

> Twelve Hispanic workers at a Grand Junction aerospace plant won a $1.25 million settlement after dropping a discrimination suit alleging they were subjected to racial slurs and taunting by white co-workers. Hamilton Sundstrand, a prime contractor for NASA, Boeing and Lockheed Martin, agreed to the payout this week to resolve a 2003 discrimination lawsuit brought by the Equal Employment Opportunity Commission. Documents filed in Denver federal court state the money is solely for "emotional distress damages." . . . Denver EEOC attorney Anjuli Kelotra said racial harassment at the Mesa County plant was tolerated by supervisors since at least 1997. "It was a day-after-day barrage," said Kelotra, referring to the ethnic name-calling. "It hurts the ears to hear it." Lead plaintiff Raymond Arellano, 45, alleged he was choked by one of the taunting workers in January 2000 and then labeled a "problem child" after reporting the attack to managers. At times, even managers used ethnic slurs when referring to Hispanic employees, said the suit. Bill Martinez, a former EEOC attorney representing Arellano, said of the roughly 250 workers at the nonunion plant, no more than 20 were Hispanic. Some of the racial hostility directed toward Hispanics seemed related to the relatively high wages the plant paid to all workers, regardless of their education and race, he said. "There is a real mentality in that town that Hispanics should be out in the fields or washing dishes in restaurants, but not taking $25 an hour machinist jobs from whites," Martinez said. (Accola, 2005)

Law enforcement professionals need to be alert to environmental risks, including workplace exploitation of Latino/Hispanic Americans, and particularly sensitive to the fear many immigrants have in reporting crimes to the police.

Discrimination Against Latino/Hispanic Americans in the Criminal Justice System

In the report supported by the National Council of the La Raza, Walker, Senger, Villarruel, and Arboleda (2004) provided a comprehensive review of the ways in which Latino/Hispanic Americans are discriminated against in the criminal justice system. This population was shown to be discriminated against in every facet of their arrest, prosecution, defense, and sentencing. Moreover, they were more likely to receive jail sentences than non-Hispanic Whites for the same offenses committed, with many of these charges related to nonviolent, low-level drug offenses (Walker et al., 2004).

Increasing Police Services to the Latino/Hispanic American Community

The Police Neighborhood Resource Center model, started in 1991 in the largely Hispanic community of Rolling Meadows, Illinois, has shown the positive results of cooperation among the police department, the Latino/Hispanic American community, and the local and regional businesses. However, given changes in the neighborhood and economic realities, the Police Neighborhood Resource Center model may have difficulties in continuing:

> City officials first established the Police Neighborhood Resource Center in the heart of the East Park Apartments in 1991 as a way to reach out to the mostly Spanish-speaking immigrant community. Currently more than 1,000 residents live in the

area, said City Manager Tom Melena. The center was also opened to reduce crime in the area—which in the early '90s was rampant, said Rolling Meadows Police Chief Steve Williams. City officials budgeted $367,606 for the resource center in 2009. The money pays for salaries of social workers, police, supplies and rent. Williams is not in favor of cutting these funds, which makes up the center's entire operating budget. "It's not a wise decision, but it's your decision," he told the council on Tuesday. "There's a reason why we opened the center in 1991. Back then there was prostitution in the alleys, burglaries and people were afraid to live there." However, Aldermen Larry Buske called the center "a money pit." "Those funds should be spread around this city," he said. "When the chief started the PNRC, it was meant to run for five to seven years. It's played itself out. Time to cut the strings." Victoria Bran, the director of the center, declined to comment on Wednesday. (Ahern, 2008)

The outreach approach of using bilingual community service officers (CSOs) who are nonsworn officers (i.e., they hold badges and wear uniforms) to serve the ethnic communities in San Diego, California, provides yet another viable model for the Latino/Hispanic American community as a whole. The CSOs provide many of the informational, referral, educational, and crime-reporting services available through the police department. The use of bilingual CSOs increases the effectiveness of law enforcement in Spanish-speaking communities. The use of Latino/Hispanic American police outreach coordinators is similar to the CSO approach:

As several players socialized after a soccer game behind Gaithersburg Middle School last month, they were approached by a group of young men wearing bandanas over their faces and wielding knives and baseball bats. They announced they were part of the MS-13 gang. The soccer players ran from the gang, and the suspects fled when they heard police sirens approaching—but not before stabbing a 30-year-old man from Gaithersburg who had to be hospitalized briefly. Soon after the incident, Officer Luis Hurtado, the Hispanic liaison in the Montgomery County Police Department's community outreach section, went to the local Spanish-language media to discuss the incident and ask anyone with information to call a police hotline. An anonymous tipster came forward. He called police after seeing the crime reported on Spanish-language station Univision and gave investigators some information, Montgomery police spokesman Derek Baliles said. Now, police are asking the same tipster to contact them again about the June 26 incident, one of numerous efforts by Montgomery investigators to combat gangs by reaching out to the Latino community. Their main goals: preventing youths from joining local gangs and cracking down on gang activity. But authorities say they also are trying to overcome language and cultural barriers to appeal to Hispanic adults, many of whom are foreign-born and reluctant to interact with law enforcement. As the Hispanic community continues attracting immigrants, efforts by police to gain its trust and cooperation against gangs must be frequently renewed, Hurtado said. "The community changes so quickly that you have to keep reinforcing the same issues over and over and over again," he said. (Cativo, 2005)

Law enforcement should be aware of the need to bridge the service gap and to reinforce the Latino/Hispanic American community with local and statewide law enforcement and public safety agencies. To this end, meetings between police executives and Latino/Hispanic American leaders of community-based and advocacy agencies have been found to be helpful:

> Philadelphia Police Commissioner Charles H. Ramsey acknowledged after a meeting yesterday with Latino leaders that the trust between police and that community "has been shaken" by allegations of misconduct by officers raiding the stores of immigrant merchants. "We obviously have a lot of work to do to mend a lot of fences with the community," he said after the hour-long meeting at City Hall. He also encouraged merchants with previously undisclosed allegations to come forward. He vowed that there would be no retaliation against anyone with a complaint against police. Members of the Latino delegation called the meeting a good first step in rebuilding trust, but said they would continue to closely follow the investigations of officers who allegedly took money and merchandise from stores while conducting raids. "We support the Philadelphia Police Department, but we do not support corruption," Danilo Burgos, president of the Dominican Business Association, told reporters after the meeting. "He listened first, and then he responded point by point to our concerns," said Pedro Rodriguez of United Neighbors Against Drugs, calling the closed-door meeting "fruitful." Councilwoman Maria Quiñones-Sánchez arranged the meeting after the Latino delegation wrote to Ramsey on Monday asking to meet him face to face. "I think he's under a cloud right now with all the different incidents," she said, referring also to an incident involving State Rep. Jewell Williams in which an officer allegedly made racially inflammatory comments. Ramsey on Monday apologized to Williams, who allegedly was roughed up during a March incident. Two officers were conducting a car stop when Williams arrived and allegedly offered to assist the officers. One of the officers ordered Williams back into his own car, and later handcuffed him and made him lie sideways in the back seat of a police cruiser. Williams was not arrested. Quiñones-Sánchez said the attendees agreed to have a public meeting in 60 days to address police-community relations. A growing number of Latino merchants have alleged that they were the subject of police raids for drug paraphernalia in which officers disabled store security cameras, then stole money and merchandise. (Moran, 2009)

Other efforts to build Latino/Hispanic police-community relationship in cities like Durham, North Carolina, have experimented with the Spanish Police Academy (Associated Press, 2003). The classes meet twice each week and mirror the regular Citizens' Police Academy, with the major difference being the use of translators. Another way to bridge the gap is to have officers learn Spanish, and some officers will attest that even "survival" Spanish-language training and "crash courses" in minority community relations (Taylor, 2000) have some degree of effectiveness.

The willingness of law enforcement officers to use Spanish phrases in their interactions with Latino/Hispanic Americans is very useful even if the officers have not attained Spanish-language fluency. The use of everyday greetings and courteous phrases in Spanish indicates officers' respect and positive attitude and is seen favorably by members of the Latino/Hispanic American community. (See Chapter 4 for a discussion of language training in police departments.)

Increasing the Number of Latino/Hispanic American Police Officers

In the past decade, Latino/Hispanic Americans have significantly increased their numbers in federal, state, and local law enforcement positions. In 2004, of the total of 105,000 full-time, federal law enforcement officers with arrest and firearm authority, Latino/Hispanic Americans comprised

17.7 percent (Reaves, 2006). For local police departments, from 2000 to 2003, the number of Latino/Hispanic American officers increased by 4,700, which brings them to 9.6 percent of the total full-time sworn and nonsworn personnel in local police departments (Hickman & Reaves, 2006a). For sheriffs' offices, during the same period, the number of Latino/Hispanic American officers increased by 1,960, which brings them to 7.4 percent of the total full-time sworn and nonsworn personnel in sheriffs' offices (Hickman & Reaves, 2006b). With respect to full-time federal officers with arrest and firearm authority, the highest percentages of Latino/Hispanic American officers are found at the Customs and Border Protection (CBP) at 36.9 percent and at the Immigration and Customs Enforcement (ICE) at 22.0 percent (Reaves, 2006). However, as noted by the U.S. Office of Personnel Management (2007), Latino/Hispanic Americans remain the only underrepresented ethnic group in the overall government workforce, when compared to their present level of percentage representation in the national Civilian Labor Force (CLF).

Latino/Hispanic Americans are still underrepresented in local police departments and sheriffs' offices. Local law enforcement's attempts to effectively serve states, cities, and community neighborhoods with large Latino/Hispanic American populations are still hampered by the proportionately small number of Latino/Hispanic American officers (given the dispersion of the Latino/Hispanic American population within the United States). A variety of reasons exist for such underrepresentation in local police departments and sheriffs' offices, including (1) history of law enforcement stereotypes and relationships with Latino/Hispanic American communities; (2) interest of Latino/Hispanic Americans in law enforcement careers; (3) image of law enforcement personnel in Latino/Hispanic American communities; (4) lack of knowledge about the different careers and pathways in law enforcement; (5) concern with and fear of background checks and immigration status, physical requirements, and the application process; (6) ineffective and misdirected law enforcement recruitment and outreach efforts within the Latino/Hispanic American community; and (7) lack of role models and advocates for law enforcement careers for Latino/Hispanic Americans.

Clearly, role models are needed to help clarify to the community what is required for a career in law enforcement. Law enforcement agencies have clearly seen the need for increasing their ability to serve the Latino/Hispanic American community with more bilingual/bicultural personnel. The following examples have been used in a variety of agencies to increase understanding of the law enforcement and criminal justice agencies, to create more favorable recruitment possibilities, and to increase understanding between law enforcement/public safety agencies and the Latino/Hispanic American community:

1. ***Red carpet mystery:***   Latino/Hispanic American families are invited to solve "crime scene" mysteries staged by the police agency and other local organizations:

> Waukesha—A 37-year-old man—is found dead on an apartment floor. Evidence of excessive drug and alcohol use is in plain view. Clearly, the death is due to an overdose. Or is it? Other clues indicate a possible violent end. In a first-of-its-kind program, the mock mystery will be solved not by police but by 30 Hispanic families who have recently immigrated to Waukesha. . . . Avila said the effort is important, because about 100 Hispanic immigrant families move to Waukesha annually and need to feel safe while adjusting to the community. "They need to learn that here police can be friends," she said. UW Extension staff, along with police and the medical examiner's office, have created a five-part series called "The Red Carpet Mystery," financed with a $191,000 federal grant aimed at stemming domestic violence. (Enriquez, 2003, p. B4)

2. ***Establishing recruitment opportunities at community festivals and events:***   The Jacksonville Sheriff's Department and other local and regional law enforcement agencies have used large-size community events as a venue for passing out recruitment brochures and scanning the crowd for potential candidates (Andino, 2002). Events like the World of Nations Festival, which represents more than 40 countries and attracts about 70,000 people across cultural, racial, and ethnic lines, provide opportunities for recruitment. "It's such a wide, diverse group that you might not otherwise get all together in one place," said Wendy Raymond Hacker, a spokeswoman for the city's special events office. Law enforcement agencies see events like this as excellent opportunities for meeting possible candidates to serve the growing Latino/Hispanic American communities.

Summary

- The label Latino/Hispanic American encompasses over 25 very diverse ethnic, cultural, and regional groups from North, Central, and South America. Law enforcement officials must be aware of the differences between the diverse groups (e.g., nationality, native cultural and regional differences and perceptions, and language dialects), as well as the within-group differences that may result from individual life experiences (e.g., sociopolitical turmoil). Since key stereotypes of Latino/Hispanic Americans by mainstream Americans are regarded as more negative than positive, it is important that peace officers make a special effort to extend respect and dignity to this community of very proud people with a culturally rich heritage. The preferred term for referring to Latino/Hispanic Americans varies with the contexts, groups, and experiences of Latino/Hispanic American individuals. Law enforcement officials must be aware of terms that are unacceptable and derogatory and terms that are currently used. When in doubt, officers have to learn to become comfortable in asking citizens which terms they prefer. Officers are advised to provide helpful feedback to their peers whenever offensive terms, slurs, labels, and/or actions are used with Latino/Hispanic Americans. Such feedback will help reduce the risk of misunderstanding and improve the working relationships of officers within the Latino/Hispanic American communities. In addition, it will help enhance the professional image of the department for those communities.
- The experience of Latino/Hispanic Americans with law enforcement officers in the United States has been complicated by the their perceptions of immigration law enforcement against undocumented immigrants and/or unauthorized migrants; by the discriminatory treatment they have received in the United States; and by community conflicts, as well as perceptions of police ineffectiveness and unresponsiveness. Some citizens may still remember this history and carry with them stereotypes of police services as something to be feared and avoided.
- The U.S. Census indicates that the Latino/Hispanic American population numbers about 45.5 million and represents 15.1 percent of the U.S. population making Latino/Hispanic Americans the largest minority group in the United States (this does not include the 3.97 million people who live in Puerto Rico). About 76.9 percent of Latino/Hispanic Americans trace their roots to Mexico, Puerto Rico, and Cuba, while the remaining 23.1 percent are from other countries of Central and South America, the Caribbean, and Spain (U.S. Census, 2007). The numerical growth of the Latino/Hispanic American population is the fastest of all American ethnic groups, with more than 10 million people

added to the U.S. population between the 1990 and 2000 censuses. Latino/Hispanic Americans are most heavily concentrated in six states: California, Texas, Florida, New York, Arizona, and Illinois.

- It is important to have an understanding about some of the myths and stereotypes of Latino/Hispanic Americans that contribute to the prejudice, discrimination, and bias this population encounters. Stereotypic views of Latino/Hispanic Americans reduce individuals within this group to simplistic, one-dimensional characters and have led many Americans to lump members of these diverse groups into one stereotypic group, "Mexicans." The key to effectiveness with any ethnic or racial group is not that we completely eliminate our myths and stereotypes, but that we are aware of them and can monitor our thinking and our behaviors when the stereotypes are not true of the persons with whom we are interacting.

- With over 25 different cultural groups making up the category we call "Latino/Hispanic American," many family differences exist among the groups in this collective. However, across all of the groups, *La familia* is perhaps one of the most significant considerations in working and communicating with Latino/Hispanic Americans. The Latino/Hispanic American family is most clearly characterized by bonds of interdependence, unity, and loyalty and includes nuclear and extended family members as well as networks of neighbors, friends, and community members. Primary importance is given to the history of the family, which is firmly rooted in the set of obligations tied to both the past and the future. Traditionally, the role of the father has been that of the disciplinarian, decision maker, and head of the household. The father's word is the law, and he is not to be questioned. The father tends to focus his attention on the economic and well-being issues of the family and less on the social and emotional issues. The mother, on the other hand, is seen as balancing the father's role by providing for the emotional and expressive issues of the family. Extended family members such as grandmothers, aunts and uncles, and godparents (*compadrazgo*) often supplement the mother's emotional support.

- Many Latino/Hispanic Americans are concerned with their inability to communicate clearly and about possible reprisal from the police, as associated with the role of law enforcement in more politically repressive countries. Peace officers must take the time needed to understand communications. They must be aware that bilingual and nonnative English speakers want to communicate effectively with them. Maintaining contact, providing extra time, using translators, and being patient with speakers encourage citizens to communicate their concerns. Cultural differences in verbal and nonverbal communication often result in misinterpretation of messages and of behaviors. Officers must recognize the nonverbal aspects of some Latino/Hispanic Americans' communication styles, such as eye contact, touch, gestures, and emotionality. Verbal aspects such as accent, mixing English with Spanish, limited vocabulary, and incorrect grammar may give the officer the impression that the individual does not understand what is communicated. As in all cases when English is the second language, it is important to remember that listening and comprehension skills with English are usually better than speaking skills.

- Latino/Hispanic Americans, because of their past experiences with law enforcement agencies, along with their own concerns about privacy, self-help, and other factors, are reluctant to report crimes and may not seek police assistance and help. It is important for law enforcement departments and officials to build relationships and working partnerships with Latino/Hispanic American communities. This effort is helped by outreach efforts such as community offices, bilingual officers, and participation of officers in community activities. Latino/Hispanic Americans tend to hold a perception of law enforcement and corrections as being severe and punishment-oriented. That is, citizens have strong views on authority and an equally strong sense of "rightness" and of punishing the criminal. Because of this perspective, law enforcement personnel must be aware that members from this community may view law enforcement as more severe than it really is. Law enforcement officials need to go out of their way to establish trust, to provide outreach efforts, and to win cooperation in order to effectively accomplish their goal to serve and protect Latino/Hispanic Americans. Building partnerships focused on community collaboration in the fight against crime is key to effectiveness.

Discussion Questions and Issues

1. *Latino/Hispanic Americans Viewing Law Enforcement as Not Sensitive*. In the historical information section of this chapter, we noted many associations made about immigration law enforcement and events that may leave Latino/Hispanic Americans with the view that law enforcement agencies are not sensitive, effective, and responsive. Suggest ways to improve such possible negative points of view.

2. *Diversity among Latino/Hispanic Americans*. Latino/Hispanic Americans consist of over 25 diverse regional, national, ethnic, and cultural groups. Which groups are you most likely to encounter in crime-fighting and peacekeeping in your work? Which groups do you anticipate encountering in your future work?

3. *Choice of Terms*. Use of the terms *Latino*, *Hispanic*, *Chicano*, *Mexican*, *La Raza*, *Puerto Rican*, and so forth is confusing for many people. How might you find out which term to use when referring to an individual if ethnic and cultural information of this kind is necessary? What would you do if the term you use seems to engender a negative reaction?

4. *Offensive Terms and Labels*. Offensive terms such as "Wetbacks," "Illegals," and "Spics" should not be used in law enforcement work at any time. Give three practical reasons for this perspective. How would you go about helping other officers who use these terms in the course of their work to become aware of their offensiveness?

5. *Effects of Myths and Stereotypes*. Myths and stereotypes about Latino/Hispanic Americans have affected this group greatly. Describe some of the Latino/Hispanic American stereotypes that you have heard of or encountered. What effect might these stereotypes have on Latino/Hispanic Americans? Suggest ways to manage these stereotypes in law enforcement. In what ways can you help an officer who uses stereotypes about Latino/Hispanic Americans to become aware of the effects of such stereotypes?

6. *Verbal and Nonverbal Communication Style Variations among Cultures*. How do you think the information in this chapter about verbal and nonverbal communication styles can help officers in their approach to Latino/Hispanic American citizens? Does understanding the cultural components of the style and behaviors help you to become more sensitive and objective about your reactions? In what ways might you use your understanding about Latino/Hispanic American family dynamics in law enforcement?

7. *Avoidance of Law Enforcement and Underreporting of Crimes*. Why do you think that many Latino/Hispanic Americans keep to their own communities and underreport crimes of violence? When are such efforts desirable? When are they ineffective? How can police agencies be of greater service to Latino/Hispanic American communities in this regard?

8. *The Future of Latino/Hispanic Americans and Law Enforcement*. The Latino/Hispanic American population is the fastest growing segment in the U.S. population. What implications do you see for law enforcement in terms of services, language, recruitment, and training?

Website Resources

Visit these websites for additional information about law enforcement contact with Latino/Hispanic Americans and related community organizations:

Federal Hispanic Law Enforcement Officers Association (FHLEOA): http://www.fhleoa.org/

This website provides information packets, special publications, and workshops and seminars when issues of national importance arise. FHLEOA provides a collective voice and representation to address law enforcement concerns before legislative bodies, regulatory agencies, and the courts.

Mexican American Legal Defense and Educational Fund (MALDEF): http://www.maldef.org/

This website provides information to bring Latino/Hispanic Americans into the mainstream of American political and socioeconomic life and highlights educational opportunities, participation, and positive visions for the future.

National Council of La Raza (NCLR): http://www.nclr.org/

This website provides information about capacity-building assistance to support and strengthen Hispanic community-based programs and information regarding applied research, policy analysis, and advocacy for Latino/Hispanic Americans.

League of United Latin American Citizens (LULAC): http://www.lulac.org

This website provides information on education, training, scholarships, and services to underprivileged and unrepresented Latino/Hispanic Americans. LULAC is the largest and oldest Latino/Hispanic organization in the United States, with over 115,000 members.

Hispanic American Police Command Officers Association (HAPCOA): http://www.hapcoa.com/

This website provides information to promote the interests of Hispanic American peace officers for recruitment, career development, promotion, and retention of qualified Hispanic police command officers.

Latin American Law Enforcement Association (LA LEY): http://www.laley.org/

This website provides law enforcement links important to the Latino/Hispanic American community in the areas of advocacy, education, and leadership, and it identifies key organizations.

Pew Hispanic Center: http://pewhispanic.org/

This website provides law enforcement links important to the Pew Hispanic Center, which is a nonpartisan research organization supported by the Pew Charitable Trusts. Its mission is to improve understanding of the U.S. Hispanic population and to chronicle Latinos' growing impact on the entire nation. The Center does not advocate for or take positions on policy issues.

Spanish Language and Latino/Hispanic Cultural Links: http://globegate.utm.edu/spanish/span.html

This website provides links to Spanish language and Hispanic culture websites. Sections: Spanish-Language Listservs, Spanish-Language Search Engines, Maps, Campus Spanish Pages, Link Sites, Organizations Supporting Spanish Teaching & Benchmarks, Spanish Grammars, On-line Courses & Lessons, Newspapers, Magazines, and Radio/TV.

U.S. Census Bureau—Facts on the Latino/Hispanic American Population: http://www.census.gov/pubinfo/www/NEWhispML1.html

This website provides statistics from the U.S. Census Bureau on Latino/Hispanic Americans. The topics include American Community Survey, Social Characteristics, Economic Characteristics, Profiles and more.

References

Accola, J. (2005, May 21). "Aerospace Firm OKs Discrimination Pact: Hispanics at Plant in Mesa Co. Sued over Racial Slurs." *Rocky Mountain News* (Denver, Colorado), p. C3.

Ahern, S. (2008, October 30). "Rolling Meadows Talks about Cutting Police Neighborhood Center's Funding." *Chicago Daily Herald*, p. 9.

Andino, A. T. (2002, April 26). "Police to Scan Ethnic Fest for Potential New Recruits." *Florida Times-Union* (Jacksonville, Florida), p. B1.

Associated Press. (2003, June 9). "Durham Civilian Police Academy Caters to Hispanics."

Associated Press. (2005, July 15). "New Study Shows Minorities Face More Stops on Some Illinois Roads."

Bernal, G., and A. Estrada. (1985). "Cuban Refugee and Minority Experiences: A Book Review." *Hispanic Journal of Behavioral Sciences*, 7, 105–128.

Bragg, R. (2000, April 23). "The Elian Gonzalez Case: The Overview: Cuban Boy Seized by U.S. Agents and Reunited with his Father." *New York Times*, p. 1.

Catalano, S. M. (2005). *Criminal Victimization, 2004.* Washington, D.C.: Bureau of Justice Statistics National Crime Victimization Survey.

Cativo, F. (2005, July 30). "Montgomery Fighting Gangs on Several Fronts; County Reaches out to Latinos to Overcome Language Barrier, Fear of Police." *Washington Post*, p. B2.

Central Intelligence Agency. (2009). *World Fact Book.* Washington, D.C.: Central Intelligence Agency.

Cohen, R. (2009, June 2). "Dreams Built in the Projects," *Washington Post*, p. A15.

Cohn, D. (2005, June 9). "Hispanic Growth Surge Fueled by Births in U.S." *Washington Post*, p. A1.

Coleman, M. (2009, February 23). "Spanish-Speaking Officers; Police Work to Ensure Language Is No Barrier; Bilingual International Affairs Unit Serves the City's Hispanic Population." *Florida Times-Union* (Jacksonville, Florida), p. A1.

Comas-Diaz, L., and E. E. H. Griffith, eds. (1988). *Cross-Cultural Mental Health.* New York, NY: Wiley.

Crawford, S. (2005, October 3). "Police Say Hispanics Not Reporting Crimes: Fear of Reprisal, Distrust of Cops Cited." *Arkansas Democrat-Gazette* (Little Rock).

Cuff, D. (2007, February 23). "Study: Bay Area Suffers from Environmental Inequality." *Inside Bay Area* (California), Section: Tri-Valley.

Delgado v. Bastrop Independent School District, 388 W. D. Texas (1948).

Enriquez, D. (2003, April 10). "Mystery Program Offers Clue about Culture: Waukesha Hispanic Families Get Lessons on Criminal Justice System." *Milwaukee Journal Sentinel*, p. B4.

Fernandex, L. F. (1970). *A Forgotten American.* New York, NY: B'nai B'rith.

Gavzer, G. (1993, March 21). "Held without Hope." *Parade.*

Gaynair, G. (2009, February 19). "Report: ICE Agents Pressured to Meet Arrest Quotas," *Associated Press*, para. 1.

Gracia, J. J. E. (2000). *Hispanic/Latino Identity: A Philosophical Perspective.* Malden, MA: Blackwell.

Hickman, M. J., and B. A. Reaves. (2006a, May). "Local Police Department, 2003." Bureau of Justice Statistics: Law Enforcement Management and Administrative Statistics.

Hickman, M. J., and B. A. Reaves. (2006b, May). "Sheriffs' Offices, 2003." Bureau of Justice Statistics: Law Enforcement Management and Administrative Statistics.

Hill, L., and R. Trapp. (2000, October 29). "African Americans and Latinos in a San Diego Study." *San Diego Union-Tribune*, p. B11.

"Hispanic Fertility Drives U.S. Population Growth." (2008, August 19). *McClatchy Newspapers*, para. 4.

"Hispanics Are the Largest Minorities in the U.S. with Purchasing Power to Exceed 1.2 Trillion by 2012," (2008, March 31). *Reuter.* para. 2.

Holmberg, M. (2006, April 5). "Robbers Preying on Hispanics." *Richmond Times Dispatch*, p. B1.

Irvin, N. (2006, February 12). "A Story of Success You Can Take to the Bank." *Winston-Salem Journal*, p. 21.

Kamb, L. (2008, February 28). "Jogger Jumped, Cuffed, Threatened. Cops at Times Use 'Obstruct' Charges as Leverage." *Seattle Post-Intelligencer*, p. A3.

Korzenny, F., and B. A. Korzenny. (2005). *Hispanic Marketing: A Cultural Perspective.* Burlington, Mass.: Elsevier Butterworth Heinemann.

Lewis, A. (2000, April 29). "Abroad at Home: Elian and the Law." *New York Times*, p. A13.

Lopez y Rivas, G. (1973). *The Chicanos.* New York, NY: Monthly Review Press.

Mendez v. Westminster, 64 F.Supp. 544 (D.C. Cal. 1946), aff'd, 161 F.2d 774 (9th Cir. 1947).

Miniter, P. C. (2007, May 8). "A Border Agent (and Immigrant) Defies Stereotypes; One Man's Work in Defending the U.S. Border Speaks Volumes about What It Means to be an American." *USA Today*, p. 21A.

Montiel, M. (1978). *Hispanic Families: Critical Issues for Policy and Programs in Human Services.* Washington, D.C.: Coalition of Spanish-Speaking Mental Health Organizations.

Morales, R., and F. Bonilla, eds. (1993). *Latinos in a Changing U.S. Economy.* Newbury Park, CA: Sage.

Moran, R. (2009, April 8). "Ramsey Acknowledges Rift with Latinos." *Philadelphia Inquirer*, p. B2.

Office of Management and Budget. (1997, October 30). "Revisions to the Standards for the Classification of Federal Data on Race and Ethnicity." *Federal Register*, 62(280), 58782–85790.

Office of Personnel Management. (2007). *Seventh Annual Report to the President on Hispanic Employment in the Federal Government.* Washington, D.C.: Office of Personnel Management.

Passel, J. S. (2005). *Unauthorized Migrants: Numbers and Characteristics.* Washington, D.C.: Pew Hispanic Center.

Passel, J. S., J. Van Hook, and F. D. Bean. (2004). *Estimates of Legal and Unauthorized Foreign Born Population for the United States and Selected States, Based on Census 2000.* Washington, D.C.: Report to the Census Bureau, Urban Institute.

Reaves, B. A. (2006, April). "Federal Law Enforcement Officers, 2004." Bureau of Justice Statistics Bulletin.

Rennison, C. M. (2002). *Hispanic Victims of Violent Crime, 1990–2000.* Washington, D.C.: Bureau of Justice Statistics Special Report.

Saslow, Eli. (2009, May 27). "The Latino Reaction: Disparate Group United in Pride." The Washington Post. Retrieved June 8, 2009, from http://www.washingtonpost.com/wp-dyn/content/article/2009/05/26/AR2009052603288.html.

Stevens, E. (1973). "Machismo and Marianismo." *Transaction-Society*, 10(6), 57–63.

Taylor, L. G. (2000, March 1). "Police Get Crash Course in Minority Relations." *Pittsburgh Post-Gazette*, p. B4.

Therrien, M., and R. R. Ramirez. (2002). "The Hispanic Population in the United States." Current Population Reports, P20-535. Washington, D.C.: U.S. Census Bureau.

Walker, N., J. M. Senger, F. Villarruel, and A. Arboleda. (2004). *Lost Opportunities: The Reality of Latinos in the U.S. Criminal Justice System.* Washington, D.C.: National Council of La Raza.

U.S. Bureau of the Census (2008). *U.S. Hispanic Population Surpasses 45 Million Now 15 Percent of Total,* Washington, D.C.: U.S. Government Printing Office.

U.S. Department of Justice (2009, March 30). "Duo Wanted for Violent Hate Crimes Arrested in Baton Rouge," *States News Service*, para. 1.

Yankelovich Monitor. (2003). *2003 Yankelovich Monitor Multicultural Marketing Study.* Chapel Hill, NC: Yankelovich Monitor.

Zarazua, J. (2009, March 5). "Suburb's Cops Won't Call Feds for ID Check," *San Antonio Express-News*, p. B1.

CHAPTER 8

Law Enforcement Contact with Arab Americans and Other Middle Eastern Groups

LEARNING OBJECTIVES

After reading this chapter you should be able to:

- List the groups belonging to the category "Middle Easterners," define "Arab" and "Muslim," and identify who the non-Arabic-speaking Middle Eastern groups are.
- Describe the reasons for Arab/Middle Eastern immigration to the United States and indicate where the largest populations of Arab Americans reside in the United States.
- Provide examples of differences among Middle Eastern groups as well as common basic Arab values.
- Explain the impact of Arab/Middle Eastern stereotypes on law enforcement and on Arab Americans and other Middle Easterners.
- Identify basic ways in which law enforcement can show respect toward the religion Islam.
- Identify selected characteristics of traditional Arab American/Middle Eastern extended family structure as it relates to law enforcement contact.
- Describe characteristics of traditional Arab/Middle Eastern communication styles and cultural practices, including taboos.
- List and discuss key issues associated with law enforcement contact with Arab American and other Middle Eastern groups.

OUTLINE

- Middle Easterners and Related Terminology Defined
- Historical Information and Arab American Demographics
- Differences and Similarities
- Stereotypes

- Islamic Religion
- Family Structure
- Communication Styles and Cultural Practices
- Key Issues in Law Enforcement
- Summary
- Discussion Questions and Issues
- Websites Resources

INTRODUCTION

Middle Easterners come to the United States for numerous reasons: to gain an education and begin a career, to escape an unstable political situation in their country of origin, and to invest in commercial enterprises with the goal of gaining legal entry into the country. People in law enforcement have continual contact with Middle Easterners from a number of different countries. Officers would benefit from having a rudimentary knowledge about past and present world events related to Middle Easterners and should be aware of stereotypes that others hold of them. Attitudes toward Middle Easterners in this country, as well as geopolitical events in the Middle East, can have implications for law enforcement.

Established Americans of Arab origin are sometimes treated as if they had just come from the Middle East and may be potential terrorists. This perception increased significantly after the terrorist attacks of September 11, 2001, and continues into the present. Stereotypes, which have long been imprinted in people's minds, can and do significantly affect people's perceptions of Arab Americans, whether they are second- or third generation or recent refugees.

MIDDLE EASTERNERS AND RELATED TERMINOLOGY DEFINED

Among the general population there is considerable confusion as to who Middle Easterners are and, specifically, who Arabs are. Although commonly thought of as Arabs, Iranians and Turks are not Arabs. Many people assume that all Muslims are Arabs, and vice versa. In fact, many Arabs are also Christians, and the world's Muslim population is actually comprised of dozens of ethnic groups. The largest Muslim population is in Asia, not in the Middle East. Nevertheless, the predominant religion among Arabs is Islam, and its followers are called *Muslims*. They are also sometimes called *Moslems*, but *Muslim* is the preferred term because it is closer to the Arabic pronunciation.

The following excerpt is from *100 Questions You Have Always Wanted to Ask about Arab Americans* (Detroit Free Press, 2001); it clears up common confusion around terminology related to Arab Americans.

> SHOULD I SAY ARAB, ARABIC, OR ARABIAN?
>
> Arab is a noun for a person and is used as an adjective as in "Arab country." Arabic is the name of the language and generally is not used as an adjective. Arabian is an adjective that refers to Saudi Arabia, the Arabian Peninsula, or the "Arabian horse." When ethnicity or nationality are relevant, it is more precise and accurate to specify the country by using Lebanese, Yemeni, or whatever is appropriate.

What all Arabs have in common is the Arabic language, even though spoken Arabic differs among countries (e.g., Algerian Arabic is different from Jordanian Arabic). The following countries constitute the Middle East and are all Arab countries with the exception of three:

- Aden
- Bahrain
- Egypt
- Iran (non-Arab country)
- Iraq
- Israel (non-Arab country)
- Jordan
- Kuwait
- Lebanon
- Oman
- Palestinian Authority
- Qatar
- Saudi Arabia
- Syria
- Turkey (non-Arab country)
- United Arab Emirates
- Yemen

There are other Arab countries that are not in the Middle East (e.g., Algeria, Tunisia, Morocco, Libya), in which the majority population shares the Arabic language (though a different variety of Arabic) and the religion Islam with people in the Arab countries of the Middle East. In this chapter we cover primarily information on refugees and immigrants from Arab countries in the Middle East. They constitute the majority of Middle Eastern newcomers who bring cultural differences and special issues requiring clarification for law enforcement. We briefly mention issues related to the established Arab American community (i.e., the people who began arriving in the United States in the late nineteenth century). We begin with a brief description of the population from the three non-Arab countries.

Iranians and Turks

Iranians use the Arabic script in their writing but for the most part speak mainly Farsi (Persian), not Arabic. Turks speak Turkish, although there are minority groups in Turkey who speak Kurdish, Arabic, Greek, and Armenian. More than 99.8 percent of Iranians and Turks are Muslim. Islam is the most common religion among people in many other Middle Eastern countries (Central Intelligence Agency, 2003). Armenians, who are largely Christian, were a persecuted minority in Turkey. The Armenian genocide, between 1915 and 1923, claimed the lives of between 1 and 1.5 million people. Animosity still exists between some Armenians and Turks. At the time of this text's writing, Turkey continues to deny that the Armenians were the victims of genocide during World War I (Armenian National Institute, 2006).

Many Iranians in the United States are Jewish or Bahai, both of which groups are minorities in Iran. Of the Muslim population in Iran, most belong to the Shi'a sect of Islam, the Shi'a version of Islam being the state religion. Persians are the largest ethnic group in Iran, making up about 50 percent of the population (Central Intelligence Agency, 2003), but there are other ethnic populations, including Kurds, Arabs, Turkmen, Armenians, and Assyrians, most of whom can be found in the United States. During the Iranian hostage crisis in 1979, many Iranians in the United States were targets of hate crimes and anti-Iranian sentiment; the same attitudes prevailed against other Middle Easterners (Arabs) and South Asians (Indians from India) who were mistakenly labeled as Iranian. Iranians and Turks are not Arabs, but some of their cultural values related to the extended family with respect to pride, dignity, and honor are similar to those in the traditional Arab world.

Many Iranian Americans and Turkish Americans came to the United States in the 1970s and were from upper-class professional groups such as doctors, lawyers, and engineers. Many of the Jewish Iranians in the United States left Iran after the fall of the Shah. In the United States, there are large Iranian Jewish populations in the San Francisco Bay Area, Los Angeles, and New York. Also, populations of Muslim Iranians are found in major U.S. cities, such as New York, Chicago, and Los Angeles.

Israelis

Israel is the only country in the Middle East in which the majority of the population is not Muslim. Approximately 20 percent of the population in Israel is made up of Arabs, both Christian and Muslim. Approximately three quarters of the Israeli population is Jewish (Central Intelligence Agency, 2006), with the Jewish population divided into two main groups: Ashkenazim and Sephardim. The Ashkenazim had descended from members of the Jewish communities of Central and Eastern Europe. The majority of American Jews are Ashkenazi, while currently the minority of Israeli Jews (by an increasingly small margin) are Sephardim, having come originally from Spain, other Mediterranean countries, and the Arab countries of the Middle East. Israeli immigrants in the United States may be either Ashkenazi or Sephardic; their physical appearance will not indicate to an officer what their ethnicity is. An Israeli may look like an American Jew, a Christian, or a Muslim Arab—or none of these.

Most of the Israeli Arabs who live within the borders of Israel are Palestinians whose families stayed in Israel after the Arab–Israeli war in 1948, following the birth of Israel as a nation. The Six-Day War in 1967 resulted in the occupation of lands that formerly belonged to Egypt, Syria, and Jordan, but where the majority of the population was Palestinian. Thus, until the signing of the Oslo 1993 peace accords between Israel and the Palestine Liberation Organization (PLO), Israel occupied territories with a population of approximately 1 million Palestinians. The Palestinian–Israeli situation in the Middle East has created a great deal of hostility on both sides. In the fall of 2000, failure to reach a negotiated settlement agreement required by the Oslo peace accords of 1993 resulted in a period of increased hostilities. The tension continued and intensified during what is referred to as the second *intifada* or Palestinian "uprising," which took place between 2001 and 2004. Hostilities continued in 2006 with the outbreak of war involving Israel and Lebanon, associated with the rocket attacks by Hezbollah and Hamas into Israel proper. Similarly, the violence in Gaza which began in December 2008, and was also associated with rocket attacks into Israel, had repercussions around the world, including in the United States. These political tensions have definite implications for law enforcement officials in the United States, especially in communities where there are large populations of Jews and Arabs, or where Israelis and Palestinians reside in large numbers (e.g., Los Angeles, New York, Chicago). All law enforcement agencies should become knowledgeable of individuals and groups with extremist views who operate in their jurisdiction and region.

Public events such as Israeli Independence Day celebrations and Israeli or Palestinian political rallies have the potential for confrontation, although the majority of these events have been peaceful. Police presence is required at such events, but as with other situations, excessive police presence can escalate hostilities. Law enforcement officials need to be well informed about current events in the Middle East as conflicts there often have a ripple effect across the world. The monitoring of world events and community trends will help police officers take a preventive posture that can ultimately help to avoid confrontation among various Middle Eastern ethnic groups in this country. Chapter 11 goes into more depth on this subject.

HISTORICAL INFORMATION AND ARAB AMERICAN DEMOGRAPHICS

Although many recent Middle Eastern immigrants and refugees in the United States have come for political reasons, not all Arab Americans left their country of origin because of these. There have been two major waves of Arab immigrants to the United States. The first wave came between 1880 and World War I, and was largely from Syria and what is known today as Lebanon (at the time these areas were part of the Turkish Ottoman Empire). Of the immigrants who settled during this wave, approximately 90 percent were Christian. Many people came to further themselves economically (thus these were immigrants and not refugees forced to leave their countries), but in addition, many of the young men wanted to avoid the military in the Ottoman Empire (Samhan, 2006). A substantial percentage of these immigrants were farmers or artisans, and they became involved in the business of peddling their goods to farmers and moved from town to town. In the way of crime statistics, not much is reported, partly because in the Arab immigrant community, people took care of their own (Samhan, 2006).

In sharp contrast to the first wave of immigrants in terms of motivation and compositional characteristics, the second wave of Arab immigrants to the United States, beginning after World War II, came in large part as students and professionals. They came seeking to escape economic instability and political unrest in their home countries. As a result, these groups brought a "political consciousness unknown to earlier immigrants" (John Zogby, 2006). The largest group of second-wave immigrants was made up of Palestinians, many of whom came around 1948, the time of the partition of Palestine, which resulted in Israel's independence. In the 1970s, after the Six-Day War between Israel and Egypt, Syria, and Jordan, another large influx of Palestinians was witnessed by the United States. In the 1980s, a large group of Lebanese came as a result of the civil war in Lebanon. Yemenis (from Yemen) have continued to come throughout the twentieth century; also many Syrians and Iraqis have made the United States their home since the 1950s and 1960s because of political instability in their countries (John Zogby, 2006). Thus, these second-wave immigrants came largely because of political turmoil in their respective home countries and have been instrumental in changing the nature of the Arab American community in the United States.

The most dramatic example of how Arab immigration has affected a U.S. city is the Detroit area in Michigan. There Arabs began to arrive in the late nineteenth century, but the first huge influx was between 1900 and 1924, when the auto industry attracted immigrants from all over the world (Woodruff, 1991). The Detroit–Dearborn area has the largest Arab community in the United States, with Arab Americans constituting about 30 percent of the population in Dearborn. A large percentage of the Detroit area's Middle Eastern population is Chaldean, Christian Iraqis who speak the Chaldean language. While they are from the heart of the Middle East, most do not identify themselves to be Iraqi, and some are deeply offended if referred to as Arab (Haddad, 2006). This is particularly true in the Detroit area, as well as in other large urban concentrations, but may be less applicable to Chaldeans in other areas (Samhan, 2006).

Selected Arab American Demographics

Immigrants from all over the Arab world continue to settle in the United States. For example, in 2000, approximately 12,000 visas (combined total) were issued to immigrants coming to the United States from Bahrain, Egypt, Iraq, Jordan, Kuwait, Lebanon, Qatar, Saudi Arabia, Syria, the United Arab Emirates, and Yemen (Samhan, 2006). According to the Migration Policy Institute (MPI), whose research is also based on U.S. Census and U.S. department of Homeland Security data, the number of Iraqi immigrants rose from approximately 32,000 in 1980 to 102,000 in 2007.

The increase of Iraqi immigrants was most dramatic in 2008 (MPI, 2009). The U.S. war in Iraq began in 2003, and it took several years for the surge of Iraqi refugees or asylees to reach the United States. As of 2007, the Iraqi immigrant population made up 0.3 percent of all immigrants in the United States (MPI, 2009).

There are approximately 3.5 to 4 million Americans of Arab ancestry in the United States, and the number of people who identified themselves as of Arab ancestry in the 2000 census was about 1.3 million (Samhan, 2006). The communities with the largest Arab American populations are in Los Angeles/Orange County, Detroit, the greater New York area, Chicago, and Washington, D.C. California has the largest "cluster" of Arab American communities (Samhan, 2006). According to Zogby International research, the five states with the largest Arab American populations in the early 2000s were California, Michigan, New York, Florida, and New Jersey (Arab American Institute, 2003). After the September 11 attacks, immigration to the United States declined significantly because of the increased security and background checks people wishing to come to America are subjected to ("Immigration Down," 2003).

DIFFERENCES AND SIMILARITIES

There is great diversity among Arab American groups. Understanding this diversity will assist officers in not categorizing Arabs as homogeneous and will encourage people to move away from stereotypical thinking. Arabs from the Middle East come from at least 13 different countries, many of which are vastly different from each other. The governments of the Arab countries also differ, ranging from monarchies to theocracies to military governments to socialist republics (Central Intelligence Agency, 2006). Arab visitors such as students, tourists, businesspeople, and diplomats to the United States from the Gulf countries (e.g., Saudi Arabia, Qatar, Oman, Bahrain, United Arab Emirates) are typically wealthy, but their Jordanian, Lebanese, and Palestinian brethren do not generally bring wealth to the United States, and in fact, many are extremely poor. Another area of difference is in clothing. In a number of countries in the Middle East, many older men wear headdresses, but it is less common among men who are younger and who have more education. Similarly, younger women in the Middle East may choose not to wear the head covering and the long dress that covers them from head to toe.

The younger generation of Arab Americans, much to the disappointment of their parents and grandparents, may display entirely different behavior from what is expected of them (as is typical in most immigrant and refugee groups). In addition, as with other immigrant groups, there are Arab Americans who have been in the United States for generations and have completely assimilated into the American culture. Consequently, they may not identify in any way with their roots. Others, even though they have also been in the United States for generations, consciously try to keep their Arab traditions alive and pass them on to their children. Officers should not treat established Arab Americans as if they were newcomers.

There are broad differences among Arab American groups associated with social class and economic status. Although many Arab Americans who come to the United States are educated professionals, a percentage comes from rural areas (e.g., peasants from southern Lebanon, West Bank Palestinians, Yemenis), and they differ in outlook and receptiveness to modernization. On the other hand, despite traditional values, many newcomers are modern in outlook. Many people have a stereotypical image of the Arab woman, yet many women of Arab descent do not adhere to this image. John Zogby, president of Zogby International, describes the modern Arab women who defy the stereotype: "Among the upper-class, educated Palestinian population, for example, you can find many women who are vocal and outspoken. You might see the young husbands wheeling the babies around in strollers while the women are discussing world events" (John Zogby, 2006).

On the other hand, certain Arab governments (e.g., Saudi Arabia) place restrictions on women, mandating that they do not mix with men, that they must always be veiled, and that they do not travel alone or drive a car. Women from less restrictive Arab countries (e.g., Egypt and Jordan) might exhibit very different behavior from those whose governments grant them fewer freedoms. Nevertheless, women in traditional Muslim families from any country typically have limited contact with men outside their family and wear traditional dress. Some implications of these traditions, as they relate to Arab women and male police officers in the United States, are discussed further in this chapter.

It is important to look at people's motivation for coming to the United States, to help avoid stereotypical thinking. Arab American police Corporal Mohamed Berro of the Dearborn, Michigan, Police Department makes a distinction between immigrants (who have "few problems adjusting to the United States") and refugees. He explains that refugees, having been forced to leave their country of origin, believe that they are here temporarily, because they are waiting for a conflict to end. As a result, they may be more hesitant to change, and relationship building may take more time (Berro, 2009).

Similarities

Despite many differences, whether apparent in socioeconomic status, levels of traditionalism, or motivation for coming to the United States, there are values and beliefs associated with Arab culture that law enforcement officials should understand in order to establish rapport and trust. Officers will recognize that some of the information listed below does not only apply to Arab culture. At the same time, the following will help officers understand deeply held beliefs that many Arab Americans would agree is key to understanding traditional Arab culture.

BASIC ARAB VALUES

1. Traditional Arab society upholds honor; the degree to which an Arab can lose face and be shamed publicly is foreign to the average Westerner. Officers recognize that dignity and respect should be shown to all individuals, but citizens from cultures emphasizing shame, loss of face, and loss of honor (e.g., Middle Eastern, Asian, Latin American) may react even more severely to loss of dignity and respect than do other individuals. People will go so far to avoid shame that they will not report crimes. "It is often difficult to get members of Arab communities to be full-fledged complainants, because they either don't complain in the first place, or do not follow through. Therefore, because of their primary concern to save face, avoid shame, and maintain harmony, it becomes more difficult to gain successful prosecution" (Haddad, 2006). Keep in mind that "shame" cultures have sanctioned extreme punishments for loss of face and loss of honor (e.g., death if a woman loses her virginity before marriage).

2. Loyalty to one's family takes precedence over other personal needs. A person is completely intertwined with his or her family; protection and privacy in a traditional Arab family often overrides relationships with other people. Members of Arab families tend to avoid disagreements and disputes in front of others, many preferring to resolve issues on their own (Haddad, 2006).

3. Communication is expected to be courteous and hospitable, and harmony between individuals is emphasized. Too much directness and candor can be interpreted as extremely

impolite. From a traditional Arab view, it may not be appropriate for a person to give totally honest responses if they result in a loss of face, especially for self or family members (this may not apply to many established Arab Americans). From this perspective, the higher goals of honor and face-saving are operative. This aspect of cross-cultural communication is not easily understood by most Westerners and is often criticized. Certainly, officers will not accept anything but the whole truth, despite arguments rationalized by cultural ideals of avoiding loss of face and shame. However, this should not lead an officer to draw attention explicitly to a face-saving style. The officer would be well advised to work around the issue of the indirect communication rather than insinuating that the citizen may not be honest.

STEREOTYPES

The Arab world has been perceived in the West in terms of negative stereotypes, and these have been transferred to Americans of Arab descent. Prejudice against Arabs based on stereotypes has been constant for decades. As with all distorted information about ethnic groups, it is important that police officers understand how stereotypes interfere with a true understanding of a people. For some people, the word *Arab* brings several images to mind: (1) wealthy sheik (despite the class distinctions in the Middle East between, for example, a wealthy Gulf Arab sheik and a poor Palestinian or Lebanese); (2) violent terrorist (the majority of Arabs worldwide want peace and do not see terrorism as an acceptable means for achieving peace); (3) sensuous harem owner; man with many wives (harems are rare and for the most part, polygamy, or having more than one wife, has been abolished in the Arab world); and (4) ignorant, illiterate, and backward (American-Arab Anti-Discrimination Committee, 2002a). Arab contributions to civilization have been significant in numerous areas, including mathematics, astronomy, medicine, architecture, geography, and language, but the West is largely unfamiliar with those contributions. Despite these stereotypes, there are high-profile Arab Americans in all sectors of the professional world. Since the first edition of this book in 1995, sizeable percentages of Arab Americans have moved out of marginal urban areas and into the suburbs (James Zogby, 2006). Organizations like the National Arab American Medical Association and the Michigan Arab American Legal Society have highly respected and substantial membership (Haddad, 2006).

Movies and Television

Perhaps the most offensive type of Arab stereotypes comes from the media; programs and movies routinely portray Arabs as evil womanizers, wealthy oil sheiks who wear turbans, thieves, and terrorists. Even films and programs aimed at children propagate this stereotype of the Arab as a villain. The original lyrics of the opening song of Disney's *Aladdin*, "Arabian Nights," sung by an Arab who has been portrayed as a stereotype, go like this: "Oh I come from a land, from a faraway place/Where the caravan camels roam/Where they cut off your ear if they don't like your face/It's barbaric, but hey, it's home" (Shaheen, 2001, p. 51).

Because many Americans do not know Arabs personally, media images become embedded in people's minds. Jack Shaheen, author of *Reel Bad Arabs: How Hollywood Vilifies a People*, writes, "By depicting Arabs solely as slimy, shifty, violent creeps, Hollywood has been not only misrepresenting the Arab world, but also creating a climate for hate" (Shaheen, 2001).

Shaheen argues that the atmosphere created by Hollywood contributed to the recorded 326 hate crimes against Arab Americans in the first month alone following the terrorist attacks in 2001.

Though military retaliations after the attacks were labeled "antiterrorist" rather than "anti-Islamic," the movie industry has continued the negative stereotyping of Arabs and Muslims. In Shaheen's view, "There certainly should be movies based on what happened, but if [images of Arabs as terrorists] are the only images we see from now on, if we continue to vilify all Muslims and all Arabs as terrorists instead of making clear this is a lunatic fringe, what are we accomplishing?" (Shaheen, 2001). He adds that the more a people are defamed, the easier it is to "deny them civil rights and no one will say anything. Look at all the hate crimes since [9/11]. Could it be that stereotypes in part played a role?" (Shaheen, 2001).

While some filmmakers and studios have become more sensitive to the potential they have in terms of perpetrating stereotypes, a number of Muslim and Arab American organizations feel that there is room for improvement.

The "Terrorist" Stereotype, Post-9/11 Backlash, and Ongoing Challenges

Images of those responsible for the attacks of September 11, 2001, were eerily similar to the terrorist image described previously. The backlash that ensued against Arab Americans, Muslim Americans, and those thought to be of Middle Eastern origin had been predicted by many organizations and individuals, including critics of the media's stereotyped image of a Middle Easterner as a terrorist. Even prior to the attacks, Arabs were labeled as terrorists. A most convincing example of the persistence of discrimination against Arabs occurred after the Oklahoma City bombing in April 1995. Immediately following the bombing, many journalists and political leaders said that the tragedy appeared to be the work of Muslim terrorists. This was the initial conclusion without any supporting evidence; the arrest and conviction of Timothy J. McVeigh proved them wrong. The paranoia that led to the conclusion of Arab involvement in the bombing gave way to Arab-bashing, including many hate calls to Arabs. The scapegoating of Arabs spread pervasively across the country.

The rage that ensued after September 11, 2001, turned into general Arab- and Muslim-bashing; thus predictions made by representatives of Arab American and Muslim American organizations became a reality. Within the first 9 weeks following the attacks, there were more than 700 reported violent crimes against Arab Americans and Muslim Americans, or those who were perceived to be. (This is discussed further in this chapter as well as in Chapter 5). Even Sikhs, who may have simply been dark-skinned and wore turbans, but were neither Muslim nor Middle Eastern, were targets and victims of hate crimes in the aftermath of the attacks.

The attacks of 9/11 were a pivotal point in the history of Arab Americans in this country. The impact, nearly a decade later, is no less important to understand as it was immediately following the attacks:

> What remained [after the attacks] was primarily a heightened self-consciousness (including a heightened sense of vulnerability) on the part of Arab Americans, and a much more widespread cognition in the rest of American society of the existence of these communities (although this recognition was . . . accompanied by a degree of antipathy). Arab American individuals and organizations would, for the foreseeable future, be placed under a microscope of intense scrutiny for disloyalty and covert sympathy with those who attacked the United States. (ADC, 2008)

Law enforcement needs to be aware of the heightened risk of threats and hate crimes toward Arab Americans when criminal acts around the world are committed by terrorists in the name of

Islam. The ADC report cited above includes two examples of global news and its impact on hate crimes against those perceived to be Arab Americans in the United States.

- Under his leadership, the late terrorist leader in Iraq Abu Mussab Al Zarqawi oversaw beheading atrocities; this resulted in a rise of hate incidents around this period.
- The July 7, 2005 bombings in London were linked to a similar increase in hate crimes.

When global events occur, fear and anger can be ignited among some highly intolerant individuals who then lash out on people who appear to be Middle Eastern. This leads to "an ongoing anxiety that Arab Americans have been and are continuing to live with" (ADC, 2008).

ISLAMIC RELIGION

Misunderstanding between Americans and Arabs/Arab Americans can often be traced, in part, to religious differences and to a lack of tolerance of these differences. Islam is practiced by most Middle Eastern newcomers to the United States as well as by many African Americans. Many Arab Americans (especially those from the first wave of Arab immigration) are Christian, however, and prefer that others do not assume they are Muslim simply because they are Arabs.

Muslims refers to the people who practice the religion called *Islam*. By and large, most Americans do not understand what Islam is and, because of stereotyping, wrongly associate Muslims with terrorists or fanatics. Many, but by no means all, Arab Muslims in the United States are religious and have held on to traditional aspects of their religion, which are also intertwined with their way of life. However, some Muslims only attend a mosque on holy days. Islam means submission to the will of God and for traditional, religious Muslims, the will of God (or fate) is a central concept. Islam religion has been called Mohammedanism, which is an incorrect name for the religion because it suggests that Muslims worship Mohammed* rather than God (Allah). It is believed that God's final message to man was revealed to the prophet Mohammed. *Allah* is the shortened Arabic word for the God of Abraham, and it is used by both Arab Muslims and Arab Christians.

The Qur'an (Koran) and the Pillars of Islam

The Qur'an is the holy text for Muslims, and is regarded as the word of God (Allah). There are five Pillars of Islam, or central guidelines, that form the framework of the religion:

1. Profession of faith in Allah (God)
2. Prayer five times daily
3. Alms giving (concern for the needy)
4. Fasting during the month of Ramadan (sunrise to sunset)
5. Pilgrimage to Mecca (in Saudi Arabia) at least once in each person's lifetime

There are several points where law enforcement officials can show respect for a Muslim's need to practice his or her religion. The need to express one's faith in God and to be respected for it is one area. Usually, people pray together as congregations in mosques, the Islamic equivalent of a church or synagogue. People, however, can pray individually if a congregation is not present. Religious Muslims in jails, for example, will continue to pray five times a day and should not be ridiculed for or prevented from doing so. Remember that prayer, five times a day, is a "pillar" of

---

* An alternate spelling is Muhammad, which is closer to the Arabic pronunciation of the name.

Islam and that strict Muslims will want to uphold this "command" no matter where they are. Call to prayer takes place at the following times:

- One hour before sunrise
- At noon
- Midafternoon
- Sunset
- Ninety minutes after sunset

Taboos in the Mosque

A police officer conveys respect to a Muslim community if he or she can avoid, where possible, entering a mosque and interrupting prayers (emergencies may occasionally make this impossible). Religion is vital in Arab life; one of the quickest ways to build rapport with the Muslim community is to show respect for Islamic customs and beliefs. Thus, other than in emergency situations, officers are advised to:

- Never step on a prayer mat or rug with shoes on.
- Avoid walking in front of people who are praying.
- Speak softly while people are praying.
- Dress conservatively (both men and women are required to dress conservatively; shorts are not appropriate).
- Invite people out of a prayer area to talk to them.
- Never touch a Qur'an, place it on the floor, or put anything on top of it.

Proper protocol in a mosque (also referred to as a *masjid*) requires that people remove their shoes before entering, but this must be left to the officer's discretion. Officer safety, of course, comes before consideration of differences.

Ramadan: The Holy Month

One of the holiest periods in the Islamic religion is the celebration of Ramadan, which lasts for one month. There is no fixed date because, like the Jewish and Chinese calendars, the Islamic calendar is based on the lunar cycle, related to the phases of the moon, with dates varying from year to year. During the month of Ramadan, Muslims do not eat, drink, or smoke from sunrise to sunset. Muslims fast during Ramadan in order to practice self-discipline and to experience and demonstrate unity with Muslims all over the world who identify with their religion. On the 29th night of Ramadan, when there is a new moon, the holiday is officially over. The final fast is broken and for up to 3 days people celebrate with feasting and other activities. Throughout the month of Ramadan, Muslim families tend to pray more often in the mosque than during other parts of the year.

For Muslims Ramadan is as important and holy as Christmas is for Christians; this fact is appreciated when others, who are not Muslim, recognize the holiday's importance. One city with a sizable Arab American population puts up festive lights in its business district during Ramadan as a gesture of acceptance and appreciation of the diversity that the Arab Americans bring to the city. The Arab American community reacted favorably to this symbolic gesture. Meanwhile, in the same city, at the end of Ramadan, while many families were in the mosque, police ticketed hundreds of cars that were parked in store parking lots across from the mosque, even though, according to some Arab American citizens, the stores were closed. When people came out of the mosque and saw all the tickets, the mood of the holiday naturally was spoiled. The perception by the Arab American citizens was that "They don't want to understand us . . . they don't know how we feel . . . they don't know what's important to us." (Readers can analyze this situation from an enforcement and community relations point of view and discuss whether the situation could have been prevented. See Question 1 in the discussion section at the end of the chapter.)

Knowledge of Religious Practices

Knowledge of religious practices, including what is considered holy, will help officers avoid creating problems and conflicts. A belief in the Islamic religion that may occasionally come to the fore in the course of police work will illustrate this point. In a suburb of San Francisco, California, police officers and a group of Muslims from Tunisia were close to violence when, in a morgue, police entered to try to get a hair sample from a person who had just been killed in a car accident. Apparently, the body had already been blessed by an *Imam* (a religious leader) and, according to the religion, any further contact would have been a defilement of the body since the body had already been sanctified and was ready for burial. The police officers were merely doing what they needed to do to complete their investigation and were unaware of this taboo. This, together with a language barrier, created an extremely confusing and confrontational situation in which officers lost necessary control. In this case they needed to explain what had to be done and communicate their needs in the form of a request for permission to handle a body that had already been sanctified. If the citizens had not granted permission, the police would then have had to decide how to proceed. Most members of the Arab American community would comply with the wishes of police officers. As in many other situations involving police–citizen communication, the initial approach sets the tone for the entire interaction.

Similarities between Christianity, Judaism, and Islam

When reading the above tenets of the Muslim faith, notice that certain practices and aspects of Islam are also found in Christianity and Judaism. All three religions are monotheistic, that is, each believes in only one God. Followers of the religions believe that God is the origin of all, and is all-knowing as well as all-powerful. Because God is merciful, it is possible for believers to be absolved of their sins, though the practices for obtaining absolution vary in the different ideologies. All three religions have a Holy Book central to the faith: Judaism has the Torah (the first five books of the Old Testament), Christianity the Bible, and Islam the Qur'an (Koran). All three religions regard their texts to be either the direct word of God or inspired by the word of God. There are similarities between the three books. For example, the concept of the Ten Commandments is present in each. All three contain stories about many of the same people, such as Adam, Noah, Abraham, Moses, David, and Solomon. Also, both the Bible and the Qur'an contain stories about Mary, Jesus, and John the Baptist. The oral reading or recitation of each book constitutes part of regular worship. Prophets exist in each tradition and are revered as those who transmit the word of God to the people. Chronologically, Judaism became a religion first, followed by Christianity and then Islam. Islam builds upon the foundations of the previous ones and believes in the authenticity of the prophets of earlier books. For example, Islamic belief sees both Moses and Jesus as rightful prophets and as precursors to Mohammed, who is believed to be the final prophet of God. As there are different interpretations of Christianity and Judaism, so do followers of Islam, too, interpret the religion in different ways. Differing readings of the Qur'an can lead to more (or less) tolerance within the religion. Lastly, both the Islamic and the Judeo–Christian traditions are said to stem from the same lineage; Abraham was father to both Isaac, whose progeny became the people of Israel, and Ishmael, who started the Arab lineage.

FAMILY STRUCTURE

Arab Americans typically have close-knit families in which family members have a strong sense of loyalty and fulfill obligations to all members, including extended family (aunts, uncles, cousins, grandparents). Traditionally minded families also believe strongly in the family's honor, and members try to avoid any behavior that will bring shame or disgrace to the family. The operating unit for Arab Americans (and this may be less true for people who have been in the United States for generations) is not the individual but the family. Hence, if a person behaves inappropriately, the entire family is disgraced. Similarly, if a family member is assaulted in the Arab world, there would be some type of retribution. For the police officer, three characteristics of the Arab family will affect his or her interaction with family members:

- Extended family members are often as close as the "nuclear family" (mother, father, children) and are not seen as secondary family members. If there is a police issue, officers can expect that many members of the family will become involved in the matter. Although officers might perceive this as interference, from an Arab cultural perspective, it is merely involvement and concern. The numbers of people involved are not meant to overwhelm an officer.
- Family loyalty and protection is seen as one of the highest values of family life. Therefore, shaming, ridiculing, insulting, or criticizing family members, especially in public, can have serious consequences.
- Newer Arab American refugees or immigrants may be reluctant to accept police assistance. Because families are tightly knit, they can also be closed "units" whereby members prefer to keep private matters or conflicts to themselves. As a result, officers will have to work harder at establishing rapport if they want to gain cooperation.

There is an important point of contact between all three of these characteristics and law enforcement interaction with members of Arab American families. Berro explains: "When we respond to a call at a home, the police car is like a magnet. Every family member comes out of the house and everyone wants to talk at once. It can be an overwhelming sensation for an officer who doesn't understand this background" (Berro, 2009).

A police officer who is not trained in understanding and responding appropriately and professionally to cultural differences could alienate the family by (1) not respecting the interest and involvement of the family members, and (2) attempting to gain control of the communication in an authoritarian and offensive manner. The consequences may be that he or she would have difficulty establishing the rapport needed to gain information about the conflict at hand and would then not be trusted or respected. To do the job effectively, law enforcement officials must respect Arab family values, along with communication style differences (the latter will be discussed shortly).

Head of the Household

As in most cultures with a traditional family structure, the man in the Arab home is overtly the head of the household and his role and influence are strong. The wife has a great deal of influence, too, but it can more often be "behind the scenes." An Arab woman does not always defer to her husband in private as she would in public. However, as mentioned earlier in the chapter, there are many women who have broken out of the traditional mold and tend to be more vocal, out-spoken, and assertive than were their mothers or grandmothers. Traditionally, in many Arab countries, some fathers maintain their status by being strict disciplinarians and demanding absolute respect, thus creating some degree of fear among children and even among wives. Once again, Arab Americans born and raised in this country have, for the most part, adopted middle-class "American" style of child raising whereby children participate in some of the decision making and are treated in an egalitarian manner just as an adult would be. In addition, as with changing roles among all kinds of families in the United States, the father as traditional head of the household and the mother as having "second-class" status is no longer prevalent among established Arab Americans in the United States. Wife abuse and child abuse are not considered respectable practices by educated Arab Americans, but the practices still occur, just as they do in mainstream American society (particularly, but not exclusively, among people on the lower socioeconomic levels).

In traditional Arab society, display of power and influence is a common male behavioral characteristic. While this can be viewed in a negative light, from certain Western perspectives, this trait can be helpful in securing the compliance of the family in important matters. The husband or father can be a natural ally of authorities. Officers would be well advised to work with both the father and the mother, for example, in matters where children are involved. On family matters the woman frequently is the authority, even if she seems to defer to her husband. Communicating with the woman, even if indirectly, while still respecting the father's need to maintain his public status, will win respect from both the man and the woman.

Children and Americanization

Americanization, the process of becoming "American" in behavior, attitudes, and beliefs, has always been an issue with refugees/immigrants and their children. Typically, children are better able than their parents to learn a language and pick up the nuances of a culture. In addition, peer influence and pressure in American society begin to overshadow parental control, especially beginning in the preteen years. Arab children, who are cherished by their parents, face an extremely difficult cultural gap with their parents if they reach a stage where they are more "American" than "Arab." Children in Arab families are taught to be respectful in front of parents and to be conscious of family honor. Parents do not consider certain aspects of Americanized behavior, in general, to be respectful or worthy of pride. When children exhibit certain behaviors that bring shame to the family, discipline can indeed be harsh.

In extreme and infrequent cases, shame to the family can result in crimes against the children, involving violence. A police officer in a Midwest police department described a case in which a father shot his daughter because she had a boyfriend (Arab women are not allowed to associate freely with men before marriage and are expected to remain virgins). This case does not suggest that violent crime, in the Arab cultural context, is an appropriate response. Mental problems or drugs and alcohol accompany most violent acts. However, when a child's (and especially a girl's) behavior involves what is seen as sexual misconduct, the family's "face" is ruined. When this happens, *all* members of the family suffer. Culturally, when a family member commits a crime, there is great shame that colors the reputation of the entire family (Ismail, 2009).

There is very little an officer can do to change the attitudes of parents who oppose their children's behavior. However, if an officer responds to calls during which he or she notices that the family has become dysfunctional because of children's behavior, it would be a service to the family to initiate some sort of social service intervention or make a referral. If a family is already at the point of needing police assistance in problems involving children and their parents, then, more likely than not, they need other types of assistance as well. At the same time, newer immigrants and refugees will not necessarily be open to social service interventions, especially if the social workers do not speak Arabic. According to Lobna Ismail, President of Connecting Cultures, a Washington, D.C. firm specializing in Arab American cross-cultural understanding, some individuals may reveal more information to people outside their own community than to people within. Refugees and immigrants are concerned about losing face or shaming the family if personal information were to be disclosed to people from their own cultural, religious, or ethnic group (Ismail, 2009).

COMMUNICATION STYLES AND CULTURAL PRACTICES

As with all other immigrant groups, the degree to which people preserve their cultural practices varies. The following descriptions of everyday behavior will not apply equally to all Arab Americans, but they do not necessarily apply only to newcomers. Immigrants may preserve traditions and practices long after they come to a new country by conscious choice or sometimes because they are unaware of their cultural behavior (i.e., it is not in their conscious awareness).

Greetings, Names, Approach, Touching

Most Arab American newcomers expect to be addressed with a title and their last name (e.g., Mr or Miss followed by the last name) although in many Arab countries, people are addressed formally by a title and their first name. Most Arab women do not change their name after they are married or divorced. They therefore may not understand the distinction between a maiden name and a married name. The usual practice for an Arab woman is to keep her father's last name for life (Boller, 1992). An Arabic name may be spelled in several different ways in English. If you see "ibn" in the middle position of a name, it means "son of," and if you seen "bint" in the same position, it means "daughter of."

Many Arab Americans who have retained their traditional customs shake hands and then place their right hand on their chest near the heart. In the Middle East, Americans are advised to do the same if they observe this gesture. This gesture signifies warmth, deep respect, and gratitude. Officers can decide whether they are comfortable using this gesture—most people would not expect it from an officer, but some might appreciate the gesture as long as the officer was able to convey sincerity. Generally, when Arabs from the Middle East shake hands, they do not shake hands briefly or firmly. (The expression "He shakes hands like a dead fish" does not apply to other cultural groups!) Traditional Arab style is to hold hands longer than other Americans do and shake hands more lightly. Older children are taught to shake hands with adults as a sign of respect. Many Arabs would appreciate an officer shaking hands with their older children. With a recent immigrant or refugee Arab woman, it is generally not appropriate to shake hands unless she extends her hand first. This would definitely apply to women who wear head coverings.

Many Arabs of the same sex greet each other by kissing on the cheek. Two Saudi Arabian men, for example, may greet each other by kissing on both cheeks a number of times. This is a very common form of greeting. Public touching of the opposite sex is forbidden in the traditional Arab world, and male officers should make every effort not to touch Arab women, even casually (discussed further under "Key Issues in Law Enforcement").

Police officers should be aware that some Arab American citizens (e.g., Lebanese) who are new to the United States may react to a police officer's approach in unexpected ways. For example, an officer who has just asked a person to give his driver's license may find the person getting out of his car to be able to talk to the officer. From the person's perspective, he or she is simply trying to be courteous (since this is done in their home country). An officer, always conscious of safety issues, may simply have to explain that in the United States, officers require citizens to remain in their cars.

Hospitality

Hospitality is a byword among Arabs, whatever their station in life. As a guest in their homes, you will be treated to the kindest and most lavish consideration. Hospitality in the Arab culture is not an option; it is more of an obligation or duty. In some parts of the Arab world, if you thank someone for his or her hospitality, he or she may answer with a common expression meaning, "Don't thank me. It's my duty." (Here the word *duty* has a more positive than negative connotation.) To be anything but hospitable goes against the grain of Arab culture. Officers need to understand how deeply ingrained the need to be hospitable is and should not to misinterpret this behavior for something that it is not. Whether in the home or in a business owner's shop or office, when an officer enters, an Arab American may very well offer coffee and something to eat. This is not to be mistaken for a bribe and, from the Arab perspective, carries no negative connotations. According to Berro (2009), most people would be offended if you did not accept their offers of hospitality. However, given police regulations, you may have to decline. If this is the case, Berro advises officers to decline graciously. On the other hand, if the decision to accept the Arab American's hospitality depends on the officer's discretion, accepting can also be good for police–citizen relations. The period of time spent socializing and extending one's hospitality gives the person a chance to get to know and see if he or she can trust the other person. Business is not usually conducted between strangers. Obviously, on an emergency call, there is no time for such hospitality. However, with the move toward increasingly community-based police organizations, officers may find that they are involved in more situations in which they may decide to accept small gestures of hospitality, if within departmental policy.

Verbal and Nonverbal Communication

Arabs in general are very warm and expressive people, both verbally and nonverbally, and appreciate it when others extend warmth to them. There are some areas in the realm of nonverbal communication in which Americans, without cultural knowledge, have misinterpreted the behavior of Arab Americans simply because of their own ethnocentrism (i.e., the tendency to judge others by one's own cultural standards and norms).

CONVERSATIONAL DISTANCE   Acceptable conversational distance between two people is often related to cultural influences. Officers are very aware of safety issues and keep a certain distance from people when communicating with them. Generally, officers like to stand about an arm's length or farther from citizens to avoid possible assaults on their person. This distance is similar to how far apart "mainstream Americans" stand when in conversation. Cultures subtly influence the permissible distance between two people. When the distance is "violated," a person can feel threatened (either consciously or unconsciously). Many but not all Arabs, especially if they are new to the country, tend to have a closer acceptable conversational distance with each other than do other Americans. In Arab culture, it is not considered offensive to "feel a person's breath." Yet many Americans, unfamiliar with this intimacy in regular conversation, have misinterpreted the closeness. While still being conscious of safety, the law enforcement officer can keep in mind that the closer than "normal" behavior (i.e., "normal" for the officer) does not necessarily constitute a threat.

When Americans travel to the Middle East, they will notice the tendency for people to stand closer to each other as compared to mainstream U.S. cultural norms. This is relevant to police officers in the United States, especially in the context of communicating with recent immigrants and refugees. (It is recommended that you not back away when an Arab stands very close while speaking to you in order to maintain rapport.) Some Arabs may stare into other people's eyes, watching the pupils for an indication of the other person's response (e.g., dilated pupils mean a positive response). Police officers, however, should avoid staring directly into a woman's eyes.

GESTURES   Many gestures used by Arabs from some countries are distinctly different from those familiar to non-Arab Americans. In a section entitled "Customs and Manners in the Arab World," Devine and Braganti (1991, p. 13) describe some commonly used gestures among Arabs:

- *What does it mean?* or *What are you saying?* Hold up the right hand and twist it as if you were screwing in a light bulb one turn.
- *Wait a minute.* Hold all fingers and thumb touching with the palm up.
- *No.* This can be signaled in one of three ways: moving the head back slightly and raising the eyebrows, moving the head back and raising the chin, or moving the head back and clicking with the tongue.
- *Go away.* Hold the right hand out with the palm down and move it as if pushing something away from you.
- *Never.* A forceful never is signaled by holding the right forefinger up and moving it from left to right quickly and repeatedly.

As with many other cultural groups, pointing a finger directly at someone is considered rude and can be taken as a sign of contempt. Arab immigrants, especially older ones, will often use their entire hand to point. The "OK" or "thumbs up" gesture is considered obscene. Again, this applies only to people who have not yet been Americanized.

Emotional Expressiveness

> When I came to my brother's house to see what the problem was [i.e., with the police], I asked, "What the hell is going on?" I held my hands out and talked with my hands as I always do. I repeated myself and continued to gesture with my hands. Later (i.e., at a trial) the police officer said that the Arab woman was yelling and screaming and acting wild, waving her arms and inciting observers to riot by her actions.*

The Arab American involved in the above situation explained that Arab women, in particular, are very emotional and that police sometimes see this emotionalism as a threat. She explained that upon seeing a family member in trouble, it would be most usual and natural for a woman to put her

---

* The names of individuals and departments have been omitted even though permission has been granted to quote. The purpose of including these incidents is not to put undue attention on any one department or individual but rather to provide education on police professionalism in interethnic relations.

hands to her face and say something like, "Oh, my God" frequently and in a loud voice. While other Americans can react this same way, it is worth pointing out that in mainstream American culture, there is a tendency to subdue one's emotions and not to go "out of control." What some Americans consider "out of control" Arabs (like Mexicans, Greeks, Israelis, and Iranians, among other groups) consider perfectly "normal" behavior. In fact, the lack of emotionalism that Arabs observe among mainstream Americans can be misinterpreted as lack of interest or involvement.

Although a communication-style characteristic never applies to all people in one cultural group (and we have seen that there is a great deal of diversity among Arab Americans), there are group traits that apply to many people. Arabs, especially the first generation of relatively recent newcomers, tend to display emotions when talking. Unlike many people in Asian cultures (e.g., Japanese and Korean), Arabs have not been "taught" that the expression of emotion is a sign of immaturity or a lack of control. Arabs, like other Mediterranean groups, such as Israelis or Greeks, tend to shout when they are excited or angry and are very animated in their communication. They may repeatedly insert expressions into their speech such as "I swear by God." This is simply a cultural mannerism.

Westerners, however, tend to judge this "style" negatively. To a Westerner, the emotionalism, repetition, and emphasis on certain statements can give the impression that the person is not telling the truth or is exaggerating for effect. An officer unfamiliar with these cultural mannerisms may feel overwhelmed, especially when involved with an entire group of people. It would be well worth it for the officer to determine the spokesperson for the group, and to refrain from showing impatience or irritation at this culturally different style. An Arab American community member made the following comment about police reactions toward Arab Americans:

> Police see Arab emotionalism as a threat. They see the involvement of our large families in police incidents as a threat. They don't need to feel overwhelmed by us and try to contain our reactions. We will cooperate with them, but they need to show us that they don't view us as backward and ignorant people who are inferior just because we are different and because we express ourselves in a more emotional way than they do. (Arab American community member)

SWEARING, OBSCENITIES, AND INSULTS   Officers working in Arab American communities should know that for Arabs, words are extremely powerful. If an officer displays a lack of professionalism by swearing at an Arab (even words like "damn"), it will be nearly impossible to repair the damage.

In one case of documented police harassment of several Arab Americans (names have been omitted in order not to single out this department), witnesses attest to officers' saying, "Mother-f_____ Arabs, we're going to teach you. Go back home!" One of the Arab American citizens involved in the case reported that officers treated him like an animal and were very insulting by asking in a demeaning tone questions such as, "Do you speak English? Do you read English?" (The man was a highly educated professional who had been in the United States for several years.) In asking him about his place of employment (he worked at an Arab American organization), the man reported that they referred to his place of employment as "the Arab Islamic shit or crap? What is that?"

Officers who understand professionalism are aware that this type of language and interaction is insulting to all persons. The choice to use obscenities and insults, especially in conjunction with one's ethnic background, however, means that officers risk never being able to establish trust within the ethnic community. This can translate into not being able to secure cooperation when needed. Even a few officers exhibiting this type of behavior can damage the reputation of an entire department for a long period of time.

ENGLISH LANGUAGE PROBLEMS   If time allows, before asking the question "Do you speak English?" officers should try to assess whether the Arab American is a recent arrival or an established citizen who might react negatively to the question. A heavy accent does not necessarily mean that a person is unable to speak English (although that can be the case). There are specific communication skills that can be used with limited-English-speaking persons (see Chapter 4), which should be applied with Arab Americans. Officers should proceed slowly and nonaggressively with questioning and, wherever possible, ask open-ended questions. An officer's patience and willingness to take extra time will be beneficial in the long run.

KEY ISSUES IN LAW ENFORCEMENT

Perceptions of and Interactions with Police

It is not possible to generalize Arab Americans' perception of the police, but it is fair to say that a large part of the Arab American community has great respect for the police. On the other hand, some of the immigrants, such as Jordanians and Palestinians, do not understand the American system and have an ingrained fear of police because of political problems in their own region of the world (James Zogby, 2006). Since they distrust the government, they are more likely to reject help from the police, and this puts them at a decided disadvantage in that they can more easily become victims. Their fear, in combination with the interdependence and helpfulness that characterize the extended family, results in families not wanting assistance from the police. Thus police will encounter some families who would prefer to handle conflicts on their own even when police intervention is clearly needed. Some of the newer immigrants and refugees feel that it is dishonorable to have to go outside the family (e.g., to police and social service providers) to get help, and, if given a choice, they would choose not to embarrass themselves and their families in this manner.

Within the Arab world of the Middle East, there are major differences among countries in the institution of policing and the manner in which citizens are required to behave with police. Immigrants from Iraq, for example, have complained that "Saddam's enforcers robbed them of their jewelry, even if it meant cutting off their fingers to get it" (Haddad, 2006). Similarly, in Saudi Arabia there is more of a fear of police than in some other countries because the punishments are stricter. For example, if a person is caught stealing, he or she will have a hand removed if a repeat offender. A Saudi Arabian woman caught shoplifting in a San Francisco Bay Area 7-11 store begged a police officer on her knees not to make the arrest because she feared being sent back to Saudi Arabia and did not know what would happen to her there. As it turned out, the officer did let her go since it was her first offense. He felt that he had some discretion in this case and decided to consider the woman's cultural background and circumstances. When it comes to interpreting cultural influences on police incidents and crimes, especially those of a lesser nature, each officer has to decide for himself or herself. (This aspect of law enforcement is discussed in Chapter 1.)

Modesty, Women's Dress, and Diversity among Women

In many parts of traditional Arab society, women do not socialize freely with men and tend to dress modestly. However, the everyday practices in the various Arab countries differ greatly. In countries such as Lebanon, Jordan, and Egypt women sometimes dress in a contemporary and modern manner and may, at the same time, cover their hair with a headscarf.

In Saudi Arabia, strict rules are maintained about public dress (e.g., the "morals police" may tap women on the ankle with a stick if their dress is too short). How some Arab women perceive the norms around their attire can differ greatly from how that same attire is perceived in the United States. For example, one of this text's coauthors (D. L.) spoke with several women in Algeria who appreciated the anonymity they could achieve with the *sefsari* (i.e., their clothing that completely covered them). The contrasts in women's attire in the Middle East are striking. Lobna Ismail of Connecting Cultures described the cover of a 2003 publication of a book entitled *Teen Life in the Middle East:*

> Two young women are talking to each other. One is wearing a black cloak or "abaya" and her hair is covered with a black scarf. The other is also wearing a black cloak, but it is open and you can see that the young woman is wearing ripped jeans and her knee cap is exposed, she has a tight shirt, and she is smoking a cigarette. (Ismail, 2009)

Ismail points out the tremendous diversity among women in the various Arab countries and the need to stay away from stereotypes based on an image of a woman in traditional Arab dress. She adds that it is not possible to draw conclusions about a woman's degree of religiosity, political affiliation, and education level just based on how she dresses. She has also observed that people often assume that an American Muslim woman who covers her hair is a newcomer to the United States and cannot speak English well. This can be quite contrary to the reality (Ismail, 2009).

Similarly, according to Ismail, there is a great deal of diversity in the United States as to how people interpret the religious preference for dressing modestly (Ismail, 2009). What a woman chooses to do differs among families. Some traditional families, even in the United States, may encourage their daughters and wives to dress modestly. In some cases, young women themselves choose to dress more modestly than their parents expect. For example, in the United States, some young women cover their hair even if their mothers do not (Ismail, 2009). In the Middle East, women may or may not wear head coverings; the choice depends on multiple factors, such as their family, age, personal preference, and background.

Modesty for a traditional Arab Muslim woman may include the need to cover her head so that men will not see her hair. In some traditional Islamic societies, a man must not see a woman's hair, and male officers should understand that asking a woman to remove her head covering (e.g., for the purpose of searching her or getting a photo identification) is analogous to asking her to expose a private part of her body. Corporal Berro, an Arab American at the Dearborn, Michigan, Police Department, advises officers to approach this matter sensitively: "Don't overpower the woman, intimidate her, or grab her head cover. Ask her to go into a private room and have her remove it or get a female officer to help with the procedure" (Berro, 2009).

American officers may have difficulty understanding the violation that a traditional Arab woman feels when her head covering is taken away forcibly. Even if a woman is arrested for something like disorderly conduct, she will be offended by any aggressive move on the part of the officer to remove her head cover or touch her in any way. When police procedures require that a head cover be removed, the officers should explain the procedure and offer some kind of an apology to show respect. Having dealt with this same issue, Immigration and Customs Enforcement (ICE) modified its regulations in the following way: "Every applicant . . . shall clearly show a three-quarter profile view of the features of the applicant with the head bare (unless the applicant is wearing a head scarf as required by a religious order of which he or she is a member)" (formerly INS Regulation 8 C.F.R. 331.1(a), 1992). Thus, ICE officials photograph Muslim women with their head coverings on. Because police departments deal with safety issues (such as concealed weapons), they may not have the liberty to accommodate this particular cultural difference in the same way as the ICE does. The matter of women and head coverings must be handled with extreme sensitivity. Similar to Berro's advice, Lobna Ismail's suggestion is that if a woman has to remove her head covering for an extensive search, the officer should first ask her to remove it herself in a private area with a female officer in attendance. Moreover, this should be done out of view of any unrelated male (Ismail, 2009). The authors of this book also recommend that law enforcement officers and corrections personnel use good judgment in this matter and not compromise their individual safety in the performance of their duties.

Arab Small Business Owners

Racial and ethnic tensions exist between Arab grocers and liquor store owners in low-income areas (such as Detroit and Cleveland) and members of other minority groups. The dynamics between Arab store-owners and African Americans are similar to those between Koreans and African Americans in inner cities. The non-Arab often views the Arab as having money and exploiting the local residents for economic gain. Dr. James Zogby explains that this perception is reinforced because, in some locales, one rarely sees a non-Arab working in an Arab-owned store. The local resident, according to Zogby, does not understand that the Arabs, for the most part, are political refugees (e.g., Palestinians) and have come to the United States for a better life. Despite stereotypes that these store owners have connections to "Arab money" (i.e., oil money), when they first arrive, the only work that they can do is operate small "marginal" businesses. Most of the small Arab-run grocery stores, liquor stores, and gas stations are family-operated businesses where two brothers, or a father and two sons, for example, are managing the operation. It would not be economically possible for them to hire outside their family (the situation is similar to Korean family-run businesses) (James Zogby, 2006). Police officers, in the midst of the conflicts between the store owners and the residents, can attempt to explain the position of the refugees, but of course, the explanation by itself cannot take care of the problem. Many poor American-born citizens harbor a great deal of animosity toward immigrants and refugees because of scarce resources.

Alcohol is forbidden in the Muslim religion, yet Arab liquor store owners sell it to their customers. There has been a debate in the Arab American community as to whether Muslim immigrants and refugees should go into this type of business. For the majority of newcomers, however, the choices are very limited. Members of other ethnic groups have also owned many of the mom-and-pop stores throughout the years.

Finally, there is another dimension to the problem of Arab store owners in inner cities. Many inner-city residents (Arab Americans and African Americans included) do not feel that law enforcement officials take the needs of the inner city as seriously as they do elsewhere. A pattern has emerged in the Arab American community whereby Arab American store owners feel that they themselves have to take on problems of crime in their stores (John Zogby, 2006). If an Arab store owner is robbed and is treated in an unsupportive or harsh way by the police, he feels that he has to defend himself and his store all by himself. In some cases, Arab store owners have assaulted shoplifters in their stores, potentially risking becoming the victims themselves. Like many other minority group members, some Arab shop owners in the inner city have given up on the police. Police officers cannot solve the social ills that plague the inner city, but, at a minimum, need to instill the confidence that they will be as supportive as possible when dealing with the crimes that immigrant/refugee store owners experience. In addition, Arab shop or gas station owners will assist their more recently arrived relatives in opening a similar business. Many of these recent immigrants do not know the system or all the regulations for running a business. There have been instances of store owners being chastised for running "illegal" businesses, when in fact they were not familiar with the complete process required for proper licensing (Haddad, 2006).

Hate Crimes against Arab Americans

Hate crimes are also discussed in Chapters 11 and 12. The following explanation deals mainly with the stereotyping and scapegoating of Arabs that often take place when a crisis in the Arab world involves Americans, or when significant events in America are linked to Arabs. Arab Americans also have a special need for protection during times of political tensions in the Middle East. As discussed in the section "The 'Terrorist' Stereotype, Post-9/11 Backlash, and Ongoing Challenges," the weeks and months following the attacks were accompanied by a huge spike in hate crimes directed at Arab Americans, Muslim Americans, and those thought to be of the same background.

There were more than 700 violent crimes against Arab Americans reported within the first 9 weeks after the tragedy of September 11, and 165 reported hate crimes from January 1, 2002, through October 11, 2002, a figure higher than most years in the previous 10 years ADC, Report, 2002b). However, the American-Arab Anti-Discrimination Committee (ADC) emphasized that this did not represent the actual total number of hate crimes; many cases were not made public because victims feared additional violence against them. Senior Deputy Chief Ronald Haddad pointed out that fear is a universally human emotion when one is victimized, and this fear factor plays an important role in why many hate crimes go unreported. In explaining the lack of reporting to police, it is also important to recognize the Arab value of saving face and maintaining harmony whenever possible (Haddad, 2006).

Prior to the terrorist attacks of 9/11, "single-bias" hate crimes (with a single motivation) against people from one ethnic or national group were the second *least* reported of the hate crimes. The initial spike in post-9/11 hate crimes declined significantly as community members and law enforcement officers worked together to curb the number of incidents. (See Exhibits 8.1 and 8.2 for the immediate post-9/11 increase in hate crimes, and Chapter 11 for further data from September 11, 2001 to 2007). Weeks before the war with Iraq, the FBI warned of a similar potential surge in hate

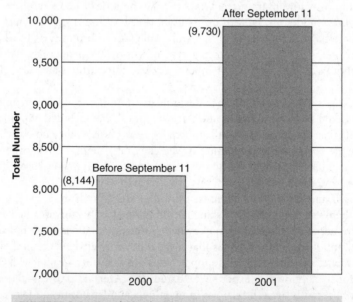

EXHIBIT 8.1   Total Single-Bias Hate Crimes before and after September 11, 2001.

Source: FBI Hate Crime Statistics.

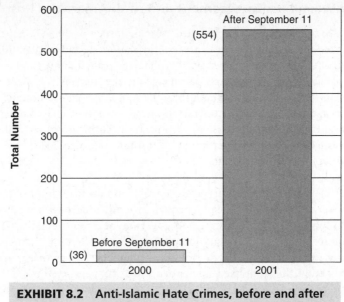

EXHIBIT 8.2   Anti-Islamic Hate Crimes, before and after September 11, 2001.

Source: FBI Hate Crime Statistics.

crimes. Top FBI officials met with Arab and Muslim leaders in the United States to assure them of the FBI's priority to prevent and investigate hate crimes. This was a step that they had *not* initially taken in the aftermath of September 11. The targeted interviews of thousands of Iraqis living in the United States were also organized in part to reassure the Iraqi community that law enforcement officials would not tolerate any ethnic backlash in the case of a war (FBI, 2003). Many Arab American agencies reported an increase in discriminatory incidents after the 2003 American invasion in Iraq, though this increase was less dramatic than what followed the terrorist attacks. Continual positive work of government and local leaders to eliminate ethnic backlash is evidenced by the May 2003 Senate resolution written by Senator Dick Durbin (D-IL) and unanimously approved, condemning violence and bigotry against Arab Americans, Muslim Americans, South Asian Americans, and Sikh Americans. (Chapter 10 touches upon some of the post-9/11 governmental actions that had an adverse effect on trust with Arab communities nationwide.)

In 2008, the ADC reported on hate crimes and discrimination against Arab Americans between the years 2003 and 2007. While the actual number of hate crimes was down as compared to the immediate post-9/11 period, there were nevertheless significant numbers of hate crimes, acts of discrimination (especially at airports and at the workplace), and border and customs issues targeted toward Arab Americans (ADC, 2008). Vandalism and destruction of property at mosques and Islamic centers were on the rise during the years 2003–2007 (ADC, 2008). Nevertheless, in the ADC's report of hate crimes during this period, praise was given to law enforcement authorities:

> Hate crimes have for the most part been thoroughly investigated by law enforcement authorities, particularly the civil rights division of the Department of Justice (DOJ). ADC commends local, state and federal law enforcement for their efforts to ensure that Arab Americans and those perceived to be Arab Americans are protected from such abuses and hate crimes. (ADC, 2008)

Relations between Law Enforcement and Arab Americans Post-9/11

According to a study released by the Vera Institute of Justice in 2006, "In the aftermath of September 11, Arab Americans have a greater fear of racial profiling and immigration enforcement than of falling victim to hate crimes." Nearly 100 Arab Americans and over 100 law enforcement personnel (FBI agents and police officers) participated in the study, which was conducted from 2003 to 2005. Interviewees in the study, both from the Arab American community and from the law enforcement agencies, felt that cooperation and trust post-9/11 had deteriorated. Arab Americans reported an "increasing sense of victimization, suspicion of law enforcement, and concerns about protecting their civil liberties" (Vera Institute of Justice, 2006).

Interview inquiries confirmed that:

> September 11 had a substantial impact on Arab American communities. In every site, Arab Americans described heightened levels of public suspicion exacerbated by increased media attention and targeted governmental policies (such as special registration requirements, voluntary interviews, and the detention and deportation of community members). Although community members also reported increases in hate victimization, they expressed greater concern about being victimized by federal policies and practices than by individual acts of harassment or violence. Among law enforcement, the most notable change was a new pressure to incorporate counter-terrorism into their work. Local police and FBI participants alike reported that this pressure had frequently resulted in policies that were poorly defined or inconsistently applied. (Vera Institute of Justice, 2006)

In addition to looking at the continued repercussions of 9/11, within both the Arab American community and the law enforcement community, the study also examined relations between these two communities post-9/11 and through 2005. While most of the FBI field offices in the study had made attempts to "reach out" to Arab American communities, many of the Arab American interviewees feared federal efforts and remained suspicious of them. In contrast, there was less fear and animosity when it came to local police departments. Furthermore, where local departments had made efforts to "cultivate goodwill," there appeared to be reduced tensions between community members and local police (Vera Institute of Justice, 2006).

The findings of the Vera Institute Study support the recommendations of the ADC that were published soon after 9/11. To build trust, the ADC recommends that law enforcement agencies and Arab Americans work closely with one another especially to foster a safe environment where citizens feel comfortable reporting hate crimes. The ADC recommends that law enforcement officials avoid stereotyping as suspects those involved in lawful political and religious activities, with the reminder that racial profiling is neither effective nor acceptable (ADC Report, 2002c).

Summary

- There is some confusion as to who Arabs and Middle Easterners are; although commonly thought of as Arabs, Iranians and Turks are not Arabs, and they do not speak Arabic. Many people assume that all Muslims are Arabs, and vice versa. Many Arabs are also Christians, and the world's Muslim population is actually comprised of dozens of ethnic groups. The largest Muslim population is in Asia, not in the Middle East. Nevertheless, the predominant religion among Arabs is Islam, and its followers are called Muslims. Israelis are also Middle Easterners; it is the only country in the Middle East in which the majority of the population is not Muslim. There are Arabs living in Israel who are Christians or Muslims. The majority of the Israeli population are Jewish, and their language is Hebrew.

• Many recent Middle Eastern immigrants and refugees in the United States have come for political reasons, but not all Arab Americans left their country of origin because of this. The first wave of Arab immigrants, largely from Syria, came between 1880 and World War I to further themselves economically. In sharp contrast to the first wave of immigrants in terms of motivation and compositional characteristics, the second wave of Arab immigrants to the United States, beginning after World War II, came in large part as students and professionals seeking to escape economic instability and political unrest in their home countries. The communities with the largest Arab American populations are in Los Angeles/Orange County, Detroit, the greater New York area, Chicago, and Washington, D.C. California has the largest "cluster" of Arab American communities.

• There is great diversity among Arab American groups. Understanding this diversity will assist officers in not categorizing Arabs as homogeneous and will encourage people to move away from stereotypical thinking. Arabs from the Middle East come from at least 13 different countries, many of which are vastly different from each other. Nevertheless, there are several basic Arab cultural values that officers should keep in mind when interacting with Arab American citizens, and these are shared across the various cultural groups. The cultural values of "face" and "saving face," which relate to dignity, reputation, and honor, are of paramount importance. Every effort should be made to protect one's "face" or honor. Family loyalty often takes precedence over other needs. Communication should be courteous and hospitable; honor and face-saving govern interpersonal interactions and relationships.

• Arab Americans have been wrongly characterized and stereotyped by the media, and as with all stereotypes, inaccurate perceptions have affected people's thinking on Arab Americans. Officers should be aware of stereotypes that may influence their judgment. Common stereotypes of Arabs include illiterate and backward, thieves, and terrorists. The Arab world has been perceived in the West in terms of these negative stereotypes, and these have been transferred to Americans of Arab descent. Prejudice against Arabs based on stereotypes has been constant for decades. The terrorist stereotype deepened after September 11, 2001. The backlash that ensued against Arab Americans, Muslim Americans, and those thought to be of Middle Eastern origin was predicted by many organizations and individuals, including critics of the media's stereotyped image of a Middle Easterner as a terrorist. Scapegoating against Arabs spread pervasively across the country in light of the existing stereotypes and the events of September 11, 2001.

• Officers can demonstrate to Muslim Arabs a respect for their religion by refraining from interrupting people in the mosque, and during prayers, unless absolutely necessary; maintaining courteous behavior in mosques, such as not stepping on prayer mats, not walking in front of people who are praying, and not touching a Qur'an. Finally, officers should attempt to work out solutions with community members regarding such issues as noise and parking associated with religious celebrations.

• The basic unit for Arab Americans, especially for recent arrivals and traditional families, is not the individual but the family, including the extended family. If a family member is involved in a police incident, officers should expect that other family members will become actively involved. Officers should not automatically assume that this involvement is an attempt to interfere with police affairs. The traditional Arab families are used to working out their conflicts by themselves; this is further reason for all members to become involved. Traditionally and outwardly, the father is the head of the household and much of the conversation should be directed toward him;

this does not mean that the officer should ignore the women.

- There are a number of specific cultural practices and taboos that officers should consider when communicating with Arab Americans who have preserved a traditional lifestyle. Be respectful of the preference of some Arab women to be modest. Male officers should not touch a woman at all, and should be mindful of her modesty in front of male officers. Traditional Arabs deeply value hospitality; it is a hallmark of culture in the Middle East. There are cultural differences in communication style that can affect officers' judgment and reactions. Becoming highly emotional (verbally and nonverbally) and speaking loudly is not looked down upon in the Arab world.

- Law enforcement needs to be continually vigilant as to the potential for hate crimes against Arab Americans and other Middle Eastern groups. In addition, some Middle Eastern immigrants bring negative perceptions of the police from their own experiences, and these contribute to the difficulty in trusting the police.

Discussion Questions and Issues

1. *Police–Ethnic Community Relations.* In the section entitled "Islamic Religion," the authors mention an incident that took place at the end of the holy month of Ramadan: officers ticketed many cars parked across the street from a mosque. According to community people, the stores adjacent to the parking lots were closed, and although parking was technically for customers only, the Arab Americans did not anticipate that there would be a problem utilizing the parking lot after hours. From a community relations point of view, the mass ticketing created some very negative feelings and a collective perception that "They (meaning the police) don't respect us; they don't want to understand us." What is your opinion regarding the way things were handled? Do you have any suggestions as to how this situation could have been prevented? Comment on what both the community and the police could have done to prevent the problem.

2. *Who Is the Head of the Household?* The stated head of the household in most traditional Arab families is the father, although the mother actually has a great deal of power within the family. Although in public many Arab women will defer decision making to their husbands, a police officer should not totally discount what the woman might have to offer in various police-related situations. How can the police officer, while respecting the status of the father, still acknowledge the mother and get input from her?

3. *Nonverbal Variations across Cultures.* When Arab Americans greet each other, they sometimes shake hands and then place their right hand on their chest near their heart. This is a sign of sincerity. In your opinion, should officers greet Arab Americans using this gesture if a person greets them in this way? What would be the pros and cons of doing this?

4. *Hospitality toward Officers: A Cultural Gesture.* Hospitality is a virtue in Arab culture and also functions to help people get to know (and see if they can trust) others with whom they are interacting. Given this cultural emphasis on being hospitable, what should an officer do if offered a cup of coffee and something to eat? If an officer has to decline the hospitality, how should it be done politely? Should department policy regarding the acceptance of hospitality be reexamined in light of this cultural tendency? Would your answer be different for departments that have adopted a community-based policing philosophy?

5. *"But It's the Custom in My Country."* In January 1991, the Associated Press reported that a Stockton, California, man originally from Jordan was arrested for investigation of "selling his daughter into slavery" because he allegedly accepted $25,000 for her arranged marriage. After police officers had taken the girl to a shelter, a police lieutenant reported on the father's protest claiming that "he was within his rights to arrange his daughter's marriage for a price." The father contacted the police and explained that it was the custom in his country and was perfectly acceptable. The police explained that he couldn't do that in this country: "It is slavery. . . ." The father

then went to the shelter where the daughter was and was arrested for creating a disturbance. If you were investigating this case, how would you proceed? How might you assess the validity of what the father was saying? If you found out that the act was indeed "perfectly acceptable in his country," how would you explain practices in the United States? Comment on the statement that the police made ("It is slavery"). From the perspective of needing cooperation from this man, what type of approach should be taken?

6. *Officer Discretion: To Let Her Go?* In the section on the perceptions of police, the authors mention an incident involving a Saudi Arabian woman who was caught shoplifting in a 7–11. She begged the officer to let her go because she feared being sent home, and there she would receive a harsh punishment (typically, in Saudi Arabia, a person's hand is cut off if he or she steals). The officer decided that since this was her first offense, he would let her go. What is your reaction to the officer's decision? What would you have done?

Website Resources

Visit these websites for additional information about law enforcement contact with Arab Americans and Middle Easterners in the United States.

American-Arab Anti-Discrimination Committee (ADC): http://www.adc.org

This website provides information about the ADC's civil rights efforts and useful summary data about cases and complaints regarding discrimination and hate crimes involving Arab Americans.

Arab American Institute Foundation (AAI): http://www.aaiusa.org

This website is dedicated to the civic and political empowerment of Americans of Arab descent. AAI provides policy, research, and public affairs services to support a broad range of community activities. In addition, the AAI also is a census information center on demographics of Arab Americans. On the website, you can access a PDF file entitled *Healing the Nation: The Arab-American Experience after September 11.*

Connecting Cultures: http://www.connecting-cultures.net

This website introduces Connecting Cultures, a consulting organization that designs and implements workshops and seminars on diversity, religion, and cross-cultural communication. It provides resources for understanding how culture and religion impact the way we communicate and work with one another. Connecting Cultures' specialty is Arab and Muslim Americans, as well as Arab culture, the Middle East, and the Muslim world.

FBI website: http://www.fbi.gov

This website provides hate crime statistics as a key feature.

United States Department of Justice: Community Relations Service http://www.usdoj.gov/crs/

The Community Relations Service is the Department's "peacemaker" for community conflicts and tensions arising from differences of race, color, and national origin. Created by the Civil Rights Act of 1964, CRS is the only federal agency dedicated to assist state and local units of government, private and public organizations, and community groups with preventing and resolving racial and ethnic tensions, incidents, and civil disorders, and in restoring racial stability and harmony. This website contains a short video entitled: "The First Three to Five Seconds"—Law Enforcement Roll Call Training Video on Arab and Muslim Cultural Awareness. This is an excellent resource for introductory training on aspects of Arab and Muslim culture.

Vera Institute of Justice: http://www.vera.org

The Vera Institute of Justice works closely with leaders in government and civil society to improve the services people rely on for safety and justice. Vera develops innovative, affordable programs that often grow into self-sustaining organizations; studies social problems and current responses; and provides practical advice and assistance to government officials around the world. They have publications on many law enforcement subjects, including a June 2006 study looking at law enforcement and Arab American community relations after 9/11.

Zogby International: http://www.zogby.com

This website provides statistics from the latest international public opinion polls covering a variety of issues, including those related to attitudes toward Arab Americans post-9/11.

References

American-Arab Anti-Discrimination Committee. (2002a). *Arab Stereotypes and American Educators* (by Wingfield and Karaman, 1995). Available: http://www.adc.org.

American-Arab Anti-Discrimination Committee. (2002b). *Report on Hate Crimes and Discrimination against Arab Americans: The Post-September 11 Backlash, Tracking Crimes from September 11, 2001 through October 11, 2002.* Available: http://www.adc.org.

American-Arab Anti-Discrimination Committee. (2002c). *ADC Fact Sheet, Condition of Arab Americans Post-9/11.* Washington, D.C.: ADC Research Institute.

American-Arab Anti-Discrimination Committee. (2008). *2003–2007 Report on Hate Crimes and Discrimination against Arab Americans. ADC Research Institute.* Washington, D.C.: ADC Research Institute. Retrieved April 16, 2009, from http://www.adc.org/PDF/hcr07.pdf.

Arab American Institute. (2003). Arab American Demographics: Full States Profiles, Demographic Data Based on Zogby International Polling. Retrieved April 19, 2009, from http://www.aaiusa.org/arab-americans/22/demographics (latest data available).

Armenian National Institute (ANI). (2006). *Frequently Asked Questions about the Armenian Genocide.* Washington, D.C.

Berro, Mohammed. (2009, February). Corporal, Dearborn, Michigan, Police Department, personal communication.

Boller, Philip J., Jr. (1992, March). "A Name Is Just a Name—Or Is It?" *FBI Law Enforcement Bulletin*, p. 6.

Central Intelligence Agency. (2003). *World Fact Book.* Agency (U.S. Govenrment). http://www.cia.gov/publications/factbook.

Central Intelligence Agency. (2006). *World Fact Book.* (U.S. Govenrment). http://www.cia.gov/publications/factbook.

Detroit Free Press. (2001). *100 Questions and Answers about Arab Americans: A Journalist's Guide.* Detroit, MI: Author.

"FBI: War Could Trigger Hate Crimes." (2003, March 12). Online at: http://www.cbsnews.com.

Haddad, Ronald. (2006, July). Senior Deputy Chief, Detroit, Michigan, Police Department, personal communication.

"Immigration Down in U.S. after 9/11." (2003, May 5). *Contra Costa Times*, p. A3.

Ismail, Lobna. (2009, April). President of Connecting Cultures, Washington, D.C., personal communication.

Mahdi, Ali Akbar, ed. (2003). *Teen Life in the Middle East.* Westport, CT: Greenwood Press.

MPI: Migration Information Source. (2009). "Iraqi Immigrants in the United States," by Terrazas, Aaron. Retrieved April 19, 2009, from: http://www.migrationinformation.org/USfocus/display.cfm?id=721\

Samhan, Helen. (2006, August). Executive Director, Arab American Institute, Foundation, Washington, D.C., personal communication.

Shaheen, Jack G. (2001). *Reel Bad Arabs: How Hollywood Vilifies A People.* New York: Olive Branch Press.

Vera Institute of Justice. (2006). *Law Enforcement and Arab American Community Relations after September 11, 2001: Engagement in a Time of Uncertainty*, by Nicole Henderson, Christopher W, Ortiz, Naomi F. Sugie, and Joel Miller.

Woodruff, David. (1991, February 4). "Letter from Detroit: Where the Mideast Meets the Midwest—Uneasily." *Business Week*, p. 30A.

Zogby, James, PhD. (2006, August). Director, Arab American Institute Foundation, Washington, D.C., personal communication.

Zogby, John, PhD. (2006, August). President, Zogby International, New York, personal communication.

CHAPTER 9

Law Enforcement Contact with Native Americans

LEARNING OBJECTIVES

After reading this chapter you should be able to:

- Describe the historical background of Native Americans especially as it relates to the dynamic between law enforcement representatives and Indians today.

- Define the terms *federally recognized tribe*, *Indian country*, and *reservations*.

- Discuss what most traditional Indian tribes share in common culturally.

- Describe characteristics of traditional Native American communication styles, including aspects of verbal and nonverbal interaction.

- Provide examples of terms, labels, and stereotypes that have been used to refer to or disparage Native Americans.

- Identify selected characteristics of the traditional Native American extended family, and acculturation problems of those who lack cultural and family support.

- List and discuss key issues associated with law enforcement contact with Native Americans.

OUTLINE

INTRODUCTION

> "It's just a bunch of Indians—let them go!"

Retired Chief Jim Cox, a Comanche Indian formerly with the Midwest City Police Department in Oklahoma, heard a police officer utter these words in the context of a traumatic moment he experienced as a youth in Oklahoma. He was riding with other Native American teenagers in an old Nash automobile. Police officers stopped the car and discovered that the teens had been drinking. Instead of taking appropriate action, which would have been to arrest the young people or at least to call the parents to pick the kids up, the officers let them go. Cox recalls to this day having heard one of the officers tell the other that Indians were not worth the time or bother: Cox interpreted this statement to mean that if the young people had killed themselves, it did not matter because they were "just Indians" (Cox, 2009). The impression of biased and prejudicial treatment of Indians* remained with him even after he had become a police officer. Dr. Peggy Bowen, Native American and Assistant Professor of Criminal Justice, expressed the sentiment that "as distasteful as the remark was then, it is absolutely still the reality today" (Bowen, 2009).

JOSE RIVERA, NATIVE AMERICAN CALIFORNIA STATE PEACE OFFICER (RETIRED)

When an officer contacts an Indian person, there is often 500 years of frustration built up. . . . Officers should be aware of the "baggage" that they bring to the encounter (Rivera, 2009).

SITTING BULL [LAKOTA], IN THE SPIRIT OF CRAZY HORSE

What treaty that the whites have kept has the red man broken? Not one. What treaty that the white man ever made with us have they kept? Not one. When I was a boy the Sioux owned the world; the sun rose and set on their land; they sent ten thousand men to battle. Who slew [the warriors]? Where are our lands? Who owns them? What white man can say I ever stole his land . . . ? Yet, they say I am a thief. What white woman, however lonely, was ever captive or insulted by me? Yet they say I am a bad Indian. What white man has ever seen me drunk? Who has ever seen me . . . abuse my children? What law have I broken? Is it wicked for me because my skin is red? (Matthiessen, 1992)

HISTORICAL INFORMATION AND BACKGROUND

Recorded history disputes the origins of the first "Indians" in America. Some researchers claim that they arrived from Asia more than 40,000 years ago; others claim that they did not arrive from anywhere else. In either case, despite their long history in North America and the fact that they were the first "Americans," traditional U.S. history books did not recognize their existence until

---

* The authors use the terms *Native American*, *American Indian*, and *Indian* interchangeably. *Native American* is often preferred as the generic name; however, government agencies often break down this overly broad category into American Indian and Alaska native. In modern usage, the term *Native Americans* can also include Native Hawaiian, Chamorros (native peoples of Guam), and American Samoans. This chapter does not include information about these cultural groups.

the European conquests, beginning with Christopher Columbus in 1492. The subject of native peoples as either nonexistent or insignificant reflects an ethnocentric and Eurocentric view of history. Even the word *Indian* is not a term that Native Americans originally used to designate their tribes or communities. Because Columbus did not know that North and South America existed, he thought he had reached the Indies, which then included India, China, the East Indies, and Japan. In fact, he arrived in what is now called the West Indies (in the Caribbean), and he called the people he met *Indians* (*Los Indios*). Eventually, this became the name for all the indigenous peoples in the Americas. However, before the white settlers came to North and South America, almost every "Indian" tribe had its own name, and despite some shared cultural values, Native Americans did not see themselves as one collective group or call themselves *Indians*. Most tribes refer to themselves in their own languages as "The People," "The Allies," or "The Friends." Some of the terms that whites use for various tribes are not even authentic names for that tribe. For example, the label *Sioux*, which means enemy or snake, was originally a term given to that group by an enemy tribe and then adopted by French traders. In many cases, a tribe's real name is not necessarily the name commonly used.

Today in public schools across the country, some educators are only beginning to discuss the nature of much of the contact with Native Americans in early American history. Traditionally, rather than being presented as part of the American people's common legacy, Native American cultural heritage is often presented as bits of colorful "exotica." Genocide, or the killing of entire tribes, is not a chapter in U.S. history on which people have wanted to focus. The reality is that Euro American and Indian relations have been characterized by hostility, contempt, and brutality. The native peoples have generally been treated by Euro Americans as less than human or as "savages," and the rich Native American cultures have been ignored or crushed. For this reason, many culturally identifying American Indians do not share in the celebrations of Thanksgiving or Christopher Columbus Day parades. To say that Columbus discovered America implies that Native Americans were not considered "human enough" to be of significance. Ignoring the existence of the Native Americans before 1492 constitutes only one aspect of ethnocentrism. American Indians' experience with the "white man" has largely been one of exploitation, violence, and forced relocation. This historical background has shaped many Native American views of Euro Americans and their culture. While most people in the United States have a sense that Native Americans were not treated with dignity in U.S. history, many are not aware of the extent of the current abuse toward them, perhaps because this group is a small and traditionally "forgotten minority" in the United States, constituting approximately 4.5 million people or 1.5 percent of the overall population (the grouping "Native American" includes "Alaska Natives") (U.S. Census Bureau News, 2008).

It would not be accurate to say that no progress at all has been made in the United States with respect to the awareness and rights of our nation's first Americans. On November 6, 2000, former President Clinton renewed his commitment to tribal sovereignty by issuing an Executive Order on consultation with tribal governments. The purpose of the Order is "to establish meaningful consultation and collaboration with tribal officials in the development of federal policies having tribal implications, to strengthen the administration's government-to-government relationship to tribes, and to reduce the imposition of unfounded mandates by ensuring that all executive departments and agencies consult with tribes and respect tribal sovereignty as they develop policies on issues that impact Indian communities" (Legix, 2000). Former President Bush, in 2002, announced in the Proclamation in Honor of National American Indian Heritage Month that by working together on important economic initiatives, "we will strengthen America . . . with hope and promise for all Native Americans" (White House, 2002). President Obama's speech to the Crow Indian Nation on their reservation in Montana acknowledged the failure of the U.S. government to keep its promises to Native Americans, referring to their "tragic history."

> Few have been ignored by Washington for as long as Native Americans—the first Americans . . . I understand the tragic history . . . Our government has not always been honest or truthful in our deals. ("Obama Adopted by Native Americans," 2008)

American Indians continue to fight legal battles over the retention of Indian lands and other rights previously guaranteed by U.S. treaties. The U.S. government has often not acted in good faith towards its Native American citizens by seriously and repeatedly disregarding Indian rights that have been guaranteed in the form of binding treaties. Consequently, individuals and tribes are reluctant to trust the words of the government or people representing "the system" because of the breach of many treaties. Whether they are aware of it or not, law enforcement agents are perceived this way and carry this "baggage" into encounters with Native Americans. Historically, the police officer from outside the reservation has been a symbol of rigid and authoritarian governmental control that has affected nearly every aspect of Indian life, especially on reservations. Officers, like most citizens, have only a limited understanding of how the government, including the criminal justice system, caused massive suffering by not allowing Indians to preserve their cultures, identities, languages, sacred sites, rituals, and lands. Because of this, officers have a responsibility to educate themselves about the history of the treatment of Indian peoples in order to deal with them effectively and fairly today. Law enforcement officers must understand Indian communities and put forth extra efforts to establish rapport. Doing so will increase the possibility of success at winning cooperation and respect from people who never before had any reason to trust any representative of government.

Native Americans and Military Service

For some American Indians, an additional phenomenon aggravates the repeated breach of trust by the federal government. There is a very proud tradition of American Indians serving in the military. For more than 200 years, they have participated with distinction in U.S. military actions. American military leaders, beginning with George Washington in 1778, have recognized American Indians to be courageous, determined, and as having a "fighting spirit" (CEHIP, 1996). American Indians contributed to the military in the 1800s and contributed on an even larger scale beginning in the 1900s. In World War I, it is estimated that 12,000 American Indians served in the military.

> More than 44,000 American Indians, out of a total Native American population of less than 350,000, served with distinction between 1941 and 1945 in both European and Pacific theaters of war. Native American men and women on the home front also showed an intense desire to serve their country and were an integral part of the war effort. More than 40,000 Indian people left their reservations to work in ordnance depots, factories, and other war industries. American Indians also invested more than $50 million in war bonds and contributed generously to the Red Cross and the Army and Navy Relief societies. . . . The Native American's strong sense of patriotism and courage emerged once again during the Vietnam era. More than 42,000 Native Americans, more than 90 percent of them volunteers, fought in Vietnam. (CEHIP, 1996)

In Desert Storm, Bosnia, and the war in Afghanistan and Iraq, Native Americans continued to serve in the U.S. Armed Forces with the estimated number having exceeded 12,000 American Indians ("First American Female and Native Soldier. . . ," 2003). According to the Defense Department, "Native Americans represent less than 1 percent of the population, yet they make up about 1.6 percent of the armed forces." The first woman soldier to die in Iraq was, Lori Pestewa, a 23-year old Hopi woman who served with the 507th Maintenance Company in Iraq ("Native Americans Back from Iraq. . . ," 2005).

> In being the first woman soldier to die in the Iraqi War and the first Native American woman to die in combat, Private First Class Lori Piestewa of the United States Army and from the Hoppi tribe served with devotion to duty. The U.S. Army reported that PFC Piestewa died fighting the enemy when her convoy was ambushed on March 23, 2003, near Nasiriyah, Iraq. PFC Piestewa died in battle along with eight other soldiers as PFC Jessica Lynch was taken prisoner and later rescued by U.S. troops on April 1, 2003. PFC Piestewa was 23 years old, a single mother of a four-year-old son and a three-year-old daughter. She carried on the tradition of her father, a Vietnam veteran, and her grandfather, a World War II veteran. Her determination shone through in a local television interview before being sent to Iraq from her hometown of Tuba, Arizona: "I am ready to go," she said, looking straight at the camera. "I learned to work with people. It's very important to me to know that my family is going to be taken care of." After her death, thanks to donations from the public, a scholarship fund was set up for Piestewa's children. Two Phoenix landmarks, Squaw Peak and Squaw Peak Freeway, have been renamed Piestewa Peak and Piestewa Freeway—a decision hailed by American Indian groups who consider the word "squaw" offensive. (Legon, 2005)

NATIVE AMERICAN POPULATIONS, RESERVATIONS, TRIBES AND IDENTITY

According to census figures, as of July 2007, the percentage estimates of Native Americans and Alaska Natives totaled 1.5 percent of the U.S. population. (This included people who indicated that they were of more than one race.) This census category is expected to comprise 2 percent of the total U.S. Population by 2050 (U.S. Census Bureau News, 2008). The three states with the largest Native American populations in 2007 were, in descending order, California, Oklahoma and Arizona (U.S. Census Bureau News, 2008). In the same year, American Indians and Alaska Natives comprised the largest racial or ethnic minority groups in the following states (U.S. Census Bureau News, 2008):

- Alaska
- Montana
- North Dakota
- Oklahoma
- South Dakota

According to Bureau of Indian Affairs (BIA) figures, there are over 562 federally recognized tribal governments in the United States (the words *tribe* and *nation* may also be used), and these include native groups of Alaskans such as Aleuts (BIA, 2009).

The federally recognized tribes each has a distinct history and culture and often a separate language. They have their own government, schools, and law enforcement and economic systems.

Indian tribe   Any tribe, band, group, pueblo, or community for which, of for the members of which, the United States holds land in trust (U.S. Code, 2007b).

With federal recognition, there is a legal relationship that exists between the tribe and the federal government. There are still many tribes that, for historical and political reasons, do not benefit from federally recognized status. Members of such tribes are not necessarily eligible for special benefits under federal Indian programs. On the other hand, fraud in this area is quite rampant whereby people falsely claim Indian ancestry to take unfair advantage of governmental benefits and other perceived opportunities. Some tribes may be state recognized or in the process of seeking federal recognition, while others may not seek recognition at all. The issue of the increasing rivalry among some Indian groups seeking recognition is reflected in the sentiment that some Indian tribes are pitted against each other over government benefits and resources.

Indian Country   "All land within the limits of any Indian reservation under the jurisdiction of the United States Government. . . , all dependent Indian communities within the borders of the United States whether within the original or subsequently acquired territory thereof, and whether within or without the limits of a state, and all Indian allotments, the Indian titles to which have not been extinguished. . . " (U.S. Code, 2007a).

An Indian reservation is land that a tribe has reserved for its exclusive use through the course of treaty-making, statutes, or executive order. It may be on ancestral lands or on the only land available when tribes were forced to give up their own territories through federal treaties. A reservation is also land that the federal government holds in trust for the use of an Indian tribe. The BIA administers and manages 66 million acres of land that, as of 2009, was held in trust for American Indians, Indian tribes, and Alaska natives. In its Fiscal Year 2005 Performance and Accountability Report, the BIA estimated there were 1.5 million Indians living on reservations (latest official information available).

The BIA uses the term *Indian Country* interchangeably with the word *reservation* in the above-noted report. At the federal level, Indian Country means all land within the limits of any Indian reservation under the jurisdiction of the U.S. government. The largest of the reservations is the Navajo reservation and trust lands, which extends into three states. Since reservations are self-governing, most have tribal police; the resulting issues of jurisdiction are discussed later in this chapter. Indians are not forced to stay on reservations, but many who leave have a strong desire to remain in touch with and be nourished by their culture on the reservations. For this reason and because of culture shock experienced in urban life, many return to reservations.

In general, the Indian population is characterized by constant movement between the reservation and the city, and sometimes relocation from city to city. In urban areas, when officers contact an Indian, they will not necessarily know how acculturated to city life that individual is. In rural areas it is easier for officers to get to know the culture of a particular tribe. In the city, the tribal background may be less important than the fact that the person is an American Indian.

Since the early 1980s, more than half of the Native American population has been living outside of reservation communities; many have left to pursue educational and employment opportunities, as life on some of the reservations can be very bleak. Although a large number return home to the reservations to participate in family activities and tribal ceremonies, many attempt to remake their lives in urban areas. A percentage of Indians do make adjustments to mainstream educational and occupational life, but the numbers are still disproportionately low. As with other culturally or ethnically defined categories of people (e.g., Asian, African American), it would be a mistake to lump all Native Americans together and to assume that they are homogeneous. For example, in Arizona alone, one finds a number of different tribes with varying traditions: there are Hopis in the northeast, Pimas and Papagos in the south, Apache in the north-central region, and Yuman groups in the west. All of these descend from people who came to what is now called *Arizona*. The relative "newcomers" are the Navajos and Apaches, who arrived about 1,000 years ago. These six tribes represent differences in culture, with each group having its own history and life experiences.

Broadly speaking, in the United States there are distinct cultural groups among Native Americans in Alaska, Arizona, California, the Central Plains (Kansas and Nebraska), the Dakotas, the Eastern Seaboard, the Great Lakes area, the Gulf coast states (Florida, Alabama, Mississippi, Louisiana, Texas), the Lower Plateau (Nevada, Utah, Colorado), Montana, Wyoming, New Mexico, North Carolina, Oklahoma, and the Northwest (Washington, Oregon, and Idaho). Every tribe has evolved its own sets of traditions and beliefs, and each sees itself as distinct from other tribes despite some significant broad similarities. It is beyond the scope of this book to delve deeply into differences among tribes. Exhibit 9.1 lists many of the tribes in North America from a historical perspective (Saltzman, 2003). The list illustrates the variety and number of historical tribes, each having similarities with and differences from other tribes. However, since the governmental removal of entire tribes from their homelands, tribes ended up spread out across the country as forced migrants from their homes. For example, as a result of the Indian Removal Act of 1830, five tribes—Cherokee, Choctaw, Chickasaw, Creek, and Seminole—were forced to relocate to Oklahoma in an area designated as Indian Territory. Some of these tribes were traditional enemies, though in current times, they have learned to coexist peacefully.*

Law enforcement officials may find themselves confused about who an American Indian is. The issue of identity is important for law enforcement because of jurisdictional laws governing which police departments, tribal or state/local, may arrest and prosecute criminals (i.e., whether Indian or non-Indian; jurisdiction is discussed later in this chapter). Individuals may claim to have "Indian blood," but tribes have their own criteria for determining tribal membership. Because the determination of tribal membership is a fundamental attribute of tribal sovereignty, the federal government generally defers to tribes' own determination when establishing eligibility criteria under special Indian entitlement programs.

Individuals may claim to be Indian when they are not. If officers have any doubt, they should ask to what tribe the person belongs and then contact the tribal headquarters to verify that person's identity. Every tribe has its own administration and authority the members of which will be able to answer questions of this nature. By verifying information with tribal authorities rather than making personal determinations of "Indianness," officers will help create a good

---

* Some readers may have heard of the "Trail of Tears," the Cherokee nation's description of their forced migration in 1838 and 1839 from Georgia, Tennessee, and North Carolina to an area in present-day Oklahoma. They called this journey the "Trail of Tears" because of the tragic effects of hunger, disease, and exhaustion on the forced march during which several thousand Cherokee men, women, and children died. The bitterness remains today among some descendents of the original people of the "Trail of Tears." While no records have been kept, there are also many stories of people who refused to go on the forced march and were killed by federal authorities (Bowen, 2009).

Northeast

Abenaki, Algonkin, Beothuk, Delaware, Erie, Fox, Huron, Illinois, Iroquois, Kickapoo, Mahican, Mascouten, Massachuset, Mattabesic, Menominee, Metoac, Miami, Micmac, Mohegan, Montagnais, Narragansett, Nauset, Neutrals, Niantic, Nipissing, Nipmuc, Ojibwe, Ottawa, Pennacook, Pequot, Pocumtuck, Potawatomi, Sauk, Shawnee, Susquehannock, Tionontati, Wampanoag, Wappinger, Wenro, Winnebago.

Southeast

Acolapissa, Asis, Alibamu, Apalachee, Atakapa, Bayougoula, Biloxi, Calusa, Catawba, Chakchiuma, Cherokee, Chesapeake Algonquin, Chickasaw, Chitamacha, Choctaw, Coushatta, Creek, Cusabo, Gaucata, Guale, Hitchiti, Houma, Jeags, Karankawa, Lumbee, Miccosukee, Mobile, Napochi, Nappissa, Natchez, Ofo, Powhatan, Quapaw, Seminole, Southeastern Siouan, Tekesta, Tidewater Algonquin, Timucua, Tunica, Tuscarora, Yamasee, Yuchi.

Plains

Arapaho, Arikara, Assiniboine, Bidai, Blackfoot, Caddo, Cheyenne, Comanche, Cree, Crow, Dakota (Sioux), Gros Ventre, Hidatsa, Iowa, Kansa, Kiowa, Kiowa-Apache, Kitsai, Lakota (Sioux), Mandan, Metis, Missouri, Nakota (Sioux), Omaha, Osage, Otoe, Pawnee, Ponca, Sarsi, Sutai, Tonkawa, Wichita.

Great Basin

Bannock, Paiute (Northern), Paiute (Southern), Sheepeater, Shoshone (Northern), Shoshone (Western), Ute, Washo.

Plateau

Carrier, Cayuse, Coeur D'Alene, Colville, Dock-Spus, Eneeshur, Flathead, Kalispel, Kawachkin, Kittitas, Klamath, Klickitat, Kosith, Kutenai, Lakes, Lillooet, Methow, Modac, Nez Perce, Okanogan, Palouse, Sanpoil, Shushwap, Sinkiuse, Spokane, Tenino, Thompson, Tyigh, Umatilla, Wallawalla, Wasco, Wauyukma, Wenatchee, Wishram, Wyampum, Yakima.

Southwest

Apache (Eastern), Apache (Western), Chemehuevi, Coahuiltec, Hopi, Jano, Manso, Maricopa, Mohave, Navaho, Pai, Papago, Pima, Pueblo, Yaqui, Yavapai, Yuman, Zuni. Pueblo could potentially be defined further: Acoma, Cochiti, Isleta, Jemez, Laguna, Nambe, Picuris, Pojoaque, Sandia, San Felipe, San Ildefonso, San Juan, Santa Ana, Santa Clara, Santo Domingo, Taos, Tesuque, Zia.

Northwest

Calapuya, Cathlamet, Chehalis, Chemakum, Chetco, Chilluckkittequaw, Chinook, Clackamas, Clatskani, Clatsop, Cowich, Cowlitz, Haida, Hoh, Klallam, Kwalhioqua, Lushootseed, Makah, Molala, Multomah, Oynut, Ozette, Queets, Quileute, Quinault, Rogue River, Siletz, Taidhapam, Tillamook, Tutuni, Yakonan.

California

Achomawi, Atsugewi, Cahuilla, Chimariko, Chumash, Costanoan, Esselen, Hupa, Karuk, Kawaiisu, Maidu, Mission Indians, Miwok, Mono, Patwin, Pomo, Serrano, Shasta, Tolowa, Tubatulabal, Wailaki, Wintu, Wiyot, Yaha, Yokuts, Yuki, Yuman (California).

EXHIBIT 9.1   **Historical Tribal Groupings and Corresponding Regions in North America.**

Source: Saltzman, 2003.

rapport between tribal members and law enforcement officials (Rivera, 2009). However, there is a great deal of numerical misinformation because of the lack of a method for verifying the accuracy of people's claims to be Native American. The term *Native American* came into popularity in the 1960s and referred to groups served by the BIA, including American Indians and natives of Alaska. Later, the term, under certain federal legislation, began to include natives from Hawaii. *Native American*, however, has rarely been accepted by all Indian groups and is seldom used on reservations. Alaska Natives, such as Eskimos and Aleuts, are separate groups and prefer the term *Alaska Native*. To know by what terms individuals or tribes prefer to be called, officers should listen to the names the members of the tribe use for themselves rather than trying to guess which one is "correct."

In the area of mislabeling, some Native Americans have Spanish first or last names (because of intermarriage) and may "look" Hispanic or Latino (e.g., the Hopis). Identification can be difficult for the officers, so they should not assume that the person is Latino just because of the name or appearance. Many Native Americans do not want to be grouped with Latinos because (1) they are not Latinos; (2) they may resent that some Latinos deny their Indian ancestry and instead identify only with the Spanish part of their heritage; and (3) many tribes have a history of warfare with the "mestizo" populations of Mexico. As an aside, the majority population in Mexico, Central America, and South America is of "Indian" ancestry. However, they adopted or were given Spanish names by the *Conquistadores* or conquerors. Many Hispanics in U.S. border communities are really of Indian, not Spanish, heritage, or they may be a mixture of the two.

SIMILARITIES AMONG NATIVE AMERICANS

Significant differences exist among the cultures, languages, history, and socioeconomic status of Native American tribes, communities, and individuals. Yet, it is still possible to talk about general cultural characteristics of Native American groups without negating their diversity. (As noted previously, this chapter does not explore differences.) The cultural characteristics described in the following sections apply to Native Americans, who are traditionally "Indian" in their orientation to life. While being aware of tribal differences, the law enforcement officer should also understand that there is a strong cultural link between the many worlds and tribes of Native Americans and their Indian counterparts throughout the American continent.

Philosophy toward the Earth and the Universe

"The most striking difference between . . . Indian and Western man is the manner in which each views his role in the universe. The prevailing non-Indian view is that man is superior to all other forms of life and that the universe is his to be used as he sees fit . . . an attitude justified as the mastery of nature for the benefit of man [characterizes Western man's philosophy]" (Bahti, 1982). Through its contrast with Western philosophy (that people have the capacity to alter nature), we can gain insight into the values and philosophies common to virtually all *identifying* Native Americans. While acknowledging the character of each Indian tribe or nation, there is a common set of values and beliefs involving the earth and the universe, resulting in a deep respect for nature and "mother earth." According to American Indian philosophy, the earth is sacred and is a living entity. By spiritual involvement with the earth, nature, and the universe, individuals bind themselves to their environment. Indians do not see themselves as superior to all else (e.g., animals, plants) but rather as part of all of creation. Through religious ceremonies and rituals, the Indian is able to transcend himself so that he is in harmony with the universe and connected to nature.

The inclination of some people who do not understand this philosophy would be to dismiss it as primitive and even backward. The costumes, the rituals, the ceremonies, and the dances are often thought of as colorful but strange. Yet from an Indian perspective, "It is a tragedy indeed that Western man in his headlong quest for Holy Progress could not have paused long enough to learn this basic truth—one which he is now being forced to recognize (with the spoilage of the earth), much to his surprise and dismay. Ever anxious to teach 'backward' people, he is ever reluctant to learn from them" (Bahti, 1982). Many non-Indians now embrace certain Native American beliefs regarding the environment; what people once thought of as primitive, they now see as essential in the preservation of our environment. Native Americans speak of "earth wisdom," a cultural legacy from their traditions that all people need to embrace for the future of the environment.

> ### An Indian prayer
> *Oh our Mother the earth, Oh our Father the sky,*
> *Your children are we, and with tired backs*
> *We bring you the gifts you love.*
> *Then weave for us a garment of brightness . . .*
> *May the fringes be the falling rain.*
> *May the border be the standing rainbow.*
> *That we may walk fittingly where birds sing . . . and where grass is green*
> *Oh our mother earth, Oh our father sky. (Author unknown)*

When law enforcement officers make contact with people who are in the midst of celebrating or praying, whether on reservations or in communities, it is vitally important to be as respectful as possible. They must refrain from conveying an air of superiority and ethnocentrism, conveying an attitude that "those rituals" are primitive. Native American prayers, rituals, and ceremonies represent ancient beliefs and philosophies, many of which have to do with the preservation of and harmony with the earth. An officer should, at all costs, try to avoid interrupting prayers and sacred ceremonies, just as one would want to avoid interrupting church services. (Officers should also be aware that taking photographs during ceremonies would constitute an interruption and is forbidden. In general, officers should seek permission before taking photos of Indians; this is true for many of the Indian tribes. Visitors to some reservations are often told that their cameras will be confiscated if they take pictures.)

In some parts of the country, people are revitalizing Native American culture rather than letting it die. For some tribes and individuals, the result is a sense of "pan-Indianism" in which there is a growing pride around ethnic Indian identity. Members of tribes or communities with very different traditions identify as a group by following certain practices that are associated with Indians. Examples include males wearing long hair, a symbol of strength and power: if you shame yourself, you cannot have long hair (Bowen, 2009); the use of the sacred pipe (i.e., the pipestone pipe, sometimes called the *peace pipe*); and participation in sweat lodges, purification rituals, and the sacred sun dance for purification. Many tribes have these elements in their traditions, and tribes practice them to varying degrees, gravitating more toward one tradition over another (Rivera, 2009).

It should be noted that the pan-Indian movement is not necessarily viewed positively by all Indians; some believe that there is a strong possibility of misusing a tradition or diluting the meaning of a ritual. There are some tribes who are reviving their own identities by emphasizing their unique customs and strengths rather than identifying with a pan-Indian movement.

LANGUAGE AND COMMUNICATION

It is possible to make some generalizations about the way a group of people communicate, even when there is great diversity within the group. The following contains information about nonverbal and verbal aspects of communication as well as tips for the law enforcement officer interacting with Native Americans. The paragraphs that follow describe patterns of communication and behavior as exhibited by some American Indians who are traditional in their outlook. No description of communication traits, however, would ever apply to everyone within a group, especially within one that is so diverse.

Openness and Self-Disclosure

Many Native Americans, in early encounters, will approach people and respond with caution. Too much openness is to be avoided, as is disclosing personal and family problems. This often means that the officer has to work harder at establishing rapport and gaining trust. In the American mainstream culture, appearing friendly and open is highly valued, especially in certain regions such as the West Coast and the South. Because different modes of behavior are expected and accepted, the non-Indian may view the Indian as aloof and reserved. The Indian perception can be that the Euro American person, because of excessive openness, is superficial and thus untrustworthy. Mainstream American culture encourages open expression of opinions, while American Indian culture does not.

Silence and Interruptions

The ability to remain quiet, to be still, and to observe is highly valued in Native American culture; consequently, silence is truly a virtue. (In mainstream American culture, it is said that "silence is golden," but this is probably more of an expression of an ideal than a description of a fact.) Indians are taught to study and assess situations and only act or participate when one is properly prepared. Indians tend not to act impulsively for fear of appearing foolish or bringing shame to themselves or to their family (Bowen, 2009). When law enforcement officials contact Native Americans, they may mistake this reticence to talk as sullenness or lack of cooperation. The behavior must not be misinterpreted or taken personally. A cultural trait must be understood as just that: a behavior, action, or attitude that is not intended to be a personal insult. The officer must also consider that interrupting an Indian when he or she speaks is seen as very aggressive and should be avoided whenever possible. As a survival skill on the reservation, Dr. Peggy Bowen, as a child, learned to remain silent and especially to avoid speaking directly to a male. Direct communication was perceived as a challenge to male authority. While this has changed to a certain extent because of the influence of the media, a reticence to talk directly to authority is still prevalent (Bowen, 2009).

Talking and Questions

Talking just to fill the silence is not seen as important. The small talk that one observes in mainstream society ("Hi, How are you? How was your weekend?" and so on) is traditionally not required by Native Americans. Words are considered powerful and are therefore chosen carefully. This cultural trait may result in a situation in which Native Americans retreat and appear to be withdrawn if someone is dominating the conversation. When law enforcement officials question Native Americans who exhibit this tendency (i.e., not being prone to talkativeness), the officer should not press aggressively for answers. Aggressive behavior, both verbal and physical, is traditionally looked down upon. Questions should be open-ended, and the officer willing to respect the silence and the time it may take to find out the needed information.

Nonverbal Communication: Eye Contact, Touching

With respect to American Indian cultures, people often make the statement that Indians avoid making direct eye contact. Although this is true for some tribes, it does not hold true for all. An officer can simply watch for this signal (i.e., avoidance of eye contact) and follow the lead of the citizen. In this section, we explain the phenomenon of avoidance of eye contact from the perspective of groups who do adhere to this behavior. Some Indian tribes believe that looking directly into another person's eyes for a prolonged period of time is disrespectful, just as pointing at someone is considered impolite. Direct eye contact can be viewed as an affront or an invasion of privacy by some tribes. Navajo tribe members tend to stare at each other when they want to express their anger. An Indian who adheres to the unspoken rules about eye contact may appear to be shifty and evasive. Officers and other law enforcement officials must not automatically judge a person as guilty or suspicious simply because that person is not maintaining direct eye contact. To put a person at ease, the officer can decrease eye contact if it appears to be inhibiting the Native American citizen. Avoidance of eye contact with the officer can also convey the message that the officer is using an approach that is too forceful and demanding. Where such norms about eye contact avoidance apply, and if an officer has to look at a person's eyes, it would help to forewarn the person (e.g., "I'm going to have to check your eyes").

With regard to their sense of space, most Native Americans are not comfortable being touched by strangers, whether a pat on the back or the arm around the shoulder. Either no touching is appropriate or it should be limited to a brief handshake. Married couples do not tend to show affection in public. In addition, people should avoid crowding or standing too close. Keep in mind that many Indian relations with strangers are more formal than those of the mainstream culture; therefore, an officer might be viewed as overly aggressive if he or she does not maintain a proper distance. Officers, therefore, who are going to pat down or search a Native American should first explain the process.

Officers may experience particular difficulty when trying to communicate with female Native Americans. Bowen recalls that until she left the reservation, she was unable to maintain direct eye contact with authority because it was never a behavior that was reinforced. As with speaking directly to males, girls and women could get into trouble if they attempted direct eye contact with men. This is still the case, to a certain extent, particularly on reservations that are more isolated than others (Bowen, 2009).

Holding back on judging cultural styles of communication is key to establishing a good rapport.

Language

Some Native Americans speak one or more Indian languages. English, for many, is a second language. Those who do not speak English well may be inhibited from speaking for fear of "losing face" because of their lack of language ability. In addition, because many Native Americans tend to speak quietly and nonforcefully, law enforcement agents must demonstrate patience and allow extra time; interaction must not be rushed. The Native American who is not strong in English needs to spend more time translating from his or her own language to English when formulating a response (this is true of all second-language speakers who are not yet fluent). As with all other languages, English words or concepts do not always translate exactly into the various Indian languages. Indian languages are rich and express concepts reflecting views of the world. It is mandatory that the utmost respect be shown when Native Americans speak their own language. Remember that the Indians have a long history of forced assimilation into the Anglo society, in which, among other things, many were denied the right to speak their native languages.

OFFENSIVE TERMS, LABELS, AND STEREOTYPES

> Native Americans are a people in transition between history and contemporary America. The challenge for [them] is to maintain their heritage, erase a stereotype and adjust recognition in society. Native Americans are too often stereotyped by antiquated and discriminatory attitudes. . . . ("Our People, Our Future," 2009)

In the interview cited in the opening of this chapter, retired chief of police Jim Cox, a Comanche Indian, described situations in which police officers told Indian jokes or used derogatory terms in his presence. Proud of his heritage, he was deeply offended by this insensitive communication. The use of racial slurs toward any group is never acceptable in crime-fighting and peacekeeping, no matter how provoked an officer may be. When officers hear disrespectful terms and stereotypical statements about Native Americans, they should speak up about this lack of professionalism and disrespect for community diversity.

There is a number of words that are offensive to Native Americans: *chief* (a leader who has reached this rank is highly honored), *squaw* (extremely offensive), *buck*, *redskin*, Indian *brave*, and *skins*. (some young Indians may use the word *skins* to refer to themselves but would be offended if others use the term.) Words such as *braves*, *chiefs*, *squaws*, and *papooses* are not native Indian terms, but have come about as mistranslations, mispronunciations, or as shortened terms, and are "perpetuated by non-Native Americans" ("Our People, Our Future," 2009). In addition, the use of Indian tribal names or references as mascots for sports teams is highly objectionable to many Native Americans.

Other terms used to refer to Native Americans are *apple* (a slightly dated term referring to a highly assimilated Indian: "red" on the outside, "white" on the inside) and *the people* (more commonly used by some groups of Indians to refer to themselves). In some regions of the country, a reservation is called a *rez* by Indians, but this word would not be appreciated when uttered by those who are not Native Americans (Bowen, 2009). It is also patronizing when non-Indians use certain kinship terms, such as *grandfather* when talking to an older man, even though other Indians may use those terms. However, as a rule of thumb, it is advisable to ask Native Americans how *they* would like to be addressed, and then respect their preference. The key is to not make assumptions about the name you use to directly call or indirectly refer to an individual (Bowen, 2009).

Other offensive and commonly used terms include *sitting Indian style* to refer to sitting in a cross-legged position on the floor; *Indian giver* to characterize someone who takes back a present or an offer; *wild Indians* to describe misbehaving children; *pow wow* to mean a discussion; or *bottom of the totem pole* to mean lowest ranking. In addition, it is worth noting that some American Indians deliberately choose not to reveal their ethnic identity in the workplace because of concerns about stereotypes about Indians. Coworkers may make comments about Indians or use offensive expressions because they do not "see one in the room." People can be deeply offended and hurt by "unintentional" references to American Indians.

Indians find it offensive when non-Indians make claims that may or may not be true about their Indian ancestry, such as "I'm part Indian—my great-grandfather was Cherokee." Although this may be an attempt to establish rapport, it rings of "Some of my best friends are Indians" (i.e., to "prove" that one does not have any prejudice). People should not assume affinity with American Indians based on novels, movies, a vacation trip, or an interest in silver jewelry. These are among the most offensive, commonly made errors when non-Indians first encounter an American Indian person or family. Another is a confidential revelation that there is an Indian "princess" in the family tree—tribe unknown, identity unclear, but a bit of glamour in the family myths. The intent may be to establish rapport, but to the Indian these types of statements reveal stereotypical thinking.

Many people growing up in the United States can remember the stereotypical picture of an Indian as a wild, savage, and primitive person. In older textbooks, including history books recounting Native American history, Indians were said to "massacre" whites, whereas whites simply "fought" or "battled" the Indians (Harris, Moran, & Moran, 2004). Hollywood has to take some responsibility for the promotion of stereotypes as well. "Native Americans have a long history of one-sided portrayals in Hollywood, including such stereotypical characters as the war whooping savage or the grunting tribesman." (NPR, 2009a [Bull]).

Other common stereotypical or disparaging statements include "All Indians are drunks" (an argument has been put forth that the white man introduced "fire water" or alcohol to the Indian as a means of weakening him); "You can't trust an Indian"; "Those damn Indians"; and "The only good Indian is a dead one"—a remark that can be traced back to a statement made by a U.S. General in 1869 (Harris, Moran, & Moran, 2004).

Despite the persistence of many social problems, progress has been made with respect to education and political participation among Native Americans. Law enforcement officials must not hold on to the stereotype of American Indians as being uneducated. There is a growing Native American population attending colleges and rising to high positions in education, entertainment, sports, and industry.

FAMILY AND ACCULTURATION ISSUES

Respect for Elders

"Nothing will anger an Indian more than them seeing [his or her] grandmother or grandfather being spoken to belligerently or being ordered around with disrespect. If that happens, that's a firecracker situation right there" (Rivera, 2009). Unlike mainstream American culture, Indian cultures value aging because of the respect they have for wisdom and experience. People do not feel that they have to cover up signs of aging because this phase of life is highly revered. The elders of a tribe or the older people in Native American communities must be shown the utmost respect by people in law enforcement. This includes acknowledging their presence in a home visit, even if they are not directly involved in the police matter at hand. In some tribes (e.g., the Cherokee) the grandmother often has the maximum power in the household and is the primary decision maker. It is advisable for people in law enforcement to include the elders in discussions so they can give their advice or perspective on a situation. The elders are generally respected for their ability to enforce good behavior within the family and tribe.

It should also be noted, however, that because of assimilation or personal preference among some Native Americans, the elders in any given household may tend to avoid interfering with a married couple's problems. And although the elders are respected to a higher degree than in mainstream culture, they may withdraw in some situations in which there is police contact, letting the younger family members deal with the problem. If in doubt, it is advisable to begin the contact more formally, deferring to the elders initially. Then officers can observe how the elders participate and whether the younger family members include them.

Extended Family and Kinship Ties

In mainstream American society, people usually think of and see themselves first as individuals, and, after that, they may or may not identify with their families or various communities and groups with which they are affiliated. In traditional Native American culture, a person's primary identity is related to his or her family and tribe. Some law enforcement agents may be in positions to make referrals when there is a problem with an individual (e.g., an adolescent) in a family. A referral for counseling for that person alone may be culturally alienating. Western-style individual counseling or therapy is a foreign way to treat problems. In addition, Native American culture is highly group oriented.

Today, some of this family and tribal cohesiveness has lessened because of forced assimilation, extreme levels of poverty, and lack of education and employment. However, many Native Americans still have large networks of relatives who are in close proximity to each other. It is not uncommon for children to be raised by someone other than their father or mother (e.g., grandmother, aunts). When law enforcement officials enter an Indian's home and, for example, ask to speak to the parents of a child, they may actually end up talking to someone who is not the biological mother or father. Various other relatives can function exactly as a mother or father would in mainstream culture. This does not mean that Indian "natural" parents are lazy about their child-rearing duties, even when the child is physically living with another relative (and may be raised by several relatives throughout childhood). The intensely close family and tribal bonds allow for this type of child-raising. The officer must not assume that something is abnormal with this type of arrangement or that the parents are neglecting their children.

Children and Separation from Parents

It is crucial that police officers understand the importance of not separating children from family members if at all possible. Many Native American families in urban areas and on reservations have memories of or have heard stories from elder family members that involved the federal government's routine and systematic removal of Indian children from their homes; in many cases, children were placed in boarding schools operated by the BIA that were often hundreds of miles away. This phenomenon, including education for the children that stripped them of their language and culture, began in the late nineteenth century. The belief was that Indians were savages and did not know how to treat children. Children were punished for speaking their own language and for saying prayers from their own religious traditions. They were basically uprooted and placed in an alien environment in an attempt by the government to eliminate the Indian population (Bowen, 2009).

Although for many families the severe trauma of children's forced separation from parents took place years ago, the aftereffects still linger (Rivera, 2009). In the early twentieth century, there was a famous case in which Hopi Indian fathers were sentenced to Alcatraz Island to hard labor. Their crime was hiding their children from BIA officials because they did not want the children to be taken to the BIA boarding schools. By hiding the children, the Hopi fathers violated federal law and were arrested and charged with sedition. This case is still talked about today (Rivera, 2009). The memory of a "uniform coming to take away a child" is an image that can be conjured up easily by some Indians. It is this "baggage" that the law enforcement officer today encounters when interacting with Native Americans. He or she may be totally unaware of the power of Native Americans' memories of these deplorable actions.

Since Native American parents can be very protective of their children, an officer is well advised to let the parents know about any action that needs to be taken with regard to the child. Law enforcement officers must become knowledgeable about the Indian Child Welfare Act (ICWA), passed by Congress in 1978. Prior to the passage of this Act, Indian children removed from their homes were placed with white foster parents. There were no Indian foster homes, and the tribes did not have any way to deal with cases involving children. With the passage of ICWA, the mandate exists to find viable homes in which to place the children, first with a tribal member, and, if that is not possible, then in an Indian home. When officers go out on calls to pick up children, there can be serious consequences if officers are not aware of this act. (Further information about the ICWA is available from the American Bar Association; its web address is listed in Website Resources.) Law enforcement officials are more likely to establish a good rapport with Indian families if they treat the children well, which includes understanding the legal rights of Indian children (Bowen, 2009).

Acculturation to Mainstream Society

People who are caught between two cultures and are successful in neither run the risk of contributing to family breakdown, often becoming depressed, alcoholic, drug dependent, and suicidal. However, Indian group members who have remained tightly identified with their culture and religion and who have close-knit extended families tend to exhibit this type of behavior less. With cultural and family support, their isolation from mainstream culture is not as pronounced as it is with individuals and families who lack this support (Bowen, 2009).

In studies on suicide and ethnicity in the United States, much has been written about patterns of what can be described as self-destructive behavior. This has been generalized to those Indian groups whose lives are characterized by despair, and, for many, a loss of ethnic identity. According to Psychologist Dr. Jon Perez, former director of the Behavioral Health Unit of the Indian Health Service (IHS):

> The intergenerational trauma, compounded by extreme poverty, lack of economic opportunity and widespread substance abuse has shattered these communities. Suicide is a single response to a multiplicity of problems. If you have these things going on, and you don't see any hope for the future, suicide seems like an option. (APA Online, 2007)

The HIS reported that the rate of suicide for Native Americans was 2.5 times higher than the national average, and that the rate for young people, ages 15–24, was triple the national average for 15–24-year olds (APA Online, 2007).

In 2005, mortality rates attributed to alcohol consumption were nearly six times higher for American Indians and Alaska Natives than for other races (IHS, 2006). Alcoholism continues to be the leading health and social problem of American Indians. The use of crystal methamphetamine on some reservations is rampant and is also creating tremendous problems whereby families experience domestic violence and neglect of children (Bowen, 2009). However, it cannot be stressed enough that the origins of the psychosocial problems that some Indians experience in mainstream society are not their own weaknesses or deficiencies. The cause of the problems dates back to the way government has handled and regulated Indian life. The dominant society in no way affirmed the cultural identity of Indians; thus many Indians have internalized the oppression that they experienced from the outside world. Furthermore, many young people feel the stresses of living between two cultural worlds. They are not fully part of the traditional Indian world as celebrated on the reservation or a community that honors traditions; they are not fully adapted to the dominant American culture. Many younger people feel alienated when it comes to their native identity. The following quote reflects the sentiments of a Native American law enforcement officer in a Southern California police department: "I know very little about my roots. My mother and grandmother were denied the opportunity to learn about their culture [forced assimilation] and nothing was passed on. I feel empty and have intense anger toward those who held the power to decide that certain traditions were not worth preserving. Forced denial of our ethnicity has resulted in extremely high alcohol, illegal drug use and suicide rates as a collective response."

KEY ISSUES IN LAW ENFORCEMENT

Perception of Police

The general distrust of police held by Native Americans stems from a history of negative relations with "the system," which can refer to federal, state, and local governments. In their view, officers represent a system that has not supported Indian rights and their tribes or communities. Most of their contact with the police has been negative in nature. Thus many Native Americans often have not had a chance to build a relationship of trust and cooperation with people in law enforcement.

Victimization Rates/Comparisons with Other Groups

According to the Bureau of Justice Statistics profile on American Indians and Crime, the rate of violent victimization of Native Americans far exceeds that of other racial or ethnic groups in the United States and is more than double the national average (BJS, 2004). These crimes affect American Indians of all age groups, geographies, economic status levels, and (both) genders. According to the National Crime Victimization Survey, between 1992 and 2001, American Indians experienced violence at rates more than twice as that of blacks, two and a half times as that of whites, and four and a half times as that of Asians (BJS, 2004). American Indians comprised 0.5 percent of the U.S. population but 1.3 percent of all violent crime victims (see Exhibit 9.2). The rate of violent crime victimization for Native American women is at least twice as that for other women (BJS, 2004). According to the Office of Juvenile Justice and Delinquency Prevention, it is twice as likely that Native American children will experience child maltreatment and victimization compared to children of all other races (U.S. Department of Justice, 2006).

EXHIBIT 9.2 Percent of Population: Violent Victimizations		
	Population (%)	**Violence Victims (%)**
Whites	84	82.2
Blacks	12.1	14.7
American Indians	0.5	1.3
Asian/Pacific Islander	3.3	1.8

Source: Bureau of Justice Statistics; National Crime Victimization Survey, 1992 to 2000.

When asked about the race of their offender, American Indian victims of violent crime primarily reported the race of the offender as white (57 percent), followed by other race (34 percent) and black (9 percent). Nearly four in five American Indian victims of rape/sexual assault indicated the offender was white. About three in five American Indian victims of robbery (57 percent), aggravated assault (58 percent), and simple assault (55 percent) described the offender as white (BJS, 2004). The less serious the offense, the higher was the percentage of American Indian victims describing the offender's race as other than black or white.

Native American Women and Rape

According to a 2006 DOJ and Centers for Disease Control study, the likelihood of a Native American woman's experiencing rape during her life is twice as that of women from all other races. (USDOJ/CDC, 2006). The epidemic of rape in Indian Country is due, in large part, to "a maze of archaic laws that prevent tribes from arresting and prosecuting offenders" (NPR, 2009c [Sullivan]). Chikasaw Nation Tribal Police Chief, Jason O'Neal explained that if a woman is Indian on Indian land and her attacker is Indian, he [O'Neal] can help her. If not, there is not much that he can do (NPR, 2009c). O'Neal describes the attackers as almost "untouchable . . . 80% of victims describe their offenders from outside the reservation" (NPR, 2009c).

> Two years ago, the Standing Rock Sioux Reservation, which straddles North and South Dakota, had five Bureau of Indian Affairs officers to patrol an area the size of Connecticut. Officials there, and on many reservations nationwide, described a rampant problem of rape where hundreds of cases were going unreported, uninvestigated and unprosecuted. According the Justice Department, 1 in 3 Native American women will be raped in her lifetime. Tribal leaders say predators believe Native American land is almost a free-for-all, where no law enforcement can touch them. (NPR, 2009c)

At the time of this text's writing, a bipartisan group of senators from the Indian Affairs Committee introduced, for the first time in American history, a bill to end the confusing maze of jurisdictional rules that allow so many rapes to be ignored. If passed, this bill would mean that tribal police could arrest and prosecute sexual assault perpetrators (and other criminals) regardless of their race or ethnicity (Govtrack.us, S. 797: Tribal Law and Order Act of 2009).

Jurisdiction

In 1885, the Major Crimes Act was passed in the United States. This gave exclusive jurisdiction to the federal government on major crimes committed on reservations. The 1994 Crime Act expanded federal criminal jurisdiction in Indian Country because of the sovereign status of federally recognized Indian tribes, which precludes most states from exercising criminal jurisdiction in Indian Country over Indian persons. Jurisdiction resides with the tribes themselves, on a limited basis, or with the federal government. Federal criminal jurisdiction in Indian Country is derived from the Federal Criminal Code, Title 18, USC 1152 (Indian Country Crimes Act) and Title 18, USC 1153 (Major Crimes Act).

FBI responsibility and jurisdiction for the investigation of federal violations in Indian Country under the Indian Country Crimes Act or Major Crimes Act is statutorily derived from Title 28 USC Section 533, pursuant to which the FBI was given investigative responsibility by the Attorney General. The resources allocated by the FBI to various locations throughout the country are based on a number of factors, including identified crime problems; jurisdictional responsibilities; and the availability of non-FBI investigative resources. Also, by virtue of the Indian Gaming Regulatory Act (IGRA) enacted in 1988, the FBI has federal criminal jurisdiction over acts directly related to casino gaming in Indian Country gaming establishments, including those locations on reservations under state criminal jurisdiction.

The FBI has established the following priorities in Indian Country in an effort to ensure that the most egregious and violent criminal acts receive priority attention by investigative personnel:

1. Homicide/Death
2. Child Sexual/Physical Abuse
3. Violent Felony Assault
4. Drugs and Gangs
5. Corruption/Fraud against the Government/Theft of Tribal Funds
6. Gaming Violations
7. Property Crimes

Indian Country programs are active in 32 FBI divisions, with 14 divisions accounting for the majority of Indian Country investigations by the FBI. The top four Indian Country Field Divisions (Albuqerque, Minneapolis, Phoenix, and Salt Lake City) accounted for 77 percent of all Indian Country case initiations by the FBI in 2005. The FBI currently has 114 special agents assigned to Indian Country matters full-time and funds 12 Safe Trails Task Forces (STTF) in Indian Country to address violent crime or identified crime problems that would normally go unaddressed if not for the existence of the STTF (FBI, 2006).

Since 1997, the Indian Country unit has conducted integrated training with FBI agents; BIA law enforcement officers; and tribal, state, county, and local police officers. In December 2003, FBI and BIA law enforcement officers fully integrated all regional training efforts (personnel and resources) and moved to standardize all Indian Country training curricula. In fiscal year 2005, over 1,000 Indian Country law enforcement officers, support personnel, and community leaders were training in FBI- and BIA-sponsored regional training (FBI, 2006).

Extract from Interview with Chief Jason O'Neal, Chief of Police Chickasaw Nation Lighthorse Police (Ada, Oklahoma) May 19, 2009*

Q. *What are the most important ways for civilian police to show respect on Indian lands?*

A. First, it is important for civilian police to understand tribal sovereignty as well as the tribes and their history. It's equally important for tribal police to understand the issues facing civilian police. This helps to build cooperation. Tribal police need to make it a priority to build relationships with all the agencies in their jurisdictions, including state and local.

Q. *What, in particular, should civilian police be learning about Indian culture?*

A. They should become familiar with religious practices, and should understand that every tribe is unique, and has it own customs and beliefs. They also need to get a basic understanding of Indian jurisdiction. We have worked with the state [of Oklahoma] to ensure that the state academy presents information of this kind. Civilian police have issues facing Indian country, and require dedicated training in this area.

(continued)

[handwritten in left margin: Comprehensive training program to ensure quality performance and ethical conduct.]

Q. *Is there anything that you can think of that Native Americans find frustrating when it comes to dealing with civilian police?*

A. It is frustrating for Native Americans and tribal police that some agencies do not recognize tribal police as equal or even perceive tribal police as police. Many of our officers attend Police Academy. We work with outside agencies to achieve common goals, and we have worked on cross-deputization agreements. We all need to recognize each other.

It can also be frustrating when civilian police are working operation in and around Indian Country, and do not coordinate with tribal police. Cooperation and mutual recognition are key. For example, we have cross-training with the Oklahoma Bureau of Narcotics and Dangerous Drugs; we have assigned an investigator to their office and vice versa.

Q. *What do Native Americans say about civilian police?*

A. We mainly receive calls from the Native public who have dealings with civilian police and who want our department to be part of the investigation. When civilian police are working in Indian country, they should consult us during an operation. We might be able to assist them or come up with an even more effective alternative to a problem.

Q. *Is there a particular message you would like to be passed on to the readers of our text regarding law enforcement interaction with Native Americans?*

A. We have to be interconnected. There is a maze of jurisdictional rules in and around Indian Country. The only way to achieve public safety is through cooperative law enforcement efforts. It benefits everyone.

Communication is the key. During any calls for service, it is critical that officers take the time to communicate with the population they serve, and in this way officers also learn how to do their jobs more effectively.

―――――
*Jason O'Neal, Chickasaw Nation Lighthorse Police Chief, was recognized for his pioneering work in cooperative law enforcement as he was awarded Chief of Police of the Year . . . at the national conference of the National Native American Law Enforcement Association (NNALEA) in Las Vegas ("Lighthorse Chief Named Police Chief of the Year," 2008).

Tribal and Civilian Police

American Indians have struggled to retain as much of their own culture and tradition within tribal police operations as possible. Within the very limited jurisdiction in which tribal police have been allowed to exercise their tribal police powers, American Indians have struggled to incorporate tribal laws and procedures. Dominant white authorities are reluctant to allow Indian police agencies to have power over their own when whites do not control the law and procedures of that agency. (Barlow, 2000)

Policing on tribal lands can cause a great deal of friction between tribal and civilian law enforcement, particularly on reservations where the lines of jurisdiction are not clear. Jurisdiction of the tribal police may be limited, and the non-Indian is not always subject to Indian tribal law. Some tribes have decriminalized their codes and taken on civil codes of law (e.g., for basic misdemeanors, civil fines may go to the tribal court), yet still conduct a trial of the non-Indian in a tribal court. Who has authority and who has responsibility can be an ambiguous area in tribal and civilian law enforcement (Setter, 2000). Police officers are put into an unusual situation when it comes to enforcing the law among Indians. They may make an arrest in an area that is considered to be "Indian land" (on which tribal police have jurisdiction). The land may be adjacent to non-Indian land, sometimes forming "checkerboard" patterns of jurisdiction. In the case of an Indian reservation on which tribal police usually have authority, civilian law enforcement agencies are challenged to know where their jurisdiction begins and ends. With the multijurisdictional agreements that many tribes have signed with local and state officials, nontribal police officers may have the right to enter reservations to continue business. It is not uncommon for a person suspected of a crime to be apprehended by a nontribal police officer on a reservation.

It is expected that civilian law enforcement agents inform tribal police or tribal authorities when entering a reservation, but this does not always happen. Going onto reservation land without prior notice and contacting a suspect or witness directly is an insult to the authority of the tribal police (Bowen, 2009). Civilian police should see themselves as partners with tribal police. Obviously, in dangerous or emergency situations, time may prevent civilian authorities from conferring with the tribal police. Where possible, it is essential that the authority of the reservation be respected. As we mentioned, on some reservations, it may not be clear who has jurisdiction, and it becomes all the more necessary to establish trusting relations.

Levels of cooperation and attitudes toward civil and tribal law enforcement partnerships differ from area to area. Retired Police Chief Cox, who also recently served as Executive Director of the Oklahoma Chiefs of Police, spoke of the progress his state has made with respect to legislation associated with jurisdictional issues and the cross-deputization of local, state, and tribal police officers (e.g., Sac and Fox, Cherokee, Creek, Comanche, and Chickasaw Nations). Most of the state's approximately 22 tribal police departments have been cross-deputized; some departments have a shared database for intelligence purposes. In the past few years, the increasing use of GPS devices has contributed to better identification of location, jurisdiction, and resources. This cross-training and cooperation are especially critical in the complex geography of the state (Cox, 2009). In Oklahoma, Indian Country spans approximately 8,000 miles, and there is no contiguous border (out of 77 counties, 63 are in Indian country). The patchwork Indian land and non-Indian land, therefore, lends itself to an uneven system of arrests and prosecutions, depending on whether a crime takes place on Indian land, with an Indian victim, and with an Indian perpetrator. The cross-deputization, which is now fairly widespread in Oklahoma, enables both the tribal and civilian police to make arrests in each other's jurisdiction. Retired Chief Cox hopes that the models and progress he has seen in Oklahoma will benefit other states as well (Cox, 2009).

Other police departments around the country, such as in New Mexico and Washington State, have also been working intensively to form relationships with local Indian tribes. Tribal police officers in Oregon are federally commissioned and state-certified police officers with full law enforcement authority. In Oregon, if a tribal police officer arrests a non-Indian, the non-Indian will be lodged in the county jail and arraigned in the county circuit court. If the same tribal police officer arrests an Indian, the Indian will be lodged in the tribal jail, usually housed in the county jail, and arraigned in tribal court. If there is a will to work cooperatively, police departments and Indian tribal departments can be of tremendous benefit to each other. Initiating this type of effort means, for both Indians and non-Indians, putting aside history and transcending stereotypes. Furthermore, individual officers should be sensitive to their own potentially condescending attitudes toward tribal police and tribal law.

Police Stops

Just as other groups such as Latinos and African Americans have routinely been victims of profiling, so have Native Americans. If a group of Native Americans is driving a large, poorly maintained car, there is the potential that they will be stopped simply because they are perceived as suspicious and because negative stereotypes are operating. Negative biases against Native Americans are strong and have persisted for generations. When there is not a legitimate reason to stop a car, the next step is for officers to check their own stereotypes of whom they think is a criminal. Like members of other ethnic groups, Indians have repeatedly reported being stopped for no reason, adding to their distrust of police.

Peyote

Many states have specific laws exempting the traditional, religious use of peyote by American Indians from those states' drug enforcement laws. Following is a definition of peyote:

> Peyote is a small turnip-shaped, spineless cactus [containing] nine alkaloid substances, part of which, mainly mescaline, are hallucinogenic in nature; that is, they induce dreams or visions. Reactions to peyote seem to vary with the social situation in which it is used. In some it may merely cause nausea; believers may experience optic, olfactory and auditory sensations. Under ideal conditions color visions may be experienced and peyote may be "heard" singing or speaking. The effects wear off within twenty-four hours and leave no ill aftereffects. Peyote is non-habit forming. (Bahti, 1982)

There have been a variety of uses associated with peyote: (1) as a charm for hunting, (2) as a medicine, (3) as an aid to predict weather, (4) as an object to help find things that are lost (the belief being that peyote can reveal the location of the lost object through peyote-induced visions; peyote was even used to help locate the enemy in warfare), and (5) as an object to be carried for protection. People have faith in peyote as a powerful symbol and revere its presence.

Peyote is carried in small bags or pouches and these can be "ruined" if touched.* Police officers may need to confiscate peyote but should do it in a way that is appropriate and respectful. It is far better to ask the Native American politely to remove the bag containing peyote rather than forcibly take it away.

In a 1990 freedom-of-religion case, the Supreme Court ruled that state governments could have greater leeway in outlawing certain religious practices. The ruling involved the ritual use of peyote by some American Indians who follow the practices of the Native American Church (NAC), which has a membership of 250,000 people (Miller, 2004). Until that time, the U.S. government allowed for the religious use of peyote among Native Americans based on the Bill of Rights' Free Exercise of Religion guarantee; in other words, peyote use was generally illegal except in connection with bona fide American Indian religious rituals.

From a law enforcement perspective, if drugs are illegal, no group should be exempt, and indeed, officers have to uphold the law. From a civil rights perspective, religious freedom applies

---

*Native Americans from many tribes across the country wear small bags called medicine bags; these are considered to be extremely sacred. The medicine bags do not carry drugs or peyote but hold symbols from nature (e.g., corn pollen, cedar, sage, tree bark), and they are believed to have certain powers. If it becomes necessary, law enforcement officers should handle these as they would handle any sacred symbol from their own religion. Ripping into the bags would be an act of desecration. The medicine contained in the bags has often been blessed and therefore must be treated with respect.

to all groups and no group should be singled out for disproportionately burdensome treatment. Historically, legal and illegal status of peyote has been complex. There have been many attempts to prohibit the use of peyote on the federal level, and many states passed laws outlawing its use. However, several states have modified such prohibitions to allow traditional American Indians to continue using peyote as a sacrament. Moreover, in some states, anti-peyote laws have been declared unconstitutional by state courts insofar as they burden the religious practice of American Indians.

This historic ambiguity on the state level, together with the 1990 ruling on the federal level, causes confusion and resentment on the part of many Native Americans. Recognizing that the existing Act of August 11, 1978 (42 USC 1996), commonly called the American Indian Religious Freedom Act, was no longer adequate in protecting Native Americans' civil rights in their traditional and cultural religious use of peyote, Congress passed, and President Bill Clinton signed into law, the American Indian Religious Freedom Act Amendments of 1994. Following are selected portions of this federal law, namely, Public Law 103-344 of the 103rd U.S. Congress, October 6, 1994:

Section 3. The Congress finds and declares that—

(1) for many Indian people, the traditional ceremonial use of the peyote cactus as religious sacrament has for centuries been integral to a way of life, and significant in perpetuating Indian tribes and cultures;

(2) since 1965, this ceremonial use of peyote by Indians has been protected by Federal regulation;

(3) while at least 28 States have enacted laws which are similar to, or are in conformance with, the Federal regulation which protects the ceremonial use of peyote by Indian religious practitioners, 22 States have not done so, and this lack of uniformity has created hardship for Indian people who participate in such religious ceremonies; and

(4) the lack of adequate and clear legal protection for the religious use of peyote by Indians may serve to stigmatize and marginalize Indian tribes and cultures, and increase the risk that they will be exposed to discriminatory treatment.

The use of peyote outside the NAC (established in 1918) is forbidden and regarded by church members as sacrilegious. If individuals use peyote under the guise of religion, they are breaking the law. Within the NAC, there are very specific rules and rituals pertaining to its sacramental use. Establishing respectful communication with the leaders of the NAC will assist officers in determining whether peyote is being abused in certain circumstances.

Law enforcement officials would do well to understand the importance and place of peyote in the culture from a Native American point of view. It is not the intent of the authors to recommend a particular course of action with regard to enforcement or lack thereof. When the use of peyote is understood from an Indian perspective, officers will be more likely to communicate a respectful attitude toward an ancient ritual that some researchers say dates back 10,000 years. If police officers suddenly enter a prayer meeting or drumming ceremony where peyote is being used and aggressively make arrests, it will be very difficult to establish trust with the community. When peyote is an issue, officers must recognize their own ethnocentrism (i.e., unconsciously viewing other cultures or cultural practices as primitive, abnormal, or inferior). Law enforcement personnel working in communities where peyote use is an issue should anticipate the problems that will occur and should discuss it with members of the Indian community. Historically, the federal government actively tried to suppress and change Native American cultures. The banning of peyote was and has been viewed by Native American groups as a failure of the Bill of Rights to truly guarantee the freedom to practice one's own religion. Officers must also understand the law and their agencies' policies on enforcement of the law.

Trespassing and Sacred Lands

In a number of states, traditional Indian harvest areas or sacred burial and religious sites are now on federal, state, and, especially, private lands. Indians continue to visit these areas just as their ancestors did to collect resources or to pray. The point of concern for law enforcement involves conflicts occurring between the ranchers, farmers, and homeowners on what Indians consider their holy ground. How the officer reacts to Indians' allegations of trespassing determines whether there will be an escalated confrontation (Rivera, 2009). When there is a dispute, the officer will alienate Indians by choosing an authoritarian and aggressive method of handling the problem (e.g., "You're going to get off this land right now"). Alternatively, he or she could show some empathy and the Native American may very well be more supportive of the officer's efforts to resolve the immediate conflict. If there is no immediate resolution, the officer can, at a minimum, prevent an escalation of hostilities.

Since police officers cannot solve this complex and very old problem, the only tool available is the ability to communicate sensitively and listen well. "The officer is put between a rock and a hard place. If the officer is sensitive, he could try to speak to the landowner and describe the situation, although often the landowners don't care about the history, claiming, 'It's my land now'. However, there have been some people who have been sensitive to the needs of the Native Americans and who have worked out agreements" (Rivera, 2009).

Native American Sites—Use of, Desecration, and Looting

The Native American Free Exercise of Religion Act of 1993 (Senate Bill 1021, introduced to the 103rd Congress), Title I—Protection of Sacred Sites, gives tribal authority over Native American religious sites on Indian lands:

a. *Right of Tribe*—All Federal or federally assisted undertakings on Indian lands which may result in changes in the character or use of a Native American religious site or which may have an impact on access to a Native American religious site shall, unless requested otherwise by the Indian tribe on whose lands the undertakings will take place, be conducted in conformance with the laws or customs of the tribe.
b. *Protection by Tribes*—Indian tribes may regulate and protect Native American religious sites located on Indian lands.

In addition to the taking over of religious sites by governmental agencies is the history of desecration and looting of sacred sites and objects. Most often, the looting has been done to make a profit on Native American articles and artifacts. Native Americans witness vandalism on their archeological sites, often without any criminal prosecution. In 1996, President Clinton signed an Executive Order (13007) protecting Indian sacred lands from anything affecting their physical integrity and preserving Indian religious practices on those sites. Congressman Nick Rahall made the following statement:

> Across the country, sites of religious importance are in danger of becoming casualties of the current Administration's push to open federal lands to development. Despite several laws in place aiming to protect the religious freedom of Native Americans, and the historic and cultural value of their lands, there is no comprehensive or approachable law to protect sacred lands from energy development and other potentially harmful activities. (Rahall, 2003)

Even more degrading to Native Americans than the violation of sacred lands is the taking of human remains (skulls and bones) from Indian reservations and public lands. Officers in certain parts of the country may enter non-Indian homes and see such remains "displayed" as souvenirs of a trip into Indian Country. The Native American Grave Protection and Repatriation Act of 1990 (NAGPRA) passed by Congress and signed by former President George H. W. Bush resulted as a response to such criminal acts. If an officer sees any human remains, he or she must investigate whether foul play might have been involved. Officers should contact state agencies established to enforce laws that protect Indian relics to determine how to proceed in such situations.

Indian Casinos and Gaming

Native American reservations in the United States are considered to be sovereign nations, and as such, leaders are responsible for providing and securing financing in order to pay for basic infrastructure and services as leaders would in any city. To date, the most successful industry on the reservations has been casinos and other types of gaming for profit. The legal wording on most documents referring to this industry uses the term *Indian gaming*. In addition, there is the National Indian Gaming Association; thus *Indian gaming* is the most common term used in publications on the subject.

Legalized gambling on reservations dates back to a landmark case in 1976 in which the Supreme Court ruled that states no longer could have regulatory jurisdiction over Indian tribes. Because of the lawsuits that followed, it was later ruled that states did not have the right to prohibit Native American tribes from organizing and participating in for-profit legalized gambling. The Indian Gaming Regulatory Act became law in 1988. For the first time, Native Americans were given the right to regulate all gaming activities on their sovereign lands.

There is a great deal of controversy around the Indian gaming industry. On the one hand, according to the National Bureau of Economic Research (NBER), "Four years after tribes open casinos, employment . . . increase[s] by 26 percent, and tribal population . . . increase[s] by about 12 percent [i.e., Native Americans return to the reservation because of the promise of work]. . . . The increase in economic activity appears to have some health benefits in that four or more years after a casino opens, mortality has fallen by 2 percent." On the other hand, according to the same 2002 NBER study, "bankruptcy rates, violent crime, auto thefts and larceny are up 10 percent in counties with a casino."

According to the National Indian Gaming Association, and the 2002 National Bureau of Economic Research (NBER), there were over 310 gaming operations of various types in more than 200 of the 550 plus tribes in the United States (NBER, 2002). About 220 were Las Vegas–style casinos with slot machines, table games, or both. Until the end of 2007, the gaming industry, in general, performed well (Standard & Poor's, 2008). American Indians made significant gains and progress through the gaming industry as it enabled a certain amount of economic self-reliance for some tribes. According to the National Indian Gaming Association (NIGA), whose motto is "Rebuilding Communities through Indian Self-Reliance," 2006 was a year in which "670,000 jobs nationwide for American Indians and [their] neighbors, direct and indirect jobs, [were] created by Indian gaming's economic multiplier effect." (NIGA, 2006)

However, since the recession beginning in 2008 the gaming industry overall has experienced a record number of defaults (Standard & Poor's, 2008). It remains to be seen how the current recession will impact the overall economic situation for tribes and reservations that rely on this industry. Jose Rivera, retired American Indian Peace Officer and specialist in Indian affairs, has spoken at a California state conference, advising people to prepare for a "post-Casino reality" because of the economic downturn (Rivera, 2009). On the other hand, in an article entitled "We Shall Remain a Sovereign (and Successful) Chickasaw Nation" Arun Rath states, "the number 1 foreign policy priority [for this Tribe] is trade. Their number 1 trading partner? Texas" (NPR, 2009b).

Fishing

"If you ever want to get into a fight, go into a local bar [e.g., in parts of Washington State] and start talking about fishing rights. The fishing issue is a totally hot issue" (Rivera, 2009).

The wording of the treaties with regard to the fishing rights of Native Americans is clear and unequivocal in English as well as in the language of the specific tribes concerned. For example, the treaty with Indians of the Northwest regarding fishing rights on the rivers gives these rights to the Indians "for as long as the rivers shall flow." The rivers in the Northwest are still flowing, and the Indians are still struggling with the state of Washington about the state's violations of the treaty's terms, even on Indian property.

Indians continue to say, "We have treaties with the government allowing us to fish here." Commercial and sports fishermen, on the forefront of trying to prevent Native Americans from exercising their treaty rights, claim that Indians are destroying the industry. From the Native Americans' perspective, they are providing sustenance to their families and earning extra money for themselves or their tribes to make it through the year. (For 150 years, there had been no industry on many, if not most, of the reservations.) Once again, the officer on the front line will be unable to solve a problem that has been raging for generations. The front-line officer's actions, in part, depend on the sensitivity of his or her department's chief executive. Admittedly, the commander is in a difficult position. He or she is between the state fish and game industry and the people trying to enforce federal treaties. Nevertheless, he or she can communicate to officers the need for cultural sensitivity in their way of approaching and communicating with Native Americans. The alternative could be deadly, as illustrated by at least one situation when, in northern California, peace officers with flack jackets and automatic weapons resorted to pursuing Native Americans with shotguns up and down the river (Rivera, 2009).

There are many complex dimensions to cases involving Native Americans "breaking the law" when, in parallel, the federal government is not honoring its treaties with them. Native Americans are frustrated by what they see as blatant violations of their rights. The history of the government's lack of loyalty to its American Indian citizens has caused great pain for this cultural group. Clearly, sensitivity and understanding on the part of the officer are required. The officer has to have patience and tact, remembering that history has defined many aspects of the current relationships between law enforcement and American Indians. Being forceful and displaying anger will alienate Native Americans and will not result in the cooperation needed to solve issues that arise.

Summary

- Historically, the police officer from outside the reservation has been a symbol of rigid and authoritarian governmental control that has affected nearly every aspect of Indian life, especially on reservations. Officers, like most citizens, have only a limited understanding of how the government, including the criminal justice system, caused massive suffering by not allowing Indians to preserve their cultures, identities, languages, sacred sites, rituals, and lands.

- Federally recognized tribes each has a distinct history and culture, and often a separate language. They have their own government, schools, and law enforcement and economic systems. Federal recognition means that a legal relationship exists between the tribe and the federal government. "Indian Country" refers to all land that is within the limits of an Indian reservation under the jurisdiction of the U.S. government, and to all dependent Indian communities within the borders of the United States. An Indian reservation is land that a tribe has reserved for its exclusive use through the course of treaty making, statutes, or executive order.

- Significant differences exist among the cultures, languages, history, and socioeconomic status of Native American tribes, communities, and individuals. Yet, there is a strong cultural link between the many worlds and tribes of Native Americans and their Indian counterparts throughout the American continent. There is a common set of values and beliefs involving the earth and the universe, resulting in a deep respect for nature and "mother earth." According to American Indian philosophy, the earth is sacred and is a living entity. By spiritual involvement with the earth, nature, and the universe, individuals bind themselves to their environment. Indians do not see themselves as superior to animals and plants, but rather as part of all of creation. Through religious ceremonies and rituals, traditional Native Americans are able to transcend themselves so that they are connected to nature and in harmony with the universe.

- Many American Indians who favor traditional styles of communication tend toward closed behavior and slow rapport building with strangers. Behaviors that appear aloof or hostile may be part of a cultural style; police officers should not automatically attribute a lack of cooperation to the behavior observed. Aggressive questioning can result in withdrawal of responses. In addition, direct eye contact for some traditional tribal members is an affront or invasion of privacy. Officers may experience particular difficulty when trying to communicate with female Native Americans. Traditionally, girls in some tribes do not maintain direct eye contact with authority. Holding back on judging cultural styles of communication is key to establishing a good rapport.

- There are many offensive terms for and stereotypes of Native Americans. The terms *chief, redskin, buck, squaw, braves,* and *skins* are examples of these, especially when used by a non-Indian. The use of Indian tribal names or references as mascots for sports teams is highly objectionable to many Native Americans.

- The traditional extended family is close-knit and interdependent, and a great deal of respect is paid to the elderly. Police officers should remember to be deferential to elders, asking for their opinion or advice, as the older family members are often the major decision makers in the family. A particularly sensitive area in family dynamics relates to the separation of children from families. This can bring back memories of times when children were forcibly taken from their parents and sent to Christian mission schools or government boarding schools far from their homes. Native Americans who have close-knit extended families, and who identify with their tribal cultures, tend to be better adjusted than those who lack family and cultural support. In the case of the latter, social and health problems can be severe, and include alcoholism, drug use, depression, and suicidal tendencies.

• Key issues for law enforcement with respect to Native Americans include the use of peyote, allegations of trespassing, sacred sites violations, fishing, Indian gaming and casinos,

victimization, and jurisdiction. Some of these involve matters in which Native Americans feel they have been deprived of their rights: in the case of peyote, the right to religious expression; in the case of trespassing, the right to honor their ancestors; and in the case of fishing, the ability to exercise their rights as guaranteed by treaties made with the U.S. government.

Discussion Questions and Issues

1. *Popular Stereotypes.* List some of the commonly held stereotypes of Native Americans. What is your personal experience with Native Americans that might counter these stereotypes? How have people in law enforcement been influenced by popular stereotypes of Native Americans?

2. *Recommendations for Effective Contact.* If you have had contact with Native Americans, what recommendations would you give others regarding effective communication, rapport building, and cultural knowledge that would be beneficial for officers?

3. *The Government's Broken Promises to American Indians.* The famous Lakota chief, Sitting Bull, spoke on behalf of many Indians when he said of white Americans, "They made us many promises . . . but they never kept but one: They promised to take our land, and they took it." There was a time when many acres of land in what we now call the United States were sacred to Native American tribes. Therefore, today many of us are living on, building on, and in some cases destroying the remains of Indian lands where people's roots run deep. How would you deal with the problem of an Indian "trespassing" on

someone's land when he or she claims to be visiting an ancestral burial ground, for example? What could you say or do so as not to totally alienate the Native American and thereby risk losing trust and cooperation?

4. *Jurisdiction.*
   a. What should law enforcement agents do when the state law is in conflict with a federal law that has been based on treaties with Native Americans signed by the federal government? How can officers who are on the front line win the respect and cooperation of Native Americans when they are asked to enforce something that goes against the treaty rights of the Indians?
   b. A special unit in the early 1990s was established by the San Diego Sheriff's department to patrol Native American reservations that were overrun from the outside by drugs and violence. Federal Public Law 280 transferred criminal jurisdiction and enforcement on reservations to some states. Research law enforcement jurisdiction issues and tribal lands in your region or state (if applicable); note whether there are still unresolved areas or areas of dispute.

Website Resources

American Indian Policy Center: http://www.airpi.org

This website provides government leaders, policy makers, and the public with information about the legal and political history of American Indian nations, and the contemporary situation of American Indians, including culturally sensitive responses to the challenges of American Indian life.

The Bureau of Indian Affairs (BIA):
http://www.doi.gov/bia

The mission of the BIA, stated on the website, is "to enhance the quality of life, to promote economic opportunity, and to carry out the responsibility to protect and improve the trust assets of American Indians, Indian tribes and Alaska Natives." This webste provides information on federally recognized Indian tribes, gaming, economic development, and education realted to Native Americans.

National Congress of American Indians (NCAI):
http://www.ncai.org

This website contains information on issues and events relevant to the organization and to Native Americans.

The National Museum of the American Indian (Washington D.C.): http://www.nmai.si.edu

This website provides links to the resources of The National Museum of the American Indian, including information on education and outreach.

National Native American Law Enforcement Association: http://www.nnalea.org

The National Native American Law Enforcement Association Newsletter is a source of information for members and the general public.

Native American Criminal Justice Resources:
http://arapaho.nsuok.edu/~dreveskr/nacjr.html-ssi

This website contains a list of criminal justice resources related to Native Americans on such topics as government data, police and victims, law and courts, crime and criminals.

Office of Tribal Justice (OTJ):
http://www.usdoj.gov/otj/

The information contained in this website pertains to the Department of Justice's involvement with Native American tribes and organizations. The office is the single point of contact within the Department for meeting responsibilities to the tribes.

Tribal Court Clearinghouse: A Project of the Tribal Law and Policy Institute: http://www.tribal-institute.org/lists/tlpi.htm

U.S. Fish and Wildlife Service: Office of Law Enforcement
http://www.fws.gov/le/Natives/NativeInfo.htm

References

American Indian Religious Freedom Act Amendment of 1994, Public Law 103-344 [H.R. 4230]; October 6, 1994, 103rd Congress.

APA Online. (2007, February). "A Struggle for Hope." *Monitor on Psychology*; *38*(2). Retrieved March 5, 2009, from http://www.apa.org/monitor/feb07/astruggle.html.

Bahti, Tom. (1982). *Southwestern Indian Ceremonials.* Las Vegas, Nev.: KC Publications.

Barlow, David. (2000). *Criminal Justice in America.* Upper Saddle River, N.J.: Prentice-Hall.

Barlow, David, and Melissa Barlow. (2000). *Police in a Multicultural Society.* Long Grove, Ill.: Waveland Press.

Bowen, Peggy. (2009, April). Assistant Professor of Criminal Justice, Alvernia College, Reading, Pa., personal communication.

Bureau of Indian Affairs (BIA). (2009). "Bureau of Indian Affairs." Retrieved May 4, 2009, from http://www.doi.gov/bia/

Bureau of Justice Statistics (BJS). (2004). *A BJS Statistical Profile, 1992–2002: American Indians and Crime.* Washington D.C.: Department of Justice.

CEHIP. (1996). "20th Century Warriors: Native American Participation in the United States Military." Prepared for the United States Department of Defense by CEHIP Incorporated, Washington, D.C., in partnership with Native American advisors Rodger Bucholz, William Fields, Ursula P. Roach. Department of Defense, 1996. Available: http://www.history.navy.mil/faqs/faq61-1.htm.

Cox, Jim. (2009, May). Retired Police Chief, Retired Executive Director of Oklahoma Chiefs of Police, Midwest City, Okla., personal Communication.

Federal Bureau of Investigation (FBI). (2006). "Indian Country Crime." Retrieved August 3, 2006, from http://www.fbi.gov/hq/cid/indian/background.htm.

"First American Female and Native Soldier Killed in Iraq War Is Remembered." (2003). *Indian Country Today* Staff Reports. Available: http://www.indiancountry.com/content.cfm?id=1050072510.

Harris, Philip R., Robert T. Moran., and Sarah V. Moran. (2004). *Managing Cultural Differences: Global Leadership Strategies for the 21st Century,* 6th ed. Oxford, U.K.: Butterworth-Heineman.

Indian Health Services (IHS). (2006). "Indian Population Trends." Retrieved July 26, 2006, from http://www.ihs.gov/publicinfo/publicaffairs/ihsbrochure/people/1_indianpoptrends-jan2006.doc.

Legix. (2000). Social and General Update: A Native American Lobbying Firm Specializing in Issues

Involving Housing, Tribal Justice, Sovereignty, Education, Economic Development, and Gaming. Available: http://www.legix.com.

Legon, Jeordan. (2005). "War in Iraq: Heroes of War." Available: http://edition.cnn.com/SPECIALS/2003/iraq/heroes/piestewa.html.

"Lighthorse Police Chief Named Police Chief of the Year." (2008, October 20). *Ada Evening News*. Retrieved May 20, 2009, from http://www.adaeveningnews.com/archivesearch/local_story_294170015.html.

Matthiessen, Peter. (1992). *The Spirit of Crazy Horse*. New York, N.Y.: Penguin Books.

Miller, Timothy. (2004). "Native American Church." Retrieved July 26, 2006, from http://religiousmovements.lib.virginia.edu/nrms/nachurch.htm.

National Bureau of Economic Research (NBER). (2002, February). "The Social and Economic Impact of Native American Casinos." NBER Working Paper No. w9198.

National Public Radio (NPR). (2009a, May 4). "For Native Americans, Old Stereotypes Die Hard," by Brian Bull. Retrieved May 5, 2009, from http://www.npr.org/templates/story/story.php?storyId=103711756

National Public Radio (NPR). (2009b, April 27). "We Shall Remain a Soverign (and Successful) Chickasaw Nation," by Arun Rath. Retrieved May 4, 2009, from http://www.npr.org/templates/story/story.php?storyId=103348033&ft=1&f=1012

National Public Radio (NPR). (2009c, May 3). "Lawmakers Move to Curb Rape on Native Lands." Article by and interview featuring Laura Sullivan. Retrieved May 3, 2009, from http://www.npr.org/templates/story/story.php?storyId=103717296

National Indian Gaming Association (NIGA). (2006). The Economic Impact of Indian Gaming in 2006. Retrieved February 8, 2009, from http://www.indiangaming.org/info/pr/press-releases-2007/NIGA_econ_impact_2006.pdf

Native American Free Exercise of Religion Act of 1993, Senate Bill 1021, introduced to 103rd Congress.

"Native Americans Back from Iraq Decry Cutback." (2005, February 17). *Washinton Post*. Retrieved May 3, 2009 from http://www.washingtonpost.com/wp-dyn/articles/A30683-2005Feb16.html.

"Obama Adopted by Native Americans." (2008, May 19). *New York Times: The Caucus*. Retrieved April 30, 2009, from http://thecaucus.blogs.nytimes.com/2008/05/19/obama-adopted-by-native-americans/

O'Neal, Jason (2009, May). Chief of Police, Chickasaw Nation Lighthorse Police, Ada, Okla., personal communication.

Rahall, Nick J. (2003, June 11). House Resources Committee, Native American Sacred Lands Act.

Rivera, Jose. (2009, November). Retired California State Peace Officer, Manager of Audience Development and Community Partnerships of Bay Area Discovery Museum, personal communication.

Saltzman, Lee. (2003). Compact History Geographic Overview. Available: http://www.dickshovel.com/up/html.

Setter, Drew. (2000, December). Legix Company, personal communication.

Seven Fires Council. (2009). "Our People, Our Future." Harrodsburg and Mercer Counties, Kentucky on line web resource. Retrieved May 1, 2009, from http://www.merceronline.com/Native/native10.htm.

Standard and Poor's. (2008, October). "U.S. Gaming Defaults Reach Record Levels: What happened to This Recession-Resistant Industry?" by Craig Pamelee, CFA and Donald Eong, CFA. Retrieved April 13, 2009, from http://www.nafoa.org/pdf/RatingsDirect

U.S. Census Bureau News. (2008, November). Facts for Features: American Indian and Alaska Native Heritage Month: November 2008. Retrieved May 2, 2009, from http://www.census.gov/Press-Release/www/releases/archives/facts_for_features_special_editions/012782.html.

U.S. Code. (2007a, January). "Indian Country Defined." Title 18; Section 1151. Retrieved May 3, 2009, from http://www.law.cornell.edu/uscode/HowCurrent.php/?tn=18&fragid=T18F00488&extid=usc_sec_18_00001151----000-&sourcedate=2008-07-07&proctime=Tue%20Jul%20%208%2004:26:27%202008

U.S. Code. (2007b, January). "Indians. Definitions." Title 25; 479a. Retrieved May 3, 2009, from http://frwebgate6.access.gpo.gov/cgi-bin/TEXTgate.cgi?WAISdocID=382958110739+9+1+0&WAISaction=retrieve

U.S. Department of Justice. (2006, March). "Juvenile Offenders and Victims: 2006 National Report—March 2006."

Office of Juvenile Justice and Delinquency Prevention. (2006, March). Retrieved March 3, 2009, from http://ojjdp.ncjrs.gov/ojstatbb/nr2006/index.html.

U.S. Department of Justice and the Centers for Disease Control and Prevention. (2006, January). "Extent, Nature, and Consequences of Rape Victimization." Retrieved April 2, 2009, from http://www.ncjrs.gov/pdffiles1/nij/210346.pdf

White House Government News Release. (2002). Available: http://www.whitehouse.gov/news/releases/2002/11/20021101-7-html.

Multicultural Law Enforcement Elements in Terrorism and Disaster Preparedness

Chapter 10   Multicultural Law Enforcement and Terrorism, Homeland Security, and Disaster Preparedness

Part Three provides information on working with multicultural communities in the areas of domestic and international terrorism. Peacekeeping efforts of homeland security and disaster preparedness within our local, state, regional, national, and global multicultural communities are addressed. Research and documented findings indicate that acts of combating terrorism and efforts toward homeland security start with key elements that are "local" in prevention, response, and implementation (Howard & Sawyer, 2004). Generally speaking, acts of terrorism in the United States usually involve local law enforcement agencies and other public safety personnel as first responders. Part Three highlights law enforcement's prevention and response strategies related to the war on terrorism, homeland security, and disaster preparedness within multicultural communities. The chapter that follows contain (1) overviews, background, and historical information with respect to law enforcement's changing roles in combating terrorism, in homeland security, and in disaster preparedness; (2) response strategies addressing local community, regional, national, and global Issues; (3) goals for homeland security and disaster preparedness in Multicultural Communities; (4) key multicultural law enforcement communication issues in dealing with terrorism, homeland security, and natural disasters; and (5) relationships and processes inherent in multijurisdictional efforts and responses related to terrorism, homeland security, and natural disaster work. The chapter ends with key concerns relevant to officers and specific challenges involved in the changing roles and practices in dealing with terrorism, homeland security, and disaster preparedness within multicultural communities.

Multicultural Law Enforcement and Terrorism, Homeland Security, and Disaster Preparedness

LEARNING OBJECTIVES

After completing this chapter you will be able to:

- Describe the role that law enforcement plays in the war on terrorism, homeland security, and disaster preparedness within multicultural communities.

- Discuss specific collaborative response strategies and how partnerships work within local, state, and federal agencies.

- Address the goals of homeland security in multicultural and diverse communities.

- Highlight the complexities of homeland security and disaster preparedness involving multijurisdictional efforts.

- Delineate recommendations for law enforcement and other emergency services personnel for actively responding to terrorism and protecting homeland security within multicultural communities.

OUTLINE

- Introduction
- Multicultural Law Enforcement Roles in Terrorism and Homeland Security
- Myths and Stereotypes about Terrorists
- Response Strategies Addressing Local-Community, Regional, National, and Global Issues
- Goals for Homeland Security and Disaster Preparedness in Multicultural Communities

- **Working with Multicultural Communities on Terrorism Prevention, Homeland Security, and Multijurisdictional Efforts**
- **Key Issues in Law Enforcement**
- **Summary**
- **Discussion Questions and Issues**
- **Website Resources**

INTRODUCTION

This chapter provides specific information on the vital role that law enforcement plays in dealing with domestic and international terrorism, homeland security, and disaster preparedness within multicultural communities. Although crimes involving terrorism affect our nation as a whole (and thus are seen as national in scope), the immediate targets, outcomes, and results are local in effect. Local law enforcement personnel and agencies are called upon to respond, provide assistance, establish order, and protect the immediate and larger community from any additional harm and danger. Multicultural knowledge and the skills required to work within diverse communities are key resources in preventing and dealing with the aftermath of terrorism, investigation of crimes, and required intelligence gathering.

The Department of Homeland Security (DHS) was created as a cabinet-level department on November 25, 2002, with the main objective of protecting the United States from terrorism. Since the establishment of the DHS, law enforcement officers and agencies have assumed many new and changing roles as well as responsibilities. These include detecting threats of terrorism, developing and analyzing information regarding threats and vulnerabilities, using information and intelligence provided, and coordinating the security efforts against terrorism. Law enforcement officers' changing roles also include assisting in the security of the transportation system, cooperating in the enforcement of immigration laws, ensuring the security of our borders, and preparing for emergencies, disasters, and community assistance in coordination with the DHS.

In this chapter, we first provide an overview of the importance of multicultural law enforcement knowledge and skills for handling terrorism, implementing homeland security, and preparing for community disasters. We then define the scope of these issues especially as they involve multicultural populations and communities. The section "Response Strategies Addressing Local-Community, Regional, National, and Global Issues" highlights the complexities in responding to and solving crimes involving terrorism. Clearly, criminal justice practices and public safety procedures already define much of the terrorism, homeland security, and disaster preparedness work and activities within law enforcement agencies. The emphasis in this chapter is on the specific aspects of multicultural law enforcement applicable to terrorism, homeland security, and disaster preparedness issues in the context of our diverse communities. We provide specific response strategies and "Key Issues in Law Enforcement" in terms of collaborative and partnership work with the variety of public safety agencies across diverse departmental levels of government. We conclude the chapter with specific recommendations for law enforcement officers and other emergency services personnel in actively responding to terrorism, homeland security, and disaster preparedness within multicultural communities.

MULTICULTURAL LAW ENFORCEMENT ROLES IN TERRORISM AND HOMELAND SECURITY

In the entire history of crime-fighting and public safety, law enforcement has never before had a challenge of the scope and complexity that it faces today with terrorism and homeland security. Today's terrorists respect neither law nor community-established practices; they honor neither law enforcement personnel nor humanitarian-service professionals. Their sole goal and mission is to inflict maximum casualty, mass destruction, and public fear, as is highlighted by the following excerpt from an al-Qaida terrorist manual found in a police raid of a cell member's home in Manchester, England:

> PLEDGE, O SISTER:
>
> . . . to make their women widows and their children orphans.
>
> . . . to make them desire death and hate appointments and prestige.
>
> . . . to slaughter them like lambs and let the Nile, al-Asi, and Euphrates flow with their blood.
>
> . . . to be a pick of destruction for every godless and apostate regime.
>
> . . . to retaliate for you against every dog who touches you with even a bad word.

Moreover, terrorists may not come to the attention of local law enforcement officers and agencies until they have committed their terrorist acts:

> Terrorism poses a fundamental challenge to the legal system. Terrorists often do nothing indictable until they commit the act. Ninety percent of the time sleepers are absolutely legal, so you can't do anything about them even if you know who they are. Terrorism challenges our categories of what is legal and what is illegal. (Ford, 2002, p. 1)

Although terrorists commit crimes to bring national and international attention to their causes and purposes, the response to terrorist attacks and the actions that might prevent them are, nevertheless, usually accomplished in local cities, neighborhoods, and communities.

> In panel after panel, the same hard truths were expressed repeatedly: With the events of 9/11, the nation entered a new and sobering era. 9/11 shocked the nation with the chilling realization that foreign enemies from both within and without are bent on destroying our institutions, our lives, our very civilization. Terrorist crime, though national in scope, is usually local in execution. In the war on terror, community police will therefore have to shoulder an increasingly heavy burden. (Bankson, 2003)

Law enforcement's knowledge of and responsiveness to local and regional issues is central to the success in the war on terrorism and homeland security. Relationships with multicultural local and regional community leaders will be an essential resource in dealing with and preventing terrorism. Law enforcement personnel have the dual role of protecting the public from acts of terrorism by those terrorists who may be hiding in multicultural communities in the United States, and protecting the members of multicultural communities who may have no ties to terrorists or criminals but are stereotyped, harassed, or discriminated against because of the biases and prejudices of others.

Definitions

As indicated in "Terrorism 2002-2005," there is no single, universally accepted, definition of terrorism (Federal Bureau of Investigation, 2007).

> **Terrorism**   "Terrorism is defined in the *Code of Federal Regulations* as 'the unlawful use of force and violence against persons or property to intimidate or coerce a government, the civilian population, or any segment thereof, in furtherance of political or social objectives' (28 C.F.R. Section 0.85)"(FBI, 2007).

The FBI defines two types of terrorism that occur in the United States:

> **Domestic terrorism**   "The unlawful use, or threatened use, of force or violence by a group or individual based and operating entirely within the United States or Puerto Rico without foreign direction committed against persons or property to intimidate or coerce a government, the civilian population, or any segment thereof in furtherance of political or social objectives"(FBI, 2007).
>
> **International terrorism**   "Involves violent acts or acts dangerous to human life that are a violation of the criminal laws of the United States or any state, or that would be a criminal violation if committed within the jurisdiction of the United States or any state. These acts appear to be intended to intimidate or coerce a civilian population, influence the policy of a government by intimidation or coercion, or affect the conduct of a government by assassination or kidnapping" (FBI, 2007).

The FBI further divides terrorist-related activities into two major categories:

> **Terrorist Incident**   "A violent act or an act dangerous to human life, in violation of the criminal laws of the United States, or of any state, to intimidate or coerce a government, the civilian population, or any segment thereof, in furtherance of political or social objectives" (FBI, 2007).
>
> **Terrorism Prevention**   "A documented instance in which a violent act by a known or suspected terrorist group or individual with the means and a proven propensity for violence is successfully interdicted through investigative activity" (FBI, 2007).

WEAPONS OF MASS DESTRUCTION (WMD)   Three types of weapons are most commonly categorized as "weapons of mass destruction" (WMD): (1) nuclear weapons, (2) biological weapons, and (3) chemical weapons. Toxin weapons are sometimes listed as a separate category or are listed as part of either biological and/or chemical weapons (see Oliver [2007] for definitions and descriptions of these and other WMD). The subcategories of WMD include activities that may be labeled as "agro terrorism," which is to harm our food supply chain, and "cyber terrorism," which is to harm our telecommunications, Internet, and computerized processes and transactions.

> **Weapons of Mass Destruction (WMD)**   "Any weapon or device that is intended, or has the capability, to cause death or serious bodily injury to a significant number of people through the release, dissemination, or impact of (a) toxic or poisonous chemicals or their precursors; (b) a disease organism; or (c) radiation or radioactivity" (Title 50, US Code, Chapter 40, Section 2302).

The FBI's (2007) definition of terrorism tends to be too specific and narrow to be used by law enforcement and with respect to other criminal justice objectives. For the purposes of this textbook, our definition of terrorism is broadened in scope to include all crimes involving terrorism, bombings, and weapons of mass destruction, whether domestic or international. It is clear that criminals who resort to terrorism and WMD, regardless of their motives, are usually not restricted by any definition and/or categories. Since the primary goal of law enforcement is to ensure public safety and security, a terrorist threat in itself is a public safety issue that can send a community into confusion and even chaos. Law enforcement is called upon to respond to threats of terrorism as well as to actual incidents and acts of terrorism. Law enforcement's knowledge, skills, resources, and sensitivity to multicultural community issues and concerns will facilitate the effectiveness of its response in the three stages of a terrorism incident: before, during, and after an act of terrorism.

Historical Information and Background

Terrorism has always been a part of organized society (Hoffman, 2006). From the earliest history of establishing order through the enforcement of laws and government, extremist groups and individuals have used property damage and violence against people to generate fear and compel "change" in society and organizations. The Department of Justice (1997), in its training manual *Emergency Response to Terrorism: Basic Concepts*, highlights some of the historical examples of terrorism over the past 300 years, and includes current events and contemporary examples.

The targets and tactics of terrorists have changed over time (Hoffman, 2006). In the past, more often the targets of terrorists were individuals. The death of a unique, single individual like a head of state, president, or prime minister would produce the major disruption that the terrorist desired. In modern times, governments and organizations have become far more bureaucratic and decentralized. Consequently, the targets of terrorists have included unique individuals, their surrounding networks, affiliated organizations and institutions, and any functions or processes associated with any targeted individual or groups. Today, terrorists attack not only prominent individuals and their organizations but also a wider range of targets that have been considered immune historically. For example, prior to modern times, terrorists had granted certain categories of people immunity from attack (e.g., women, children, elderly, disabled, and doctors). By not recognizing any category of people as excluded from attack, terrorists today have an unlimited number of targets for attack. The apparent randomness and unpredictability of terrorist attacks make the work of law enforcement and other public safety officers extremely challenging, and solutions require a high level of sophistication. (See Oliver [2007] for a timeline and history of terrorist attacks in the United States.)

As a result of the greater range of potential victims and the demographic background of terrorists, multicultural knowledge, skills, and resources constitute critical elements in the (1) preparation of local communities for safety and security with regard to terrorism, (2) prevention of possible terrorists' crimes and incidents, (3) participation in emergency response to terrorism, (4) investigation and information gathering involving terrorists, and (5) follow-up actions and prosecution of crimes involving and/or resulting from terrorism.

MYTHS AND STEREOTYPES ABOUT TERRORISTS

Knowledge of the concerns, diversity, and historical backgrounds of various multicultural communities will facilitate the public safety and peacekeeping mission of law enforcement officers in dealing with terrorism. It is important to have an understanding about some of the myths and stereotypes that are held of groups associated with terrorism and how these stereotypes might contribute to prejudice, discrimination, and biased encounters with members of these populations. Stereotypic views of multicultural groups who might be potential terrorists reduce individuals within those groups to simplistic, one-dimensional caricatures and as either "incompetent cowards" who can't fight face to face or "suicidal bogey persons" who can't be stopped. It is important for law enforcement officers to be aware of the different stereotypes of potential terrorists. The key to effectiveness in multicultural law enforcement with any group is to intelligently discern the myths and stereotypes about that group. Further, we need to be aware of these stereotypes and be able to monitor our thinking and our behaviors when the stereotypes do not apply to the persons with whom we are interacting.

Some of the current stereotypes that might affect law enforcement officers' perceptions of terrorists include the following:

1. ***Arab and Middle Eastern Nationality or Muslim Religious Background:***   As a result of high-profile attention to terrorist incidents such as the September 11, 2001, attacks by al-Qaida and the foiled terrorist plot to down 10 (or even more) trans-Atlantic flights using components of bombs assembled on board during the summer of 2006, it is easy to stereotype terrorists as having Arab and Middle Eastern nationality or Muslim religious backgrounds. Terrorists can be foreign or domestic, and clearly the majority of the domestic terrorist incidents and attacks in the United States has not come from groups or individuals of Arab and Middle Eastern nationality or Muslim religious backgrounds. In "Terrorism 2002–2005," the FBI (2007) highlights the long-standing trend that the vast majority of the terrorism attacks in the United States is conducted by Americans (domestic extremists) against other Americans. During the period covered in the report, 23 of the 24 recorded terrorism incidents were perpetrated by special interest extremist groups (i.e., 22 of the 24 incidents were by animal rights and environmental movement groups and one by a white supremacist group) (FBI, 2007). Corley, Smith, and Damphousse (2005), in their research on the Changing Face of American Terrorism, reviewed the files of the American Terrorism Study (ATS), a project that included demographic data on persons indicted under the FBIs Counterterrorism Program since the 1980s. In the 1980s, of the 215 terrorists indicted, 79 percent were Americans (48 percent in the right-wing category and 31 percent in the left-wing or environmental categories) and only 21 percent were international terrorists. Similar findings were noted for their 1990s findings: of the 231 terrorists indicted, 70 percent were Americans (45 percent in the right-wing groups and 25 percent in the left-wing or environmental groups) and 30 percent were in the international terrorist groups.

   Foreign terrorist groups include (examples from Howard & Sawyer, 2004):

   • Abu Nidal Organization (Libya)
   • Aum Shinrikyo, Aleph (Japan)
   • Harakat ul-Mujahidin (Pakistan)
   • Sinn Fein (Ireland)
   • Euzkadi Ta Askatasuna (Spain)
   • Red Army Faction (Germany)
   • Red Brigade (Italy)
   • Popular Front for the Liberation of Palestine (PLO)
   • Sendero Luminoso (Peru)

- Black Tigers (Sri Lanka)
- November-17 (Greece)
- Interahamwe (Africa)
- Abu Sayyaf (Philippines)
- AUC (Colombia)
- People's War (Nepal)
- Free Aceh (Indonesia)
- Cosican Army (France)

Any of the current terrorist organizations around the world could combine forces or utilize operatives from other organizations to "look different" than expected or stereotyped. As highlighted by Howard et al. (2009), "we have seen a threat posed by non-state actors spanning the globe that exploit open societies, porous borders and differences in state legal structures and international laws to perpetrate their acts" (p. 118).

2. ***Insane and/or Behave Like Automatons:***   Unlike the movie industry's portrayal of terrorists, these individuals are usually not insane, although their actions may appear insane or irrational (Dershowitz, 2002). According to Malcolm W. Nance, a 20-year veteran of the U.S. intelligence community's Combating Terrorism Program and author of *The Terrorist Recognition Handbook*, most terrorists are generally intelligent, rational, decisive, and clear-thinking. In the heat of an attack, terrorists may focus on and harness their energies to accomplish their mission with dedication, motivation, ruthlessness, and commitment that may appear to outsiders as "insanity."

3. ***Not as Skillful or Professional as U.S. Law Enforcement Officers and Personnel:***   As would be obvious, terrorists are not all similar in skills, training, and background. They vary in terrorist-training background, from foreign-government-trained professionals who make up the foreign intelligence agencies of countries like Libya, Cuba, Iran, and North Korea to the novice, untrained civilian militia, vigilante, and criminals. The training and experience of some of the terrorists render them as skillful in their craft as any law enforcement professional in the United States. On the other hand, others have skill levels similar to petty criminals on the street. The use of intelligence information (i.e., not assumptions or stereotypes) to assess the skill and ability levels of terrorists or terrorist groups is central to homeland security. Howard (2007) notes, "Al-Qaeda's training is very eclectic and comprehensive; its tacticians and trainers have taken much from the special operations forces of several nations, including the U.S., U.K., and Russia. Indeed, Al-Qaeda fighters are as well or better trained than those of many national armies" (p. 121).

Throughout this text, the authors have emphasized attitudes and skills required of law enforcement officials in a multicultural society to include (1) respecting cultural behaviors that may be different from one's own, (2) observing and understanding behaviors important to diverse communities, and (3) analyzing and interpreting diverse behaviors for application within multicultural communities. Similarly, multicultural skills and knowledge are also elements that can contribute to detecting and predicting terrorist actions and activities for homeland security when coupled with an intelligence-based approach. Just as it is important to understand one's own biases and stereotypes about multicultural communities in order to effectively serve those communities, law enforcement officers need to change their perceptions of who the terrorists are before they can effectively detect terrorist activities.

Tips to Detect Terrorist Behavior

1. *Anyone Could Be a Terrorist:*   Law enforcement officers who start to look for specific groups may be blinded and may overlook a group or individuals who may actually be the real terrorists sought. For example, if one were going by Arab descent or nationality, one would have missed Richard C. Reid, the shoe bomber (i.e., who was of British citizenship), and Jose Padilla, the alleged plotter for releasing a "dirty bomb" in the United States (born in Chicago, of U.S. citizenship and Puerto Rican descent). If one thought that terrorists were inferior and not intelligent, one would have missed apprehending Theodore Kaczynski, the Unabomber, who was a professor at several major universities.

2. *Learn to Acknowledge the Terrorist's Motivation, skills, and Capabilities:*   Because of the actions of terrorists, law enforcement officers may view terrorists with contempt along with other negative stereotypic descriptors like "crazies," "camel jockeys," "suicidal," "scum of the earth," and "rag heads." Such contempt and disdain for terrorists may indeed be the perspective that blinds law enforcement officers and others to the lethal actions and goals of terrorists. Law enforcement officers must, with clear insight and perceptions, acknowledge terrorists for what they are: motivated, ruthless human beings who use destruction, death, and deceit to meet their lethal goals. For example, prior to the bombing of the Alfred P. Murrah Federal Building in Oklahoma City, one law enforcement and intelligence stereotype held that U.S. domestic terrorists were not capable of mass destruction but were merely a criminal nuisance element of society (Heymann, 2001).

3. *Analyze and Utilize Intelligence and Other Source Information:*   Law enforcement officers are trained to gather and use information from various sources in a criminal investigation. For homeland security, key sources of information include not only local, state, and federal intelligence sources, but also knowledge, relationships, and networks developed within the local multicultural communities. As noted by Nance (2003), "Terrorism against America can only be defeated through careful intelligence collection, surveillance, cooperative efforts among law enforcement and intelligence agencies, and resolving the root complaints of the terrorist-supporting population."

4. *Observe and Interpret Street-Level Behaviors:*   Law enforcement officers are trained to observe and interpret street-level criminal behaviors, and such skills are applicable to recognizing some of the behaviors of terrorists. Terrorists are not invisible "ghosts" (i.e., terrorists' behaviors and actions are usually visible to the trained observer); however, stereotypes based on race, ethnicity, gender, age, nationality, and other demographic dimensions may inhibit a law enforcement officer from observing and correctly interpreting the actions and behaviors of possible terrorists. Racial profiling would be one of the actions that could hamper law enforcement efforts in detecting a terrorist's intent. The only time that one could appropriately use racial profiling alone to detect a terrorist is when one has already had specific intelligence on a specific person as a terrorist (Howard & Sawyer, 2004).

Without proper intelligence, it is almost impossible to effectively interpret behaviors that one observes. For example, three of the September 11, 2001, terrorists were involved in traffic stops by the police for speeding on three separate occasions prior to the terrorists' attacks:

• Mohammed Atta, the al-Qaida 9/11 skyjacker who piloted the American Airlines Flight 77 into the North Tower of the World Trade Center, was stopped in July 2001 by the Florida State Police for driving with an invalid license. A bench warrant was issued for his arrest because he ignored the issued ticket. Atta was stopped a few weeks later in Delray Beach,

Florida, for speeding, but the officer was unaware of the bench warrant and let him go with a warning (Kleinberg & Davies, 2001, p. A1).

• Zaid al-Jarrah, the al-Qaida 9/11 skyjacker who investigators believe was a pilot on United Airlines Flight 93, which crashed in Pennsylvania, was stopped and cited by the Maryland State Police on September 9, 2001, for driving 90 miles per hour in a 65-mph zone near the Delaware state line (a $270 fine). Trooper Catalano, who made the stop, reported that he looked over the car several times, videotaped the entire transaction, and said that the stop was a "regular, routine traffic stop" ("A Nation Challenged," 2002, p. A12).

• Hani Hanjour, one of the al-Qaida 9/11 skyjackers aboard the plane that crashed into the Pentagon, was stopped for speeding within a few miles of the military headquarters 6 weeks before the attack and was ticketed by the Arlington, Virginia, police for going 50 miles per hour in a 35-mph zone. Hanjour surrendered his Florida driver's license to the police officer who stopped him but was allowed to go on his way (Roig-Franzia & Davis, 2002, p. A13).

In the case of Timothy McVeigh, the Oklahoma City bomber, law enforcement officials properly interpreted information, which led to his arrest at a traffic stop. McVeigh was stopped by Trooper Charles Hanger of the Oklahoma Highway Patrol about 90 minutes after the bombing of the Alfred P. Murrah Federal Building. Trooper Hanger was looking for suspicious vehicles headed his way given the approximate travel distance to his location and time of the bombing.

> Oklahoma Highway Patrol Trooper Charles Hanger pulled over McVeigh's yellow Mercury Marquis on I-35 about 63 miles north of Oklahoma City because his car was missing a rear license plate. Hanger told the jury he took shelter behind the door of his cruiser as McVeigh got out of the car and walked toward him. As McVeigh reached for his camouflage wallet, Hanger said he noticed a bulge under his light windbreaker. "I told him to take both hands and slowly pull back his jacket," Hanger said. "He said, 'I have a gun.' I pulled my weapon and stuck it to the back of his head." As Hanger searched and cuffed him, McVeigh told the trooper he was also carrying a knife and a spare clip of ammunition. In the chamber of the pistol, Hanger found a round of Black Talon ammunition, bullets designed to inflict maximum damage on a shooting victim. Hanger then arrested McVeigh for carrying a concealed pistol in a shoulder holster. Three days later, McVeigh was tied to the blast as he waited for a court hearing on the gun charge. ("Trooper Describes Arrest," 1997, p. A2)

RESPONSE STRATEGIES ADDRESSING LOCAL-COMMUNITY, REGIONAL, NATIONAL, AND GLOBAL ISSUES

The targets and methods of terrorists have become more diverse and more difficult to predict. Howard (2009) notes that "not only are targets selected to cause casualties without limit, they are selected to undermine the global economy" (p. 118).

> Whereas the violent global jihadist movement manifested itself primarily in terrorism preventions in the United States from 2002 through 2005, internationally the movement claimed major attacks against U.S. and Western targets that resulted in American casualties. Most of these incidents were perpetrated by regional jihadist groups operating in primarily Muslim countries, and included attacks committed by Indonesia-based Jemaah Islamiya and al-Qa'ida in the Arabian Peninsula. The

coordinated suicide bombing of London's mass transit system by homegrown jihadists, however, brought the violent jihadist movement and the tactic of suicide bombing to a major European capital. (FBI, 2007)

Often, clues surrounding the terrorist incident and/or attack will reveal whether domestic or international terrorism was involved and will point toward possible motives and the perpetrators behind the incident. Clues that might be helpful, surrounding a terrorist event, include the following:

Timing of the event may be significant to the terrorist group or individual. For many years to come, September 11 will be a day on which all U.S. facilities around the world will operate at a heightened state of security and awareness because of the al-Qaida's simultaneous terrorist attacks. Within the United States, April 19 will continue for some time to be a day of heightened alert because it is the anniversary of both the bombing of the Alfred P. Murrah Federal Building in Oklahoma City and the fire at the Branch Dividian compound in Waco, Texas. The more the law enforcement works with a community-policing model to understand the makeup of a multicultural community, the greater the likelihood that officers will have the knowledge to predict potential terrorist targets within communities.

Occupancy, location, and/or purpose related to the target include the following types of elements:

- Controversial businesses are those that have a history of inviting the protest and dislike of recognized groups that include one or more components of extremist elements. For example, controversial businesses include abortion clinics, logging mills, nuclear facilities, and tuna fishing companies.
- Public buildings and venues with large numbers of people are seen by terrorist as opportunities for attention-getting with mass casualties and victims. For some terrorists, causing massive destruction and casualties in targeted public buildings or in venues containing large numbers of people is linked to the identity of the operator/owner of the building or venue. Examples of such targets are the World Trade Center, World Bank, entertainment venues, athletic events, tourist destinations, shopping malls, airports, and convention centers.
- Symbolic and historical targets are links the terrorists make regarding the relationship of the target and the organization, event, and/or services that specifically offend extremists. Examples of symbolic and historical targets include the offices of the Internal Revenue Service (IRS) for tax resisters, the offices of the Bureau of Alcohol, Tobacco and Firearms (ATF) for those who oppose any form of gun control, and African American churches and Jewish synagogues for those who are members of white supremacist groups.
- Infrastructure systems and services include those structures and operations that are vital for the continued functioning of our country. Throughout the United States, these targets include communication companies, power grids, water treatment facilities, mass transit, telecommunication towers, and transportation hubs. Terrorists' attacks on any of these targets have the potential for disabling and disrupting massive areas and regions, resulting in chaos, especially with respect to huge numbers of injuries and fatalities across large geographical areas. Law enforcement officers' and agencies' knowledge of possible targets linked to occupancy, location, and/or purpose of an organization within the local, multicultural communities will enhance the ability to prevent and to prepare for a terrorist incident. For any of the noted indicators of a terrorist incident or attack, law enforcement officers would nearly always be among the first responders to the scene (IACP, 2001).

The First-Response Challenge for Law Enforcement

Law enforcement officers as first responders to a terrorism attack confront tremendous challenge, risk, and responsibility. The terrorist attack or crime scene is complicated by the confusion, panic, and casualty of the attack as well as any residual effects in the event that Weapons of mass destruction were used. Moreover, it has been quite typical for terrorists to deliberately target responders and rescue personnel at the crime scene. Terrorists have utilized "secondary devices" to target law enforcement and other public safety personnel responding to a terrorist's attack. For example, in the 1997 bomb attack at an Atlanta abortion clinic, a second bomb went off approximately one hour after the initial explosion and was very close to the command post established for the first bomb attack.

> As we are the first responders in any natural disaster or terrorist attack that takes place in our communities, we know quite well that the role of law enforcement is key to the nation's homeland security. This is what we have been trained to do. We take steps to improve our community's safety. We handle crises. We deal with emergencies. We reduce vulnerability to known threats and hazards. We provide oversight of police training to deal with unusual circumstances. And we coordinate with other emergency management and law enforcement agencies. This is the core of our profession. (Chief R. Gil Kerlikowske, Seattle Chief of Police, remarks given at the Washington Association of Sheriffs and Police Chiefs Conference, Spokane, Wash., May 21, 2003)

As in all hazardous law enforcement situations, officer safety and self-protection are top priorities. However, in some terrorist attacks, as in the September 11, 2001, multiple-site scenario, no amount of self-protection at the scene would have prevented the deaths of the 69 police, fire, and port officers from New York and New Jersey who were killed in the attack. Neither could the U.S. Secret Service agent, FBI agent, and the U.S. Fish and Wildlife Service agent aboard Flight 93 that crashed in rural Pennsylvania have protected themselves from becoming victims (Oliver, 2007).

Law enforcement personnel, as first responders to terrorists' crimes, need to know that the forms of self-protection can be defined in terms of the principles of time, distance, and shielding. Law enforcement personnel must have sufficient cross-cultural language skills to communicate the importance of these principles for effective action and response within multicultural communities during a terrorist incident:

1. *Time* is used as a tool in a terrorist crime scene. Spend the shortest amount of time possible in the affected area or exposed to the hazard. The less time one spends in the hazard area, the less likely one will become injured. Minimizing time spent in the hazard area will also reduce the chances of contaminating the crime scene.
2. *Distance* from the affected terrorist area or hazardous situation should be maximized. The greater the distance from the affected area while performing one's functions, the less the exposure to the hazard. Maintaining distance from the hazard areas will also ease the evacuation of the injured, allow for other emergency personnel requiring immediate access, and facilitate crowd control by law enforcement officers.
3. *Shielding* can be used to address specific types of hazards. Shielding can be achieved through buildings, walls, vehicles, body armor, and personnel protective equipment including chemical protective clothing, fire protective clothing, and self-contained breathing apparatus.

Law enforcement officers must understand the various types of danger and harm that may result from a terrorist situation not only for their own self-protection but in order to understand the reactions of affected victims and to be able to provide effective assistance to those affected by terrorist activities. Law enforcement personnel need to be aware that many people who are from multicultural communities may have had prior experiences (or have heard of prior experiences) with WMD incidents within their home countries (e.g., Vietnamese Americans' experience with thermal harm during the napalm bombing of their villages; Iraqi Americans' experience with chemical harm from mustard gas attacks within their communities).

Response Strategies: Detecting and Preventing Attacks of Terrorism

Law enforcement officers spend years studying criminal behaviors in order to prevent crimes and to capture and prosecute criminals. Public safety roles for law enforcement agencies now require the use of some of these same skills in identifying the criminal behaviors of potential terrorists. As noted by Hoffman (2006) and others, the most difficult and critical component of homeland security is to recognize and prevent a terrorist attack. As such, criminal justice officers need to be competent in recognizing the Terrorist Attack Pre-incident Indicators (TAPIs), a term used by the intelligence community to describe actions taken and behaviors exhibited by terrorists before they carry out an attack (Nance, 2003). We discuss in Chapter 13 one source of TAPIs, which includes the tools of "profiling" used in law enforcement today. For example, Secret Service officers are trained to watch for individual behaviors, compiled as a profile, which may serve as indicators for possible actions toward those whom the officers are protecting. El Al, the Israeli airline, has used very successfully a behavior-recognition profile to detect individuals who might be potential skyjackers of its airliners (Howard & Sawyer, 2004).

Law enforcement officers, with training in observing and working with cultural differences and diverse communities would benefit by applying their skills and training to recognizing terrorist's behaviors. As will be noted in Chapter13, public safety officers must avoid a stereotype-based approach to detecting criminals; this holds equally true in detecting terrorists. Stereotypes alone do not help in the detection and prevention of terrorism regardless of whether they are based on race or on the notion of what constitutes a "terrorist." Stereotyping will obscure law enforcement officers' perceptions of the real dangers and issues in providing for our homeland security. For example, several of the September 11, 2001, terrorists behaved in ways that threw off any surveillance based on cultural and religious stereotypes: more than one skyjacker was seen in nightclubs and strip bars. Such behaviors would be contrary to the American stereotype of devout Muslim fundamentalists who would be averse to alcoholic beverages, nightclub exotic dancers, and overt sexual behaviors of men and women at bars. Although it is beyond the scope of this chapter to detail the development of law enforcement skills for recognizing terrorists' behaviors, it is critical to emphasize that the application of stereotyping, racial profiling, and biased perceptions will not lead to the detection and capturing of terrorists. (See Nance [2003] for additional information on developing skills and tools with TAPIs.) The following incident exemplifies the use of law enforcement skills and intelligence in homeland security:

> Four homegrown Muslim terrorists on a mission from hell were arrested last night as they planted what they thought were high-powered plastic explosives at two Bronx synagogues, authorities said. The men were also allegedly plotting to use a Stinger missile to shoot a military plane out of the sky in upstate New York immediately after the bombings. "This is America's finest hour. The best resources of the Police

Department, Homeland Security and the FBI kept us safe," said Jonathan Rosenblatt, a rabbi at the targeted Riverdale Jewish Center . . . They planted what they thought were explosives in a parked car outside the house of worship. One acted as a lookout, while the other three allegedly drove up the block to the Riverdale Jewish Center and planted two more bags of "explosives" in cars. Unbeknownst to them, their explosives were duds—supplied by authorities who had been monitoring their plan for more than a year. Cops swooped in and arrested them right after they allegedly planted the last of the phony bombs. (Weiss, Calabrese, & Fermino, 2009)

Incident Command and Emergency Operations Centers for Coordination of Multiple Response Agencies

Homeland Security Presidential Directive Number 5 (2003) establishes the National Incident Management System (NIMS) and the Incident Command System (ICS) for all emergency operations to include terrorism incidents, homeland security, and community disasters. The goal of the NIMS is to ensure that all law enforcement and emergency responding entities and jurisdictional levels are capable of working together to manage domestic emergencies, crises, and incidents under a common framework. All police command and decision processes related to a terrorism and homeland security incident or a community disaster are coordinated through the Incident Command System (ICS). (For the full scope of these operations, see Oliver [2007].)

Multijurisdictional Action

In our discussion about coordinating efforts for terrorism prevention, homeland security, and disaster preparedness, a variety of diverse federal, state, and local agencies and organizations are involved in multijurisdictional actions for combating a terrorist incident or attack. Some of the key elements ensuring success for law enforcement agencies and officers in such incidents include the following:

1. Preparation and planning provide some of the best avenues for successful crisis management and subsequent recovery from a terrorist incident. The following planned steps are critical:
   - Develop pertinent plans and policies for terrorist incidents and attacks
   - Establish multijurisdictional plans/protocols and mutual-aid agreements
   - Ensure availability of multicultural law enforcement personnel with language expertise
   - Implement, as much as possible, preventive procedures and plans
   - Train law enforcement personnel as first responders and as members of multijurisdictional teams involved in a terrorist incident
   - Provide background information about the makeup of the different multicultural communities and their prior experiences as victims of terrorism
   - Rehearse possible events and incidents
   - Acquire the necessary protective and communication equipment
   - Establish multidiscipline community service teams (and, again, where possible, provide for the range of language expertise required by the community)
   - Establish a network of multicultural leaders and communities for communication, intelligence, and response implementation
2. Cost and deployment of resources have been highlighted by most local governments with respect to the degree of burden and expenditure needed to be borne by local law

enforcement and by other public safety agencies involved in combating possible terrorism incidents.

> Government resources increasingly have been thrown into the fight against terrorism, and that endangers community policing, Los Angeles Police Chief William J. Bratton declared at a public forum yesterday. Community policing caused a downward trend in crime nationally in the 1990s, but crime is beginning to rebound because less money and attention is being devoted to community policing in this decade, he said. Many of those resources have been siphoned to prevent terrorism, and there has been a general disinvestment in policing, he said. In the previous decade, 100,000 additional police were hired and $3 billion was spent on research, including the application of DNA evidence, and on the equipping of police forces. Bratton called for a balancing of the expenditures so that both policing and terrorism are addressed. (Smith, 2006)

Since local tax-based funds are insufficient to address the enormity of costs involved in the planning, prevention, and deployment of resources to address terrorism concerns and issues, one of the key concerns within multicultural communities is the diversion of funds from community-policing activities to the war on terrorism.

3. Access to intelligence and informational databases provides the information necessary for the prevention of and response to terrorist threats. The best prevention against terrorist incidents and acts at the local community level is to ensure coordination with federal and state intelligence sources and access to ongoing intelligence-gathering capacity from the federal level. On the local level, it is important that law enforcement officers and agencies develop critical relationships and networks with the local multicultural communities. Developing such relationships requires both ongoing efforts and constant renewal of the relationships through clear communication and trust between law enforcement and community members. For example, in the foiled terrorist plot to down trans-Atlantic British airlines with explosives, the tip to the local police department came from a person in the Muslim community who had been concerned about the activities of an acquaintance after the July 7, 2005, terror attacks in London (Arena, 2006).

4. Multijurisdictional training and rehearsals have been identified as critical elements in the successful implementation of terrorist incident management and recovery. Clearly, there are few opportunities to develop the relationships, awareness, communication and processes required for a coordinated effort ahead of an incident's occurring. As illustrated in the following example, the involvement of these multijurisdictional agencies and their personnel in rehearsals provide valuable lessons for any possible real terrorist incidents.

> A massive cloud of lethal gas, dozens of agonizing deaths by asphyxiation, an unknown number of hidden nuclear devices, executions, a ship full of hostages, and an enemy mine bobbing in the harbor: If any of it had been real, it would have been an absolutely horrible couple of days at the Port of Hueneme. Fortunately, the series of catastrophes was part of an anti-terrorism exercise, an elaborate two-day drama staged Tuesday and Wednesday with the help of the Navy, the Coast Guard, some 140 FBI agents, 81 officers from the Ventura County Sheriff's Department—in all, representatives from 18 military and law-enforcement agencies. . . . Along the way, the participating agencies picked up

lessons they will use to streamline some of their procedures. "There won't be wholesale changes," said Banks, of the warfare center. "But even an hour saved could be a crucial hour." The Ventura County sheriff's SWAT team learned that storming a ship is a lengthier process than taking over a home, said department spokesman Eric Nishimoto. With the FBI taking the lead in the antiterrorist operations, officers also realized that dealing with a hierarchy of agents from all over the U.S. was not equivalent to dealing with operatives from the local office. "It's a totally different dynamic," Nishimoto said. Simply communicating with other agencies was sometimes difficult. "Everyone's enmeshed in their own acronyms," said Tom Netzer, who coordinated the exercise for the Center for Asymmetric Warfare. "It helped when we got everyone to just speak English." (Chawkins, 2003, p. M1)

Training for terrorist incidents that are multijurisdictional in nature would allow for the rehearsal and practices necessary for effective overall terrorism response efforts. As in any simulated practice exercise, not all components of a terrorist incident can be anticipated or incorporated. Nonetheless, such training and rehearsal would allow for a timelier implementation of the response strategies important to a terrorist incident, as will be noted in the next section. Training in responding to terrorism, to date, has included limited scenarios related to multicultural community elements. In time, emphases upon language expertise, bilingual communications, and interpreter participation need to be added to training exercises.

Building Community Networks and Resources

In order to detect and deter terrorist incidents and attacks, the development of strong community networks, relationships, and resources is critical. The ability to obtain critical information from a community assessment depends on ongoing, positive, and trusted relationships within the multicultural communities.

In Boston police's new anti-terror strategy, some of the frontline recruits will be neighborhood watch groups. Police Commissioner Kathleen M. O'Toole is planning to spend federal homeland security money to help watch groups spot possible terrorists, an initiative designed at the same time to rebuild the city's once nationally recognized community policing program. "There's no bright line between terrorism and ordinary inner-city crime," O'Toole told the Globe. "The federal government has made it very clear that if we launch homeland security initiatives that also have some benefit via ripple effect on other aspects of policing, then that's OK." The Department of Homeland Security advises the US Justice Department on a program called Citizen Corps, which includes a national neighborhood watch program incorporating terrorism awareness education with crime prevention. "It serves as a way to bring residents together to focus on emergency preparedness and emergency response training," said Steven Llanes, a Homeland Security spokesman. (Smalley, 2005)

Part Two, "Cultural Specifics for Law Enforcement," includes discussion of ways to enhance communication, develop relationships, and widen community networks within multicultural communities. All of those strategies will ultimately assist in effective detection and deterrence of terrorism within those communities, and will contribute to homeland security and disaster preparedness responses.

Using Ethnic and Multicultural Media as a Resource

For any terrorist and homeland security incident or community disaster, law enforcement agencies must help to provide a constant flow of credible information to the local community. Clearly, if positive relationships have been formed with the diversity of residents and the multicultural community leaders, the law enforcement agency's credibility would not be suspect and/or in question. Media sources used for the release of information should include the ones used by most populations, as well as those used by specific multicultural groups, especially those broadcast or print in the languages of the key multicultural groups of the community. Some public safety agencies may be concerned about not having their information already prepared and translated into the language of the diverse ethnic and cultural groups; however, given the nature and importance of the information, most ethnic media will do the translation in order to provide critical information to their audiences.

Policies, procedures, and mechanisms need to be in place for releasing information to enable the safety and security of all community residents. This means that the involvement of ethnic and multicultural media is critical; the ready availability of translations and interpretations is key in ensuring appropriate responses, alleviating any unnecessary fears or concerns, and providing assurances that public safety agencies and officers are in control of the situation. The media have been shown to be the most efficient and reliable means to disseminate information rapidly to the community regarding a terrorist incident and to notify community residents of the subsequent response by the public safety agencies. Strategic media events should be held to continuously inform the public that the incident is well under control, the personnel are well prepared and trained to handle the incident, and the community's recovery is fully expected.

Whether dealing with a terrorist incident or an everyday event, the basis for effective communications with the community through the media is a strong partnership and established positive relationships with the media. Law enforcement agencies need to understand that whether in crisis management or in daily peacekeeping, the media have a dual role: to obtain information, stories, and perspectives on the incident for news-reporting objectives and to inform the community efficiently of impending dangers and threats stemming from the incident. Good media relations allow for the strategic communication of critical incident information to the communities served by the law enforcement agencies. To reach multicultural communities, police officers must go beyond the conventional and mainstream media sources and become familiar with all media, in English and in other languages, that will reach the broadest populations in the shortest amount of time.

GOALS FOR HOMELAND SECURITY AND DISASTER PREPAREDNESS IN MULTICULTURAL COMMUNITIES

Oliver (2007) summarized the process and major steps taken to develop a national strategy for homeland security by the police, which include some of the following key research studies and reports:

1. "National Strategy for Homeland Security" (Office of Homeland Security, 2002), which details the broad array of strategies and issues for the United States
2. "From Hometown Security to Homeland Security" (IACP, 2005), which highlights the role of local police in homeland security and the "best practices" for achieving a national strategy for homeland security and disaster preparedness

3. *Homeland Security: Best Practices for Local Government* (Kemp, 2003), which identifies best practices from local law enforcement for homeland security
4. "Protecting Your Community from Terrorism: Strategies for Local Law Enforcement" (Murphy and Plotkin, 2003), a joint effort by the Police Executive Research Forum (PERF) and the office of COPS, which provides the insights of national, state, and local law enforcement leaders on homeland security strategies.

Chief Kerlikowske (2003) of the Seattle Police Department highlighted the critical areas that local law enforcement officials and departments need to address as part of the national strategy for homeland security and disaster preparedness:

1. Intelligence and Warning
2. Border and Transportation Security
3. Domestic Counterterrorism
4. Protecting Critical Infrastructure and Key Assets
5. Defending against Catastrophic Threats
6. Emergency Preparedness and Response

In the following sections, we address several of the six critical areas noted above and highlight the key factors important to multicultural communities within each area for multicultural law enforcement.

Intelligence and Warning

The IACP (2005) report "Hometown Security is Homeland Security" notes that there are over 700,000 officers involved in daily law enforcement and public safety efforts. Police departments and their officers have close knowledge of their constituencies and have developed valuable relationships within their diverse communities. The strengths of such day-to-day law enforcement efforts in local communities enable state, local, and tribal law enforcement officials to develop unique relationships within their communities to: (1) assess and gather intelligence and information; (2) identify, investigate, and apprehend suspected terrorists; and (3) provide and disseminate information and warnings to the local communities (IACP, 2005).

Since the establishment of the DHS, law enforcement agencies have been receiving a variety of intelligence information, advisories, warnings, and other pertinent communications regarding efforts and activities to be implemented in local communities. Local law enforcement agencies and officers, because of their community knowledge and networks, have been called upon to aid in intelligence data gathering regarding possible terrorists. Such efforts have often sparked a mixed reception by law enforcement agencies. From one perspective, this puts a strain on the established relationships of community policing within multicultural communities. Public confidence and trust in law enforcement agencies are essential for the effective prevention of and response to terrorism and for homeland security. Residents in diverse communities must be able to trust that they will be treated fairly and protected as part of homeland security. This is of particular importance where there may be perceptions, assumptions, and/or stereotypes among community residents as to who might be a "terrorist amongst us." When local law enforcement agencies and officers are called upon to provide assistance, the tasks of information gathering and interviewing possible terrorist suspects within multicultural communities involve the following critical steps:

1. *Contact with Community Leaders:* Law enforcement officers need to work closely with community leaders in order to establish a cooperative plan for gathering necessary information. Community leaders can effectively inform their multicultural communities as to

why information gathering is taking place and what the associated processes are. In addition, community leaders can, for example, work with the community relations offices of law enforcement agencies to develop a communication plan for the effective dissemination of information.

2. *Utilize a Communication Plan:*   It is essential to have a well-developed and pilot-tested communication plan to ensure that the proper messages are disseminated to multicultural communities. This is particularly important when language translations and interpretation are necessary. A carefully pre-tested core message regarding data-gathering procedures and interviews has more chance of success than on-the-spot messages: unplanned messages would be subject to the momentary interpretation of those who first hear such information.

3. *Clearly Explain the Implications of Participation in the Data-Gathering Process:*   When it comes to accusations of terrorism and/or fears related to homeland security, members of multicultural communities who might be stereotyped as "terrorists," or have experienced prejudice by others in this regard, would naturally be quite cautious of any contact with law enforcement agencies and officers. Clearly defined procedures and information about data gathering and interviews are extremely important. In addition, if there are federal-agency consequences (e.g., being reported to the ICE for a visa violation), these elements should be clearly stated to ensure an ongoing relationship of trust with the community.

4. *Utilize Law Enforcement Personnel, Interpreters from Similar Backgrounds:*   Use, whenever possible, law enforcement personnel (and interpreters) from the same or similar ethnic/cultural background as that of the communities involved; this contributes to relationship building and the trust necessary for information-gathering attempts. Clearly, the availability of bilingual personnel can make a significant difference to speakers of other languages.

Using Information and Intelligence Provided

Law enforcement agencies receive intelligence and information from many resources for their work related to homeland security. Such information generally is packaged by the different U.S. intelligence agencies and distributed by the FBI. The FBI's Strategic Information Operations Center (SIOC) is one of the key centers for homeland security and the war on terrorism (FBI, 2008). Agents from the FBI, CIA, Defense Department, Customs, ATF, Secret Service, and NSA work side-by-side to consolidate the interagency intelligence work.

The Terrorist Threat Integration Center (TTIC), which opened in January 2003 and functions under the CIA's direction, incorporates intelligence from both foreign and domestic sources regarding terrorists identified by the DHS, the FBI's Counterterrorism Division, the CIA's Counterterrorism Center, and the Department of Defense. The extent to which law enforcement agencies are able to take action prior to a terrorist act or incident presents legal and jurisdictional dilemmas. As noted by Norwitz (2002), because "the objective of a criminal investigation is successful prosecution, all law enforcement efforts must withstand judicial scrutiny at trial. Provision of Articles IV, V, and VI of the U.S. Constitution, as well as the Bill of Rights, offer powerful protections against law enforcement excess, which, by extension, applies to international terrorists operating on our soil."

Moreover, law enforcement must continue to maintain positive police–community relationships in order to properly serve the diverse society and multicultural communities within its jurisdiction. Such services include protecting those who might be wrongly accused or incorrectly stereotyped as terrorists (or both).

Border and Transportation Security

As noted by DHS "The United States shares a 5,525 mile border with Canada and a 1,989 mile border with Mexico. Our maritime border includes 95,000 miles of shoreline and navigable waterways as well as a 3.4 million square mile exclusive economic zone. All people and goods legally entering into the United States must be processed through an air, land, or sea port of entry. Many international airports are dispersed throughout the United States. Each year, more than 500 million people legally enter our country. Some 330 million are non-citizens; more than 85 percent enter via land borders, often as daily commuters" (Office of Homeland Security, 2002). Police and local law enforcement agencies are central to the border and transportation security operations. Two key issues are: (1) racial profiling within the context of homeland security, and (2) collaborative and enforcement efforts with ICE.

Racial Profiling within the Context of Homeland Security

The issue of racial profiling, as will be noted in Chapter 13, is a major problem and concern for African Americans, Arab Americans, and Latino/Hispanic Americans, and for members of other groups, as well. Individuals from different cultural and racial backgrounds believe that the determining factor in whether peace officers exercise their discretion in stopping a vehicle has to do with the driver's race and ethnicity. In the area of homeland security, current federal policy prohibits the use of racial profiling except under narrow circumstances. Law enforcement officers should be cautious in the use of racial profiling for detecting terrorists and in homeland security matters. Hoffman (2006) has documented that terrorists will "do whatever it will take" to avoid detection and accomplish a mission. Even though the use of racial profiling in circumstances involving terrorism is legal and justifiable, its use may not actually result in detecting the terrorist because the terrorist is knowledgeable about the racial profiling used.

Working with Immigration and Customs Enforcement (ICE)

In 1996, Congress passed legislation that expanded the role of local and state law enforcement agencies in federal immigration enforcement to enter into written agreements (known as Memoranda of Understanding) with ICE to carry out the functions of immigration officers such as investigation, apprehension, and detention. The ICE's 287(g) program allows local law enforcement agencies to collaborate with federal immigration authorities in a wide range of activities (as discussed in Chapter 1). As highlighted by the Police Foundation (2009), "Police executives have felt torn between a desire to be helpful and cooperative with federal immigration authorities and a concern that their participation in immigration enforcement efforts will undo the gains they have achieved through community oriented policing practices, which are directed at gaining the trust and cooperation of immigrant communities" (p. 5). In addition, police departments have to consider the impact of local enforcement of immigration law on already inadequate local resources.

As part of the ICE's ACCESS (an acronym for Agreements of Cooperation in Communities to Enhance Safety and Security), local and state law enforcement agencies may form partnerships with ICE to address specific issues related to undocumented immigrants in their communities coming to the attention of those agencies. The ICE 287(g) program is a key component of the ICE ACCESS programs available for assistance to local and state law enforcement officers. The conclusions of the Police Foundation (2009), a nonpartisan research and think-tank organization dedicated to "Supporting innovation and improvements in policing," indicated the following concerns about the ICE 287(g) program (p. 5):

- The costs of participating in the ICE's 287(g) program outweigh the benefits.
- Police officers should be prohibited from arresting and detaining persons to solely investigate immigration status in the absence of probable cause of an independent state criminal law violation.
- If a local agency nevertheless enters the 287(g) program, its participation should be focused on serious criminal offenders and should be limited to verifying the immigration status of criminal detainees as part of the 287(g) Jail Enforcement Officer program.
- Local and state authorities participating in federal immigration enforcement activities should develop policies and procedures for monitoring racial profiling and abuse of authority. In order to preserve the trust that police agencies have built over the years by aggressively engaging in community-oriented policing activities, local law enforcement agencies should involve representatives of affected communities in the development of local immigration policies.
- There is a need for empirical research on ICE's 287(g) program and other methods of police collaboration with federal immigration authorities so that we have more objective data by which to better understand the way in which these programs are carried out in the field and their impact on public safety and civil liberties.
- Local law enforcement agencies should employ community-policing and problem-solving tactics to improve relations with immigrant communities and resolve tension caused by expanding immigration.
- Local law enforcement leaders and policing organizations should place pressure on the federal government to comprehensively improve border security and reform the immigration system, because the federal government's failure on both issues has had serious consequences in cities and towns throughout the country.

One of the key conclusions of the Police Foundation (2009) survey is:

> Local police must serve and protect *all* residents regardless of their immigration status, enforce the criminal laws of their state, and serve and defend the Constitution of the United States. As police agencies move away from their core role of ensuring public safety and begin taking on civil immigration enforcement activities, the perception immigrants have of the role of police moves from protection to arrest and deportation, thereby jeopardizing local law enforcement's ability to gain the trust and cooperation of immigrant communities. "How can you police a community that will not talk to you?" asked one police chief participating in the project. Without the cooperation of immigrant witnesses and victims of crime, local law enforcement's ability to identify, arrest, and prosecute criminals is jeopardized. (p. 5)

Given the ICE 287(g) program, one of the key challenges for a law enforcement agency involves decision making as to where the local public safety agencies and departments become involved in enforcing and working with ICE. The ramifications for multicultural community relationships and network building are significant. The decision making and strategic responses to terrorism within these collaborative and possible joint efforts are not always clear-cut, nor "given," for any law enforcement agency, as exemplified by the following law enforcement departmental stance:

> Roswell police have stopped detaining undocumented immigrants for the Border Patrol. Police Chief Rob Smith told a Police Council Committee meeting Wednesday that recent conversations with the Border Patrol and Immigration and Customs Enforcement cast doubt on the practice. "The legal people are saying, 'Well, we're not sure,' and I think the reason they're not sure is it's never been challenged," he said. Smith said the Roswell department has detained suspected undocumented immigrants since he became an officer 32 years ago. The American Civil Liberties Union has argued that holding undocumented immigrants without a criminal charge constitutes unlawful detention. Being in the country without proper documents is a civil violation. Smith told officers in a memo May 14 the department no longer would incarcerate undocumented immigrants if their legal status in the country was the only charge. (Associated Press, 2009)

However, the general argument supporting leaving undocumented immigrants alone (unless they have committed a criminal act or are creating a disturbance) is based on the perspective that tracking down and deporting undocumented workers is technically the job of ICE, not the police, as noted in Chapter 1 (and within the discussion on the ICE 287(g) program in this Chapter). Central to the clarity of roles required by the officer in the field is that police agencies have to create policies related to determining, reporting, and turning in undocumented immigrants to ICE. Sometimes the trust of the entire community (unauthorized migrants and legal immigrants) is at stake with multicultural communities.

As noted by the Police Foundation (2009) survey report, many law enforcement agencies will most likely not participate in the ICE 287(g) program. The following recommendations apply to local law enforcement agencies that have decided not to be part of the ICE 287(g) program in working with multicultural communities concerning legal and undocumented immigration status. (A more detailed version with specific examples is provided in Chapter 7 for the Latino/Hispanic American community.)

1. *Develop Agency and Departmental Policies with Regard to Reporting and Working with ICE:* Law enforcement agencies must have clear policies and procedures to address the circumstances in reporting to ICE. The policy must include: (1) the circumstances under which a person will be reported to ICE; and (2) that no person will be reported or referred to ICE where no laws have been violated.
2. *Contact with the Multicultural Community Leaders:* Law enforcement officers need to work closely with community leaders to establish a cooperative plan to inform them of the agency's policies and their implementation. Community leaders could, for example, work with law enforcement agencies' community relations offices to develop a communication plan for the effective dissemination of information about its policy in working with ICE.
3. *Utilize a Communication Plan:* It is essential to have a well-developed communication plan to ensure that the proper messages are provided to the specific multicultural communities regarding when a person may or may not be reported or referred to ICE. This is particularly important when language translations and interpreting are necessary.
4. *Clearly Define and Spell out the Implications for Any Contact with the Law Enforcement Agency and Possible Reporting to ICE:* When it comes to the possibility that contact with

the local police department may result in a person being questioned by ICE and/or being involved in deportation procedures, members from multicultural communities tend to be quite cautious. The fear that they might be stereotyped as illegal (or the possibility that they have experienced prejudice by others in this regard) would naturally make any contact with law enforcement agencies and officers tenuous.

5. *Train All Sworn and Nonsworn Personnel on the Agency or Departmental Policy with Regard to Working with ICE:* Law enforcement agencies need to provide training and education to enable officers to utilize legal enforcement tools effectively so they can perform their work professionally within today's multicultural communities. Training that provides accurate information concerning groups about which officers might have stereotypes is one approach that will help to ensure implementation of a department's policy in working with ICE.

6. *Utilize Law Enforcement Personnel and Translators/Interpreters from the Same or Similar Communities:* To the extent that it is possible, the use of law enforcement personnel who are from the same or similar ethnic communities would add to developing and sustaining the trust that is needed between law enforcement and those communities.

7. *Ensure Community Outreach Services:* Every police–community interaction requires a strong, ongoing link to community groups and advocacy organizations. A link is established when community task forces are assembled to address issues, especially those involving possible police interactions with undocumented immigrants and/or unauthorized migrants.

8. *Provide Real-Time Information and Referral to Community-Based Advocacy Services:* Police departments may want to provide real-time information and referral to the resources and services available from specific multicultural community-based advocacy services related to undocumented immigration issues.

Immigration and Customs Enforcement cooperation with local law enforcement agencies is of particular concern for multicultural communities where there has been a history of undocumented immigration as well as legal immigration (e.g., Latino/Hispanic American, Asian/Pacific American, Arab and Middle Eastern American). Indeed, some multicultural community members will be prosecuted and deported. As indicated by Decker, Lewis, Provine, and Varsanyi (2008), the vast majority of Police Departments will check Immigration Status and/or contact ICE when encountering possible unauthorized immigrants in the following situations: (1) Arrested for a violent crime (more than 85 percent), (2) Detained for parole violation or failure to appear in court (more than 65 percent), (3) Arrested for domestic violence (more than 60 percent), (4) Interviewed as possible victims of human trafficking (more than 50 percent), and (5) Arrested for a nonviolent crime, with no prior record (about 50 percent). However, where no wrong has been committed, law enforcement must keep a check on potential stereotyping and the prejudicial act of singling out individuals based on those stereotypes.

To assist local law enforcement agencies in developing policies and procedures in working with ICE, the Major Cities Chiefs (MCC, 2006) developed a nine-point position-and-guidance statement. At the time of the writing of this publication, the administration was in the process of reevaluating the ICE 287(g) program (see Chapter 1).

1. *Securing the Borders:* Illegal immigration is a national issue and the federal government should first act to secure the national borders to prevent illegal entry into the United States.

2. *Enforcing Laws That Prohibit the Hiring of Illegal Immigrants:* The federal government and its agencies should vigorously enforce existing immigration laws prohibiting employers from hiring illegal immigrants. Enforcement and prosecution of employers who

illegally seek out and hire undocumented immigrants or turn a blind eye to the undocumented status of their employees, will help to eliminate one of the major incentives for illegal immigration.

3. *Consulting and Involving Local Police Agencies in Decision Making:*   MCC and other representatives of the local law enforcement community such as the International Association of Chiefs of Police and local district attorneys and prosecutors should be consulted and brought in at the beginning of any process to develop a national initiative to involve local police agencies in the enforcement of federal immigration laws.

4. *Ensuring Completely Voluntary Participation of Agencies:*   Any initiative by local police agencies to be involved in the enforcement of immigration laws should be completely voluntary. The decisions related to how local law enforcement agencies allocate their resources, direct their workforce, and define the duties of their employees to best serve and protect their communities should be left in the control of state and local governments.

5. *Creating Incentive-Based Approaches with Full Federal Funding:*   Any initiative to involve local police agencies in the enforcement of immigration laws should be an incentive-based approach with full federal funding to provide the necessary resources to local agencies that choose to enforce immigration laws.

6. *Maintaining Current Assistance Funding without Reductions and/or Shifting of Funds:*   The funding of any initiative to involve local police agencies in the enforcement of immigration laws should not be at the detriment of current funding or consist of a reduction either directly or indirectly in any current federal funded program focused on assisting police agencies with local policing or homeland security activities.

7. *Clarifying the Authority and Limitation of Liability:*   The authority of local police agencies and their officers to become involved in the enforcement of immigration laws should be clearly stated and defined. The statement of authority should also establish liability protection and an immunity shield for police officers and police agencies that take part in immigration enforcement as authorized by clear federal legislation.

8. *Ensuring of the Removal of Civil Immigration Detainers from the NCIC [National Crime Information Center] System:*   Until the borders are secured and vigorous enforcement against employers who hire illegal immigrants has taken place, federal agencies should cease placing civil immigration detainers in NCIC and remove any existing civil detainers currently within the system. Moreover, local law enforcement agencies have concerns regarding the lack of authority and the uncertainty over the authority of local agencies to enforce immigration laws. The inclusion of civil detainers within the system has created confusion for local police agencies and subjected them to possible liability for exceeding their authority by arresting a person upon the basis of a mere civil detainer.

9. *Continuing Enforcement against Criminal Violators Regardless of Immigration Status:* Immigrants, documented and/or unauthorized, who commit criminal acts will find no safe harbor or sanctuary from their criminal violations within any major city, but will instead face the full force of criminal prosecution.

Domestic Counterterrorism

Office of Homeland Security (2002) defined its "law enforcement mission to focus on the prevention of all terrorist acts within the United States, whether international or domestic in origin, using all legal means—both traditional and nontraditional—to identify, halt, and, where appropriate, prosecute terrorists in the United States . . . DHS will utilize the full range of its legal authorities to pursue, not only the individuals directly engaged in terrorist activity, but also their sources of support (to include the people and organizations that knowingly fund the terrorists) and those that provide them with logistical assistance."

A key component of the DHS legal arsenal is the USA Patriot Act signed into law by the president on October 26, 2001, to improve government coordination in law enforcement, intelligence gathering, and information sharing. The official title for this act was "the U.S.A. P.A.T.R.I.O.T. Act," in which the acronym stands for, "Uniting and Strengthening America by Providing Appropriate Tools Required to Intercept and Obstruct Terrorism" (Doyle, 2002). In this text, we refer to this act by its common reference, the Patriot Act, which has ten Titles that provide for additional powers for government to use against terrorists. Key parts of the Patriot Act that have raised concern within multicultural communities include the power of law enforcement officers to (1) question, detain, and remove potential foreign terrorists within our borders; (2) enhance surveillance methods to track and intercept communications without customary court orders; and (3) increase information sharing for key infrastructure protection by allowing for cooperation between federal, state, and local law enforcement agencies through the expansion of the Regional Information Sharing System (RISS). The Patriot Act expired in 2005 (Doyle, 2005), but most of its components and titles have been renewed in 2006.

The key component of the Patriot Act that has caused the maximum concern in multicultural communities, especially within Arab and Middle Eastern communities, is the power of law enforcement officials to question, detain, and remove possible terrorists from the country. The FBI and DHS have requested the assistance of state and local law enforcement and public safety agencies in data-gathering and interviewing efforts for homeland security purposes under the provisions of the Patriot Act.

Law enforcement agencies must be concerned about how they participate in homeland security data-gathering efforts in order to avoid possible negative effects on their relationships with multicultural communities. Clearly, as ours is a nation built on the rule of law, DHS must utilize federal laws to win the war on terrorism while always protecting the civil liberties of those individuals within multicultural communities and within the larger national communities as a whole. DHS uses our federal immigration laws and customs regulations to protect our borders and ensure uninterrupted commerce, and encourages state and local governments to strengthen their codes and regulations to protect our public welfare, to prosecute terrorists, and to be partners in countering the domestic and global threat of terrorism.

Protecting Critical Infrastructure and Key Assets

As noted by DHS (2002), "terrorists are opportunistic, and they exploit vulnerabilities we leave exposed, choosing the time, place, and method to attack weaknesses they observe or perceive. Increasing the security of a particular type of target, such as aircraft or buildings, makes it more likely that terrorists will seek a different target." While DHS and local law enforcement agencies cannot assume to be able to prevent all terrorist attacks, preventing attacks on the critical infrastructure in the following sectors would be most important:

- Agriculture
- Food
- Water
- Public Health
- Emergency Services
- Government

- Defense Industrial Base
- Information and Telecommunications
- Energy
- Transportation
- Banking and Finance
- Chemical Industry
- Postal and Shipping Services

Community Assessment

Preventing, limiting, and reducing a community's vulnerability to attack requires a careful and ongoing community assessment to locate and measure the risks involved in the particular community. Such assessments would involve reviewing and analyzing all the localities that are likely targets for terrorism and working to improve the security of these locations. Some law enforcement agencies have developed a rating system and have cataloged their possible problem areas into different priority levels. The following four priority level assessment categories could be used in a community assessment or in a particular law enforcement department or agency (U.S. Department of Justice, 1997):

1. First Priority Level—Fatal: These are processes and functions the failure of which would result in death, severe financial loss, massive legal liabilities, or catastrophic consequences. Such processes and functions would include all essential mission-critical elements such as electrical power, communications, information systems, and command and leadership functions.
2. Second Priority Level—Critical: These would be processes and functional units of the agency, department, or organization that are critical to its operations and would be difficult to do without for any long period of time. Some examples of "critical" functional units might include computer terminals, elevators, perimeter security lights, and heat/air conditioning in the building. Examples of critical processes might include building entry/exit security and two-way communication radio network.
3. Third Priority Level—Important: These would include processes and functional units that are essential but not critical to the department, agency, or organization such as facsimile, copier, videotape player, video camera, and tape recorders. Some examples of "important" processes would include files and record access, administrative training, and new-hire orientation.
4. Fourth Priority Level—Routine: These would include processes and functional units that are not strategically mission-important (although their failure may cause some inconvenience) to the agency, department, or organization, such as coffeemakers, microwave ovens, and room thermostats. Nonessential and routine processes might include providing parking lot stickers and duty lists for staff personnel and providing information at the reception area.

Community assessments of functional units and processes should be ongoing and scheduled routinely so that information of possible terrorist targets can be updated on a regular basis.

Defending against Catastrophic Threats

As noted by DHS (2002), "the expertise, technology, and material needed for building the most deadly weapons known to mankind—including chemical, biological, radiological, and nuclear weapons—are proliferating. If our enemies acquire these weapons, they are likely to try to use them, and the consequences of such an attack could be far more devastating than those we suffered on September 11, 2001. Attacks using weapons of mass destruction, or WMD (which include chemical, biological, radiological, or nuclear weapons) in the United States, could cause large numbers of casualties, mass psychological disruption, and contamination, and could over-whelm local medical capabilities." Of greatest vulnerability would be many of the multicultural communities in our nation. Such multicultural community vulnerabilities were evident in natural disasters such as hurricanes Katrina and Rita.

Emergency Preparedness and Response

Regional and local law enforcement and public safety agencies must prepare to minimize the damage and to recover from any future terrorist attacks that may occur despite our best efforts at prevention. Past experience has shown that preparedness efforts are key in providing an effective response to major terrorist incidents and natural disasters. As such, we need a comprehensive national system to bring together and command all necessary response assets quickly and effec-tively. DHS has been building on the strong foundation already laid by the Federal Emergency Management Agency (FEMA), and plans to lead our national efforts to create and employ a system that will improve our response to all disasters, manmade and natural.

Following some of the past concerns raised by multicultural groups, FEMA has imple-mented its Diversity Outreach Program. For example, as part of the Diversity Outreach Program, the State of Florida and FEMA have proactively worked with affected families and individuals to provide assistance for damages caused by the four major hurricanes that devastated the state in prior hurricane seasons (FEMA, 2004). Another FEMA news release (2009) shows the Diversity Outreach Program as follows:

> One aspect of this comprehensive effort is the established relationship with Native American tribal associations in the declared counties. FEMA and state officials met with 21 tribes across the declared counties, from the Lummi and Nooksack in Whatcom County in the northern part of the state, to the Cowlitz in Cowlitz County in the south, to the Jamestown S'kallam, Lower Elwha Klallam, Makah and Quileute in Clallam County in the west. There are also several teams of multi-lingual representa-tives prepared to meet with members of these particular communities. These repre-sentatives have the ability to speak 8 languages: Vietnamese, Laotian, Cambodian, Thai, Hmong, Spanish, Korean, and Chinese. Many flyers have been printed up in not only these languages but also in Croatian, Ukrainian, Arabic, Japanese, Russian and Tagalog. Multilingual members have also been invited to speak at various forums, from Spanish speaking radio stations to Buddhist congregations. (FEMA, 2009)

WORKING WITH MULTICULTURAL COMMUNITIES ON TERRORISM PREVENTION, HOMELAND SECURITY, AND MULTIJURISDICTIONAL EFFORTS

In an earlier section we quoted Nance (2003), who highlighted a key element for homeland security and for winning the fight against terrorism that must include "cooperative efforts among law enforcement and intelligence agencies, and resolving the root complaints of the terrorist-supporting population." Clearly, law enforcement agencies are not in a position to resolve the root complaints involved with any terrorist-supporting nation or community. Law enforcement agencies are, however, in an excellent position to prevent the erosion of positive community–policing relationships with the multicultural communities that might include community members who hold concerns of root complaints and other issues of unfairness, bias, and discrimination.

Training Law Enforcement Agencies in Multicultural Community Homeland Security Issues

Law enforcement professionals have recognized that prejudices left unchecked, and actions based on them, can result in not only humiliation and citizen complaints, but also missed opportunities for building long-term police–community relationships important for homeland security. Social scientists have noted that stereotypes and prejudices become more pronounced when fear, danger, and personal threat enter the picture, as may happen in possible terrorism incidents.

Educating Multicultural Communities on Homeland Security

Most cities and states currently host websites and online information on homeland security for their communities. However, information and education regarding homeland security–specific actions for the prevention of terrorism are not available to most communities in the United States. This lack of information is even more pronounced for some of the multicultural communities with recent immigrants and refugees (including those from South and Central America, Asia, Eastern Europe, and the Middle East). The role of law enforcement officers in providing such information offers another viable avenue for developing positive relationships with multicultural communities and for community-policing efforts. Clearly, all communities are interested in acquiring specific information regarding activities of homeland security.

Law enforcement agencies may also want to include in their Citizen's Police Academies' curriculum information regarding homeland security and ways that the multicultural communities could participate and provide assistance to the public safety departments. In addition, law enforcement agencies might utilize the nonsworn and CSO personnel to provide such information in a bilingual mode to ensure proper information to communities with large populations of immigrants and refugees. Community-based presentations at familiar neighborhood centers, associations, churches, mosques, and temples may facilitate greater multicultural population attendance and participation. Likewise, collaborative programs of law enforcement agencies and community-based organizations have resulted in positive dissemination of information and an ongoing building of trust with multicultural communities (e.g., see IRCO and Dial-911 in Chapter 1 and Spanish Police Academy in Chapter 7).

KEY ISSUES IN LAW ENFORCEMENT

1. *Reluctance to Report Crimes and Participate in Homeland Security Efforts:*   Multicultural groups that have been stereotyped as possible terrorists (e.g., Arab and Middle Eastern Americans, Muslims, South Asians, Central Asians) may be reluctant to report crimes related to these stereotypes and may not seek police assistance and help for violations of their civil rights. Moreover, many may avoid contact with law enforcement agencies entirely with respect to homeland security efforts. Many of the multicultural groups may come from countries with extensive terrorism problems and may remember how police in their home countries have brutalized and violated them and others (in quelling terrorism). Sensitivity to

the experiences of these multicultural groups and a knowledge of their history of being victimized by terrorists will be of positive value in gaining participation and cooperation in homeland security efforts. Another key challenge to effective cooperation with multicultural communities on homeland security issues is to help allay the fears and concerns expressed by community members with regard to their multiple interactions with law enforcement officers. Inquiries relating to homeland security, for example, may coexist with the investigation into other crimes and code enforcements like immigration, health, sanitation, housing, and welfare.

2. *Victimization:*   Law enforcement agencies protect the safety and security of citizens in multicultural communities where harassment and discrimination resulting from being stereotyped as a terrorist may lead to victimization. Documentation of such crimes against Asian/Pacific Americans and Arab and Middle Eastern Americans are provided in Chapters 5 and 8, respectively, and in Chapter 13 in this text. Some victims are harassed and attacked because of their attire or their appearance. Victimization also includes unfair accusations of being a terrorist. Those accused, or so identified, must have the trust that the police and other public safety personnel are not against them. Furthermore, they must believe that their well-being and safety are just as important as those of others who are not subject to these perceptions, assumptions, or stereotypes. Moreover, residents who are discriminated against or stereotyped as terrorists must be able to trust that prosecutors, judges, parole, and probation will utilize their full armamentarium to deter and jail terrorists, as well as those who unjustly terrorize, discriminate, and/or harass other citizens who are unfairly stereotyped as terrorists.

3. *Differential Treatment:*   In this chapter, as well as in the culture-specific chapters, we have provided examples of how members of multicultural communities have been treated unfairly because of law enforcement officers' perceptions that they are threats to homeland security or possible terrorists. Especially if a target is a possible terrorist, expressions of bias and prejudice by law enforcement agencies may go unchallenged because of the tremendous fear of the potential terrorist threat, as well as the need to rally around the issues of homeland security. Often such bias and prejudice are expressed via inappropriate language and disrespectful terms such as, "rags," "suicidal rag-heads," "A-rabs," "Arab-bombers," and "Muslim fanatics." Under such circumstances, both law enforcement executive leadership and officers' professionalism will determine whether such bias and prejudices go unchecked or whether the treatment of a possible terrorist suspect will be fair and justifiable. Clearly, should the suspect not be a terrorist, then an injustice had occurred because of differential treatment. Moreover, the multicultural community of which the suspect is a member will begin to question their trust and reliance on the police agency that shows such bias and prejudice. Should the suspect indeed have been correctly identified as a possible terrorist, then any stereotypic and differential treatment may jeopardize the prosecution of the case as well.

4. *False Tips from Informants:*   As with any information-gathering and intelligence operations, there will always be the need to determine the validity, reliability, and trustworthiness of information received. Law enforcement agencies have always depended on informants as sources of critical information as part of any investigative process. In a terrorism incident, some of these informants would be very much connected with the criminal and often the most notorious elements within the community. Moreover, some of these informants may be keenly aware of what is "on the street" but may have ulterior or personal motives for providing information. Both standard interviewing and incident interview skills and tools

need to be used to sort out false information and to confirm the credibility of sources important to the facts of a terrorist incident.

5. *Training to Heighten Awareness:* Until recently, issues of terrorism and weapons of mass destruction were primarily the domain of the federal law enforcement agencies, with minor involvement of local law enforcement personnel. The awareness of terrorism cues, situations, and warnings of possible acts are not part of the everyday experience of local law enforcement personnel and their agencies. Terrorist-related awareness training has been used as an approach to heighten the awareness and skill levels of local law enforcement officers.

6. *Extension of Community Policing Approaches:* Community-based policing has been proven to be a valuable approach to working with multicultural community groups and to learning about their needs, concerns, and problems (Oliver, 2001). Chapter 14 discusses some of the key concepts, principals, and practices for community-oriented policing within multicultural communities. In this chapter, we highlight the importance of using those same community-policing concepts, tools, and practices for information gathering as well as for information dissemination following a terrorism incident. As will be noted in the following example, the process of community policing could provide the "eyes and ears" for our country in the war on terrorism:

> To stop terrorists before they strike, the Department of Homeland Security should implement some of the preventative policing initiatives that were used to combat crime in the 1990s, Flynn said. "What did we learn in the 1990s, when we got federal assistance to deal with crime? We learned about community policing, problem solving, prevention, partnerships with the community. . . . And doing all those things helped us produce the greatest crime decreases in American history. All those attributes apply to terrorism. . . . It's a false dichotomy to separate homeland security from criminal justice. It's the same fabric." (Deleo, 2005)

Summary

- The experience of law enforcement agencies involved in homeland security and the war on terrorism within multicultural communities is evolving. Likewise, the new and changing roles as well as functions for law enforcement in homeland security and disaster preparedness present many challenges for the day-to-day work within the criminal justice system and the local, regional, and national plans against terrorism. Homeland security challenges for law enforcement agencies include the following: (1) detecting and preventing attacks of terrorism; these can be made more complex within multicultural communities because of the past histories of those communities with law enforcement in the United States, as well as in their native homelands; (2) avoiding stereotypes and possible biased perceptions based on ethnicity, culture, race, and religion that may be evoked within multicultural communities; and (3) working with multicultural community leaders regarding their perceptions of police actions and efforts in homeland security. Officers should realize that some citizens may have been both victimized by terrorism within their native homeland and harmed by the antiterrorism efforts in the United States (while being innocent of any involvement with terrorism). These citizens carry with them stereotypes of police services as something to be feared and avoided. Law enforcement officials need to go out of their way to work with multicultural communities to establish trust, to provide outreach efforts, and to win cooperation in order to effectively accomplish their goals for homeland security efforts. Building partnerships focused on community collaboration in the fight against terrorism is important locally and nationally.

• The DHS has been providing law enforcement agencies a variety of intelligence information, advisories, warnings, and other pertinent communications regarding the efforts and activities to be implemented within local communities. Local law enforcement agencies and officers, because of their knowledge of the existing multicultural communities and networks, have been called upon to aid in data gathering and development of useful intelligence regarding possible terrorists. Such efforts have often produced a mixed reception by law enforcement agencies. Local law enforcement agencies and officers are often requested to provide assistance for homeland security information gathering and the interviewing of possible terrorist suspects. In addition, participation in the ICE 287(g) program involving the partnership of local and state law enforcement agencies with ICE has presented opportunities and challenges in working within multicultural communities.

• The Department of Homeland Security (DHS) was created as a cabinet-level department on November 25, 2002, with the main objective of protecting the United States from terrorism. With the development of the DHS, law enforcement officers and agencies have faced many new and changing roles as well as responsibilities. These include detecting threats of terrorism, developing and analyzing information regarding threats and vulnerabilities, using information and intelligence provided, and coordinating the security efforts against terrorism. Some multicultural community members, because of their past experiences with law enforcement, may be reluctant to participate in homeland security efforts. It is important for law enforcement departments and officials to build relationships and working partnerships with multicultural communities to ensure effective participation in combating terrorism and implementing homeland security.

• Coordination of efforts for terrorism, homeland security, and disaster preparedness requires a variety of diverse federal, state, and local agencies and organizations to be involved in multijurisdictional actions. Some of the key elements/issues for law enforcement agencies and officers involved in such incidents include the following: (1) Preparation and planning provide some of the best avenues for successful crisis management and subsequent recovery from a terrorist incident; and (2) Cost and deployment of resources have been highlighted by most local governments with respect to the degree of burden and expenditure needed to be borne by local law enforcement and by other public safety agencies involved in combating possible terrorism incidents.

• Law enforcement agencies today have an emerging and vital role in the war on terrorism, homeland security, and disaster preparedness that involves the critical step of building key relationships and networks within multicultural communities, including ethnic and multicultural media sources. Multicultural knowledge and skills of local law enforcement can contribute to uncovering key information, resources, and tools in dealing with the prevention and criminal investigation of terrorism, including intelligence-gathering needs. Until recently, issues of terrorism and weapons of mass destruction were primarily the domain of the federal law enforcement agencies, with minor involvement of local law enforcement personnel. The awareness of terrorism cues, situations, and warnings of possible acts are not part of the everyday experience of local law enforcement personnel and their agencies. Terrorist-related awareness training has been used as an approach to heighten the awareness and skill levels of local law enforcement officers.

Discussion Questions And Issues

1. *Terrorist Targets in Your Local Community*: The chapter provided a four- level priority approach to implementing a community assessment of possible terrorist targets. Review the possible terrorist targets in your community using the four-level priority categorization. List the special challenges involved in protecting the top two priority levels of possible terrorist targets in your community. List some of the unique challenges in working with multicultural communities in this regard (either within your community or in a nearby community with multicultural neighborhoods).

2. *Ethnic and Multicultural Media as a Resource*: The authors identified media resources as an effective way to communicate and disseminate information to community residents. What media resources might you use for communicating a terrorist incident involving Weapons of Mass Destruction (WMD) materials in your city or town? Provide some examples of multicultural media resources that might be used in your area. What approaches might you use to develop positive and effective relationships between these media resources and your local law enforcement agency?

3. *Utilizing Law Enforcement Personnel from Similar Backgrounds*: Select an area in your city or town that would have the greatest diversity of languages spoken. How would you plan for and ensure adequate bilingual personnel or other language resources to assist these community residents in the case of a terrorist incident?

4. *Working with Multicultural Groups on Homeland Security and Disaster Preparedness*: The authors recommended some guidelines and approaches for collaborative efforts in information gathering and in implementing homeland security efforts within multicultural communities. Select one or more multicultural groups that are part of your community (or a part of a nearby community). How would you apply the suggested guidelines and approaches to working with these multicultural groups?

5. *Victimization including being unfairly accused or identified as a possible terrorist*: What are ways to prevent and to help multicultural communities so members would not be the recipients of unjust accusation and victimization? What approach would you suggest for your local law enforcement agencies to prevent such victimization? What would you suggest that your multicultural community agencies do to prevent discrimination and harassment for those who are unfairly stereotyped?

Website Resources

Visit these websites for additional information about multicultural law enforcement issues in dealing with terrorism, homeland security, and disaster preparedness:

Association of Former Intelligence Officers (AFIO):
http://www.afio.com

This website provides the Weekly Intelligence News, which summarizes some of the homeland security issues from the perspectives of the AFIO.

Central Intelligence Agency—Factbook:
http://www.cia.gov/cia/publications/factbook/index.html

This website provides background and current information about groups and countries affecting the homeland security of the United States.

Department of Homeland Security (DHS):
http://www.dhs.gov/index.shtm

This website provides extensive information regarding the DHS, as well as about the threat level for the United States at any point in time. Suggestions and tips are provided for local communities in their preparation for homeland security.

Department of State—Travel Warnings and Consular Information:
http://travel.state.gov/travel/cis_pa_tw/tw/tw_1764.html

This website highlights countries and areas around the world that might be of a terrorist threat to citizens of the United States and its homeland security.

Federal Bureau of Investigation: http://www.fbi.gov/

This website provides the latest annual report of terrorism incidents in the United States.

Federal Bureau of Investigation, Explosive Unit:
http://www.fbi.gov/hq/lab/html/eu1.htm

This website provides the latest information about bombing incidents in the United States as well as international incidents affecting U.S. citizens.

Federal Bureau of Investigation Disaster Squad:
http://www.fbi.gov/hq/lab/disaster/disaster.htm

This website provides information about the FBI Disaster Squad, which is currently made up of approximately 40 people—four agents and the rest latent fingerprint specialists—all from the Forensic Analysis Branch in the FBI Laboratory.

Federal Emergency Management Agency:
http://www.fema.gov/

This website provides a range of useful information related to the management of community, state, and national emergencies.

Homeland Security Information Center (HSIC):
http://www.ntis.gov/hs/

This website provides a range of useful information related to resources for national emergencies, homeland security, and natural disasters.

Transportation Security Administration (TSA):
http://www.tsa.gov/

This website provides information on the Transportation Security Administration (TSA), which oversees security for the highways, railroads, buses, mass transit systems, ports, and the 450 U.S. airports.

U.S. Army Medical Research Institute of Chemical Defense: http://ccc.apgea.army.mil/

This website provides both general as well as research-oriented information and findings on chemical weapons of mass destruction.

U.S. Bomb Data Center:
http://www.atf.gov/aexis2/index.htm

This website provides a national collection center for information on arson- and explosives-related incidents throughout the United States. The U.S. Bomb Data Center databases incorporate information from various sources such as the Bureau of Alcohol, Tobacco, Firearms, and Explosives; the Federal Bureau of Investigation; and the United States Fire Administration. Information maintained by the National Repository is available for statistical analysis and investigative research by the academic and the law enforcement community.

U.S. Department of Defense Chemical, Biological, Radiological and Nuclear Defense Information Analysis Center (CBRNIAC):
http://www.cbrniac.apgea.army.mil/Pages/default.aspx

The website provides information from the Chemical, Biological, Radiological and Nuclear Defense Information Analysis Center (CBRNIAC), formerly known as the Chemical and Biological Defense Information Analysis Center (CBIAC). CBRNIAC is a full service arm of the Department of Defense (DoD) Information Analysis Center (IAC) under contract to the Office of the Secretary of Defense and administratively managed by the Defense Technical Information Center (DTIC) and serves as the focal point for DoD Chemical, Biological, Radiological and Nuclear (CBRN) Defense scientific and technical information.

U.S. Coast Guard (USCG):
http://www.uscg.mil/default.asp

The U.S. Coast Guard is responsible for the protection of all our ports and waterways within the DHS. The website highlights many of the specific aspects of homeland security for a law enforcement agency.

References

"A Nation Challenged: The Terrorists; Hijacker Got a Speeding Ticket." (2002, January 9). *New York Times*, p. A12.

Arena, K. (2006, August 11). "Officials: Plot Suspects Met Alleged al Qaeda Bomber." CNN.com, at http://www.cnn.com/2006/WORLD/europe/08/11/terror.plot/index.html.

Associated Press. (2009, May 28). "Roswell Police Ends Policy of Holding Immigrants."

Bankson, R. (2003). "Terrorism: National in Scope, Local in Execution." *Community Links*. Washington, D.C.: Community Policing Consortium.

"Burdens of Security: Omaha-Area Agencies Are Cooperating Well in Guarding against Attacks by Terrorists." (2003, June 16). *Omaha World Herald*, p. B6.

Chawkins, S. (2003, November 6). "Agencies Get a Taste of Terrorism in Action: Simulated Attacks at the

Port of Hueneme Help Build Teamwork among Emergency Groups." *Los Angeles Times.*

Corley, S. H., B. L. Smith, and K. R. Damphousse. (2005). "The Changing Face of American Terrorism." In L. L. Snowden and B. C. Whitsel (Eds.), *Terrorism: Research, Readings, and Realities.* Upper Saddle River, NJ: Pearson/Prentice Hall.

Decker, S. H., P. G. Lewis, D. M. Provine, and M. W. Varsanyi. (2008, August 21–22). "Immigration and Local Policing Results from a National Survey of Law Enforcement Executives." Paper presented at the Police Foundation conference, The Role of Local Police: Striking a Balance between Immigration Enforcement and Civil Liberties, Washington, D.C.

Deleo, D. (2005, August 5). "Call for Broader Anti-Terror Effort." *Patriot Ledger*, p. 11.

Dershowitz, A. M. (2002). *Why Terrorism Works: Understanding the Threat, Responding to the Challenge.* New Haven, Conn.: Yale University Press.

Doyle, C. (2002, April 18). "The USA PATRIOT Act: A Sketch." CRS Report for Congress.

Doyle, C. (2005, June 29). "The USA PATRIOT Act Sunset: Provisions that Expire on December 31, 2005." CRS Report for Congress.

Federal Bureau of Investigation. (2007, November). *Terrorism 2002–2005.* Washington, D.C.: U.S. Department of Justice.

Federal Bureau of Investigation. (2008, December). *An SICO Milestone: Ten Years in Protecting the Nation.* Washington, D.C.: U.S. Department of Justice.

Federal Emergency Management Agency (FEMA). (2004, December 7), "FEMA's Diversity Outreach Program a Success." News Release Number: 1539-303.

Federal Emergency Management Agency (FEMA). (2009, March 9), "Reaching Washington's Many and Diverse Communities." News Release Number: 1817-047.

Ford, P. (2002, March 27). "Legal War on Terror Lacks Weapons." *Christian Science Monitor*, Section 4, p. 1.

Heymann, P. B. (2001). *Terrorism and America: A Commonsense Strategy for a Democratic Society.* Cambridge, MA: MIT Press.

Hoffman, B. (2006). *Inside Terrorism.* New York, NY: Columbia University Press.

Howard, R. D. (2007). "The New Terrorism." In Howard, R. D., Sawyer, R. L., and Bajema, N. E. (Eds.). *Terrorism and Counterterrorism: Understanding the New Security Environment,* 3rd ed. New York, NY: McGraw-Hill.

Howard, R. D., Sawyer, R. L., and Bajema, N. E. (Eds.) (2009). *Terrorism and Counterterrorism: Understanding the New Security Environment,* 3rd ed. New York, NY: McGraw-Hill.

Howard, D. R., and R. L. Sawyer. (Eds.). (2004). *Terrorism and Counterterrorism: Understanding the New Security Environment.* Guilford, CT: McGraw-Hill/Dushkin.

International Association of Chiefs of Police (IACP). (2001). *Leading from the Front: Project Response: Terrorism.* Alexandria, VA: Author.

International Association of Chiefs of Police (IACP). (2002). *Project Response: The Oklahoma City Tragedy.* Alexandria, VA: Author.

International Association of Chiefs of Police. (2005). *From Hometown Security to Homeland Security: IACP's Principles for a Locally Designed and Nationally Coordinated Homeland Security Strategy.* Alexandria, VA: Author.

Kemp, R. L. (2003). *Homeland Security: Best Practices for Local Government.* Washington, D.C.: International City/County Management Association (ICCM).

Kerlikowske, R. G. (2003, May 21). "Remarks Given at the Washington Association of Sheriff and Police Chiefs Conference," Spokane, WA, Seattle Chief of Police.

Kleinberg, E., and D. Davies. (2001, October 19). "Delray Police Stopped Speeding Terror Suspect." *Palm Beach Post* (Florida), p. A1.

Major City Chiefs. (2006, June). "M.C.C. Immigration Committee Recommendations for Enforcement of Immigration Laws by Local Police Agencies." Adopted by the Major Cities Chiefs.

Murphy, G. R., and M. R. Plotkin. (2003). "Protecting Your Community from Terrorism: Strategies for Local Law Enforcement." In *The Strategies for Local Enforcement Series, Volume 1: Improving Local-Federal Partnerships.* Washington, D.C.: PERF and COPS.

Nance, M. W. (2003). *The Terrorist Recognition Handbook.* Guilford, Conn.: Lyons Press.

Norwitz, J. H. (2002, August). "Combating Terrorism: With a Helmet or a Badge?" *Journal of Homeland Security.* Available: http://www.homelandsecurity.org/journal/Search.aspx?s=norwitz.

Office of Domestic Preparedness. (2003, June). *The Office of Domestic Preparedness Guidelines for Homeland Security, June 2003: Prevention and Deterrence.* Washington, D.C.: DHS.

Office of Homeland Security. (2002). *National Strategy for Homeland Security.* Washington, D.C.: GPO.

Office of Homeland Security. (2004). *Securing Our Homeland: U.S. Department of Homeland Security Strategic Plan.* Washington, D.C.: GPO.

Oliver, W. M. (2001). *Community-Oriented Policing.* Upper Saddle River, NJ: Prentice-Hall.

Oliver, W. M. (2007), *Homeland Security for Policing.* Upper Saddle River, NJ: Prentice Hall.

Police Foundation. (2009). *The Role of Local Police: Striking a Balance between Immigration Enforcement and Civil Liberties.* Washington, D.C.: Police Foundation.

Roig-Franzia, M., and P. Davis. (2002, January 9). "For Want of a Crystal Ball; Police Stopped Two Hijackers in Days before Attacks." *Washington Post*, p. A13.

Smalley, S. (2005, May 30). "Terror Plan Relies on Watch Groups." *The Boston Globe*, p. B1.

Smith, G. (2006, March 2). "Community Policing Guru Issues Warning," *The Providence Journal* (Rhode Island), p. C01.

Snowden, L. L. and B. C. Whitsel. (Eds.). (2005). *Terrorism: Research, Readings, and Realities.* Upper Saddle River, NJ: Pearson/Prentice Hall.

"Trooper Describes Arrest 90 Minutes after Bombing." (1997, April 28). *Deseret News* (Salt Lake City), p. A2.

U.S. Department of Justice Office of Justice Programs. (1997). Emergency Response to Terrorism: Basic Concepts. Washington, D.C.: U.S. Department of Justice.

Weiss, M., E. Calabrese, and M. Fermino. (2009, May 21). "Chilling Terror Plot Thwarted–4 Set to 'Bomb' Synagogues; Eyed Plane 'Shootdown' Upstate." *New York Post*, p. 7.

Response Strategies for Crimes Motivated By Hate/Bias and Racial Profiling

Part Four provides a detailed explanation of strategies for preventing, controlling, reporting, monitoring, and investigating crimes that are based on hate or bias caused by the victim's race, ethnicity, national origin, religion, or sexual orientation. Criminal cases of these types have come to be known as bias or hate crimes; noncriminal cases are referred to as incidents. Some agencies refer to these acts as civil rights violations. The next two chapters contain policies, practices, and procedures for responding to these types of crimes or incidents. We recognize that other groups, such as women, the elderly, the homeless, and the disabled, are sometimes victimized. However, in this book we focus primarily on hate crimes and incidents wherein the motivation was related to the victim's race, ethnicity, national origin, religion, or sexual orientation. The reasons for collecting data on crimes and incidents motivated by hate/bias committed by individuals or organized groups are included in Chapter 12. The end of that chapter provides examples to help students, members of the criminal justice system, and the community to develop sensitive and workable programs for handling these crimes and incidents. The recommended policies, training, practices, and procedures outlined in this text are currently in operation in most law enforcement agencies across the nation and are based on studies and recommendations by the U.S. Department of Justice's Community Relations Service. The Commission on Peace Officer Standards and Training, found in all states of the nation, is another major source of materials. The final chapter in Part Four provides information about racial profiling for members of the criminal justice system. The type of policing reviewed in this unit is a civilizing process that will contribute to multicultural coexistence and cooperation. All law enforcement professionals should have a good working knowledge of the guidelines that follow.

CHAPTER 11

Hate/Bias Crimes: Victims, Laws, Investigations, and Prosecutions

LEARNING OBJECTIVES

After reading this chapter you should be able to:

- Describe the scope of the hate crime problem, including historical perspectives.
- Define as well as differentiate between hate crimes and hate incidents.
- Explain hate crime and incident source theories.
- Discuss response strategies to hate crimes and appropriate victim assistance techniques.
- Identify hate crimes related to anti-Semitism, sexual orientation, race, ethnicity, and national origin.
- Explain hate crime laws, investigative procedures, and offender prosecution.

OUTLINE

- Introduction
- The Hate/Bias Crime Problem
- Definition of Hate Crime and Hate Incident
- Hate Crime Source Theories
- Jews and Anti-Semitism
- Lesbian, Gay, Bisexual, and Transgender Victimization
- Hate Crime Laws
- Hate/Bias Crime and Incident Investigations
- Hate/Bias Crime Prosecution
- Hate/Bias Crime and Incident Victimology
- Summary

- **Discussion Questions and Issues**
- **Website Resources**

INTRODUCTION

Crimes motivated by hate/bias have occurred in the United States for generations. Most of the immigrant groups that have come to America, including the Irish, Italian, Chinese, Polish, and Puerto Rican, to name a few, have been victimized. Even though they are indigenous peoples, Native Americans also have not been immune to hate crimes. The descendents of African slaves continue to be victims of bias, discrimination, and crimes motivated by hate. This chapter, however, addresses only crimes motivated by hate in which the victims are Jewish or gay, lesbian, bisexual, or transgender individuals. Additional examples of specific racial, ethnic, and religious groups hate/bias crimes are discussed in the culture-specific chapters (Chapters 5 through 9).

THE HATE/BIAS CRIME PROBLEM

The criminal justice system as well as every community must address the problem of hate/bias crimes and incidents. As far as the magnitude of the problem is concerned, consider the following:

> In a recent Center [Southern Poverty Law Center (SPLC)] survey, a startling majority of respondents reported witnessing some form of bias or bigotry within the last 12 months. One of the survey's most dramatic results came when respondents were questioned about their personal experience with prejudice. An overwhelming majority, 70 percent, reported having personally witnessed an incident of everyday bigotry such as racial stereotyping or the use of derisive names for people of a given color, gender, or sexual identity over the last year. Finally, nearly all who responded to the survey believe that race continues to divide the country. (SPLC Report, 2006, p. 8)

Victims of hate/bias crimes are particularly sensitive and unsettled because they feel powerless to alter the situation, since they cannot change their racial, ethnic, or religious background. Furthermore, the individual involved is not the sole victim, because often fear of similar crimes can affect an entire group of citizens. A physical attack on a person because of race, religion, ethnic background, or sexual orientation is a particularly insidious form of violent behavior. Verbal assaults on persons because of others' perceptions of their "differences" are equally distressing to both the victim and the society. And, unfortunately, these kinds of incidents can also occur in the law enforcement workplace among coworkers. When law enforcement treats such occurrences seriously, it sends a message to community members that the local police agency will protect them. Doing the same within the law enforcement organization and correctional system sends a vitally important message to all employees.

The criminal justice system, and especially local law enforcement agencies, will become the focus of criticism if attacks are not investigated, resolved, and prosecuted promptly and effectively. A hate/bias crime can send shock waves through the ethnic or racial community at which the act was aimed. These acts create danger, frustration, concern, and anxiety in our communities. Law enforcement and corrections personnel must have some perspective on both the global and the local situations when it comes to hatred and bias within the population they serve or within which they work. Criminal justice system practitioners must be trained to counteract hate crimes and violence as well as addressing their inhumane impact. The importance of local law enforcement officials' monitoring of such world events is discussed in Chapter 12. This is a major undertaking as we begin the twenty-first century because the United Nations is currently actively involved in peacekeeping efforts in many different countries. There are also ongoing internal conflicts in many countries that have had repercussions in the United States.

Many studies over the years have determined that a large number of hate crime perpetrators are youthful thrill-seekers, and the same research statistics indicate that as many as 60 percent of offenders committed crimes for the thrill associated with the victimization. The second most common group responsible for hate crimes is reactive offenders who feel that they are answering an attack by their victims. The least common perpetrators, according to reports, are hard-core fanatics who are driven by racial or religious ideology or ethnic bigotry. These individuals are often members of or potential recruits for extremist organizations. Some perpetrators of hate crimes live on the U.S. borders and are petrified by what they consider to be "brown hordes" of Mexicans, South and Central Americans, Cubans, and Haitians who enter the United States both legally and illegally. They feel that if they cease their militant rhetoric and violence toward these immigrants, the country will be inundated with immigrants. It is a fact that Mexicans are the largest immigrant group in the country. Their visibility makes them a magnet for antiimmigrant sentiment including discrimination and hate crimes. There are also many racists living near Native American reservations; their aim is to challenge, through violence, the few remaining treaty rights granted to native people.

Community awareness of hate violence grew rapidly in the United States during the late 1980s and the 1990s. Many states commissioned special task forces to recommend ways to control such violence, and new legislation was passed. Despite the abundance of rhetoric deploring acts of bigotry and hate violence, however, few communities have utilized a **holistic** approach to the problem. Typically, efforts to prevent and respond to such crimes by local agencies have not been coordinated. Indeed, there are many effective programs that deal with a particular aspect of bigotry or hate in a specific setting; however, few models weave efforts to prevent hate violence into the fabric of the community.

> **Holistic**   View that the integrated whole has a reality independent and greater than that of the sum of its parts.

In 2006, a series of deadly racial attacks in jails and prisons, especially in California, cast a spotlight on long-simmering but little-discussed tensions between blacks and Latinos. According to interviews with teachers, students, politicians, researchers, government officials, civil rights lawyers, police officers, correctional officers, and businesspeople:

> [I]n almost every arena of public life—schools, politics, hospitals, housing, and the workplace—blacks and Latinos are engaged in an edgy competition. The racial attacks and competition highlight a nationwide issue, or trend between the two groups. Unlike in the past when whites were involved in the lion's share of hate crimes, 73 percent of the identified suspects in anti-black hate crimes are Latino. And in anti-Latino crimes, 80 percent of the suspects are black, according to a report by the county's [Los Angeles] Commission on Human Relations. ("Jail brawls," 2006, p. A8)

Hate crimes are the most extreme and dangerous manifestation of racism. Law enforcement professionals, including neighborhood police officers (the best sources of intelligence information), must be aware of the scope of the hate/bias crime problem from both historical and contemporary perspectives. The same is true of the correctional officers who work directly with the inmate population.

A U.S. Commission on Civil Rights, Intimidation, and Violence (1990) report identified several factors, still true today, that contribute to racial intimidation and violence, including the following:

- Racial integration of neighborhoods, leading to "move-in violence" (explained later in the chapter)
- Deep-seated racial hatred played on by organized hate groups
- Economic competition among racial and ethnic groups
- Poor police response to hate crimes

The unprecedented numbers of Latin American and Asian immigrants moving into neighborhoods that were unprepared for the social, economic, political, and criminal justice system consequences of multicultural living has also been a factor in some communities.

Beginning during the 2008 presidential campaign, and continuing briefly into the presidency of Barack Obama, the nation witnessed what has been described as a backlash against the election of the first black president in U.S. history. Across America, law enforcement agencies documented a range of alleged hate crimes and incidents, ranging from threats, verbal insults, and vandalism to physical attacks. Most of these crimes were committed not by gangs or hate groups, but by individuals motivated by their biases. "There have been 'hundreds of incidents since the election, many more than usual,' said Mark Potok, director of the Intelligence Project at the Southern Poverty Law Center, which monitors hate crimes" ("Obama Election Spurs Race Crimes around Country," 2008).

The Scope of Hate Crimes Nationally

Tracking hate crimes, which are typically underreported, did not begin in earnest until 1992. The federal Hate Crime Statistics Act of 1990 encourages states to collect and report hate crime data to the Federal Bureau of Investigation (FBI). The FBI, in partnership with local law enforcement agencies, began collecting data on hate/bias incidents, offenses (see later in this chapter definitions of hate/bias incidents and offenses), victims, offenders, and motivations. The FBI publishes an annual report as part of the Uniform Crime Reporting (UCR) Program. The UCR Program collects data for crimes motivated by biases against race, religion, sexual orientation, ethnicity/national origin, or disability. Each bias type is then broken down into more specific bias. For example, when a law enforcement agency determines that a hate crime was committed because of bias against an individual's race, the agency may then classify the bias as anti-white, anti-black, anti-American Indian/Alaskan Native, anti-Asian/Pacific Islander, or anti-multiple races group, which describes a group of victims in which more than one race is represented. Most hate/bias crime statistics are, by definition, "single-bias incidents" (i.e., those that involve one type of bias). Multiple-bias incidents are those that involve two or more offense types motivated by two or more biases.

The UCR Program is a nationwide cooperative statistical effort of more than 17,700 city, county, state, federal, tribal, university, and college law enforcement agencies. The collection of hate crime information reported in the UCR is voluntary, however, and not all law enforcement agencies gather or submit data to the FBI. During 2007 (the most recent year for which data are available), law enforcement agencies active in the UCR Program represented 94.6 percent of the total population, a vast improvement from when the program first began ("Hate Crime Statistics 2007," 2008). The report indicates that in 2007, 2,025 law enforcement agencies documented 7,621 single-bias hate

EXHIBIT 11.1 Five-Year Comparison of FBI Hate Crime Statistics (2003–2007).

	2003	2004	2005	2006	2007
Participating Agencies	11,909	12,711	12,417	12,620	13,241
Total Hate Crime Incidents Reported	7,489	7,649	7,163	7,722	7,624
Number of States, Including D.C.	50	50	50	50	50
Percentage of U.S. Population Represented by Participating Agencies	82.8%	86.6%	82.7%	85.2%	94.6%

Source: UCR Hate Crime Statistics—2003 to 2008.

crime incidents and 8,999 single-bias offenses. This indicates a slight decrease overall from 2006. A 5-year comparison of FBI hate crime statistics (2003–2007) is displayed in Exhibit 11.1.

The FBI's annual hate crime report is an essential tool for understanding our nation's hate crime problem; however, it alone does not provide a clear picture of the extent and nature of hate/bias crime. The FBI simply compiles state statistics, which are not an accurate reflection of the actual number of hate crimes. This is because of the voluntary nature of the reporting system on the part of law enforcement agencies and the failure of many victims to report crimes to police. Even though there have been gains in the number of agencies reporting hate crimes, there were still more than 4,000 that did not participate in the program in 2007. Over 15 percent of those that did participate reported no hate crime incidents in their jurisdictions that year. Thus, although the report gives some insight into the trends in hate crimes, it is not entirely reflective of the total problem ("Variables Affecting Crime, 2007," 2008).

This becomes clear when comparing the FBI numbers with those found in a 2005 study by the Department of Justice's Bureau of Statistics. Whereas the FBI has reported national hate crime totals of about 6,000 to 10,000 per year since it began publishing the numbers, the study, based on detailed and highly accurate National Crime Victimization Surveys (NCVS), found that the real annual level of hate crime in America averaged some 191,000 incidents—in other words, about 20 to 30 times higher than the numbers reported by the FBI ("Variables Affecting Crime, 2007," 2008, p. 3). The NCVS study also highlighted several other key points about hate crimes, including the fact that per capita rates of victimization "varied little by race or ethnicity: about 0.9 per 1,000 whites, 0.7 per 1,000 blacks, and 0.9 per 1,000 Hispanics." Perhaps more important, the study concluded that hate crimes were vastly more violent than others—almost 84 percent of hate crimes included violence ranging from rape to assault, while only 23 percent of nonhate crimes did ("Variables Affecting Crime, 2007," 2008).

The data in the FBI annual report also provide little information about the characteristics of crimes, victims, offenders, or arrests. Recognizing these deficiencies, the FBI created the National Incident-Based Reporting System (NIBRS). NIBRS staff interview persons about their experience with crime, both reported and not reported, which results in more details on more categories of crime, including concurrent offenses, weapons, injury, location, property loss, and characteristics of the victims, offenders, and arrestees, including their gender, race, and age. The information is analyzed annually and becomes the NCVS report previously mentioned. The information is combined with the statistics collected by the FBI as part of the UCR Program and results in a more thorough report and analysis of the data. To make the data comparable between the UCR Program and the NCVS, only those crimes in which an individual was the victim are included in this report. A comparison of UCR and NCVS data provides some striking similarities but also some major differences between the two. The data collected by NCVS indicate that only about 44 percent of hate crimes are reported to the police.

The authors used UCR reports covering the period 2003 through 2007 to examine trends in reported hate crime incidents and offenses in the United States. These data are shown in Exhibits 11.2 and 11.3. The data illustrate that there was little change year to year over the 5-year period studied in the numbers reported in each category. Not shown is the tremendous increase in bias-motivated crimes involving ethnicity or national origin following September 11, 2001. Anti-Islamic bias was 2 percent in 2000, skyrocketed to 27 percent in 2001, and dropped to 11 percent in 2002. Many Muslims, or those who appeared to be Arab, became the targets of hate/bias crimes because of their perceived or actual ethnicity or national place of origin. See Chapter 8 for further details.

The Exhibits 11.2 and 11.3 show that African Americans comprised by far the largest group of victims of bias/hate crime as they have been since the FBI began gathering hate crime statistics. Hate crimes against African Americans averaged 67 percent of the total number of crimes motivated by racial bias over the 5 years studied. After African Americans, the most

EXHIBIT 11.2   Hate Crime: Single-Bias Incidents and Offences (2003–2007).

Hate Crimes	2003	2004	2005	2006	2007
1. Incidents	7,485	7,642	7,160	7,720	7,621
Offenders Bias:					
Racial	51%	53%	55%	52%	51%
Religious	18%	18%	17%	19%	18%
Sexual Orientation	17%	16%	14%	16%	17%
Ethnic/National Origin	14%	13%	13%	13%	13%
2. Incidents by Category					
Against Persons	63%	57%	57%	57%	58%
Against Property	36%	44%	42%	43%	42%
3. Offenses	8,706	9,021	8,380	9,076	8,999
Offenders Bias:					
Racial	52%	54%	56%	53%	53%
Religious	16%	16%	16%	18%	16%
Sexual Orientation	16%	16%	14%	16%	16%
Ethnic/National Origin	14%	13%	14%	14%	14%
4. Offences by Category					
Against Persons	61%	63%	63%	60%	60%
Against Property	39%	37%	37%	40%	40%

Source: UCR Hate Crime Statistics—2003 to 2008.

Notes:

1. Columns might not total to 100% due to rounding off.

2. Disability bias and crimes against society are not included because they are less than 1 percent of the total in each category.

EXHIBIT 11.3   Hate Crime: Single-Bias Offences—Specific Bias Motivation (2003–2007).

	2003	2004	2005	2006	2007
Racial Bias:	4,574	4,863	4,691	4,737	4,724
Anti-Black	66%	68%	68%	66%	69%
Anti-White	21%	21%	20%	21%	18%
Anti-Asian/Pacific Islander	6%	5%	5%	5%	5%
Anti-American Indian	2%	2%	2%	2%	2%
Anti-Multiple Racial Groups	5%	5%	5%	6%	6%
Religious Bias:	1,426	1,480	1,314	1,597	1,477
Anti-Jewish/Semitic	69%	68%	69%	64%	68%
Anti-Islamic	11%	13%	11%	12%	9%
Anti-Other	8%	12%	8%	9%	10%
Anti-Catholic	6%	4%	5%	5%	4%
Anti-Protestant	4%	3%	4%	4%	4%
Sexual Orientation:	1,430	1,406	1,171	1,415	1,460
Anti-Male Homosexual	62%	61%	61%	62%	59%
Anti-Homosexual	21%	21%	20%	21%	25%
Anti-Female Homosexual	15%	14%	15%	14%	13%
Anti-Heterosexual/Bisexual	1%	4%	2%	2%	2%
Ethnicity/National Origin:	1,236	1,201	1,144	1,233	1,256
Anti-Hispanic	43%	51%	58%	62%	62%
Anti-Other	57%	49%	42%	38%	38%

Source: UCR Hate Crime Statistics—2003 to 2008.

Notes:

1. Columns might not total to 100 percent due to rounding off.

2. Anti-Jewish/Semitic as a percentage of total religious bias.

victimized groups were Jews, Hispanics, and gay men. The Bureau of Justice Statistics released a report indicating that American Indians experience the highest level of hate crimes per capita, according to data from the NCVS. The NCVS study discovered that the overall rate of violent victimization (excluding homicide) for American Indians is 118.8 per 1,000, which is at least twice the rate for any other racial group (Rennison, 2001, p. 10). The FBI-UCR reports for the period studied also showed that, on average, 61 percent of hate crimes offences were committed against people and 39 percent against property (see Exhibit 11.2).

Offenders' reported motivations for the 5 years studied are shown in Exhibit 11.4. The statistics for hate/bias crimes motivated by disability and those against society (government buildings, for example) are not shown because they each amount to less than 1 percent of the total. Also, not shown in the exhibits but highlighted in the UCR reports is the fact that white people were the most common offenders in hate crimes.

The Southern Poverty Law Center reported a trend that the organization had seen regarding Latinos. Between 2003 and 2007, according to FBI statistics, hate crimes against Latinos experienced a 40 percent rise, which the Center attributes to "anti-immigrant propaganda increasing on both the

EXHIBIT 11.4 Offenders' Reported Motivations in Percentage of Incidents (2003–2007).

	2003		2004		2005		2006		2007	
Racial Bias	3,844	51.3%	4,402	57.5%	3,919	54.7%	4,000	51.6%	3,870	50.8%
Anti-Black	2,458	34.0%	2,731	35.7%	2,630	36.7%	2,640	34.2%	2,658	34.9%
Anti-White	830	11.1%	829	10.8%	828	11.6%	890	11.5%	749	9.8%
Anti-Asian/Pacific Islander	231	3.1%	217	2.8%	199	2.8%	181	2.3%	188	2.5%
Religious Bias	1,343	17.9%	1,374	18.0%	1,227	17.1%	1,462	18.9%	1,400	18.4%
Anti-Semitic	927	12.4%	954	12.5%	848	11.8%	967	12.5%	969	12.7%
Anti-Semitic as Percentage of Religious Bias	69%		69%		69%		66%		69%	
Anti-Islamic	149	2.0%	156	2.0%	128	1.8%	156	2.0%	115	1.5%
Ethnicity/National Origin	1,026	13.7%	972	12.7%	944	13.2%	984	12.7%	1,007	13.2%
Anti-Hispanic	426	5.7%	475	6.2%	522	7.3%	576	7.5%	595	7.8%
Sexual Orientation	1,239	16.5%	1,197	15.6%	1,017	14.2%	1,195	15.5%	1,265	16.6%

Source: Anti-Defamation League's Washington Office from information collected by the FBI.

Notes:

1. Columns might not total to 100 percent due to rounding off.

2. Disability bias and crimes against society are not included because they are less than 1 percent of the total in each category.

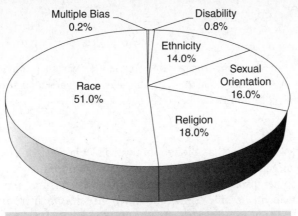

EXHIBIT 11.5   Hate Crime: Bias-Motivated Offenses, Average Percent Distribution (2000–2007).

Source: UCR Hate Crime Statistics—2000 to 2008.

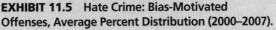

EXHIBIT 11.6   Hate Crime: Bias-Motivated Murders (2003–2007).

	2003	2004	2005	2006	2007
Murders	14	5	6	3	9
Motivation:					
Racial	5	3	3	3	2
Sexual Orientation	6	1	0	0	5
Ethnic/National Origin	2	0	3	0	2
Religion	0	1	0	0	0
Disability	1	0	0	0	0

Source: UCR Hate Crime Statistics Reports—2003 to 2008.

margins and in the mainstream of society [so that] hate violence has risen against perceived 'illegal aliens'" ("Hate Crimes—Anti-Latino Hate Crime Up for Fourth Year," 2008).

Exhibit 11.5 shows the average percent distribution of bias-motivated offenses for an 8-year period, and Exhibit 11.6 shows the number and bias motivation for murders for a 5-year period.

DEFINITION OF HATE CRIME AND HATE INCIDENT

Hate Crime

The federal definition of hate crime addresses civil rights violations under Title 18 U.S.C. Section 245. Although state definitions vary, in general a hate crime is considered to be:

- a criminal act or attempted act,
- against a person, institution, or property,
- that is motivated in whole or in part by the offender's bias against a
  - race,
  - color,
  - religion,
  - gender,

- ethnic/national origin group,
- disability status, or
- sexual orientation group.

Definitions of hate crime often incorporate not only violence against individuals or groups but also crimes against property such as arson or vandalism, in particular those directed against government buildings, community centers, or houses of worship.

Hate Incident

Hate incidents involve behaviors that, though motivated by **bias** against a victim's race, religion, ethnic/national origin, gender, age, disability, or sexual orientation, are not criminal acts. Hostile or hateful speech, or other disrespectful or discriminatory behavior, may be motivated by bias but is not illegal. Such incidents become crimes only when they directly incite perpetrators to commit violence against persons or property or if they place a potential victim in reasonable fear of physical injury (IACP, 1999).

> **Bias**   Preference or an inclination to make certain choices that may be positive (bias toward excellence) or negative (bias against people), often resulting in unfairness.
>
> **Bias-based policing**   The act (intentional or unintentional) of applying or incorporating personal, societal, or organizational biases and/or stereotypes in decision making, police actions, or the administration of justice.

HATE CRIME SOURCE THEORIES

Urban Dynamics Theories

The relationships among the clustering of new immigrant groups, the economy, move-in violence, and hate/bias incidents and crimes in cities are well documented. It is important to understand that hate incidents and crimes often do not occur in a vacuum but are part of a larger social and economic interchange.

CLUSTERING AND TARGET ZONE THEORY   Studies have shown that initially new immigrants tend to locate or cluster where people of their own ethnic and racial background are already established. They tend to congregate in the same areas of the country or within a city to be near relatives or friends; to have assistance in finding housing and jobs and in coping with language barriers; and to find the security of a familiar religion and social institutions. One study on new immigrant grouping by Steven Wallace for the University of California, Berkeley, which is still valid today, noted that

> for the first generation or two, ethnic communities are helpful because they provide a sense of continuity for immigrants while easing subsequent generations into American values and society. . . . The existence of an ethnic or immigrant community is obvious evidence that a group has not assimilated. A community represents a place where immigrants are able to associate with others like themselves. An immigrant community provides a safe place to engage in those activities that deviate from dominant norms such as speaking a language other than English, honoring "foreign"

symbols of pride, and exhibiting other non-Anglo behavior. Commonly located in low-rent districts, ethnic communities are functionally found where members can afford to live while they work at low wage jobs. (Wallace, 1987, pp. 88–89)

These core areas are typically where low-socioeconomic-class whites, blacks, Hispanics, and established immigrants have settled because housing is cheap (or government subsidized), employment or welfare services are available, and there is a great deal of comfort derived from living with people of one's own race or culture. These areas are often impoverished ghettos, with substandard, older housing, and they are frequently overcrowded, with a high incidence of social conflict and crime, including drug and gang activity. As new immigrants and members of varied racial and cultural groups move into the core area, they come into conflict with existing members of that community—a phenomenon that has been going on for generations. The newcomers and the established community members compete for housing, jobs, financial resources (e.g., welfare, food stamps), and education. When there is a collapse of affordable health services, lack of affordable housing, and reductions in benefits (cuts in social programs by federal and state authorities), as occurred in the 1990s, 2003, and again in 2008–2009, conflicts escalate between racial and ethnic groups. Conflicts also take place due to the influx of illegal immigrants into communities across the nation. As these circumstances intensify, incidents of discrimination, bias, and hate violence increase. Those who are more established want to move out, not just to improve their lot but also to escape the conflict.

Wallace indicates that the rewards of better education and jobs tend to come with assimilation into mainstream society. Some groups of immigrants can be seen as "temporary inhabitants" of the inner city; they work toward and achieve their goal of moving into the suburbs as they improve their economic situation. As they gain wealth and education, they acquire the same economic and educational advantages as long-time Americans (Wallace, 1992).

THE ECONOMY AND HATE VIOLENCE   Poor economic times contribute greatly to hate violence. In many areas of the country, when major industries such as steel and auto manufacturing have downturns, go out of business, or relocate, the likelihood of economic distress among low-skilled and unskilled workers increases. Scapegoating often results when blue-collar jobs are unavailable. The distress that accompanies unemployment and rising prices is often directed toward immigrants and minorities and manifests itself as harassment and violence.

Sociologists indicate that hate frequently stems from being deprived or having one's needs unsatisfied, so the poor despise the rich, the uneducated ridicule the intellectual, and the established ghetto inhabitant hates the new immigrant or refugee who moves into the area. Social scientists argue that the government definition of poverty does not measure the experience of being poor or the changes taking place in inner cities: not only has the number of ghetto poor increased but also has the severity of economic deprivation among them. Ghetto poverty and concentrations of diverse populations in one area often lead to conflict in these neighborhoods. The stresses of urban life, especially in inner cities, give rise to increased incidents of violence, especially in depressed economic conditions and reduced space.

MOVE-IN VIOLENCE   Move-in violence can occur when people of one ethnicity or race move into a residence or open a business in a neighborhood composed of people from a different race or ethnicity. It can also take place when the new resident is of the same ethnicity or race—for example, a Cuban moving into a Mexican neighborhood or a Caribbean black moving into an African American community. Changing diversity and demographics can have a significant impact on a community because of hostility based on both perceived and real group differences.

However, the presence of new migrants or immigrants in a racially or ethnically different neighborhood does not automatically result in intergroup conflict or violence.

Historically, most cases of move-in violence have involved black, Hispanic, or Asian victims who locate housing or businesses in previously all-white suburbs or neighborhoods. Whites have not been the sole perpetrators, however; they have also been victims. For example, in Worcester, Massachusetts (in 1999), and in Sacramento, California (in 2000), Russian immigrants had moved into nonwhite neighborhoods and community conflict had occurred. Historically, new residents or business owners have moved into areas that are primarily black, Hispanic, or Asian and have experienced friction with the original residents. According to the U.S. Department of Justice's Community Relations Service, there have been cases of Hispanic migration or immigration into communities that had been presided over for many years by black leaders. In some of these new mixed communities, such as the Los Angeles area neighborhoods of Lakewood, Watts, and Pomona, Hispanic/Latino community members have sometimes perceived that their concerns are being ignored. Other cases of conflict have involved communities with new immigrants from the Middle East and South Asia. For the past three decades, Middle Easterners have made up one of the fastest-growing immigrant groups in the country, their numbers increasing sevenfold since 1970 as compared to a tripling of the overall immigrant population during that period. Nationwide, the largest newcomer groups from the Middle East consist of Iranians and Israelis, but there has also been a large number of Pakistanis from south Asia.

Targets of Hate Crimes

The psychocultural origin of hate crimes stems from human nature itself. To hate means to dislike passionately or intensely—to have an extreme aversion to or hostility toward another person, idea, or object. Hate can have a benign manifestation, such as when one hates evil, or bad weather, or certain foods, or it can have an abnormal expression when it becomes obsessive or is wrongly directed at someone who has done no harm. People can be culturally conditioned to hate those who are different from them because of their places of origin, looks, beliefs, or preferences. As the song in the musical *South Pacific* reminds us, "We have to be taught to hate and fear/We have to be taught from year to year." Crimes and acts of hate serve as frightening reminders to vulnerable citizens that they may not take safety for granted. Collectively, they begin to develop a mentality that hate crimes can take place anywhere—in streets, in neighborhoods, at workplaces, and even in their homes. Not all crimes motivated by prejudice or bias involve hate. Many nonviolent incidents are committed impulsively, or as acts of conformity, or as deliberate acts of intimidation designed to achieve specific ends of the perpetrator that do not necessarily involve hate.

There are innumerable examples of hate/bias crimes that have victimized blacks, Asians, and Hispanics. Clearly, such hate goes back for many generations. These are discussed in Part Two, "Cultural Specifics for Law Enforcement." The following sections address Jews and lesbian, gay, bisexual, and transgender people as victims of hate or bias crimes.

JEWS AND ANTI-SEMITISM

Jews

Jews belong to a religious and cultural group, although they have sometimes been incorrectly labeled as constituting a separate racial group. Jews have experienced discrimination, persecution, and violence throughout history because their religious beliefs and practices often set them apart from the majority. Even when they were totally assimilated (i.e., integrated into society), as was true in Germany in the early twentieth century, they were still not accepted as full citizens and eventually experienced the ultimate hate crime—genocide. The term *anti-Semitism* means "against Semites," which literally includes Jews and Arabs. Popular use of this term, however, refers to anti-Jewish sentiment.

European anti-Semitism had religious origins: Jews did not accept Jesus Christ as the son of God and were portrayed as betrayers and even killers of Christ. This accusation gave rise to religious anti-Semitism and what Christians saw as justification for anti-Jewish acts. In the past few decades, there have been great strides made by religious leaders to eliminate centuries of prejudice. For example, a 1965 Roman Catholic decree (the Nostra Aetate) stated that the church did not hold Jews responsible for the death of Christ. The decree, written by the Second Vatican Council under the leadership of the pope, encouraged people to abandon blaming Jews and instead work for stronger links and increased understanding between the religions. But despite some progress in ecumenical relations, there are still individuals who, 2,000 years after the birth of Christ, believe that Jews of today are responsible for Christ's death. Abraham Foxman, National Director of the Anti-Defamation League (ADL), said in 2005:

> of great concern is the persistence of two of the most insidious manifestations of anti-Semitism: The beliefs that Jews are more loyal to Israel than to America, and that Jews were responsible for the death of Jesus. Since so much of the history of anti-Semitism relates to the charges that Jews are always aliens in the societies in which they live and are Christ-killers, these realities should not be taken lightly. In our recent survey, 33 percent of those polled said American Jews were more loyal to Israel than America, a remarkably consistent finding that goes back four decades. Thirty percent of Americans said Jews were responsible for the death of Jesus. (Foxman, 2005)

According to Foxman, anti-Semitism also increased because of the United States' war in Iraq. In the same article he said:

> What happened in our country shortly before the start of fighting in Iraq was a reminder. The old canard espoused by Charles Lindbergh before WWII—that Jews, because of their narrow self-interest, were bringing the country to war—was now *being updated* to blame neo-conservative Jews. Unlike when Pat Buchanan accused Jews of causing the first Gulf War, this time the accusations took on a life of their own. (Foxman, 2005)

A 2005 survey by the ADL found that 14 percent of Americans had anti-Semitic attitudes, which was a dramatic decline since their initial survey in 1964 when 29 percent of Americans were deemed to possess anti-Semitic attitudes. The 2005 survey report indicates that their findings are generally consistent with what they found over the last decade, with some variation: in 1998, the number was 12 percent; in 2002 it was 17 percent (Foxman, 2005). Another type of anti-Semitism falls under what some would label as anti-Zionism (i.e., against the establishment of the state of Israel as a homeland for Jews). Although politically oriented, this type of anti-Semitism still makes references to "the Jews" and equates "Jews" with the suppression of the Palestinian people.

The 2006 terrorist attacks by Hezbollah operating from Lebanon resulted in extreme unrest in the Middle East and severe criticism of Israel. From the Israeli perspective, the Hezbollah as well as Hamas (responsible for rocket attacks from the Gaza strip) had never formally accepted Israel's right to exist as a nation. Israel was directly threatened by Hezbollah's widespread presence, especially in South Lebanon where attacks directly into Israel could occur. The Arab world and some of the non-Arab world criticized Israel for what they believed to be extreme military actions in Lebanon in which infrastructure was destroyed and attacks lasted longer than was expected. This 2006 Middle East conflict resulted in demonstrations in the United States by both pro-Palestinian and pro-Israeli contingents.

Police officers must be aware of the potential fallout in the United States when conflicts arise in the Middle East, particularly between Israelis and the Palestinians. Anti-Israel attitudes are sometimes expressed as anti-Zionist and anti-Jewish sentiments, despite the fact that Jewish political identification with Israel varies greatly. For example, in January 2009, five Chicago Jewish institutions were tagged with anti-Israel and anti-Semitic graffiti, in apparent response to the conflict in Israel and Gaza. Lonnie Nasatir, Chicago ADL Regional Director, issued a statement:

> These acts of anti-Semitic vandalism against our local Jewish institutions are despicable and cowardly and clearly have no place in Chicago. We applaud law enforcement for taking these incidents seriously and treating them as hate crimes, and we hope that the perpetrators will be brought to justice. Together, we must send a message that our community stands united against the haters and that acts of intimidation will not be tolerated. We saw a similar spike in anti-Israel and anti-Semitic incidents in Chicago and across the country during the Lebanon campaign in 2006 and following the outbreak of the second Palestinian intifada in 2000. It is a sad statement that events taking place across the globe can reverberate in acts of hate in our local community. ("ADL Decries the Anti-Semitic Vandalism of Five Jewish Institutions in Chicago," 2009)

Prevalence of Anti-Semitic Crimes

The ADL produces an annual "Audit" report on the number of anti-Semitic incidents, which is compiled from official crime statistics from, as of 2008, 44 states and the District of Columbia as well as information provided to ADL's regional offices by victims, law enforcement officials, and community leaders. The numbers in the Audit consistently exceed those collected by the FBI for the UCR report produced each year. The Audit identifies both criminal and noncriminal incidents of harassment and intimidation, including distribution of hate literature, threats, and slurs. It includes incidents such as physical and verbal assaults, harassment, property defacement, vandalism, and other expressions of anti-Jewish sentiment. Exhibit 11.7 is a national Audit of anti-Semitic incidents year by year, with totals from 1986 to 2007. The graph shows that the number of anti-Semitic incidents declined in 2007 for the third consecutive year after a most recent peak in 2004. The reason for the spikes of Anti-Semitic hate crimes seen in the graph in certain years has already been discussed. Seven states continued the trend of reporting the largest numbers of anti-Semitic incidents. They are those with the largest Jewish populations and thus the most vulnerable targets—New York, California, New Jersey, Massachusetts, Pennsylvania, Connecticut, and Florida.

Anti-Semitic Groups and Individuals

Several types of groups in the United States have exhibited anti-Semitic attitudes, and some of the most extreme groups have committed hate crimes against Jews. The most glaringly anti-Semitic organizations are white supremacist groups, such as the Ku Klux Klan (KKK), the Aryan Nation, White Aryan Resistance (WAR), the Order, the Posse Comitatus, the Covenant and the Sword, the

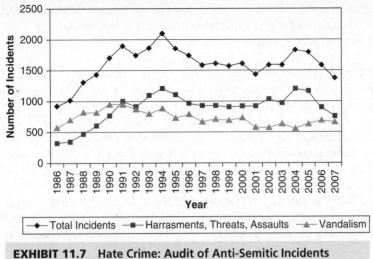

EXHIBIT 11.7 Hate Crime: Audit of Anti-Semitic Incidents (National Totals 1986–2007).

Source: Annual ADL Audit of Anti-Semitic Incidents in U. S. (2008) Anti-Defamation League.

Arm of the Lord, and neo-Nazi skinheads (discussed further in Chapter 12). These groups tend to hate all who are different from them but focus a great deal of attention on blacks and Jews. Some messianic individuals who believe that Armageddon (the end of the world) is imminent have been known to threaten Jews by phone or mail, but rarely have these threats been carried out. These people believe that Jews need to repent and see themselves as instruments of God, connected to the coming of the end of the world. Those who argued that it was the United States' support of Israel that led to the September 11, 2001, attacks have demonstrated another aspect of anti-Semitism. Some hate groups used this argument to stir up anti-Jewish feelings and to erode sympathy and support for Jews and for Israel at their organizations' rallies and within the general public. In addition, those who are vehemently pro-Arab and anti-Israel may exhibit strong anti-Jewish attitudes. While it is not as common for anti-Zionist attitudes to result in acts of violence against Jews in the United States as it is in Europe, Jewish Americans, like Arab Americans, can nevertheless become targets during Middle Eastern crises. Finally, in times of recession, Jews are often blamed for the economic decline, and the notion of Jewish "influence" (i.e., the baseless charge that Jews control the media, the banks, and even the world economy) provides a convenient scapegoat. It is not within the scope of this section to delve into these myths, but we point out that there is widespread harmful misinformation about Jews that anti-Semites continue to spread.

In May 2009, four men were arrested after a year-long investigation by the FBI and the New York Police Department in connection with an alleged plot to bomb two synagogues in the Riverdale section of the Bronx. They were also charged with plotting to use Stinger missiles to destroy military aircraft at the Air National Guard base at Stewart airport in Newburgh, New York ("FBI, NYPD Arrest 4 in Alleged Plot to Bomb NY Synagogues," 2009).

According to NBC, the four men were all Muslim, one a born Muslim of Afghan descent and three who converted to Islam in prison. "The leader of the group, James Cromitie, was concerned about deaths at the hands of the U.S. military in Afghanistan, and also expressed anti-Jewish sentiment, Joseph Demarest the head of the New York FBI said. According to the criminal complaint, Cromitie said 'I hate those f-ing Jewish bastards.' He bragged that it would be a 'piece of cake' to bomb a Jewish Center in Riverdale, according to the complaint" ("FBI, NYPD Arrest 4 in Alleged Plot to Bomb NY Synagogues," 2009).The same suspect allegedly said, in essence, he wanted to "do jihad" and die as a martyr because of the U.S. military's involvement against Muslims in Iraq and Afghanistan.

> "The bombing plot uncovered by law enforcement is another reminder of the extreme lengths violent anti-Semites will go to act on their hatred. According to the police complaint, the suspects in the attempted Riverdale bombings were motivated by a deep-seated hatred of Jews, and were so determined to attack synagogues that they allegedly engaged in surveillance of the potential targets, and sought for nearly a year to obtain the weapons and bombs to bring the attack to fruition. The arrests illustrate how law enforcement continues to play a critical role in ensuring the safety and security of the Jewish community and in protecting all of its citizens from terrorism. We have long known that Jews remain a prime target for would-be terrorists, and we must always remain vigilant in the face of this threat." ("ADL Applauds Law Enforcement for Arrests of Homegrown Terrorists in Plot to Blow Up New York City Synagogues," 2009)

Jewish Community Concerns

Around the holiest days of the Jewish year (Rosh Hashanah and Yom Kippur, occurring in the early fall), there can also be heightened anxiety among some community members regarding security. Indeed, many synagogues hire extra security during times of worship over this 10-day holiday period. Acts of defilement can occur in synagogues and other Jewish institutions at random times as well. These acts and manifestations of prejudice bring back painful memories for Jews who experienced violent expressions of anti-Semitism in other countries, especially for those who lived through the Holocaust; some of the memories and fears have been passed on to subsequent generations. At the same time, some people may overreact to an insensitive remark that stems from ignorance on the part of the speaker rather than from malicious anti-Semitism. Some people may not understand that a swastika painted by teenagers on a building does not necessarily precede any acts of anti-Jewish violence. Yet a swastika almost always evokes a fearful reaction among many Jewish community members because of the historical significance of the symbol.

Police officers must understand that different segments of the Jewish community feel vulnerable to anti-Semitism, and therefore officers are advised to listen to and take seriously Jews' expressions of concern and fear. At the same time, they need to explain that sometimes acts of vandalism are isolated and are not targeting any group in particular (e.g., many skinheads or "thugs" are unhappy with their lot in life and tend to hate everyone). Finally, officers who take reports from citizens should reassure those citizens that their local law enforcement agency views hate crimes and incidents seriously and that extra protection will be provided if the need arises.

What Law Enforcement Can Do

By discussing the concerns and fears of some Jewish community members, we do not imply that all Jewish citizens are overly concerned for their safety. In fact, a large percentage of American Jews does not even identify as Jews and does not share a collective or community consciousness with other Jews. At the other extreme are people who interpret events or remarks as anti-Semitic rather than as ignorance or insensitivity. Whatever the case, police officers should be aware that anti-Semitism has a long and active history, and even if some fears appear to be exaggerated, they have a basis in reality.

Officers can take some steps to establish rapport and provide protection in Jewish communities when the need arises:

1. When an officer hears of an act that can be classified as a hate crime toward Jews, it should be investigated, tracked, and dealt with as such. Dismissing acts of anti-Semitism as petty crime will result in a lack of trust on the part of the community.
2. When hate crimes and incidents are perpetrated against other groups in the community (e.g., gay, African American, Asian American groups), officers should alert Jewish community leaders immediately. Their institutions may be the next targets.
3. Officers should be aware of groups and individuals who distribute hate literature on people's doorsteps or vehicle windshields. Publications such as *Racial Loyalty*, for example, target Jews and "people of color" and accuse Jews of poisoning the population. A book published by the same organization, *On the Brink of a Bloody Racial War*, has been left on many Jews' doorsteps. Even if no violence occurs, the recipients of such hate literature become very fearful.
4. In cooperation with local organizations (e.g., Jewish community relations councils, ADL), officers can provide information through joint meetings on ways that individuals can heighten the security of Jewish institutions (e.g., information on nonbreakable glass, lighting of facilities in evenings).
5. Law enforcement officials should be familiar with the important dates of the Jewish calendar, especially when the High Holidays (Rosh Hashanah and Yom Kippur) occur. Some people are concerned about safety and protection during events at which large groups of Jews congregate.
6. Finally, officers may contact a Jewish umbrella organization in the community to assist them in sending necessary messages to local Jewish institutions and places of worship. Two organizations in particular are worth noting: the national JCRC (Jewish Community Relations Council) and the ADL. The JCRC has representative organizations in almost every major city in the United States. This organization, the regional ADL organizations, and the Jewish Federations can be of great assistance to law enforcement in disseminating information to members of the Jewish community.

Because of their history, some Jews expect anti-Semitic incidents, and the reality is that there are still anti-Semites in our society. An officer has to be responsive to generated fears and community concerns. An officer's ability to calm fears as well as to investigate threats thoroughly will result in strong relations between law enforcement officials and Jewish community members.

LESBIAN, GAY, BISEXUAL, AND TRANSGENDER VICTIMIZATION

According to Mitchell Grobeson, a retired LAPD sergeant who is gay,

> When members of the gay community sought respectability within society, there was no word that did *not* carry a derogatory connotation for non-heterosexuality. The term "**homosexual**" carried negative connotations because the American Psychiatric Association used this as a medical diagnosis for a psychiatric illness until 1993. As such, various gay leaders tried to replace this with the term "**homophile**" and subsequently, "**gay**." Because "**lesbians**" sought distinctiveness, the phrase "gay and lesbian" became more common. Other discriminated classes sought out their own unique identification, so the terms "**bisexual**" and "**transgender**" were added as these persons sought recognition within the larger community. (Grobeson, 2009)

Bisexual   Of or relating to sexual attraction to both men and women

Gay   A male homosexual

Homophile   Same as homosexual

Homosexual   Characterized by sexual attraction to those of the same sex as oneself

Lesbian   A homosexual woman

Transgender   Covers a range of people, including heterosexual cross-dressers, homosexual drag queens, and transsexuals who believe they were born in the wrong body. This term includes those who consider themselves to be both male and female, or intersexed, as well as those who take hormones to complete their gender identity without a sex change.

A related term that is important to understand is *phobia*, which is defined in Webster's Dictionary as an irrational, excessive, and persistent fear of some particular thing or situation. Gays and Lesbians Initiating Dialogue for Equality (GLIDE) defines *homophobia* as "an irrational fear, hatred, ignorance, or general discomfort with gay, lesbian, bisexual, or transgender persons, topics, or issues." Sometimes, homophobia results in homophobic acts, which can run the full spectrum from antigay jokes to physical battery resulting in injury or death. In this text, as in government reporting systems, homophobic acts are referred to as anti–sexual orientation or gender identity bias incidents and offenses. LGBT is an initialism or acronym referring collectively to lesbian, gay, bisexual, and transgender people. The authors use those initials throughout this textbook.

Hate crimes targeting LGBT individuals are distinct from other bias crimes because they target a group made up of every other category discussed in this textbook. In the United States today, there are organizations whose membership includes gay Jews, Catholics, Mormons, Buddhists, Armenians, Latinos/as, African Americans, Asians and Pacific Islanders, and virtually every other ethnic, racial, and religious group. Every year in the United States, thousands of LGBT persons are harassed, beaten, or murdered solely because of their sexual orientation or gender identity.

Hate Crime Laws Specific to LGBT Persons as Victims

As of April, 2009, 45 states and the District of Columbia have hate crime statutes criminalizing various types of bias-motivated violence or intimidation ("Strengthen Hate Crime Laws," 2009). A few states have created laws specific to crimes that are directed against LGBT persons because of their sexual orientation or gender expression. There are no federal laws either protecting victims of crimes based on sexual orientation or gender identity or providing for an additional penalty enhancement for such crimes. The Hate Crimes Sentencing Act, which applies only to federal offenses, allows judges to consider homophobia as a motive only during sentencing. For many years, the U.S. Congress has considered legislation to deal with sexual-orientation or gender identity hate incidents and offenses. The legislation, known as the "Local Law Enforcement Hate Crimes Prevention Act" (LLEHCPA), was passed by the House of Representatives and the Senate and was sent to the White House for final approval in October 2009 when this text book was being revised. If passed and signed into law, the LLEHCPA would provide for the following ("Local Law Enforcement Hate Crimes Prevention Act of 2007," 2009):

- Extend existing federal protections to include "gender identity, sexual orientation, gender, and disability,"
- Allow the Justice Department to assist in hate crime investigations at the local level when local law enforcement is unable or unwilling to fully address these crimes,

- Mandate that the FBI begin tracking hate crimes based on actual or perceived gender identity, sexual orientation, gender, and disability,
- Remove limitations that narrowly define hate crimes as violence committed while a person is accessing a federally protected activity, such as voting or going to school,
- Provide $10 million in funding to help State and local agencies pay for investigating and prosecuting hate crimes,
- Require the FBI to track statistics on hate crimes against transgender people (statistics for the other groups are already tracked).

Many civil rights, professional, civic, education, and religious groups and state attorneys general have expressed support for the bill. The same is true of national law enforcement organizations, including the International Association of Chiefs of Police, the Major Cities Chiefs Association, the National District Attorneys Association, the National Organization of Black Law Enforcement Executives, the National Sheriffs' Association, and the Police Executive Research Forum ("Strengthen Hate Crime Laws," 2009).

One reason the legislation has not passed is the lobbying effors of groups that oppose it, such as the Traditional Values Coalition (TVC). According to the group's website, "the Traditional Values Coalition deplores all acts of violence against innocent victims of bias-motivated violent crimes directed at anyone including homosexuals or gender confused individuals. . . . However, TVC strongly opposes any legislation that puts fundamental religious liberties at risk. Our laws should not provide extra legal protections for someone simply because of the way he/she engages in sex" ("S.1105—The So-Called Hate Crimes Bill", 2007). The TVC describes itself as an interdenominational public policy organization located in Washington D.C. that speaks on behalf of 43,000 churches.

LGBT Persons as Victims of Hate/Bias Incidents and Offenses

THE SCOPE OF LGBT VICTIMIZATION   The FBI-UCR hate crime report covering 2007 indicates that there were 7,621 single-bias incidents reported, and of those that were based on sexual orientation (16.6 percent), there were 1,265 incidents and 1,460 offenses ("Hate Crime Statistics 2007," 2008). Refer to Exhibits 11.2 and 11.3 for the breakdown by category. However, the UCR statistics, as in previous years, continue to fall well short of the number of incidents and offenses reported to the National Coalition of Anti-Violence Programs (NCAVP) and other such organizations. The NCAVP is a network of over 35 antiviolence organizations that monitor, respond to, and work to end incidents of hate and domestic violence and other forms of violence affecting LGBT communities. The coalition produces a report each year documenting the number of bias-motivated incidents targeting LGBT individuals in the United States. "The total number of victims reporting anti-LGBT violence to NCAVP in 2007 was 2,430, which represents a 24 percent increase over the total number of victims reported in 2006" ("Anti-Lesbian, Gay, Bisexual and Transgender Violence in 2007," 2008).

The number of LGBT victims reporting bias-motivated incidents to the NCAVP is significantly higher than to the FBI. Researchers and gay rights groups, therefore, question the validity, findings, and implications of the FBI-UCR reports. Recall that law enforcement compliance with the Hate Crime Statistics Act of 1990 is voluntary and many agencies in the United States do not report hate bias incidents and offenses to the FBI.

The data shown in Exhibits 11.2 and 11.3 for the period covered seem to indicate that of the total of hate crime incidents and offenses reported each year, the average related to sexual-orientation bias was 16 percent. A look at Exhibit 11.3 and 11.4, showing the specific motivation for sexual-orientation bias offenses, shows that anti–male homosexual bias had the highest percentage for each year of the study period.

Increases noted in sexual orientation, antihomosexual bias crimes occurred during the years when gays and lesbians were trying to legally marry and gain adoption rights, which resulted in movements in some states as well as on the national level to block these efforts (i.e., the controversial issues of "same-sex marriage" and adoption of children). In short, LGBT persons and communities had garnered more visibility, both positive and negative, during the years in question. Both statistical and anecdotal evidence clearly demonstrates that when LGBT issues are in the limelight, LGBT communities and individuals are targeted for violence. Many of the driving political and cultural forces behind the era of violence described in 2004 were not nearly as prominent during 2005. In short, events both specific and ancillary to LGBT communities help create an environment that fosters increased violence against LGBT persons (NCAVP, 2006).

LGBT VICTIM PROFILES   The distribution of LGBT victims across various demographics remains fairly constant over the years. In 2007, of the 2,430 reported incidents, victims of African descent comprised 13 percent whose race or ethnicity was known. Latinos and Latinas were 16 percent, and whites were 38 percent of the victims. Arab/Middle Eastern persons as victims made up about 1 percent as did Indigenous/Native American people. The race/ethnicity of victims for the year 2007 is displayed in Exhibit 11.8.

Anti-LGBT murders are often easily distinguishable from other murders by the level of brutality involved. LGBT murder victims are often dismembered, stabbed multiple times, or severely bludgeoned. See Exhibit 11.9 for a year-to-year analysis of known anti-LGBT murders in the years 1997 through 2007 according to the NCAVP ("Anti-Lesbian, Gay, Bisexual and Transgender Violence in 2007," 2008). The exhibit indicates that, according to NCAVP data, there were 181 murders during the period. A study conducted by the NCAVP determined that almost

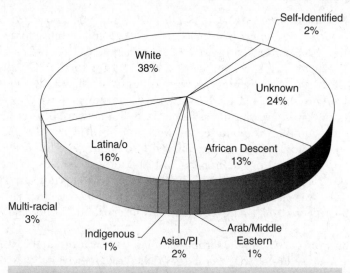

EXHIBIT 11.8   Race/Ethnicity of LGBT Hate/Bias Crime Victims for 2007.

Source: National Coalition of Anti-Violence Programs, 2008, Release Edition.

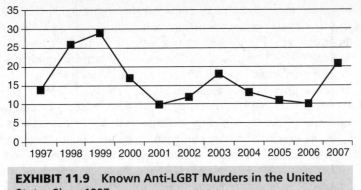

EXHIBIT 11.9   Known Anti-LGBT Murders in the United States Since 1997.

Source: National Coalition of Anti-Violence Programs, 2008, Release Edition.

60 percent of anti-LGBT murders involve "extraordinary violence." Clarence Patton, executive director of the nation's largest antiviolence project, based in New York, makes reference to the "extraordinary levels of violence involved" in such anti-LGBT crimes, saying that "many bias-motivated physical assaults against gay, bisexual, HIV-positive, and transgender persons are extremely violent and brutal" ("Gay and Lesbian Anti-Violence Project," 2006). The following are just a few examples of this phenomenon across the nation:

- *New Mexico:* Following an attack in a Santa Fe motel parking lot, where five men beat two gay men while yelling antigay epithets, one victim spent 8 days in a coma and had to learn to walk and talk again ("Two Defendants in Gay Bashing Case Avoid Prison," 2006, p. 36).
- *Alabama:* Three suspects beat, stabbed, and strangled an 18-year-old gay man, then burned his body in the woods near his mobile home in Bay Minette ("New Call for Hate Crime Change," 2005, p. 35).

In a 2-month span, from June to July of 2008, the NCAVP documented a few of the many LGBT murders ("Pattern of Severe Anti-LGBT Violence Nationwide," 2008).

- *Tennessee:* The body of a transgender, African American woman is found near a daycare center in Memphis.
- *Colorado:* The body of an 18-year-old transgender Latina is found in Greeley beaten to death with a fire extinguisher.
- *Tennessee:* Two people killed and seven wounded in a shooting that took place at a Unitarian church in Knoxville. Shooting appears to be at least partially antigay motivated.

The Phenomenon of Underreporting Anti–Sexual Orientation Incidents and Offenses

Various reasons have been postulated for the phenomenon of LGBT hate crimes being seriously underreported to law enforcement, including the following:

1. *Law enforcement is not required to collect and report LGBT hate/bias crimes:* Under the Hate Crimes Statistics Act, local law enforcement agencies are not required to report hate crimes to the FBI, and some do not. An additional criticism is that of the agencies that do

submit data, many do not include hate crime statistics, either denying these sorts of crimes occur in their community or not classifying them as such.

2. *LGBT individuals do not report being victimized:* Unwillingness to "come out" (be identified as LGBT) by reporting these crimes to authorities is thought to be the most common reason that some victims do not report a crime. If this were the only factor, however, then the phenomenon would not remain constant within metropolitan areas with large, open LGBT populations and organizations that provide outreach on such issues. In fact, data from the Los Angeles Gay and Lesbian Center, the primary agency that provides victim services and documentation of homophobic hate violence for L.A. County (including the independent city of West Hollywood, whose population comprises approximately 35 percent LGBT residents), clearly demonstrate that the underreporting of hate crimes is continuing into the new century. The truth is that many members of the LGBT community remain mistrustful of the police or suspect that their reporting of such incidents will not result in any significant action by law enforcement ("Stonewalled," 2005).

The NCAVP 2005 report listed the following reasons why victims of anti-LGBT bias hesitate to report their experiences, either to police or to organizations within their own community. The victim:

a. fears reprisal from the offender(s).

b. fears embarrassment or abuse from police.

c. would be ostracized from family, friends, or coworkers and would possibly lose employment, custody of children, or housing.

d. at the urging of family members, friends, and coworkers does not to report the incident.

e. is so emotionally impacted by the experience that he or she wishes to "forget" it and "move on" and not deal with reporting the occurrence.

f. blames himself or herself for being in the "wrong" place, saying the "wrong" thing, or acting in the "wrong" way.

g. either does not believe anything can be done about the situation or believes the police will not do anything about the situation.

h. dismisses hate incidents (versus hate offenses/crimes) such as eggs or lit cigarettes being thrown at him/her as not being serious enough to report.

i. is not aware of national or local antiviolence programs or other alternatives to the police (or the victim believes the organizations will not help if he or she does not make an official police report).

Differences in culture and language, along with gender, age, and class, often lead to perceptions that advocacy organizations may not be sensitive to the victim's own background. The NCAVP strongly believes that the incidence of anti-LGBT bias crime affecting younger and older people, immigrants, people of color, people in the military, and those within other marginalized populations is *grossly* underreported (NCAVP, 2006, p. 35).

3. *Other reasons for anti–sexual orientation crimes being underreported:*

a. *Mixed motive or pick-up crimes.* According to Grobeson, though victims' advocates believe that a crime in which bias was a *primary* motivation should be classified as a hate crime, law enforcement officers are often unwilling to do so if there is any other motive in addition to bias (Grobeson, 2009). These advocates point out that law enforcement personnel have a practice of looking for "pick-up crimes." That is, some law enforcement personnel tend to drop the hate bias motivation of any incident or offense in which an element of *any* other crime is involved (e.g., assault with a deadly weapon or robbery). Amnesty International confirms this practice in a study that revealed that in some instances, any indication of "mixed motives" for a crime, (e.g., although homophobic slurs were used, the victim was also robbed) means that the case is discounted as a hate crime (e.g., and classified as a robbery) ("Stonewalled," 2005, p. 38).

b. *Conflicting police training policies and practices.* Another facet of the issue of underreporting is that law enforcement personnel who receive training in the handling of hate crimes are often instructed *not* to ask about a person's sexual orientation, so assaults and batteries motivated by homophobia are often not classified as hate crimes. The reluctance of some LGBT victims to reveal the homophobic component of a crime to police, for reasons already discussed, leads to low criminal justice figures on homophobic hate crime (Grobeson, 2009). Law enforcement is a key component in combating violence against lesbian, gay, bisexual, and transgender people, and victims expect appropriate action and professionalism when reporting an assault.

TRANSGENDER PERSONS AS VICTIMS OF SEXUAL ORIENTATION HATE CRIMES   Statistically, transgender people, per capita, are 16 times more likely to be murdered than the general population and three times more likely than African American males, the next closest category ("Literary Stereotyping," 2003, p. 88). Of transgender murder victims in the United States, nonwhite youths are disproportionately represented (Manley, 2006). The Los Angeles Commission on Human Relations released a report that showed that hate crimes against transgender people had the greatest likelihood of violence of any victim group: 88 percent involved violence compared to 58 percent for hate crimes against gay and lesbian people (Felsenthal, 2004).

Though there have been numerous hate crimes against transgender individuals throughout the United States, few garnered the national media attention of the murder of Gwen Araujo:

> Three Bay Area men were convicted of killing transgender teenager Gwen Araujo. The 17-year-old Araujo, who was biologically male, was slapped, punched, kicked and hit with a soup can and a frying pan, bound with rope and strangled. The body was buried in a remote location near South Lake Tahoe. ("Killers Get Maximum," 2006, p. A1, A6)

TOOLS FOR LAW ENFORCEMENT (TRANSGENDER PROTOCOL)   Most law enforcement personnel are unlikely to have had any significant contact with members of the transgender community prior to or even during their careers, depending upon where they work. Most problems for police officers in their encounters with transgender individuals involve a lack of experience, education, training, department policy and procedure, or protocol. Consider the following:

- *Washington, D.C.:*   A transgender woman, arrested in a domestic dispute, was placed in a male cell-block at the D.C. Superior Court after authorities determined that they had no procedure for changing her gender from male to female in the court's criminal record system even though she had identification that had been legally corrected to reflect her gender ("Stonewalled," 2005, p. 61).
- *Texas:*   An African American transgender woman told Amnesty International that she was dressed in "drag" when they detained her in "the tank" with males at the Bexar County Jail, San Antonio (p. 60).

A protocol for law enforcement or corrections should include the following:

1. Officers should refer to the transgender person either by the name on the identification, the person's adopted name, or in the gender pronoun for which he or she is dressed or seeking to be perceived. (e.g., refer to a transgender man in woman's attire as "miss" or "ma'am.").

2. In investigative circumstances, an officer may respectfully ask gender- and name-related questions. Once those questions have been answered, an officer should refer to that person by the name the individual regularly uses.

3. If a frisk or search is necessary, under governing legal standards and barring exigent circumstances, two officers of the gender requested by the transgender individual should search the person. The frisk or search should be consistent with maintenance of not only physical integrity and human dignity of the person, but also officer safety. If a transgender individual does not specify a preference, then officers of the same gender presentation should conduct the search (e.g., a transgender female who expresses no preference should be searched by female officers).

4. Officers should avoid any behavior that harasses transgender persons.

5. If incarcerated, transgender persons should be housed in the appropriate location according to his or her gender identification.

6. A narrative report, in its first paragraph, should indicate the gender the individual is living as and should state that he or she is transgender. The person should thereafter be referred to throughout the report by the adopted name or appropriate pronoun based upon gender presentation.

7. Statistical or booking pages are based upon the legal name and gender (genitalia) of the individual.

Sources: San Francisco Police Department Protocol; Amnesty International; Grobeson, 2009.

It is important that hate crime reports document the perspective of the perpetrator as well as of the victim in attacks on transgender individuals. Most homophobic incidents targeting transgender individuals include epithets such as "You fucking queer." It is important for reporting, investigating, and collecting accurate statistical data that these incidents be documented as targeting persons because they are gay, transgender, or both (Manley, 2006).

It is suggested that large police agencies have personnel specifically assigned to investigate hate crimes against LGBT individuals. Most agencies assign hate crimes to investigators, often to those assigned to handle "crimes against persons," as a corollary duty. "If you assign a robbery detective to investigate hate crimes, you will wind up with a robbery filing," says Grobeson. At the very least, agencies should ensure that those who investigate such crimes receive appropriate training.

Mini Case Study

How should this situation have been handled by the police department?

Officers respond to a call at a motel and are met by a nude, intoxicated individual who has breasts but also male genitalia. The individual is arrested for public intoxication. All indications are that the individual is living as a woman, but because of the male genitalia, the individual is placed in the all-male jail. Officers learn that she is a "pre-op" transsexual, a person who is in the process of becoming, in this case, a woman.

Perpetrators of Crime Related to Sexual Orientation

Grobeson suggests that many gay-bashing suspects fit specific profiles, such as being a gang member or member of a white supremacist group. Sometimes gangs incorporate gay-bashing into their new-member initiation. White supremacists (including neo-Nazi, skinheads, and the like) advocate violence against LGBT persons. It is important to note that those who engage in homophobic acts almost always engage in actions that discriminate against other groups as well.

Another view of offender profiles is found in a research paper submitted to the American Psychological Association. The report found that 32 percent of young college students had engaged in verbal anti-LGBT harassment, and 18 percent had made threats or committed actual physical violence ("Stonewalled," 2005). While this one study showed that the perpetrators were fairly ordinary young adults, not prone to joining gangs or hate groups, the most commonly cited anti-LGBT offenders have been classified into categories of "thrill seekers," "moral ideologues," or "turf defenders." In 2005, the offenders were predominately male (82 percent). Of the offenders whose age was known, they were almost equally divided among ages 17 and under, 18 to 29, and 30 to 49. In comparison with prior years, the most significant growth (+67 percent) was among older offenders, aged 50 to 59. Of those offenders whose race/ethnicity was known in 2005, most were Caucasian (39 percent), followed by African descent (27 percent), and Latino/a (24 percent). The largest group of offenders (63 percent) had no prior relationship to their victims. When categorized by those offenses *for which relationship information was available*, the percentage of offenders unknown or stranger to the victim was 37 percent in 2005; an equal number of offenders were known by the victim (37 percent). The proportion of offenders who had some type of prior contact with the victim has shown a trend of increase in recent years (NCAVP, 2006).

Sexual Orientation Hate/Bias Crimes and the Military

The military does not recruit or retain persons known to be homosexual. The military, however, has a "don't ask, don't tell" policy put into place under former President Bill Clinton, which means that if a homosexual is recruited or already in the military and the fact has not come to the attention of authorities (who are not to ask), then there is no action taken. There are, however, a large number of gay and lesbian individuals discharged each year from all branches of the armed forces. As mentioned in Chapter 2, in late 2008 and early 2009, military commanders testified before Congress and addressed both President Bush and President Obama asking that they recall the "Don't Ask, Don't Tell" policy. They claimed that the arbitrary nature of the policy has not only caused hardships for individuals, but has unnecessarily hampered military efforts, readiness, and mission ("Admirals, Generals: Repeal 'Don't Ask, Don't Tell,'" 2008).

It is important that FBI agents, military police, and law enforcement agencies that have adjacent military installations become familiar with organizations such as Servicemembers Legal Defense Network (SLDN) as well as with the updated policies issued by the Department of Defense (DoD). Military police officers should have an action plan to address relevant (anti-LGBT) issues, including eliminating mistreatment, harassment, and inappropriate comments or gestures; training; reporting of harassment; enforcement of policies prohibiting harassment; and measurement of antiharassment program effectiveness.

Sexual Orientation Hate/Bias Crimes and School Campuses

Campus police need to be aware that many states have enacted "Safe Schools" laws mandating environments that are free of harassment and discrimination, where no student is subjected to abuse or a hostile learning environment. There are many cases nationwide wherein students who were not protected by administrators or were subjected to unequal restrictions have sued their schools. Most of the court decisions found school administrators liable for failing to provide an environment free of hostility and resulted in expensive verdicts.

Bullying, discrimination, and assaults for any reason are a serious problem in today's schools. The effects can be detrimental to a child's self-esteem and social and academic success. Parents must learn the common characteristics of bullies and victims, and how parents can support and empower their child to develop bully-resistance skills. Also, parents must learn ways to intervene and provide guidance for children who are bullying others. There are courses on these skills available in most communities.

As of 2007, only 11 states and the District of Columbia have comprehensive antibullying laws that specifically address bullying and harassment based on sexual orientation, and only three of these have laws that mention gender identity. Nine other states have "generic" antibullying laws that do not provide specific definitions or define protected classes. On a federal level, it has been ruled that the effects of "bullying" students perceived to be gay cannot be dismissed, and that school districts can be held liable should they deny the impact of "bullying" on students ("Alito's Landmark Ruling," 2005).

A study in 2007 determined that of LGBT students, 86 percent reported being verbally harassed, 44 percent reported being physically harassed, and 22 percent reported being physically assaulted at school because of their sexual orientation. More than half (61 percent) of students reported that they felt unsafe in school because of their sexual orientation, and more than a third (38 percent) felt unsafe because of their gender expression ("2007 National School Climate Survey: Nearly 9 out of 10 LGBT Students Harassed," 2008). The students reported they often skipped classes or school because they felt unsafe or uncomfortable, which affected their grades. LBGT teens, according to the U.S. Department of Health and Human Services, account for 30 percent of all teen suicides, 28 percent of all dropouts, and 40 percent of homeless teens ("Gay Miami Teen Gets Accolades," 2005). There are cases of gay students getting seriously injured or even killed because of their sexual orientation. One example occurred in Oxnard, California, in 2008 when a gay eighth-grader was shot to death by a 14-year-old fellow student while in the computer lab at their junior high school. According to the *Contra Costa Times*, "The slaying of the 15-year-old boy has alarmed gay rights activists and led to demands that middle schools do more to educate youngsters about discrimination on the basis of sexual orientation. [The boy's] death has drawn national attention and outraged many gays" ("Gay Killing Draws Call for Change," 2008, p. A7).

It is important to note that law enforcement, particularly campus police, is becoming more involved in campus situations such as sexual-orientation bias crimes. They are expected to complete official documentation regarding alleged violations and physical assaults based on a student's perceived or actual sexual orientation or gender identity. It is particularly important for campus police to be vigilant because most LGBT teens do not report that they are victims of bias incidents or crimes at school, fearing that school officials will tell their parents about their real or perceived sexual orientation and/or that school officials will not do anything to stop the abusers.

Carolyn Laub, executive director of the Gay-Straight Alliance Network, commenting on the murder of the Oxnard student, said that "with young people coming out at younger ages, our schools—especially our junior highs and middle schools—need to be proactive about teaching respect for diversity based on sexual orientation and gender identity" ("Gay Killing Draws Call for Change," 2008). It is obvious that school officials, including campus police, where they exist, must take steps to alter the negative experiences of LGBT students, so they are not harassed or assaulted in school.

Police Relations with Gay and Lesbian Communities

Historically, in most cities and counties in the United States, relations between the police and the gay and lesbian communities have been strained. The strained relationships are sometimes caused by how the community members, as individuals or as a group, have been mistreated or abused by law enforcement officers. Many LGBT persons believe that the police regard them as deviants, criminals, and second-class citizens who are unworthy of protection or equal rights. Because of this perception, many gay and lesbian victims do not report the crimes to the police or cooperate with investigations. Even though negative attitudes and stereotypes will probably continue, progressive police departments and law enforcement officers who are professionals have found that communication and mutual respect between the department and gay and lesbian communities are in the best interests of all concerned.

Examples of police departments in which outreach and communication have resulted in cooperation between the agencies and the gay community include San Francisco, Boston, New York, and Baltimore. These departments have observed a noticeable difference in reporting by lesbian and gay crime victims, fewer complaints of police abuse, and a general improvement in relations between law enforcement and gay and lesbian communities. It is also important that community-based policing principles and protocol be utilized in LGBT communities. Officers should recognize issues and concerns not only about sexual-orientation bias crimes but also about domestic violence within the LGBT community. Domestic violence, although virtually invisible in LGBT communities, is commonplace and should be investigated following the same guidelines and policies as those used for heterosexual relationships.

Researcher Kevin Berrill observed that there are numerous ways to improve relationships between the justice system and gay and lesbian groups. One of the keys to good relations, according to Berrill, is regular, institutionalized communication at the department, in committees and councils, and in public forums. In addition, he mentions the following (Berrill, 2006):

1. The creation of task forces and councils to establish ongoing dialogue and networking on important issues.
2. Public forums that allow police officials to meet the LGBT community and help officials to recognize that they are a constituency with legitimate needs and concerns.
3. The appointment of a police official to be a liaison with the LGBT community to respond to complaints and requests.
4. The involvement of prosecutors in the development of policies, procedures, communications, and awareness training to improve relations between the criminal justice system and LGBT groups and individuals.

Almost every community has extremist and even militant segments, and the LGBT community is no exception. Some activists or activist groups may require additional attention and special interaction with local law enforcement. The goal of the agency liaison and its management should be to avoid costly litigation and to communicate effectively with persons representing such groups. Departments should have an assigned liaison officer meet with these groups in an attempt to agree on acceptable behavior before any public demonstration occurs. Some groups obtain press coverage by orchestrating arrests by the police; in such cases, liaison and close monitoring by field supervisors, a press relations officer, a police video unit, and a department manager would be an absolute necessity. This methodology has been successful with agencies in the San Francisco Bay Area, resulting in no physical confrontation with groups, no negative press or photos, and no legal action. However, even the best police outreach efforts may prove ineffective. For example, some activist groups have refused to communicate with police during their "actions." Nevertheless, police officers should not permit negative publicity from previous incidents with any group to stop them from attempting to make positive contact prior to scheduled public events. The willingness of the police to work with any community group, particularly LGBT activist groups, always results in positive publicity for the law enforcement agencies and the cities or counties they serve (Grobeson, 2009).

The handling and investigation of hate crimes require specialized and unique expertise. The epidemic of hate crimes will continue unabated as long as law enforcement management does not address it proactively. It is important for law enforcement administrators to realize that they can be subjected to litigation and even punitive damages for the actions of their subordinates if they fail to provide proactive policies or take affirmative stances in regard to officer training or discipline (vicarious liability). It is equally important that military and campus police officers know the laws and establish protocol for preventing and investigating crimes motivated by hate against anyone, including LGBT individuals.

HATE CRIME LAWS

Federal Laws

Federal laws provide criminal and civil causes of action for victims of hate crimes in the United States, regardless of whether they are citizens. Federal law does not prohibit all acts of hate violence, however. Federal statutes forbid violence by private parties only when there is intent to interfere with a federally protected right—that is, one specifically guaranteed by a federal statute or by the U.S. Constitution. Federal authorities can intervene only when a crime is motivated by race, religion, or national origin and, when at the time the crime is committed, the victim is engaged in a "federally protected activity." Such activity includes voting, serving on a jury, going to work, or enrolling in or attending public school. Nevertheless, these rights are broadly interpreted when a perpetrator's motive is tainted by racial hatred. Federal legislation is currently [2009] pending which, if passed, would add gender, sexual orientation, gender identity, and disability to this list. It would also remove the prerequisite that the victim be engaging in a federally protected activity. See previous discussion in this chapter under the heading "Hate Crime Laws Specific to LGBT Persons as Victims."

A victim of a hate/bias crime that violates a federal law can initiate criminal prosecution by reporting the crime to a local office of the FBI. That office then assigns an investigator to the case. A victim may also contact the local U.S. attorney's office or the criminal section of the Civil Rights Division at the U.S. Department of Justice in Washington, D.C. In addition to criminal prosecution, a victim can pursue a civil suit if the facts support a civil action under the federal statutes. The victim can seek both damages and injunctive relief in civil action against the perpetrator of violence that is motivated by racial, sexual orientation, gender, or disability hatred.

In general, the federal criminal statutes are intended to supplement state and local criminal laws. Procedurally, the U.S. Department of Justice (DOJ) will not become actively involved in prosecuting a particular action until local authorities have concluded their case. After a person is convicted or acquitted in state courts, the DOJ evaluates the result before determining whether to prosecute under federal statutes. There is no set time within which the Justice Department makes its decision.

State Laws

As of April, 2009, as mentioned earlier, 45 states and the District of Columbia have hate crime statutes criminalizing various types of bias-motivated violence or intimidation ("Strengthen Hate Crime Laws," 2009). However, a significant number of those statutes do not include coverage of crimes based on sexual orientation or gender identity.

Many states have enacted "penalty-enhancements" statutes, which were upheld unanimously by the U.S. Supreme Court in June 1993 in its decision in a Wisconsin case (*Wisconsin v. Mitchell*, 508 U.S. 476, 1993). Penalty enhancements are legal when the defendant intentionally selects his or her victim based on the victim's race, religion, national origin, sexual orientation, gender, or disability. Many states have also enhanced criminal penalties for vandalism aimed at houses of worship, cemeteries, schools, and community centers.

Why Special Laws and Penalty Enhancements?

There are those, including some law enforcement leaders, who argue that there is no need for special laws dealing with hate/bias crimes because there are already statutes covering specific crimes. For example, an assault by one person on another is prosecutable in all jurisdictions. Therefore, the argument runs, why would such an assault be prosecuted differently even if it is motivated by a person's hate or bias toward victims because of their color, ethnic background, religion, sexual orientation, gender, or disability? Localities and states headed by leaders with this perspective have no system for identifying, reporting, investigating, and prosecuting hate/bias crimes. Thus, there are deficiencies in the way some law enforcement agencies and prosecutors process hate crimes.

First, incidents are not classified by racial, ethnic, sexual orientation, disability, or religious motivation, making it virtually impossible to tabulate acts of hate violence, spot trends, perform analyses, or develop response strategies. Second, an inaccurate characterization of certain types of hate violence crimes occurs. For example, cross burnings are variously classified as malicious mischief, vandalism, or burning without a permit. Swastika paintings are often classified as graffiti incidents or malicious mischief.

There are also some key differences that make hate/bias crimes more serious than standard offenses, justifying the establishment of special laws and sentence enhancements. "Hate crimes differ from other forms of interpersonal violence in three important ways. They are more vicious, extremely brutal, and frequently perpetrated at random on total strangers (commonly a single victim) by multiple offenders (usually groups of white, working-class male teenagers)" (National Coalition of Anti-Violence Programs, 2006). Compared to nonbias assaults, hate/bias crimes have been found, through statistical studies, to be about three times more violent, twice as likely to cause injury, and four times more likely to result in hospitalization. Another justification for the enhancement of penalties is that "bias crimes have been found by criminologists to be irrational in nature, particularly disruptive and threatening both to victims and to the community compared to those [crimes] which have some rational cause. Similar findings are that bias crimes are far more likely to be committed randomly against victims by complete strangers than conventional crimes" ("The Severity of Crime," 1984, p.16). The irrational nature of bias crimes, the studies conclude, makes them highly socially disruptive, because "whole groups of citizens are placed in constant fear of random violence from attackers with whom they have no direct connection" ("The Severity of Crime," 1984, p. 9). Crimes of this sort deny the free exercise of civil rights, sometimes frightening the victim out of exercising freedom of speech, association, and assembly. Often, the attacks are acts of terrorism intended to punish the victim for being visible (i.e., a person who looks or acts different is easy for a bigoted person to single out). Finally, these acts against individuals are also often meant to terrorize entire communities.

"Bias crimes are also at least twice as likely to involve multiple offenders acting in concert, often against a single victim. Nationally, approximately 25 percent of violent crimes are committed by two or more offenders" ("The Severity of Crime," 1984, p. 21). Hate/bias crimes require more police resources for investigation, community response, and victim assistance than most other crimes. There is, therefore, a national consensus that such crimes justify special laws and enhanced penalties for offenders. They send a clear message to the perpetrator and the public that these crimes will not be tolerated and will be treated as serious offenses.

HATE/BIAS CRIME AND INCIDENT INVESTIGATIONS

Criminal justice agencies must make hate/bias crimes a priority for response, from the initial report through prosecution. To ensure that all personnel treat such crimes seriously, each agency must have written policies and procedures that establish protocol for a quick and effective response. Only when policies and procedures as well as feasible community programs, are in place, will society begin to control and reduce hate crimes.

Law enforcement agencies must provide investigators with training that includes such critical elements as understanding the role of the investigator, identifying a hate/bias crime, classifying an offender, interviewing a victim, relating to a community, and prosecuting an offender. When hate/bias crimes occur, they require investigators' timely response, understanding, and vigilance to ensure a careful and successful investigation. Investigators must have a comprehensive knowledge of the general elements and motivations behind hate/bias crimes and must recognize the potential of these crimes to affect not only the primary victim, but also the victim's family, other members of the victim's group, and the larger community.

There are general and specific procedures and protocols that should be used in response to crimes and incidents motivated by the victim's race, religion, ethnic background, or sexual orientation (RRES). These include actions to be taken by each of the following categories of personnel:

- Assigned officer/first responder
- Patrol field supervisor
- Watch commander
- Assigned investigator or specialized unit
- Crime prevention, community relations, or specialized unit
- Training unit

The actual guidelines may vary among jurisdictions, but the basics are the same. Specific guidelines are available from federal and state organizations or police and sheriffs' departments. Some law enforcement agencies have model protocols that could be secured and used in the classroom or by departments who have not developed their own procedures.

Models for Investigating Hate/Bias Crimes

The following are suggested guidelines for law enforcement agencies without standardized protocol for follow-up of hate/bias crimes and incidents. The suggested formats are based on the size of the department.

SMALL DEPARTMENT (AGENCIES OF 1 TO 100 SWORN)   A small department may not have the staffing depth to have a specialized unit or investigator who can deal solely with hate crimes. Officers in small departments are usually generalists, meaning that they carry any type of case from the initial report through the investigation and submission to the district attorney. Therefore, all personnel should receive awareness training on cultural and racial issues and learn the requirements of handling crimes and incidents motivated by hate. The officer who takes the crime or incident report must have it approved by his or her supervisor. Some small departments have allowed patrol officers to specialize in the investigation of certain crimes; they might be involved in either providing advice and direction or actually taking the case and handling it to its conclusion. These officers are usually the ones allowed to attend training and conferences that will teach and update them on the investigations of these crimes and incidents. Some departments have a patrol supervisor perform the follow-up investigation and submit the case to the prosecutor's office. It is important that the officer and his or her supervisor keep command officers informed of major cases. Small agencies with a detective follow-up investigations unit must make sure that unit members are trained in aspects of dealing with crimes motivated by hate.

MEDIUM-SIZED DEPARTMENT (AGENCIES OF 100 TO 500 SWORN)   The following is a model suggested for a medium-sized department with a crimes-against-persons investigations unit and an administration unit responsible for community relations or affairs. The format follows this protocol: The responding patrol officer takes the initial report, decides if what occurred was indeed a crime or incident motivated by hate or bias, and then completes a preliminary investigation. Then the officer documents the findings on the department offense report form and follows the policy and procedure as established by the agency. The officer's supervisor and watch commander approve the report (which may or may not already be classified as a hate/bias or civil rights violation, depending on department policy). Then it is forwarded to the investigations unit that follows up on such cases (usually the crimes persons unit). The investigations unit supervisor reviews the report and again evaluates whether a crime or incident took place. If it is decided that it is a hate/bias crime, the report is assigned to a crimes persons investigator *who specializes in this type of investigation*.

A copy of the report is also forwarded (through the appropriate chain of command) to the administration or community relations unit for follow-up. The staff of the latter unit is also trained to handle hate/bias and civil rights violations investigations and to provide victim assistance. The administrative follow-up would include:

- Investigations required
- Referrals and support for the victim
- Conducting of public meetings to resolve neighborhood problems
- Conflict resolution
- Liaison with the diverse organizations in the community and victim advocates

Some cases may require that the criminal investigator and the administrative officer work jointly to resolve the crime or incident under investigation.

LARGE DEPARTMENTS (AGENCIES OF 500-PLUS SWORN)   Most large departments have enough staff that they can have a specialized unit. There are many advantages to having a specialized unit that focuses on crimes motivated by hate/bias or civil rights violations. The investigators become familiar and experienced with the law and special procedures required and can handle more complex, sensitive cases. Investigators who are allowed to specialize can form networks with victim advocate organizations, other police agencies, and community-based agencies. They work closely with the district attorney's office (probably with a special bias unit within that agency), establishing the working relationships and rapport important to successful prosecutions. The investigators develop a sense of pride in their efforts and a commitment to provide a competent investigative and victim assistance response. Since the primary function of the unit is hate/bias crime investigations, officers can sometimes develop knowledge of individuals and groups that commit such offenses and become more aware of where the incidents occur.

Detectives who handle a multitude of cases do not have the time to track and monitor these crimes and therefore may not spot trends. Specialized units can evaluate the field performance of the patrol officers who have handled such crimes and can provide suggestions for improvement or commendations when the response has been effective or innovative.

There are also disadvantages to specialized units. Often, when there is a specialized unit, patrol officers believe that what is happening in the neighborhood in which they work is not their problem—it is the problem of the specialized unit. The officer takes reports and then transfers responsibility for resolution of problems. Patrol officers may be unaware of a problem or its magnitude or even what resources are being marshaled to resolve it unless there is good communication between them and the members of the specialized unit. These disadvantages are surmountable, however, especially if the department uses community-oriented policing strategies, which usually involve a higher degree of communication among agency units and with the community.

Hate crimes that fit certain criteria, to be discussed later, are investigated at the federal level by the FBI's Bias Crimes Unit and the Bureau of Alcohol, Tobacco and Firearms (BATF), and church arson and explosives experts. BATF investigators also focus on regulating the illegal sale to and possession of firearms by potential perpetrators of hate crimes.

HATE/BIAS CRIME PROSECUTION

District Attorneys' or Prosecutors' Office

Many district attorneys' offices in the United States now have attorneys and/or units that specialize in hate crime prosecution. These agencies have established policies and procedures designed to prosecute such crimes effectively and efficiently. There are compelling reasons for district attorneys to devote special attention and resources to these crimes. A prosecutor has discretion to influence, if not determine, what might be called the public safety climate that citizens in the communities he or she serves will experience. Establishing a public safety climate that fosters the full enjoyment of civil and political rights by the minority members of our communities requires a focused political will directed to that end, as well as resources and capacity. The most effective and successful approaches to building a climate of public safety have been those that:

- Established specialized hate crimes or civil rights violations units.
- Standardized procedures to prosecute hate crime cases (this standardization should include vertical prosecution of cases).
- Appointed attorneys to be liaisons with various ethnic, racial, religious, and sexual orientation groups in the community.
- Provided all attorneys on staff with cultural awareness or sensitivity training.
- Provided alternative sentencing programs aimed at rehabilitating individuals who commit hate-motivated crimes. (One example is the ADL's "The Juvenile Diversion Program: Learning about Differences," a 9-week series for students and sometimes parents on civil rights law, racism, anti-Semitism, the Holocaust, and the legacy of discrimination against minorities in America.)

District attorneys can play a major role in educating judges on the nature, prevalence, and severity of hate crime and in encouraging effective sentences for this offense. They can also be very effective in their working relationships with and encouragement of police officers investigating these crimes. The effort involves each member of the criminal justice system, but the prosecutor has one of the most important roles.

Special Problems in Prosecuting Hate/Bias Crimes

Prosecutors confront an array of issues when considering a potential hate crime. Ascertaining the real motivation for someone's behavior is difficult, and actually proving that a person took an action because of hate can be an arduous task. Hate crime charges are the only ones for which proving motive becomes as important as proving modus operandi. Juries can often find it impossible to conclude with certainty what was going on in a suspect's mind during the crime. Attorneys who handle hate/bias crimes indicate that there are four potential obstacles to successful prosecutions:

1. Proving the crime was motivated by bias
2. Uncooperative, complaining witnesses
3. Special defenses
4. Lenient sentences

Prosecutors, given these obstacles, sometimes have difficulty deciding whether to file hate crime charges. It is often difficult to accurately identify hate-motivated crimes or incidents. Usually, no single factor is sufficient to make the determination, and sometimes the perpetrator disguises the incident so that it does not appear to be a hate/bias crime. Even cases that have been well investigated may lack sufficient evidence to prove that the crime was motivated, beyond a reasonable doubt, by hate or bias. Generally, prosecutors follow established guidelines for determining whether a crime was bias related. Their criteria include:

- Plain common sense
- Perceptions of the victim(s) and witnesses about the crime
- Language used by the perpetrator
- Background of the perpetrator
- Severity of the attack
- Lack of provocation
- History of similar incidents in the same area
- Absence of any apparent motive

The National District Attorneys Association developed a comprehensive desk manual for prosecutors for identifying, responding to, and preventing hate violence. The desk manual, titled *Hate Crime: A Local Prosecutor's Guide for Responding to Hate Crime*, contains information about working with outside agencies and organizations, case screening and investigation, case assignment and preparation, victim and witness impact and support, trial preparation, sentencing alternatives, and prevention efforts. The manual could be useful in the development of a training curriculum specifically designed for prosecutors. The association's website, which is listed at the end of this chapter, provides information on how to order the desk manual.

Objective Evidence: Bias Motivation

It is important that first responders and investigators properly identify and classify bias-motivated crimes. Officers unsure about identifying a potential hate/bias crime should consult with a supervisor or an expert (even outside the agency) on the topic. To help investigators determine whether an incident meets sufficient objectively determined criteria to be classified as a hate/bias crime, the U.S. Department of Justice developed a document, "Summary Reporting System: Hate Crime Data Collection Guidelines," which contains a series of examples related to the reporting of hate crime incidents. These examples are intended to ensure uniformity in reporting data to the state and the FBI's UCR Section. The following are a few examples of guidelines:

- The offender and the victim were of different racial, religious, ethnic/national origin, or sexual orientation groups. For example, the victim was black and the offenders were white.
- Bias-related oral comments, written statements, or gestures were made by the offender that indicated his or her bias. For example, the offender shouted a racial epithet at the victim.
- Bias-related drawings, markings, symbols, or graffiti were left at the crime scene. For example, a swastika was painted on the door of a synagogue.
- The victim was visiting a neighborhood where previous hate crimes had been committed against other members of his or her racial, religious, ethnic/national origin, or sexual orientation group and where tensions remain high against his or her group.
- Several incidents have occurred in the same locality, at or about the same time, and the victims are all of the same racial, religious, ethnic/national origin, or sexual orientation group.
- A substantial portion of the community where the crime occurred perceives that the incident was motivated by bias.

For a complete list of guidelines recommended by the Department of Justice, the website where "Summary Reporting System: Hate Crime Data Collection Guidelines" can be ordered is listed at the end of this chapter.

Because of the difficulty of knowing with certainty that a crime was motivated by bias, the Hate Crimes Statistics Act stipulates that bias is to be reported only if the investigation reveals sufficient objective facts that would lead a reasonable and prudent person to conclude that the offender's actions were motivated, in whole or in part, by bias. The specific types of bias to be reported are as follows (U.S. Department of Justice, 1990, p. 15):

Racial Bias

Antiwhite

Antiblack

Anti-American Indian or Alaskan Native

Anti-Asian/Pacific Islander

Antimultiracial group

Religious Bias

Anti-Jewish

Anti-Catholic

Anti-Protestant

Anti-Islamic (Muslim)

Anti–other religion (Buddhism, Hinduism, Shintoism, etc.)

Anti–multireligious group

Anti-atheist or anti-agnostic

Ethnicity/National Origin Bias

Anti-Arab

Anti-Hispanic

Anti–other ethnicity/national origin

Sexual Orientation Bias

Anti–male homosexual (gay)

Anti–female homosexual (lesbian)

Antihomosexual (gays and lesbian)

Antiheterosexual

Antibisexual

Antitransgender

Training is available to help criminal justice agency personnel make decisions regarding hate/bias crimes. A few of those sources are:

- Office for Victims of Crime (OVC)
- Bureau of Justice Assistance (BJA)
- Office of Juvenile Justice and Delinquency Prevention (OJJDP)

All three sponsor grants to agencies to fund the development of programs and to provide training seminars and technical assistance to individuals and local agencies regarding hate crimes. OVC is working to improve the justice system's response to victims of hate crimes, and OJJDP funds agencies to develop training for professionals and to address hate crimes through preventive measures and community resources. BJA has a training initiative for law enforcement agencies designed to generate awareness and to help in identifying, investigating, and taking appropriate action for bias crimes, as well as arming agencies with tools for responding effectively to incidents. Websites for all three agencies are listed at the end of this chapter.

In 2002, the Southern Poverty Law Center and Auburn University at Montgomery initiated an innovative online hate crime–training program. The two organizations teamed up to develop the course "Introduction to Hate and Bias Crimes," which is offered to law enforcement officers from the United States and Canada. Such training has been being offered for years through a variety of agencies, both public and private, but constraints such as the expense of travel, time away from work, and the low priority given to the matter by many police agencies have hampered officers' efforts to pursue it. The online course is a way to reach law enforcement officers in small towns and rural areas. Using material from the Federal Law Enforcement Training Center (FLETC), it introduces officers to the basics of hate crime, terminology, and categories of offenders. The course uses video clips, discussion boards, and online chats with veteran hate crime experts. Completion of the course earns students either one semester hour of college credit or 10 continuing education units. Information about the course schedule, future courses, and scholarship opportunities is available online at a website listed at the conclusion of this chapter.

Mini Case Study

You decide: Are federal, state, or local laws violated in the incident described below? Can officials order the offending effigy to be taken down? Could this be considered a hate crime? Is the display, while offensive, protected by the First Amendment? 1) Apply what you learned in this chapter and discuss in class how the incident should be handled. 2) Would this case be handled differently if the effigy were of a black person?

It is Halloween of 2008, and you are a police officer who receives 60 different calls from persons offended by a display of an effigy showing the likeness of Republican vice presidential nominee Sarah Palin. The effigy is hanging by a noose from a tree on the front lawn of a home. (This actually occurred in October, 2008, in West Hollywood, California).

HATE/BIAS CRIME AND INCIDENT VICTIMOLOGY

Meaningful assistance to victims of major crimes became a priority only in the 1980s. The growth of a body of "victimology" literature (President's Task Force on Victims of Crime created by President Reagan in 1982; the Omnibus Victim and Witness Protection Act of 1982; and the Comprehensive Crime Control Act of 1984, to name a few) and the emergence of numerous victim advocate and rights organizations began at about that time, reflecting a growing concern about crime, the victims of crime, and their treatment by the criminal justice system. The public mood or perception had become (and may still be) that the criminal justice system cares only about the defendant. The perception was that the defendant's rights were a priority of the system, while the victim was neglected in the process. As a result of the task force recommendations, state and federal legislation, and research by public and private organizations (most notably the National Institute of Justice), improvements were made in victim services and treatment as well as in the criminal justice system.

Law Enforcement and the Victim

For the most part, perpetrators of hate crimes commit them to intimidate a victim and members of the victim's community so that the victims feel isolated, vulnerable, and unprotected by the law. Many victims do not report their attacks to police out of fear and believe their best defense is to remain quiet. Other reasons for this behavior, in addition to those outlined earlier in this chapter, include:

- fear of revictimization or retaliation
- fear of having privacy compromised
- for gays, lesbians, bisexual, or transgender individuals, fear of repercussions from being "outed" by family, friends, and employers
- fear of law enforcement and uncertainty about the criminal justice system responses
- for aliens, fear of jeopardizing immigration status, being reported to INS, or deportation
- humiliation or shame about being victimized
- lack of support systems within the community
- cultural and language barriers

In the law enforcement field, courses in recruit academies and advanced in-service officer programs typically include training about victimization that covers such topics as sociopsychological effects of victimization, officer sensitivity to the victim, victim assistance and advocacy programs, and victim compensation, restitution criteria, and procedures for applying. Classes normally stress the importance of keeping victims informed of their case status and of the criminal justice process. How patrol officers and investigators of such crimes interact with victims affects the victims' immediate and long-term physical and emotional recovery. Proper treatment of victims also increases their willingness to cooperate in the total criminal justice process. Because of such training programs, the victims of hate crimes began receiving special attention and assistance in progressive cities and counties all over the country.

Victims of hate/bias violence generally express three needs: (1) to feel safe, (2) to feel that people care, and (3) to get assistance. To address the first two needs, law enforcement agencies and all personnel involved in contacts with victims must place special emphasis on victim assistance to reduce trauma and fear. Such investigations sometimes involve working with people from diverse ethnic backgrounds, races, and/or sexual orientation. Many victims may be recent immigrants with limited English and unfamiliar with the American legal system, or may have fears of the police, courts, or government rooted in negative experiences from their countries of origin. In many Asian countries, for example, there is a history of police corruption. Often, immigrants who are victims of crimes in the United States think that reporting of a crime may not only be futile but could invite unwanted and costly attention because of their experiences in their own countries.

Therefore, the officer or investigator must be not only a skilled interviewer and listener but also sensitive to and knowledgeable about cultural and racial differences and ethnicity. He or she must have the ability to show compassion and sensitivity toward the victim and his or her plight while gathering the evidence required for prosecution. As when dealing with other crime victims, officers involved in the investigation must:

- approach victims in an empathic and supportive manner and demonstrate concern and sensitivity;
- attempt to calm the victim and reduce the victim's alienation;
- reassure the victim that every available investigative and enforcement tool will be utilized by the police to find and prosecute the person or persons responsible for the crime;
- consider the safety of the victim by recommending and providing extra patrol and/or providing prevention and precautionary advice;
- provide referral information to entities such as counseling and other appropriate public support and assistance agencies;
- advise the victim of criminal and civil options.

The stress experienced by victims of hate/bias crime or incidents may be heightened by a perceived level of threat or personal violation. Just like the victims of rape or abuse, many become traumatized when they have to recall the details of what occurred. Sometimes the victim, because of what happened to him or her, transfers his or her anger or hostility to the officer—a psychological reaction called *transference*. The officer must be prepared for this reaction and must be able to defuse the situation professionally without resorting to anger. It is imperative that investigators and officers make every effort to treat hate crime victims with dignity and respect so that they feel that they will receive justice. Insensitive, brash, or unaware officers or investigators may not only alienate victims, witnesses, or potential witnesses, but also create additional distrust or hostility and cause others in the community to distrust the entire police department.

Addressing the victim's need to get assistance requires that the community have established resources that can assist the victim and the victim group (e.g., gays, Hispanics). Few communities have the resources necessary to offer comprehensive victim services. Even where resources are available, victims are often unaware of them because of poor public awareness programs or the failure of the criminal justice system to make appropriate referrals because of a lack of training or motivation. A key resource is the availability of interpreters for non-English-speaking victims and witnesses. Ideally, jurisdictions with large populations of non-English-speaking minorities should recruit and train an appropriate number of bilingual employees. If the jurisdiction does not have an investigator who speaks the same language, an interpreter system should be in place for immediate callout. Victims of hate-motivated incidents are encouraged to report the circumstances to the National Hate Crimes Hotline (1-800-347-HATE).

Readers wishing additional information about how to deal with victims can refer to *Victims of Crime*, by Jerin and Moriarty (1997). It is a well-developed textbook for the field of victimology that has many criminal justice applications. Another resource for first responders, *Bringing Victims into Community Policing*, was developed by the National Center for Victims of Crime and the Police Foundation. The publication, available on the NCVC website, provides guidelines for dealing with specific types of crime victims.

Summary

- The federal Hate Crime Statistics Act of 1990 encouraged states to collect and report hate crime data to the Federal Bureau of Investigation. The FBI, in partnership with local law enforcement agencies, collects data on hate/bias incidents, offenses, victims, offenders, and motivations and publishes an annual report as part of the Uniform Crime Reporting (UCR) Program.

- In the United States, crimes motivated by hate have historically been directed against immigrant groups. Native Americans, African Americans, Jews, gays, lesbians, and bisexual and transgender individuals, as well as people of Arab or Middle Eastern descent continue to be victims of bias, discrimination, and crimes motivated by hate.

- The federal definition of hate crime falls under Title 18 U.S.C. Section 45. Although state definitions and statutes vary, in general a hate crime is considered to be a criminal act, or attempted act, against a person, institution, or property, that is motivated in whole or in part by the offender's bias against a race, color, religion, gender, ethnic/national origin group, disability status, or sexual orientation group. The prevalence of hate/bias crimes and incidents is often attributed to changing national and international conditions, immigration, and demographic changes translated to a local environment. Urban dynamic theories attempt to explain hate crime and hate incidents as occurring due to the relationships among the clustering of new immigrant groups, the economy, and move-in violence.

- Jews belong to a religious and cultural group that has experienced discrimination, persecution, and violence throughout history because their religious beliefs and practices often set them apart from the majority.

- The acronym or initials LGBT refers to lesbian, gay, bisexual, and transgender people. Hate crimes targeting LGBT individuals are distinct from other bias crimes because they target a group made up of every other category discussed within this textbook. Every year, in the United States, thousands of LGBT persons are harassed, beaten, or murdered solely because of their sexual orientation or gender identity.

- Criminal justice agencies must make hate/bias crimes a priority for response, from the initial report through prosecution. All law enforcement personnel must treat such crimes seriously. Law enforcement agencies must provide all responders and investigators with training on the various protocols relating to hate/bias crimes. It is also sometimes necessary for the agency to establish liaisons with diverse organizations in the community and with victim advocates.

- District attorneys' offices have established policies and procedures designed to prosecute hate/bias crimes effectively. This is necessary in order to establish a public safety climate that fosters the full enjoyment of civil and political rights by minority members of communities.

- Meaningful assistance to victims of hate/bias crimes should be a priority for members of the criminal justice system that investigate and prosecute perpetrators. Perpetrators of hate crimes commit them to intimidate a victim and members of the victim's community so that the victims feel isolated, vulnerable, and unprotected by the law. Criminal justice agency employees dealing with the victims of hate/bias crimes must be aware of and sensitive to the sociopsychological effects of victimization.

Discussion Questions and Issues

1. **Hate/Bias Crimes and Incident Reduction.** Make a list of important elements in the design of a community-based program to reduce the number of hate/bias crimes and incidents in your area.

2. **Move-in Violence.** Discuss, in a group setting, what strategies might be used by a community to reduce the impact of move-in violence on a new immigrant.

3. *Victims of Hate/Bias Crimes or Incidents.* Have you been the victim of a hate/bias crime or incident? Share the experience with others in a group setting: the circumstances, the feelings you experienced, how you responded, and what action was taken by any community-based agency or organization.

4. *Victim Resources.* Find out what resources exist in your community to assist victims of hate/bias crimes.
   a. Which groups provide victim assistance?
   b. Which coalition groups exist, and what types of community outreach programs are offered?

c. What types of pamphlets or other written materials are available?
d. Which groups have speakers' bureaus?
e. Which groups are working with local law enforcement agencies with regard to response programs or cultural awareness training?
f. Which groups are working with the district attorney's office?
g. What types of legislative lobbying efforts are taking place, and who is championing the work?

Website Resources

Visit these websites for additional information about hate crimes and victim assistance:

American-Arab Anti-Discrimination Committee (ADC): http://www.adc.org

This website offers information about the ADC's civil rights efforts and useful summary data about cases and complaints regarding hate crimes and discrimination involving Arab Americans.

Anti-Defamation League (ADL): http://www.adl.org

The ADL provides a source of model policies and procedures for the investigation and tracking of crimes motivated by hate.

Bureau of Justice Statistics (BJS):
http://www.ojp.usdoj.gov/bjs

This website contains data about crimes reported by law enforcement agencies across the nation to the FBI. BJS is also a resource center for justice topics such as training, technical assistance, publications, and grants.

Community Relations Service (CRS):
http://www.usdoj.gov/crs/

The Community Relations Service is the Department of Justice's "peacemaker" for community conflicts and tensions arising from differences of race, color, and national origin. CRS assists communities in developing local mechanisms, conducting training, and instituting other proactive measures to prevent or reduce racial/ethnic tension.

National District Attorneys' Association:
http://www.ndaa.org

This website is a resource for information on many subjects. The association produced a guide titled *Hate Crime: A Local Prosecutor's Guide for Responding to Hate Crime*, which covers several

issues that arise during hate crime prosecutions. By highlighting model protocols and procedures from offices around the nation, the resource guide will help prosecutors' offices develop policies and procedures on handling hate crime investigations and prosecutions. It will also provide a comprehensive roadmap to individual prosecutors who handle hate crime cases. Both prosecutors who are working on their first hate crime case and the more experienced prosecutors of bias crimes will find the resource guide helpful.

National Gay and Lesbian Task Force (NGLTF):
http://www.ngltf.org

NGLTF gathers and studies information about lesbian, gay, bisexual, and transgender individuals as victims of crimes motivated by hate.

Office for Victims of Crime (OVC):
http://www.ojp.us.doj.gov/ovc

The site provides information about victims of crime and models for providing victim services. It also provides resources for training, publications, research, statistics, program funding, and grants pertaining to victims of crime.

International Association of Chiefs of Police:
http://www.theiacp.org

This website provides an online resource for law enforcement issues publications including *Recruitment/Retention of Qualified Police Personnel: A Best Practices Guide*, December 7, 2001.

Minorities in Law Enforcement (MILE):
http://www.mile4kids.com

The Minorities in Law Enforcement organization is a culturally diverse, nonprofit coalition of law enforcement professionals working in concert with elected officials and the private sector to give at-risk urban youth better alternatives to crime, violence, gangs, and drugs. Membership is not limited to law enforcement officers.

National Conference for Community and Justice (NCCJ): http://www.ncjj.org

NCCJ's programming facilitates community and interfaith dialogues and provides workplace consultations, youth leadership development, and seminarian and educator training. Its nationally recognized research provides data and analysis results to the evolving study of intergroup relations, and its public policy arm works with government leaders and advocates policies that reflect understanding and respect.

National Congress of American Indians (NCAI): http://www.ncai.org

NCAI addresses a broad range of policy matters in its efforts to advocate on behalf of American Indian and Alaska Native tribal governments.

National Council of La Raza (NCLR): http://www.nclr.org

NCLR is the largest national Hispanic civil rights and advocacy organization in the United States. The private, nonprofit, nonpartisan organization works to improve opportunities for Hispanic Americans. NCLR conducts research, policy analysis, and advocacy, providing a Latino perspective in five key areas: assets/investments, civil rights/immigration, education, employment and economic status, and health.

National Office of Victim Assistance (NOVA): http://www.nova.org

NOVA is a good resource for victim assistance networks. The organization is based in Washington, D.C., and can be reached at (202) 393-6682.

Office of Juvenile Justice and Delinquency Prevention (OJJDP): http://www.ojjdp.ncjrs.org

OJJDP is a resource center for programs, publications, training, and grants regarding juvenile justice and delinquency prevention.

The Prejudice Institute: http://www.prejudiceinstitute.org

A resource for activists, lawyers, and social scientists, the Prejudice Institute is devoted to policy research and education on all dimensions of prejudice, discrimination, and ethnoviolence.

Simon Wiesenthal Center: http://www.wiesenthal.com

The Simon Wiesenthal Center is an international Jewish human rights organization dedicated to preserving the memory of the Holocaust by fostering tolerance and understanding through community involvement, educational outreach, and social action. The Center confronts important contemporary issues including racism, anti-Semitism, terrorism, and genocide.

Southern Poverty Law Center (SPLC): http://www.splcenter.org

SPLC is an excellent resource for information about and statistics concerning hate organizations. As mentioned in this chapter, SPLC offers an online training course, "Introduction to Hate and Bias Crimes," for law enforcement officers from the United States and Canada. Information about the course is available at http://www.intelligence-project.org.

U.S. Department of Justice (DOJ): http://www.doj.gov

The U.S. Department of Justice developed a document, "Summary Reporting System: Hate Crime Data Collection Guidelines," which contains a series of examples related to the reporting of hate crime incidents. These examples are intended to ensure uniformity in reporting data to the state and the FBI's UCR section. The Guidelines can be ordered via the website. The FBI offers training for law enforcement officers and administrators on developing data-collection procedures. For more information, contact the FBI at 1-888-UCR-NIBR. See also *Hate/Bias Crimes Train-the-Trainer Program*, conducted by the National Center for State, Local and International Law Enforcement Training, Federal Law Enforcement Training Center (FLETC), and U.S. Treasury Department. Also available from the DOJ is "Twenty Plus Things Law Enforcement Agencies Can Do to Prevent or Respond to Hate Incidents Against Arab-Americans, Muslims, and Sikhs." The document lists a number of ways law enforcement agencies can prevent or respond to hate incidents against these persons. These include community assessments, patrol practices, community outreach, conducting training, and departmental policies and procedures review. The website for this particular document is http://www.usdoj.gov/crs/twentyplus.htm

Vera Institute of Justice: http://www.vera.org

The Vera Institute of Justice works closely with leaders in government and civil society to improve the services people rely on for safety and justice. Vera develops innovative, affordable programs

that often grow into self-sustaining organizations, studies social problems and current responses, and provides practical advice and assistance to government officials around the world. It has publications on many law enforcement subjects.

References

"ADL Applauds Law Enforcement for Arrests of Homegrown Terrorists in Plot to Blow up New York City Synagogues." (2009, May 21). ADL on-line. Retrieved May 27, 2009, available at www.adl.org/PresRele/ASUS_12/5532_12.htm.

"ADL Decries the Anti-Semitic Vandalism of Five Jewish Institutions in Chicago." (2009, January 12). ADL on-line. Retrieved April 20, 2009, available at www.adl.org.

"Admirals, Generals: Repeal 'Don't Ask, Don't Tell.' " (2008, November 18). *ABC News.* Retrieved May 27, 2009, available at abcnews.go.com/US/wireStory?id=6274139.

"Alito's Landmark Ruling Supports Bullied Gay Students." (2005, November 11). *Gay & Lesbian Times*, p. 38.

"Anti-Lesbian, Gay, Bisexual and Transgender Violence in 2007." (2008). A Report of the National Coalition of Anti-Violence Programs, 2008 Release Edition. New York, NY.

"Audit of Anti-Semitic Incidents 1987 to 2007." (2008). ADL on-line. Retrieved April 20, 2009, available at www.adl.org.

Berrill, K. (2006). National Gay and Lesbian Task Force, personal communications.

"FBI, NYPD Arrest 4 in Alleged Plot to Bomb NY Synagogues." (2009, May 21). NBC Universal on-line. Retrieved May 28, 2009, available at www.nbc-newyork.com/news/local/FBI-Bust-Plot-Foiled.html.

Felsenthal, A. (2004, June 14). "Hate Crimes Bill Passes Senate." *IN Magazine*, p. 13.

Foxman, A. (2005, April 22). "After 350 Years, Still a Lot to Do." *Haaretz*, p. 1.

"Gay and Lesbian Anti-Violence Project Releases Data on 2005 Hate Incidents." (2006, May 22). AVP Media Release, on-line: Anti-Violence Project, El Paso, Tex. Available: www.lambda.org.

"Gay killing draws call for change." (2008, March 29). *Contra Costa Times*, p. A7.

"Gay Miami Teen Gets Accolades for Inspiring Peers." (2005, January 6). *Gay & Lesbian Times*, p. 28.

Grobeson, M. (2009). Sergeant (Ret.), Los Angeles Police Department, personal communication.

"Hate Crimes—Anti-Latino Hate Crime Up for Fourth Year." (2008, Winter). Intelligence Report, Southern Poverty Law Center. Retrieved April 20, 2009, available at www.splcenter.org/intel/intelrep;ort/intrep.isp.

"Hate Crimes Statistics 2007." (2008, October). Bureau of Justice Statistics Special Report, U.S. Department of Justice, Office of Justice Programs, Washington, D.C. Available at: www.ojp.usdoj.gov/bjs

International Association of Chiefs of Police (IACP). (1999). "Responding to Hate Crimes: A Police Officer's Guide to Investigation and Prevention." Publications online: www.theiacp.org

"Jail Brawls Reflect Larger Race-Relations Problems." (2006, February 21). *Washington Post*, p. A8.

Jerin, Robert A., and Loura J. Moriarty. (1997). *Victims of Crime.* Chicago, Ill.: Nelson-Hall.

"Killers Get Maximum Prison Time." (2006, January 28). *Contra Costa Times*, p. A1, A6.

"Literary Stereotyping." (2003, January). *The Blade—Transitions: Transgender News & Commentary*, p. 88.

"Local Law Enforcement Hate Crimes Prevention Act of 2007." (2009). Retrieved April 16, 2009, available at GovTrack.us. (database of federal legislation): http://www.govtrack.us/congress.

Manley, R. (2006, March). Columnist, Transgender Activist (National Transgender Action Coalition), personal communications with Mitchell Grobeson.

National Coalition of Anti-Violence Programs. (2006). "Anti-Lesbian, Gay, Bisexual and Transgender Violence in 2005."

"2007 National School Climate Survey." (2008, October 8). Gay, Lesbian and Straight Education Network. Retrieved April 20, 2009, available at www.glsen.org.

"New Call for Hate Crime Change in Alabama." (2005, December 15). *Gay & Lesbian Times*, p. 35.

"Obama Election Spurs Race Crimes Around Country." (2008, November 16). *ABC News.* Retrieved

April 20, 2009, available at abcnews.go.com/US/wireStory?id=6263743.

"Pattern of Severe Anti-LGBT Violence Nationwide." (2008, August 4). National Coalition of Anti-Violence Programs. Retrieved April 20, 2009, available at www.ncavp.org.

Rennison, C. (2001). "Violent Victimization and Race, 1993–98." Washington, D.C.: National Institute of Justice.

"S.1105—The So-Called Hate Crimes Bill." (2007). Retrieved April 20, 2009, available at http://www.traditionalvalues.org.

"Strengthen Hate Crime Laws." (2009, April). *The Philadelphia Inquirer.* Retrieved April 20, 2009, available at www.adl.org.

"Stonewalled: Police Abuse and Misconduct against Lesbian, Gay, Bisexual, and Transgender People in the U.S." (2005). New York, NY: Amnesty International USA.

"The Severity of Crime." (1984, January). Bureau of Justice Statistics, Bulletin No. NCJ-92326, pp. 9, 16, 17 and 21. U.S. Department of Justice, Office of Justice Programs, Washington D.C. Available at: www.ojp.usdoj.gov/bjs

"Two Defendants in Gay Bashing Case Avoid Prison." (2006, June 22). *Gay & Lesbian Times*, p. 36.

U.S. Commission on Civil Rights, Intimidation, and Violence. (1990, September). Racial and Religious Bigotry in America (Clearing House Publications No. 96). Washington, D.C.: U.S. Government Printing Office.

U.S. Department of Justice. (1990). Summary Reporting System: Hate Crime Data Collection Guide Lines. Washington, D.C.: U.S. Government Printing Office.

"Variables Affecting Crime, 2007." (2008, October). Bureau of Justice Statistics, U.S. Department of Justice, Office of Justice Programs, Washington D.C. Available at: www.ojp.usdoj.gov/bjs

Wallace, S. (1987). "Elderly Nicaraguans and Immigrant Community Formation in San Francisco." Unpublished doctoral dissertation, University of California, San Francisco.

Wallace, S. (1992, November 9). personal communication.

CHAPTER 12

Hate/Bias Crimes: Reporting, Monitoring, and Response Strategies

LEARNING OBJECTIVES

After reading this chapter you should be able to:

- Discuss the nationwide reporting system for hate crime data collection.
- Explain the need for standardized and comprehensive statistics for the analysis of trends related to hate crimes and bias.
- Identify extremist hate groups and organizations that monitor them.
- Develop community response strategies to reduce hate crimes and incidents.
- Understand the scanning methodology and approaches for hate/bias crimes in multicultural communities.

OUTLINE

INTRODUCTION

Changing demographics in almost every part of the United States require that all localities deal with issues of intergroup relations. The ideal of harmony in diversity is offset by increased stress on the social fabric of a community, stress that often leads to bigoted or violent acts. Newspaper headlines across the country provide convincing examples of disharmony on a daily basis. Hate/bias crimes are not a new phenomenon; they have been present for generations. It is crucial for law enforcement to maintain accurate and thorough documentation of such crimes.

Data must be collected at local levels and sent in a standardized fashion to state and national clearinghouses so that proper resources may be allocated to hate/bias crime investigations, prosecutions, and victim assistance. Such a system provides information necessary not only to the criminal justice system but also to public policymakers, civil rights activists, legislators, victim advocates, and the general public. The data, if comprehensive and accurate, provide a reliable statistical picture of the problem. Agencies collecting data have also been able to use the statistics to strengthen their arguments and rationale for new hate crime penalty enhancements. In addition, the information is used in criminal justice training courses and in educating communities on the impact of the problem. Another, and possibly the most important, rationale for expending energy on tracking, analyzing, investigating, and prosecuting these crimes is that a single incident can be the tragedy of a lifetime to its victim and may also be the spark that disrupts an entire community.

Increased public awareness of and response to such crimes have largely been the result of efforts by community-based organizations and victim advocate groups. By documenting and drawing public attention to acts of bigotry and violence, these organizations laid the groundwork for the official action that followed. It is extremely important that hate groups across the United States be monitored by criminal justice agencies. Documenting and publicizing a problem does not guarantee it will be solved, but is a critical part of any strategy to create change. It also raises consciousness within the community and the criminal justice system. It is a simple but effective first step toward mobilizing a response.

HATE/BIAS CRIMES REPORTING

Purpose of Hate/Bias Crime Data Collection

Establishing a good reporting system within public organizations (e.g., human relations commissions) and the justice system is essential in every area of the country. Hate/bias crime data are collected to help police:

- Identify current and potential problems (i.e., trends)
- Respond to the needs of diverse communities
- Recruit a diverse force
- Train criminal justice personnel on the degree of the problem and the reasons for priority response

When police have information about crime patterns, they are better able to direct resources to prevent, investigate, and resolve problems pertaining to them. Tracking hate/bias incidents and crimes allows criminal justice managers to deploy their resources appropriately when fluctuations occur. Aggressive response, investigation, and prosecution of these crimes demonstrate that police are genuinely concerned and that they see such crimes as a priority. As departments show their commitment to addressing hate/bias crime, the diverse communities they serve will be more likely to see police as responsive to their concerns. A secondary benefit for a responsive agency is that blacks, Asians, Hispanics, lesbians, gays, and women would be more apt to consider law enforcement as a good career opportunity.

The Boston Police Department began recording and tracking civil rights violations in 1978, when it created its Civil Disorders Unit. Boston was probably the first law enforcement agency in the United States to record and track such crimes. The Maryland State Police Department was also a forerunner when it began to record incidents on a statewide, systematic basis as part of a pioneering government-wide effort to monitor and combat hate violence in 1981. Agencies that implemented policies and procedures to deal with hate/bias crimes during the 1980s proved to be leaders in the field; in addition to Boston and Maryland, New York, San Francisco, and Los Angeles had forward-looking programs. The policies and procedures of these agencies have been adopted as models by other organizations.

Congressional Directive: Federal Hate Crime Legislation

In response to a growing concern and in an attempt to understand the scope of the hate crime problem, the U.S. Congress enacted the federal Hate Crimes Statistics Act (HCSA) of 1990 and subsequent acts that amended the directive. The Act requires the attorney general to establish guidelines, and to collect and publish data on the prevalence of crimes motivated by bias or hate. The U.S. Attorney General delegated his agency's responsibilities under the Act to the FBI. The Uniform Crime Report (UCR) section of the FBI was assigned the task of developing the procedures for and managing the implementation of the collection of hate crime data. The national clearinghouse for hate/bias crime data enables the criminal justice system to monitor and respond to trends in those localities that voluntarily submit the information.

Uniform Crime Report System

The approach adopted by the U.S. Department of Justice incorporated a means of capturing hate crime data received from law enforcement jurisdictions into the already established nation-wide UCR program. As part of the UCR Program, the FBI publishes statistics annually in *Hate Crime Statistics.* The U.S. Department of Justice encouraged law enforcement agencies to follow the spirit of the federal legislation and to collect data voluntarily. The first UCR data were published in 1992 with participation from 6,200 law enforcement agencies. More than 17,700 city, county, state, federal, tribal, university, and college law enforcement agencies, representing 50 states and the District of Columbia, took part in the UCR program in 2007 ("Hate Crime Statistics 2007," 2008), the most recent report available. Although there was not 100 percent participation, the statistics represented over 94.6 percent of the nation's population, a vast improvement from when the program first began. As part of the attorney general's Hate Crime Initiative, the Bureau of Justice Statistics has examined ways to improve participation by law enforcement agencies in collecting hate crime statistics and reporting it to the FBI, and in profiling local responses to hate crime. The findings will assist the federal government in improving the accuracy of hate crime statistics and reporting practices and in developing a model for hate crime reporting. FBI hate crime statistics can be found on a website cited at the end of Chapter 11.

Almost all states lack a central repository for police intelligence on hate crimes. That means an investigator working in one city might not even know about a critical piece of information gathered in another location within the same state during a different incident. In 2000, California unveiled what it called the first high-tech database in the country aimed at combating hate crimes. The state implemented a computer system allowing police departments statewide to call up names, mug shots, and even the types of tattoos that identify particular individuals or groups linked to hate crimes.

HATE/BIAS CRIMES MONITORING

Monitoring Hate Groups

Monitoring extremist groups is an important obligation of law enforcement. A nationwide criminal justice reporting system tracks these groups, and their activities are also monitored through nongovernmental organizations such as:

Southern Poverty Law Center (SPLC): SPLC Report (formerly Klanwatch) and SPLC Intelligence Project: The SPLC Report and Intelligence Project are two products of the nonprofit Southern Poverty Law Center located in Montgomery, Alabama. The SPLC's Intelligence Project monitors and investigates organizations and individuals whom it deems "hate groups" and "extremists" and publishes a quarterly *Intelligence Report.* The organization considers the monitoring of white supremacist groups on a national scale and the tracking of hate crimes among its primary responsibilities. They also offer free legal services to victims of discrimination and hate crimes. The organization publishes e-mail newsletters "Hatewatch Weekly," "Mix It up Monthly," "Tolerance.org," and "Teaching Tolerance," and, in 2006, added "Immigration Watch" to report on and monitor hate and extremism in the anti-immigration movement. The Center, which began as a small civil rights law firm in 1971, is now internationally known for its hate/bias publications, tolerance education programs, legal victories against white supremacist groups, and tracking of hate groups.

Over the years, SPLC has won lawsuits against many supremacist groups, including White Aryan Resistance, Church of the Creator, Christian Knights of the KKK, Aryan Nations, and Imperial Klans of America (IKA). The legal actions resulted in the taking of those groups' assets, which crippled or ended their operations. In some cases, the assets have included homes of white supremacists and the land and/or compounds they used for meetings. A court action against IKA, the second-largest Klan organization in America, was brought in November 2008. The suit is against five members who committed an unprovoked attack on a 16-year old boy of Panamanian descent at the Meade County Fairgrounds in Brandenburg, Kentucky. The attack resulted in serious injuries to the boy. ("No. 2 Klan group on trial in KY teen's beating," 2008, p.2)

Anti-Defamation League (ADL): The Anti-Defamation League (ADL) was founded in 1913 "to stop the defamation of Jewish people and to secure justice and fair treatment to all citizens alike." The ADL has been a leader of national and state efforts in the development of legislation, policies, and procedures to deter, investigate, and counteract hate-motivated crimes. The organization is also respected for its research publications and articles dealing with such crimes. The ADL developed a recording system that has served as a model of data collection nationwide since its launch in 1979.

National Gay and Lesbian Task Force (NGLTF) and NGLTF Policy Institute: The NGLTF works to eradicate discrimination and violence based on sexual orientation and Human Immunodeficiency Virus (HIV) status. The NGLTF was founded in 1973, to serve its members in a manner that reflects the diversity of the lesbian and gay community. In 1991, the task force was restructured into two organizations—the NGLTF and the NGLTF Policy Institute—to improve its lobbying efforts and expand its organization and educational programs.

Center for Democratic Renewal: The Center for Democratic Renewal (CDR; formerly the National Anti-Klan Network) has tracked bias activity since 1982. CDR's strategy to end bigoted violence focuses on tracking bias activity, educating society through publications, and assisting victims through various programs.

Simon Wiesenthal Center: The Simon Wiesenthal Center, based in Los Angeles, is a human rights group named after the famed Nazi hunter. It monitors the Internet worldwide for tactics, language, and symbols of the high-tech hate culture. The center shares its information with affected law enforcement agencies. The organization, in some states, also operates Holocaust exhibits that are used as shocking examples of atrocities committed against Jewish people during World War II. Police academies and in-service, advanced officer training courses often use the exhibits for training on hate violence.

ORGANIZED HATE GROUPS

Knowledge of hate groups is essential when policing in a multicultural society. It is imperative for the criminal justice system to investigate (using methods including informants, surveillance, and infiltration), monitor, and control organized hate groups. Aggressive prosecution and litigation against these groups are also critical.

THE WHITE SUPREMACIST MOVEMENT   "The white supremacist movement is composed of dozens of organizations and groups, each working to create a society totally dominated by white Christians, where the human rights of lesbians and gay men and other minorities are denied. Some groups seek to create an all 'Aryan' territory; others seek to re-institutionalize Jim Crow segregation" (Center for Democratic Renewal, 1992). While most of these organizations share a common bigotry based on religion, race, ethnicity, and sexual orientation, they differ in many ways. They range from seemingly innocuous religious sects or tax protesters to openly militant, even violent, neo-Nazi skinheads and Ku Kluxers. No single organization or person dominates this movement. Frequently, individuals are members of several different groups at the same time. An SPLC Intelligence Report asserts that for the last several years white supremacist groups have focused their attention on Latino immigrants, and in particular on those who are in the country illegally. The supremacists had historically targeted blacks and Jews. These hate groups have exploited the controversy surrounding illegal immigration in order to recruit more members, especially in the states bordering Mexico. The same report, however, indicates that hate groups increasingly have turned their attention to the subprime mortgage crisis and resulting recession, which they blame on minorities ("Hate Crimes—Anti-Latino Hate Crime Up for Fourth Year," 2008).

NUMBERS OF HATE GROUPS IN THE UNITED STATES   The SPLC, as previously mentioned, tracks active hate groups in the United States. They identify hate groups by gathering information from their publications, citizens' reports, law enforcement agencies, field sources, and news

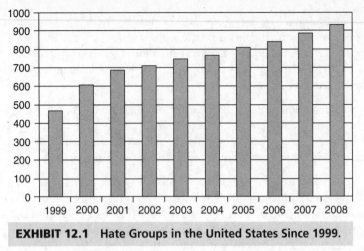

EXHIBIT 12.1 **Hate Groups in the United States Since 1999.**

Source: Southern Poverty Law Center, Special Report, March 2009.

reports. The number of groups known to be active fluctuates and is determined by surveying marches, rallies, speeches, meetings, leafleting, published literature, and criminal acts. Some white supremacist groups consist of only a few members, while others have tens of thousands. In 2009, the annual Intelligence Report of the Southern Poverty Law Center reported that there were 926 active hate groups in the United States, compared with 888 in 2007 and 602 in 2000. This is an increase of 54 percent since 2000 (see Exhibit 12.1). California had 84 active hate groups, followed by Texas with 66 and Florida with 56 ("The Year in Hate," 2009). These numbers are likely due to high illegal immigrant populations in these states, a circumstance that historically has contributed to a rise in hate groups. In addition to immigration issues, the SPLC report ascribes the increase in the number of hate groups to the economic recession and the election of the first African American president. The report explains that bigoted extremists emerge in greater numbers during bad economic times, and they focus blame for the downturn on specific groups of people. For example, they blame illegal immigrants for the subprime mortgage meltdown as already mentioned. The SPLC points out that President Barack Obama received more threats than any president did in history and that there were numerous cases of beatings, graffiti, and threats toward other African American citizens following his election.

Hate groups are categorized by the Center as Ku Klux Klan, Neo-Nazi, Racist Skinhead, Christian Identity, Black Separatist, Neo-Confederate, and Other. The "Other" category includes groups, vendors, and publishing houses endorsing a hodgepodge of racist doctrines. Although the numbers of white supremacists in the United States are small in comparison with the total population, Loretta Ross, program research director of the CDR, explains why they should be taken seriously:

Because the percentage of whites who actually belong to white supremacist groups is small, there is a general tendency to underestimate their influence. What is really significant is not the number of people actually belonging to hate groups, but the number who endorse their messages. Once known primarily for their criminal activities, racists have demonstrated a catalytic effect by tapping into the prejudices of the white majority. (Ross, 1995, p. 7)

The following is a partial list of hate groups with brief descriptions.

Neo-Nazis and Klans

The reason for concern about the activities of neo-Nazis and Klans is obvious from their history of criminal activities, and plots to launch race wars and kill officials who oppose them.

The largest of the neo-Nazi and Klan groups include the following:

Neo-Nazi-Type Groups	Klan-Type Groups
Aryan Nations	Alabama White Knights of the KKK
Knights of Freedom	America's Invisible Empire Knights
National Alliance	of the KKK
Nationalist Socialist Movement	American Knights of the KKK
World Church of the Creator	Imperial Klans of America
(Creative Movement)	Invincible Empire Knights of the KKK
	Knights of the White Kamellia
	New Order Knights of the KKK
	White Shield Knights of the KKK

The ideology of Klan members, neo-Nazis, and other white supremacists has been clear since the formation of these groups. They commonly advocate white supremacy, anti-Semitism, homophobia, and racism.

The most violent groups are the neo-Nazis, and their movements are growing in the United States and in countries such as Germany and Austria. Young people ages 13 to 25 who wish to join these organizations are required to commit a hate crime as part of the induction process. They openly idealize Hitler, and have committed murders and hundreds of assaults as well as other violent crimes; most of their victims are African Americans, Latinos, Asian Americans, gays, lesbians, bisexuals, transgender individuals, and even the homeless.

WORLD CHURCH OF THE CREATOR OR CREATIVE MOVEMENT   The World Church of the Creator (WCOTC), classified as a neo-Nazi-type group, was founded in 1973 by Ben Klassen, who wrote the organization's manifesto, *The White Man's Bible.* The organization's existence ended in mid-1990 following the suicide of Klassen and the imprisonment of other leaders. In 1996, however, the WCOTC was reborn and, according to authorities, has again become America's most dangerous white supremacist group. The group's rallying cry is "Rahowa," which stands for Racial Holy War. The group is also violently anti-Christian. A judge of the U.S. District Court in Chicago, ruled in December 2002 that the WCTOC, founded in Illinois, would have to surrender the name because an Oregon-based religious group already had a trademark on it. The group now calls itself the Creative Movement and has moved its headquarters to Riverton, Wyoming. The organization has not only a large membership that is active in many states but also one of the largest white prison gang memberships. It has been tough to control because of its religious facade, which allows its members to gather for meetings in prison.

ARYAN NATIONS   The group Aryan Nations was formed in the early 1970s and operates out of northern Idaho. It is considered primarily an identity group but also embraces neo-Nazi philosophy. The organization preaches that God's creation of Adam marked "the placing of the White Race upon this earth," that all nonwhites are inferior, and that Jews are the "natural enemy of our Aryan (white) race" (Berkowitz, 1999).

THE NATIONAL ALLIANCE   The neo-Nazi group, National Alliance, believes it is part of nature and subject to nature's laws only; therefore, members are able to determine their own destiny regardless of laws imposed by the government. They profess that those who believe in a divine control over mankind absolve themselves of responsibility for their fate. They also believe they are members of the Aryan (or European) race and are superior to other races.

Racist Skinheads

Membership of young adults in Racist Skinhead groups has grown considerably since the group's inception in 1986. According to a 2006 report by the ADL, the United States has seen a "significant and troubling" resurgence of Racist Skinhead activity. The report indicates that the increase in number of Racist Skinhead groups, in all parts of the country, has been accompanied by a rise in violent hate crimes carried out by them against Jews, African Americans, Hispanics, gays and lesbians, and immigrants ("ADL Reports Resurgence of Racist Skinheads," 2006). Racist Skinheads have been behind several attempted acts of terrorism; for example, in 2005, a racist skinhead was convicted for plotting to firebomb an Oklahoma City synagogue.

The ADL report cites several factors for the resurgence in racist skinhead activity:

- Alienated white youth have found a welcome reception on the Internet from white supremacists hungry for new recruits. The Internet has made it very easy for young people to be exposed to online message forums and social networking websites prevalent in the racist skinhead subculture.
- The white power music industry, around which the Racist Skinhead subculture revolves, has experienced a substantial growth in online promotion and sales.
- Racist Skinhead groups such as Hammerskin Nation and Blood & Honor have expanded globally using the Internet to create a network of international white supremacist sites and giving haters in different parts of the country—indeed, the world—the ability to connect online.;
- Less competition exists from the major established white supremacist groups, whose activity has diminished because of the arrests or deaths of leaders and serious factional infighting.

Racist Skinheads, easily recognized by their closely shaven heads, are transient and sometimes do not join with Skinhead groups. SPLC indicates their numbers are hard to assess because of this fact.

The influence of adult white supremacist groups on Racist Skinheads and neo-Nazi skinheads has been substantial. The youth participate in adult hate group rallies and show a great deal of solidarity with them. Skinhead groups have developed their own leadership and appeal distinct from adult Klan and neo-Nazi groups. The adult hate groups seek to replenish their membership ranks from the Racist Skinhead groups. Prominent skinheads established several new hate music vendors in 2005, which allowed these groups to capture profits from the white power music trade (SPLC Report, 2006).

In October 2008, two men from a rural county in Tennessee, described as neo-Nazi skinhead white supremacists, were arrested by federal authorities. They were charged with possessing an unregistered firearm, conspiring to steal firearms from a federally licensed gun dealer, and, more seriously, plotting to kill 88 people with plans for beheading 14 of them. The killing spree was to have included a black school and ultimately targeted the Democratic candidate for President, Barack Obama. According to a newspaper account of the incident, "the numbers 14 and 88 are symbols in skinhead culture . . . referring to a 14-word phrase attributed to an imprisoned white supremacist: 'We must secure the existence of our people and a future for white children' and to the eighth letter of the alphabet, H. Two '8's or 'H's stand for 'Heil Hitler'" Authorities stated that "there did not appear to be any formal assassination plan, [but they] took the threats seriously" ("Obama Assassination Plot Foiled," 2008).

Identity

Identity describes a religion that is fundamentally racist, anti-Semitic, and antihomosexual. According to SPLC, the active Identity groups across the United States are organized under different names but with similar ideologies. The goal of Identity groups is to broaden the influence of the white supremacist movement under the guise of Christianity. They form their views of diverse people based on a particular interpretation of the Bible. For example, "[Identity] teaches that people of color are pre-Adamic, that is not fully human and are without souls; that Jews are children of Satan and that white people of northern Europe are the Lost Tribes of the House of Israel" ("World Church," 1992, pp. 42–44). The movement takes the position that white Anglo-Saxons—not Jews—are the real biblical "chosen people," and that blacks and other nonwhites are "mud people" on the same level as animals and therefore are without souls (Berkowitz, 1999). Identity followers believe that the Bible commands racial segregation, interpreting racial equality as a violation of God's law.

CHRISTIAN IDENTITY   Followers of this sect, founded in California by Wesley Swift after World War II, use the Bible as the source of their ideology. It is a quasi-theological movement of small churches, tape and book distribution businesses, and radio ministries.

POSSE COMITATUS   Another Identity group is Posse Comitatus, which means "power of the country" in Latin. The group is anti-tax and anti–federal government. The Posse believes that all government power is rested in the county rather than at the federal level.

CHRISTIAN PATRIOTS   The followers of this Identity group belong to many different organizations, all of which espouse white supremacy. Their core beliefs are as follows:

- White people and people of color are fundamentally two different kinds of citizens, with different rights and responsibilities.
- The United States is not properly a democracy, but a republic in which only people with property should vote.
- Democracy is the same as "mobocracy," or mob rule.
- The United States is a Christian republic, with a special relationship between Christianity and the rule of law.
- Internationalists (usually identified as Jews) and aliens (sometimes identified as Jews, sometimes as immigrants or people of color) are attempting to subvert the U.S. Constitution and establish one-world socialism or, alternatively, the New World Order.
- The Federal Reserve banking system is unconstitutional and a tool of the "International Jewish Banking Conspiracy" (Center for Democratic Renewal, 1992).

Black Separatists

The SPLC has identified black separatist groups active in the United States under two different names: the House of David and the Nation of Islam. Black separatist groups are organizations whose ideologies include tenets of racially based hatred. Black separatist followers share the same agenda as white supremacists: racial separatism and racial supremacy. The two movements also share a common goal of racial purity and a hatred of Jews. One example of a black separatist militant organization espousing hatred of Jews is the Black African Holocaust Council (BAHC). BAHC, based in Brooklyn, New York, was established in 1991. Membership is restricted to African Americans and Native Americans. The organization publishes a monthly magazine, the *Holocaust Journal*, which is replete with anti-Semitic and anti-white rhetoric. BAHC holds monthly meetings and conducts weekly lectures and study groups on anti-white or anti-Semitic issues.

Despite the differences between black extremist and white supremacist groups, and their mutual contempt, these groups are able to join rhetorical forces to demean and slander Jews.

RESPONSE ALTERNATIVES TO ORGANIZED HATE GROUPS

Law enforcement agencies must actively work to fight and control organized hate groups, tracking their activities, establishing when they are responsible for crimes, and assisting in their prosecution. Intelligence gathering is crucial to the efforts to reduce and prevent hate/bias crimes. Equally important is networking and sharing hate group information with other criminal justice agencies. Many have called this approach a cross-disciplinary coalition against racism. It involves statewide and regional commitments by criminal justice agencies to work with other public and private entities, including the Internal Revenue Service. All the institutions jointly develop and implement components of multitiered intervention strategies targeting enforcement, education, training, victim assistance, media relations, political activism and advocacy, and ongoing self-evaluation.

The fight begins with an assessment of the size and scope of the various supremacist groups, their movements, their leaders, and their publications. When hate crimes are perpetrated against one group in the community, law enforcement must immediately alert any other organizations that are potential targets. For example, if a synagogue is the object of an arsonist, law enforcement should notify not only other synagogues, but also the National Association for the Advancement of Colored People (NAACP), National Council of La Raza, and other minority organizations in the region, state, and adjoining states. The investigating agency should notify other law enforcement agencies (i.e., city, county, state, and federal) in their county and region of the incident as well.

TRENDS AND PREDICTIONS FOR ORGANIZED HATE GROUPS

Some experts predict that white supremacists will continue to commit traditional crimes (e.g., cross burnings, vandalism) but will also venture into high-tech activities such as computer system infiltration and sabotage. Their political activism will include "white rights" rallies, protests, and demonstrations; election campaigns by racist candidates; and legislative lobbying. These activities are expected to incite countermovements and will create very labor-intensive situations for law enforcement to handle.

Observers of hate groups have also noted the shift in tactics of white supremacists in the United States. Discovering that supremacists could no longer effectively recruit members using the ideology of open racism with the focus on persons of color, Jews, immigrants, and the like, they are now targeting lesbians and gays. According to those who study hate groups, supremacists find that while many whites may share their racial, religious, and ethnic prejudices, most are no longer willing to act on them openly. Thus a new strategy is being employed that combines old hatreds with new rhetoric. This new approach does not imply that supremacists no longer hate people of color, Jews, and so on. Rather, it means they are refocusing their energies; they are exploiting white fear of change; and they have adopted as a prominent part of their new agenda not only homophobia but also antiabortion, anti-immigration, and the so-called pro-family and pro-American values, in addition to their traditional racist and anti-Semitic beliefs. Ross (1995) says the broadening of issues and the use of conservative buzzwords have attracted the attention of whites who may not consider themselves racist but do consider themselves patriotic Americans concerned about the moral decay of "their" country.

One disturbing trend is observed in the age and gender of new members of supremacist groups: there are more younger members than in the past (including teenagers), and many are young women. Organized hate is no longer the exclusive domain of white men over 30 years of age. Organizations and officials tracking hate groups have offered other predictions on the evolution and future of hate groups. These experts believe groups that have traditionally shunned or actively opposed each other for ideological reasons will join forces against their "common enemies." For one example among many, although neo-Nazis have long despised Arabs and Muslims, they have increasingly allied with Arab and Muslim extremists against common enemies, most often Jews. American neo-Nazis have also been increasingly cooperating with their counterparts in Europe.

The Internet and Hate Groups

As noted above, the Internet has become the medium of choice for recruiting young members to hate groups and for disseminating hate dogma and racist ideology. The Internet enables people to spread hate around the world instantaneously, in a cheap, easy, and anonymous manner. The medium provides hate groups the ability to send unsolicited mass e-mailings simultaneously into millions of homes, some of them seeking to recruit today's affluent and educated youth to their cause. Their hundreds, or possibly thousands, of websites entice viewers with online games, comic strips, and music, or simply a friendly pitch from another kid. College and university sites are being bombarded with messages and lures from hate groups. In some areas the Internet is also being used to provide tips on how to target groups' opponents with violence. SPLC tracks hate sites and have developed its own website with a special online campaign, "Hate Hurts," about the impact of hate. Internet companies must work with the police, within the realm of freedom-of-speech requirements, to enforce their own standards and to block hate dogma websites or hate e-mail within their system.

HATE/BIAS CRIME AND INCIDENT CONTROL

Hate/bias crimes and incidents can be controlled only through the combined efforts of the community (schools, private organizations, government agencies, churches, service organizations, and families), federal and state legislatures, and the criminal justice system—a holistic approach. It is important to profile communities to determine whether they are at risk of strife or conflict caused by the social, economic, and environmental conditions that can result in hate crimes and incidents.

Identifying Communities at Risk

COMMUNITY PROFILING   Law enforcement agencies experiencing demographic changes in their communities are well advised to perform an analysis of what is taking place: community profiling. It is important to know if the numbers of any group are increasing and why. The assessment should include estimates of the number of those who might be in the country illegally. Such a profile must include a sense of timing: what can the community and law enforcement personnel expect from profiled groups with regard to the observance of holidays and religious or cultural ceremonies?

> **Community profiling**   It involves a demographic analysis of the community with regard to the ethnicity/national origin, race, religion, and sexual orientation of groups whose members work or reside there.

Progressive agencies send their patrol officers lists of religious and cultural holidays and world crisis events that could affect the area they serve. If officers wait to identify at-risk communities until after hate crimes are committed, they are not fulfilling their professional responsibilities. Knowing how to identify at-risk communities and then committing resources to resolve problems before they escalate is proactive police work, which is crucial to preventing conflict. While this involves more departmental time and personnel initially, the ultimate savings through the prevention of community disruption is well worth the effort.

NEIGHBORHOOD AND POLICE PARTNERSHIP   Neighborhoods (citizens and all those local institutions encompassed by the term) working together with the police provide the best means of identifying communities at risk. How does a city determine if a neighborhood is at risk? Who is responsible for the assessment? What strategies can be utilized to mitigate the at-risk status? The best approach is community policing, described in Chapters 14 and 15, whereby police help the community protect itself and enhance the quality of life of its members. Officers and citizens meet to discuss the neighborhoods' most serious problems and work together to resolve them.

> **At-risk Communities**   Communities having a high level of criminal activity or disorder and usually a higher number of incidents of civil rights violations—hate/bias crimes, discrimination, racism, and bigotry.

Community policing encourages officers to delve into observations and feelings to determine not only what is happening, but also who is involved, what their motivation is, and where they are from. Officers should consider themselves as first-line intelligence assets for their community. For example, they should watch for graffiti and/or other materials posted on walls, fences, telephone poles, and buildings. These markings could signal a racist operation in progress or a locally active hate group. In addition, to be effective, officers who patrol highly diverse areas must have some degree of cultural awareness and ability to engage in cross-cultural communication. It has been said that if officers are scrambling to understand communities only after a crime is committed, it is a terrible indictment of their lack of professionalism.

In addition, officers must know neighborhood leaders and ways to locate them quickly if they are needed to provide general assistance or to help control rumors or people. Neighborhood leaders can also provide invaluable help when it comes to dealing with victims who distrust police. A problem-focused approach provides officers with a solid understanding of social, economic, and environmental problems in the community. There are limits to what the police can do without community help. In many communities, however, police first have to overcome their traditional role identification as crime fighters independent of the community before they can become an integral part of a team that works together to solve local problems. When officers patrol neighborhoods daily, they can interact with citizens to engender trust and can monitor their activities. Herman Goldstein, University of Wisconsin law professor and the architect of the problem-oriented policing (POP) concept, said that "the police department, more than any other agency of government, must have a bird's eye view of the dynamics within its community, including the demographics, agendas of various groups, and an in-depth understanding of the hopes, aspirations and frustration of various groups. This will give the police a feel for the mood and tensions that exist within a community" (Parker, 1991, p. 13).

ROLE OF HUMAN RELATIONS COMMISSIONS (HRCs)   Many cities and counties nationwide have established community HRCs. Created as independent agencies, they are responsible for fostering equal opportunity and eliminating all forms of discrimination. These objectives are accomplished by means of investigating, mediating, and holding public hearings on problems that arise from discrimination prohibited by federal, state, and local laws. Most HRCs will not investigate incidents of discrimination where such a function is preempted or prohibited by state or federal legislation. In cases where there is a violation of state or federal law, the HRC refers the complainant to the appropriate agency. It then monitors the progress of the complaint. Each HRC has established procedures that govern how it receives, investigates, holds hearings on, and mediates and resolves complaints. Confidentiality is a protected right of the complainant in discrimination cases reported to HRCs. As established by state or federal law, the names of the parties may not be made public, with a few exceptions, without the written consent of both parties involved. Human relations commissions should also be part of the community–police partnership, in which they all take responsibility for educating their community about its diversity. This includes serious and sustained efforts to bring people together for dialog.

COMMUNITY RELATIONS SERVICE (CRS)   The CRS, an arm of the U.S. Department of Justice, is a specialized federal conciliation service available to state and local officials to help prevent and resolve racial and ethnic conflict, violence, and civil disorder. When governors, mayors, police chiefs, and school superintendents need help to defuse racial or ethnic crises, they turn to CRS. This service helps local officials and residents tailor locally defined resolutions when conflict and violence threaten community stability and well-being. Created by the Civil Rights Act of 1964, CRS is the only federal agency dedicated to preventing and resolving racial and ethnic tensions, incidents, and civil disorders. CRS gathers data in seven areas: demographic balance, administration of justice (particularly police–community relations), employment, education, housing, health and welfare, and community relationships. The statistical data is then used to assess six critical factors:

1. Relationship of minorities to the administration of justice system
2. Impact of the economy
3. Level of minorities' inclusion in and/or exclusion from the system, and the number of minorities serving as elected officials
4. Quality of intergroup relationships

5. Current level of violence in the community/neighborhood and/or city

6. Basic demographic influences

It is time consuming to perform this type of analysis and to develop a program based on the findings. Police departments have access to the same kind of data and they possess a great deal of the experience and expertise necessary to complete the same type of analysis within neighborhoods, if they choose to do so.

TRENDS TO MONITOR: STEEP TYPOLOGY

Trend Monitoring in Multicultural Communities

Monitoring conditions in a community provides useful information for forecasting potential negative events and preparing accordingly. The framework for evaluating any predictions should include an analysis of economic circumstances, social and cultural conditions, as well as the political environment within the community.

The acronym STEEP stands for social, technological, environmental, economic, and political. There is often a connection between the economy, social conditions, and politics and the numbers of hate/bias crimes that occur. This relationship is explained in Chapter 11. It is important for agency personnel and officers involved in community-oriented policing to understand the basic economic, social, and political issues contributing to social unrest.

Economic Circumstances

Crime, social unrest, riots, and disturbances have often occurred during depressed economic times. Waves of immigrants (both legal and illegal) also add to the scramble for available jobs and services. Internationally, poverty, overcrowding, and wars have been pressuring more people to migrate than ever before, laying the conditions for what the United Nations called "the human crisis of our age." In Florida, for example, refugees from Cuba and Haiti flooded the state in the 1980s and 1990s. Many areas experienced real conflict as established residents who were already struggling now had masses of people competing with them for services and jobs. California continually experiences legal and illegal immigration from Mexico and Central and South America. The new immigrants (the weakest group) become the target for people's frustrations as their own sense of well-being decreases. The established ethnically and racially mixed groups in neighborhoods see what they perceive as preferential treatment for the newcomers and react accordingly.

Federal decisions that lead to settlement of immigrants into economically depressed communities have frequently been made without regard to the adequacy of local resources to handle the influx. Subsequent polls reflect an increase in anti-immigrant attitudes. Eventually, police and community problems evolve as a consequence of these well-meaning national policies that have not been thoroughly worked through.

Tracking influxes of immigrants into communities, plus an awareness of political decisions, should keep law enforcement executives and officers alert to relocation and acculturation problems of newcomers in their communities. Tracking also provides an opportunity to work with the community to develop transition management plans as well as preventive programs for keeping the peace. National immigration policies and politics have a tremendous impact on cities and counties, and therefore criminal justice agencies must monitor them and plan accordingly.

Henry DeGeneste and John Sullivan wrote the following in *Fresh Perspectives*, a Police Executive Research Forum publication in 1997, and clearly it is still true today:

> Urban tensions are fueled by a combination of . . . wealth disparity and the pressures of large scale migration, which are present not only in American cities, but in cities worldwide. . . . [Robin] Wright [a journalist for the Los Angeles Times] notes, "[T]ensions in cities are often complicated by another dimension—racial or ethnic diversity." . . . [M]inorities are increasingly left stranded in urban outskirts—slums or squatter camps—excluded politically and financially. Their ensuing frustrations contribute to the volatility of urban life. Conflict (such as riots) resulting from urban decay, overcrowding, poor social services and ethnic tension has occurred in cities world-wide and can be expected to continue, particularly as swelling migrant populations flock to cities. (DeGeneste and Sullivan, 1997, p. 2)

Political Environment

Executives of criminal justice agencies must monitor legislation, sensitive court trials, and political events that affect not only the jurisdictions they serve, but also the nation and the world. Often what goes on outside of the United States has an impact on local populations. Law enforcement must be aware of foreign political struggles and their potential to polarize ethnic and racial groups in the local community, leading to conflict. Police must have the ability to recognize potential problems and strive to prevent or mitigate intergroup conflict. Only by acknowledging their primary role in preventing and mediating conflict in the community can peace officers begin to remediate long-standing and emerging tensions. The criminal justice system cannot operate in a vacuum.

Social and Cultural Conditions

Typically, poverty and frustration with the system, the perception of racism, and unequal treatment are conditions for social unrest. Diverse peoples living in close proximity can also create potentially unstable social conditions. Furthermore, on familial level, a decline in the cohesiveness of the nuclear family (including divorce) adds to stresses within micro units in the society. Unemployment, especially among youth, is another social condition with potentially dangerous consequences.

Finally, gangs and the heavy use of illegal drugs and their impact on neighborhoods lead to social and cultural conditions ripe for explosive events. None of these elements alone, however, account for community violence. But all these factors, in combination with political and economic conditions, contribute to discontent. Officers frequently are frustrated because they cannot undo decades of societal precursors that set the stage for upheavals.

LAW ENFORCEMENT RESPONSE STRATEGIES

Public confidence and trust in the criminal justice system, and law enforcement in particular, are essential for effective response to hate/bias crimes. Residents in communities where people of a race, ethnic background, religion, or sexual preference different from their own reside must be able to trust that they will be protected. They must believe that the police are not against them, that the prosecutors are vigorously prosecuting, that the judges are invoking proper penalties, and that parole, probation, and corrections are doing their share to combat crimes motivated by hate or bias. If people believe they have to protect themselves, tensions build, communication breaks down, and people try to take the law into their own hands.

Community Programs to Reduce and Control Hate Crimes

Some solutions to reduce hate/bias crimes involve going back to basics, involving grassroots institutions such as families, schools, workplaces, and religious organizations. Partnerships between the criminal justice system and these institutions are often more successful in instituting crime reduction programs than is the criminal justice system alone. However, some institutions that once built positive values or exercised some control over people are no longer working or have diminishing influence. The broken or dysfunctional family, for example, contributes significantly to society's problems, including the increase in criminal activity.

An effort must be made to reinstitute values that reinforce noncriminal behavior; law enforcement must be an integral part of that movement. The status quo policing approach (reactive) will not work anymore. "People have clearly begun to recognize that our strict law enforcement arrest approach isn't getting the job done," notes Darrel Stephens (2006), former executive director of the Police Executive Research Forum. Progressive criminal justice executives and communities realize that crime has multiple and complex causes and that police departments are neither the first nor the only line of defense. If crime is to be controlled, there must be a community alliance or partnership and the causes must be attacked on multiple fronts.

Generic Community Resources and Programs

Community resources and programs that are available or can be established include:

- *Victims' hotline:* Similar to those available for domestic violence and rape victims, and suicide prevention. The staff is trained to provide victim assistance in terms of compassion, advice, referrals, and a prepared information package.
- *Human relations commission:* The staff provides assistance to victims of hate crimes or incidents, holds hearings, and provides recommendations for problem resolution.
- *United States Department of Justice Community Relations Service:* The CRS, with headquarters in Washington, D.C., has 14 regional and field offices and provides services to every state. The Justice Department has trained staff who, when notified of a problem, will participate in and mediate community meetings in an attempt to resolve conflicts. Many states have similar justice agencies that perform these services.
- *Conflict resolution panels:* Specially trained staff of a city or county who can assist agencies and/or victims (including groups) in the resolution of conflict, such as that caused by hate or bias.
- *The media:* Cooperation in building public awareness of the problem of hate/bias violence via articles on causes and effects, resources, and legal remedies is essential.
- *Multilingual public information brochures:* These can be provided by government agencies on the rights of victims, services available, and criminal and civil laws related to hate and bias.
- *Police storefronts:* Police substations, established in the neighborhoods of communities with high concentrations of ethnic minorities, which are staffed by bilingual officers and/or civilians. The staff takes reports and provides assistance to the members of that community.
- *Community resource list:* List of organizations that specialize in victim assistance. Examples are the Anti-Defamation League of B'nai B'rith, Black Families Associations,

Japanese American Citizens Leagues, the NAACP, and the Mexican American Political Association, to name a few. National organizations that might be contacted as a resource are listed in Appendix C. The importance of establishing networks with minority leaders and organizations cannot be overstressed. These networks are extremely important for criminal justice agencies and should be identified and cultivated in advance so the leaders will be available and willing to assist in a timely fashion with investigations, training, victim aid, and/or rumor control. If an agency experiencing serious hate/bias problems does not react quickly and effectively, victims and their community groups gain media attention when they publicly question an inadequate response or resolution. If a system involving trust and respect is already in place, such a network proves its worth when violence occurs in the agency's community. A good relationship with representatives of diverse communities is essential because it can help broaden the department's understanding of different cultures, ethnicities, and races. The same is true of members of gay and lesbian groups. When community members are utilized within departments, they can also help convince reluctant victims and/or witnesses to cooperate with investigators. Furthermore, they can encourage more victims to report incidents.

The key to a successful law enforcement response to hate crimes is building a partnership with victimized communities. There are many components and processes in building such a partnership. Other activities and events characterizing such a joint effort would include educating the public at large, providing organizational networking opportunities, monitoring the media, and implementing federal, state, and county programs. The activities for each are described in the following sections.

EDUCATING THE PUBLIC AT LARGE   Prejudice and bias, which can ultimately lead to violence, are often the result of ignorance. In many cases the biased individual has had little or no firsthand exposure to the targeted group; thus the bias may be due to learned stereotypes and negative media images.

One key to combating ignorance is to educate the public as well as criminal justice system employees about the history, diversity, cultures, languages, and issues of concern of the various groups within the community. This can be accomplished through neighborhood forums, workshops, and speakers' bureaus. The speakers' bureaus should be composed of people who are well versed on the issues and are available to speak at community meetings, schools, and other forums. Criminal justice employees, of course, would be trained in the workplace and/or through in-service or academy-based training courses. Most cities and counties have organizations that represent community groups that can assist in developing and implementing such education at local elementary and secondary schools, in churches, and on college and university campuses. To check the accuracy of material presented, organizers of educational programs should have at least two or three minority community members provide input on the content of the program to be delivered. Preferably, they would represent the different subgroups within the community. Neighborhoods and community residents should be encouraged to observe their various heritages through the celebration of holidays and other special days via fairs and festivals. Calendars show that there are more holidays for different religions and cultures in the United States than anywhere else in the world.

ORGANIZATIONAL NETWORKING   National and local organizations must network to share information, resources, ideas, and support regarding crimes motivated by hate. The list of potential organizations would include the NAACP, the ADL, the Committee against Anti-Asian Violence, the NGLTF, the SPLC, and the National Institute against Prejudice and Violence. Such advocacy organizations can construct an invaluable bridge to victim populations and assist in urging citizens to come to the police with information about hate crimes. Most of these organizations have publications and reports covering such topics as how to respond to bigotry, trends in racism, and community organizing. Through networking, organizations or groups learn who their allies are, increase their own resources and knowledge about other minority groups, and form coalitions that make a greater impact on the community and the criminal justice system. They can also assist criminal justice agencies in dealing with community reactions to hate violence and help the victims of violence cope with the experience.

The Phoenix, Arizona, Police Department offers a good example of organizational networking still used today. In 1994, a hate crimes advisory board with representation from most of Phoenix's ethnic groups was created. The knowledge that members have and share about their communities, cultures, and potential hot spots is highly beneficial. The organization expanded into the Central Arizona Hate Crime Advisory Board to reflect its growth, and more recently changed its name to Arizona Citizens Hate Crime Advisory Board. The board has become Arizona police departments' conduit to their many different communities. Such partnerships between human rights groups, civic leaders, community leaders, and law enforcement can advance police–community relations by demonstrating a commitment to be both tough on those responsible for hate crimes and aware of the special needs of hate crime victims.

MONITORING THE MEDIA   Minority organizations and the criminal justice system must monitor the media, which can be a foe or an ally. The media must be used strategically for education and publicity about hate/bias crimes and incidents, about multicultural and multiracial workshops, and about festivals and other cultural events. They must be monitored in terms of accuracy of reporting and must be asked to publish corrections when warranted. Negative editorials or letters to the editor pertaining to an affected group should be countered and rebutted by an op-ed piece from within management of the involved criminal justice agency. Organization leaders or their designated spokespersons should make themselves available as the primary sources of information for reporters to contact.

FEDERAL, STATE, AND COUNTY PROGRAMS   Police executives should seek out every source of federal, state, and county law enforcement assistance programs and make the information available to investigators and/or task forces investigating or preventing hate crimes.

CHURCHES, MOSQUES, AND SYNAGOGUES   Where the usual support organizations (e.g., ACLU, NAACP, ADL) do not exist and sometimes even where they do, churches, mosques, and synagogues often are advocates for people facing discrimination and/or who are victims of a hate incident or crime. For example, the Concord, California Hispanic Ministry acts frequently as an advocate for Latinos with tenant–landlord problems in addition to providing Spanish-language masses, family counseling, and religious classes.

Communities with Special Programs

Some jurisdictions have used a community approach to decrease the numbers of crimes and incidents of all types, including those motivated by hate/bias. Some exemplary programs include the following:

- *Block watch volunteers program:*   The Northwest Victim Services (NVS), a nonprofit organization created in 1981 in Philadelphia, formed a partnership with police in the city's highest-crime-rate districts (the 14th and 35th) that utilizes an organized block watch program. Carefully selected, screened, and trained block watch volunteers perform not only the usual functions of neighborhood watch (crime prevention) but also a vital victim assistance role. The volunteer program has expanded and now provides assistance to citizens throughout the city. They provide emotional support for victims who are often frightened or unfamiliar with the criminal justice process, and volunteers accompany the victims to the courtroom for the various stages of the trial.

• *Task force on police–Asian relations:*   In localities that have large Asian populations, task forces have been created that consist of criminal justice members, educators, victim/refugee advocates, volunteer agency representatives, and representatives from each Asian group living or working in the community. The purposes are several: to train criminal justice employees on communication techniques that improve relations and make them more effective in dealing with the Asian community; to prepare Asians on what to expect from the various criminal justice components, especially the police; to open lines of communication between law enforcement and Asians; and to encourage Asians to report crimes and trust the police. Agencies in California that have created such task forces and could be contacted for additional details are the San Francisco, Westminster, Garden Grove, Anaheim, Fresno, San Jose, and Huntington Beach Police Departments. These task forces could certainly be adapted to other ethnic and racial groups as well. The city of Boston and other cities have effectively used the task force approach to resolve neighborhood problems, and have found them to be effective for exchanging information and curtailing rumors; identifying problems and working on solutions; and, perhaps most important, allowing citizens to help with and approach problems on a joint basis.

• *Network of Neighbors:*   The Office of the Human Relations Commission (OHRC) in Montgomery County, Maryland, has a "memorandum of understanding" with the police that when a hate crime occurs, the police department immediately notifies the commission. The commission in turn contacts the volunteer of the Network of Neighbors who lives closest to the victim. The network member visits the victim as soon as possible to assure the person of community support and to assist with other needs. The volunteers receive training on victim assistance and referrals. The New York City Police Department modeled a similar Good Neighbor Program after Montgomery County's. The county also has three other networking programs established by mutual agreements between the police department and the OHRC: (1) Network of Teens; (2) Partnership Board; (3) Committee on Hate Violence. All are linked to the police department and hold monthly briefings reviewing hate incidents and crimes. The Network of Teens includes the STOP program, which educates juvenile perpetrators of hate violence about the impact of their behavior both on the victims and on the entire community. The program, which began in 1982, sends first offenders to the STOP program instead of through the court system. The OHRC requires that juvenile perpetrators and their parents attend five 2.5-hour sessions. Sessions include written and experiential exercises, discussions, films, and homework relating to their specific incident and the impact of hate and violence in general. Juveniles are also required to perform 40 hours of community service.

• *School Programs:*   The Maine Office of the Attorney General's Civil Rights Team Project, created in 1996 with the help of a U.S. Department of Justice, Bureau of Justice Administration grant, uses teams of students and faculty members to promote awareness of bias and prejudice in its public high schools, middle schools, and elementary schools. Their stated mission is that no students in the state should have to experience anxiety, fear, or terror in school because of their color of the skin, religion, gender, sexual orientation, or disability, or any other aspect of themselves that makes them different from other students. Law enforcement works together with teachers and administrators to empower students to stand up for civility and respect. The teams are made up of three or four students per grade, plus two or three faculty advisers. The teams have two formal responsibilities: (1) to promote awareness of bias and prejudice within their schools and (2) to organize forums for students to talk about harassment. If a team receives information about harassment, it is charged with forwarding that information to a responsible teacher or administrator. The Attorney General's office assigns a community adviser to each team to serve as liaison between the team and the Office. Annually, the Attorney General's office provides full-day training for new and returning civil rights teams and for faculty and community advisers. This training includes:

- a presentation on the type of hate crimes committed in Maine schools
- interactive exercises on the role of degrading language and slurs in escalating a situation to serious harassment and violence
- a presentation by a Holocaust survivor or a victim of bias and prejudice
- role playing exercises on how to run effective civil rights team meetings
- small-group work using real-life scenarios

All participating schools agree to host Attorney General's office staff for a half-day workshop for faculty, administrators, and staff. The workshop gives teachers and other school staff a better understanding of the destructive impact of degrading language and bias-motivated harassment and teaches them how to intervene when students engage in such behavior. A similar project within the schools was created in Massachusetts.

Such community models, including those of churches and synagogues, can play a vital role in reducing violence in neighborhoods, schools, and the workplace. Successfully implemented programs can reduce individual violence, ranging from street crime to domestic abuse to drug-related crimes. Civil unrest, which can often include gang violence and open confrontations between various segments of society, can also be reduced. Building bonds of trust between the police and the community also allows community-oriented policing to contribute to the goal of promoting color-blind policing, where citizens and their police form new partnerships that offer the promise of reducing the potential for civil unrest.

Stephen Wessler, for the Bureau of Justice Administration (BJA), prepared a research paper,

"Addressing Hate Crimes: Six Initiatives That Are Enhancing the Efforts of Criminal Justice Practitioners." The monograph highlights six BJA-funded projects that demonstrate the creativity and deep commitment of local, state, and federal law enforcement agencies in leading the nation's effort to combat bias-motivated crime. It identifies projects that support police and prosecutorial agencies in responding to hate crimes and supplies sources for additional information. To obtain a copy of this monograph (NCJ 179559), contact the National Criminal Justice Reference Service at www.ncjrs.gov.

Mini Case Study: Lewiston, Maine, 2001 to the Present

The ongoing, changing relationship between the people of Lewiston, Maine, and its Somali population can be used as a case study, illustrating the strategies suggested in this text.

After reading the case study below, consider these questions:

1. What other methods could be employed in Lewiston to address the tensions and ease the Somalis' assimilation into that community?
2. Could Lewiston have predicted the arrival of more Somalis and prepared for them? What strategies have you learned that could be used?

In the year 2000, the census of the small city of Lewiston, Maine, counted approximately 35,000 people, including 361 black residents, none of whom were Somali. Then refugees from that African country began to arrive to escape civil war, poverty, and political or religious persecution. Many had been waiting for years in refugee camps in Kenya for an opportunity to come to America. Some of the newcomers came to Lewiston from Somali communities elsewhere in the United States, looking for cheaper housing, better schools, and a better social environment. They were also seeking more generous government assistance programs than those in the metropolitan areas from which they moved. The Somalis wanted to protect their children from exposure to gangs, drugs, and violence as well as racial predjudice they found in the big cities. After September 11, 2001, however, the Somalis' decision to move to Maine became easier when employers and the general public in the big cities became suspicious of them and many lost their jobs.

At first these immigrants were welcomed to Lewiston. Over the years, as their numbers increased, tension at times ran high. Friction occurred as the city's resources (jobs, schools, welfare, housing) were overwhelmed and competition for them increased; language problems were also a factor. Some in the community began to react in racist and discriminatory ways toward the Somalis.

In early 2003, the World Church of the Creator (WCOTC) and the National Alliance planned a rally at a local college to exploit these reactions to the growing Somali community. These two groups saw the friction in Lewiston as an opportunity to organize the community against the Somalis. But the city and its police department responded by creating a steering committee for a new group, the "Many and One Coalition," which had 200 members. Taking advice from the SPLC (especially its publication *Ten Ways to Fight Hate: A Community Response Guide*) and other local and national human rights groups, they planned the community's response to the impending rally. An outreach coordinator for the SPLC Tolerance Project came to Lewiston days prior to the rally to help the town organize its efforts. The day before the rally, the college hosted a forum on issues of tolerance and diversity. The following day, about 5,000 townspeople showed up for a separate rally in support of diversity and the Somali community. Only 30 people turned out for the hate rally.

As of the beginning of 2009, Lewiston had the largest percentage of Somalis of any U.S. city—approximately 3,500. Although not every problem associated with the Somalis has been resolved, over the years the city has made many accommodations. The city hired an English-speaking Somali to work as a liaison officer and added an AT&T language translation line for Somali callers. Schools implemented adult education and "English as a second language" programs. Cultural exchange programs were established in which residents could learn about the Somali culture, and Somalis, about American. Most Somalis have assimilated into the community and are accepted by the local population.

Sources: SPLC Report, 2003. "A Collision of Cultures Leads to Building Bridges in Maine," 2005. "Tensions Flare over Somalis in Lewiston," 2007. "Tension over Somali Refugees in Maine," 2009.

Summary

- The U.S. Congress enacted the federal Hate Crimes Statistics Act (HCSA) of 1990. The collection of hate/bias crime data enables the criminal justice system to monitor and respond to trends in those localities that voluntarily submit the information.
- Standardized and comprehensive statistics for hate/bias crimes provide information to law enforcement agencies so they can monitor and respond to trends. The tracking of these crimes allows criminal justice managers to deploy their resources appropriately when fluctuations occur. Aggressive response, investigation, and prosecution demonstrate that police are genuinely concerned and that they see such crimes as a priority.
- The criminal justice system must be proactive and react swiftly to crimes by hate groups. It will let the hate groups know that their actions will result in apprehension and prosecution. A result of proactive enforcement is that other members of the community will also become sensitive to the impact of hate/bias crimes on victims and how the criminal justice system responds. A secondary benefit is that blacks, Asians, Hispanics, Native Americans, lesbians, gays, women and any other victimized group would be more apt to consider law enforcement as a good career opportunity.
- Knowledge of hate groups is essential when policing in a multicultural society. It is imperative within the criminal justice system that organized hate groups be investigated, monitored, and controlled. Aggressive prosecution of these groups is also critical. It is equally important that criminal justice agencies develop a method for networking in order to share information about hate groups.

- Extremist hate groups are categorized as Ku Klux Klan, Neo-Nazi, Racist Skinhead, Christian Identity, Black Separatist, Neo-Confederate, and Other. The "Other" category includes groups, vendors, and publishing houses that endorse racist doctrines.
- Hate/bias crimes and incidents can be controlled only through the combined efforts of the community. This includes schools, private organizations, government agencies, churches, service organizations, families, federal and state legislatures, and the criminal justice system. It is important to profile communities to determine whether they are at risk of strife or conflict caused by the social, economic, and environmental conditions that can result in hate crimes and incidents. Monitoring conditions in a community provides useful information for forecasting potential negative events and for preparing accordingly.
- The framework for evaluating any predictions should include an analysis of economic circumstances, social and cultural conditions, as well as the political environment within the community. Some solutions for reducing hate/bias crimes involve grassroots institutions such as families, schools, workplaces, and religious organizations. Partnerships between the criminal justice system and these institutions are often more successful in instituting crime reduction programs than is the criminal justice system alone.
- Progressive criminal justice executives and communities realize that crime has multiple and complex causes and that police departments are neither the first nor the only line of defense. The key to a successful law enforcement response to hate crime is a strong partnership between law enforcement and the victimized communities.

Discussion Questions and Issues

1. *Hate Crimes Monitoring Systems:* Does your law enforcement agency (where you work or in the community in which you reside) have a system in place for monitoring hate/bias crimes and incidents? If yes, obtain a copy of the statistics for at least the past 5 years (or for as many years as are

available) of the hate/bias crimes and determine the following:

a. What trends are noticeable in each category?

b. Do the categories measure essential information that will assist your law enforcement agency in recognizing trends?

c. What would improve the data collection method to make it more useful in measuring trends and making predictions?

d. Has your law enforcement agency actually used the data to track the nature and extent of such crimes and incidents? Did it deploy resources accordingly? Provide the class with examples.

2. *Trend Monitoring:* Make a list of specific community social, economic, and political conditions and events occurring within the law enforcement jurisdiction in which you work or live. Which ones, if any, could potentially be connected to crimes motivated by hate? For each condition listed, make a "Comments" column. Suggest what specific factors a peace officer or criminal justice practitioner should look for in the community that would assist the agency in forecasting trends and events.

3. *Resources:* Find out what resources exist in your community to assist victims of hate/bias crimes.

a. Which groups provide victim assistance?

b. Which coalition groups exist, and what types of community outreach programs are offered?

c. What types of pamphlets or other written materials are available?

d. Which groups have speakers' bureaus?

e. Which groups are working with local law enforcement agencies with regard to response programs or cultural awareness training?

f. Which groups are working with the district attorney's or prosecutor's office?

4. *Role of Your District Attorney's Office:* Assess the role of your district attorney's or prosecutor's office by determining the following:

a. Does it have a special hate crimes or civil rights unit?

b. Do hate crime cases receive special attention?

c. Are misdemeanor and felony hate crimes prosecuted differently?

d. How does the office determine if it will prosecute a hate crime case?

e. What types of training do assistant district attorneys receive regarding hate crimes?

f. What types of community outreach does the district attorney's office provide regarding hate crimes?

5. *Victim Assistance:* Identify avenues of victim assistance in your area. Research and document the following:

a. Does your state have a crime victims' assistance program? Does it offer victim compensation? What about a victim's bill of rights?

b. What services does the local department of mental health staff offer?

c. Do any community groups, rape crisis centers, or crime victim services agencies in the area offer counseling to hate crimes victims?

d. Are any mental health care professionals willing to donate their services to victims of hate crimes?

6. *Human Relations Commission:* What is the role of the human relations commission (HRC), if one exists in your area?

a. Does it have a specific task force on hate crimes?

b. Does it have any type of tracking system for recording statistics on hate crimes?

c. What is its relationship with local law enforcement agencies and district attorneys' offices regarding hate crimes?

d. What is its relationship with community organizations concerned with hate crimes? Has it produced any brochures, pamphlets, or other materials on hate crimes?

e. Does it provide multicultural workshops or sensitivity training regarding different ethnic, racial, and lifestyle groups?

f. Have there been occasions when the HRC has gone beyond the scope of its charter or stated goals that resulted in negative exposure or media attention? Describe the circumstances.

Website Resources

Visit these websites for additional information about hate crimes and victim assistance:

American-Arab Anti-Discrimination Committee (ADC): http://www.adc.org

It is a resource for information about civil rights efforts and includes useful summary data about cases and complaints regarding hate crimes and discrimination involving Arab Americans.

Anti-Defamation League (ADL): http://www.adl.org

This website is a resource for information on organized bigotry. The League collects and assesses a vast amount of information on anti-Semites, racists, and extremists. After carefully evaluating information, ADL disseminates that information through books, periodicals, reports, and other materials. The ADL pioneered the development of a model statute with enhanced penalties for bias-motivated crimes.

National Asian Pacific American Legal Consortium: http://www.napalc.org

The Consortium monitors and documents hate-motivated incidents, publishes an annual anti-Asian violence audit, represents victims of hate-motivated violence, advocates for the passage of strict hate crime laws, and educates the Asian Pacific American community, law enforcement, policy makers, and the general public about the problem of hate-motivated violence.

The National Association for the Advancement of Colored People (NAACP): http://www.naacp.org

The NAACP is the oldest and the largest civil rights organization in the United States. Its principal objective is to ensure the political, educational, social, and economic equality of minority group citizens in the United States.

(NCCJ): www.nccjctwma.org

This organization, founded in 1927 as The National Conference of Christians and Jews, is a human relations organization dedicated to fighting bias, bigotry, and racism in America. NCCJ promotes understanding and respect among all races, religions, and cultures through advocacy, conflict resolution, and education.

The National Organization for Women (NOW): http://www.now.org

Now is the largest feminist organization in the United States, with over 500,000 contributing members. Since NOW was founded in 1966, it has struggled to end the injustice and inequality women face daily.

The National Council of La Raza (NCLR): http://www.nclr.org

NCLR is a private, nonprofit, nonpartisan, tax-exempt organization established in 1968 to reduce poverty and discrimination, and to improve life opportunities for Hispanic Americans. NCLR is the largest constituency-based national Hispanic organization, serving all Hispanic nationality groups in all regions of the country.

The Southern Poverty Law Center (SPLC): http://www.splcenter.org

The SPLC combats hate, intolerance, and discrimination through education and litigation. It tracks the activities of hate groups in the United States.

References

"A Collision of Cultures Leads to Building Bridges in Maine." (2005, March 13). *St. Petersburg Times.* Available at: http://www.sptimes.com, p. 1A.

"ADL Reports Resurgence of Racist Skinheads in U.S. and Launches New Online Racist Skinhead Project." (2006, February 7). Anti-Defamation League. New York, NY.

Berkowitz, H. (1999, September 14). Hate on the Internet, Congressional Testimony.

Bureau of Justice Statistics. (2008). "Hate Crime Statistics, 2007." U.S. Department of Justice, Office of Justice Programs, Washington, D.C.

Center for Democratic Renewal. (1992). *When Hate Groups Come to Town: A Handbook of Effective Community Responses.* Atlanta, GA: Author.

DeGeneste, Henry I., and Sullivan, John P. (1997, July). "Policing a Multicultural Community." *Fresh Perspectives,* Police Executive Research Forum, Washington D.C.

"Hate Crimes—Anti-Latino Hate Crime Up for Fourth Year." (2008, winter). *Intelligence Report,* Southern Poverty Law Center.

"No. 2 Klan Group on Trial in KY Teen's Beating." (2008, November 11). *New York Examiner,* p. 2.

"Obama Assassination Plot Foiled." (2008, October 28). *Contra Costa Times,* p. 1, 13.

Parker, Patricia A. (1991, December). "Tackling Unfinished Business: POP Plays Valuable Position in Racial Issues." *Police, 19,* pp. 5–9.

Ross, L. (1995). "White Supremacy in the 1990s." *Public Eye,* pp. 1–12.

SPLC Report. (2003, March). "Maine Town's Diversity Rally Outdraws Hate-Group Gathering." Vol. 33, No. 1, p. 8.

SPLC Report. (2006, March). "Hate Group Numbers Top 800," Vol. 36, No. 1, p. 1.

Stephens, Darrel W. (2006). Chief of Police, Charlotte-Mecklenburg Police Department, Charlotte, NC, personal communication.

"Tensions Flare over Somalis in Lewiston." (2007, May 13). *Contra Costa Times,* p. A18

"Tension over Somali refugees in Maine." (2007, May 11). *Vail Daily*. Retrieved May 11, 2009, available at: www.vaildaily.com.

"The Year in Hate." (2009, spring). Special Issue of *Intelligence Report*, Issue 133. Southern Poverty Law Center.

"World Church of the Creator-America's Most Dangerous Supremacist Group." (1992, September 21). *Southern Poverty Law Center Newsletter*, pp. 42–44.

CHAPTER 13

Racial Profiling

LEARNING OBJECTIVES

After reading this chapter you should be able to:

- Explain the historical background of the term *racial profiling*.
- Define *racial profiling* and explain the problems associated with using inconsistent definitions.
- Explain the challenges involved in the use of profiling in the war on terrorism.
- Identify seven approaches used by police departments to prevent racial profiling.
- Discuss the rationale for and against collection of racial profiling data.
- Explain the differences between "racial profiling" and the legitimate use of "profiling" in law enforcement.

OUTLINE

INTRODUCTION

Actual or perceived racial profiling by law enforcement officers affects blacks, Hispanics, Arab Americans, and other minority groups from every walk of life, every vocation, and every level of the socioeconomic ladder. The extent to which race, ethnicity, and/or national origin can be used as factors in targeting suspects for stops, searches, and arrests has been a concern of citizens and law enforcement for some time. The controversy over racial profiling is compounded by the unsupported assumption that the officer making traffic and field-interrogation stops of non-white citizens is making a race-based decision rooted in racial prejudice. These concerns became even more critical since the "War on Terrorism" began on September 11, 2001.

DEFINITIONS

Since the issues of biased policing came to the attention of the public and to law enforcement in the 1990s, racial profiling has been discussed and defined in hundreds of articles and publications. However, no single definition dominated the national conversation about this issue. The debate troubled not only those involved in the criminal justice system, but also concerned citizens and communities, scholars, researchers, civil rights organizations, and legislators. With no agreed-upon criteria for what does or does not constitute racial profiling, it was difficult to clarify, address, and develop approaches to prevent the practice. Variation among definitions means interested parties are often talking at cross-purposes, unwittingly discussing different types of police practices, behavior, and stops. For this reason, proposals to prohibit racial profiling were difficult to develop and carry out. Eventually, the U.S. government, federal and state legislatures, law enforcement organizations, and community advocacy institutions addressed the problem of definition and reached some agreement.

Racial Profiling

The authors will use the definition developed by the U.S. Department of Justice and the National Organization of Black Law Enforcement Executives (NOBLE). According to these organizations, racial profiling is any police-initiated action that relies on the race, ethnicity, or national origin rather than on the behavior of an individual or on information that leads the police to a particular individual who has been identified as being, or having been, engaged in criminal activity. Racial profiling, also known as "Driving While Black or Brown (DWB)," has been ruled illegal by the courts and is considered improper police practice by law enforcement officers and agencies.

Profile: Formal and Informal

A formal profile is typically a document that contains explicit criteria or indicators that is issued to officers to guide them in their decision making. It is usually based on data collected and interpreted to signify a trend or suggest that given a particular set of characteristics (behavioral or situational commonalties), a person could believe that something may result based on that particular cluster of characteristics. A profile relies upon expert advice provided to law enforcement agencies to identify perpetrators of criminal activities. It can be an outline or short biographical description, an individual's character sketch, or a type of behavior associated with a group. It is a summary of data presenting the average or typical appearance of those persons or situations under scrutiny. Officers use these indicators of behavioral or situational commonalties to develop reasonable suspicion or probable cause to stop subjects. An informal profile represents the "street sense," personal experiences, and strongly held beliefs of the officers who use them (Harris, 2002). Informal profiles are more common in law enforcement than formal ones.

Profiling

Any police-initiated action that uses a compilation of the background, physical, behavioral, and/or motivational characteristics for a type of perpetrator who leads the police to a particular individual who has been identified as being, could be, or having been engaged in criminal activity.

Race, Ethnicity, and Minority

Race, ethnicity, and minority refer to individuals of a particular descent, including Caucasian, African, Hispanic, Asian/Pacific, or Native American. In the text, the term *black* is used to describe all individuals with black skin, regardless of their national origin or ethnicity, and includes African Americans. The term *Latino/Hispanic* is used to describe an individual's ethnicity. The terms *minority* or *minorities* are used within the text to describe groups of individuals who represent a numeric minority within a racial or ethnic population.

Reasonable Suspicion

A police officer may briefly detain a person for questioning or request identification only if the officer has a reasonable suspicion that the person's behavior is related to criminal activity. The officer, however, must have specific facts that must be articulated to support his or her actions; a mere suspicion or "hunch" is not sufficient cause to detain a person or to request identification. Reasonable suspicion can be based on the observations of a police officer combined with his or her training and experience, and/or reliable information received from credible outside sources.

Suspect-Specific Incident

An incident in which an officer is lawfully attempting to detain, apprehend, or otherwise be on the lookout for one or more specific suspects who have been identified or described in part by national or ethnic origin, gender, or race is called a "suspect-specific" incident.

HISTORICAL BACKGROUND OF THE TERM *RACIAL PROFILING* IN LAW ENFORCEMENT

During the 1990s, concerns about police use of racial profiling as a pretext to stop, question, search, and possibly arrest people became a major focus of minority individuals and communities, politicians, law enforcement administrators, scholars, and researchers. National surveys in the last decade revealed that the majority of Americans, white as well as black, believed racial profiling was commonly used in the United States, but 80 percent of those surveyed opposed the practice. They believed that police were routinely guilty of bias in their treatment of racial and ethnic minorities, and also that such behavior had been going on for a long time.

What is the source of racial profiling as both a term and as a law enforcement practice? Before addressing that question, it is useful to examine how people use prior events or information to make decisions in everyday life.

People routinely form mental images or tentative judgments about others and the surrounding circumstances or situation, both consciously and subconsciously, which is also a form of stereotyping. This sort of stereotyping, or looking for what one perceives to be indicators, provides a preliminary mental rating of potential risk to a person encountering a particular event or person.

It involves conscious and unconscious thought processes whereby an individual: (1) makes observations and selects data born out of that person's past experiences, (2) adds cultural and personal meaning to what he or she observes, (3) makes assumptions based on the meanings that he or she has attributed to the observation, (4) draws conclusions based on his or her own beliefs and, finally, (5) takes action (see Senge's "Ladder of Inference" discussed later in this chapter). This process comprises, for all people, basic decision making in their lives, and it guides a person's interpretation of events. A person's socialization, including the person's upbringing by his or her parents, plays a major role in determining decisions and the actions taken as a result of these decisions in both professional and personal settings.

Profiling in law enforcement is used by officers to look for characteristics that indicate the probability of criminal acts, or factors that tend to correlate with dangerous or threatening behavior. For officers, most of these characteristics have been internalized based on experience and training. If they have had dangerous encounters while on duty, such experiences prepare them for similar future events—as the old saying goes, *better safe than sorry!* The professional training that leads to the development of indicators or common characteristics comes from many sources, beginning with the police academy and in-service training under the supervision of a field-training officer. Informal education may include mentoring by an older partner and pressure from peers on how to do the job, and more formal training continues via advanced officer courses on various subjects. All of these help establish the common practice of profiling. If an official profile of a suspect is used by an agency, and the perpetrator is caught, we say, "He or she fits the profile," thus validating this perspective. When serial bombing suspect Eric Robert Rudolph was finally apprehended in June 2003, for example, FBI profiling experts immediately confirmed that the notorious fugitive did indeed "fit their profile." Training and experience provide officers with indicators to look for not only to prevent harm to them, but also to identify those people or events that are suspicious and warrant closer attention. This attention then helps civilians and police officers decide what action is prudent to take when confronted by a similar person or situation. This does not necessarily mean the person using profiling in this way is biased or prejudiced. Fulbright professor Ira Straus, in an article for United Press International, suggests that some degree of profiling can be appropriate and even necessary as long as it is not abusive. In the article, he is not using the term *profiling* to mean the same as the definition used in this textbook, but is using "profiling" to mean stereotyping:

> Profiling is universal. Every person relies on it for a preliminary rating of their risks with each person they run into. If people do not profile explicitly, they do it implicitly. If they do not do it consciously, they do it unconsciously. But they go on doing it. They could not live without it.
>
> Do police do it too? Of course they do. All police and investigative efforts involve working from two ends, direct and indirect. The direct end means following the trail of specific leads and informants. The indirect end means profiling; that is, finding a social milieu or pool to look in and ask around in—a milieu where there are more likely to be informants, leads, and criminals answering to that crime.
>
> To profile is morally risky. The dangers of unfair and unreasonable profiling— that is, profiling based on unfounded prejudices such as racism—are well known. They are widely discussed, guarded against, and proscribed. (Straus, 2002, pp. 1–2)

Professor Straus implies that profiling (or in his context, stereotyping) is not always based on accurate information or data. When the meanings placed on observations are faulty or biased, the assumptions and conclusions, therefore, may be incorrect, thereby leading to inappropriate attitudes, behavior, and actions.

Law enforcement officers, airport security personnel, customs and border patrol agents, and members of some other occupations use profiles. In the absence of conclusive or specific details, it is the only way to narrow the amount of information from which to make decisions, including whether or not to stop a person for further investigation.

Although there are other historical examples of racial profiling, the first use of the term appears to have occurred in New Jersey, where troopers were trying to stem the flow of illegal drugs and other contraband into and across their state. In the early 1990s, the Drug Enforcement Administration (DEA) and the New Jersey State Police (NJSP) developed a relationship: the DEA provided training to the NJSP on what it had determined to be common characteristics of drug couriers along Interstate 95 from Miami through New Jersey. The characteristics included the types of cars preferred (Nissan Pathfinders), the direction of travel, and the use of rental vehicles from another state. In addition, it was common to find that a third party had rented the vehicle, that the driver was licensed in a state different from the one in which the rental took place, and that there were telltale behavioral cues (such as nervousness or conflicting stories). The profile also noted that the national origin of those involved in drug trafficking organizations was predominantly Jamaican, thus implying dark skin.

The NJSP used "pretextual stops" (i.e., using some legal pretext, such as failing to signal a lane change or having a missing license plate or faulty brake light) on I-95 to determine the potential criminality of a car's driver and occupants. The officer(s) would then attempt to establish a legal basis to search for illegal drugs. Many argued, and the courts agreed, that these pretextual stops were also based on the fact that the cars' drivers and occupants were black or dark-skinned. In other words, they had been racially profiled—targeted because of the color of their skin. The resultant studies determined that blacks and Hispanics on I-95 were stopped with a frequency disproportionate to their numbers on that road. Due to the controversy, and the subsequent court decision and punitive judgment against the NJSP, they no longer distribute a typical felony offender profile to their officers "because such profiles might contribute to what the state's attorney general calls 'inappropriate stereotypes' about criminals" (Will, 2001). New Jersey, like other states, has also created legislation making racial profiling illegal, with criminal sanctions for officers practicing it.

PROFILING CHALLENGES IN THE WAR ON TERRORISM

Prior to September 11, 2001, the use by law enforcement agencies of profiles that included race, ethnicity, or national origin, or the act of profiling using the same criteria, had come to be generally frowned upon, or even condemned, in the United States. But an attitude change occurred after the horrendous attacks on the World Trade Center in New York City and the Pentagon. One outcome of that event was the establishment of the U.S. Department of Homeland Security (DHS) and the attempt to coordinate law enforcement agencies and the military in defense of the nation's citizenry and infrastructure. The scope of the state of emergency created by the hijackers altered both public opinion and government policy concerning profiles and profiling based on national origin and ethnicity, especially regarding both the legitimacy and necessity of the practices. Given the ongoing and complex conflicts in the Middle East, plus the global terrorist threat from al-Qaida, Taliban, and other Islamic extremists, the issue became more charged and complicated. Police at the national and local level had to develop strategies for detecting and apprehending terrorists. Tentative profiles were quickly developed on the basis of obvious characteristics and experience.

Since all the terrorists involved in the September 11 incidents were Islamic males from the Middle East, the issue became whether law enforcement and security personnel could target or profile suspicious men with similar backgrounds for stops, searches, or increased questioning. Profiling, using those criteria, began to be employed on the basis of several factors common to these particular terrorists, who were:

- young males, Arab in appearance
- primarily citizens of Saudi Arabia
- trained in fundamentalist religious and/or al-Qaida training camps in Afghanistan or Pakistan
- adherents of Islam who had been inspired to religious extremism by fundamentalist clergy, especially with regard to **Al-jihad**
- harboring a deep hatred, in general, of Western decadence, materialism, and immorality, which they perceived as undermining the values and stability of their societies, and, in particular, of America for its interference in Middle Eastern affairs.

Al-jihad or Jihad   Struggle (literal translation of Arabic). The term has also been used by some to mean "holy war" against infidels or nonbelievers.

Chapter 8, Law Enforcement Contact with Arab Americans and Other Middle Eastern Groups. This subject is covered in more detail in chapter 8, Law Enforcement Contact with Arab Americans and other Middle Eastern Groups.

Initially there was little outcry among the general public against these actions and others. Recall that prior to "September 11," 80 percent of Americans opposed racial profiling. Polls taken soon after the attack showed 70 percent of Americans believed that some form of profiling was necessary, and acceptable, to ensure public safety. It is apparent that the public was willing to give up certain freedoms in exchange for helping the government reduce the opportunity for terrorists to operate in the United States. Members of the American Association for Public Opinion Research, at a May 2002 meeting, offered a historical perspective. They said that while civil liberties usually have broad public support, the public has been willing to tolerate substantial limits on those freedoms when there are serious threats to security and safety within the United States and to Americans abroad. Their report cited the decline in support for civil liberties after Pearl Harbor and again at the height of the Cold War. Other than the American Civil Liberties Union (ACLU) and the National Association of Arab Americans, there were few who spoke out against detentions of Middle Easterners and South Asians at security areas in airports and elsewhere after "September 11." These organizations questioned the use of what appeared to them to be racial profiling and abuse of civil rights, generally and specifically. However, many citizens argued that proactive law enforcement and enhanced security measures at airports were necessary to prevent or reduce opportunities for terrorist acts and to investigate and bring to justice those involved. Discovering terrorists and their missions, prior to another attack, became a matter of urgency. The researchers added, however, that support for civil liberties has always resumed when the threat subsided. This certainly was the case as time passed after "September 11" without additional terrorist acts in the United States.

The use of profiles and profiling in law enforcement requires a balancing of morality, legality, efficiency, equality, liberty, and security concerns. It has the potential to affect millions of innocent people in the United States who are or may appear to be of Muslim, Arab, Middle Eastern or South Asian descent, or Sikh. It is important that law enforcement officials and security agents avoid hasty judgments and not condemn all Muslims, those of the Islamic faith, or Middle Easterners for the crimes of a few. Officers, agents, and those who protect airports and other public facilities should seek to learn more about both Islam and Arab civilization (see Chapter 8).

POLICE AND CITIZEN PERCEPTIONS OF RACIAL PROFILING

How does law enforcement balance the need to reduce crime, and especially terrorism, against the potential for accusations of discrimination, race biased policing, and stereotyping? It is a challenging and complex problem for officers, especially for those strongly committed to nonbiased practices who believe in proactive policing. The real questions associated with any type of law enforcement profiling or the development of profiles are:

1. Who is doing the profile construction and on what basis?
   • Does that person have some expertise (e.g., in behavioral science)?
   • Is the profile creator objective, unbiased, and nonjudgmental in formulating a particular profile?
2. Who is interpreting the profile?
   • Is that person sufficiently trained in its application?
3. Is the officer who is using profiling doing so legally?
   • Is it based on departmental policy rather than on his or her personal biases, attitudes, and beliefs?

Criminal justice agencies face major challenges regarding the issue and impact of the use of profiles and profiling. Law enforcement personnel are entrusted with (1) protecting the rights of those who are the subject of stereotyping, harassment, and discrimination (i.e., those who are *misidentified* as a result of profiles or profiling); (2) identifying and bringing to justice those who are terrorists or criminals (i.e., those who are *correctly identified*); (3) not missing terrorists and/or criminals who do not fit a particular profile or stereotype; and (4) not being so hampered by their personal stereotypes, attitudes, beliefs, perceptions, and knowledge (or lack thereof) that innocent people are detained and terrorists are not apprehended in the course of law enforcement.

Myth, Misperception, or Reality?

There are some police officers, government administrators, and others who maintain that racial profiling is a myth or a misperception. They argue that the majority of officers does not stop or detain people based on their race, ethnicity, or national origin, but on their behavior, location, circumstances, and other factors. Officers contend that those who are stopped often do not understand police procedures or are overly sensitive, or are using the allegation that bias was involved in their stop, questioning, search, and/or arrest to cast aspersions on the action taken in an attempt to nullify it.

There has been over a decade of reform measures by agencies to eliminate racial profiling or the perception thereof. Sometimes the reforms were compelled by a class action lawsuit or legislation. Regardless of the motivations for reform, have these measures resulted in perceptible change? Are law enforcement agencies still being accused of racial profiling? Various organizations, including the Vera Institute of Justice, the ACLU, Amnesty International, colleges and universities, and the U.S. Department of Justice have studied allegations of racial profiling in cities and counties across the nation since the phenomenon became a glaring media issue in the 1990s. The conclusion of the research on the subject, however, seems to indicate that although there has been some improvement, "no jurisdiction in the U.S. has addressed racial profiling in an effective and comprehensive way" (Amnesty International, 2004, pp. 28–29). Some examples illustrate the continued concern with this issue:

- *Oregon:*   In 2006 the Portland Police Bureau was accused by local media, based upon an ACLU complaint, of stopping Latinos and African Americans at a rate disproportionate to their numbers in the community. African Americans represented 6 percent of the city's population, but 14 percent of all traffic stops that year. Latinos represented 6 percent of the population, but 9 percent of traffic stops. Based on these figures, the argument was that African Americans were more than twice as likely to be stopped as were whites, and Latinos, more than one and a half times. That particular year, more than 10 percent of African Americans and Latinos stopped by the police were subjected to discretionary searches, while only 5 percent of whites were subjected to such searches. Evidence of criminal activity was found in a higher percentage of searches of whites (31 percent) than of African Americans (27 percent) or Latinos (25 percent) ("ACLU of Oregon Analysis of Key Data Related to Portland Police Bureau Traffic Stops in 2006," 2007).
- *Missouri:*   In 2007, it was the 8th year in a row that data on traffic stops were submitted to the Attorney General's office to address allegations of racial profiling, as mandated by a state law enacted in 2000. According to an analysis of the data, the disparity index for African American drivers continued to be of concern, rising from 1.49 in 2006 to 1.58 in 2007. The index is a measure that compares a racial or ethnic group's proportion of total vehicle stops to its proportion of the driving-age population. Values above 1 indicate overrepresentation. African Americans represent 10.7 percent of Missouri's population, yet account for 16.9 percent of all vehicle stops ("Racial Profiling Data Released for '07," 2008, p. 1).
- *California:*   In 2007, the San Francisco Chronicle reported that, according to an ACLU representative (Mark Schlosberg), the city's police department had not complied with a 2001 mandate from the Police Commission to collect data on all traffic stops. The mandate was because of citizen and ACLU concerns that the police were targeting African Americans. The Commission had ordered that "the city's officers file reports on the race, sex and age of motorists they stopped and whether their vehicles were searched" ("SFPD Stops Collecting Traffic Stop Racial Data," 2007, p. A1). The ACLU, after studying 27 months of summaries covering about 180,000 traffic stops, found that African Americans and Hispanics were 2.5 times more likely to be searched than were whites. The ACLU representative quoted in the Chronicle concluded that "racial profiling is a significant problem."
- *Arizona:*   In 2008, the Arizona Department of Public Safety implemented policies requiring highway patrol officers to document their reasons for searching vehicles they stop and to obtain motorists' consent for a search. Consent was to be verified by the driver's signature on a form or by using a video or audio recording of the driver giving permission. Department policy and training now also state that "officers must have a 'reasonable suspicion of criminal activity' before requesting consent for a search" ("Ariz. DPS Tightens Search Rules to Avoid Profiling," 2008). The changes were recommended by an advisory board created by

the governor as a result of a class action suit brought by the ACLU in 2001 alleging racial profiling on northern Arizona interstate highways.

- *New York:*   The New York Police Department (NYPD) was criticized in 2009 by civil rights groups because officers had stopped, questioned, and frisked more than a half a million people the previous year. The contention, based on data collected and released by the NYPD, was that a disproportionate number of these individuals were African Americans and Latinos. According to the Center for Constitutional Rights, the raw data indicated that more than 80 percent of those stopped were young African American or Latino men ("NYCLU Analysis Reveals NYPD Stopped Nearly 2 Million Innocent New Yorkers; Most are Black & Latino," 2009). Civil rights advocates had sued the NYPD in 2006 over the same issue, a year when the department data also indicated they had stopped over 500,000 persons. Despite these figures, however, the RAND Corporation, an independent research agency hired to analyze the same data, found no racial profiling in its examination, and "warned against the kind of simplistic comparisons made by the civil rights groups" ("New York: Analysis of Racial Disparities in the New York City Police Department's Stop, Question, and Frisk Practices," 2007).

Although these anecdotes highlight departments that still need imporvement, there have been success stories as well. For example, the *New York Times* reported in 2007 that federal monitors from the U.S. Department of Justice had found that the New Jersey State Police had made so much progress in eliminating racial profiling that it no longer needed their supervision. This was only 8 years after that agency acknowledged that troopers were focusing on black and Hispanic drivers at traffic stops ("New Jersey Police Win Praise for Efforts to End Profiling," 2007, p. C13). In a consent decree signed in 1999, the state had agreed to allow the federal Department of Justice to oversee how traffic stops were conducted, along with other State Police activities. After the implementation of approriate remedies, the *Times* reported, "compliance requirements in all areas are now at 100 percent levels, [and] it appears the ultimate goal has been attained. Ample evidence exists to suggest that the agency has become self-monitoring and self-correcting to a degree not often observed in American law enforcement" ("New Jersey Police Win Praise for Efforts to End Profiling," 2007).

It appears, therefore, that despite laws, court orders, and agency policies and procedures that prohibit officers from using race or ethnicity as a decision-making factor, the practice still takes place. However, it is difficult to analyze the degree to which this is the case, because the data collected by law enforcement agencies are often fraught with methodological problems. This is discussed later in this chapter.

As indicated, most police officers and city or county administrators deny the existence of racial profiling. They claim that those who believe they have been the victims of profiling may not be aware of other factors that the officer took into consideration. A traffic stop is the most common situation leading to complaints of racial profiling. A 2005 nationwide survey regarding police contact with the public established that speeding was the most common reason for being pulled over, accounting for 56 percent of all traffic stops. The report indicates that in 2002 and 2005, white, black, and Hispanic drivers were stopped by police at similar rates, but blacks and Hispanics were more likely than whites to be searched by police (see Exhibit 13.1). In 2005, 86 percent of those stopped believed it was for a legitimate reason ("Contacts between the Police and the Public, 2005," 2007).

Researchers studying allegations of racial profiling must also explore discretionary decision making of individual officers, a subject that has long been the object of study by those doing research in the criminal justice field.

EXHIBIT 13.1   Contacts Between Police and the Public, 2005.

White, black, and Hispanic drivers were stopped by police at similar rates; blacks
and Hispanics were searched by police at higher rates than were whites.

Race/Hispanic origin of resident	Percent of drivers stopped by police (%)		Percent of stopped drivers searched by police (%)	
	2002	2005	2002	2005
Total	8.8	8.8	5.0	4.8
White	8.8	8.9	3.5	3.6
Black/African American	9.2	8.1	10.2	9.5
Hispanic/Latino	8.6	8.9	11.4	8.8

Source: Bureau of Justice Statistics, Special Report—April 2007 NCJ 215243.

Most of the research on criminal justice has documented that the impact of racial
prejudice on criminal justice agents' decision-making has been decreasing in prevalence and importance for at least 30 years. Prior to the 1970s, racial prejudice was
still the basis for many state and local laws. Since that time, police departments have
made continuing serious managerial efforts to reduce and eliminate prejudicial
behavior by police officers, and recent research is no longer consistent with earlier
research on the extent to which race per se directly influences police decisions. This
recent research suggests that police officers' behavior is predicted primarily by legal
and situation-specific factors and that the influence of race and other extra-legal
factors is diminishing. (Engel, Calnon, and Bernard, 2002, pp. 251–252)

Police Perceptions

What are the police officers' perceptions of allegations that all race-based decision making by
them is motivated by their own prejudice?

Most law enforcement officers would maintain they are not biased, prejudiced, or using
racial profiling in their policing methods. Proactive policing sometimes involves using legitimate
profiling based on officer experience and training or using profiles provided by their agency.
Sometimes, however, officer experience can mean a lot of things. If the experience leads to faulty
assumptions and conclusions, then the officer might engage in inappropriate behavior and take
the wrong action. (See the section "Education and Training" of this chapter for a discussion of the
sources of officers' beliefs and attitudes.)

Officers use profiling (behavioral commonalities or indicators) or written profiles to identify those whom they should investigate to determine if they are committing or about to commit a
crime. Profiling is done on a daily basis by police officers, not just in high-crime areas where gangs
congregate or highway corridors where drug runners operate, but in all communities. It also takes
place in predominantly white communities when officers see out-of-place or suspicious-looking
members of minority groups. The officer in this situation would argue that he or she would find
reason to check out anyone, regardless of color, who did not seem to fit the area or time of day,
especially if he or she were acting suspiciously. Profiling also takes place when an officer sees a
white person in a predominantly minority area, especially if the area is one in which drug sales or

prostitution takes place. The officer checks out the individual if reasonable suspicion is present that a crime might be taking place. Most officers would emphatically deny they are biased or prejudiced when using such profiling.

Officers also insist that both their agency and the community in which they work pressure them to reduce crime in the neighborhoods, and that profiling (not racial profiling) is a tool to accomplish a reduction in some crimes. For example, the *New York Times* reported that on November 11, 2008, a young man was shot and killed not far from the Queens home of Dennis Walcott, Deputy Mayor of New York. Residents in the predominantly Caribbean neighborhood demanded what the *Times* described as "a vigorous police presence." Soon there were complaints about young men being stopped, but at the same time, street violence diminished. "We struggle with the duality of wanting a safe neighborhood and police who are respectful of our children," the deputy mayor said. "It's an inherent challenge and I'm not sure there is an easy answer" ("Police Polish Image, but Concerns Persist," 2009, p. 21).

Also, if officers believe that their agency supervisors and managers want them to be aggressive on the streets by stopping vehicles and pedestrians to determine if there is potential criminal activity leading to a search and arrest, officers will do so, especially if this behavior is rewarded within their organization. Reward structures within agencies include such things as favorable evaluations, shifts, and assignments, and even promotions. Unfortunately, if officers come to believe that minority citizens are more likely to be involved in criminal activity of some sort and that aggressively stopping their vehicles will result in more searches and arrests, they are more likely to stop them (referred to as the expectancy theory), especially if the department encourages and rewards the practice.

The Police Executive Research Forum (PERF) undertook an extensive study of racial profiling. They chose to avoid the term *racial profiling*, preferring *racially biased policing*. They indicate in their report that racial profiling was defined so restrictively that the term does not fully capture the concerns of both police and citizens. For example:

> Racial profiling is frequently defined as law enforcement activities (e.g., detentions, arrests, searches) that are initiated *solely* on the basis of race. Central to the debate on the most frequently used definitions is the word "solely." In the realm of potential discriminatory actions, this definition likely references only a very small portion. Even a racially prejudiced officer likely uses more than the single factor of race when conducting biased law enforcement. For example, officers might make decisions based on the neighborhood and the race of the person, the age of the car and the race of the person, or the gender and the race of the person. Activities based on these sample pairs of factors would fall outside the most commonly used definition of racial profiling. ("Racially Biased Policing," 2001, p. 3)

Using this common definition of racial profiling, then, provides a very narrow meaning for the term. "Those who define the practice so narrowly (i.e., race as the only reason for stopping, questioning or arresting someone) that we can imagine only the most extreme bigots engaging in it. Using such a definition, racial profiling is easy to both denounce and deny" (Barlow and Barlow, 2002).

In the PERF study, staff conducted meetings around the country with citizens and police line and command staff regarding occurrences and perceptions of biased policing. The subsequent report, "Racially Biased Policing: A Principled Response," revealed that the police in the study were using the narrow definition of racial profiling (stops based *solely* on race or ethnicity) and thus could declare vehemently that police actions based solely on race, national origin, or ethnicity were quite rare. The citizens in the study, however, were using a broader definition, one that included race as one among several factors leading up to the stop of the individual.

> Many of our law enforcement participants did express skepticism that "racial pro-
> filing" was a major problem, exacerbating some citizens' frustration. It became
> clear to staff that these differing perceptions among citizens and police regarding
> racial profiling's pervasiveness were very much related to the respective definitions
> they had adopted. The citizens equated "racial profiling" with all manifestations of
> racially biased policing, whereas most of the police practitioners defined "racial
> profiling" as stopping a motorist based *solely* on race. Presumably, even officers
> who engage in racially biased policing rarely make a vehicle stop based *solely* on
> race (often ensuring probable cause or some other factor is also present). ("Racially
> Biased Policing," 2001, p. 15)

OTHER FACTORS IN POLICE STOPS   Those concerned about racial profiling must also recognize that when a stop or detention by officers is not self-initiated, it was most likely to have been initiated because a witness or victim had provided a description of a person or event that they felt required police action—a suspect-specific incident or one due to computer-generated information. This is the case in the majority of contacts police make with citizens. If the complainant describes a suspect of a certain race, ethnicity, or national origin, that is what the officer will search for. For example, if police receive a report of possible criminal activity, and reliable information indicates that he is 5 foot 8 inches, lean, long-haired, and Asian, then "Asian" may be considered, along with the other demographics, in developing reasonable suspicion or probable cause to detain. If, however, the citizen is reporting the activity of a minority because of his or her own biases, the police should attempt to ensure the legitimacy of the complaint and not be an agent of what might be racially charged paranoia. In Brooksfield, Wisconsin, dispatchers are trained to gather more information from callers to determine if the call is legitimate. If not, they then can explain this fact to the caller and not trigger a potentially volatile police–citizen encounter.

Some allegations of racially motivated stops are clearly not reasonable. In some cases, officers cannot discern the race or ethnicity of the driver and/or occupant(s) prior to the stop. For example, some cars have tinted or darkened windows or a head rest on the back of the seats, making it impossible to determine the race, ethnicity, or even gender of the occupant(s). When officers use radar, it is another example of an electronic device determining which vehicle to stop and not the race, ethnicity, or national origin of the driver. Obviously at nighttime, it is challenging to identify drivers or passengers in detail. (Readers of this textbook should try to identify the occupants of a vehicle in front of them to test this argument.)

Policing during the 1990s and into the present day has been driven by two forces: (1) data developed and analyzed by specialists (crime analysts) that provide officers with predictions on where crimes might occur (including time of day and even generalized suspect information), and (2) POP or COP approaches, wherein neighborhood representatives tell officers about problems, including potential suspects, in their communities. In the latter case, members of the community demand that officers take enforcement action against drug dealers, prostitutes, gang members, those disturbing the peace, and suspicious persons, regardless of their race or ethnicity.

Another example of urban policing using race-neutral, data-driven technology and methods is New York's innovative **CompStat**—or COMPSTAT—(short for **Comp**uter **Stat**istics or COMParative STATistics). It refers to the New York Police Department's personnel and resource management system, the purpose of which is crime reduction. It uses Geographic Information

Systems (GIS) technology to map crime and identifies problems in the city. Crime data are forwarded every week to the chief of the department's CompStat Unit. Based on this information, precinct commanders and members of top management deploy manpower and resources to most effectively reduce crime and improve police performance.

Officers are held accountable for reducing specific crime in targeted areas. If robberies are up in a certain precinct, officers are deployed to locate and arrest those responsible. If the neighborhood to which they are assigned is a minority part of the city, those contacted will likely be members of that minority group. Race is irrelevant to this sort of policing. When Russian immigrants in New York dominated the Ecstasy trade, law enforcement efforts targeted (profiled) them, and ultimately their illegal activities were reduced. Arrests are most often the result of criminal intelligence, computer-generated data, and good police work, not racism. The CompStat system, which began in 1994, has since been replicated in many other departments, including Los Angeles, Philadelphia, and Baltimore under different names or acronyms.

There are some who argue that the use of racial profiling is justified and should be legal because the demographics of crime demonstrate a relationship between the numbers of blacks and Hispanics stopped, searched and arrested, and incarcerated, and the numbers of crimes committed—that is, members of those minority groups do commit more crime than do whites or Asians (MacDonald, 2001). Others argue this sort of rationalization perpetuates the problem through a vicious cycle. Studies have been used both to prove and to disprove this hypothesis. It is open to question whether officers stop minorities because they believe this hypothesis, because they are biased, or both.

Victim and Civil Rights Advocates' Perceptions

The claims and counterclaims about the existence and prevalence of racial profiling have been made for years, and they should not be dismissed as misperceptions or misunderstandings. We have to regard them as indicators of a very real social phenomenon.

Blacks are not the only Americans who say they have been the targets of racial or ethnic profiling by law enforcement. Hispanic men reported they were more likely than white men to question why they were stopped and how they were treated (Lundman and Kaufman, 2003). Also, just as DWB has been used by civil rights advocates to demonstrate racial profiling of African Americans or Hispanics, in recent years, "flying while Arab" has been used to describe the targeting of Arabs, South Asians, and Middle Easterners. The complaints of racial profiling are most often heard at airports and other places where there is a concern about the potential for terrorist attack. Civil rights advocates say that Arabs, South Asians, and Middle Easterners, most of them loyal American citizens, have become victims of the new war on terrorism. It is a difficult issue and one in which officers and security agents are damned if they do and damned if they don't. Minorities complain that they are not only more likely to be stopped than whites, but they are also often pressured to allow searches of their vehicles.

There are many accounts by people who have been stopped by police on questionable grounds and subjected to disrespectful behavior, intrusive questioning, and disregard for their civil rights. In fact, a study by Amnesty International (AI), United States estimates there are 32 million victims of racial profiling and that 87 million individuals are at high risk of victimization during their lifetimes (AI, 2004). The study involved a series of nationwide hearings and public testimony from individuals alleging to be victims of racial profiling while driving, walking, shopping, traveling through airports, and during other activities. These accounts lend credibility to the reality of the practice. Data collected by police departments to refute such claims often reveal that, without further analysis and interpretation, minority drivers are stopped in numbers out of proportion to their presence on the road.

It is not uncommon for white officers to downplay the existence and scope of racial profiling during departmental training programs on the topic. However, upon hearing fellow officers describe their own experiences as members of a minority group, the white officers typically respond with surprise, but are then more receptive to the suggestion that there is a problem ("Racially Biased Policing," 2001, p. 15). In a 2002 study, the findings of which are still relevant today, David and Melissa Barlow surveyed African American police officers in Milwaukee to determine whether they felt they had ever been racially profiled, and, if so, to what extent. The researchers wanted to learn how black officers felt about the legality of the circumstances under which they had been stopped by police. Because the subjects of the survey were themselves police officers, their views could not be easily dismissed.

The survey defined racial profiling as "when race is used by a police officer or a police agency in determining the potential criminality of an individual" (Barlow and Barlow, 2002, p. 14). Of the 2,100 sworn personnel of the Milwaukee Police Department, 414 were designated as black. The response rate to this survey was 38 percent (158 officers). Over 99 percent were over 25 years of age and had been sworn police officers for at least 1 year. The percentage of male respondents was 83.5, while the percentage of female respondents was 16.5.

Exhibit 13.2 shows that the majority of those who responded to the survey believed that they had been racially profiled. Note that the percentages drop off rapidly as the survey proceeded from questions about being stopped and questioned to questions about being arrested. The researchers suggest that the numbers fall off rapidly because the officers would have identified themselves as such upon being stopped and thus avoided further action. It should be noted that some of those surveyed reported that they were on duty but in plain clothes when they were stopped. From their findings, the Barlows conclude that black men are more likely to be the victims of racial profiling than were black women by a ratio of three to one.

In their research, the Barlows also asked the sworn police officers of the Milwaukee Police Department whether they personally used racial profiling in the performance of their job. They found that most (90 percent) of the respondents do not use racial profiling nor believe it is a necessary or legitimate tool for law enforcement. The researchers concluded: "Although many white Americans, members of law enforcement and government officials deny the existence of

---

EXHIBIT 13.2   Racial Profiling Survey.

Question: In your professional opinion, do you believe you have ever been stopped, questioned, searched, ticketed, or arrested as a result of racial profiling?

	Yes (%)	*No* (%)
Stopped	69	31
Questioned	52	60
Searched	19	81
Ticketed	21	79
Arrested	7	93

Source: Barlow and Barlow, 2002, p. 14.

racial profiling or racially biased policing, the findings from the study suggest it is a reality" (Barlow and Barlow, 2002, p. 15).

The following mini-case studies involve descriptions of fictional events but are based upon similar, actual occurrences. The issues and implications of each should be discussed in class, especially the question of whether the police behavior is proper, justified, legal, or necessary.

Mini Case Studies: Culture and Crime

You Decide—Racial Profiling?

A well-dressed young Hispanic male is driving through a predominantly white community early in the morning on his way to work in a new BMW. He is pulled over for speeding and the officer, instead of simply asking for a driver's license and writing a speeding ticket, calls for backup and is joined by another officer. The young man is told to leave his vehicle and the officers search it. "Hey, where did you get the money for something like this?," one officer asks mockingly as he starts the process of going through every inch of the BMW. One of the officers pulls off an inside door panel, and more dismantling of the vehicle follows. They say they are looking for drugs, but in the end find nothing. After ticketing the driver for speeding, the two officers casually drive off.

1. Do you believe police officers do in fact pull over and search the vehicles of minorities disproportionately to their numbers?
2. Are there racial or ethnic characteristics on which officers can legitimately focus during an investigation or to prevent criminal activity?
3. Should profiling only include the actions, behavior, and activities of the person(s) observed by the officer?
4. How can law enforcement leadership and trainers teach officers to distinguish between behavioral profiling and racial profiling?
5. Are those who argue that the "demographics of crime" justify racial profiling using data that are biased? Does this sort of rationalization perpetuate the problem through a vicious cycle?

Does the War on Terrorism Give License to Law Enforcement to Engage in Racial Profiling?

An Arab American says he was recently a victim of racial profiling at an airport in Washington, D.C., while on his way to Detroit. He was pulled out of line, questioned, and searched. He reported that this was done in front of everyone else in line and was humiliating. He thought that the authorities at the airport were doing this so non-Arab Americans could see that they are doing something about security. He felt he had been racially profiled.

Discuss the following:

1. Passengers who appear "Arab-looking," which has included South Asians and Latinos, have been asked to leave airplanes because fellow passengers and crew members refuse to fly with them. How can airline security and management justify these actions?
2. Sikh men have been denied the right to board aircraft because they refuse to fly without their turban, which equates to asking an individual to fly without a basic article of clothing.
3. Has the war on terrorism or the conflict in the Middle East provided the opportunity for officers and security personal to use racial profiling tactics?
4. What options are available for officers and security personnel to provide security and safety to the public they serve?

Racial bias, or the perception of same, distorts attitudes toward civil authority. It also impacts the victims' quality of everyday life. In addition to actual bias, the perception of bias is a substantial barrier to good police–community relations. The victims of racial profiling maintain that police use this practice because there are officers who believe that having black or brown skin is an indication of a greater risk of criminality and they therefore view minorities as potential criminals. The victims believe, therefore, that skin color becomes evidence every time they engage in the most common and prototypically American act—driving.

PROFILING AS A LEGAL TOOL OF LAW ENFORCEMENT

Profiling and profiles have long been used as legitimate law enforcement tools to look for signs of potential criminal activity. They are tools utilized by law enforcement in almost every country in the world, although the people profiled will vary by country. For example, the constabularies in Northern Ireland and England have profiles that help them identify extremists among members of the Irish Republican Army (IRA). Religion and national origin would be factors in this profile, not race or ethnicity. In Israel, the police have profiles of Palestinian terrorists. Now the criminal justice community in many parts of the world is using profiles to locate and arrest members of Al-Qaida. In the United States, a potential terrorist's profile used by airport and homeland security agents might include such factors as (1) a man in his 20s or 30s who comes from Saudi Arabia, Egypt, or Pakistan (2) who is probably living in one of six states: Texas, New Jersey, California, New York, Michigan, or Florida; and (3) who is likely to have engaged in some sort of suspicious activity, such as taking flying lessons, traveling in areas of possible targets, or getting a U.S. driver's license. Meeting some of these criteria—not necessarily having a certain skin color— is enough to instigate questioning by law enforcement authorities.

PERF created policy intended for adoption by police departments across the nation. The policy clearly delineates what is legal profiling. The policy discusses the U.S. Constitution Fourth Amendment provision that officers shall *not consider* race/ethnicity to establish reasonable suspicion or probable cause except when based on trustworthy, locally relevant information that links a person or persons of a specific race/ethnicity to a particular unlawful incident(s). The policy:

- disallows use of race as a general indicator for criminal behavior
- disallows use of stereotypes/biases
- allows for the consideration of race *as one factor* in making law enforcement decisions if it is based on trustworthy and locally relevant information that links specific suspected unlawful activity to a person(s) of a particular race/ethnicity
- relies on *descriptions* of actual suspects, not general *predictions* of who may be involved in a crime.

For example, an officer observes the following: (1) the tail light is burned out on a vehicle with a white driver; (2) it is midnight; (3) the car is in a minority neighborhood where drugs are known to be sold; (4) the driver pulls up to the curb and talks briefly to someone standing there; (5) an exchange takes place; (6) the driver drives away; (7) the driver makes furtive movements as if hiding something under the seat when police pull him over. Although not a representative example because the driver is white, race was used as a part of the decision to pull the driver over.

PERF recommends that the following principle be applied: "Race/ethnicity should be treated like other demographic descriptors. Police can use race/ethnicity as one factor in the same way that they use age, gender and other descriptors to establish reasonable suspicion or probable cause." The organization recommends that the best test for officers to use include two questions: (1) Would I be engaging this particular person but for the fact that this person is white? (2) Would I be asking this question of this person but for the fact that this person is [fill in the demographic descriptor] ("Racially Biased Policing," 2001).

What is necessary in assessing the use of profiles and profiling is a combination of common sense and fairness, a balance between effective law enforcement and protection of civil liberties. The authors believe that profiles and profiling will not upset such a balance if they are used judiciously, fairly, and within the law. Most officers understand that profiling, not racial profiling, is an acceptable form of proactive law enforcement, and the courts agree. The U.S. Customs Service, the U.S. Border Patrol, and the DEA have long used profiles as a tool to detain and investigate persons fitting the "drug courier profile." Such a profile is based on behaviors, actions, traits, demeanor, intelligence information, carrier routes, statistical evidence, and other factors (not just a single characteristic like race or ethnicity). The U.S. Border Patrol obviously links race to incidence of crime on the border with Mexico. It is only logical to assume that most people attempting to enter the country illegally from Mexico are of Hispanic/Latino or Mestizo descent. The use of profiles in this context appears to be legal and acceptable. A border patrol profile, however, not only includes the ethnicity of the individual but also such factors as their proximity to the border, erratic driving, suspicious behavior, and the officers' previous experience with alien traffic.

Currently, airport police and security agents [Transportation Security Administration (TSA)], and other officials within the Department of Homeland Security (DHS) use profiles to try to identify those who might be a threat to security in their respective jurisdictions. For example, the CAPPS system (CAPPS I), implemented in 1998, relied on what is known as a Passenger Name Record (PNR). CAPPS stands for Computer Assisted Passenger Prescreening System. It was first implemented and administered by the FBI and the Federal Aviation Administration (FAA) in response to terrorist incidents in the United States and abroad. When a person books a plane ticket, certain identifying information is collected by the airline, including name, birth date, address, and phone number. This information is checked against other data such as the TSA's No-Fly list and the FBI's 10 most wanted fugitive list. The traveler is then assigned a terrorism "risk score." High scores require the airline to conduct extended baggage and/or personal screening, and, where appropriate, to contact law enforcement. In November 2001, control of the CAPPS I system was transferred from the FBI and FAA to the TSA. The CAPPS I system also screens passengers based on their destination and how they purchased their tickets—not on how they look. None of the profile information specifically involves the race, ethnicity, or national origin of the persons checked.

In 2003, the TSA presented a proposal for an expanded system to be called CAPPS II, but the request was canceled in 2004 by the DHS because of opposition from Congress and civil liberties groups. TSA immediately announced a successor program called Secure Flight, which would work much the same way as CAPPS II, but it too was blocked by Congress until it can pass tests for accuracy and privacy protection. The CAPPS II system checks a passenger's information against commercial databases (credit reports and consumer transactions) to determine if his or her identity is authentic. Critics of CAPPS II and Secure Flight see the systems as having the potential for unconstitutional invasions of privacy and government snooping. They also are concerned that people may be falsely identified as terrorists. TSA began operational testing of Secure Flight at the end of 2008 for domestic passenger vetting, with full implementation expected in 2010.

Legitimate Use of Race/Ethnicity

An important question is whether race can *ever* be a valid consideration when conducting law enforcement activity. In the *Travis* opinion, the majority concluded that "race or ethnic background may become a legitimate consideration when investigators have information on the subject of a particular suspect" (Travis, 62 F. 3rd at 54). Simply put, the suspect described and being sought is of a certain race or ethnicity (refer to the definition of suspect-specific incident in this chapter). Court decisions have allowed officers to consider the totality of the circumstances surrounding the subject of their attention in light of their experience and training, which may include "instructions on a drug courier profile" (*Florida v. Royer*, 460 U.S. at 525, note 6). Actually, many courts have upheld the use of drug courier profiles as the sole determinant of a stop or cause for suspicion. Therefore, profiles combined with other facts and circumstances can establish reasonable suspicion or probable cause. Race or color may be a factor to consider during certain police activity (*U.S. v. Brignoni-Ponce*, 442 U.S., 837, 887, 1975). The *Whren* (*Whren v. United States*) decision by the Supreme Court enhanced the already extensive power of police to detain individual citizens under the banner of the war on drugs by allowing pretext stops through the "objective" standard test (Bast, 1997; Harris, 1999).

Some see the *Whren* decision "objective standard" ruling as opening the door for police abuse. They argue that in the *Whren* case, it did not matter to the court that the officers lied about their intent, that they were violating departmental policy to make the stop, or that they really wanted to stop the car because it contained two African American men who sat at a stop sign for 20 seconds in an area known for drug dealing. They are concerned that the *Whren* decision clearly opens the door for racial profiling because it allows police officers to stop anyone without reasonable suspicion or probable cause, thus providing a mechanism for circumventing the Fourth Amendment requirements of the U.S. Constitution. Because minor traffic violations are numerous, they argue, to limit stops to the observation of traffic violations is no limitation at all. If a police officer wants to stop a car but does not have the legal authority to do so, all the officer has to do is to follow it until the driver gets nervous and at some point turns right without a turn signal, drifts across the center line, or simply fails to come to a complete stop at a stop sign. Upon observing a minor traffic violation, the police officer can stop the driver and attempt to pressure him or her into giving consent for the car to be searched. Under this "objective" standard, the motivation of the officer and previous enforcement patterns become irrelevant (Barlow and Barlow, 2000). It is important to note that the Court's decision in *Whren* did not create the practice of pretextual stops. Instead it validated this long-standing police practice that is even encouraged by police administrators. Neither was the *Whren* decision unpredictable. It is the result of more than a decade of decisions wherein the courts were unwilling to consider the legality of the use of race in law enforcement decision making (Withrow, 2006).

The courts said the burden that "brief detentions" place on law-abiding minority citizens is a minor and necessary inconvenience in the war on crime, suggesting that little damage is done by the practice of profiling. However, those who advocate making the standard for brief detentions more restrictive insist that these court decisions have failed to acknowledge that these detentions grow into regular occurrences, breeding resentment and anger both in the citizens stopped and in the police officers who confront hostile persons of color. Police officers who use race, ethnicity, gender, sexual orientation, or national origin as a factor in criminal profiling based on presumed statistical probabilities then contribute to the very statistics upon which they rely.

The Supreme Court has made it clear that as long as the government can show that police searches and seizures are objectively reasonable (i.e., based on probable cause or reasonable suspicion), they do not violate the Fourth Amendment, regardless of the officer's subjective (actual) motivation for the search or seizure. That does not mean, however, that objectively reasonable searches and seizures can never violate the Constitution. Officers motivated by prejudice who lawfully search or seize only members of certain racial, ethnic, religious, or gender groups are still subject to claims of constitutional violations (i.e., racial profiling).

Police officers who undertake searches of persons or vehicles not incident to an arrest must have reasonable suspicion or probable cause to perform such a search. An officer who does not have reasonable suspicion may ask for a consent to search (except in those states or localities where it is illegal) and even have the motorist sign a waiver to that effect. Sometimes, however, evidence of racial bias may be discovered when there is a repeated pattern of minorities being subjected to consent searches much more often than whites. Law enforcement agencies must monitor the data they collect on discretionary consent searches to ensure that the discretion is not applied more often to minorities. One explanation for the disparity, according to some researchers, is that minorities may be more nervous around police and officers may misinterpret that as suspicious behavior.

Far-reaching authority for searches was granted to law enforcement when, on October 26, 2001, President George W. Bush signed the Patriot Act Presidential Executive Orders into law. The law gave sweeping new powers to both domestic law enforcement and international intelligence agencies. The provisions of the law, aimed at terrorism, expanded surveillance capabilities (in effect, searches) and allowed for nationwide wiretaps under certain circumstances. Many aspects of the new law were questioned by those concerned about the potential for government intrusion into the lives and civil rights of innocent people. The Patriot Act was renewed by congress on March 9, 2006, following an intense debate regarding protection of civil liberties. Proponents were able to show that in the 4 years since the Act was passed, there were no verified civil-liberties abuses, and the new bill added more than 30 new significant civil liberties safeguards. The USAPA is discussed more fully in Chapter 10.

Illegitimate Use of Race/Ethnicity

Courts have held that matching a profile *alone* is not the equivalent of the reasonable suspicion or probable cause necessary to conduct an investigative detention or arrest (see, e.g., *Reid v. George*, 448 U.S. 438, 1980, and *Royer* at 525, note 6). There are no circumstances under which officers may stop citizens based solely on their race, ethnicity, gender, religion, national origin, or any other demographic feature. Officers must base their stops of persons, whether in a vehicle or on foot, on reasonable suspicion or probable cause that a violation of the law has been or is about to be committed based on facts and information that they can articulate.

Some states, via legislation, have banned consent searches where there is no clear reason for suspicion. The mere nervousness of the motorist or occupant(s) is not sufficient reason to ask for a consent search. The Fourth (banning unreasonable search and seizure) and the 14th (equal protection of the laws) Amendments to the U.S. Constitution provide a framework for the protection of drivers from being indiscriminately targeted by the police via traffic stops. To prove this type of claim, the claimants must produce facts or statistics showing that they were targeted solely because of their race, ethnicity, gender, religion, or national origin. The burden then shifts to the police to provide evidence that they did not act solely on the basis of any of these factors.

In 2003, the U.S. Department of Justice banned all racial profiling by federal agents in a directive entitled "Guidance Regarding the Use of Race by Federal Law Enforcement Agencies." Critics of the directive complain that it is inadequate and ineffective because it does not provide criteria that define racial profiling, is merely advisory and not legally binding, and contains no legal remedies for those who think they have been racially profiled.

The United States Congress since 2001 has been considering legislation that would ban federal, state, and local law enforcement agencies from using racial profiling. One such bill, the "End Racial Profiling Act," was introduced in the 110th Congress but had not become law as of the revisions to this text. The legislation would allow the United States, or individuals injured by racial profiling, to bring civil actions for declaratory or injunctive relief. It would require federal law enforcement agencies to maintain policies and procedures for eliminating racial profiling and to end existing practices that permit racial profiling. It would require state, local, and Indian tribe governments applying for federal law enforcement assistance grants to certify that they have done the same, and to establish an administrative complaint procedure and independent auditor program for addressing complaints. The bill would also require the Attorney General to undertake a 2-year demonstration project to collect data on hit rates for stops and searches by law enforcement agents, make grants to develop and implement best-practice systems to eliminate racial profiling, and issue regulations for reporting on racial profiling (United States Senate Online, 2009).

In recent years, over 20 states have enacted laws that require law enforcement agencies to develop and enforce policies to prevent racial profiling. Twelve of those states also require law enforcement officials to collect data on the race and gender of each driver stopped by police and what actions were taken ("Jurisdictions Currently Collecting Data," 2007).

Weeding out the illegitimate uses of profiles or profiling by police officers is the only way law enforcement can maintain credibility within the communities they serve. The authors believe that the majority of officers know not to base their actions on any prejudices they might hold.

PREVENTION OF RACIAL PROFILING IN LAW ENFORCEMENT

To formulate measures to prevent the practice of racial profiling and inappropriate behavior and actions on the part of officers, the criminal justice system should consider the following seven areas:

- Accountability and supervision
- Agency policy to address racial profiling
- Recruitment and hiring
- Education and training
- Minority community outreach
- Professional traffic stops
- Data collection on citizens' race/ethnicity

Accountability and Supervision

Preventing the use of racial profiling or biased policing in law enforcement is critical. Police executives must reflect seriously on this and respond to both the reality and the perceptions of biased policing. Law enforcement executives, managers, and supervisors must send a clear message to all personnel that using race, ethnicity, or national origin alone as the basis for any investigative stop is not only unacceptable conduct but also illegal. It can lead to termination from employment and possibly to prosecution. If convicted, the officer(s) could be fined and/or incarcerated depending on the laws of the particular state.

Police managers and supervisors, in order to identify officers who might be biased, should monitor such indicators as: (1) high numbers of minority citizen complaints; (2) high numbers of use-of-force or resisting incidents involving minorities; (3) large numbers of arrests not charged because prosecutors find improper detentions and/or searches; (4) perceptible negative attitude toward minorities; (5) negative attitudes toward training programs that enhance police–community relations or cultural awareness.

Prevention of racial profiling also involves other components of the criminal justice system such as prosecutors and courts. Legislators are also an integral part of the process. For example, in New Jersey it is a crime for the police to use race as the primary factor in determining whom to stop and search, punishable by 5 years in prison and a $15,000 fine. Supervision, legislation, and documenting the race/ethnicity of drivers stopped alone will not root out rogue officers who use racial profiling tactics. A program that reviews other contacts officers have with residents should also be instigated to help reduce such incidents. Law enforcement agencies must convey to their communities that they, the citizens, will be protected from such abuses and that abuse is not tolerated or advocated. Preventing the use of racial profiling by law enforcement officers not only is crucial to maintaining credibility within the community, but also reduces exposure to civil liability on the part of the departments and officers. Law enforcement managers might use the following self-assessment to evaluate their agency's policies and practices to determine if any of them could lead to a negative image of the department in the community or possible civil liability.

Self-Assessment

1. Has your law enforcement agency taken a proactive stance regarding bias-based traffic law enforcement?
2. How many civil rights complaints has your department received during the past year? What percentage is related to traffic stops?
3. Has your department been negatively portrayed in the media regarding community relations or bias-based traffic enforcement?
4. Do you collect data on the race, ethnicity, gender, and national origin of those your agency's police officers have stopped, detained, searched, and arrested?
5. Have you authorized departmentwide use of in-car video systems?
6. Is there an effective citizen complaint system in place and is the department responsive?
7. Do you have supervisory control that can identify (early alert) officers who may have patterns of bias-based traffic enforcement?
8. Does your agency have disciplinary policies and training established for officers with patterns of bias-based traffic enforcement?
9. Has your agency instituted proactive measures to build positive relations with the minority community (e.g., meetings with community leaders and neighborhood associations) before problems surface? ("Understanding Bias-Based Traffic Law Enforcement," 2003)

The authors of this text believe the majority of law enforcement officers, supervisors, and managers within agencies across the country are hardworking men and women who are committed to serving all members of our communities with fairness and respect. These professionals know racial profiling is unacceptable and conflicts with the standards and values inherent in ensuring all people are treated equally regardless of their race or ethnicity. They know racial profiling can expose a police department to costly lawsuits and ruin minority relations. They are intolerant of the use of racial profiling and willingly partner with their communities to address the issues involved. These professionals develop approaches to eradicate both confirmed acts of racial profiling and the perception that it is taking place within their agency or jurisdiction.

Agency Policies to Address Racial Profiling

Law enforcement agencies must have clear policies and procedures to address racial profiling and the perceptions thereof. As of 2003, according to the Bureau of Justice Statistics, 63 percent of departments had written policies concerning racial profiling by officers (see Exhibit 13.3). This included about 9 in 10 agencies serving populations of 250,000 or more residents (Bureau of Justice Statistics Report, 2006). Many departments in the United States have developed such general orders to cover not only traffic stops but also the temporary detentions of pedestrians

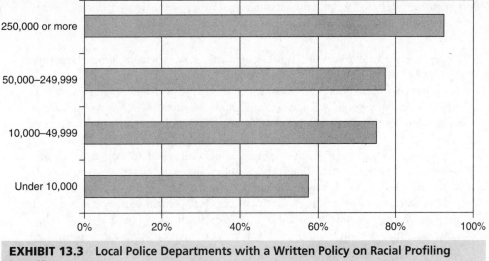

EXHIBIT 13.3 **Local Police Departments with a Written Policy on Racial Profiling by Officers, 2003.**

Source: Bureau of Criminal Statistics, May 2006, NCJ 210118.

and even bicyclists. The policies usually address the Fourth Amendment requirement that investigative detentions, traffic stops, arrests, searches, and property seizures by officers must be based on a standard of reasonable suspicion or probable cause which officers can support with specific facts and circumstances. The policy must include the following: (1) no motorist, once cited or warned, shall be detained beyond the point where there exists no reasonable suspicion of further criminal activity; (2) no person or vehicle shall be searched in the absence of probable cause, a search warrant, or the person's *voluntary* consent. The policy should specify that in each case where a search is conducted, this information shall be recorded, including the legal basis for the search and the results. It is strongly recommended that consent searches only be conducted with written consent utilizing the agency forms provided. Some agencies now require that an officer's verbal request for consent to search an individual or vehicle be documented by a video or audio recording at the scene. According to Professor Brian Withrow, "Some police chiefs are considering imposing Miranda-like restrictions on the consent search. This will make the consent search process more onerous (i.e., expensive) so that hopefully the police will be more judicious in its use" (Withrow, 2009).

According to the International Association of Chiefs of Police (IACP), departments without a policy should look at as many models addressing racial profiling as possible before they select one that meets their needs. Agencies should also involve community members, especially minorities and civil rights advocates, in the development and implementation of the policy. The policy must communicate a clear message to law enforcement personnel and the people they serve that racial profiling and other forms of bias-based policing are not acceptable practices. The statement should include what discipline (including criminal prosecution where such laws exist) could result if officers violate the provisions of the policy.

The San Francisco Police Department created a general order that outlines their policy for policing without racial bias. It states that "To maintain that trust, it is crucial for members of our Department to carry out their duties in a manner free from bias and to eliminate any perception of policing that appears racially biased." The general order clarifies the circumstances in which officers can consider race, color, ethnicity, national origin, gender, age, sexual orientation, or gender identity when making law enforcement decisions.

> *Policy:* Investigative detentions, traffic stops, arrests, searches, and property seizures by officers will be based on a standard of reasonable suspicion or probable cause in accordance with the Fourth Amendment of the U.S. Constitution. Officers must be able to articulate specific facts and circumstances that support reasonable suspicion or probable cause for investigative detentions, traffic stops, arrest, nonconsensual searches, and property seizures. Department personnel may not use, *to any extent or degree*, race, color, ethnicity, national origin, age, sexual orientation or gender identity in conducting stops or detentions, or activities following stops or detentions *except* when engaging in the investigation of appropriate suspect-specific activity to identify a particular person or group. Department personnel seeking one or more specific persons who have been identified or described in part by any of the above listed characteristics may rely on them in part only in combination with other appropriate identifying factors. The listed characteristics should not be given undue weight:
>
> • Except as provided above, officers shall not consider race, color, ethnicity, national origin, gender, age, sexual orientation, or gender identity in establishing reasonable suspicion or probable cause.
> • Except as provided above, officers shall not consider race, color, ethnicity, national origin, gender, age, sexual orientation, or gender identity in deciding to initiate even those consensual encounters that do not amount to legal detentions or to request consent to search. (San Francisco Police Department General Order 5.17, 07/17/03)

In 1979, the IACP, NOBLE, the National Sheriffs' Association, and the PERF created the Commission on Accreditation for Law Enforcement Agencies (CALEA). The primary purpose of the Commission is to improve law enforcement service by creating a national body of standards developed by law enforcement professionals. Furthermore, it recognizes professional achievements by establishing and administering an *accreditation* process through which a law enforcement agency can demonstrate that it meets those standards. "Participation in the CALEA accreditation program is voluntary, but successful completion provides a law enforcement agency with a nationally recognized award of excellence and professional achievement. Additional benefits of obtaining CALEA accreditation may include more favorable liability insurance costs and increased governmental *and community support*" (see CALEA website: www.calea.org.).

CALEA in 2001 issued Standard 1.2.9 regarding bias-based profiling. The standard requires that CALEA accredited agencies have a written policy governing bias-based profiling and, at a minimum, include the following provisions: (1) a prohibition against bias-based profiling in traffic contacts, in field contacts, and in asset seizures and forfeiture efforts; (2) training agency enforcement personnel in bias-based profiling issues including legal aspects; (3) corrective measures if bias-based profiling occurs; and (4) an annual administrative review of agency practices including citizen concerns. CALEA does not require mandatory collection of traffic stop data even though there is a growing demand for such action. The Commission's position is that not all law enforcement agencies must collect traffic stop data when other successful measurement systems are in use and/or the situation in the community served does not indicate there is a concern about police bias (Bureau of Justice Statistics Report, 2006).

Recruitment and Hiring

Police agencies can reduce racial bias by recruiting and hiring officers who can police in a professional way. Within legal parameters, the department should hire a workforce that reflects the community's racial and ethnic demographics. Those hired should be expected to carry out their duties with fairness and impartiality. Having such a workforce increases the probability that, as a whole, the agency will be able to understand the perspectives of its racial/ethnic minorities and communicate with them effectively.

The officers that departments should be recruiting are those who are aware of and capable of managing their own ethnic, racial, and cultural stereotypes and biases in a professional way. These qualities are essential to reducing bias in policing. The multiple testing stages that applicants for law enforcement positions go through help weed out those who are unable to control their biases. Interviews, polygraphs, psychological tests, and background investigations are all intended to identify those who are biased to the point that they might act based on their prejudices (see Chapters 1 and 3). It should be noted that the possibility of bias is not limited to white officers. Members of minority groups can have biases against white people, against members of other minority groups, or even against members of their own race/ethnic group. In 2003, the *Boston Globe* analyzed 20,000 citations by Boston police; it was discovered that "minority officers here are at least as tough as whites on minority drivers, and sometimes tougher" ("Boston to Track All Stops by Police," 2003, p. A1). Police recruitment messages, verbal and written, must emphasize that those who are prejudiced, regardless of their race or ethnicity, and who cannot distinguish between appropriate and inappropriate behavior and actions, will not be hired. As mentioned earlier in this chapter, no one is completely free of bias, but the recruitment effort should be targeted at those who understand and control their biases.

Education and Training

Law enforcement agencies need to provide training and education to enable officers to utilize legal enforcement tools so they can perform their work professionally and effectively within today's multicultural communities. Some departments have utilized interactive simulation training exercises to train officers on professional traffic stop procedures, especially those involving agitated citizens. Clearly, most law enforcement officers know not to act based on the prejudices and stereotypes they might hold. However, the nature of prejudice is such that some people are not aware of their own prejudices or biases. Therefore, they make inferences and take actions toward certain groups based on these biased perceptions. Training that provides accurate information concerning groups about which officers might have prejudices and stereotypes is one of the approaches police departments should use to prevent racial profiling.

What is the mental process that takes place when an officer makes a stop based on race, ethnicity, or national origin? Officers who have a biased belief system observe and collect certain data that in turn reinforce that belief system. Meanings are added to make sense of the observations ("I notice minorities more and stop them more because of my biased beliefs about them"). Based on these meanings, assumptions are made that fill in for missing data ("This motorist is carrying drugs on him"). The officer draws conclusions (based on beliefs) and then takes action (decides to stop African American and Hispanic motorists much more frequently than whites). These steps in our thinking take place very quickly. Most of us are not aware that this process goes on all the time (see the section in Chapter 1 on prejudice in law enforcement).

In their book *The Fifth Discipline Fieldbook: Strategies and Tools for Building a Learning Organization*, management specialist Peter Senge and his coauthors provide a clear and simple model called the "Ladder of Inference," which illuminates most people's typical patterns (and flaws) of thinking. The authors discuss thinking and decision-making processes using the ladder to describe, from the bottom up, how people select data, add meanings, make assumptions, draw conclusions, adopt beliefs, and ultimately take action (see Exhibit 13.4). They maintain that:

> We live in a world of self-generating beliefs that remain largely untested. We adopt those beliefs because they are based on conclusions, which are inferred from what we observe, plus our past experience. Our ability to achieve the results we truly desire is eroded by our feelings that:
>
> - Our beliefs are the truth
> - The truth is obvious
> - Our beliefs are based on real data
> - The data we select are the real data. (Senge, Kleiner, Roberts, Ross, and Smith, 1994, p. 242)

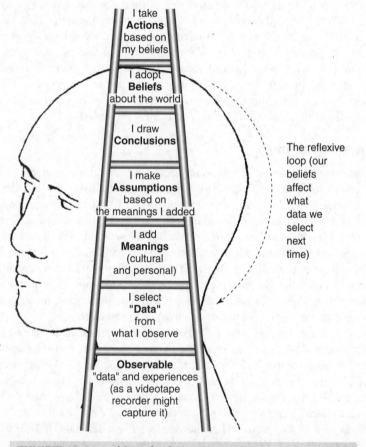

EXHIBIT 13.4   Ladder of Inference.

Source: Senge et al., 1994, pp. 242–246. Reproduced with permission of Peter Senge.

The authors explain that most people no longer remember where their attitudes and beliefs came from (i.e., what data or experiences led to their assumptions and conclusions). Therefore, they may not understand the basis of the actions they take. Senge and his coauthors discuss "leaps of abstraction" in which:

> our minds literally move at lightning speed . . . because we immediately "leap" to generalizations so quickly that we never think to test them. . . . [L]eaps of abstraction occur when we move from direct observation (concrete "data") to generalization without testing. Leaps of abstraction impede learning because they become axiomatic. What was once an assumption becomes treated as a fact. (Senge et al., 1994, pp. 192–193)

The authors say that we then treat generalization as fact.

> How do you spot leaps of abstraction? First, by asking yourself what you believe about the way the world works. . . . Ask "what is the 'data' on which this generalization is based?" Then ask yourself, "Am I willing to consider that this generalization may be inaccurate or misleading?" It is important to ask this last question consciously, because, if the answer is no, there is no point in proceeding. (Senge et al., 1994, p. 194)

In intensive training conducted by Senge nationwide, police and other corporate executives are able to learn about the models above and relate them to issues and challenges in their own organizations. The models provide some insight into what may be going on in officers' minds as they stop members of minority groups. Thus the models can help officers better understand their actions vis-à-vis racial profiling. It is natural for people to substitute assumptions for what is not known, but in the case of racial profiling, this is a very dangerous proposition. Officers have to recognize when they are converting their biases into "facts" and when their assumptions substitute for real data.

Training and education provide departments an opportunity to inform officers of the penalties for not adhering to policies and laws on the subject. Many state legislatures have created laws barring law enforcement officers from engaging in racial profiling. Such legislation also requires that every law enforcement officer participate in expanded training regarding racial profiling. This training is typically coordinated, monitored, and controlled by the Commission on Peace Officer Standards and Training (POST), an agency that is found in every state. These state commissions should, if they haven't already, integrate the topic of racial profiling into their diversity training for both entry-level and in-service programs. Law enforcement agencies should consult local chapters of their community's minority group organizations to obtain accounts and examples of actual or perceived racially biased policing for use in training programs. Such programs should also cover:

1. Definitions of key terms involved, such as profile, profiling, racial profiling, racially biased policing, probable cause, and reasonable suspicion.
2. Identification of key indices and perspectives that signal cultural differences among residents in a local community.
3. The negative impact of biases, prejudices, and stereotyping on effective law enforcement, including examination of how historical perceptions of discriminatory enforcement practices have harmed police–community relations.

4. History and role of the civil rights movement and its impact on law enforcement.
5. Specific obligations of officers in preventing, reporting, and responding to discriminatory or biased practices by fellow officers.
6. Various perspectives of local groups and race relations experts regarding cultural diversity and police–community relations.

Training should also involve constitutional law and ethics. Every state will have different requirements, but here is an example from the Commission on POST of Missouri:

1. All commissioned, licensed peace officers, who have the authority to enforce vehicle/traffic laws, must attend a minimum of 1 hour of racial profiling training each year.
2. Individuals who have *no authority* to make traffic stops are *exempt* from this annual requirement.
3. All racial profiling training used to meet the requirement must be obtained from a licensed training center, an approved provider of continuing education, or a course approved by POST.

The law enforcement community is more capable now than ever before of effectively addressing biased policing. In the past few decades, there has been a revolution in the quality and quantity of police training, the standards for hiring officers, and accountability.

Minority Community Outreach

Every police–community interaction requires a strong, ongoing link to community groups and civil rights organizations. Links might be established when community-oriented policing, which became popular in the 1990s, is used to address neighborhood problems. A link is also established when community task forces are assembled to address issues, especially of racial profiling and the perception thereof. These steps demonstrate respect for the minority community and create shared responsibility for whatever action is taken. The police hold primary responsibility for community outreach on every level, but the community is also responsible for becoming involved in activities that form positive relationships with the police. Policing within the community can function only in an environment of mutual engagement and respect. In the context of racial profiling or biased policing, outreach to the community is imperative. For constructive dialog to take place, therefore, police executives must remain open to discussions of racial profiling or the perception thereof within their jurisdictions. Sometimes, data on traffic stops and people searched can be used as a springboard for dialog and communications between law enforcement and the community. It is an opportunity for the clarification and open discussion of the raw data. An individual who has been trained in the analysis of such data and the use of appropriate statistical benchmarks should moderate the discussions.

Although there are many examples of police departments collaborating with the minority community to discuss and resolve issues pertaining to racial profiling or racially biased policing, the Chicago Police Department could serve as a positive example. Historically, since 2000, Chicago's police superintendent has sponsored a series of meetings between the police and residents of the minority community to address racial tensions and concerns about police racial bias. The forums included community activists, and staff of all ranks represented the police department. Prior to the first meeting, participants were surveyed for their opinions, perceptions, and observations about racial profiling and racially biased policing. The questionnaire also asked them to rate the department's strengths and weaknesses regarding minority outreach and solicited their ideas about how to improve police–minority relations and resolve issues. The forums were moderated by an independent facilitator. At the first meeting, community members shared their thoughts, experiences, and concerns, and police staff was asked to listen but not respond. Later in the day, the police shared their thoughts and reactions to the morning session, and the citizens were instructed to listen and not respond. During the final session of the day, all participants joined in a discussion of the issues and ideas raised earlier. The meetings continued over a period of time until the participants identified specific actions to be taken by both the police and community members to address the issues that had been raised ("Racially Biased Policing," 2001).

PROFESSIONAL POLICE TRAFFIC STOPS

The reason for every stop made by a law enforcement officer must be legally defensible and professional. Professional traffic stops involve four key elements:

- *Organizational/agency policy.* Agencies must develop a well-structured policy concerning professional traffic stops, outlining the conduct of officers and the prohibition of discriminatory practices.
- *Officer training.* Agencies should include a component on racial profiling into existing in-service training programs. Special workshop discussions on the issue of racial profiling can also be scheduled.
- *Data collection.* Agencies must collect traffic stop data when the situation in the community served indicates that there is a concern about police bias.
- *Accountability/supervision.* Law enforcement supervisors and managers must hold officers accountable for adhering to the policy. They must personally take the message to employees, as well as to the public, that biased policing will not be tolerated and could result in discipline, possibly including prosecution or termination. Managers, supervisors, and the entire workforce must embrace and adhere to the policy.

Deputy Chief Ondra Berry (Reno, Nevada, Police Department), now retired, in diversity training he conducts nationwide (and as he formerly did in communications with his own officers), offers the following advice: "When contemplating stopping a motorist, ask yourself, 'Is there a possibility that I may be making an assumption about this driver based on race? Am I moving from my own personal "data" and making a leap of extraction about this vehicle or about this person?'" Officers must recognize that this is a possibility. Berry further advises, "Do not take race into account when deciding who to stop. Use your good policing skills. Again, if you are normal, you have unbalanced views about people who are different from you" (Berry, 2009). The IACP, after significant study, identified the components that constitute a "professional traffic stop." The organization's publication "Recommendations from the First IACP Forum on Professional Traffic Stops" (2003) should be referred to for additional information.

DATA COLLECTION ON CITIZENS' RACE/ETHNICITY

When racial profiling became an issue throughout the United States, many law enforcement jurisdictions began collecting data on the race/ethnicity of people stopped and/or searched by police. Some did so voluntarily while others did so because of court decrees or community pressure. The purpose of collecting data is to address racially biased policing and the perceptions thereof and to determine whether it is taking place. The use of data collection requires officers to complete a form following each traffic stop.

Research by PERF ("Racially Biased Policing," 2001) examined the arguments for and against data collection:

Arguments in Favor of Data Collection

Data collection helps agencies:

1. Determine whether racially biased policing is a problem in the jurisdiction
2. Convey a commitment to unbiased policing
3. "Get ahead of the curve"
4. Effectively allocate and manage department resources

Collecting data and interpreting them, if done correctly, reflects accountability and openness on the part of the agency. The process helps to improve police–community relations. Departments doing so identify problems and search for solutions. The data can be informative to department management about what types of stops and searches officers are making. Managers and supervisors can then decide not only whether these practices are the most efficient allocation of department resources but also whether biased policing is taking place. Without the collection and analysis of data, departments can have a difficult time defending their practices if challenged in court.

Arguments against Data Collection

1. Data collection does not yield valid information regarding the nature and extent of racially biased policing
2. Data could be used to harm the agency or its personnel
3. Data collection may impact police productivity, morale, and workload
4. Police resources might be used to combat racially biased policing and the perceptions thereof in more effective ways

Many departments still resist record keeping. They argue, for one, that the mere collection of "racial" statistics may imply that biased policing is taking place. These agencies maintain that the raw data, when first collected and before analysis and comparison with benchmarks, could reinforce or increase the public's negative perceptions of the agency at the cost of both the morale and the effectiveness of officers. At the same time, some departments have expressed concern that any data they do collect could be used against them in court. These law enforcement executives question the ability of data collection systems to provide valid answers about the nature and extent of racially biased policing within their departments. The simple collection of data will neither prevent racial profiling nor accurately identify if it is taking place. The process alone does not protect agencies from public criticism, scrutiny, and litigation because the data collected are open to interpretation. The raw data collected represent meaningless numbers unless put into a relevant context using statistical benchmarks (to be discussed later) to provide a legitimate means of comparison. Standing alone, the data collected can be used to make or defend any position that someone may adopt about racial profiling. Law enforcement agencies, therefore, must take additional steps to ensure that the numbers they collect accurately reflect reality. Each department must evaluate its specific circumstances. For agencies that have had no community complaints and/or already closely monitor officer behavior in other ways, undertaking data collection may not be the most efficient use of resources.

Another argument used against data collection has been the observation that, within some law enforcement agencies, officers discontinued or reduced the number of self-initiated traffic stops and pedestrian contacts they made when data collection became a requirement. Officers resentful or concerned about being monitored ceased to initiate stops in order to avoid the possibility of being perceived as racially biased. Some agencies do not require the officer to reveal his or her identity on the data form. The identity of the individual(s) detained is never documented on the form. Some city/county administrators and law enforcement executives are also concerned about the time and costs associated with the collection and analysis of data.

Thus, data collection has its advantages, disadvantages, and limitations. PERF recommends that police agency executives, in collaboration with citizen leaders, review the pros and cons of the practice. They must factor in the agency's political, social, organizational, and financial situation to decide whether or not to either initiate data collection or allocate available resources to other approaches to address racially biased policing and the perceptions thereof.

DATA COLLECTION ELEMENTS The basic elements for data collection that both the U.S. DOJ Resource Guide and PERF recommend to law enforcement agencies are:

- Date/time/location
- Characteristics of the individual(s): Age/gender, race/ethnicity/national origin
- Reason for stop: penal or vehicle code violation or infraction; reactive (call for service) or self-initiated
- Search or no search: if search, the search authority (including consent [if consent involved]) and results (what, if anything, was recovered)
- Disposition: arrest, citation, verbal warning, written warning, or no action

There is a rationale and justification behind each of the recommended elements. They are designed to determine not only whom the police are stopping, but also the circumstances and context of the stops. "In effect, we are trying to collect 'circumstantial' data to tell us the real reasons citizens are being stopped—which should reflect the motivations of the officers and/or the impact of agency policies and practices" ("Racially Biased Policing: A Principled Response", 2001, p. 121). In completing the section of the form pertaining to race, ethnicity, or national origin, officers are expected to use their best judgment, based on their observations, training, and experience, and not ask the person detained. PERF, COPS, and the U.S. Department of Justice have developed protocols and guidelines for the collection, analysis, and interpretation of vehicle stop data. These detailed how-to guides should be referred to by those involved in developing a system or methods of tracking vehicle stops and trying to measure racial bias in policing. The materials available from these agencies (see Website Resources at the end of this chapter) provide information on what activities to target for data collection.

Most agencies collect data only on traffic stops (moving or mechanical violations) because of their frequency and also because that is where there is the greatest potential for police racial bias (or perception thereof) to occur. Another source of data is vehicle stops or general investigative stops of drivers. This sort of stop involves officer discretion (wherein the officer should have reasonable suspicion or probable cause to conduct an investigative stop) and is also an important source of information to analyze. Collecting data on *detentions* encompasses not only traffic and vehicle stops, but also pedestrian or bicyclist stops. A fourth source of data is *nonconsensual encounters*, in which an officer is not detaining the citizen, but is questioning him or her. PERF recommends that agencies collect data on all vehicle and traffic stops. Their recommendation does not include pedestrian stops or nonconsensual encounters that do not amount to detentions. Exhibit 13.5 shows a series of concentric circles that represent the types of activities police departments might target for data collection.

Data collection would be different for municipal and highway policing. The job of city police and county sheriffs are mostly responsive in nature in that they answer to calls for service from victims or witnesses to events. The officers' enforcement patterns depend on the character

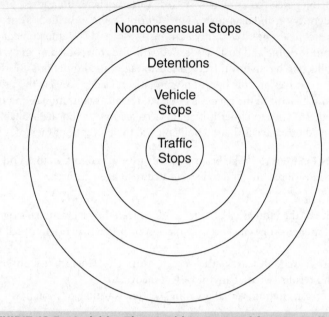

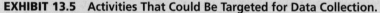

EXHIBIT 13.5   Activities That Could Be Targeted for Data Collection.

Source: PERF report, 2001, p. 121.

of the neighborhoods in which they serve, and thus the race/ethnicity of the persons they contact will vary accordingly. This must be taken into account during data analysis and interpretation. Comparative benchmarks must be utilized for each differing community and area of the city or county. Highway policing, in contrast, involves more self-initiated activity and more discretion on the part of officers. Moreover, distinguishing between low- and high-discretion stops may prove useful for data collection and analysis.

The Montgomery County, Maryland, Police Department, as part of an agreement with the Fraternal Order of Police and the Department of Justice in 2000, began to collect data on all traffic stops, using electronic media rather than paper. All traffic stops result in the officers' entering specific information into a handheld computer (with special software); the information is later downloaded into the department's central database.

The Bureau of Criminal Statistics reported that, as of October 2004, the most recent study available as of the revision of this edition, 29 of the nation's 49 state law enforcement agencies required their officers to record the race or ethnicity of motorists stopped for traffic violations. Twenty-two state agencies required officers to record race or ethnicity data for all officer-initiated stops, and seven, in more limited circumstances. The 22 state police agencies collecting race or ethnicity data for all traffic stops represent an increase of 6 states since 2001 and 13 states since 1999. Among the 20 agencies that did not require traffic patrol officers to collect race or ethnicity data in 2003, 14 agencies had previously reported collection of race or ethnicity data in 2001. The report indicates that most agencies (27) relied on their officers' observations of the driver's race or ethnicity as the method of determining the race or ethnicity of the motorist ("Traffic Stop Data, 2004," 2005).

There are some local law enforcement agencies that collect data on traffic stops voluntarily while others do so in response to state statute, injunction, Attorney General requirement, or court order. At the end of each year, these agencies report their findings to whatever entity requires it and include recommendations for any needed changes.

STATISTICAL BENCHMARKS   Statistical benchmarks are the comparative populations or groups against which the data collected are going to be analyzed and interpreted. In other words, they are the estimates of the proportions of individuals available to be stopped by race or ethnicity within the area studied. Racial profiling analysis requires developing and using an appropriate benchmark. The selection and development of benchmarks is a very complicated process often requiring the assistance of specialists in the field so the correct interpretation of the data is achieved. There are different types of benchmarks, but three are most common:

1. *Resident population of the community* that is policed by the department under consideration, that is, the demographics of the geographic area to be studied. This method is probably the most commonly used.
2. *Field observation of drivers* at randomly selected sites during randomly selected times. Normally field observers attempt to identify the race or ethnicity and approximate age of each driver.
3. *Accident records for not-at-fault drivers* to estimate the qualitative features (e.g., racial composition) of actual roadway users. Information arising from accident statistics is commonly used by traffic engineers to develop qualitative benchmarks of actual road users.

There are advantages and disadvantages to each of the types of benchmarks mentioned, and there is no agreement among experts on which is the most reliable. None of these benchmarks is universally adaptable to every racial profiling evaluation, and the advantages and disadvantages of each must be taken into consideration when deciding which one to use. However, one criminal justice researcher, Brian Withrow, maintains that:

> A benchmark comparison alone cannot measure the factors that influence a police officer's decision to initiate a traffic stop. We cannot even determine whether or not the officer even knew the race of the individual prior to the stop. In other words, benchmark comparisons only tell us who gets stopped, not why. (2004, p. 23)

The benchmarks selected must be able to help measure whether individuals are being stopped on the basis of their race, ethnicity, or national origin. One question to be asked is, in a similar situation, would a person who was not a member of a minority group have been stopped? In other words, the correct comparison is not to the people living in the neighborhood or driving on the highway who did not engage in the same conduct as the person stopped, but to those who did engage in the same conduct but were not stopped because they were not of a minority race (U.S. Department of Justice, 2000). One can see how difficult a task it is to develop statistical benchmarks.

Unfortunately, most research and analysis of collected data on traffic and field interrogation stops (detentions) does not take into consideration the decision-making processes of the officers involved. Most data collection efforts have neglected the need to explain how and why officers make decisions pertaining to traffic or other stops when studying racial profiling. Research designs should also allow for the investigation of officers' decision making after stops have been initiated (Engel et al., 2002, p. 261). One strategy recently developed to do this is the Internal Benchmarking method, which involves conducting routine, ongoing racial profiling surveillance of certain law enforcement officers and comparing their behavior or performance with similarly situated peers. The term *similarly situated* refers to officers who work the same assignment (e.g., patrol), in the same geographical area, and during the same time period. The method was developed by Professor Samuel Walker (Walker, 2003) from the University of Nebraska, and tested using data collected at the Wichita, Kansas, Police Department in 2001 by Professor Withrow (Withrow, 2009). The goal was to construct an internal benchmark that would identify officers on an individual level who actually stop substantially higher numbers of racial minorites. The method is a "data-driven administrative tool for identifying employees with performance problems and providing some kind of intervention to correct the problematic behavior" (Withrow, 2009, p. 5).

An agency using the Internal Benchmark strategy to determine if a suspected officer is using racial profiling practices would also incorporate other performance indicators into the investigation. For example, is the officer receiving an above-average number of citizen complaints or excessive-force allegations? Professor Walker describes performance indicators as part of what can be a comprehensive early warning system that agencies can use to evaluate the behaviors of their officers. According to Professor Withrow, however, although the Internal Benchmark method is an encouraging strategy, it is not a panacea. He indicates that:

> the number of variables necessary to define similarly situated officers may be problematic. It is because policing is a dynamic process. When properly developed, however, the advantages of an early warning system for racial profiling surveillance can be substantial. The analysis based on these data is free from the error known to exist within the traditional benchmarking strategies. The results are more credible and less subject to conjecture or debate. Also, the information provides insight into officer performance at the individual level. This allows the department to focus its attention on the individual officers who appear to be performing errantly or at the very least ineffectively. (Withrow, Dailey, and Jackson, 2009, p. 15–16)

Unfortunately, no benchmarking strategy has proven to be universally acceptable, and there is considerable disagreement amongst practitioners, scholars, and researchers on their reliability and validity. In general, benchmarking strategies fail to completely measure the population of individuals who are actually observed by the police but not stopped. At best, benchmarks estimate the population of individuals who *might* or *should* be observed by the police, and thus available to be stopped (Withrow, 2007). The benchmark sets the stage for responding to the most important question asked in a racial profiling study: Do the police stop a disproportionate number of racial and ethnic minorities? "Inevitably, the answer to this question comes from comparing a numerator (the proportion of individuals actually stopped by race or ethnicity) with a denominator (the proportion of individuals estimated to be available to be stopped by race or ethnicity)" (Withrow et al., 2009, p. 6).

An example of the use of benchmarks is found in a 2006 study by the RAND Corporation. The New York City Police Department (NYPD) had stopped half a million pedestrians for suspected criminal involvement. The RAND report indicated that the raw statistics for these encounters suggested large racial disparities—89 percent of the stops involved nonwhites. The report asked the following questions:

1. "Do these statistics point to racial bias in police officers' decisions to stop particular pedestrians?
2. Do they indicate that officers are particularly intrusive when stopping nonwhites?"

The NYPD asked the RAND Corporation to help it understand this issue and come up with recommendations for addressing potential problems. Researchers analyzed data on all street encounters between NYPD officers and pedestrians in 2006. They compared the racial distribution of stops to external benchmarks. Using these benchmarks, the researchers attempted to construct what the racial distribution of the stopped pedestrians would have been if officers' decisions had been racially unbiased. They then compared each officer's stopping patterns with an internal benchmark constructed from stops in similar circumstances made by other officers. Finally, they examined stop outcomes, assessing whether stopped white and nonwhite suspects had different rates of frisk, search, use of force, and arrest. They found small racial differences in these rates and made communication, recordkeeping, and training recommendations to the NYPD for improving police–pedestrian interactions ("New York: Analysis of Racial Disparities in the New York City Police Department's Stop, Question, and Frisk Practices," 2007).

DATA ANALYSIS AND INTERPRETATION   Once data have been collected, what do they show? The most difficult part of the process is the analysis and interpretation of the statistics compiled. Ultimately, the problem with interpreting results is that the traffic and field interrogation data have been collected without the guidance of any theoretical framework. Researchers have simply counted things such as the number of traffic stops, citations, and searches conducted by police on white and nonwhite suspects. Instead, the research should be conducted under the larger theoretical context of explaining behavior. Problems with the interpretation of empirical data are caused, in part, by data collection efforts that have not addressed why officers might engage in decision making based on citizens' race (Engel et al., 2002).

Robin Engel and her coauthors state in their report that research on racial profiling should include consideration of three dependent variables:

1. *The behavior of the individual police officer:*
   a. Why do police officers in general stop more black citizens than white citizens? How and why do officers make decisions?
   b. Why do some officers exhibit more racial disproportionality, while others exhibit less?
   c. Have there been changes in racial disproportionality over time?
2. *The behavior of different police departments:*   Do some police departments have high rates of racial profiling and others have low rates? If so, what explains these differences?
3. *The aggregate rates of officer and departmental behavior:*   Has race-based decision making been transformed in the past 40 years from one based primarily on individual racial prejudice to one based mainly on race-based departmental policies? (Engel et al., 2002, p. 261)

As explained, statistical benchmarks must be developed for comparison with the raw data collected by agencies. Among the decisions that must be made are:

1. Are the statistics collected compared with the city's racial makeup as determined by the nationwide census?
2. Are they compared with licensed drivers living in the city's jurisdiction?
3. Are they compared with the racial composition of the drivers on the roads, if that could be determined?
4. Are situational characteristics (e.g., suspects' characteristics, characteristics of the police–citizen encounter, and legal characteristics) considered and collected?
5. Are officers' characteristics (e.g., sex, race, experience, and attitudes) considered and collected?

6. Are organizational characteristics (e.g., formal and informal policies and attitudes and preferences of administrators and first-line supervisors) considered and collected?
7. Are community characteristics (e.g., demographic, economic, and political) considered and collected?

Data interpretation can be done internally by the law enforcement agency involved if the community political climate is good and there is trust that the analysis will be credible. However, since a positive community political climate is not usually the case, and to avoid the perception that the findings are suspect, most agencies obtain the services of an independent analyst. It is important that the analyst not only have some general knowledge of law enforcement procedures, but also be knowledgeable on the selection and development of statistical benchmarks or base rates. COPS, in conjunction with the Department of Justice (DOJ), has produced a document entitled "How to Correctly Collect and Analyze Racial Profiling Data: Your Reputation Depends on It." This provides recommendations on the methodology for data collection and analysis. This 2002 document can be downloaded from their website at www.cops.usdoj.gov. Another helpful document, published in 2005, by PERF in collaboration with COPS and DOJ, is "Understanding Race Data from Vehicle Stops: A Stakeholder's Guide," by Lorie Fridell. (See the Website Resources under PERF at the end of this chapter).

COMMUNITY TASK FORCES FOR DEVELOPMENT AND IMPLEMENTATION Citizen input is critical to the success of data collection and interpretation. Community group representatives must be involved with police personnel of all ranks to form a task force. The task force members, including in most cases an independent analyst, work together to decide: (1) if data will be collected about the race/ethnicity of persons contacted by officers, (2) the design of benchmarks to utilize in the interpretation of the data, and (3) the response or action to be taken based on the interpretation. Representatives might include members of local community groups such as the NAACP, the Urban League, the ACLU, the Latino Unity Coalition, and Pan Pacific Asian representatives. Police departments should take their input and implement the appropriate recommendations in subsequent phases of the project. Task forces and community-oriented policing are beneficial to a department's efforts to investigate and solve problems associated with allegations of racial profiling. Task forces not only help ensure that the process addresses specific concerns of the community, but also help improve police–community relations. PERF suggests how to get started:

1. Unless mandated, decide, with citizen input, whether data collection should be one component of the jurisdiction's overall response to racially biased policing and the perceptions thereof.
2. Communicate with agency personnel as soon as a decision is made to start collecting data. The executive should provide a rationale for data collection and address anticipated concerns.
3. Set up a process for listening to the concerns of personnel, and have personnel help to develop constructive ways to address them.
4. Develop a police–citizen group to serve in an advisory capacity.
5. Develop the data collection and analysis protocol. Ensure that the interpretations will be responsible, based on sound methodology and analysis.
6. Field test the data collection system for 3 to 6 months, and use that test to make modifications before implementing the system jurisdictionwide. ("Racially Biased Policing," 2001, pp. 143–144)

UNINTENDED RESULTS OF DATA COLLECTION   In some agencies, when mandatory data collection was instituted, the number of traffic tickets dropped precipitously as officers, wary of being accused of racial profiling, stopped fewer people. This occurred, for example, in Houston and Cincinnati. In some other agencies, officers refused to fill out the forms or made mistakes, which made the data unusable. The officers complained that the collection process was a waste of time and that the data collected might be used against them. Some argued that officers who use racial profiling because they are prejudiced will never fill out the form. There are examples of cities in which police officers are so fearful of the possibility of being accused of being racist if they stop a person of color that they avoid making contact even if a violation or minor crime is being committed. If accusations begin to control policing, public safety suffers. Some agencies have equipped their patrol vehicles with video cameras and audio recording devices to provide evidence of the actions of their officers in the event of complaints.

Summary

- Although the term *racial profiling* was first used in association with the New Jersey State Police stopping individuals along Interstate 95 in the early 1990s, there have been complaints about this practice for decades in the United States.
- When the issue of racial profiling came to the attention of the public and of law enforcement in the 1990s, there was no agreement on a definition, so it was difficult to develop approaches to prevent the practice.
- Prior to September 11, 2001, use of profiles that included race, ethnicity, or national origin were condemned by most U.S. citizens, but this attitude changed after the attacks on the World Trade Center and the Pentagon. As time has passed from those events, profiling has again become controversial. This has become a challenge in the national response to terrorism.
- Some police officers, government administrators, and others maintain that racial profiling is a myth or a misperception. An abundance of anecdotes and government reports, organizational studies, and statistics indicate that the racial profiling of African Americans and Latinos (and some other races and ethnicities) persists, however, despite efforts to end the phenomenon.
- Many police and sheriffs' departments across the nation as well as federal law enforcement agencies have adopted policies that address racial profiling. These policies cover accountability and supervision; recruitment and hiring; education and training; outreach to the minority community; professional traffic stops; and data collection on race and ethnicity.
- To be legally defensible and professional, traffic stops must be part of a well-structured organizational policy that prohibits discriminatory practices; officer training must include a component on racial profiling; traffic stop data must be collected if there is a community concern about police bias; and officers must be held accountable by their supervisors. Any data collected must be analyzed using appropriate benchmarks.
- Citizen discontent and lawsuits can originate as a result of racial profiling or the use of any profiling that appears to have been based on bias. Law enforcement professionals must be critical and introspective when analyzing the problem of racism and prejudice in the profession, and must be aware of the strong feelings the topic of profiling engenders.

Discussion Questions and Issues

1. *Law Enforcement Agency Policy on Racial Profiling.* The student can determine if a police department in the area meets recommended standards regarding policies pertaining to racial profiling:
   a. Does the policy clearly define acts constituting racial profiling using the definition provided at the beginning of this chapter?
   b. Does the policy strictly prohibit peace officers employed by the agency from engaging in racial profiling?
   c. Does the policy provide instructions by which individuals may file a complaint if they believe they were a victim of racial profiling by an employee of the agency?
   d. Does the agency provide public education relating to the complaint process?
   e. Does the policy require appropriate corrective action to be taken against a peace officer employed by the agency who, after an investigation, is shown to have engaged in racial profiling in violation of the agency's policy?
   f. Does the agency require the collection of data relating to traffic stops in which a citation is issued and to arrests resulting from those traffic stops, including information relating to:
      1. The race or ethnicity of the individual detained?
      2. Whether a search was conducted and, if so, whether it was based on the consent of the person detained?
   g. Does the agency's policy require it to submit a report on the findings and conclusions based on the data collected to a governing body of the county or state for review and monitoring purposes? What benchmarks are utilized and who interprets the data?

2. *Actual Incident for Discussion.* In a city in Indiana, an African American police officer driving an unmarked police car was pulled over by an officer not from his agency. The officer was wearing his uniform at the time, but he was not wearing his hat, which would have identified him as a police officer when viewed from outside the car. According to a complaint filed, the trooper who pulled the man over appeared shocked when the officer got out of the car. The trooper explained that he had stopped the man because the stopped officer had three antennas on the rear of his car. Discuss the following:
   a. Do you think the officer who pulled over a colleague was guilty of racial profiling?
   b. Do you think the officer was being honest when he said the reason for the stop was the multiple antennas? Is having multiple antennas a crime?
   c. Can complaints of being racially profiled be dismissed as the exaggerations of hypersensitive minorities or people who do not understand the job of a police officer?

Website Resources

Visit these websites for additional information about racial profiling and related issues:

American-Arab Anti-Discrimination Committee (ADC): http://www.adc.org

This website provides information about the ADC's civil rights efforts and useful summary data about cases and complaints regarding discrimination involving Arab Americans.

American Civil Liberties Union (ACLU): http://www.aclu.org

This website contains multiple locations for information about many issues, including racial profiling.

Americans for Effective Law Enforcement (AELE): http://www.aele.org/traffic.html

This website offers publications, research, and education on a variety of criminal justice issues. Available online is an article "Specimen Directive," which prohibits discriminatory stops, searches, and enforcement action.

Asian American Legal Defense and Education Fund (AALDEF): http://www.aaldef.org

This website provides information about civil rights issues concerning Asian/Pacific Americans and highlights issues of immigration, family law, government benefits, anti-Asian violence and police misconduct, employment discrimination, labor rights, and workplace issues.

Commission on Accreditation for Law Enforcement Agencies (CALEA): http://www.calea.org

CALEA was conceived in 1979 by the International Association of Chiefs of Police, the National Organization of Black Law Enforcement Executives, the National Sheriffs' Association, and the Police Executive Research Forum. The website contains information about the organization and the standards law enforcement agencies must adopt in order to be accredited.

Institute on Race & Poverty: http://www1.umn.edu.irp

This website, affiliated with the University of Minnesota, provides access to various studies, including those dealing with race and poverty, components of racial profiling legislation, and racial profiling. The website offers two studies of particular interest. "Report on Traffic Stop Data in St. Paul" (2001, May 24) documents the University's analysis data on traffic stops—a study requested by the St. Paul Police Department. The report confirmed a disproportional number of minorities being stopped and searched and against whom action was taken. "Components of Racial Profiling Legislation" (2001, March) is a research paper presenting the essential elements of effective racial profiling legislation.

International Association of Chiefs of Police (IACP): http://theiacp.org

This website provides a resource for law enforcement issues publications, including "Bias-Free Policing" by the 2001 Civil Rights Committee, which contains a policy statement for agencies concerning the prohibition of bias-based policing, and "Condemnation of Bias-Based Policing" by the 2001 Narcotics and Dangerous Drugs Committee.

Mexican American Legal Defense and Education Fund (MALDEF): http://www.maldef.org

This website is a good source of information on Latino civil rights issues and publications.

National Organization of Black Law Enforcement Executives (NOBLE): http://www.noblenatl.org

This website is a good source of information on many subjects, including recommended police policy and procedure, NOBLE publications, press releases and training material, resources, and classes. "Perspective: Racial Profiling—A Symptom of Bias-Based Policing" is an online primer on the subject of racial profiling.

Police Executive Research Forum (PERF): http://policeforum.org

This website provides an abundance of information about racial profiling and model programs. PERF has produced a free video and guide to facilitate police–citizen discussions on racially biased policing. They have also produced a helpful guide, "Racially Biased Policing: A Principled Response."

References

"ACLU of Oregon Analysis of Key Data Related to Portland Police Bureau Traffic Stops in 2006." (2007, November 13). Retrieved January 13, 2009, available at www.aclu.org.

Amnesty International USA. (2004). "Threat and Humiliation: Racial Profiling, Domestic Security and Human Rights in the United States." New York, NY: Amnesty International USA.

"Ariz. DPS tightens search rules to avoid profiling." (2008, December 30). My Fox Phoenix Local News online. Retrieved January 13, 2009, available at www.myfoxphoenix.com.

Barlow, David E., and Melissa Hickman Barlow. (2002). "Racial Profiling: A Survey of African American Police Officers." *Police Quarterly*, 5(3), 334–358.

Barlow, David E., and Melissa Hickman Barlow. (2000). *Police in a Multicultural Society: An American Story.* Prospect Heights, IL: Waveland Press.

Bast, Carol M. (1997). "Driving While Black. Stopping Motorists on a Subterfuge." *Criminal Law Bulletin*, 33, 457–486.

Berry, O. (2009). Retired Deputy Chief, Police Department, Reno, Nev, personal communication.

"Boston to Track All Stops by Police." (2003, July 20). *Boston Globe*, p. A1.

Bureau of Justice Statistics Report. (2006, May). U.S. Department of Justice, Bureau of Justice Statistics, NCJ 210118.

Commission on POST, Missouri. Available at www.dps. mo.gov/post/main/index.htm.

"Contacts between the Police and the Public, 2005." (2007). U.S. Department of Justice, Bureau of Justice Statistics, NCJ 215243.

Engel, Robin S., Jennifer M. Calnon, and Thomas J. Bernard. (2002). "Theory and Racial Profiling: Shortcomings and Future Directions in Research." *Justice Quarterly*, 19(2), 249–273.

Harris, D. A. (1999). "Driving While Black. Racial Profiling on Our Nation's Highways." American Civil Liberties Union. Available: www.aclu.org/prfiling/report/index.

Harris, D. A. (2002). "Profiles in Injustice: Why Racial Profiling Cannot Work." New York, NY: New York Press.

"Jurisdictions Currently Collecting Data." (2007). Institute on Race and Justice, Northeastern University. Available at: www.racialprofilinganalysis.neu.edu/background/jurisdictions.php.

Lundman, Richard J., and Robert K. (2003, February). "Driving While Black: Effects of Race, Ethnicity, and Gender on Citizen Self-Reports of Traffic Stops and Police Actions." *Criminology*, 41, 195–220.

MacDonald, H. (2001, Spring). "The Myth of Racial Profiling." *City Journal*, 11(2), pp. 1–5.

"New Jersey Police Win Praise for Efforts to End Profiling." (2007, September 6). *The New York Times*, p. C13.

"New York: Analysis of Racial Disparities in the New York City Police Department's Stop, Question, and Frisk Practices." (2007). RAND Corporation. Available at: www.rand.org.

"NYCLU Analysis Reveals NYPD Stopped Nearly 2 Million Innocent New Yorkers; Most are Black & Latino." (2009, February 11). New York Civil Liberties Union. Available at: www. nyclu.org.

"Police Polish Image, but Concerns Persist." (2009, January 4). *New York Times*, p. 21.

"Racially Biased Policing: A Principled Response." (2001). Police Executive Research Forum. Washington, D.C.

"Racial Profiling Data Released for '07." (2008, July 3). *Cassville (Missouri) Democrat*, p. 1.

"Recommendations from the First IACP Forum on Professional Traffic Stops." (2003). International Association of Chiefs of Police. Available: www.theiacp.org.

Senge, Peter, Art Kleiner, Charlotte Roberts, Richard Ross, and Bryan J. Smith. (1994). *The Fifth Discipline Fieldbook: Strategies and Tools for Building a Learning Organization.* New York, NY: Currency Doubleday.

"SFPD Stops Collecting Traffic Stop Racial Data." (2007, March 7). *The San Francisco Chronicle*, p. A1, A11.

Straus, I. (2002, October). "Commentary: Profile to Survive." United Press International. Available: www.upi.com.

"Traffic Stop Data Collection Policies for State Police, 2004." (2005, June). U.S. Department of Justice, Bureau of Justice Statistics Fact Sheet, NCJ 209156.

"Understanding Bias-Based Traffic Law Enforcement." (2003, July). National Highway Traffic Safety Administration. Available: http://www.nhtsa.dot.gov.

United States Senate online. (2009). Retrieved March 24, 2009, available at www.senate.gov.

U.S. Department of Justice. (2000). *A Resource Guide on Racial Profiling Data Collection Systems: Promising Practices and Lessons Learned.* Washington, D.C.

U.S. v. Brignoni-Ponce, 442 U.S., 837, 887. (1975). Retrieved April 14, 2009, available at www.supreme.justia.com/us/422/873/.

Walker, S. (2003, March 8–9). "Internal benchmarking for traffic stop data: An early intervention system approach." Presented at Racial Profiling in the 21st Century: New Challenges and Implications for Racial Justice. Northeastern University, Boston, Mass.

Will, George F. (2001, April). "Exposing the 'Myth' of Racial Profiling." *Washington Post*, p. A19.

Withrow, B. (2004, March). "A Comparative Analysis of Commonly Used Benchmarks in Racial Profiling: A Research Note." Unpublished paper submitted to the Academy of Criminal Justice Sciences, Wichita State University, School of Community Affairs, Wichita, Kansas.

Withrow, B. (2006). *Racial Profiling from Rhetoric to Reason.* Upper Saddle River, NJ: Pearson-Prentice Hall.

Withrow, B. (2007). "When *Whren* Won't Work: The Effects of a Diminished Capacity to Initiate a Pretextual Stop on Police Officer Behavior." *Police Quarterly*, 10(4), 351–370.

Withrow, B. (2009, February). personal communication.

Withrow, B., J. Dailey, and H. Jackson. (2008). "The Utility of an Internal Benchmarking Strategy in Racial Profiling Surveillance." *Justice Research and Policy* 10(2), 19–47.

Cultural Effectiveness for Peace Officers

Chapter 14 Community Policing and Multicultural Response Strategies for Gangs, the Homeless and the Mentally Ill

Chapter 15 Emerging Strategies, Roles, and Technology for Peace Officers in Multicultural Law Enforcement

Part Five concludes this text, highlighting some of the themes from previous chapters and presenting broad concepts on the emerging role of peace officers within a twenty-first-century multicultural society.

Chapter 14 discusses community policing and multicultural response strategies for officers and agencies in their dealings and interactions with gangs, the homeless, and the mentally ill—groups represented in the majority of America's multicultural cities and communities. This chapter raises awareness of the problems and issues that arise with gangs, the homeless, and the mentally ill, and provides officers with insight into dealing with these groups effectively.

Chapter 15 considers many of the changing and emerging issues confronting peace officers in their peacekeeping roles as well as in the use of high technology in multicultural law enforcement. Peace officers need to be competent in dealing with broader roles in multijurisdictional crime-solving efforts. Moreover, the role of peace officers also demands competencies needed for post-disaster responses, including responses to terrorism incidents. Assisting and communicating with members of multicultural communities after a disaster require additional resources, skills, and the use of new law enforcement tools and technology. Modern law enforcement also requires improved interagency communication as well as positive relations with multicultural communities.

In addition to the Instructor's Manual for this text, Appendix E, Listing of Gangs and Characteristics That Identify Them, includes further resource material on topics dealt with in Part Five.

CHAPTER 14

Community Policing and Multicultural Response Strategies for Gangs, the Homeless, and the Mentally Ill

LEARNING OBJECTIVES

After reading this chapter you should be able to:

- Assess the relevance of community policing to all multicultural communities.
- Describe the three types of major gangs and their level of criminal activity.
- Describe a youth gang and causation.
- Identify strategies law enforcement can use to reduce the gang problem.
- Define homelessness and its impact on homeless people and multicultural peacekeeping.
- Identify response strategies law enforcement can use to mitigate the homelessness problem in multicultural communities.
- Define mental illness and the challenges for people with mental illness in multicultural communities.
- Explain police protocol for encounters with mentally ill people and appropriate response strategies for managing these encounters.

OUTLINE

- Law Enforcement Strategies to Reduce Youth Gang Problems
- Homelessness and Its Impact on Peacekeeping
- Peacekeeping Strategies to Mitigate the Homelessness Crisis
- Mental Illness Challenges in Multicultural Communities
- Police Protocol in Encounters with People Who Have Mental Illness
- Response Strategies Between Police and People with Mental Illness
- Summary
- Discussion Questions and Issues
- Website Resources

INTRODUCTION

Gangs, homeless persons, and people with mental illness are groups that are represented in the majority of America's multicultural cities and communities. Law enforcement officers have continual contact with these groups for various reasons: gangs—suspected criminal activity; homeless people—loitering complaints by businesses; and people with mental illness—public nuisance complaints. Police officers need to recognize that there is a great amount of diversity among gangs, the homeless, and people with mental illness. Learning about the backgrounds of these groups can safeguard against negative stereotypes and biases, which can often lead to prejudicial law enforcement treatment.

Law enforcement's responsiveness to gang problems and the challenges of homelessness and people with mental illness is an essential component of developing strategies for peacekeeping in a diverse society. Ongoing relationships with multicultural community leaders, nonprofit organizations, and other government entities are needed resources in dealing with these societal issues. How community policing interplays with these multicultural groups and communities is pivotal to the success or failure of every police department's stated mission.

COMMUNITY POLICING

A.L. "Skipper" Osborne, Founder/CEO of TAJFA (Truth and Justice for All) and former Chapter President of NAACP, Portland, Oregon, in a personal communication to one of the authors reports:

> The police must meet with the community on a regular basis—not when there is a crisis but before there is a crisis. It is important that the police and community are honest and accountable to each other to build a relationship of trust. The police and community must share a common goal of respect, cooperation and justice for all if community policing is to work in a free and multicultural society. (Osborne, 2009)

Community policing is one of several terms that police agencies across the nation use to refer to working partnerships with communities. Other commonly used terms are problem-oriented policing (POP), community-based policing (CBP), service-oriented policing (SOP), and community-oriented policing (COP). The concept of and practices associated with community policing are central to any discussion on multicultural groups and immigrant populations. The legislative basis of what became known as Community Oriented Policing Services (COPS, Title 1 of the Violent Crime Control and Law Enforcement Act of 1994) became law under the Clinton Administration and directed the U.S. Department of Justice to create the Office of Community

Oriented Policing Services. From 1995 to 2008, the COPS Office invested $12.4 billion to help law enforcement advance the practice of community policing and facilitated more than 13,000 state, local, and tribal agencies to hire more than 117,000 police officers and deputies (COPS Office, 2008b). The major goals of the COPS Office are:

1. Awarding grants to tribal, state, and local law enforcement agencies to hire and train law enforcement officers
2. Awarding grants to tribal and local law enforcement agencies to purchase and use crime reduction technologies
3. Awarding grants to tribal and local law enforcement agencies to develop and test innovative policing strategies
4. Providing training and technical assistance to advance community policing to all levels of law enforcement and to other criminal justice components
5. Providing training and materials to state and local government leaders and the citizens in those communities to foster problem solving and police officers' interaction with communities

Community Policing   A partnership between the police and the local community that identifies strategies to reduce crime, increase traffic safety, and deal with all other public safety problems.

Today's police officers are increasingly comfortable with contemporary community policing described as a problem-solving approach. Community policing enables police officers to work with citizens outside the conventional channels by meeting with community groups and learning of their concerns. It also allows community members to understand the "culture" of law enforcement and helps them grasp the reasons police officers make the decisions they do. It encourages new strategies and creative ways of dealing with crime and peacekeeping at the neighborhood level and allows for a change of image of the traditional law enforcement officer. This is especially true in certain immigrant neighborhoods or ethnic conclaves where citizens have traditionally feared the police.

A great deal of literature is available to law enforcement agencies on community policing. Community policing depends on a strong partnership with the various communities that make up a city or jurisdiction. The partnership ensures dialogue and provides the mechanism that allows a police department to be aware of current and relevant issues in the community as they relate to crime, public safety, public nuisance, and the use of "order maintenance." The following description of a police department without a community-policing approach, though dated, is a graphic example of how world events and the influx of refugees have to be monitored in a communty policing partnership approach.

Order Maintenance   The police handling of incidents that are not crimes but public nuisance matters about which the police officer uses discretion to decide a course of action.

This dramatic example involves the case of a medium-sized police department in Garden Grove, California, that exemplifies the problems associated with not using community policing. Neither the management of the department nor the city was aware that the ethnic community had been changing significantly. Only two years after startling events began to take place did patrol officers begin to pay attention to the changes, most of which occurred suddenly following the fall of Saigon in 1975. After the withdrawal of American forces from Vietnam, the United States changed its immigration policy to relocate people in jeopardy from Southeast Asia. Police officers were performing their "crime fighter" role, but, because there was no partnership with the community, there was no reason or incentive to monitor and report the changes they were noticing. This particular community, therefore, was not prepared for the increase in racial disputes and violence on the streets and in the schools, nor was it prepared for the increasing needs in government, infrastructure, and social services. Police officers recognized that it took much longer to answer calls involving Vietnamese citizens than it did with those in the Anglo community because of language and cultural differences. Police officer and management frustrations resulted. Community policing would have had a plan in place for that neighborhood transition. Why? Had community policing been in place, the department, including all local government institutions, and the neighborhoods would have been working together closely.

Community policing allows for collaboration with the community. The police are unable to know the community as well as the community knows itself (Berry, 2009). Community policing represents a more democratic style of policing, allowing for openness and dialogue between the police and citizens to deal with strategies to combat crime. The following information, for example, illustrates how the implementation of community policing in Chicago, Illinois, was the definitive factor in the overall decrease of violent crimes and property crimes in a 10-year period.

Similar to other major cities and communities in the early 1990s, Chicago also witnessed a rise in crime rates; however, the Chicago Police Department acted differently from most other police departments when it decided to initiate a new experiment known as "community policing" in April 1993. The experiment was called CAPS—Chicago Alternative Policing Strategy. It was based on the hypothesis that if the police, residents, and other city agencies work together, they can reduce crime. This was a mammoth-sized project and required a long-term commitment, but the decision to embrace the mechanics of community policing paid off immediately and continues to do so today. In the 10 years from 1998 through 2007, the Chicago Police Department reported that the overall decline in violent crimes, such as murder, criminal sexual assault, robbery, and aggravated assault/battery, and property crimes, such as burglary, theft, motor vehicle theft, and arson, was 34.4 percent, or 4.6 percent on a compounded annual basis. Noteworthy to the success of CAPS are the ongoing meetings and activities with citizens and the following organizational details:

> Chicago is divided into 25 police districts. Each police district contains between 9 and 15 police beats, with a total of 281 beats throughout the city. It is at the beat level that the Department's strategy of police–community partnership and problem-solving is carried out. Each police district is led by a district commander. In addition to uniformed beat and rapid response officers, each district has teams of civilian-dressed tactical and gang tactical officers. Each district also offers a Community Policing Office which helps coordinate police–community partnership and problem-solving at the beat level and provides special services to senior citizens. ("Chicago Police Department 2007 Annual Report," 2007, p. 33)

Storefront Offices and Other Temporary Offices

Minority groups, neighborhoods, schools, and businesses appreciate the outreach efforts of the police to build and maintain positive relationships. However, the police must remind themselves that, in order to maintain goodwill relationships with citizens in their communities, they must have ongoing contact with the people they are sworn to protect and to serve. Different types of temporary offices known as "storefront," "schoolfront," and "neighborhood" offices afford this ongoing contact.

> **Storefront Office**   A temporary office located in a business office or shopping center where the police officer conducts routine business.
>
> **Schoolfront Office**   A temporary office located in a school where the police officer conducts routine business. Schools that have a regular police school resource officer are not considered schoolfront offices.
>
> **Neighborhood Office**   A temporary office located in a neighborhood, usually an apartment/business office complex where the police officer conducts routine business.

Each temporary office has a unique purpose for businesses, schools, and neighborhood multicultural communities, but they also possess similar characteristics and benefits:

- In the storefront office, for example, which is not a new concept, police work at a desk in an office inside a business location during a day or swing shift. Schoolfront and neighborhood offices serve the same function.
- When police officers show up at any of the facilities (business, school, or apartment complex) and park their patrol cars, they provide visibility to the public. Inside, the officer completes reports, returns telephone calls, or visits with the facility's staff or occupants.
- At the storefront, schoolfront, or neighborhood office, people in the community see the police on a frequent basis. This interaction creates a more positive and personal relationship.
- The police at storefront, schoolfront, and neighborhood offices provide interventions for problem business customers and school students, resources for school counselors, and safety-related classes to students and neighborhood organizations.

The Police Executive Research Forum (PERF) looked for commonalities among various community-policing programs across the country and conducted thorough research on community policing. The researchers outlined four major categories of community-policing activities within agencies throughout the United States (PERF, 2004):

1. *Citizenship participation:*   This involves citizens attending police–community meetings and helping police identify and resolve problems; attending citizen police academies; and participating in neighborhood watch programs and other volunteer programs.
2. *Police partnership outreach:*   Police conduct regularly scheduled meetings with community groups; sponsor youth programs; work with victim assistance programs; and reach out to other special needs organizations.
3. *Police problem solving:*   Police collaborate with external resources such as community groups, other police departments, businesses, nonprofit organizations, and government agencies; enforce criminal and traffic laws; and work with other nonpolice code enforcement agencies.
4. *Police organizational change:*   The organization uses different styles of leadership and empowerment; uses scientific methods for assignment to patrol areas or beats; reviews classification and prioritization of calls; uses crime analysis and crime solvability; uses progressive methods for recruiting sworn and nonsworn personnel; and uses citizen participation, partnership outreach, and different methods of problem solving.

All of these activities and tasks require opening a dialogue between the police and diverse community groups so that groups can identify their peacekeeping concerns and the police can respond to them. Departments typically mix a variety of community-policing activities together; however, the common thread within all tasks is that the police assist the community in policing and protecting itself in many societal ways. To do so, the police must engage the community in the duty of policing. The police are dependent on a relationship and partnership with the community to perform these important tasks. This is sometimes referred to as "building bridges." The community identifies problems with the encouragement, direction, and ongoing participation of the police.

Even with the attention community policing has been receiving in Criminal Justice College programs and police departments throughout the United States, more instruction on this topic would benefit everyone. For example, in 2006, the majority of state and local law enforcement training academies offered only eight hours of community policing in their basic police training programs to new police officers (U.S. Department of Justice, 2009a).

Mini Case Study: What Would You Do?

You are a patrol sergeant, and an apartment manager, who also serves as the community leader for new immigrants from Nigeria, approaches you at a community meeting. He requests your police department open up a neighborhood office in his apartment complex. He indicates that there are at least 40 families with small children and teenagers from Nigeria in the large complex. He asks you to provide, in addition to the police presence at the neighborhood front office, some workshops on crime prevention and traffic laws for the 12 new families who just arrived in the United States one month ago. Further, he tells you that there are at least 10 children in the apartment complex who need bicycle helmets. Describe what steps you will take to establish a neighborhood office and how you will operate it. Also, outline how you will organize and present your workshops to these new immigrants, and obtain bicycle helmets for the children who need them.

At the beginning of the chapter, we mentioned the connection between gangs, the homeless, and the mentally ill in being part of the diversity of the community. We now look at gangs, including their multicultural facets, in detail. The focus on community policing not only encompasses ethnic, racial, and national groups, but also all other subcultural groups as well. The more knowledge and familiarity officers have with all groups in our diverse society, the more skilled they will be in using the right kind of communication and response strategies.

TYPES OF GANGS AND CRIMINAL ACTIVITY

In 1982, only 27 percent of U.S. cities with populations of 100,000 or more had a reported gang problem (Miller, 1982). In the mid-1980s criminal gangs started expanding from urban cities to suburban areas to rural America. The following information provided by the U.S. Department of Justice National Gang Intelligence Center's (NGIC) National Gang Threat Assessment shows the more recent relative increases in gang numbers (NGIC, 2009):

- In 2008, 58 percent of state and local law enforcement agencies reported that criminal gangs were active in their jurisdictions, compared with 45 percent in 2004.
- Approximately 1 million gang members, belonging to more than 20,000 gangs across all the 50 states and the District of Columbia, were criminally active in 2008.

- From 2005 to 2008, there was a 200,000 person increase in gang membership; 900,000 gang members reside in local communities and 147,000 are incarcerated in local, state, and federal correctional facilities.

In law enforcement these numbers represent the three most common types of gangs: street gangs, prison gangs and outlaw motorcycle gangs. To help mitigate the growth of gangs and their criminal activity, the FBI facilitated creation of the National Gang Intelligence Center (NGIC) in 2005. The NGIC compiles gang intelligence from federal, state, and local law enforcement on the growth, migration, criminal activity, and association of gangs, which pose a significant threat to the United States. Its mission is to support law enforcement by disseminating timely information and by providing strategic/tactical analysis of intelligence (FBI, 2009a).

Criminal Activity

Gang criminal activities and threats report by NGIC for criminal justice study and review describes (NGIC, 2009):

- Local street gangs remain a significant threat because they are the largest in number nationwide and most use violence while committing various crimes.
- Gang members are moving from urban areas to suburban and rural communities for a variety of reasons, including expanding drug distribution territories, increasing illicit revenue, and recruiting new members.
- In many communities, up to 80 percent of the crimes are committed by gangs. Crimes include alien smuggling, armed robbery, assault, vehicle theft, drug trafficking, extortion, fraud, home invasions, identity theft, murder, and weapons trafficking.
- Gang members are the primary retail-level distributors of most illicit drugs. They distribute wholesale-level quantities of marijuana and cocaine in most urban and suburban communities.
- Some gangs traffic illicit drugs at the regional and national levels; several are capable of competing with U.S.-based Mexican drug trafficking organizations.
- Gang members illegally cross the U.S–Mexico border for the purpose of smuggling illicit drugs and illegal aliens from Mexico into the United States.
- Many gangs use the Internet to recruit new members and to communicate with members in other parts of the United States and in foreign countries.
- Street gangs and outlaw motorcycle gangs pose a threat to law enforcement along the U.S. borders of Canada and Mexico. They associate with Canadian- and Mexican-based gangs and criminal organizations to facilitate various criminal activities.

Mexican Drug Cartels

United States law enforcement officials at federal, state, and local levels have been combating the flow of illegal drugs from Mexico's drug cartels across the border into the U.S. border states of California, Arizona, New Mexico, and Texas for years. It remains an ongoing problem, and U.S. law enforcement agencies have responded by using drug interdiction and other practices, which have netted in countless arrests and drug seizures. As of 2009, drug trafficking, human trafficking, and, most noticeably, the violence from these criminal activities have spilled over into local U.S. communities across the Mexico border and beyond.

Since establishing the specialized home invasion unit in 2008, the city police department of Tucson, Arizona, has investigated more than 200 home invasions, with more than three-quarters of the invasions linked to the drug trade. One incident involved intruders breaking into the wrong house, shooting and injuring a woman. Another incident involved a man who was suspected of being a drug dealer, who was kidnapped from his home at gun point and has not been found since. The increased violence from drug cartel gang wars has spread from Mexico throughout the United States and even into Canada. Law enforcement officials suspect Mexican drug cartels were responsible for numerous shootings in Vancouver, British Columbia; kidnappings in Phoenix, Arizona; aggravated assaults in Birmingham, Alabama; and many more violent crimes in other states and communities (Archibold, 2009). Sadly, law enforcement officials in Mexico and the United States agree that the United States is the source of the guns used in the violent drug cartel wars in Mexico. In one of the many strategic responses to this crisis, the Obama administration hopes increased security measures at the border will detect firearms from being smuggled in cars from the United States into Mexico.

National and Regional Gangs

The NGIC has identified the approximate number of gangs in seven regions of the United States where there are thousands of gang members (some of whom operate in multiple regions). (See Exhibit 14.1.) State, county, and city law enforcement agencies are more aware of local gangs in

EXHIBIT 14.1   Gangs By Region, 2009.

Region	Gangs	Members	Gangs with Significant Activity
New England: VT, NH, ME, MA, CT, and RI	640	17,250	Hells Angels, Latin Kings, Tiny Rascal Gangster Crips, Surefios 13, Trinitarios, and United Blood Nation
East: NY, PA, NJ, DE, MD, DC, WV, and VA	2,900	73,650	Black Guerilla Family, Crips, Latin Kings, MS13, Ñeta, and United Blood Nation
Central: ND, SD, NE, KS, MN, IA, MO, WI, IL, MI, IN, OH, and KY	5,800	222,400	Bandidos, Chicago-based Gangster Disciples, Latin Kings, Native Mob, Outlaws, Vice Lords, and Black P. Stones
Southeast: AR, LA, TN, MS, AL, GA, NC, SC, and FL	9,871	172,360	Bandidos, Crips, Gangster Disciples, Latin Kings, and M13
Southwest: UT, CO, OK, AZ, NM, and TX	5,297	111,000	Aryan Brotherhood, Bandidos, Barrio Azteca, Hermanos de Pistoleros Latinos, Latin Kings, Mexican Mafia, Mexikanemi, Tango Blast, and Texas Syndicate
Pacific: CA, NV, and HA	6,900	237,000	Aryan Brotherhood, 18th Street, Bandidos, Black Guerrila Family, Bloods, Crips, LaEme, Mexican Mafia, Nuestra Familia, Hells Angels, and M13
Northwest: WA, OR, ID, MT, and WY	2,093	36,650	Bloods, Brown Pride, Crips, (74 Hoover and Rolling 60s) Florencia 13, Gangster Disciples, LaEme, Noretenos, Surenos, and Varrio Locos 13

Source: NGIC, January 2009.

their multicultural jurisdictions. See Appendix E for a listing of national and regional gangs and their specific characteristics, for the three major types of gangs.

Gangs in the Military

It is not uncommon to find gang membership among military personnel and their dependents in the U.S. Armed Forces. According to the NGIC, members from all three major types of gangs have been identified in the U.S. military on both foreign and domestic installations. Even though the actual numbers are unknown, military personnel and military veterans who are gang members pose a risk to law enforcement, particularly if these gang members, trained in weapons and tactics, pass this instruction on to other gang members (NGIC, 2009).

Street Gangs

National, regional, and local street gangs are the largest and control the greatest geographic area. They are represented in urban and rural communities and Indian Country. Street gangs are active in crime and violence. Most youth join street gangs. However, 67 percent of gang members identified by law enforcement agencies are 18 years or older compared to 33 percent who are under 18 years of age (NYGC, 2006). Exhibit 14.2 shows a listing of national and regional street gangs.

EXHIBIT 14.2   National and Regional Street Gangs, 2009.

Gang (National or Regional)	Region	Primary Race/Ethnicity
18th Street (National)	44 cities in 20 states	Mexican
Almighty Latin King and Queen Nation (National)	15 cities in 5 states	Mexican and Puerto Rican
Asian Boyz (National)	28 cities in 14 states	Asian
Black P. Stone (Regional)	Chicago	African American
Bloods (National)	123 cities in 33 states	African American
Crips (National)	221 cities in 41 states	African American
Florencia 13 (Regional)	5 states	Mexican
Fresno Bulldogs (Regional)	California	Hispanic
Gangster Disciples (National)	110 cities in 31 states	African American
Latin Disciples (Regional)	Chicago	Puerto Rican
Mara Salvatrucha (National)	5 states	Hispanic
Sueños and Norteños (Regional)	California	Hispanic
Tango Blast (Regional)	Texas	Hispanic
Tiny Rascal Gangsters (National)	Southwest, Pacific and Eastern states	Asian
United Blood Nation (Regional)	West Coast	African American
Vice Lord Nation (National)	74 cities in 28 states	African American

Source: NGIC, January 2009.

Gangs in Indian Country

Most street gangs that operate on reservations are local gangs and are primarily composed of Native American youth. Some Indian Country street gangs are regional, such as the Native Mob, located on and off the reservation. According to the National Youth Gang Center (NYGC), the Native Mob is identified as one of the largest and most violent Native American street gangs for criminal activity and has gangs operating in Minnesota, Michigan, Wisconsin, North Dakota, and South Dakota. Similar to other gangs, the Native Mob is involved with the retail-level distribution of illegal drugs (primarily marijuana and methamphetamine) and its members commit crimes such as auto theft, assault, robbery, drive-by shootings, and homicide (NYGC, 2009).

Prison Gangs

National, regional, and local prison gangs are prevalent throughout the federal and state prison system in the United States. They are highly structured and organized networks, having an influence in prison operations and in street gang crime. According to the NGIC, national-level prison gangs pose a major crime threat since most maintain some form of relationship with drug trafficking organizations. Prison gangs are controlled by established internal rules and codes of conduct that are strictly enforced by gang leaders. For example, California-based Mexican Mafia (La Eme) uses fear and intimidation to control Hispanic street gangs whose members are in prison and on the street in California. Such control gives La Eme command over 50,000 to 75,000 members (NGIC, 2009). See Appendix E for the listing of prison gangs and their specific characteristics.

Outlaw Motorcycle Gangs

According to the NGIC, outlaw motorcycle gangs (OMGs) number more than 20,000 in membership and are a serious domestic threat because of their strong associations with transnational drug trafficking organizations (Canada and Mexico borders) and other criminal enterprises. There are more than 300 active OMGs in the United States, with chapters such as the Hells Angels Motorcycle Club (Hells Angels), the Bandidos Motorcycle Club (Bandidos), and the Outlaws Motorcycle Club (Outlaws) performing the majority of cross-border drug smuggling operations with major international drug trafficking organizations (U.S. Department of Justice, 2009b). The NGIC also reports that national-level OMGs maintain criminal networks of regional and local motorcycle clubs, commonly referred to as "support," "puppet," or "duck" clubs, whose members conduct criminal activities in support of the larger OMGs, and who are a source for new members. It is reported that some members of support clubs have obtained employment with private businesses or government agencies, which allows them to provide national-level OMGs with business, government, and financial information that can be used to protect their criminal enterprises (NGIC, 2009). See Appendix E for the listing of OMGs and their specific characteristics.

Racial and Ethnic Composition of Gangs

In a five year period from 1996 to 2001, race and ethnicity of gang members were determined in four NYGC Surveys (NYGC, 2006). The report findings showed stability in gang members' race and ethnic composition across survey years; however, the percentages were disproportionately high for the general population of Hispanic/Latino Americans and African Americans, and extremely low for white Americans in the United States (see Exhibit 14.3). Examine Appendix E for the racial and ethnic characteristics of all three types of gangs. Readers need to keep in mind

EXHIBIT 14.3 Race/Ethnicity of Gangs, 2006.

Race/Ethnicity	1996	1998	1999	2001
Hispanic/Latino	45%	47%	48%	49%
African American	36%	33%	31%	34%
Caucasian/White	12%	12%	13%	10%
Asian	5%	6%	7%	5%
Other	2%	2%	1%	2%

Source: NYGC, July 2006.

that even though the numbers are reported to be low for white membership in these three major types of gangs, white membership is among the highest in hate/bias groups in the United States as referenced in Chapter 12.

Gang-Related Homicides

Homicides by drive-by shooting and by other means have occurred in almost every city where there are criminal gangs. Multiple gang-related homicides usually occur more often in larger cities and suburban counties than in smaller cities and rural counties. The NYGC survey analysis highlights gang-related homicides for the period of 2002 to 2005 (NYGC, 2007):

1. Approximately two-thirds of all homicides in the Uniform Crime Reports (UCR) and about three-fourths of all gang-related homicides occurred in cities with populations more than 50,000 between 2002 and 2004 annually.
2. In 2005, more than half of the nearly 1,000 homicides in Los Angeles and Chicago combined were considered to be gang related.
3. In 2005, the reported number of gang-related homicides was slightly below the 10-year average of about 800.

Gun Use by Gangs

Law enforcement officers know that firearms play a major role in gang violence and that gang members are more likely to carry guns and use them. In a Rochester, New York, study, the rate of gun possession for gang members was about 10 times higher compared to nongang juvenile offenders (Thornberry, Krohn, Lizotte, Smith, and Tobin, 2003). Also, gang members who carried firearms committed violent crimes about 10 times more often (NYGC, 2009). Law enforcement officers must always be alert and watchful to the potential threat of violence directed against them when encountering gang members; however, they must be professional and not overreact in their contacts with gang members.

YOUTH GANGS AND CAUSATION

The terms *youth gang* and *street gang* are commonly used interchangeably, but the use of the term *street gang* for *youth gang* often results in confusing youth gangs with adult criminal organizations (NYGC, 2009). To eliminate the confusion, it is important to remember that street gangs are composed of juveniles and young adults as we mentioned earlier in the section on street gangs.

Youth under 18 years of age represent 33 percent of street gangs, and those 18 years or older account for 67 percent of street gang membership (NYGC, 2006).

Definition of Youth Gang

The definition of *youth gang* varies among most law enforcement agencies and jurisdictions at the federal, state, and local levels in the United States. The NYGC, a branch of the Office of Juvenile Justice and Delinquency Prevention of the U.S. Department of Justice, provides an excellent definition for criminal justice professionals and educators, and it is the definition we use in this section.

> **Youth Gang**   A self-formed association of peers having four characteristics: (1) three or more members, generally ages 12 to 24; (2) a name and some sense of identity, generally indicated by such symbols as style of clothing, graffiti, tattoos, and hand signs; (3) some degree of permanence and organization; and (4) an elevated level of involvement in delinquent or criminal activity (NYGC, 2006).

Genderwise Membership in Gangs

The majority of gang members are males, but within the early adolescent members nearly one-third are females (Esbensen and Winfree, 1998; Gottfredson and Gottfredson, 2001).

Of the two genders, females leave gang membership at an earlier age than do the majority of males (Gottfredson and Gottfredson, 2001; Thornberry et al., 2003). Some observers attribute this early departure to maturity, and others, to pregnancy. Additional research has indicated that the gender composition of the gang is associated with gang delinquency. Another study showed that females in all-female gangs, or in a gang with a majority of females, demonstrated the lowest delinquency rates, whereas males and females in co-ed gangs exhibited the highest delinquency rates, often higher than that of males in all-male gangs (Peterson, Miller, and Esbensen, 2001).

Risk Factors for Gang Membership

All law enforcement and criminal justice professionals should be aware of the risk factors that make young people vulnerable to gang membership. The following five risk factors were identified by the combined efforts of Thornberry (1998); Esbensen (2000); Hill, Lui and Hawkins (2001); and Howell and Egley (2005):

- Prior delinquency in violence and alcohol/drug use.
- Poor family management and problematic parent–child relations.
- Low school attachment and academic achievement, and negative labeling by teachers.
- Association with peers who engage in delinquency.
- Disorganized neighborhoods where large numbers of youth are in trouble and where drugs and firearms are readily available.

LAW ENFORCEMENT STRATEGIES TO REDUCE GANG PROBLEMS

In 1992, the FBI developed a National Gang Strategy designed to incorporate the investigative and prosecutorial practices proven successful in the Organized Crime/Drug Program National Strategy. By promoting coordination and information sharing between federal, state, and local law enforcement agencies, the FBI's Safe Streets and Gang Unit is able to identify violent gang enterprises that pose a significant threat and to pursue these criminals with coordinated investigations that support successful prosecutions. The FBI's Safe Streets and Gang Unit administers 152 Violent Gang Safe Streets Task Forces through out the United States (FBI, 2009c). Likewise, state and local law enforcement agencies have been responding to the gang threat since their inception but have not always maintained a consistent level of responsiveness. This is owing to any one or a combination of several reasons, which are a lack of budget funding, lack of political support, and lack of effective resources, or dealing with a formidable and relentless gang threat.

U.S. Department of Justice Office of Community Oriented Policing (COPS)

The COPS Office recognizes that street gangs can take on many forms and offers guides and reports on major training modules that are resources for law enforcement officials, educators, and parents to address specific types of crimes committed by gangs. These resources provide details of community-policing solutions to youth crime and school violence. The COPS Office encourages law enforcement agencies to analyze their local gang problem and use these resources when appropriate. The following five training modules are voluminous in size and contain numerous subtopics that provide substantive value (COPS, 2008a):

1. The COPS Toolkit for Addressing Specific Gang Problems
2. Law Enforcement Responses for Addressing Gang Activity
3. Gang Activity in Specific Populations
4. Criminal Behaviors of Gangs
5. Statistics and Research on Gangs

Cross-Cultural Gang Violence

Law enforcement agencies are well aware of cross-cultural gang violence motivated by hate, retaliation, and turf wars. In 2008, cross-cultural gang violence escalated between Bloods and Crips for control of retail-level drug distribution in the New England Region; and in the Southeast Region, Hispanic gangs and African-American gangs had violent confrontations for control of gang territories (NGIC, 2009). In addition to such violence, gangs have been known to commit hate crimes and murder police officers.

Largest Gang Arrest in the U.S. History

On May 21, 2009, in the City of Hawaiian Gardens and nearby communities, just southeast of Los Angeles, California, approximately 1,400 federal, state, county, and city law enforcement officers arrested 88 Latino gang members. According to the Department of Justice, the multiagency operation was connected to the murder of a sheriff's deputy, racially motivated attacks on African Americans, and illicit drug trafficking. Called "Operation Knock Out," the largest gang arrest in the U.S. history led to federal indictments against 147 members and associates of the Latino gang Varrio Hawaiian Gardens, whose members have ties to the Mexican Mafia. The investigation of the gang began in 2005 after Los Angeles County Sheriff's Deputy Jerry Ortiz was fatally shot by Varrio Hawaiian Gardens' gang member Jose Orozco, while Deputy Ortiz was attempting to arrest Orozco in connection with the shooting of an African American male. After the shooting, Orozco was arrested for murder, convicted, and placed on death row. Prior to the massive arrests, 10 defendants were already in custody and 49 were still at large as fugitives or waiting to be located. Charges included violation of the federal RICO (Racketeer Influenced and Corrupt Organizations) Act, murder, attempted murder, drug trafficking, carjackings, extortion, kidnapping, and witness intimidation. Seventeen SWAT teams helped make the arrests, and police seized 105 firearms and 31 pounds of methamphetamines. Twenty-six children were taken into protective custody (FBI, 2009b; Glover and Winton, 2009).

This major multiagency gang operation illustrates the need for law enforcement officers, especially in certain regions of the country, to familiarize themselves with the cultural, racial, and ethnic dimensions of gangs. Budgets permitting, training academies and department management need to sustain a focus on cross-cultural gang activity, updating their training content on this topic on a regular basis.

Resources for Law Enforcement

The authors have identified resources and strategies to assist federal, state, and local law enforcement agencies to mitigate the gang threat in our multicultural nation. The following agencies are of key importance in this process:

Boys & Girls Clubs of America Gang Prevention/Intervention Target Outreach

The Boys & Girls Clubs of America developed special gang prevention and intervention initiatives targeting youth ages 6 to 18. Through referrals from schools, courts, law enforcement, and community youth service agencies, the tested and proven Targeted Outreach Program identifies and recruits delinquent or at-risk youth into club programs and activities. The initiative is sponsored by the Office of Juvenile Justice and Delinquency Prevention (OJJDP) of the U.S. Department of Justice (Boys & Girls Club of America, 2008).

Gang Awareness Training Education (G.A.T.E.)

G.A.T.E. is a school based classroom curriculum instructed by law enforcement officers and prevention specialists. G.A.T.E.'s goals are the prevention of gang activity, youth violence, and drug use among young people. Lessons focus on life skills, societal norms, and critical thinking to teach young people how to solve problems and avoid delinquent behavior (G.A.T.E., 2009).

Gang Resistance Education and Training (G.R.E.A.T.) Program

The G.R.E.A.T. program is a school-based, law enforcement officer-instructed classroom curriculum. The program's primary objective is prevention, and it is intended as an immunization against delinquency, youth violence, and gang membership. G.R.E.A.T. develops partnerships with the Boys & Girls Clubs of America and the Police Athletic League. It also has five regional training centers to train police officers across the United States (G.R.E.A.T., 2009).

Police Athletic League (PAL)

PAL is a charitable, nonprofit, and national organization, whose mission is to make a positive difference in the lives of young people and contribute to the overall quality of life in chapter cities throughout the United States. PAL provides educational, athletic, and cultural after-school programs in a safe environment. PAL teaches life skills and provides experiences essential for youth to become successful and productive citizens. PAL activities are supervised by full-time police officers who nurture strong and positive relationships among the youth, their communities, and the police department (PAL, 2008).

Mini Case Study: What Would You Do?

You are a police officer who has just been reassigned to a new neighborhood. You are meeting with a group of parents in a multicultural neighborhood gathering this evening. The neighborhood has misgivings toward your agency because of some police officers' use of profanity toward citizens and disrespect toward African American teenage males at traffic stops. There are a few street gangs in the neighborhood, and one of the biggest complaints from parents is that even good kids are being treated by the police as if they are gang members. What would you say at this meeting? How would you respond to the parents' allegations?

HOMELESSNESS AND ITS IMPACT ON PEACEKEEPING

Dealing with the homeless is not a new task for law enforcement in America. In repeated acts of humane and compassionate treatment, the Philadelphia Police Department offered their station precincts as shelter to more than 100,000 homeless people a year during the 1880s (Monkkonen, 1981). Almost a century later, in the 1980s, U.S. cities started noticing a significant increase of homeless people and blamed the recession as one of the major causes. In 1994, Christopher Jencks estimated the homeless population at about 400,000 people, but advocates for the homeless disagreed saying this was a low estimate as compared to government sources, who said this was a high number (Jencks, 1994). In its 2007 annual report, the National Law Center on Homelessness and Poverty (NLCHP) estimated 3.5 million people, including 1.35 million children, had experienced homelessness (NLCHP, 2007).

Race, Ethnicity, and Family Status

In 2006, the U.S. Conference of Mayors estimated the homeless population to be 42 percent African American, 39 percent white, 13 percent Hispanic, 4 percent Native American and 2 percent Asian. With reference to family status, officials estimated that, of the homeless population, on average, single men comprised 51 percent, families with children 30 percent, single women 17 percent, and unaccompanied youth 2 percent (U.S. Conference of Mayors, 2006).

Quality-of-Life Concerns

In America, the homeless are constantly in need of food, water, and shelter, so it is not uncommon for many homeless people to panhandle for food or money. Poor health, an unsatisfactory diet, bad personal hygiene, and sleep deprivation are common problems homeless people deal with. The following 2006 data show the quality-of-life concerns for the homeless as noted by NLCHP (2007):

1. *Shelter:* 29 percent of shelter requests by homeless families were unmet, an increase of 5 percent from the previous year. Reported federal funding for low-income housing fell by 56 percent from 1976 to 2007. In 1976, federal housing funding was $87 billion, and 435,362 new affordable units were built. In 2007, funding had dropped to $38 billion, and no new housing units were built.

2. *Homelessness:*   On any given night there are approximately 840,000 homeless people in the United States.
3. *Poverty:*   Almost 37 million people live in poverty.
4. *Working Class:*   Each month, 44 percent of adults work, and still do not make enough to afford housing.
5. *Veterans:*   26 percent of homeless adults are veterans.
6. *Substance Abuse:*   37 percent of homeless single adults and 10 percent of homeless adults in families with children have substance abuse issues.
7. *Mental Health Issues:*   22 percent of homeless single adults and 8 percent of homeless adults in families with children have mental health issues.
8. *Life Span:*   The average life expectancy for a homeless adult is 42 to 52 years, compared to 73 to 76 for the general population.

Federal Law Definitions of Homelessness

The authors refer to two definitions for homelessness under federal law. One is a general definition of homelessness for adults and the second definition specifically applies to homeless children and youth. These definitions are delineated in the federal law known as the McKinney-Vento Act; both definitions are under U.S Code, Title 42: The Public Health and Welfare, chapter 119. The key elements are highlighted in both definitions.

Homeless Adult Person   (1) a person who lacks a fixed, regular, and adequate nighttime residence; (2) a person who resides in a public or private temporary shelter/transitional housing (Subchapter 1: General Provisions Section 11302).

Homeless Children and Youths   Have similar residency and shelter/transitional housing as a homeless adult, but includes sharing the housing of other persons due to loss of housing; living in motels, hotels, trailer parks, or camping grounds; or abandoned in hospitals (Subchapter VI: Education and Training, Part B: Education for Homeless Children and Youth, Section 11434a).

Critics of the Federal Law Definitions

Many advocates for the homeless believe the federal law definitions of homelessness are too narrow in scope and complicate the methodology for accurately tracking the homeless number. One such critic is the National Coalition for the Homeless (NCH), which indicates that most studies are limited to counting people who are in shelters or on the streets. The NCH argues that this approach may yield useful information about the number of people who use services such as shelters and soup kitchens or are easy to locate on the street; however, it can too often underestimate the number of homeless. The NCH maintains that many people who lack a stable, permanent residence have few shelter options because shelters are filled to capacity or are unavailable (NCH, 2008a).

A study conducted by the U.S. Conference of Mayors in 2007 found that 12 of the 23 cities surveyed had to turn away people in need of shelter due to a lack of adequate capacity. Ten of the cities found an increase in households with children seeking access to shelters and transitional housing, while six cities noted an increase in the number of individuals seeking these resources.

Of the total population of the surveyed cities, 1–3 percent used a shelter or transitional housing in the past year. Singles and unaccompanied children remain homeless an average of 4.7 months, while 5.7 months is the average for families with children in the 23 surveyed cities (U.S. Conference of Mayors, 2007). In addition, a study of homelessness in 50 cities found that in nearly every city, the city's officially reported estimate of the number of homeless people greatly exceeded the number of emergency shelter and transitional housing spaces (National Law Center on Homelessness and Poverty, 2004). Moreover, there are few shelters in rural areas of the United States, where the homeless population is reported to be 9 percent and relies on church groups and volunteers for help (Archibold, 2006).

Methods Used in Counting the Homeless Population

The NCH ranks the earlier cited 2007 NLCHP estimate of 3.5 million as the best approximation on the number of people who are likely to experience homelessness in a given year. Their findings are based on estimates from a study of service providers across the country at two different times of the year in 1996. The NCH points out that on a given night in October, 444,000 people (in 346,000 households) experienced homelessness; for a given night in February, the figure was 842,000 (in 637,000 households)—this translates to almost 10 percent of the population living in poverty. The NCH further comments that on converting these estimates into an annual projection, the numbers that emerge are 2.3 million (based on the October estimate) and 3.5 million people (based on the February estimate). This translates to approximately 1 percent of the U.S. population experiencing homelessness each year, with 38 (in October) to 39 percent (in February) of them being children (Urban Institute, 2000). The NCH concludes that not all people experiencing homelessness use service providers, so the actual number of people experiencing homelessness is likely higher than those found in the study (NCH, 2008a).

Causes for Homelessness

There are many interrelated causes for people's experiencing homelessness. History shows that a poor economy, coupled with high unemployment, contributes to increased poverty and housing shortages. Personal bankruptcy, chronic alcohol and drug abuse, domestic violence, family breakups, lack of family or government support, and mental illness are contributing factors as well. Being an undocumented immigrant or a runaway can also be a cause for homelessness. The lack of affordable housing, poverty, and unemployment were the primary causes leading to homelessness and hunger for families according to a 2008 survey by the U.S. Conference of Mayors. Regarding individuals, the top three reasons for homelessness were substance abuse, lack of housing, and mental illness (U.S. Conference of Mayors, 2008). Domestic violence was the immediate cause for women to leave their abusive spouses and become homeless (National Alliance to End Homelessness, 2007). Exhibit 14.4 lists other findings from the U.S. Conference of Mayors.

When There Are No Shelters

People who experience homelessness become creative and adaptive when they need temporary shelter. Safety is a concern for homeless people when they sleep, and shelter is important in extreme (cold, wet, or hot) weather. Exhibit 14.5 shows the locations where homeless people sleep and congregate.

1. Cities reported a 12 percent increase in homelessness from 2007 to 2008.
2. The majority of cities reported an increase in the number of homeless families.
3. Sixty-three percent of the cities reported an increase of homelessness because of the foreclosure crisis.
4. Tenants of rental units where the landlord faced foreclosure were the most vulnerable to becoming homeless.
5. Requests for emergency food assistance went up in nearly every city surveyed with the demand outpacing the supply in 20 cities.
6. Fifty-nine percent of the requests for food assistance were coming from families—many for the first time.
7. Most cities reported that, at times over the past year, the demand for homeless assistance exceeded the availability of shelter.

EXHIBIT 14.4   Findings of Survey on Homelessness, 2008.

Source: U.S. Conference of Mayors, 2008.

Homeless people are continually forced to leave from most, if not all, of these temporary locations by the police, business owners, or other government representatives. When homeless people do not leave, they are subjected to arrest by police officers for trespassing or disorderly conduct offenses. Advocates for the homeless from all across the United States are uniting with homeless people to resolve this dilemma through public awareness, in legislation, and in the courts.

Crime Victimization

The homeless are extremely vulnerable to person and property crimes. The NCH indicated that from 1999 to 2007 there were 774 acts of violence against homeless people resulting in 215 murders and 557 victims of assault in 235 cities across 45 states and Puerto Rico (NCH, 2008b). They also reported that the ages of the suspects ranged from 10 years to 75 years; the victims' ages ranged from 4 months to 74 years; and the gender composition of the victims was 463 males and 66 females (NCH, 2008b). Exhibit 14.6 shows the number of homicides classified as hate crimes against homeless people.

1. Abandoned buildings	12. Parks
2. Alleys	13. Patios
3. Awnings	14. Picnic Tables
4. Benches	15. Rest Areas
5. Bus Stations	16. Sidewalks
6. Cardboard Boxes	17. Subway Stations
7. Cars	18. Tarps
8. Construction Sites	19. Tents
9. Covered Bus Stops	20. Train Stations
10. Homeless Camps	21. Vacant Buildings
11. Overpasses	22. Vacant Houses

EXHIBIT 14.5   When There Is No Shelter, 2009.

Source: Olson, 2009.

EXHIBIT 14.6 Hate Crimes against Homeless People, 2007.

Year	Homicides Classified as a Hate Crime	Fatal Attacks on Homeless People
1999	17	48
2000	19	42
2001	10	17
2002	11	14
2003	14	8
2004	5	25
2005	6	13
2006	3	20
2007	0	28
	Total 85	Total 215

Source: NCH, 2007.

The authors recognize that individual crimes committed against homeless people are not coded and classified by most local, state, and federal law enforcement agencies because the FBI's Uniform Crime Report does not collect homelessness status in its crime victimization and suspect statistics. Further, homelessness status is not protected by federal hate/bias crime laws; however, the 2009 House of Representatives, 111th Congress, introduced a bill to protect homeless citizens.

State Laws Protecting the Homeless from Hate Crimes

On May 7, 2009, Maryland became the first state in the United States to adopt hate-crimes protection for homeless people. Maryland state lawmakers referenced cases like the one in south Baltimore in 2001, where a group of young men attacked and beat to death three homeless men. Three men were sentenced to prison for the brutal crimes, and one of them called their actions "bum stomping" (Nuckos, 2009). California, Florida, Ohio, and Texas are considering similar hate-crime legislation to protect the homeless. According to Michael Stoops (2009), Executive Director of the NCH, in 2006 Maine passed a law that allows judges to increase penalties for people who attack the homeless, and in 2008 Alaska passed a similar law. "We need to send a symbolic and practical message that attacks against the homeless will not be tolerated," Stoops said.

PEACEKEEPING STRATEGIES TO MITIGATE THE HOMELESSNESS CRISIS

Public trust and confidence in government and law enforcement agencies are essential for effective responses to the homelessness crisis. Homeless people in communities must believe they will be protected and treated with respect by the police, before relationships can develop. They must sense that the police are sincere in their efforts to help them and there is no risk of being harassed or assaulted. Further, homeless people and their advocates must see positive behavior from the police that matches their rhetoric to help. Chapter 13 discussed humane law enforcement strategies for responding to hate/bias crimes and the same strategies identified have value for people experiencing homelessness.

Seven Tips for Encounters with a Homeless Person on the Street

1. Take precautions for your safety.
2. Offer food, water, or meal vouchers.
3. Never give cash to a homeless person.
4. If you choose, provide cash or other donations to a soup kitchen, shelter, rescue mission, or other non-profit organization to help the homeless.
5. Treat the homeless person with respect.
6. Don't argue with them.
7. Remember, homeless people are individuals and come from diverse backgrounds.

EXHIBIT 14.7   **Seven Tips for Encounters with a Homeless Person on the Street.**

Source: Olson, 2009.

Education and Training

Awareness training on homelessness in law enforcement academies and departments nationwide for all officers should be mandatory. The content should include the causes and solutions to homelessness along with how to interact with homeless people in a humane and respectful manner. Some law enforcement and public safety training programs already include this topic in their cultural diversity courses and its addition has proven useful. In the teaching experience of one of the authors (Olson), criminal justice college students greatly benefit from homelessness awareness instruction. Some practical tips that can be included in such instruction and in community meetings are listed in Exhibit 14.7.

Soup Kitchens

Soup kitchens, located in many cities throughout the entire United States, provide meals to those who are hungry, poor, and homeless. Many churches, mosques, and synagogues help in providing emergency shelter during extreme weather periods. When law enforcement officers and criminal justice students volunteer their time at soup kitchens that serve the disadvantaged, they have an opportunity to get to know the homeless in their community, and conversely, the homeless get to know them.

Mini Case Study: What Would You Do?

Consider the following case study picturing two scenarios: (1) the individuals involved are U.S. born, and speak English fluently; (2) the individuals involved are immigrants and are limited–English speaking. Describe the challenges in each scenario, as you answer the questions following the case study.

You are a police officer on duty and you are having lunch with another police officer at a family style restaurant in your patrol district. A homeless adult male with a small child walks into the restaurant, and both approach you and the other officer at your table. The man tells you he is homeless and that he and his nine year old daughter are looking for temporary shelter and haven't had a meal in 24 hours. The man tells you he was laid off from his part-time job one month ago and was evicted from his apartment one week ago. He mentions he has no family and friends to turn to for assistance, and suddenly his nine year old daughter looks at you and starts crying, pleading "please help me and my daddy."

• How do you feel about this situation?
• What are you going to say to the child and her father?
• How are you going to help these two individuals with your current knowledge, skills, and resources?

MENTAL ILLNESS CHALLENGES IN MULTICULTURAL COMMUNITIES

In any given year, an estimated 26.2 percent of Americans ages 18 and older suffer from a diagnosable mental disorder or mental illness and about 6 percent, 1 in 17, suffer from a serious mental illness (National Institute of Mental Health, 2009).

> **Mental Illness**   A mental-health disorder characterized by alterations in thinking, mood, or behavior associated with distress and/or impaired functioning (U.S. Surgeon General's Report, 1999).

For a police officer in America these percentages are significant because an estimated 7 percent of police contacts in jurisdictions with 100,000 or more people involve the severely mentally ill (U.S. Department of Justice, 2006a). People with severe mental illness can include anyone—children, teenagers, adults, and senior citizens. Mental illness transcends race, ethnicity, gender, and sexual orientation. Serious mental illness includes major depression, schizophrenia, bipolar disorder, obsessive compulsive disorder (OCD), panic disorder, post traumatic stress disorder (PTSD), and borderline personality disorder (National Alliance on Mental Illness, 2009). Most trained and experienced law enforcement officers are familiar with these disorders and the term "psychotic episode," as they have had encounters with people with mental illness. Police officers know that psychotic episode is a critical period of time for the person with a mental illness. Stabilization of the person without injury or loss of life should always be the primary objective in these encounters.

> **Psychotic Episode**   A period of time when a person with a serious mental illness is impaired and at risk of endangering himself or herself, or others.

It is mandatory that law enforcement officers acquire knowledge and skills in the area of mental health. The following information reflects the volume of contacts that two different police departments reported on mental-health incidents over the course of 1 year.

- The Lincoln, Nebraska, Police Department found that it handled more than 1,500 mental health investigation cases in 2002, and that it spends more time on these cases than on injury traffic accidents, burglaries, or felony assaults (Lincoln Police Department, 2004).
- The New York City Police Department responds to about 150,000 "emotionally disturbed person" calls per year (Waldman, 2004).

Mental illness is a problem for police, medical services, and social services, and places a burden on the local community as well. Since there is a large potential for miscommunication and misunderstanding when dealing with those afflicted with a mental illness, many encounters can quickly turn negative. Police officers must be prepared when dealing with people who have mental illness, and studying the types of calls involving people with mental illness will prove invaluable for them.

Types of Calls

Regardless of the time of the day or the size of the agency, law enforcement officers encounter people with mental illness in a variety of situations. According to the U.S. Department of Justice, these types of calls involve criminal offenders, disorderly persons, missing persons, complainants, victims, and persons in need of care. Exhibit 14.8 shows examples for each role.

EXHIBIT 14.8   Roles of People with Mental Illness in Law Enforcement Encounters.

Role	Examples
Offender	• A person with mental illness commits a person or property crime. • A person with mental illness commits a drug crime. • A person with mental illness threatens to commit suicide. • A person with mental illness threatens to injure someone else in the delusional belief that the other person poses a threat to him or her. • A person with mental illness threatens to injure police as a means of forcing police to kill him (commonly called "suicide by cop").
Disorderly person	• A family or community member reports annoying or disruptive behavior by a person with mental illness. • A hospital, group home, or mental health facility calls for police assistance in controlling a person with mental illness. • A police officer on patrol encounters a person with mental illness behaving in a disorderly manner.
Missing person	• A family member reports that a person with mental illness is missing. • A group home or mental health institution reports that a person with mental illness walked away and/or is missing.
Complainant	• A person with mental illness calls the police to report real or imagined conditions or phenomena. • A person with mental illness calls the police to complain about care received from family members or caretakers.
Victim	• A person with mental illness is the victim of a person or property crime. • A family member, caretaker, or service provider neglects or abuses a person with mental illness.
Person in need of care	• Police are asked to transport a person with mental illness to a hospital or mental health facility. • Police encounter a person with mental illness who is neglecting his or her own basic needs (food, clothing, shelter, medication, etc.).

Source: "People with Mental Illness," U.S. Department of Justice, Office of Community Oriented Policing Services, May 2006.

Individually and collectively, law enforcement officers are trained to handle different types of incidents in various types of scenarios. Likewise, police officers will benefit from studying and formulating response strategies to the five most frequent types of people-with-mental-illness scenarios, which are (Peck, 2003):

1. A family member, friend, or other concerned person calls the police for help during a psychiatric emergency.
2. A person with mental illness feels suicidal and calls the police as a cry for help.
3. Police officers encounter a person with mental illness behaving inappropriately in public.
4. Citizens call the police because they feel threatened by the unusual behavior or the mere presence of a person with mental illness.
5. A person with mental illness calls the police for help on account of imagined threats.

Even though these are the five most frequent scenarios law enforcement officers may have with people with mental illness, no two contacts or encounters are ever the same. Further, it is worth mentioning that police officers will continually have such types of contacts at places such as parks, schools, colleges, businesses, care facilities, and any other locations where there are people. Law enforcement officers must always be attentive and sensitive to the behavior and needs of each mentally ill person.

POLICE PROTOCOL IN ENCOUNTERS WITH PEOPLE WHO HAVE MENTAL ILLNESS

Law enforcement officers exercise a great amount of discretion when they have an encounter with a person who has a mental illness. Generally, there are three options: (1) arrest, (2) hospitalization, and (3) informal disposition. Arrest is based on a crime that has been committed. The police officer then takes the mentally ill person into custody and transports him or her to jail where the arrested person is booked for the crime and later released, similar to any other person under the same circumstances. The authors discourage the arrest of a mentally ill person for the sole reason of getting the person treatment for his or her mental illness. Some officers may believe that arresting a mentally ill person may result in treatment for that person in a correctional facility. In almost all cases this is not the reality in the criminal justice system. All arrests should be made on the probable cause that a crime has been committed and law enforcement officers should always follow the due process protection guarantees of the U.S. Constitution.

Hospitalization of a person with mental illness is accomplished through voluntary and involuntary commitments. Often law enforcement officers will become involved with helping family members who need assistance in the voluntary commitment of another family member who consents to be taken to a hospital or clinic for mental health treatment. The police officer generally will stand by until the ambulance arrives to transport the person, or, depending on the law enforcement agency's protocol and the totality of the circumstances, make the transport themselves to the hospital or clinic. If the person with mental illness in this scenario refuses to a voluntary commitment, the police officer must then decide if the individual is a danger to himself or herself, or to others. When it is determined that the mentally ill person is indeed a danger to himself or herself, or others, then the police officer can legally place a police officer hold on the person to make it an involuntary commitment. In this case, the police officer would take the person into custody and transport to a local hospital that treats and accommodates people with mental illness. Law enforcement officers should follow mental health professionals' guidelines, local laws, and their agency's procedures when making a voluntary or involuntary commitment on any person.

Informal disposition is the third alternative to arrests or hospitalizations in encounters between law enforcement officers and persons with mental illness. Usually there is no written report by the police officer as required in an arrest or hospitalization. Commonly, the only documentation of the informal disposition is in the police officer's notebook and in the 911 Center's Computer Aided Dispatch (CAD). Informal dispositions can range from calming down a mentally ill person and having a responsible family member or friend watch over, to doing nothing at all. The following study provides data and insight on informal dispositions:

> Seventy-five percent of encounters between law enforcement officers and mentally ill persons are handled through informal disposition. This usually involves the police officer using informal tactics to calm or settle a person down. Some people have called this practice as "psychiatric first aid." (Lamb, Weinberger, and DeCuir, 2002)

Use of Force

Police interactions with people with mental illness have the potential of being dangerous, but usually are not. According to the U.S. Department of Justice, there were 982 police officers assaulted and 15 police officers feloniously killed between 1993 and 2002 by "mentally deranged" assailants. These assaults and murders are tragic, but these attacks by people with mental illness represent one out of every 59 assaults on officers and one out of every 42 officers killed. For the person with severe mental illness, it is estimated that he or she is four times more likely to be killed by the police in encounters than are other citizens (U.S. Department of Justice, 2006a). Unfortunately for the person who has a severe mental illness, he or she is vulnerable to excessive force by police officers who may not possess the mental health training and skills to diffuse a potentially dangerous contact. Too often in every city, county, and state there are reports of a mentally ill person either injured or killed by a police officer who did not use alternate methods in the encounter. On September 17, 2006, one such tragedy occurred in Portland, Oregon, when James P. Chasse Jr. had a fatal encounter with the police.

Chasse, a 42-year-old white male who suffered from schizophrenia, ran from two Portland police officers and a Multnomah County Deputy Sheriff. The police were chasing Chasse because he was seen acting strange and urinating behind a tree in the Pearl District of Portland, Oregon. One of the police officers grabbed Chasse and pushed him to the ground. While on the ground, a scuffle ensued, and police allege that Chasse bit one of the police officers on the leg and attempted to bite another. In reaction, one police officer kicked Chasse in the chest and another struck Chasse in the head with his fists. Police tasered Chasse and then placed him in maximum restraint, meaning his ankles were bound to his wrists, which were cuffed behind his back to keep him from kicking. Chasse became unconscious, and medical personnel were dispatched to the scene. An ambulance medic checked Chasse out and indicated he was okay to be taken to jail by the police. When Chasse arrived at the jail his feet were wedged under the backseat of the patrol car, and two police officers and jail staff removed him from the patrol car. Chasse screamed and spat at them, and the jail staff placed a "spit sock" of nylon material over his head. He was then placed in an isolation jail cell and moments later observed in an unconscious state. A jail nurse noticed that Chasse looked like he was having a seizure and had blood around his mouth, but never called 911 for medical help. Instead, the arresting officer and his partner put Chasse into the backseat of their patrol car and took off to Portland Adventist Hospital, a hospital that the police department contracts with. While en route to the hospital Chasse's physical condition became worse, and the police officers took the 33rd Avenue exit off of I-84. The handcuffs were removed from Chasse, and the police attempted CPR on him. An ambulance arrived and took Chasse to the hospital where moments later he was pronounced dead (Bernstein, 2006).

A Multnomah County grand jury found no criminal wrongdoing by police or others in the death of Chasse. The decision came after a Portland Police Bureau inquiry concluded that Chasse died from multiple rib fractures when an officer pushed him to the ground and accidentally fell on top of him. According to Oregon State Medical Examiner Dr. Karen Gunson, Chasse died from broad-based, blunt-force trauma to his chest suffered early in his encounter with police. Dr. Gunson also called Chasse's death "accidental." An autopsy disclosed he had 26 breaks in 16 ribs, some of which punctured his left lung and caused massive internal bleeding. Two days before Chasse's death, mental health specialists from Project Respond called for police to help them at Chasse's apartment because he was urinating in the hallway and was off his medication. By the time police arrived, Chasse had run out of the door (Bernstein, 2006).

Certainly, police officers must always be alert to their own safety when there is any resistance to an arrest, but the Chasse incident illustrates the need for the police to approach a person with mental illness in a calm and nonthreatening manner. Furthermore, police officers, when they have exhausted all other means, should only use the minimum amount of force necessary to physically restrain any person. Unfortunately, the average number of classroom hours that recruits spend on mental illness issues in the police academies nationwide is a shockingly low 6.5 hours and sometimes, though not guaranteed, maybe one or two hours at in-service training (Hails and Brorum, 2003). The Police Executive Research Forum recommends a minimum of 16 hours of training on mental illness issues at the police academy level. In the meantime, police departments across the United States need to examine what practices have worked well for police officers who have had encounters with persons with mental illness and highlight these effective methods in their training programs. Exhibit 14.9 lists recommendations for police officers who have contact with mentally ill persons.

Mentally Ill Persons in the Corrections System

In a 2006 study, it was reported that 56 percent of state prisoners, 45 percent of federal prisoners, and 64 percent of local jail inmates were identified to have a mental health condition (U.S. Department

---

Recommendations for Police Officers Who Have Contact with Mentally Ill Persons

1. Make an initial assessment of the situation or type of incident.
2. Follow the appropriate procedures as to how you will handle the situation, leading to final disposition or outcome of the contact.
3. Communicate in a respectful manner.
4. Speak in a calm and nonthreatening voice.
5. Be direct in your inquiries and requests.
6. Rephrase your inquiries and requests if needed.
7. Be patient and take the extra steps to communicate.
8. Do not talk down or belittle the person with mental illness.
9. Do not make threats toward the person with mental illness.
10. Protect the person with mental illness, others, and yourself from any physical injuries.
11. If the person with mental illness is having a psychotic episode and requires physical restraint, use the appropriate techniques to minimize any physical injuries to him or her.
12. Only use the minimum amount of force necessary, and justified, if the person with mental illness becomes violent to you or others.
13. Always seek medical treatment for a person with mental illness if they are physically injured.
14. Notify a supervisor and, at a minimum, document in your police report any use of physical force against a person with mental illness.

EXHIBIT 14.9   Recommendations for Police Officers Who Have Contact with Mentally Ill Persons.

Source: Olson, 2009.

of Justice, 2006b). The following data is from the U.S. Department of Justice Bureau of Justice Statistic's 2006 report (U.S. Department of Justice, 2006b):

- Jail inmates
    Symptoms of mania: 54 percent
    Major depression: 30 percent
    Psychotic disorder: 24 percent
- State prisoners
    Symptoms of mania: 43 percent
    Major depression: 23 percent
    Psychotic disorder: 15 percent
- Federal prisoners
    Symptoms of mania: 35 percent
    Major depression: 16 percent
    Psychotic disorder: 10 percent

Noted in the same study was the prevalence of violence associated with criminal activity. An estimated 61 percent of state prisoners and 44 percent of jail inmates who had a mental health problem had a prior violent offense. In addition, inmates with a mental health problem had high rates of substance dependence or abuse in the year before their admission. Those who were dependent on or abusing drugs/alcohol accounted for 74 percent of state prisoners and 76 percent of local jail inmates (U.S. Department of Justice, 2006b).

Among inmates who had mental health problems, 27 percent of state prisoners and 24 percent of jail inmates were victims of physical or sexual abuse. Those receiving mental health treatment since being incarcerated amounted to about one in three state prisoners, one in four federal prisoners, and one in six local jail inmates. Those receiving a prescribed medication were the most common type of treatment receivers, with 27 percent in state prisons, 19 percent in federal prisons, and 15 percent in local jails (U.S. Department of Justice, 2006b).

RESPONSE STRATEGIES BETWEEN POLICE AND PEOPLE WITH MENTAL ILLNESS

In June 1999, President Bill Clinton's administration convened the first Conference on Mental Health to address ways of reducing the stigma of mental illness and discrimination against people with mental disorders. The Attorney General chaired a session on mental health and the criminal justice system. The purpose was to address the recurring cycle of people with mental disorders being incarcerated for crimes (often minor offenses) and receiving minimal or no treatment for their underlying mental health problems. The session focused on legislative proposals to address these issues, including a mental health court proposal and other proposed legislation to improve services to the mentally ill within correctional settings. Following up on the Conference on Mental Health, the Office of Justice Programs and the Department of Health and Human Services (DHHS) Center for Mental Health Services hosted a conference in July 1999 on the treatment of people with mental disorders within the justice system. Issues included the challenges of integrating criminal justice and mental health systems, diverting mentally ill offenders to appropriate treatment through mental health court programs, improving mental health services in the juvenile justice system, and creating community partnerships to respond to the needs of people with mental illness.

One of the many benefits that resulted from the 1999 Clinton administration conferences on mental illness and other similar conferences is the ongoing awareness that respect and civil rights protection of people with mental illness must always be a priority as it is essential with all multicultural groups. Government and specifically the criminal justice system must be responsive and adaptive, and make changes in how it deals with people who have mental illness. Law enforcement agencies should follow four strategies to deal with the problem of people with mental health issues:

1. Partnerships with multicultural community leaders, local faith-based organizations, and other community-based agencies (e.g., homeless shelters, food banks, social services, hospitals/clinics) to provide a network of support for people with mental health problems.
2. Assistance to local ethnic business organizations that wish to work voluntarily with mental health issues within the community.
3. Creation of specific police training programs and continuing education for encounters with people with mental health problems.
4. Development and updating of policies, procedures, and practices within the law enforcement agency for dealing with mental health problems (e.g., crisis intervention teams).

Professional law enforcement officers should encourage the development of and participation in community task forces and committees on mental health issues. Police officers need to become involved with these task forces and brainstorm ideas and strategies on how to eliminate the stigma of mental illness and promote the well-being of people with mental health problems. This can be accomplished through positive support services and community connectedness, which are critical in task force effectiveness (Human Rights Watch, 2003; Sentencing Project, 2002).

Mini Case Study: CIT (Crisis Intervention Team)

The characteristics of the CIT model explained below are impressive. After reading about the specifics of the CIT in Memphis, Tennessee, identify and explain at least two barriers that could possibly prevent a police department from adopting the CIT model. After you identify the barriers, discuss ways of overcoming these obstacles so that the model becomes a more feasible one for a police department.

Memphis, Tennessee

In recent years, the most effective approach to improving police response to incidents involving people with mental illness, and especially crisis incidents, has been specialization. More departments have seen the value of having trained officers or even specialized units dispatched to handle these situations. The Memphis, Tennessee, Crisis Intervention Team (CIT) model is a team of selected patrol officers (10 to 20 percent of those assigned to patrol) who receive extra training, 40 hours initially, and then serve as generalists/specialists. These specialists perform the full range of regular patrol duties, but respond immediately whenever crisis situations involving people with mental illness occur. In those situations, these officers assume on-scene command

as soon as they arrive. They are trained to handle the crisis situations as well as facilitating the delivery of treatment and other services. The specialists quickly become knowledgeable about voluntary and involuntary commitments, and they develop good working relationships with professionals in the mental health community (U.S. Department of Justice, 2006a).

Research indicates that the CIT model works effectively in Memphis, Tennessee (Reuland and Margolis, 2003). Response times were generally under 10 minutes; the CIT officers handled 95 percent of all mental disturbance calls; regular patrol officers have been assigned to support the program; police time spent waiting for mental health admissions has dramatically decreased; arrest rates of people with mental illness have been reduced; referrals to treatment have increased; police-related injuries suffered by people with mental illness have been lowered; officer injury rates have been lowered; and call-outs for the Special Weapons and Tactics team were down. Numerous police departments throughout the United States have embraced the CIT model and have achieved similar results (U.S. Department of Justice, 2006a).

Summary

- *Community policing* is a term frequently used by law enforcement officers, criminal justice educators, elected officials, and community leaders. It refers to a style of policing in which law enforcement agencies and communities form partnerships to help problem solve crime and public safety issues. It (or the lack of it) is pivotal to the success (or failure) of every law enforcement agency's stated mission. Public safety and quality-of-life concerns are important to all of America's multicultural cities and communities. Both police and multicultural communities benefit when there is citizenship participation and relevant activities that build bridges for ongoing relationships.

- There are three major types of gangs: (1) Street gangs, (2) Prison gangs, and (3) Outlaw motorcycle gangs. Typical gang-related crimes include alien smuggling, armed robbery, assault, automobile theft, drug trafficking, extortion, fraud, home invasions, identity theft, murder, weapons trafficking, and hate crimes. There are approximately one million criminal gang members in the United States. Street gangs have the largest membership and most members are 18 years and older, but the majority of youth who join a gang belong to a street gang. The next largest group of gangs is prison gangs, followed by outlaw motorcycle gangs.

- Street gangs that are composed of young people between the ages of 12 and 24 are commonly referred to as youth gangs. Causation variables for youth gang membership include five risk factors which are: (1) prior delinquency in violence and alcohol/drug use; (2) poor family management and problematic parent–child relations; (3) low school attachment and academic achievement, and negative labeling by teachers; (4) association with peers who engage in delinquency; (5) and disorganized neighborhoods where large numbers of youth are in trouble and where drugs and firearms are readily available.

- By promoting coordination and information sharing between federal, state and local law enforcement agencies, the FBI has been able to and continues to identify violent gang enterprises that pose a significant threat. The FBI has also been able to pursue these criminals with coordinated investigations that support successful prosecutions. State and local law enforcement agencies have been responding to the gang threat since their inception but have not always maintained a consistent level of responsiveness. Major multiagency gang operations involving federal, state, county, and city law enforcement officers illustrate the need for law enforcement officers, especially in certain regions of the country, to familiarize themselves with the cultural, racial, and ethnic dimensions of gangs. Organizations such as COPS (Community Oriented Policing Services), an office of the U.S. Department of Justice, continue to provide excellent resources to law enforcement to mitigate the gang threat.

- A homeless person is an individual who lacks a regular and adequate nighttime residence. Homelessness is a growing problem in the United States that impacts all multicultural groups. The main causes for homelessness include a poor economy, unemployment, poverty, and a lack of shelter. People who are homeless are targeted victims of hate crimes. On May 7, 2009, Maryland became the first state in the United States to include hate crimes protection to homeless people.

- Before the police can be effective in responding to mitigate homelessness problems, homeless people must perceive that they will be protected and treated with respect by the police. Law enforcement officers need to demonstrate compassion to the homeless and be unbiased in their treatment to homeless people. Law enforcement officers need to be knowledgeable about organizations that help the homeless.

- Mental illness is characterized by alterations in thinking, mood, or behavior associated with distress and/or impaired functioning. There are many challenges faced by people with mental illness when they are in the roles of criminal offenders, disorderly persons, missing persons, complainants, victims, and persons in need of care. Unfortunately, due to their mental illness they are at an unfair disadvantage and are often treated with bias and disrespect.

• Most police officers have limited training on dealing effectively with mental health issues. Officers need to be aware that the use and level of force directed against a person with mental illness may be unnecessary unless there is a risk to the officer's safety. Other methods of dealing with the mentally ill are available to law enforcement, and more training is needed on the local, state, and national levels. Law enforcement must be responsive and adaptive, and make changes in how it deals with people who have mental illness. Strategies include: (1) partnerships with the leadership of ethnic and racial communities, local faith-based organizations, and other community-based services (i.e., hospitals/clinics) to provide a network of support for people with mental health problems; (2) assistance to local ethnic business organizations that voluntarily wish to work with mental health issues within the community; (3) creation of specific police training programs and continuing education for encounters with people with mental health problems; and (4) development and updating of policies, procedures, and practices within the law enforcement agency for dealing with mental health problems.

Discussion Questions and Issues

1. **Community Policing.** Why is community policing in minority, ethnic, and immigrant communities especially crucial to the success of law enforcement in any given city or rural community? Discuss the two examples presented in this section of the chapter (i.e., the police department in Garden Grove, California, without community policing in place [at the time of the fall of Saigon] and the Chicago Police Department whose community policing efforts resulted in a dramatic decline of violent crimes and property crimes in the city). What lessons can you extract from these two examples that may be applicable to your jurisdiction?

2. **Types of Gangs.** Make a list of the specific street gangs and outlaw motorcycle gangs within the law enforcement jurisdiction that you work or live in. Research information regarding each gang's membership and reported criminal activity. After compiling this information, discuss three strategies a police department could use to curtail each gang's membership and criminal activity.

3. **Homelessness.** Compile a list of the homelessness conditions and causes in the law enforcement jurisdiction that you work or live in. Research the number of people who are homeless and indicate their race, ethnicity, age, and gender. Identify the number of temporary emergency shelters, rescue missions, and soup kitchens in the area. Also, refer to Exhibit 14.5: "When There Is No Shelter" and identify all of the 22 types of places homeless people stay in your area. Upon completing these tasks, identify strategies you could take individually, and collectively with other people, to help people who are homeless in your multicultural community.

4. **Police Encounters with Mental Illness.** Select a city, county, or state law enforcement agency in your community and collect the following information:
   a. How many hours of training do police recruits receive at the academy on mental health issues?
   b. How many hours a year do police officers receive for mental health issues at in-service training?
   c. Review the police department's written policy, procedures, and practices for encounters with people who have mental illness.
   d. Does the police department track and keep record of all police officer contacts with people who have mental illness?
   e. Does the police department follow the four response strategies law enforcement should use to deal with problems of people with mental health issues?

Website Resources

Visit these websites for additional information about community policing, gangs, people who are homeless, and people who have mental illness:

Gang Resistance Education and Training (GREAT): http://www.great-online.org

The GREAT Program is a school-based, law enforcement officer-instructed classroom curriculum. The program's primary objective is prevention and is intended as an immunization against delinquency, youth violence, and gang membership.

Federal Bureau of Investigation (FBI) National Gang Information Center (NGIC): http://www.fbi.gov/hq/cid/ngic/violent_gangs.htm

The website is a component of the FBI's National Gang Information Center and provides information on gangs; the threats posed by gangs; how to help spot and prevent gang activity; and resource material for parents, educators, and police.

National Alliance on Mental Illness (NAMI): http://www.nami.org/

NAMI is the nation's largest grassroots organization for people with mental illness and their families. Founded in 1979, NAMI has affiliates in every state and in more than 1,100 local communities across the country.

National Alliance to End Homelessness (NAEH): http://www.endhomelessness.org

The NAEH is a nonpartisan, mission-driven organization committed to preventing and ending homelessness in the United States. They conduct research and provide data to policymakers and elected officials to inform debates and educate the public and opinion of leaders nationwide.

National Institute of Mental Illness (NIMI): http://www.nimh.nih.gov

NIMH is part of the National Institute of Health, a component of the U.S. Department of Health and Human Services. The mission of NIMH is to transform the understanding and treatment of mental illnesses through basic and clinical research, paving the way for prevention, recovery, and cure.

National Law Center on Homelessness and Poverty (NLCHP): http://www.nlchp.org

The mission of NLCHP is to prevent and end homelessness by serving as the legal arm of the nationwide movement to end homelessness. To achieve its mission, the organization pursues three main strategies: impact litigation, policy advocacy, and public education.

National Youth Gang Center (NYGC): http://www.iir.com/nygc

The response to America's gang problem by the Office of Juvenile Justice and Delinquency Prevention (OJJDP) involves five major components, one of which is the implementation and operation of the National Youth Gang Center (NYGC). To accomplish this mission, the Center conducts assessments of the scope and characteristics of youth gang activity in the United States, develops resources and makes them available to the field, and provides training and technical assistance in support of community-based prevention, intervention, and suppression efforts.

Office of Community Oriented Policing (COPS): http://www.cops.usdoj.gov

The website is a component of the Justice Department, and its mission is to advance the practice of community policing as an effective strategy to improve public safety. Their online Resource Information Center (RIC) offers publications, DVDs, CDs, and training materials on a wide range of law enforcement concerns and community policing topics (e.g., Crisis Intervention Teams).

References

Archibold, Randal C. (2006, October 11). "Far From Big City, Hidden Toll of Homelessness." *The New York Times*. Retrieved April 3, 2009, from http://www.nytimes.com/2006/10/11/us/11homeless.html.

Archibold, Randal C. (2009, March 22). "Mexican Drug Cartel Violence Spills Over, Alarming U.S." *The New York Times*. Retrieved May 13, 2009, from http://www.nytimes.com/2009/03/23/us/23border.html?_r=

2&scp=1&sq=mexican%20drug%20cartel%20violence&st=cse

Bernstein, M. (2006, October 18). "No Indictment in Chasse Death." *The Oregonian*. Retrieved May 11, 2009, from http://blog.oregonlive.com/oregonianextra/2006/10/no_indictment_in_chasse_death.html

Berry, O. (2009, March). Retired Assistant Chief, Reno Police Department, and Training Consultant, Reno, Nev., personal communication.

Brown, L. (2002, April 7). "On the Outside", in News and Record. Available at: http://www.naehcy.org/conf/dl/2008/vissing_issues.doc.

Boys & Girls Club of America (BGCA). (2008). "Boys and Girls Club Gang Prevention through Targeted Outreach." Retrieved May 9, 2009, from http://www.findyouthinfo.gov/cf_pages/programdetail.cfm?id=304

Chicago Police Department. (2007). "Chicago Police Department 2007 Annual Report," p. 33.

Community Oriented Policing Services (COPS). (2008a). "Gangs: Guides and Reports." Retrieved March 27, 2009, from http://www.cops.usdoj.gov/default.asp?Item=1594#stats

Community Oriented Policing Services (COPS). (2008b). "About Cops." Retrieved May 8, 2009, from http://www.cops.usdoj.gov/default.asp?Item=35

Department of Health and Human Services (DHHS). (1999). "Mental Health: A Report of the Surgeon General," p. 5.

Esbensen, F. A. (2000). *Preventing Adolescent Gang Involvement*. Youth Gang Series. Washington, D.C.: U.S. Department of Justice, Office of Juvenile Justice and Delinquency Prevention.

Esbensen, F. A., and L. T. Winfree, Jr. (1998). "Race and Gender Differences between Gang and Non-Gang Youth: Results from a Multi-Site Survey." *Justice Quarterly*, *15*, 505–525.

Federal Bureau of Investigation (FBI). (2009a). "Violent Gangs." Retrieved March 26, 2009, from http://www.fbi.gov/hq/cid/ngic/violent_gangs.htm.

Federal Bureau of Investigation (FBI). (2009b). "Massive Racketeering Case Targets Hawaiian Gardens Gang Involved in Murder of Sheriff's Deputy, Attacks on African-Americans and Widespread Drug Trafficking." Retrieved May 28, 2009, from http://losangeles.fbi.gov/dojpressrel/pressrel09/la052109.htm.

Federal Bureau of Investigation (FBI). (2009c). "Violent Gang Task Forces." Retrieved September 28, 2009, from http://www.fbi.gov/hq/cid/ngic/natgangtfs.htm.

Gang Awareness Training Education (G.A.T.E.). (2009). "Welcome." Retrieved May 9, 2009, from http://openthegate.org/

Gang Resistance Education and Training (G.R.E.A.T.). (2009). "Welcome." Retrieved May 9, 2009, from http://www.great-online.org/

Glover, S., and R. Winton. (2009, May 22). "Dozens arrested in crackdown on Latino gang accused of targeting blacks." *L.A. Times*. Retrieved May 28, 2009, from http://www.latimes.com/news/local/la-me-gang-sweep22-2009may22,0,6857156.story

Gottfredson, G. D., and D. C. Gottfredson. (2001, October). *Gang Problems and Gang Programs in a National Sample of Schools*. Ellicott City, Md.: Gottfredson Associates, Inc. Available: http://www.gottfredson.com/gang.htm.

Hails, J., and R. Borum. (2003). "Police Training and Specialized Approaches to Respond to People with Mental Illnesses." *Crime and Delinquency*. 49: 1. P.52–61.

Hill, K. G., C. Lui, and J. D. Hawkins. (2001). *Early Precursors of Gang Membership: A Study of Seattle Youth*. Bulletin. Youth Gang Series. Washington, D.C.: U.S. Department of Justice, Office of Juvenile Justice and Delinquency Prevention.

Howell, J. C., and A. Egley, Jr. (2005). "Moving Risk Factors into Developmental Theories of Gang Membership." *Youth and Juvenile Justice*, *3*(4), 334–354.

Human Rights Watch. (2003). *United States: Mentally Ill Mistreated in Prison-More Mentally Ill in Prison than in Hospitals*. Washington, D.C.: Human Rights Watch.

Jencks, Christopher. (1994). *The Homeless*. Cambridge, MA: Harvard University Press.

Lamb, R., L. Weinberger, and W. DeCuir. (2002). "The Police and Mental Health," *Psychiatric Services*, *53*(10), 1266–1271.

Lincoln Police Department. (2004). "Emergency Protective Custody Issues for the Police." Mimeo.

Miller, W. (1982). *Crime by Youth Gangs and Groups in the United States*. Washington, D.C.: Government Printing Office.

Monkkonen, Eric H. (1981). *Police in Urban America, 1860–1920*. Cambridge, England: Cambridge University Press.

National Alliance to End Homelessness. (2007, June). "Domestic Violence." Retrieved April 3, 2009, from http://www.endhomelessness.org/content/article/detail/1647

National Alliance on Mental Illness. (2009). "About Mental Illness." Retrieved April 6, 2009, from http://www.nami.org/template.cfm?section=About_Mental_Illness

National Coalition for the Homeless. (2008a, June). *How Many People Experience Homelessness?* NCH Fact Sheet No. 2. Washington D.C.

National Coalition for the Homeless. (2008b, November). "Hate Crimes against People Who Are Homeless." NCH Fact Sheet #21. Washington D.C. Available: http://www.nationalhomeless.org/publications/facts/hatecrimes.html

National Gang Intelligence Center (NGIC). (2009). *National Gang Threat Assessment.* Product No. 2009-M0335-001. Retrieved March 12, 2009, from http://www.usdoj.gov/ndic/pubs32/32146/32146p.pdf

National Institute of Mental Health. (2009, February). "The Numbers Count: Mental Disorders in America." Retrieved April 4, 2009, from http://www.nimh.nih.gov/health/publications/the-numbers-count-mental-disorders-in-america/index.shtml#Intro

National Law Center on Homeless and Poverty. (2007). *2007 Annual Report.* Washington D.C. Available: http://www.nlchp.org/content/pubs/2007_Annual_Report2.pdf

National Law Center on Homeless and Poverty. (2004, January). "Homelessness in the United States and the Human Right to Housing." Washington, D.C. Available: http://nlchp.org

National Youth Gang Center (NYGC). (2006). National Youth Gang Survey, 1999–2001. NCJ 209392. Available: http://www.ncjrs.gov/pdffiles1/ojjdp/209392.pdf

National Youth Gang Center. (2007). *National Youth Gang Survey Analysis.* Retrieved March 27, 2009, from http://www.iir.com/nygc/nygsa/measuring_the_extent_of_gang_problems.htm#homicidesnumber

National Youth Gang Center (NYGC). (2009). "What Is A Youth Gang?" Retrieved March 27, 2009, from http://www.iir.com/nygc/faq.htm#q1

Nuckos, B. (2009, May 8). "Attacks on Homeless Become Hate Crime in Maryland." *Associated Press.* Retreived May 13, 2009, from http://www.google.com/hostednews/ap/article/ALeqM5j8c5otLB8fe_IQaaBhvnhGQ5u8pAD981MCEO0

Olson, Aaron T. (2009, May). Cultural Diversity in Criminal Justice Professions Instructor at Portland Community College, Portland, Oregon and retired police supervisor with the Oregon State Police, personal communication.

Osborne, A. L. (2009, May). "Skipper." Founder/CEO of TAJFA (Truth and Justice for All) and Former President of NAACP, Portland, Ore., personal communication.

Peck, L. (2003). "Law Enforcement Interactions with Persons with Mental Illness." *TELEMASP Bulletin, 10*(1), 1–12.

Peterson, D., J. Miller, and F. Esbensen. (2001). "The Impact of Sex Composition on Gangs and Gang Delinquency." *Criminology, 39*(2), 411–439.

Police Athlethic League (PAL). (2008). "Welcome to National PAL." Retrieved May 9, 2009, from http://www.nationalpal.org/

Police Executive Research Forum (PERF). (2004). "Community Policing: The Past, Present, and Future." Washington, D.C. Available: CommunityPolicingReduced_570119206_12292005152352

Reuland, M., and G. Margolis. (2003). "Police Approaches That Improve the Response to People with Mental Illnesses: A Focus on Victims." *The Police Chief, 11*, 35–39.

Sentencing Project. (2002). *Mentally Ill Offenders in the Criminal Justice System.* Washington, D.C.: The Sentencing Project.

Stoops, Michael. (2009, April) Executive Director of the National Coalition for the Homeless, Washington, D.C., personal communication.

Thornberry, T. P. (1998). "Membership in Youth Gangs and Involvement in Serious and Violent Offending." In R. Loeber, and D. P. Farrington (eds.), *Serious and Violent Juvenile Offenders: Risk Factors and Successful Interventions,* Thousand Oaks, Calif.: Sage Publications.

Thornberry, T. P., M. D. Krohn, A. J. Lizotte, C. A. Smith, and K. Tobin. (2003). *Gangs and Delinquency in Developmental Perspective,* New York, NY: Cambridge University Press.

Urban Institute. (2000, December 1). *America's Homeless II: Populations and Services* 2100 M Street NW, Washington, D.C. Available: http://www.urban.org/UploadedPDF/900344_AmericasHomelessII.pd

U.S. Conference of Mayors. (2006, December). *A Status Report on Hunger and Homelessness in America's Cities*: A-23 Survey. U.S. Conference of Mayors, 1620 Eye St., NW, 4th Floor, Washington, D.C. Available: http://www.usmayors.org/hunger-survey/2006/report06.pdf

U.S. Conference of Mayors. (2007, December). *A Status Report on Hunger and Homelessness in America's Cities*: A-23 Survey. U.S. Conference of Mayors, 1620 Eye St., NW, 4th Floor, Washington, D.C. Available: http://www.usmayors.org/HHSurvey2007/hhsurvey07.pdf

U.S. Conference of Mayors. (2008, December 12). *The U.S. Conference of Mayors Release 2008 Hunger and Homelessness Survey Results*. Press Release. Available: http://www.usmayors.org/pressreleases/documents/hungerhomelessness_121208.pdf

U.S. Department of Justice. (2006a). Office of Community Oriented Policing Services: "People with Mental Illness." Available: http:www/cops.usdoj./gov.mimie/open.pdf

U.S. Department of Justice. (2006b). Office of Justice Programs, Bureau of Justice Statistics: "Study Finds More than Half of All Prison and Jail Inmates Have Mental Health Problems." Available: http://www.ojp.usdoj.gov/bjs/pub/press/mhppjipr.htm.

U.S. Department of Justice. (2009a). Office of Justice Programs, Bureau of Justice Statistics: "State and Local Law Enforcement Training Academies, 2006" Special Report, February 2009, NCJ222987. Available: http://www.ojp.usdoj.gov/bjs/pub/pdf/slleta06.pdf

U.S. Department of Justice. (2009b). "About Violent Gangs: Outlaw Motorcycle Gangs." Retrieved March 26, 2009, from http://www.usdoj.gov/criminal/gangunit/about/omgangs.html.

U.S. Surgeons's Report. (1999). "Chapter 4: Adults and Mental Health" Retrieved September 28, 2009 http://www.surgeongeneral.gov/library/mentalhealth/toc.html#chapter4

Waldman, A. (2004, March 17). "Police Struggle with Approach to the Mentally Ill: Recent Killings Have Led to Calls for Better Tracking and Treatment of the Mentally Ill and More Training for Officers." *The Christian Science Monitor*. Available: www.csmonitor.com2004/0317/p11s02-usju.htm.

CHAPTER 15

Emerging Strategies, Roles, and Technology for Peace Officers in Multicultural Law Enforcement

LEARNING OBJECTIVES

After completing this chapter you will be able to:

- Identify emerging issues in peace officer strategies within the context of a multicultural society.
- Discuss the need for police officers to have a professional and positive self-image.
- Define and understand the interwoven concepts of leadership, professionalism, and synergy.
- Describe the peace officer's role in working with multicultural communities and interagency efforts in response to global and regional events.
- Explain how curtailing litigation against law enforcement agencies is a key challenge.
- Review the need for law enforcement to adapt to innovations and advanced technology.

OUTLINE

- Introduction
- The Future of Peacekeeping Strategies in Multicultural Communities
- Impact of Image on Human Behavior and the "Peace Officer" Image
- Police Leadership in Professionalism and Synergy
- Multicultural Communities and Interagency Efforts in Response to Global and Regional Events

INTRODUCTION

This chapter focuses on emerging and changing issues in the strategies and roles confronting the peace officer in multicultural law enforcement today. Awareness of the changing role and image of peace officers will result in increased cultural competence and community effectiveness in law enforcement. Given the impact of greater diversity on both peacekeeping and law enforcement, we explore how cultural understanding can be translated into more effective community policing. To increase cultural awareness, readers are provided with a simple model for a quick analysis of differences in various cultures, ethnic groups, and generations. Improved police performance and professionalism are dependent on cross-cultural skills and sensitivity among peace officers. Peace officers need to be able to manage and adapt to innovations and advanced technology within their increasing roles in local community policing and in multijurisdictional crime-solving efforts such as terrorism, homeland security, and disaster preparedness. The role of peace officers has increased in functions to encompass assistance to and communication with multicultural communities in disasters, terrorism, and controlling possible community confrontations resulting from global/regional events. Curtailing litigation against law enforcement agencies is a key challenge for law enforcement leaders and officers, requiring changes in police policies, training, and practices. Training and preparation of future law enforcement personnel will require changes in the curriculum of the police academies, as well as the ongoing and continuing education of law enforcement officers.

Perhaps the greatest challenge facing law enforcement officers and leaders is to develop law enforcement organizations and services that can (1) effectively recognize, relate to, and operate within the multicultural communities and the global shifts in culture, (2) utilize technological advances, and (3) adapt to community/governmental expectations. As highlighted by the First Leadership Conference of the International Association of Chiefs of Police (IACP):

> Forces in the community, the police agency, local government, and global trends are profoundly altering expectations and requirements for leading police agencies successfully. Today's law enforcement organizations must embrace innovations and technological advances through appropriate organizational change, training, education, and preparation of its officers. This is particularly important in the training curricula and processes within the police academies. Emphasis is critically needed in the area of working with multicultural communities and in the overall knowledge bases of diversity, basic psychology, interpersonal relations, and communications. (IACP, 1999)

The themes highlighted by the IACP's First Leadership Conference are as important to law enforcement today as they were approximately a decade ago. Russell B. Laine, Chief of Police,

Algonquin, Illinois, and the 115th President of the IACP, made the following statement on global cooperation and police leadership:

> I am pleased to say that the IACP's International Policing Division continues to prosper, but there is much work ahead: this will be a big year for our international activities . . . This growth is essential because it is clear that successfully confronting the challenge posed by transnational criminal and terrorist organizations requires that the international law enforcement community establish and maintain effective working relationships that allow us to pool our information and our resources . . . We need to ensure that we plan for the future of our profession by providing opportunities for leadership growth. The IACP has embraced this concept and has developed incredible programs focused on leadership development. The Center for Police Leadership and the Police Chief Mentoring Project offer programs and training courses that should be used as a basis for developing the next generation of police leadership. (Laine, 2008)

THE FUTURE OF PEACEKEEPING STRATEGIES IN MULTICULTURAL COMMUNITIES

Those who would uphold law and order in the twenty-first century will need to be more proactive and less reactive (Thibault, Lynch, and McBride, 2001). The new generation of peace officers must not only increase their knowledge in such matters, but also promote positive law enforcement innovations. In this chapter we focus on a few strategies for agencies to consider in their efforts to keep community peace in a multicultural society.

Within multiracial communities facing the myriad challenges of transition and integration, economic constraints, and the complexity of crimes, representatives of the justice system need to act proactively, sensitively, and knowledgeably. If social order is not to be replaced by chaos, law enforcement representatives of all types not only need to be culturally sensitive but also must actively avoid racist, sexist, and homophobic behavior that may trigger violent social protest. Clearly, the diverse images of law enforcement as held by the multicultural communities rest upon the professionalism that today's peace officers display with regard to cultural competence, technical knowledge, and communication skills. The image of law enforcement projected to the public by police officers, their organizations, and the media is especially important within multicultural venues (Hancock and Sharp, 2000).

IMPACT OF IMAGE ON HUMAN BEHAVIOR AND THE "PEACE OFFICER" IMAGE

People create both accurate and inaccurate images, of themselves and others, as well as images of their roles. Our behavior is then influenced by these mental pictures, and others respond to what we project, which may not necessarily reflect reality. The most powerful of these images is the one we have of ourselves, followed by those formed about our multiple roles. Similarly, we also create images of our organizations and the criminal justice system and its activities.

According to Norman Boehm, former director of the California Commission on Peace Officer Standards and Training, police officers today are both knowledge and service workers who must focus on effective performance. Thus, he believes, police departments must become both learning organizations and enforcement agencies. Boehm maintains that the former have the responsibility to provide officers with new knowledge, skills, and behaviors to be effective on the job. "Smart cops," in every sense of the word, are becoming the norm (Barlow, 2000; White, 2007).

Such an image of peacekeepers may explain why so many justice agencies are mandating a 2- or 4-year college degree for entering recruits. Carter and Wilson (2006) describe in detail the benefits of an educated officer: "Researchers, practitioners, commissions, and even police agencies themselves have been calling for increased education requirements for police officers for many reasons. Some point out that police work has become increasingly complex and, as a result, education requirements for police officers should be increased. Others suggest that better educated police officers will be 'more rounded thinkers and exhibit a greater humanistic bent.' " Brainpower, not brawn, is what will make for effectiveness in the vastly changing world.

Exhibit 15.1 differentiates between perceptions of the disappearing and the emerging police work culture. Contrasting the two views helps to explain why, within the criminal justice field, a different image of law enforcement must be created for the peace officer and then

EXHIBIT 15.1   Law Enforcement and Role Transitions.

TRADITIONAL WORK CULTURE	EVOLVING WORK CULTURE
Attitude Reactive; preserve status quo	Proactive; anticipate the future
Orientation Enforcement as dispensers of public safety	Enforcement and peacekeeping as helping professionals
Organization Paramilitary with top-down command system; intractable departments and divisions; centralization and specialization	Transitional toward more fluid, participative arrangements and open communication system; decentralization, task forces, and team management
Expectations Loyalty to your superior, organization and buddies, then duty and public service; conformity and dependency	Loyalty to public service and duty, and one's personal and professional development; demonstrate leadership competence and interpersonal skills
Requirements Political appointment, limited civil service; education—high school or less	Must meet civil service standards; education—college and beyond, lifelong learning
Personnel Largely white males, military background and sworn only; all alike, so structure workload for equal shares in static sharply defined slots	Multicultural without regard to sex or sexual preference; competence norm for sworn and unsworn personnel; all different, so capitalize on particular abilities, characteristic, potential
Performance Obey rules, follow orders, work as though everything depended on your own hard efforts toward gaining the pension and retirement	Work effectively, obey reasonable and responsible requests; interdependence means cooperate and collaborate with other; ensure financial/career future
Environment Relatively stable society where problems were somewhat routine and predictable, and authority was respected	Complex, fast-changing, multicultural society with unpredictable problems, often global in scope, and more disregard of authority, plus more guns/violence even among juveniles

projected to the public. This is but a synopsis of the transition underway in the world of work and law enforcement, which in turn alters our views of various justice roles. In the latter, the shift and trends seem to be away from the traditional approaches—from reactive to proactive; from just enforcement and crime fighting toward prevention and detection of criminal activity, toward preserving the public peace and service, and toward protecting life and property; and from just public-sector policing to synergistic security services by both the public and the private sectors working in cooperation (Hunter, Barker, and Mayhall, 2008).

Image Projection

Within this larger context, comprehending the significance and power of image and its projection becomes critical for would-be peacekeepers. Image is not a matter of illusion or mere public manipulation of appearances. Behavioral scientists have long demonstrated the vital connection between image and identity, between the way we see ourselves and our actual behavior. Realists among us have always known that life's "losers," many of them convicted felons, lack an adequate sense of identity and suffer from feelings of poor self-worth. Some people raised in dysfunctional families go so far as to engage not only in self-depreciation and abuse but in self-mutilation as well. Aware of these factors, one state (California) established a special commission to promote self-esteem among school youth, so as to curb crime and delinquency.

Behavioral communication may be understood in terms of senders and receivers of messages. Exhibit 15.2 suggests that we view the multiple images we form in terms of concentric or

Multiple Images

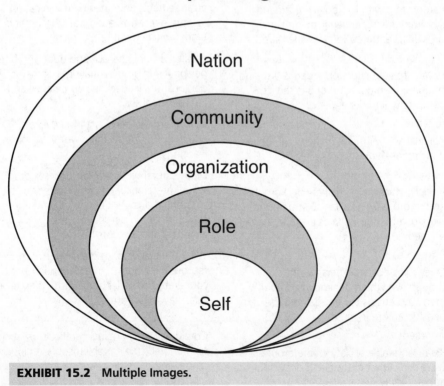

EXHIBIT 15.2   **Multiple Images.**

spiraling circles, centered on the all-important self-image at the core (Leary, 1996). As we see ourselves, we project an image to which people respond. Normally, we are in control of the reactions and treatment we receive by the image we project. Our self-concept has been long in development, the outcome not just of life experience but of others' input to us. If a child continuously receives negative feedback from parents and teachers, he or she begins to believe in personal worthlessness. Usually, such young people fail to achieve unless an intervention calls into question their distorted concept of self. Such persons are likely to project weak images that often prompt others to take advantage of them. On the other hand, if they have self-confidence and project a positive image, both verbally and nonverbally, an acceptable response from others is probable. (The exception would be with bigoted persons who reflect an inner bias and refuse to accept people different from themselves as with, for example, frustrated youth known as skinheads. In this case, the problem and conflict are caused by feelings of low self-worth). The best antidote to underachievement or even racism is for a person to have a healthy self-image.

Furthermore, if a person is confused about identify, as is often the situation with adolescents, people tend to respond in an uncertain way toward that person. Therefore, in the selection of police candidates, law enforcement officials seek those with a strong self-image and self-appreciation. Police academy training should reinforce, not undermine, this self-confidence. Police supervisors are advised to provide regular positive reinforcement of their officers' sense of self.

We play many roles in the course of life—male or female, married or single, child or parent, student or mentor. However, our concern here is specifically on work and professional roles within the criminal justice system and the changing images projected by its practitioners. In terms of behavioral communication theory, police officers project an image to the public based on how they see themselves, and citizens usually respond to that image (Langworthy and Travis, 1999).

Two examples—one old, and one new—illustrate this point. In 1829 Sir Robert Peel established the London Metropolitan Police, projecting an image of a paid, professional force, to which the British public responded positively, calling them "peelers" or "bobbies." Rejecting the old adage "employ a thief to catch a thief," he recruited these new police from the military (rather than from criminal backgrounds, as was then the custom) and compensated them with adequate salaries, so they would be less inclined to accept bribes or indulge in other irregularities (Gilbert, 1990).

Since then the role of police has evolved as society has changed its perceptions of values and priorities, justice and criminality, and law and enforcement (Carter and Radalet, 1999; Champion and Rush, 1997; White, 2007). Currently, for example, the average citizen seems less concerned about police enforcement of vice and traffic laws and more concerned about their combating gang and domestic violence, especially physical abuse of children, spouses, and the aged, and, even more recently, terrorism and threats to homeland security. Understandably, the North American public today, particularly the minorities and the disenfranchised, have high expectations about being treated humanely and fairly when encountering police in an economically developed country. However, new arrivals to the United States and Canada, whether through documented or undocumented entry, come with their own cultural perceptions and perspectives from their homeland. These can include negative images of police there, which may be that of oppressors and bribe takers. For these citizens, professional police in the new homeland may need to go out of their way to help them overcome the mental barriers they carry due to their cultural background.

The second example involves how modern media have a powerful influence on how the public perceives police. It begins with fictional police and crime scene investigators as depicted in novels and mystery stories, expands to reports of police activities in newspapers and magazines, and extends to radio, television, and Internet broadcasts about policing. Today U.S. movies and television "cop shows" are viewed internationally. The range of media impact on images of law enforcement is extensive.

With information age and its associated high-tech communication technologies, we have seen that local police actions can, in a second, become international incidents. With the help of satellites, television, and the internet, the inhabitants of our planet react as a global village. On a daily basis, we see embarrassment to law enforcement's image occurring locally, nationally, and worldwide. With instant communications, including video capacity on cell phones, the reality is that criminal justice representatives will continue to be subject to extra scrutiny and accountableness.

The principal lesson to be learned from any controversial police action is that the organizational image of a reasonable and effective agency can be undermined by the unprofessional and illegal actions of a relatively small percentage of officers (Palmiotto, 2001). It is not enough for a peace officer to be a competent professional; he or she must also assist the department by preventing or reporting wrongdoing by colleagues.

Peace Officer Image

Adopted in various American states, the term *peace officer*, which we use interchangeably with *police officer*, is a concept that might offset and reverse negative publicity. Law enforcement personnel must take pride in the term and internalize its meaning. By projecting this image and its corresponding behavior, police are more likely to make a favorable impression on people. Interestingly, it is the terminology that was very popular in the old West and often used in old cowboy movies. This term is also in use nationally within the U.S. Department of Justice, as well as within certain regions. For example, the California code (Section 830) defines a peace officer as including sheriffs, police, marshals, constables, inspectors, investigators, district attorneys, state highway patrol and police, state university and college police, and designated personnel in the departments of justice, corrections, fish and game, parks and recreation, and forestry. This broad definition applies to members of the National Guard when on duty during states of emergency, as well as to U.S. federal marshals. It can encompass a wide range of related criminal justice occupations, such as arson investigators; park rangers; coroners; investigators of child support and fraud; security officers in municipal and public utilities; harbor, port, and transportation security officers; and public housing security. Similarly, in the state of Texas, the term peace officer is in widespread use; its Commission on Law Enforcement Standards and Training uses the term for constables, sheriffs, city police, specialized police, and the Texas Rangers. But do practitioners appreciate the implications of this nomenclature by which they are widely known?

Within this wide spectrum of peace officers, the image is strengthened by their being "sworn" to uphold the law, their adherence to standards and training, their badge and weapon, and sometimes their uniforms and insignia. But the true significance of the words *peace officer* is yet to be fully realized by most of who operate under the umbrella term.

Influencing the Public Positively

Psychologists remind us that the image we have of our role affects not only our behavior but also the behavior of those to whom we project this image. The U.S. Marine Corps, for example, is currently undergoing a change of image from warriors to peacekeepers and humanitarians (DeFilippis, 2008; McMillen, 2008). What if all those described previously under the definition of peace officer actually saw themselves as such, thus projecting that image to the public? What if they were actually to become peace practitioners rather than symbolic enforcers of authority? A change in role image and actions among agents of the law might prompt the majority of the law-abiding community to perceive them more positively—as peace officers in fact as well as in name. Rather than fear police, citizens would turn to them as resourceful problem solvers. Neighborhood police who interact with the community are more likely to improve public perception of law enforcement, in contrast to police who rarely leave their squad cars or come into difficult areas as members of special units. Manning (1997), in describing police organizations, indicates that the police understand the importance of being active in their construction of a positive image and do take great care to emphasize the positive and limit access to negative events and actions.

Changing Police Cultures

In the article "Taking Police Culture Seriously," law professor Andrew Goldsmith of Melbourne, Australia, makes these astute observations:

> Police culture tends to be seen negatively, as a contrary and perverse influence on "proper" exercise of police discretion. It is seen as often subversive of the ideals and demands of legality. Yet most modern societies are essentially dependent upon rule-based forms of police accountability. Police culture needs to be approached more positively, as a potential resource in the formulation of rules governing police powers and practices. This requires that police administrators and officers participate in negotiated rulemaking, a process similar to collective bargaining, in which police cultural perspectives are drawn upon. (Goldsmith, 1990)

Traditional police cultures need to transition away from the more rigid military and bureaucratic cultures of the past to a more flexible, corporate-like, proactive, and high-tech culture (White, 2007). Law enforcement leaders become change agents in this twenty-first century process. To facilitate the changeover, many police administrators and managers apply methods of cultural analysis to their own unique work environment.

Ways of Analyzing Cultures

There are many ways to study a culture, such as a systems approach that would analyze it in terms of kinship, education, economics, politics, religions, associations, health, and pastimes. However, Harris and Moran (2000) provide a simple model that will enable those in law enforcement to get a grasp of a culture, whether on a large or a small scale, regardless of the grouping. These 10 benchmarks can be used to better comprehend a foreign organizational or local culture, especially that of a minority or ethnic group. Exhibit 15.3 summarizes these characteristics for cultural analysis, first in terms of cultures in general and then specifically in the context of police culture.

A police officer in emergency situations is obviously not going to have the time to do an in-depth cultural analysis. However, especially in community-policing types of situations, the officer can undertake some preparation before beginning an assignment in a given area where citizens will largely be from unfamiliar ethnic groups. Most people have preconceived notions or only a stereotypical understanding of cultural groups with which they have not previously had contact. The categories listed in Exhibit 15.3 are areas where one often finds predictable cultural variations. The more information an officer or agent can gather about the cultural patterns of a distinctive community group, the less likely he or she is to make false assumptions about people. Knowledge of these cultural patterns would help the officer understand the behavior and actions of groups and contribute to an overall ability to establish rapport and gain trust.

1. **Sense of self and space.** Examine how people in this cultural group perceive themselves and distance themselves from others. Culture not only helps to confirm one's identity but provides a sense of space, both physical and psychological. Such cultural conditioning of behavior may dictate a humble bearing in one culture or macho posturing in another. Some cultures support rugged individualism and independent action, while others teach that self-worth is attained in group conformity and cooperation. In some cultures, such as American, the sense of space dictates more physical distance between individuals, while in Latin/Asian cultures, less distance is desirable. Some cultures are very structured and formal, while others are more flexible and informal. Some cultures are very closed and determine one's place very precisely, while others are more open and dynamic. Each culture validates self in unique ways.

Police culture, for example, expects officers to project a sense of authority and assertiveness, to be respected and in control, to be curious and suspicious, to act with social appropriateness and a sense of duty, to uphold the law, and to serve the common good. Sense of space is experienced in terms of a precinct or district, a patrol area ("beat"), or a neighborhood in community-based policing.

2. **Communication and language.** Examine the communication system in the culture, both verbal and nonverbal. Apart from the national or regional language that might be spoken, study the dialects, accents, slang, jargon, graffiti, and other such variations. For example, there are differences in the way the English language is spoken in England and within the British Isles and Commonwealth nations; in North America, between the Canadians and the Americans (and within the latter between regions and groups, such as black English). Levine reminds us to go Beyond Language to comprehend the full communication by seeking the meanings given to body language, gestures, and signals.

The police culture has its own jargon and code system for communicating rapidly within the field of law enforcement; organizational communications dictate a formal system for reporting, for exchanges with superior ranks, for dealing with public officials and the media. A code of silence may exist about speaking to outsiders concerning police business and personnel.

3. **Dress and appearance.** Examine the cultural uniqueness relative to outward garments, adornments, and decorations or lack thereof; the dress or distinctive clothing demanded for different occasions (e.g., business, sports, weddings or funerals); the use of color and cosmetics; the hair and beard styles, or lack thereof; body markings.

In police culture, policy, regulations and even custom may determine a uniform with patches and insignia of rank, plus certain equipment to be worn and even the length of hair permissible. Exceptions may be permitted for those in administration, detective, or undercover work.

4. **Food and eating habits.** Examine the manner in which food is selected, prepared, presented, and eaten. According to the culture, meat, like beef or pork, may be prized or prescribed, or even forbidden all together—one person's pet may be another's delicacy. Sample national dishes, diverse diets, and condiments for tastes do vary by culture (realize that cultural groups can be conditioned to accepting some food or seasoning that your own body would not tolerate without reactions. Feeding habits may range from the use of hands or chopsticks to the use of utensils or cutlery (e.g., Americans and Europeans do not hold and use the fork in the same manner). Subcultures can be studied from this perspective (as in soldier's mess, executive dining rooms, vegetarian restaurants, prescriptions for females, etc.). Even drinking alcohol differs by culture—in Italy, it is more associated with eating a meal, while in Japan and Korea it is ritualized in the business culture as part of evening entertainment and strengthening business relations, sometimes done to excess.

EXHIBIT 15.3 Characteristics for Culture Analysis.

In police culture, the emphasis has been on fast foods, hearty meals (preferably "complimentary," although official regulations require payment by officers for all such services); customs include that the patrol car sets the eating time for both partners, as well as off-duty relaxation and comradery in a "cop's drinking hole," sometimes marked by too much alcoholic consumption. The new generation of police is more concerned about healthy foods, keeping physically fit, and stress management—including diet, exercise, no smoking, and no substance abuse.

5. **Time and time consciousness.**   Examine the time sense as to whether it is exact or relative, precise or casual. In some cultures, promptness is determined by age or status (e.g., at meetings—subordinates arrive first, the boss or elder last). Is the time system based on 12 or 24 hours? In tribal and rural cultures, tracking hours and minutes is unnecessary, for timing is based on sunrise and sunset, as well as the seasons, which also vary by culture (e.g., rainy or dry seasons vs. fall/winter/spring/summer). Schedules in the postindustrial work culture are not necessarily 8 hours; businesses may operate on a 24-hour basis because of telecommunications and electronic mail. Chronobiologists are concerned under such circumstances about the body's internal clock and performance, so analyze body temperature and composition relative to sleepiness, fatigue, and peak periods (e.g., as with jet fatigue when passing through time zones).

The police culture operates on a 24-hour schedule with sliding work shifts that do affect performance; some departments adopt the military time-keeping system of 24 hours. Normally, promptness is valued and rewarded; during police operations, timing is precise, with watch synchronization of all involved.

6. **Relationships.**   Examine how the culture fixes human and organizational relationships by age, sex, status, and degree of kindred, as well as by wealth, power, and wisdom. In many cultures, marriage and the family unit are the most common means for establishing relations between the sexes and among parents, children, and other relatives. In the Far East, this is accomplished through an extended family that may involve aunts, uncles, and cousins living in the same household. Many cultures also operate with the male head of household as the authority figure, and extend this out from home to community to nation, explaining the tendency in some countries to have dictators. In traditional cultures, custom sets strict guidelines about boy—girl relations prior to marriage, about treatment of the elderly (in some cultures, they are honored, in others ignored), about female behavior (wearing veils and appearing differential to males in contrast to being considered an equal). "Underworld" or criminal cultures sometimes adopt a family pattern with the "godfather" as the head and various titles to distinguish roles.

In police culture, organizational relations are determined by rank and protocol, as well as by assignment to different departmental units. Although policy may dictate that all fellow officers and citizens be treated equally, unwritten practice may differ. The partnership system usually forgoes close relations and trust between individuals whose life and welfare is dependent upon the other. Postindustrial policing is moving more toward developing team relationships.

7. **Values and norms.**   Examine how the culture determines need satisfaction and procedures, how it sets priorities, and values some behavior while decrying other practices. Thus cultures living on a survival level (e.g., homeless) function differently from those which are affluent. In some Pacific Island cultures, for instance, the more affluent one becomes, the more one is expected to share with the group. Cultural groupings with high security needs value material things (e.g., money and property), as well as law and order. In the context of the group's value system, the culture sets norms of behavior within thatsociety or organization. Acting upon a unique set of premises, standards of membership are established

affecting individual behavior—for example, the conventions may require total honesty with members of one's own group but accepts more relaxed behavior with those from other groups. Other standards may be expressed in gift-giving customs, rituals for birth/marriage/death, and guidelines for showing respect, privacy, and good manners. The culture determines what is legal or illegal behavior through a codified system or custom; what may be legal in one culture may be illegal in another.

In police culture, for instance, subordinates are expected to show respect for officers of superior rank, while the reverse may be tolerated for those who have broken the law. Publicly and by departmental regulations, a code of ethics is in place in which bribery and corruption are punishable offenses. A department of internal affairs ensures that alleged transgressors of such norms are investigated and tried or exonerated. This culture also espouses traditional American values of duty, loyalty, patriotism, and so on.

8. **Beliefs and attitudes.**   Examine the major belief themes of a people and how this affects their behavior and relations among themselves, toward others, and what happens in "their world." A cultural "universal" seems to be a concern for the supernatural, evident in religious adherence and practices, which are often dissimilar by group. "Primitive" or tribal cultures are described as "animists" because they experience the supernatural in nature (e.g., "Indians" or Native Americans)—a belief to which modern environmentalists resonate. The differences are apparent in the Western cultures with Judeo-Christian traditions, as well as Islamic, in contrast to Eastern cultures, dominated by Buddhism, Confucianism, Taoism, and Hinduism. Religion, or the lack of it, expresses the philosophy of a people about important realities of life's experiences. Some cultural groups are more fundamentalist and rigid in their religious beliefs, while others are more open and tolerant. The position of women in a society is one manifestation of such beliefs—in some, the female is enshrined, in others treated like an equal by the male; in others, she is subservient to the male and treated like chattel. A people's belief system is often dependent on their cultural stage of human development—hunting, farming, industrial, or postindustrial; advanced technological societies seems to substitute a belief in science or cosmic consciousness for more traditional beliefs.

In police culture, for example, there has been a strong belief in group loyalty, pragmatism, power, and public service. God and religion have been acknowledged in oaths, in religious societies of police officers, by appointment of department chaplains, and during burial ceremonies of officers who die in the line of duty. Until recently, the law enforcement culture tended to be "chauvinistic," but that is changing with the introduction of more female officers and education of the workforce on diversity issues.

9. **Mental processes and learning.**   Examine how some cultures emphasize one aspect of brain, knowledge, and skill development over another, thus causing striking differences in the way their adherents think and learn. Anthropologist Edward Hall suggests that the mind is internalized culture and involves how a people organize and process information. Life in a particular group or locale defines the rewards and punishments for learning or not learning certain information or in a certain way. In some cultures, the emphasis is on analytical learning—abstract thinking and conceptualization, while in others it is upon rote learning or memorization; some cultures value logic, while others reject it; some cultures restrict formal education only to males or the wealthy, while others espouse equal education for all. While reasoning and learning are cultural universals, each culture has a distinctive approach. However, the emergence of the computer and telecommunications as learning tools are furthering the globalization of education.

In police culture, recruit academies and other forms of in-service training may differ by locality as to content, instructional emphasis, and method. Anti-intellectualism among some police is being undermined by professional development and standards established by the federal/state governments and their credentialing processes, as well as by criminal justice curricula in higher education. As a result, modern police are moving from a more reactive, pragmatic, action-oriented behavior based on feelings and experience toward a proactive, thoughtful, analytical, and informed response. Professional competence is judged now by high performance and level of learning, not just by years on the job and connections.

10. **Work habits and practices.**   Another dimension for examining a group's culture is their attitude toward work, the types of work, the division of work, the dominant work habits and procedures, and the work rewards and recognitions that are provided. Some cultures adopt a work ethic that says it is desirable for all to be so engaged in worthwhile activities— even sports and the arts, while others preclude labor for income. Work worthiness is measured differently by cultures as to income produced, job status, or service to the community. In Japan, for example, cultural loyalty is transferred from the family to the organization, which is dependent upon the quality of individual performance. Classification of vocational activity is somewhat dependent on the culture's stage of development—a people can be characterized primarily as hunters, farmers, or factory or knowledge/service workers, with the trend away from physical labor toward use of mental energy aided by new technologies. The nature of work, as well as the policies, procedures, and customs related to it, are in transition. In the postindustrial culture, there is more emphasis on the use of advanced technologies, such as automation and robotics, as well as upon quality of working life—from compensation and benefits to stress management or enhancement of one's potential on the job. In conjunction with work, a culture differs in the manner and mode of proffering praise for good and brave deeds, outstanding performance, length of service, or other types of accomplishment. Promotions, perks, and testimonials are all manifestations.

In police culture, a hierarchial structure has organized work into specializations, divisions, and other such operational units engaged primarily in law enforcement and crime fighting. Job performance varied from "workaholics" to those who just put in time. Today the trend is toward peacekeeping and crime prevention, toward teamwork and community-based policing, toward obtaining citizen cooperation. Rewards and recognitions in the past have been largely commendations, advancement in rank, and retirement dinners, but now are being expanded to include assignments for professional development, interagency exchanges, and even sabbatical leaves for educational advancement.

Source: Excerpted with permission from Philip R. Harris and Robert T. Moran. (2000). *Managing Cultural Differences* (5th ed.). Boston, Mass.: Butterworth-Heinemann. This parent book with *Instructor's Guide* is part of the 12 titles in the MCD Series of volumes available from Butterworth-Heinemann (225 Wildwood Ave, Woburn, MA 01801; 781-904-2500; Web site: www.BH.com).

Admittedly Exhibit 15.3 offers only 10 general classifications for cultural analysis, whether it is a nation, an organization, a profession, a group, a generation (e.g., youth or seniors), or an ethnic or racial group. There are other dimensions of culture, but the categories provided here are the ones that will help peace officers more quickly and systematically comprehend cultures such as those described in Part Two of this book. The same approach can also be applied to study the "underworld" or criminal culture and its various subcultures (e.g., bank robbers, car thieves, hijackers, drug pushers, or sexual perverts). Further, during international travel, whether on duty or vacation, these same major characteristics can be observed to make the intercultural experience more meaningful. When law enforcement officers from other countries visit, these guidelines are useful for encouraging them to talk about their national or police cultures. All the aspects of culture noted are interrelated; there is a danger in trying to compartmentalize this complex concept and miss the sense of the whole.

Using Culture to Create Positive Police Images

If the representatives of law enforcement are more culturally aware and sensitive, they are more likely to project to the public a positive image as peacekeepers. Following are examples of actual newspaper headlines affecting the image of the department involved. Although the media do not always accurately report what happened, we know that there are still instances of police insensitivity and that even inaccurate news reports leave deep impressions in the minds of readers. Some negative headlines have included statements such as the following:

- "Cops Get Booted for Sex Offenses and Booze Violations" (Carlisle, 2009)
- "NYC Man Sues Police for $220M over Alleged Assault" (Associated Press, 2009)
- "City Settles Cop's Suit for $500,000; Sex Harassment Alleged" (MacInnes, 2009)
- "Police Brutality Lawsuit Settled; City Agrees to Pay $48,750 in Case" (Caywood, 2009)
- "Cop Seen Bashing Cyclist in Video Fired by NYPD, May Face Jail Time" (Gendar, 2009)

More positively, there are numerous reports of law enforcement agencies engaged in constructive cross-cultural communication with the communities they seek to protect. Some positive headlines have included statements such as the following:

- "Virginia Police View Success of Cleanup of City Neighborhood" (Malinowski, 2009)
- "Phoenix Police Recognized for Revitalization Efforts" (State News Service, 2009)
- "Fewest Homicides Since '76: Stockton Killings Drop for 3rd Year in a Row" (Burkin, 2009)
- "Reflecting the Community: Police Try to Increase Diversity in Ranks" (Patriot News, 2009)
- "Police, Community Partnership Marks Its Seventh Anniversary" (Cima, 2008)

If police are culturally sensitized, they will more likely achieve their goals with positive interactions. Throughout this book the underlying message to law enforcement has been that patrolling or observing on the basis of one's own cultural background may result in distorted perceptions. Instead, peace officers should try to better understand the unique world of the community being served.

POLICE LEADERSHIP IN PROFESSIONALISM AND SYNERGY

Lack of professionalism and inadequate personnel development can be very costly to any organization. But when it occurs within the public sector, it can prove damaging to both individuals and their careers, as well as to agencies and society. The following subsections cover three key concepts, which will be defined especially because of their implications for law enforcement and peacekeeping within a multicultural society (see Barlow, 2000; Dantzker, 2000; Hunter, Barker, and Mayhall, 2008; White, 2007).

Leadership

Leadership   Is exercised when one takes initiative, guides, or influences others in a particular direction, and demonstrates how a process or procedure is performed.

Leaders are said both to possess a good balance of conceptual, technical, and professional competence and to demonstrate judgment and people skills. Leaders are not only creative change agents but practical futurists, exercising foresight and the capacity for the "big picture" and the "long view"

(White, 2007). Today as we transition into a new information age and multicultural work environment, leaders need to be both transformational and transcultural. That is, such high performers advance innovations in the following initiatives (Kennedy, 2008):

- Transforming work places from the status quo to appropriate environments
- Renewing organizations and becoming role models by transmitting intellectual excitement and vision about their work
- Helping personnel to manage change by restructuring their mind-sets and values
- Helping to improve their organizations by preparing the next generation of supervisors and professionals. They do this primarily through the human resource development program that they initiate and/or supervise. At a more personal level, they become mentors and coaches to high-performing personnel with organizational potential.

In terms of multicultural diversity and inclusion aspects, such leaders deal with all persons fairly, regardless of gender, race, color, religion, or cultural differences. A leader seeks to empower a more diverse workforce in law enforcement to be reflective of the communities they serve. Furthermore, culturally sensitive leaders cut across cultural barriers while combating prejudice, bigotry, or racism wherever found in the organization and community (Kennedy, 2008). Police supervisors, for example, exercise this leadership through anticipatory thinking, strategic planning, creative decision making, and effective communications (White, 2007). Similarly, chiefs of police provide leadership when they annually present their departmental goals, both orally and in writing, for the benefit of the city council and their agency workforce, ensuring over the year that these goals are systematically achieved.

Professionalism

Professionalism Approaching an activity, such as one's occupation or career, with a sense of dedication and expertise.

In contrast to an amateur, a professional is a committed high performer. A professional possesses integrity and demonstrates competence—regardless of the role, career activity, or sport in which he or she is engaged. Following is a description of some of the characteristics of professionalism, particularly as relevant to law enforcement. A professional in criminal justice systems is concerned about:

- Doing an effective job or rendering an effective service
- Developing and maintaining his or her career skill or competency level
- Exhibiting ethical and sensitive behavior and ensuring that other departmental members do the same
- Capitalizing on diversity in people and organizations and seeking to develop human potential with regards to diversity
- Being aware of the latest developments in the criminal justice field

In law enforcement, professionals make it a point to understand the law and legal system in which they work, as well as key issues in the criminal justice field. To increase their competence, these professionals are familiar with aspects of criminal and deviant behavior. Whether writing a report, conducting an investigation or an interview, or commanding a police action, professional peace officers do the work consistently well (White, 2007). They are high performers who meet their own goals and targets, not just for self-advancement or to please command officers, but because of the important nature of their duties. Their performance observes the code of ethics expected of public employees. With growing multiculturalism both in the community and in the workforce, law enforcement professionals support policies and programs that promote collaboration among people of diverse backgrounds (Kennedy, 2008). Furthermore, they work with colleagues or the community to rectify any divisiveness, intolerance, discrimination, and even violence in the workplace. As is noted later in this chapter, competence in emerging computer technology, digital communication, and research tools is necessary in law enforcement today.

Synergy

> **Synergy** Implies cooperation and the integration of separate parts to function as a whole and to achieve a common goal.

Synergy occurs through working together in combined action, attaining a greater total effect than the sum of the individual parts. Cultural synergy builds on the differences in people to promote mutual growth and accomplishment. Through such collaboration, similarities, strengths, and diverse talents are shared to enhance human activities and systems. For team management and teamwork, synergistic relations are essential (Harris and Moran, 2000; Gehl, (2004), Kennedy, 2008). In law enforcement, synergistic leaders:

- Facilitate interagency and interprecinct cooperation
- Create consensus, which enables disparate people and groups to work together by sharing perceptions, insights, and knowledge
- Promote participation, empowerment, and negotiation within an organization or community, so that members work for mutual advantage and are committed to teamwork and the common good over personal ambition or need
- Demonstrate skills of facilitating, networking, conflict resolution, and coordination
- Are open-minded, effective cross-cultural communicators

Synergistic leaders give priority to the professional development of subordinates, especially through training and team building (Justice and Jamieson, 1999).

Thus leadership, professionalism, and synergy are three powerful, interrelated concepts. When combined within the criminal justice system in general, or law enforcement and peacekeeping in particular, they may alter one's role, image, and performance. Leadership, professionalism, and synergy are illustrated at both the organizational and the individual levels in the context of the new work culture (Gido, 2009).

MULTICULTURAL COMMUNITIES AND INTERAGENCY EFFORTS IN RESPONSE TO GLOBAL AND REGIONAL EVENTS

Society and communities today are so complex and interdependent that individual departments can best deal with certain enforcement challenges and crime problems through cooperation among criminal justice entities at all levels of government. This is especially true with such enforcement challenges as terrorism, homeland security, catastrophic disasters, and crime problems that are multijurisdictional in nature (e.g., identity theft and human trafficking). Although cooperation is certainly more efficient and effective, for many traditional public safety agencies, it may require a paradigm shift in the thinking of its members. Effecting change means exercising a type of law enforcement leadership that actively promotes specific information interchanges, joint ventures, and task forces that operate on a statewide or regional basis. It would be contrary-thinking and unprofessional behavior to avoid working with another agency because of jurisdictional jealously and the fear as to who receives credit for success in the operation. Similarly, the distorted desires to protect one's agency territory or budget can interfere with a view of the big picture and interrelationships required to address certain issues. The overriding concern should be the public good with agencies working together to prevent and counter criminality in the community.

Within the larger criminal justice system, there are already many commissions, councils, and other structures for promoting interagency collaboration. Law enforcement leaders with a sense of professionalism and synergy would ensure that all their command is committed to such collaborative action. As a case in point, many matters of police training are best dealt with at a statewide or regional level, but with local agency input and participation. Probably the greatest area for improvement of synergistic relations is between and among federal, state, and local law enforcement as illustrated in current law enforcement collaborative efforts in the areas of terrorism, homeland security, and disaster preparedness (see Chapter 10).

Agency representatives come from differing organizational cultures. Therefore, any interagency collaboration or merger requires the practice of the kind of cross-cultural communication skills described in Chapter 4. Another illustration directly related to the theme of this book is a border city with a twin urban area in another country. For the United States, this synergy could be along the northern border with Canada or the southern border with Mexico, requiring international cooperation among public agencies that have similar missions but different cultural contexts and legal systems. In such situations, local police departments of both nations should routinely share information and should cooperate in combating crime or facilitating cross-border traffic. This cooperation might contribute to more humane treatment of U.S., Mexican, and Canadian citizens who break the law when on the other side of the border. Under Mexican law, based on the Napoleonic law system, the supposed transgressor is considered guilty until proven innocent, the opposite of the U.S. legal system, which is based on English Common Law. Another example of this is discussed at length in Chapter 9: Native American tribal police and local or state police have established, in a few areas of the country, interdependent relationships whereby cross-training and cross-deputization are taking place.

For American, Canadian, and Mexican police and tribal police, there are numerous other ways to be mutually supportive, ranging from information exchanges on criminology and specific criminals and groups to promotion of better bilateral relations and border law enforcement management. These objectives can be achieved when there is cooperation of law enforcement in all the countries involved and with tribal police. To overcome cross-cultural barriers, police jurisdictions and their personnel in adjoining countries (or in Indian country) have more to gain by thinking in terms of synergy across borders. One place to begin is to learn about the differences in each nation's legal system. Therefore, something is to be gained by joint training projects, such as a collaborative effort of customs service or border patrol agents of two or all three nations, especially during these times with the problems of international terrorism and homeland security on the rise.

Police Professionalism, Ethics, and Diversity

Police professionalism, according to Hunter, Barker, and Mayhall, (2008), requires self-awareness and a positive self-image. The late Pamela D. Mayhall, coauthor of *Police Community Relations and the Administration of Justice (7th Ed.)*, advocated not only greater technical skill training but also higher educational attainments, along with the setting of goals for career development. This is one important way that professionalism can be encouraged and grow. To reduce stress within the working environment of modern police, this criminal justice professor advocated an atmosphere of improved intraagency communication, as well as supportive relations with the community (Anderson, Swenson, and Clay, 1995).

POLICE PROFESSIONALISM   The principal purpose of criminal justice education, whether in universities, colleges, or academies, is to improve performance and to increase professionalism among those in law enforcement. What are the characteristics of a police professional? Many answers have been provided throughout this book, including in an earlier section of this chapter discussing the concept of professionalism in general. A law enforcement professional is:

- One who is properly educated and public service oriented
- One whose behavior and conduct on the job is appropriate and ethical, avoiding clear conflict of interests
- One who respects the dignity and humanity of everyone contacted in the course of his or her duties by treating all fairly and with equal justice
- One who is culturally sensitive to the differences and potential of others
- One who is aware of the impact of agency culture on the professional behavior of officers
- One who is a lifetime learner concerned about personal and career development for both self and others

POLICE ETHICS   As a concept, ethics is closely associated with professionalism. Codes of ethics are vital to guide the behavior of practitioners of the learned professions (e.g., law or medicine) and to punish those who do not adhere to the agreed, enunciated conduct of behavior for those vocations. For peace officers, such codes promote self-regulation and discipline within a law enforcement agency (Boyd, 1993). Often these codes are written and summarized within an agency mission statement. Being a professional implies not only competence and expertise, but adherence to higher standards of professional conduct (White, 2007).

In the best sense, professionalism implies having more than technical skills and refers to the moral contributions that professionals make in a complex, democratic society—the ethic of the calling. The ethical person is perceived as someone who has courage and integrity, and is willing to resist corruption and unprincipled people by upholding humanity, justice, and civility. Such a peace officer tries to be loyal to his or her own conscience and avoids unprofessional behavior (e.g., use of excessive force, succumbing to the "blue code of silence" during investigations, biased policing or expressions of bias and bigotry, or acceptance of bribery).

POLICE AND DIVERSE COMMUNITY GROUPS   Nowhere is law enforcement's sense of professionalism and ethics challenged more than in the manner in which they treat diverse ethnic and racial group members, whether citizens or visitors. Apart from indigenous Native Americans, everyone else in America came as immigrants or slaves. Today, the newcomers are primarily from South and Central America, Asia, the Middle East, and the Eastern European countries of the former Soviet Union. For every first generation of immigrants, the process of acculturation is extremely challenging.

Any new group integrating into the United States will present new law enforcement challenges that require changes in police tactics and behavior. For law enforcement organizations, human resource development (HRD) starts with recruitment and selection of qualified candidates. Apart from meeting basic qualifications, future peace officers must have a stable personality, be willing to receive further education and training, be career oriented, and, in some cases, be representative of the multicultural communities in which they serve. In previous chapters, we have reviewed these challenges.

Organizational Trends in Law Enforcement

In concluding this section, it is useful to present two organizational trends that effect increasingly important changes to law enforcement agencies. Change must come from within the department before all personnel can demonstrate effectiveness and sensitivity in the community.

Trend One: Transforming the Organizational Culture

The culture of law enforcement agencies must internalize changes and accept diversity within both the department and the community. In the past this culture typically was dominated by white males, principally of Irish or Italian backgrounds, who were often military veterans. With the influx of a multicultural workforce into the criminal justice fields, system change is necessary if the organizational culture is to reflect the needs and concerns of this new generation from a culturally diverse society (Prosser, 2007).

One of the nation's leading diversity consultants, Elsie Y. Cross, has been in the forefront of articulating the reality of organizations' need to change. Over her more than 20 years of working with many large corporate clients, this consultant helped people become aware that most corporate cultures have actually been white male cultures, in which the majority controlled the power in the organization. This control manifested in the form of domination at meetings, key decision making, the establishment of exclusive information loops, and the choosing of their own successors. To change the organizational culture and to increase organizational effectiveness, Elsie Y. Cross Associates recommends the following strategies for managing diversity and valuing differences (Cross, 2000; White, 1992):

- Introduce culture change to overhaul policies and procedures by means of focus groups and workshops that define basic assumptions, written codes, and rituals; incorporate this feedback into a revised mission statement that becomes a proclamation of the "new organizational culture vision and values."
- Identify the barriers that block individual or group diversity goals; identify the champions capable of building broad, internal coalitions around cultural awareness and group action against discrimination and for planned change.
- Require that the top command make at least a 5-year commitment of resources to redefining the agency culture toward more effective management of diversity.
- Hold managers accountable for implementing the diversity changes through regular evaluation of their efforts.
- Confront the pain of racism and sexism at the personal and group level in the organization.

This management model has proven successful, and Cross (2000) credits the National Training Laboratories for Applied Behavioral Sciences with helping her to develop it. The strategy is invaluable to law enforcement leaders in a multiracial and multicultural society.

Trend Two: Organizations Moving beyond Awareness to Meet Today's Multicultural Challenges

Law enforcement leaders should ask themselves this question: does our agency provide adequate training for officers in cultural awareness? When a law enforcement agency has provided the basic training in cultural awareness and implemented effective diversity and inclusion policies, it is time to adopt another strategic plan that moves the agency toward cultural competence. George F. Simons, internationally known consultant on diversity, believes we must move beyond mere avoidance of ethnic, racial, and gender discrimination or sexual harassment. Police supervisors and managers should not have to "walk on eggs" while at work trying not to offend women and minorities. For managing or training in a multicultural environment, this expert counsels that advanced diversity training that teaches people the skills to communicate and collaborate effectively with each other as colleagues, especially in mixed-gender, mixed-ethnic, and mixed-racial groups, should be conducted. Dr. Simons (2009) offers the following advice:

- Organizational policy should be developed that supports productive partnerships and creative sharing among diverse membership of representatives from majority and minority groups.
- Executives and other leaders should participate in special coaching programs that include assessment, mind management, and communications training that enables them to develop model behavior and values that inspire their associates to work ingeniously with differences.

To further promote police officer professionalism and peacekeeping strategies in a diverse society, officers must be able to look up to leaders who are not ethnocentric and biased in their manner of leading their agency and responding to the communities they serve. For a peace officer to reflect cultural awareness and understanding of all peoples, as well as applying the principle of fair treatment to every police action and communication, he or she must have role models at all levels of the chain of command, especially at the level of police chief. The police chief should explicitly demonstrate pluralistic leadership and, ideally, be "an ambassador for diversity" within his/her department. Attaining a pluralistic outlook cannot happen consistently without direction from the top. For this reason, we reprint in Exhibit 15.4 a list of characteristics and attributes of a pluralistic leader developed by MGH Consulting (Hernandez, 2008).

Pluralistic leaders:

1. Look for ways to serve as catalysts for changing the work environment and community to welcome and value diverse people
2. Are committed to eliminating all the various "isms" (racism, sexism, etc.) that exist in their immediate work environment or neighborhood and speak to the greater concerns for equality, fairness, and other democratic ideals
3. Help diverse people to be seen fairly and to be valued in the work environment and broader community
4. Accept feedback about how to improve their relationships with those who are different by remaining open to change and growth
5. Acknowledge their own prejudices or stereotypes and see the limitations that these will bring to their work
6. Take time to assess their individual progress toward achieving the qualities and characteristics of a pluralistic leader
7. Mentor others who need to gain sensitivity toward diversity
8. Value differences among people and cultures as one of the great treasures of the human family and global community

---

EXHIBIT 15.4   Police Pluralistic Leaders.

Source: MGH Consulting, © 1993, reprinted with permission of MGH Consulting, 2454 Cameron Drive, Union City, CA 94587.

CURTAILING LITIGATION AGAINST POLICE AGENCIES AND OFFICERS

Much innovation is necessary so that police responses will satisfy citizens rather than provoke them to initiate lawsuits against officers and their departments, especially in multicultural communities. Nonviolent peacekeeping is particularly necessary in ethnic, immigrant, and racially diverse communities, where misperception and miscommunication may occur because of language barriers, as well as differences in body language and nonverbal interactions. The principal problem in this regard relates to the use of force by law enforcement at the time of arrest—that is, whether it is perceived as excessive or deadly. Agencies that analyze citizen complaints against officers usually find that this area receives the most negative community feedback, especially from persons who feel disenfranchised.

America is a very litigious society. Throughout the United States, the last decade of the twentieth century witnessed a dramatic increase in individual and class action suits against law enforcement agencies for mistreatment and killing of citizens by police officers. The scope of this national problem can be appreciated by citing statistics from the city of Detroit. Between 1997 and 2000, that municipality had to pay $32 million because of lawsuits brought against the police. A city council analysis showed that 78 percent of the money so expended involved cases with only a small number of officers; 261 officers were named in more than one suit. The issue is what the city administration should do with such repeat offenders. Furthermore, are the officers guilty of unprofessional behavior and maltreatment or simply the victims of legal strategies by lawyers?

The City of Los Angeles had to pay $14,658,075 in 1991 as a result of settlements, judgments, and awards related to excessive-force litigation against its police. Then, in 1994, a jury awarded Rodney King $3.8 million to compensate for police actions. A federal judge ruled on August 28, 2000, that the Los Angeles Police Department (LAPD) can be sued as a racketeering enterprise in the so-called Rampart corruption scandal. This unprecedented decision, subject to judicial review by higher courts, could open this municipality to scores of lawsuits capable of bankrupting the city. U.S. District Judge William Rea ruled from the bench on a civil suit brought against the LAPD by a man who claimed he was beaten and framed in 1997 for a crime by rogue police officers in the LAPD's Ramparts Division. Such illegal actions by officers within the Ramparts Division caused 100 cases to be dismissed, resulting in five officers being charged with both conspiracy and even attempted murder. This latest ruling cleared the plaintiff to pursue the case under the federal racketeering statutes against conspiracies. His lawyers maintain that the innocent man was a victim of a police conspiracy to deny him of his lawful rights as a citizen. The LAPD has been under a Federal consent decree for 8 years with progress shown in lowering the number of litigated cases against it (Rosenbaum and Bibring, 2009); however, other reforms may still be needed:

> The department still shows disturbing and unjustifiable racial patterns in the way it does its policing. A report prepared last fall for the ACLU of Southern California by Yale economist Ian Ayres examined detailed data on more than 800,000 cases in which the LAPD stopped pedestrians or drivers between July 2003 and June 2004. It found racial disparities that could not be justified by any legitimate rationales evident in the data, such as differences in crime rates in the neighborhoods where the stops occurred, the time of day or the age and gender of the people stopped. Ayres also found that while African Americans and Latinos are frisked and asked to submit to consent searches much more often than whites, those searches were less likely to turn up drugs, weapons or other evidence of crime. What's more, the latest raw

numbers available on the LAPD's website reveal, disturbingly, that racial disparities in how people are treated when stopped have increased, rather than declined, over the last five years. Consider these figures: When stopped, African Americans drivers were asked to exit their vehicles 2.41 times more often than whites between July and December 2003. That figure grew to 3.49 times more often for the same period in 2008. For Latinos, the numbers grew from 2.37 in 2003 to 3.68 in 2008. Similar increases are evident in the disparities in which African Americans and Latinos are stopped, frisked and searched. (Rosenbaum and Bibring, 2009)

Many lawsuits against police agencies and their members are frivolous or unsubstantiated and are thus thrown out of court or are decided in favor of law enforcement. However, too many lawsuits result from inadequately screened or trained officers whose behavior on the job is not just unprofessional and unethical but outright biased and criminal. With greater public access to improved communications technology and increased information, citizens are fighting back when police abuse their human or civil rights. When they win these legal suits, taxpayers ultimately have to pay for the insufficiencies or mistakes of their public servants in the criminal justice system.

Some analysts believe the problem is exacerbated because personnel in too many agencies operate more like soldiers than like peace officers (e.g., growth of Special Weapons and Tactics [SWAT] teams in departments). For 150 years, police departments have been organized based on the military model. As noted in the Police Leadership in the 21st Century Conference, "The transition to participatory management seems irreversible. It is, less and less, a choice that the chief executive can control. In the empowerment environment of contemporary organizations, chiefs are less able to function entirely through hierarchical structures, especially to effect change" (IACP, 1999). In the twenty-first century, the move toward organization in which power is increasingly shared and accountability required at all levels of the law enforcement agency will continue to be emphasized because of increasing public dissatisfaction with law enforcement agencies, highlighted by legal settlements against officers. Public dissatisfaction, in turn, is reflected in jury decisions, as exemplified by the following excessive-force case:

A Harris County jury on Monday awarded $3 million to the Houston mother of a schizophrenic man who was shocked, hogtied and later died as Precinct 1 constable's deputies took him into custody on a mental health warrant four years ago. After a three-week trial, the jury concluded by a 10–2 vote that three of the four deputies named in Shirley Nagel's lawsuit used unreasonable and excessive force as the deputies detained Nagel's son, Joel Don Casey, on Feb. 18, 2005. Casey's death was ruled a homicide. An autopsy found the 52-year-old man died of psychotic delirium with physical restraint associated with heart disease. He also suffered fractures to his seventh cervical vertebrae and the left horn of his thyroid cartilage, believed to have occurred when one deputy dropped a knee on Casey's neck and pulled Casey's head back, said the dead man's attorney, Kent Spence. After $4\frac{1}{2}$ hours of deliberations that began Friday and continued Monday, the jury awarded $2.4 million to Nagel and $600,000 to her son's estate, which she represents. (O'Hare, 2009)

On the other hand, what of the officer's rights when accused of misconduct during a legal action? Brian Harris, a homicide detective of the Houston Police Department, noting that in our judicial system the accused is presumed to be innocent until proven guilty, argued that under such circumstances, the public should afford sworn officers the same rights as afforded to the supposed victim. Until the evidence is presented and an inquiry commission or court has rendered a verdict, the public and media should not presume guilt. Furthermore, there is the issue of intent. When an officer's life or well-being is threatened, he or she may not intend to hurt a perpetrator while defending himself or herself. Again, this is where training comes in, so that discipline and control are maintained in very difficult situations that police increasingly find themselves in while patrolling and seeking to ensure law and order in the community. Detective Harris concludes that training in basic police practice and its implementation by supervisors are the key to effective performance on patrol: "When police create time and distance between themselves and the suspect, then they can conduct a safer encounter."

EMERGING TECHNOLOGY AND MULTICULTURAL LAW ENFORCEMENT INNOVATIONS

Attempts are being made by the new generation of law enforcement leaders to develop innovative strategies, structures, and services that meet the changing needs of communities (Foster, 2005; IACP, 1999; Office of Justice Programs, 1999; Taylor, Caeti, Loper, Fritsch, and Liederbach, 2006). As noted by Buerger (2004), "Most police training curricula and most traditional, social science-based criminal justice programs lack the ability to prepare students to deal with technology-based crime or with financial crime. Those skills are taught in business and computer science programs in universities and elsewhere." These skills need to be incorporated within law enforcement curriculum. Moreover, each year new technologies emerge, such as using biometric procedures for rapid computerized identification of possible terrorists at U.S. borders through their fingerprints (the Immigration and Customs Enforcement's US-VISIT Program) and the identification of people by their eyes, smell, and other body characteristics ("New Ways," 2000, pp. 85–91) as well as DNA profiles as evidence (Dwyer, Neufeld, and Scheck, 2000). As these new opportunities for improved law enforcement unfold, the importance of government and law enforcement agencies working in parallel becomes even more critical. As highlighted by Boyd, Melis, and Myers (2004), "To build a stronger, more seamless, and more supportive partnership between all facets of law enforcement and the FBI, the Futures Working Group (FWG) formed on April 2, 2002. The FWG represents a partnership between the FBI and the Society of Police Futurists International (PFI), with its noble and ambitious goals that include the development of forecasts and strategies to ethically maximize the effectiveness of local, state, federal, and international law enforcement bodies as they strive to maintain peace and security in the 21st century."

New models for law enforcement officers' training and education need continuous development, implementation, and review. As noted by Buerger (2004), current criminal justice education has developed a three-step program for law enforcement officers: (1) high school diploma or GED, (2) police training academy, and (3) 2- or 4-year undergraduate college education focusing upon the basic law enforcement certification curricula (2-year programs) and the criminal justice major for the undergraduate degree (4-year programs).

The future will create new training needs not currently standard in either college programs or police training academies. New developments in technology will create a need for investigators who can cope with the criminal uses of those technologies. The sheer volume of financial crimes perpetrated via computer hacking and identity theft will exceed the capacity of federal agencies to investigate. If local police do not adapt to the need, private resources likely will fill the gap or leave local jurisdictions and their constituents without legal recourse?. With all of these factors in mind, what can the law enforcement and academic communities do to improve the balance between educating and training future police officers? Three main models—creating a new model of interdisciplinary criminal justice degree; modifying the existing social science curricula to similar effect; and placing greater emphasis at the point of hiring upon the course of study, rather than on mere possession of a degree—demonstrate some possible approaches. (Buerger, 2004)

Law enforcement officers and their organizations need to pay attention to ongoing technology and scientific advances to work within all communities. Advancement in technology often requires law enforcement agencies to abandon some of their tried-and-true methods.

Foster (2005), in his book *Police Technology*, highlights the following areas as emerging and future technologies:

1. Personal Locator Beacon (PLB) will allow people to be able to find each other in public places and under emergency conditions.
2. Transponder technology will facilitate greater numbers of house arrest arrangements, which could lessen the use of prison by 20 percent at a cost savings of up to $8 billion per year.
3. Magnetic Gradient Measuring and Passive Millimeter Wave (PMW) Imaging, which will improve the technology for detecting metal objects and contrabands in people and will allow for security screening in places such as airports and governmental facilities.
4. "Dataviellance" includes technology that will allow for better use of the massive amounts of data collected in homeland security monitoring efforts and activities.
5. Biometrics will enhance individual identity confirmation and improve access technologies.
6. Less-Lethal Use of Force devices will focus on a variety of tools and technologies that can be used to incapacitate offenders without causing injuries.

Some agencies have established an innovation task force made up of the most creative officers from all units of the department. In this approach, the chief asks the group to discover ways for police to encourage a "climate of understanding within the community, and combat a climate of fear." To that end, the innovation team, along with community focus groups, might study new ideas of promise and develop action plans to implement them. The following are some examples of such innovations:

- Ongoing contact, structured and unstructured, with leaders of all minority and immigrant community organizations such as churches, businesses and civic bodies, and schools. The ongoing nature of the program must be emphasized because, typically, law enforcement only meets with community leaders after a crisis.
- Bicycle or scooter bike patrols in problem and recreational areas; officers then interact with community members, especially where there are large concentrations of minority and immigrant youth.
- Crises management strategies not only for emergencies and disasters, but also for homeland security and working with neighborhoods at risk (see Chapters 10).
- Neighborhood or shopping mall storefront police substations.
- Police concentration on repeat offenders and repeat locations of criminal activities.

- Law enforcement strategies with the homeless and those with mental health problems.
- Teams consisting of officers from diverse backgrounds regularly meeting with inner-city youth, engaging them in such activities as sports, mentoring, and finding new ways to become role models.
- Preventative programs with schools to reduce school violence. For example, a Federal Bureau of Investigation (FBI) report (O'Toole, 2000), "The School Shooter: A Threat Assessment Perspective," lists personal traits in teenagers that may lead to violence. Police and educators need to use this profile to help identify high-risk youth who manifest poor coping skills, access to weapons, drug and alcohol abuse, alienation and narcissism, inappropriate humor, and no parental or guardian monitoring of television or Internet use. In addition to these characteristics, be alert to dysfunctional family situations, as well as poor interactions in school, on the part of the troubled youngsters.
- Development of neighborhood child protection plans to reduce incidents of child abuse. Such plans should include constructive opportunities for youth to network with each other and with positive adult role models in their community. Such plans should also include business, civic, and religious organizations and the adoption of a particular high-risk neighborhood in which the police, community leaders, and family members make a commitment to protecting their youth.
- Innovative strategies by police to counteract hate crimes within their communities (see Chapters 11 and 12).

Police supervisors, in their respective departments, should actively encourage the innovations described in this chapter, as well as police innovators who contribute to cultural synergy and peacekeeping. For example, agencies might have an award system for the Innovative Officer of the Month and display the person's picture in the squad room with a description of his or her innovative practice on or off duty. Central to the use of innovation in multicultural law enforcement is the ability of officers and leaders to manage the forces of change as noted by Covey (2008):

"The police are the public and the public are the police and the test of police efficiency is the absence of crime and disorder, not the visible evidence of police action in dealing with it." Expressing the essence of the needed paradigm shift in the world, this quote is from Sir Robert Peel, considered by many to be the father of the modern concept of urban policing—and he said it over 150 years ago. Thus what we will call the "new" mind-set is not really new. The new mind-set is about partnering for a sustainable civil society, representing a paradigm shift toward a community justice system—for victims, for offenders, for the police, for judges, and for society at large. In such a model, everyone is responsible for bringing about justice. Solutions come from various pockets of the community, not just from those whose formal role is to provide protection. This move requires a quantum leap by both individuals and communities. Communities must leave behind reactive systems and initiate proactive systems. Command-and-control models must be discarded in favor of empowering individuals. The new paradigm or mind-set is made up of three powerful ideas: initiative, partnership, and prevention. Imagine these three components as the critical threads that must be woven through the fabric of society. (Covey, 2008)

Summary

- Professional law enforcement leaders must take the initiative to guide their departments to cultural competence. Also, leaders must capitalize on the diversity of people within the organization and community, establish synergy, and seek to develop human potential for the betterment of both. The challenges for law enforcement in particular are to recognize and appreciate diversity within both the community and the workforce, while using such insights advantageously. Human diversity must become a source of renewal rather than tolerable legislated requirements within our agencies, communities, and society. To accomplish this goal within criminal justice systems, multicultural awareness and skills training must become an integral part of the human resource development of peacekeepers.

- Awareness of the changing role and image of peace officers will result in increased cultural competence and community effectiveness in law enforcement. To increase cultural awareness, readers are provided with a simple model for a quick analysis of differences in various cultures, ethnic groups, and generations. With respect to images, people create both accurate and inaccurate images of themselves and their roles, and of others. Our behavior is then influenced by these mental pictures, and others respond to what we project, which may not necessarily reflect reality. The most powerful of these images is the one we have of ourselves, followed by those formed about our multiple roles. Similarly, we also create images of our organizations, our nation, and the criminal justice system and its activities. The diverse images of law enforcement as held by the multicultural communities rest upon the professionalism that today's peace officers display with regard to cultural competence, technical knowledge, and communication skills. The image of law enforcement projected to the public by police officers, their organizations, and the media is especially important within multicultural venues.

- Leadership, professionalism, and synergy are three powerful, interrelated concepts. When combined within the criminal justice system in general, or law enforcement and peacekeeping in particular, they may alter one's role, image, and performance. For professionals in any facet of the criminal justice system, change first begins with leadership modeling the role, and then with the practitioners' image of their role. Finally this image is projected to the public. In the evolving new work culture, adhering to the image of peace officer is appropriate and requires that those in public service become more culturally sensitive in their outlook and approach. Effectively dealing with all diversity issues within the field of law enforcement then becomes a means for exercising leadership that demonstrates a respect for all differences. A lack of professionalism and inadequate personnel development can be very costly to any organization. But when it occurs within the public sector, it can prove damaging to both individuals and their careers, as well as to agencies and society. The type of peacekeeping advocated in this chapter also requires competent supervision and management within police administration. It is also important that departments, regionally or statewide, work together to prevent and counter criminality in the community at the same time promoting the common good and civility. There must be interagency collaboration and synergy, not only with respect to fighting crime, but also as it relates to training, information exchange, and recruitment within a multicultural and diversity context.

- Society and communities today are so complex and interdependent that individual departments can best deal with certain enforcement challenges and crime problems through cooperation among criminal justice entities at all levels of government. This is most certainly true with enforcement challenges like terrorism, homeland security, catastrophic disasters, and crime problems that are multijurisdictional in nature, like identity theft and human trafficking. Although cooperation is certainly more efficient and effective, for many traditional public safety agencies, it may require a paradigm shift in the thinking of its members. Effecting change means exercising a type of law enforcement leadership that actively promotes specific information exchanges, joint ventures, and task forces that operate on a statewide, regional, national, or global basis.
- America is a very litigious society. In recent years, there has been an increase in lawsuits against law enforcement officers. The principal problem in this regard relates to the use of force by law enforcement at the time of arrest—that is, whether it is perceived as excessive or deadly. Agencies that analyze citizen complaints against officers usually find that this area receives the most negative community feedback, especially from persons who feel disenfranchised. When citizens win these legal suits, taxpayers ultimately have to pay for the insufficiencies or mistakes of their public servants in the criminal justice system.
- Attempts are being made by the new generation of law enforcement leaders to develop innovative strategies, structures, and services that meet the changing needs of communities. Law enforcement officers and their organizations will need to continually update and increase their sophistication with advanced technology and scientific innovation to work with all communities. Some agencies have established innovation task forces made up of the most creative officers from all units of a department. New models for law enforcement officers' training and education need continual development and review. Current criminal justice education has developed a three-step program for law enforcement officers: (1) high school diploma or GED, (2) police training academy, and (3) 2- or 4-year undergraduate college education focusing upon the basic law enforcement certification curricula (2-year programs) and the criminal justice major for the undergraduate degree (4-year programs). Future multicultural law enforcement training needs will dictate new standards for training in either college programs or police training academies.

Discussion Questions and issues

1. *Emerging Technology and Multicultural Law Enforcement Innovations.* Law enforcement officers and agencies need to embrace and utilize the innovations and emerging advanced technologies that are available for effective work in multicultural communities. Using the list of innovations given in the chapter as a starting point, brainstorm other innovations and advanced technology that you think would be important to multicultural law enforcement. In what ways will the items in your list have a positive impact on multicultural communities? Could there be any negative impact on those communities?

2. *Curtailing Litigation against Police Agencies and Officers.* Innovation and thoughtfulness are necessary so that a police response will satisfy citizens rather than provoke them to initiate lawsuits against officers and their departments, especially in multicultural communities. Select one or more multicultural groups that are part of your community (or part of a nearby community) and discuss how nonviolent peacekeeping is particularly critical in ethnic, immigrant, and racially diverse communities. What does it mean to say that police officers should do their duties with honor and integrity?

Website Resources

Visit these websites for additional information about strategies and roles related to emerging innovation and technology issues in multicultural law enforcement:

IACP Technology Clearinghouse:
http://www.iacptechnology.org/

This website provides information on the application of automated data collection, information management, and transportation technology for law enforcement organizations, including the impact the use of such technology has on multicultural communities and the diverse society as a whole.

International Association of Chiefs of Police (IACP):
http://www.iacp.org

This website provides information and reports by the IACP highlighting emerging law enforcement issues and technology that might have an impact on multicultural communities.

New Police Technology:
http://www.newpolicetechnology.com/

This website was developed by the innovation officers of the Dutch police to promote new technology and transfer of knowledge for police services globally. New Police Technology scans the world for new inventions, innovations, and applications in law enforcement, investigate these for a positive business case in policing, and pilot them in the real law enforcement practice.

Police Executive Research Forum (PERF):
http://www.policeforum.org/

This website provides information for improving policing and advancing professionalism through research and involvement in public policy debate.

Social Technology Future Consortium:
http://www.socialtechnologies.com/

This website provides information for keeping up with and anticipating new developments in science and technology as these affect organizational strategies.

References

Anderson, W., Swenson, D., and Clay, D. (1995). *Stress Management for Law Enforcement Officers.* Upper Saddle River, NJ: Prentice Hall.

Associated Press. (2009, May 28). "NYC Man Sues Police for $220M over Alleged Assault." Associated Press.

Barlow, H. D. (2000). Criminal Justice in America. Upper Saddle River, NJ: Prentice-Hall.

Boyd, T. (1993). "A Model for Development of Police Officers' Understanding and Adherence to Ethical Standards" (Order 16-0313). POST Commission, Sacramento, Calif.

Boyd, S., A. Melis, and R. Myers. (2004). "Preparing for the Challenges ahead." *FBI Law Enforcement Bulletin,* 73(1), 2–11.

Buerger, M. (2004). "Educating and Training the Future Police Officer." *FBI Law Enforcement Bulletin,* 73(1), 26–32.

Burkin, C. (2009, January 13). "Fewest Homicides Since '76: Stockton Killings Drop for 3rd Year in a Row." *The Record* (Stockton, CA).

Carlisle, N. (2009, June 4). "Cops Get Booted for Sex Offenses and Booze Violations," *Salt Lake Tribune.*

Carter, D. L., and L. A. Radalet. (1999). *The Police and the Community.* Upper Saddle River, NJ: Prentice-Hall.

Carter, L., and M. Wilson. (2006). "Measuring Professionalism of Police Officers." *The Police Chief,* 73(8). Available: http://policechiefmagazine.org/magazine/index.cfm?fuseaction=display_arch&article_id=971&issue_id=82006.

Caywood, T. (2009, May 23). "Police Brutality Lawsuit Settled; City Agrees to Pay $48,750 in Case." *Telegram & Gazette* (Massachusetts), p. A1.

Champion, D. J., and G. E. Rush. (1997). *Policing in the Community.* Upper Saddle River, NJ: Prentice Hall.

Cima, G. (2008, April 4). "Police, Community Partnership Marks Its Seventh Anniversary." *The Pantagraph* (Bloomington, Ill.), p. A5.

Covey, S. R. (2008, December). "A Whole New Mind-Set on Fighting Crime." *The Police Chief,* 75(12). Available: http://policechiefmagazine.org/magazine/

index.cfm?fuseaction=display_arch&article_id=168
7&issue_id=122008.

Cross, E. Y. (2000). *Managing Diversity—The Courage to Lead*. Westport, Conn.: Quorum Books.

Dantzker, M. L. (2000). *Understanding Today's Police*. Upper Saddle River, NJ: Prentice-Hall.

DeFilippis, R. (2008, March 27). "Sea-Based Marines Deliver Humanitarian Supplies to Liberians." Available: www.mfr.usmc.mil/MFRNews/2008/2008.03/LiberianSupplies.asp.

Dwyer, J., P. Neufeld, and B. Scheck. (2000). *Actual Innocence*. New York, NY: Doubleday.

Foster, R. E. (2005). *Police Technology*. Upper Saddle River, NJ: Pearson Prentice Hall.

Gehl, A. R. (2004). "Multiagency Teams: A Leadership Challenge." *The Police Chief*, *70*(10). Available: http://policechiefmagazine.org/magazine/index.cfm?fuseaction=display_arch&article_id=1395&issue_id=102004.

Gendar, A. (2009, February 20). "Cop Seen Bashing Cyclist in Video Fired by NYPD, May Face Jail Time." *Daily News* (NY), p. 8.

Gido, R. L. (2009). "The World Is Flat: Globalization and Criminal Justice Organizations and Workplaces in the Twenty-First Century." In R. Muraskin and A. R. Roberts, *Visions for Change: Crime and Justice in the Twenty-First Century*, 5th ed. Upper Saddle River, NJ: Prentice Hall.

Gilbert, E. L, ed. (1990). *The World of Mystery Fiction*. Bowling Green, Ohio.: Bowling Green State University Popular Press.

Goldsmith, A. (1990). "Taking Police Culture Seriously." *Policing and Society*, *1*(2), 91–114.

Hancock, E. W., and P. M. Sharp. (2000). *Public Police: Crime and Criminal Justice*, Upper Saddle River, NJ: Prentice Hall.

Harris, P. R., and R. T. Moran. (2000). *Managing Cultural Differences Instructor's Guide*. Boston, Mass.: Gulf Publications Series/Butterworth-Heinemann.

Hernandez, M. G. (2008, April), MGH Consulting, Personal Communication.

Hunter, R. D., T. D. Barker, and P. D. Mayhall. (2008). *Police Community Relations and the Administration of Justice*, 7th ed. Upper Saddle River, NJ: Prentice-Hall.

International Associations of the Chiefs of Police (IACP). (1999). Police Leadership in the 21st Century: Achieving and Sustaining Executive Success. Recommendations from the President's First Leadership Conference. Available: http://www.theiacp.org/document/

Justice, T., and D. Jamieson (1999). *The Complete Guide to Facilitation: Enabling Groups to Succeed*. Amherst, Mass.: Human Resource Development Press.

Kennedy, D. (2008). *Putting Our Differences to Work: The Fastest Way to Innovation, Leadership, and High Performance*. San Francisco, Calif.: Berrett-Koehler

Laine, R. B. (2008). "President's Message: Challenges and Opportunities in the Year Ahead." *The Police Chief*, *75*(11). Available: http://policechiefmagazine.org/magazine/index.cfm?fuseaction=display_arch&article_id=1661&issue_id=112008.

Leary, M. R. (1996). *Self-Presentation: Impression Management and Interpersonal Behavior*. Boulder, Colo.: Westview Press.

Langworthy, R. H., and Travis, L. P. III (1999). *Policing in America: A Balance in Forces*, 2nd ed. Upper Saddle River, NJ: Prentice Hall.

MacInnes, A. (2009, May 22). "City Settles Cop's Suit for $500,000; Sex Harassment Alleged." *Herald News* (Passaic County, NJ), p. B01.

Malinowski, Z. (2009, May 22). "Virginia Police View Success of Cleanup of City Neighborhood." *Providence Journal-Bulletin* (Rhode Island), p. 1.

Manning, P. K. (1997). *Police Work: The Social Organization of Policing*, 2nd ed. Prospect Heights, Ill.: Waveland Press.

McMillen, M. (2008, August). "Transforming the MEU: Design a MEU to Conduct Tactical Diplomacy." *Marine Corps Gazette*, p. 55. Available: www.marinecorpsgazette-digital.com/marinecorpsgazette/200808/?pg=55

"New ways of identifying people." (2000, September 9). *Economist*, pp. 85–91.

Office of Justice Programs. (1999). "Enhancing Technology's Use in Addressing Crime," Fiscal Year 1999 Annual Report, Chapter 8. Available: http://www.ojp.usdoj.gov/99anrpt/chap8.htm.

O'Hare, P. (2009, March 3). "Excessive Force $3 Million Verdict in Death Tied to Taser Schizophrenic Man Died after He Was Shocked and Hogtied by Pct. 1 Deputies' Taser: County Found at Fault." *Houston Chronicle*, p. A1.

O'Toole, M. E. (2000). The School Shooter: A Threat Assessment Perspective. Washington, D.C.: FBI.

Palmiotto, M. J. (2001). *Police Misconduct: A Reader for the 21st Century*. Upper Saddle River, NJ: Prentice-Hall.

Patriot News. (2009, January 6). "Reflecting the Community: Police Try to Increase Diversity in Ranks." Harrisburg, Pa., p. B1.

Prosser, M. A. (2007, January). "Policing a Diverse Community." *The Police Chief,* 74(1). Available: http://policechiefmagazine.org/magazine/index.cfm?fuseaction=display_arch&article_id=1088&issue_id=12007.

Rosenbaum, M., and P. Bibring. (2009, June 4). "LAPD—It's Not Quite Reformed." *Los Angeles Times,* p. 27.

Simons, George F. (2009, June). International Diversity Consultant, Personal Communication.

State News Service. (2009, May 22). "Phoenix Police Recognized for Revitalization Services."

Taylor, R. W., T. J. Caeti, D. K. Loper, E. J. Fritsch, and J. Liederbach. (2006). *Digital Crime and Digital Terrorism.* Upper Saddle River, NJ: Pearson Prentice Hall.

Thibault, E. A., L. M. Lynch, and R. B. McBride. (2001). *Proactive Police Management.* Upper Saddle River, NJ: Prentice-Hall.

White, M. D. (2007). *Current Issues and Controversies in Policing.* Boston, Mass.: Allyn and Bacon.

White, J. P. (1992, August 9). "Elsie Cross vs. the Suits: One Black Woman Is Teaching White Corporate America to Do the Right Thing." *Los Angeles Times Magazine,* pp. 14–18, 38–42.

APPENDIX A

Multicultural Community and Workforce: Attitude Assessment Survey*

The first set of questions ask for your opinions about how certain segments of the community view the police. Using the response sheets (Attitude Assessment Survey Response Sheet) on pages 493–496, put the number of the response that you think best describes each group's perception. Remember, give the response based on how you feel each group would answer the statements.

1. In your opinion, how would this group rate the job this police department does? (See response sheet.)

2. This group generally cooperates with the police.

3. Overall, this group thinks that police department acts to protect the rights of individuals.

4. Which of the following, this group feels, describes the current relationship between the police and the community?

5. Overall, this group feels this department responds to citizen complaints about officers in an objective and fair manner.

6. This group thinks most contacts with police are negative.

The next set of questions ask for your opinions about procedures and practices within the police department.

7. Overall, police supervisors in this department respond to citizens' complaints about employees in an objective and fair manner.

8a. Most police officers in this department are sensitive to cultural and community differences.

8b. Most civilian employees in this department are sensitive to cultural and community differences.

9a. This department adequately prepares officers to work with members of the community who are of a different race or ethnicity than the majority of the population.

9b. This department adequately prepares civilian employees to work with members of the community who are of a different race or ethnicity than the majority of the population.

10. The police administration is more concerned about police–community relations than it should be.

11a. Special training should be given to officers who work with community members who are of a different race or ethnicity than the majority population.

11b. Special training should be given to civilian employees who work with community members who are of a different race or ethnicity than the majority population.

---

* Adapted with permission from the Alameda, California Police Department.

12. Special training should be given to assist officers in working with each of the following segments of the community.

13. How often are racial slurs and negative comments about persons of a different race or ethnicity expressed by personnel in this department?

14a. Persons of a different race or ethnicity in this city are subject to unfair treatment by some officers in this department.

14b. Persons of a different race or ethnicity in this city are subject to unfair treatment by some civilian employees in this department.

15a. Prejudicial remarks and discriminatory behavior by officers are not tolerated by line supervisors in this department.

15b. Prejudicial remarks and discriminatory behavior by civilian employees are not tolerated by line supervisors in this department.

16. Transfer policies in this department have a negative effect on police–community affairs.

17. Citizen complaint procedures in this department operate in favor of the citizen, not the employee.

18. Internal discipline procedures for employee misconduct are generally appropriate.

19. The procedure for a citizen to file a complaint against a department employee should be which of the following?

20. With regard to discipline for misconduct, all employees in this department are treated the same in similar situations, regardless of race or ethnicity.

21. What kind of discipline do you think is appropriate for the first incident of the following types of misconduct? (Assume intentional.)

This section examines your views about police–community relations training and community participation. Please circle the response that best describes your opinion.

22. Do you think training in police–community relations was adequate to prepare you to work with all segments of the community?

23. How often do you have opportunities to participate in positive contacts with community groups?

24. Do you think this department has an adequate community relations program?

25. What subject areas related to community relations would be helpful on an in-service training basis?

26. What do you think is the most important thing that citizens need to understand about the police?

27. How can the police department best educate the public about police policies and practices?

28. Listed are steps that police departments can take to improve police services as they relate to community relations. How important you think each of them should be to this administration?

Attitude Assessment Survey Response Sheet

Place the number that corresponds to your response in each column.

	Business community	Minority residents	Community leaders	Most residents	Juveniles
Question 1:					
(1) Very good					
(2) Good					
(3) Fair					
(4) Poor					
(5) Very Poor					
Question 2:					
(1) Most of the time					
(2) Sometimes					
(3) Rarely					
(4) Never					
Question 3:					
(1) Strongly agree					
(2) Agree					
(3) Disagree					
(4) Strongly disagree					
Question 4:					
(1) Very good					
(2) Good					
(3) Fair					
(4) Poor					
(5) Very poor					
Question 5:					
(1) Strongly agree					
(2) Agree					
(3) Disagree					
(4) Strongly disagree					
Question 6:					
(1) Strongly agree					
(2) Agree					
(3) Disagree					
(4) Strongly disagree					

Place check in column corresponding to your response for each question.

	Strongly agree	Agree	Disagree	Strongly disagree	Don't know
Question 7:					
Question 8a:					
Question 8b:					

(*continued*)

	Strongly agree	Agree	Disagree	Strongly disagree	Don't know
Question 9a:					
Question 9b:					
Question 10:					
Question 11a:					
Question 11b:					

Check one response for each group.

Question 12:

	Strongly agree	Agree	Disagree	Strongly disagree
African American/black (includes Caribbean, Haitian, and so forth)				
Asian				
Hispanic				
Homosexual				

Circle your response.

Question 13:   (1) Often   (2) Sometimes   (3) Rarely   (4) Never

Place check in column corresponding to your response for each question.

	Strongly agree	Agree	Disagree	Strongly disagree	Don't know
Question 14a:					
Question 14b:					
Question 15a:					
Question 15b:					
Question 16:					
Question 17:					
Question 18:					

Circle one response.

Question 19:
(1) Citizen sends complaint in writing to department.
(2) Citizen telephones complaint to department.
(3) Citizen comes to department.

(4) Any of the above is an acceptable means.

(5) None of the above is an acceptable means.

  Please explain.

_____

_____

Circle your response.

Question 20: (1) Strongly agree (2) Agree (3) Disagree (4) Strongly disagree

Check one response for each.

Question 21:

Type of misconduct	Verbal warning	Training/ counseling	Oral reprimand	Formal reprimand	Suspension	Termination
Excessive force						
False arrest						
Discrimination						
Use of racial slurs						
Criminal conduct						
Poor service						
Discourtesy to citizen						
Improper procedure						

Please circle the response that best describes your opinion.

Question 22:   (1) Yes   (2) No   (3) Did not receive training
            If no, please describe why the training was not satisfactory.
            Please explain._____

_____

_____

Question 23:   (1) Frequently   (2) Sometimes   (3) Rarely   (4) Never

Question 24:   (1) Yes   (2) No   (3) Don't know
            Please explain._____

_____

_____

Question 25:   _____

_____

_____

Question 26:   _____

_____

_____

Question 27:

Circle one only.

(1) Through patrol officer contacts with citizens

(2) Through public meetings

(3) Through the media

(4) Selected combinations of the responses above

(5) Other (explain): _____

_____

_____

(6) Don't know

Check one response for each

Question 28:

	Somewhat important	Important	Not at all important
Hire more police			
Focus on more serious crimes			
Improve response time			
Increase salaries			
Provide more training			
Raise qualifications for potential applicants			
Be more courteous to public			
Increase foot patrols			
Reduce discrimination			
Provide dedicated time for community involvement			

APPENDIX B

Cultural Diversity Survey: Needs Assessment*

ANONYMOUS QUESTIONNAIRE

There has been a great deal of discussion in recent years about whether the job of police officer has been changing. Some of the discussion revolves around issues related to contact with people from different cultural, racial, or ethnic groups. Please check or enter one answer for each question.

1. Comparing the job of an officer today with that of an officer a few years ago, I think that today the job is

    ( ) a lot more difficult
    ( ) somewhat more difficult
    ( ) about the same in difficulty
    ( ) somewhat easier
    ( ) a lot easier

2. When I stop a car with occupant(s) of a different racial or ethnic group than mine, I must admit that I am more concerned about my safety than I would be if I stopped a car with the same number of occupant(s) of the same racial or ethnic group as mine.

    ( ) strongly agree
    ( ) agree
    ( ) disagree
    ( ) strongly disagree

3. If an officer notices a group of young people gathering in a public place and the young people aren't known to the officer, they should be watched very closely for possible trouble.

    ( ) strongly agree
    ( ) agree
    ( ) disagree
    ( ) strongly disagree

4. If an officer notices a group of young people from another racial or ethnic group gathered in a public place, the officer should plan on watching them very closely for possible trouble.

    ( ) strongly agree
    ( ) agree
    ( ) disagree
    ( ) strongly disagree

5. How often do you think it is justifiable to use derogatory labels such as "scumbag" and "dirtbag" when dealing with possible suspects?

    ( ) frequently
    ( ) some of the time

---

* Adapted with permission: police department wishes to remain anonymous. Editor: This should appear on page 1.

( ) once in a while
( ) never

6. When I interact on duty with civilians who are of a different race, ethnicity, or culture, my view is that

( ) they should be responded to a little more firmly to make sure that they understand the powers of the police
( ) they should be responded to somewhat differently, taking into account their different backgrounds
( ) they should be responded to the same as anyone else

7. When I encounter citizens of a different race, ethnicity, or culture who have committed a violation of the law, my view is that

( ) they should be responded to a little more firmly to make sure they understand the powers of the police
( ) they should be responded to somewhat differently, taking into account their different backgrounds
( ) they should be responded to the same as anyone else

8. When interacting on duty with civilians who have a complaint or a question and who are of a different race, ethnicity, or culture, I try to be very aware of the fact that my usual gestures may frighten or offend them.

( ) strongly agree
( ) agree
( ) disagree
( ) strongly disagree

9. When interacting on duty with offenders who are of a different race, ethnicity, or culture, I try to be very aware of the fact that my usual behavior may frighten or offend them.

( ) strongly agree
( ) agree
( ) disagree
( ) strongly disagree

10. How often have you run into a difficulty in understanding what a civilian was talking about because of language barriers or accents?

( ) frequently
( ) once in a while
( ) hardly ever
( ) never

11. How often have you run into difficulty in understanding what an offender was talking about because of language barriers or accents?

( ) frequently
( ) once in a while
( ) hardly ever
( ) never

12. How often have you run into some difficulty in making yourself clear while talking to a civilian because of language barriers or accents?

    (   ) frequently
    (   ) once in a while
    (   ) hardly ever
    (   ) never

13. How often have you run into some difficulty in making yourself clear while talking to an offender because of language barriers or accents?

    (   ) frequently
    (   ) once in a while
    (   ) hardly ever
    (   ) never

14. How important is it that the police department provide training to make its members aware of the differences in culture, religion, race, or ethnicity?

    (   ) extremely important
    (   ) very important
    (   ) fairly important
    (   ) not too important
    (   ) not important at all

15. Personally, I believe that the training I have received on group differences is

    (   ) far too much
    (   ) somewhat too much
    (   ) about the right amount
    (   ) too little
    (   ) virtually nothing

16. The training in the area of group differences has been

    (   ) extremely helpful
    (   ) very helpful
    (   ) somewhat helpful
    (   ) not too helpful
    (   ) not helpful at all

17. My own view is that our department's quality of service could be improved by

    (   ) placing greater emphasis on hiring on the basis of the highest score obtained on the entrance exam, making no attempt to diversify by race, ethnicity, or gender
    (   ) placing greater emphasis on diversity by race, ethnicity, or gender and somewhat less emphasis on the numerical rank obtained on the entrance examination
    (   ) giving equal weight to both the score obtained on the entrance examination and diversification by race, ethnicity, or gender

18. What percentage of civilian or internal complaints against employees is adjudicated equitably?

    (   ) over 80 percent
    (   ) between 60 and 80 percent

(   ) between 40 and 60 percent
(   ) between 20 and 40 percent
(   ) less than 20 percent

19. Some civilian or internal complaints are adjudicated more favorably toward people from diverse groups rather than toward the majority population.

(   ) strongly agree
(   ) agree
(   ) disagree
(   ) strongly disagree

20. I think that employees of a different race or ethnicity receive preferential treatment on the job.

(   ) strongly agree
(   ) agree
(   ) disagree
(   ) strongly disagree

21. The racial diversity of my coworkers has made it easier for me to see issues and incidents from another perspective.

(   ) strongly agree
(   ) agree
(   ) disagree
(   ) strongly disagree

22. To think that employees of a different race or ethnicity than mine receive preferential treatment on this job

(   ) bothers me because I do not think it is justified
(   ) does not bother me because I think it is justified
(   ) is fair only because it makes up for past discrimination
(   ) I do not believe minorities get preferential treatment

23. In certain situations, having a partner of a different race or ethnicity than mine is more advantageous than having a partner of my same race or ethnicity.

(   ) strongly agree
(   ) agree
(   ) disagree
(   ) strongly disagree

24. I have received negative feedback from members of the community regarding the conduct of other officers.

(   ) strongly agree
(   ) agree
(   ) disagree
(   ) strongly disagree

25. I have received negative feedback from members of the community regarding the conduct of officers who are of a different race or ethnicity in particular.

(   ) strongly agree
(   ) agree

( ) disagree

( ) strongly disagree

26. I have received more negative feedback from members of the community regarding the conduct of officers from different races and ethnic backgrounds than about the conduct of white officers.

( ) strongly agree

( ) agree

( ) disagree

( ) strongly disagree

27. In terms of being supervised

( ) I would much rather be supervised by a man

( ) I would somewhat rather be supervised by a man

( ) I would much rather be supervised by a woman

( ) I would somewhat rather be supervised by a woman

( ) It does not make a difference whether a man or a woman supervises me

28. In terms of being supervised by a man

( ) I would much rather be supervised by a nonminority

( ) I would somewhat rather be supervised by a nonminority

( ) I would much rather be supervised by a minority

( ) I would somewhat rather be supervised by a minority

( ) It does not make a difference to which group my supervisor belongs

29. In terms of being supervised by a woman

( ) I would much rather be supervised by a nonminority

( ) I would somewhat rather be supervised by a nonminority

( ) I would much rather be supervised by a minority

( ) I would somewhat rather be supervised by a minority

( ) It does not make a difference to which group my supervisor belongs

If this questionnaire is being used for a training class, please check the one answer in the following questions that best applies to you.

30. What is your sex?

( ) male

( ) female

31. What is your race?

( ) white

( ) African American or black

( ) Hispanic

( ) Native American

( ) Asian American

( ) other

32. How many years have you been employed by the police department?

( ) 0–5 years

( ) 6–10 years

( ) 11–20 years
( ) more than 20 years

33. What is your current rank?

( ) officer
( ) sergeant
( ) lieutenant
( ) captain or commander
( ) deputy chief
( ) chief

34. What is the highest academic degree you hold?

( ) high school
( ) associate's degree
( ) bachelor's degree
( ) master's degree

APPENDIX C

Listing of Consultants and Resources

The following is a partial list of professional consultants and resources that may be useful to law enforcement agencies (current as of June 2009). Please note that we are not endorsing the services of these consultants but are making our readers aware of their specialized multicultural and cross-cultural training and consultation. We recommend searching the internet for a more detailed listing.

CROSS-CULTURAL DIVERSITY CONSULTANTS AND RESOURCES

Aaron T. Olson, Organization and Training Services Consultant, P.O. Box 345, Oregon City, OR 97045. Telephone: (971) 409-8135. Co-author of *Multicultural Law Enforcement: Strategies for Peacekeeping in a Diverse Society and Multicultural and Diversity Strategies for the Fire Service.* Provides training on cultural diversity and other topics, including on-call and travel to worksites, for staff development to businesses and government organizations. Website: http://www.atolson. com. E-mail: information@atolson.com

The Backup Training Corporation. 701 E. Front Avenue, Suite 301, Coeur d'Alene, ID. 838314. Telephone: (800) 822-9398 or (208) 765-8062. Specializes in the production and delivery of customized digital training, which is interactive and computer-based, for law enforcement. Such courses include cultural diversity, community policing, use of force, and more. Website: http://www. thebackup.com.

ChangeWorks Consulting (CWC). 28 South Main Street, #113, Randolph, MA 02368. Telephone: (781) 986-6150. CWC staff use an innovative philosophy and framework to address diversity, inclusion, antiracism, and organizational change. From education and training to strategic planning, from assessments to diversity councils, from planning diversity initiatives to writing insightful articles, they work with clients to provide services that help create more equitable and respectful environments. Website: http://changeworksconsulting.org

Deena Levine & Associates. LLC, P.O. Box 582, Alamo, CA 94507. Telephone: (925) 947-5627. Co-author of *Multicultural Law Enforcement: Strategies for Peacekeeping in a Diverse Society.* Provides cross-cultural consulting, with a network of associates, for businesses and a variety of other organizations. Website: http://www.dlevineassoc.com. E-mail: deena_levine@astound.net

Elsie Y. Cross Associates, Inc. 7627 Germantown Avenue, Philadelphia, PA 19118. Telephone: (215) 248-8100. Provides organization development in planning and implementing diversity initiatives. Offers a quarterly e-journal, on a broad range of issues that affect anyone interested or engaged in diversity initiatives and programs. While its focus is primarily on the workplace, it also covers topics such as health care and criminal justice, just to name a few. Website: http://www. diversityinc.com/public/3617.cfm

George Simons International (Also known as Diversophy). 236 Plateau Avenue, Santa Cruz, CA 95060. Telephone: (831) 531-4706. Provides consulting, coaching, training, e-learning and customized tools to empower organizations and their people to work, communicate, and negotiate effectively across cultures. Website: http://www.diversophy.com

The GilDeane Group, Inc. 13751 Lake City Way, NE, Suite 210, Seattle, WA 98125. Telephone: (206) 362-0336. Is a consulting and training firm that helps people and their organizations work effectively across cultural borders. They believe "cultural intelligence" is the key to this effectiveness. Website: http://www.gildeane.com

Guardian Quest. 900 Lakewood Place, Aurora, IL 60506. Telephone: (630) 363-5119. Provides training and consulting on organizational assessments, diversity, ethics, and leadership, and train the trainers to businesses and government and public safety agencies. Retired Deputy Chief Ondra Berry from the Reno Police Department is cofounder of the organization. Website: http://guardianquest.com

Herbert Z. Wong & Associates. 245 First Street, Suite 1800, Cambridge, MA 02142 and 111 Deerwood Road, Suite 200, San Ramon, CA 94583. Telephone: (925) 837-3595. Dr. Herbert Z. Wong is co-author of *Multicultural Law Enforcement: Strategies for Peacekeeping in a Diverse Society* and *Multicultural Law Enforcement: Concepts and Tools in Practice.* Herbert Z. Wong & Associates' consultants engage in organizational surveys, cultural assessments, and workforce diversity training. The consulting firm specializes in diversity and cultural competency training and the assessment of organizational culture for implementing the strategic advantages of diversity. Federal law enforcement and regulatory agency diversity assessment and training are also provided.

Loden Associates, Inc. 14 Aviara Ct, Napa, CA 94558. Telephone (415) 435-8507. Loden Associates takes a comprehensive approach to the design and implementation of diversity initiatives that maximize synergy with strategic business goals and support for organizational culture change. All client consultation and program development are based on proven behavioral science principles that facilitate broad acceptance of change. Website: http://www.loden.com

ODT Inc. P.O. Box 134, Amhurst, MA 01004. Telephone: (800) 736-1293. A web store source of alternative information on maps, corporate diversity materials, and books. Offers an array of fascinating and thought-provoking resources to expand your view of the world. Website: http:// www.odt.org

Simulations Training Systems. P. O. Box 910, Del Mar, CA 92014. Telephone: (800) 942-2900 and (858) 755-0272. Produces simulation training programs for businesses, schools, government agencies, and nonprofit organizations dealing with the areas of cross-cultural relations, diversity, empowerment, team building, the use and abuse of power, ethics, and sexual harassment. Website: http://www.simulationtrainingsystems.com

Sounder, Betances and Associates, Inc. 5448 North Kimball Avenue, Chicago, IL 60625. Telephone: 773-463-6374. Works with public and private organizations of all sizes in providing consultation and training services on diversity awareness, diversity competency, diversity mentoring, leadership, and many other areas. Has a special program customized for law enforcement agencies. Website: http://betances.com

ANTI-BIAS ORGANIZATIONS AND GOVERNMENT AGENCIES

U.S. Commission on Civil Rights, 624 9th Street N.W., Washington, D.C. 20425. Telephone: (202) 376-8312. The U.S. Commission on Civil Rights (a) investigates complaints alleging that citizens have been deprived of their right to vote as a result of discrimination; (b) studies and collects information relating to discrimination on the basis of race, color, religion, sex, age, disability, or national origin; (c) reviews federal laws, regulations, and policies with respect to discrimination and equal protection under the law; and (d) submits reports to the President and to Congress on civil rights issues. Website: http://www.usccr.gov

Arab American Institute (AAI)
1600 K Street, NW, Suite 601
Washington, DC 20006
(202) 429-9210
Website: http://www.aaiusa.org

American-Arab Anti-Discrimination Committee (ADC)
1732 Wisconsin Ave, NW
Washington, D.C. 20007
(202) 244-2990
Website: http://www.adc.org

Anti-Defamation League (ADL)
605 3rd Ave.
New York, NY 10158
(212) 684-6950
Website: http://www.adl.org

U.S. Department of Justice
Bureau of Justice Statistics
810 Seventh Street, NW
Washington, D.C. 20531
(800) 732-3277
Website: http://www.ojp.usdoj.gov/bjs

Asian American Justice Center (Formerly the National Asian Pacific American Legal Consortium)
1140 Connecticut Avenue, NW, Suite 1200
Washington, DC 20036
Phone: 202-296-2300
http://www.advancingequality.org

Center for Democratic Renewal National Office (CDR)
P.O. Box 50469
Atlanta, GA 30302-0469
(404) 221-0025
Website: http://www.thecdr.org

Coalition against Anti-Asian Violence
c/o Asian American Legal Defense and Education Fund
99 Hudson Street, 12th Floor

New York, NY 10013
(212) 966-5932
Website: http://www.aaldef.org/

Congress of Racial Equality (CORE)
National Headquarters
817 Broadway 3rd Floor
New York, New York 10003
(212) 598-4000 or (800) 439-2673
Website: http://www.core-online.org

U.S. Equal Employment Opportunity Commission (EEOC)
131 M Street, NE
Washington, DC 20507
Phone: (202) 663-4900
Website: http://www.eeoc.gov

Gay & Lesbian Alliance against Defamation (GLAAD)
150 West 26th Street, Suite 503
New York, NY 10001
(212) 629-3322
Website: www.glaad.org

Jewish Council for Public Affairs
443 Park Avenue South, 11th Floor
New York, NY 10016
(212) 684-6950
Website: http://www.jewishpublicaffairs.org

Museum of Tolerance
9786 W. Pico Blvd
Los Angeles, California 90035
(310) 553-8403
http://www.museumoftolerance.com

**National Association for the Advancement
of Colored People (NAACP)**
National Headquarters
4805 Mt. Hope Drive
Baltimore, MD 21215
(410) 580-5777 or (877) NAACP-98
Website: http://www.naacp.org

National Conference for Community and Justice
328 Flatbush Avenue
Box 402
Brooklyn, NY 11217

Phone: 718 783-0044
Website: http://www.nccj.org

National Congress of American Indians (NCAI)
1516 P Street NW,
Washington, DC 20005
(202) 466-7767
Website: http://www.ncai.org

National Council of La Raza (NCLR)
Raul Yzaguirre Building
1126 16th Street, N.W.
Washington, D.C. 20036
(202) 785-1670
Website: http://www.nclr.org

National Gay and Lesbian Task Force
1325 Massachusetts Ave NW, Suite 600
Washington, D.C. 20005
(202) 393.5177
Website: http://www.thetaskforce.org

National Organization for Women (NOW)
1100 H Street NW, 3rd floor
Washington, D.C. 20005
(202) 628-8669
Website: http://www.now.org

National Organization of Black Law Enforcement Executives (NOBLE)
Hubert T. Bell Jr. Office Complex
4609-F Pinecrest Office Park Drive
Alexandria, VA 22312-1442
(703) 658-1529
Website: http://www.noblenatl.org

The Prejudice Institute
2743 Maryland Ave.
Baltimore, MD 21218
telephone: (410) 243-6987
(410) 243-6987
Website: http://www.prejudiceinstitute.org

Southeast Asia Resource Action Center (SEARAC)
1628 16th Street, NW, 3rd Floor
Washington, D.C. 20009

(202) 667-4690
Website: http://www.searac.org

Southern Poverty Law Center
400 Washington Avenue
Montgomery, AL 36104
334-956-8200
Website: http://www.splcenter.org

U.S. Department of Justice Community Relations Service Headquarters
600 E. Street, N.W., Suite 6000
Washington, DC 20530
(202) 305-2935
(202) 305-2935
Website: http://www.usdoj.gov/crs

APPENDIX D

Self-Assessment of Communication Skills in Law Enforcement: Communications Inventory

The following is adapted for law enforcement from Dr. Phil Harris's Communications Inventory in High Performance Leadership: HRD Strategies for the New Work Force Culture (HRD Press, Amherst, MA, 1995). As you answer the questions, think about your cross-cultural communication with both citizens and coworkers in your department. (Many of these questions also apply to communication with people of the same background.) Find your areas of strength and your areas of weakness and make it a point to improve those areas. To check whether your perceptions of your communication are correct, have a coworker or partner fill out the questionnaire for you. Part of knowing where to improve involves self-awareness and an honest appraisal of your strengths and weaknesses.

Instructions: Circle the word that best describes your approach to the communication process.

1. In communicating, I project a positive image of myself (e.g., voice, approach, tone).

   Seldom   Occasionally   Often   Always

2. When appropriate, I try to show my "receiver" (the person with whom I am communicating—for example, victims, citizens making complaints, suspects, witnesses, and coworkers) that I understand what is being communicated from his or her point of view. I do this by restating this point of view and by showing empathy and concern.

   Seldom   Occasionally   Often   Always

3. I am sensitive to culturally different usages of eye contact, and I establish eye contact where appropriate, but avoid intense eye contact with people for whom less eye contact is more comfortable.

   Seldom   Occasionally   Often   Always

4. I am aware of when my own emotions and state of mind affect my communication with others. (e.g., I know my own needs, motives, biases, prejudices, and stereotypes).

   Seldom   Occasionally   Often   Always

5. I refrain from using insensitive and unprofessional language while on the job (including language used in written and computer communications).

   Seldom   Occasionally   Often   Always

6. I try not to let the person with whom I am communicating push my "hot buttons," which would negatively affect my communication (e.g., cause me to go out of control verbally).

   Seldom   Occasionally   Often   Always

7. When speaking with individuals from groups that speak English differently from the way I do, I try not to imitate their manner of speech in order to be "one of them."

   Seldom   Occasionally   Often   Always

8. With non-native speakers of English, I try not to speak in an excessively loud voice or use incorrect English (e.g., "You no understand me?") in an attempt to make myself clear.

   Seldom   Occasionally   Often   Always

9. I am aware that many immigrants and refugees do not understand police procedures and I make special efforts to explain these procedures (including their rights).

   Seldom   Occasionally   Often   Always

10. I check in a supportive manner to see if people have understood my message and directions, and I encourage people to show me that they have understood me.

    Seldom   Occasionally   Often   Always

11. With non-native speakers of English, I make a special point to simplify my vocabulary, eliminate the use of slang and idioms, and try to use phrases that are not confusing.

    Seldom   Occasionally   Often   Always

12. I make extra efforts to establish rapport (e.g., show increased patience, give more explanations, show professionalism and respect) with individuals from groups that have typically and historically considered the police their enemies.

    Seldom   Occasionally   Often   Always

13. I am sensitive to cultural or gender differences between me and the receiver.

    Seldom   Occasionally   Often   Always

14. I convey respect to all citizens while on duty, regardless of their race, color, gender, or other difference from me.

    Seldom   Occasionally   Often   Always

15. When using agency communication channels or media, I communicate professionally, avoiding inappropriate or derogatory remarks.

    Seldom   Occasionally   Often   Always

[*Source*: Adapted with permission from the Alameda, California, Police Department]

APPENDIX E

Listing of Gangs and Identifying Characteristics

The following information lists national and regional gangs and their specific characteristics for the three major types of gangs presented in Chapter 14:

> Section I: Street Gangs
>
> Section II: Prison Gangs
>
> Section III: Outlaw Motorcycle Gangs

This material does not include all gangs in the United States. Individual state, county, and city law enforcement agencies should be contacted for information on local and regional gangs in their jurisdictions. This listing was adapted and reproduced with permission from the National Drug Intelligence Center of which the *National Gang Threat Assessment for the National Gang Intelligence Center* is a part. Both centers are part of the U.S. Department of Justice. This information was published in 2009, and was current as of the writing of this text's fifth edition.

SECTION I: STREET GANGS

18th Street (National)

Formed in Los Angeles, 18th Street is a group of loosely associated sets or cliques, each led by an influential member. Membership is estimated at 30,000 to 50,000. In California, approximately 80 percent of the gang's members are illegal aliens from Mexico and Central America. The gang is active in 44 cities across 20 states. Its main source of income is street-level distribution of cocaine and marijuana and, to a lesser extent, heroin and methamphetamine. Gang members also commit assault, auto theft, carjacking, drive-by shootings, extortion, homicide, identification fraud, and robbery.

Almighty Latin King and Queen Nation (National)

The Latin Kings street gang was formed in Chicago in the 1960s and consisted predominantly of Mexican and Puerto Rican males. Originally created with the philosophy of overcoming racial prejudice and creating an organization of "Kings," the Latin Kings evolved into a criminal enterprise operating throughout the United States under two umbrella factions: Motherland, also known as KMC (King Motherland Chicago), and Bloodline (New York). All members of the gang refer to themselves as Latin Kings and, currently, individuals of any nationality are allowed to become members. Latin Kings associating with the Motherland faction also identify themselves as "Almighty Latin King Nation (ALKN)," and make up more than 160 structured chapters operating in 158 cities across 31 states. The membership of Latin Kings following KMC is estimated to be 20,000 to 35,000. The Bloodline was founded by Luis Felipe in the New York State correctional system in 1986. Latin Kings associating with Bloodline also identify themselves as the "Almighty Latin King and Queen Nation (ALKQN)." Membership is estimated to be 2,200 to 7,500, divided among several dozen chapters operating in 15 cities across five states. Bloodline Latin Kings share a common culture and structure with KMC and respect them as the Motherland, but all chapters do not report to the Chicago leadership hierarchy. The gang's primary source of income is the street-level distribution of powder cocaine, crack cocaine, heroin, and marijuana. Latin Kings continue to portray themselves as a community organization while engaging in a wide variety of criminal activities, including assault, burglary, homicide, identity theft, and money laundering.

Asian Boyz (National)

Asian Boyz is one of the largest Asian street gangs operating in the United States. Formed in southern California in the early 1970s, the gang is estimated to have 1,300 to 2,000 members operating in at least 28 cities across 14 states. Members primarily are Vietnamese or Cambodian males. Members of Asian Boyz are involved in producing, transporting, and distributing methamphetamine as well as distributing MDMA and marijuana. In addition, gang members are involved in other criminal activities, including assault, burglary, drive-by shootings, and homicide.

Black P. Stone Nation (National)

Black P. Stone Nation, one of the largest and most violent associations of street gangs in the United States, consists of seven highly structured street gangs with a single leader and a common culture. It has an estimated 6,000 to 8,000 members, most of whom are African American males from the Chicago metropolitan area. The gang's main source of income is the street-level distribution of cocaine, heroin, marijuana and, to a lesser extent, methamphetamine. Members are also involved in many other types of criminal activity, including assault, auto theft, burglary, carjacking, drive-by shootings, extortion, homicide, and robbery.

Bloods (National)

Bloods is an association of structured and unstructured gangs that have adopted a single-gang culture. The original Bloods were formed in the early 1970s to provide protection from the Crips street gang in Los Angeles, California. Large, national-level Bloods gangs include Bounty Hunter Bloods and Crenshaw Mafia Gangsters. Bloods membership is estimated to be 7,000 to 30,000 nationwide; most members are African American males. Bloods gangs are active in 123 cities across 33 states. The main source of income for Bloods gangs is street-level distribution of cocaine and marijuana. Bloods members are also involved in transporting and distributing methamphetamine, heroin, and PCP (phencyclidine), but to a much lesser extent. The gangs also conduct other criminal activity including assault, auto theft, burglary, carjacking, drive-by shootings, extortion, homicide, identity fraud, and robbery.

Crips (National)

Crips is a collection of structured and unstructured gangs that have adopted a common gang culture. Crips membership is estimated at 30,000 to 35,000; most members are African American males from the Los Angeles metropolitan area. Large, national-level Crips gangs include 107 Hoover Crips, Insane Gangster Crips, and Rolling 60s Crips. Crips gangs operate in 221 cities across 41 states. The main source of income for Crips gangs is the street-level distribution of powder cocaine, crack cocaine, marijuana, and PCP. The gangs are also involved in other criminal activity such as assault, auto theft, burglary, and homicide.

Florencia 13 (Regional)

Florencia 13 (F 13 or FX 13) originated in Los Angeles in the early 1960s; gang membership is estimated at more than 3,000. The gang operates primarily in California and increasingly in

Arkansas, Missouri, New Mexico, and Utah. Florencia 13 is subordinate to the Mexican Mafia (La Eme) prison gang and claims Sureños (Sur 13) affiliation. A primary source of income for gang members is the trafficking of cocaine and methamphetamine. Gang members smuggle multikilogram quantities of powder cocaine and methamphetamine obtained from supply sources in Mexico into the United States for distribution. Also, gang members produce large quantities of methamphetamine in southern California for local distribution. Florencia members are involved in other criminal activities, including assault, drive-by shootings, and homicide.

Fresno Bulldogs (Regional)

Fresno Bulldogs is a street gang that originated in Fresno, California, in the late 1960s. Bulldogs are the largest Hispanic gang operating in central California, with membership estimated at 5,000 to 6,000. Bulldogs are one of the few Hispanic gangs in California that claim neither Sureños (Southern) nor Norteños (Northern) affiliation. However, gang members associate with Nuestra Familia (NF) members, particularly when trafficking drugs. The street-level distribution of methamphetamine, marijuana, and heroin is a primary source of income for gang members. In addition, members are involved in other criminal activity, including assault, burglary, homicide, and robbery.

Gangster Disciples (National)

The Gangster Disciples street gang was formed in Chicago, Illinois, in the mid-1960s. It is structured like a corporation and is led by a chairman of the board. Gang membership is estimated at 25,000 to 50,000; most members are African American males from the Chicago metropolitan area. The gang is active in 110 cities across 31 states. Its main source of income is the street-level distribution of cocaine, crack cocaine, marijuana, and heroin. The gang is also involved in other criminal activity, including assault, auto theft, firearms violations, fraud, homicide, operation of prostitution rings, and money laundering.

Latin Disciples (Regional)

Latin Disciples, also known as Maniac Latin Disciples and Young Latino Organization, originated in Chicago in the late 1960s. The gang is composed of at least 10 structured and unstructured factions with an estimated 1,500 to 2,000 members and associate members. Most members are Puerto Rican males. Maniac Latin Disciples are the largest Hispanic gang in the Folk Nation Alliance. The gang is most active in the Great Lakes and the southwestern regions of the United States. The street-level distribution of powder cocaine, heroin, marijuana, and PCP is a primary source of income for the gang. Members are also involved in other criminal activity, including assault, auto theft, carjacking, drive-by shootings, home invasion, homicide, money laundering, and weapons trafficking.

Mara Salvatrucha (National)

Mara Salvatrucha, also known as MS 13, is one of the largest Hispanic street gangs in the United States. Traditionally, the gang consisted of loosely affiliated groups known as cliques; however, law enforcement officials have reported increased coordination of criminal activity among Mara Salvatrucha cliques in the Atlanta, Dallas, Los Angeles, Washington, D.C., and New York metropolitan areas. The gang is estimated to have 30,000 to 50,000 members and associate members worldwide, 8,000 to 10,000 of whom reside in the United States. Members smuggle illicit drugs, primarily powder cocaine and marijuana, into the United States and transport and distribute the drugs throughout the country. Some members also are involved in alien smuggling, assault, drive-by shootings, homicide, identity theft, prostitution operations, robbery, and weapons trafficking.

Sureños and Norteños (National)

As individual Hispanic street gang members enter prison systems, they put aside former rivalries with other Hispanic street gangs and unite under the name Sureños or Norteños. The original Mexican Mafia members, most of whom were from southern California, considered Mexicans from the rural, agricultural areas of northern California weak and viewed them with contempt. To distinguish them from the agricultural workers or farmers from northern California, members of Mexican Mafia began to refer to the Hispanic gang member prisoners who worked for them as Sureños (Southerners). Inmates from northern California became known as Norteños (Northerners) and are affiliated with Nuestra Familia. Because of its size and strength, Fresno Bulldogs are the only Hispanic gang in the California Department of Corrections (CDC) that does not fall under Sureños or Norteños but remains independent. Both the Sureños and the Norteños gang members' main sources of income are retail-level distribution of cocaine, heroin, marijuana, and methamphetamine within prison systems and in the community and extortion of drug distributors on the streets. Some Sureños members have direct links to Mexican DTOs and broker deals for Mexican Mafia as well as for their own gang. Both Sureños and Norteños gangs are also involved in other criminal activities such as assault, carjacking, home invasion, homicide, and robbery.

Tango Blast (Regional)

Tango Blast is one of largest prison/street criminal gangs operating in Texas. Tango Blast's criminal activities include drug trafficking, extortion, kidnapping, sexual assault, and murder. In the late 1990s, Hispanic men incarcerated in federal, state, and local prisons founded Tango Blast for personal protection against violence from traditional prison gangs such as the Aryan Brotherhood, Texas Syndicate, and Texas Mexican Mafia. Tango Blast originally had four city-based chapters: Houstone, Houston, Texas; ATX or La Capricha, Austin, Texas; D-Town, Dallas, Texas; and Foros or Foritos, Fort Worth, Texas. These four founding chapters are collectively known as "Puro Tango Blast" or "The Four Horsemen". From the original four chapters, former Texas inmates established new chapters in El Paso, San Antonio, Corpus Christi, and the Rio Grande Valley. In June 2008 the Houston Police Department (HPD) estimated that more than 14,000 Tango Blast members were incarcerated in Texas. Tango Blast is difficult to monitor. The gang does not conform to either traditional prison/street gang hierarchical organization or gang rules. Tango Blast is laterally organized, and leaders are elected sporadically to represent the gang in prisons and to lead street gang cells. The significance of Tango Blast is exemplified by corrections officials reporting that rival traditional prison gangs are now forming alliances to defend themselves against Tango Blast's growing power.

Tiny Rascal Gangsters (National)

Tiny Rascal Gangsters are one of the largest and most violent Asian street gang associations in the United States. It is composed of at least 60 structured and unstructured gangs, commonly referred to as sets, with an estimated 5,000 to 10,000 members and associates, who have adopted a common gang culture. Most members are Asian American males. The sets are most active in the southwestern, Pacific, and New England regions of the United States. The street-level distribution of powder cocaine, marijuana, MDMA, and methamphetamine is a primary source of income for the sets. Members are also involved in other criminal activity, including assault, drive-by shootings, extortion, home invasion, homicide, robbery, and theft.

United Blood Nation (Regional)

Bloods is a universal term that is used to identify both West Coast Bloods and United Blood Nation (UBN). While these groups are traditionally distinct entities, both identify themselves by "Blood," often making it hard for law enforcement to distinguish between them. United Blood Nation (UBN) started in 1993 in Rikers Island GMDC (George Mochen Detention Center) to protect its members from the threat posed by Latin Kings and Ñetas, who dominated the prison. United Blood Nation (UBN) is a loose confederation of street gangs, or sets, that once were predominantly African American. Membership is estimated to be between 7,000 and 15,000 along the U.S. eastern corridor. UBN derives its income from street-level distribution of cocaine, heroin, and marijuana; robbery; auto theft; and smuggling drugs to prison inmates. UBN members also engage in arson, carjacking, credit card fraud, extortion, homicide, identity theft, intimidation, prostitution operations, and weapons distribution.

Vice Lord Nation (National)

Vice Lord Nation, based in Chicago, is a collection of structured gangs located in 74 cities across 28 states, primarily in the Great Lakes region. Led by a national board, the various gangs have an estimated 30,000 to 35,000 members, most of whom are African American males. The main source of income is street-level distribution of cocaine, heroin, and marijuana. Members also engage in other criminal activity such as assault, burglary, homicide, identity theft, and money laundering.

SECTION II: PRISON GANGS

Aryan Brotherhood

Aryan Brotherhood, also known as AB, was originally ruled by consensus but is now highly structured with two factions—one in the CDC and the other in the Federal Bureau of Prisons (BOP). The majority of members are white males, and the gang is active primarily in the southwestern and Pacific regions of the United States. Its main source of income is the distribution of cocaine, heroin, marijuana, and methamphetamine within prison systems and on the streets. Some AB members have business relationships with Mexican DTOs that smuggle illegal drugs into California for AB distribution. AB is notoriously violent and is often involved in murder for hire. Although the gang has been historically linked to the California-based Hispanic prison gang Mexican Mafia (La Eme), tension between AB and La Eme is increasingly evident, as seen in recent fights between whites and Hispanics within CDC.

Barrio Azteca

Barrio Azteca is one of the most violent prison gangs in the United States. The gang is highly structured and has an estimated membership of 2,000. Most members are Mexican national or Mexican American males. Barrio Azteca is most active in the southwestern region, primarily in federal, state, and local corrections facilities in Texas, and outside prison in southwestern Texas and southeastern New Mexico. The gang's main source of income is smuggling heroin, powder cocaine, and marijuana from Mexico into the United States for distribution both inside and outside prisons. Gang members often transport illicit drugs across the U.S.–Mexico border for DTOs. Barrio Azteca members are also involved in alien smuggling, arson, assault, auto theft, burglary, extortion, intimidation, kidnapping, robbery, and weapons violations.

Black Guerrilla Family

Black Guerrilla Family (BGF), originally called Black Family or Black Vanguard, is a prison gang founded in the San Quentin State Prison, California, in 1966. The gang is highly organized along paramilitary lines, with a supreme leader and central committee. BGF has an established national charter, code of ethics, and oath of allegiance. BGF members operate primarily in California and Maryland. The gang has 100 to 300 members, most of whom are African American males. A primary source of income for gang members is cocaine and marijuana distribution. BGF members obtain such drugs primarily from Nuestra Familia/Norteños members or from local Mexican traffickers. BGF members are involved in other criminal activities, including auto theft, burglary, drive-by shootings, and homicide.

Hermanos de Pistoleros Latinos

Hermanos de Pistoleros Latinos (HPL) is a Hispanic prison gang formed in the Texas Department of Criminal Justice (TDCJ) in the late 1980s. It operates in most prisons and on the streets in many communities in Texas, particularly Laredo. HPL is also active in several cities in Mexico, and its largest contingent in that country is in Nuevo Laredo. The gang is structured and is estimated to have 1,000 members. Members maintain close ties to several Mexican DTOs and are involved in trafficking quantities of cocaine and marijuana from Mexico into the United States for distribution.

Mexikanemi

The Mexikanemi prison gang (also known as Texas Mexican Mafia or Emi) was formed in the early 1980s within the Texas Department of Criminal Justice (TDCJ). The gang is highly structured and is estimated to have 2,000 members, most of whom are Mexican nationals or Mexican American males living in Texas at the time of incarceration. Mexikanemi poses a significant drug trafficking threat to communities in the southwestern United States, particularly in Texas. Gang members reportedly traffic multikilogram quantities of powder cocaine, heroin, and methamphetamine; multiton quantities of marijuana; and thousand-tablet quantities of MDMA from Mexico into the United States for distribution inside and outside prison. Gang members obtain drugs from associates or members of the Jaime Herrera-Herrera, Osiel Cárdenas-Guillén, and/or Vicente Carrillo-Fuentes Mexican DTOs. In addition, Mexikanemi members maintain a relationship with Los Zetas, a Mexican paramilitary/criminal organization employed by the Cárdenas-Guillén DTO as its personal security force.

Mexican Mafia

The Mexican Mafia prison gang, also known as La Eme (Spanish for the letter M), was formed in the late 1950s within the CDC. It is loosely structured and has strict rules that must be followed by the 200 members. Most members are Mexican American males who previously belonged to a southern California street gang. Mexican Mafia is primarily active in the southwestern and Pacific regions of the United States, but its power base is in California. The gang's main source of income is extorting drug distributors outside prison and distributing methamphetamine, cocaine, heroin, and marijuana within prison systems and on the streets. Some members have direct links to Mexican DTOs and broker deals for themselves and their associates. Mexican Mafia is also involved in other criminal activities, including controlling gambling and homosexual prostitution in prison.

Ñeta

Ñeta is a prison gang that began in Puerto Rico and spread into the United States. Ñeta is one of the largest and most violent prison gangs, with about 7,000 members in Puerto Rico and 5,000 in the United States. Ñeta chapters in Puerto Rico exist exclusively inside prisons; once members are released from prison they are no longer considered part of the gang. In the United States, Ñeta chapters exist inside and outside prisons in 36 cities across nine states, primarily in the Northeast. The gang's main source of income is retail distribution of powder and crack cocaine, heroin, marijuana and, to a lesser extent, LSD, MDMA, methamphetamine, and PCP. Ñeta members commit assault, auto theft, burglary, drive-by shootings, extortion, home invasion, money laundering, robbery, weapons and explosives trafficking, and witness intimidation.

SECTION III: OUTLAW MOTORCYCLE GANGS

Bandidos

Bandidos Motorcycle Club, an OMG with 2,000 to 2,500 members in the United States and 13 other countries, is a growing criminal threat to the nation. Law enforcement authorities estimate that Bandidos is one of the two largest OMGs in the United States, with approximately 900 members belonging to more than 88 chapters in 16 states. Bandidos is involved in transporting and distributing cocaine and marijuana and producing, transporting, and distributing methamphetamine. Bandidos is most active in the Pacific, southeastern, southwestern, and west central regions and is expanding in these regions by forming new chapters and allowing members of support clubs to form or join Bandidos chapters. The members of support clubs are known as "puppet" or "duck" club members. They do the dirty work for the mother club.

Hells Angels

Hells Angels Motorcycle Club (HAMC) is an OMG with 2,000 to 2,500 members belonging to more than 250 chapters in the United States and 26 foreign countries. HAMC poses a criminal threat on six continents. U.S. law enforcement authorities estimate that HAMC has more than 69 chapters in 22 states with 900 to 950 members. HAMC produces, transports, and distributes marijuana and methamphetamine and transports and distributes cocaine, hashish, heroin, LSD (lysergic acid diethylamide), MDMA, PCP, and diverted pharmaceuticals. HAMC is involved in other criminal activity, including assault, extortion, homicide, money laundering, and motorcycle theft.

Mongols

Mongols Motorcycle Club is an extremely violent OMG that poses a serious criminal threat to the Pacific and southwestern regions of the United States. Mongols members transport and distribute cocaine, marijuana, and methamphetamine and frequently commit violent crimes, including assault, intimidation, and murder, to defend Mongol's territory and uphold its reputation. Mongols have 70 chapters nationwide, with most of the club's 800 to 850 members residing in

California. Many members are former street gang members with a long history of using violence to settle grievances. Agents with the ATF have called Mongols Motorcycle Club the most violent and dangerous OMG in the nation. In the 1980s, the Mongols OMG seized control of southern California from HAMC, and today Mongols club is allied with Bandidos, Outlaws, Sons of Silence, and Pagan's OMGs against HAMC. The Mongols club also maintains ties with Hispanic street gangs in Los Angeles.

Outlaws

Outlaws Motorcycle Club has more than 1,700 members belonging to 176 chapters in the United States and 12 foreign countries. U.S. law enforcement authorities estimate that the Outlaws have more than 94 chapters in 22 states with more than 700 members. The Outlaws are also known as the American Outlaws Association (AOA.) and Outlaws Nation. Outlaws are the dominant OMG in the Great Lakes region. Gang members produce, transport, and distribute methamphetamine, and transport and distribute cocaine, marijuana and, to a lesser extent, MDMA. Outlaws members engage in various criminal activities, including arson, assault, explosives operations, extortion, fraud, homicide, intimidation, kidnapping, money laundering, prostitution operations, robbery, theft, and weapons violations. It competes with HAMC for membership and territory.

Sons of Silence

Sons of Silence Motorcycle Club (SOSMC) are one of the largest OMGs in the United States, with 250 to 275 members among 30 chapters in 12 states. The club also has five chapters in Germany. SOSMC members have been implicated in numerous criminal activities, including murder, assault, drug trafficking, intimidation, extortion, prostitution operations, money laundering, weapons trafficking, and motorcycle and motorcycle parts theft.

GLOSSARY*

Acculturation: The process of becoming familiar with and comfortable in another culture. The ability to function within that culture or environment, while retaining one's own cultural identity.

Affirmative action: Legally mandated programs whose aim is to increase the employment or educational opportunities of groups that have been disadvantaged in the past.

Alien: Any person who is not a citizen or national of the country in which he or she lives.

Al-Jihad: Struggle (literal translation in Arabic). The term has also been used by some to mean "holy war" against infidels or nonbelievers.

Al-Qaida: Also spelled al-Qaeda. A multinational group that funds and orchestrates the activities of Islamic militants worldwide. It grew out of the Afghan war against the Soviets, and its core members consist largely of Afghan war veterans from all over the Muslim world. Al-Qaida was established around 1988 by the Saudi militant Osama bin Laden. Bin Laden used an extensive international network to maintain a loose connection between Muslim extremists all over the Arab world, as well as in Europe, Asia, the United States, and Canada.

Anti-Semitism: Latent or overt hostility toward Jews, often expressed through social, economic, institutional, religious, cultural, or political discrimination and through acts of individual or group violence.

Assimilation: The process by which ethnic groups that have emigrated to another society begin to lose their separate identity and culture, becoming absorbed into the larger community.

Asylee: A foreign-born individual in the United States or at a port of entry who is found to be unable or unwilling to return to his or her country of nationality, or to seek the protection of that country because of persecution or a well-founded fear of persecution. Persecution or the fear thereof must be based on the indivudal's race, religion, nationality, membership in a particular social group, or political opinion. (Adapted from Department of Homeland Security, Definition of Terms, 2008)

Awareness: Bringing to one's conscious mind that which is only unconsciously perceived.

Bias: Preference or an inclination to make certain choices that may be positive (bias toward excellence) or negative (bias against people), often resulting in unfairness.

Bias-based policing: The act (intentional or unintentional) of applying or incorporating personal, societal, or organizational biases and/or stereotypes in decision making, police actions, or the administration of justice.

Bigot: A person who steadfastly holds to bias and prejudice, convinced of the truth of his or her own opinion and intolerant of the opinions of others.

B-NICE incident: An acronym for any terrorist incident involving Biological, Nuclear, Incendiary, Chemical, and/or Explosive weapons of mass destruction.

Bisexual: Of or relating to sexual attraction to both men and women.

Community policing: A partnership between the police and the local community that identifies strategies to reduce crime, increase traffic safety, and deal with all other public safety problems.

Consent decree: An out-of-court settlement whereby the accused party agrees to modify or change behavior rather than plead guilty or go through a hearing on charges brought to court. [*Source*: CSIS Project Glossary @ (http://csisweb. aers.psu.edu/glossary/c.htm)]

Cosmopolitan: Literally, "a citizen of the world." A person capable of operating comfortably in a global or pluralistic environment.

Cross-cultural: Involving or mediating between two cultures.

Culture: Beliefs, values, habits, attitudes, patterns of thinking, behavior, and everyday customs that

---

* Glossary, except where indicated otherwise, is adapted in part from Simons, G., C. Vazquez, and P. Harris. (1993). *Transcultural Leadership: Empowering the Diverse Workforce.* Houston, TX: Gulf Publishing Company. Permission granted by authors.

have been passed on from generation to generation. Culture is learned rather than inherited and is manifested in largely unconscious and subtle behavior. Culture is passed on from generation to generation.

Cultural competence: A developmental process that evolves over an extended period of time; both individuals and organizations are at various levels of awareness, knowledge, and skills along a continuum of cultural competence. Culturally competent organizations place a high value on the following: (1) Developing a set of principles, attitudes, policies, and structures that will enable all individuals in the organization to work effectively and equitably across all cultures; and (2) developing the capacity to acquire and apply cross-cultural knowledge and respond to and communicate effectively within the cultural contexts that the organization serves. [*Source*: Adapted from Cross, T., B. J. Bazron, K. W. Dennis, and M. R. Isaacs. (1989). *Toward a Culturally Competent System of Care. Volume 1: Monograph on Effective Services for Minority Children Who Are Severely Emotionally Disturbed*. Washington, D.C.: CASSP Technical Assistance Center, Georgetown University Child Development Center].

Department of Homeland Security (DHS): The cabinet-level federal agency responsible for preserving the security of the United States against terrorist attacks. This department was created as a response to the 9/11 terrorist attacks.

Discrimination: The denial of equal treatment to groups because of their racial, ethnic, gender, religious, or other form of cultural identity.

Diversity: The term used to describe a vast range of cultural differences that have become factors needing attention in living and working together. Often applied to the organizational and training interventions in an organization that seek to deal with the interface of people who are different from each other. Diversity has come to include race, ethnicity, gender, disability, and sexual orientation.

Domestic terrorism: Involves groups or individuals whose terrorist activities are directed at elements of government, organizations, or population without foreign direction.

Dominant culture: Refers to the value system that characterizes a particular group of people that dominates the value systems of other groups or cultures. See also **Macroculture/majority or dominant group.**

Émigré: An individual forced, usually by political circumstances, to move from his or her native country and who deliberately resides as a foreigner in the host country.

Ethnic group: Group of people who conceive of themselves, and who are regarded by others, as alike because of their common ancestry, language, and physical characteristics.

Ethnicity: Refers to the background of a group with unique language, ancestral, often religious, and physical characteristics. Broadly characterizes a religious, racial, national, or cultural group.

Ethnocentrism: Using the culture of one's own group as a standard for the judgment of others, or thinking of it as superior to other cultures that are merely different; an attitude of seeing and judging all other cultures from the perspective of one's own culture.

Gay: A male homosexual.

Heterogeneity: Dissimilarity; composed of unrelated or unlike elements. A heterogeneous society is one that is diverse, and frequently refers to racial and ethnic composition.

Hierarchy: Deeply embedded system of societal structure whereby people are organized according to how much status and power they have.

Glass ceiling: An invisible and often perceived barrier that prevents some ethnic or racial groups and women from becoming promoted or hired.

High context/low context communications: Frameworks of communication, largely but not exclusively influenced by culture, related to how much speakers rely on messages other than from words to convey meaning; explicit and specific communications is valued in the low-context style, and conversely, an intuitive and relatively indirect style characterizes high-context communication.

Holistic: View that the integrated whole has a reality independent and greater than the sum of its parts. (*Source*: *Webster's New World Dictionary*).

Homeland security: Federal and local law enforcement programs for gathering, processing, and application of intelligence to provide the United States with a blanket of protection against terrorist attacks.

Homeless adult person: Includes: (1) a person who lacks a fixed, regular, and adequate nighttime residence; and (2) a person who resides in a public or private temporary shelter/transitional housing. (*Source*: U.S. Code, 2007).

Homeless children and youth: Has similar residency and shelter/transitional housing as an adult, but includes sharing the housing of other persons due to loss of housing or are living in motels, hotels, trailer parks, or camping grounds, or are abandoned in hospitals (*Source*: U.S. Code, 2007).

Homophile: Same as homosexual.

Homosexual: characterized by sexual attraction to those of the same sex as oneself.

Immigrant: Any individual admitted to the United States as a lawful permanent resident; also referred to as "permanent resident alien." (*Source*: Department of Homeland Security, Definition of Terms, 2008).

Indian Country: "All land within the limits of any Indian reservation under the jurisdiction of the United States Government; . . . , all dependent Indian communities within the borders of the United States whether within the original or subsequently acquired territory thereof, and whether within or without the limits of a state, and all Indian allotments, the Indian titles to which have not been extinguished . . ." (*Source*: U.S. Code, 2007).

Indian tribe: Any tribe, band, group, pueblo, or community for which, or for the members of which, the United States holds land in trust (*Source*: U.S. Code, 2007).

Informal networks: A system of influential colleagues who can, because of their position or power within an organization, connect the employee with information, resources, or other contacts helpful to his or her promotion or special assignment prospects.

Institutional racism: The failure of an organization (public or private) to provide goods, services, and opportunities to people because of their color, culture, ethnic origin.

International terrorism: Involves groups or individuals whose terrorist activities are foreign-based and/or directed by countries or groups outside the United States or whose activities transcend national boundaries.

Jihad: See **Al-Jihad.**

Lesbian: A homosexual woman.

Macroculture/majority or dominant group: The group within a society that is largest and/or most powerful. This power usually extends to setting cultural norms for the society as a whole. The term majority is falling into disuse because its connotations of group size are inaccurate in certain cities or regions of the country.

Mental illness: A mental health disorder characterized by alterations in thinking, mood, or behavior associated with distress and/or impaired functioning (*Source*: U.S. Surgeon General's Report, 1999).

Mentor: "A trusted counselor or guide" (*Source*: Webster's New World Dictionary). A mentor is usually a more experienced person who helps a less experienced one. The mentor provides information, advice, support, and encouragement to someone who is usually an apprentice, protégé, or a less experienced person. It involves leading, developing, and guiding by example in his or her area of success.

Minority group: A group which is the smaller in number of two groups that constitute a whole; part of the population that differs in certain ways from the majority population and is sometimes subjected to differential treatment.

Multiculturalism: The existence within one society of diverse groups that maintain their unique cultural identity while accepting and participating in the larger society's legal and political system.

Neighborhood office: A temporary office located in a neighborhood, usually an apartment business office complex where the police officer conducts routine business.

Order maintenance: The police handling of incidents that are not crimes, but public nuisance matters about which the police officer uses discretion to decide a course of action.

Paradigm shift: What occurs when an entire cultural group begins to experience a change that involves the acceptance of new conceptual models or ways of thinking and results in major societal transitions (e.g., the shift from agricultural to industrial society).

Parity: The state or condition of being the same in power, value, rank, and so forth; equality.

Pluralistic: The existence within a nation or society of groups distinctive in ethnic origin, culture patterns, religion, or the like. A policy of favoring the preservation of such group with a given nation or society.

Prejudice: Judgment or opinion formed before facts are known, usually involving negative or unfavorable thoughts about groups of people.

Profile: A "profile" is typically a document that contains explicit criteria or indicators issued to officers to guide them in their decision making. It is usually based on data collected and interpreted to signify a trend or suggest that, given a particular set of characteristics (behavioral or situational commonalties), a person could believe that something may result based on that particular cluster of characteristics. A profile relies on using expert advice provided to law enforcement agencies to identify perpetrators of criminal activities. It can be an outline or short biographical description, an individual's character sketch, or a type of behavior associated with a group. It is a summary of data presenting the average or typical appearance of those persons or situations under scrutiny. Officers use these indicators of physical, behavioral, or situational commonalties to develop reasonable suspicion or probable cause to stop subjects.

Profiling: Any police-initiated action that uses a compilation of the background, physical, behavioral, and/or motivational characteristics for a type of perpetrator that leads the police to a particular individual who has been identified as being, could be, or having been engaged in criminal activity.

Psychotic episode: The period of time when a person with a serious mental illness is impaired and at risk of endangering himself or herself, or others.

Race: A group of persons of (or regarded as of) common ancestry. Physical characteristics are often used to identify people of different races. These characteristics should not be used to identify ethnic groups, which can cross racial lines.

Racially biased policing: Occurs when law enforcement inappropriately considers race or ethnicity in deciding with whom and how to intervene in an enforcement capacity.

Racial profiling: Any police-initiated action that relies on the race, ethnicity, or national origin rather than the behavior of an individual or information that leads the police to a particular individual who has been identified as being, or having been, engaged in criminal activity.

Racism: Total rejection of others by reason of race, color, or, sometimes more broadly, culture.

Racist: One with a closed mind toward accepting one or more groups different from one's own origin in race or color.

Refugee: Any person who is outside his or her country of nationality who is unable or unwilling to return to that country because of persecution or a well-founded fear of persecution. Persecution or the fear thereof must be based on . . . race, religion, nationality, membership in a particular social group, or political opinion. (*Source*: Department of Homeland Security, Definition of Terms, 2008). An individual can also be an "economic refugee," fleeing conditions of poverty for better opportunities elsewhere.

Scapegoat: To blame one's failures and shortcomings on innocent people or those only partly responsible.

Stereotype: To believe or feel that people are considered to typify or conform to a pattern or manner, lacking any individuality. Thus a person may categorize behavior of a total group on the basis of limited experience with one or a few representatives of that group. Negative stereotyping classifies people in a group by slurs, innuendoes, names, or slang expressions that depreciate the group as a whole and the individuals in it.

Schoolfront office: A temporary office located in a school where the police officer conducts routine business. Schools that have a regular police school resource officer are not considered schoolfront offices.

Storefront office: A temporary office located in a business office or shopping center where the police officer conducts routine business.

Subculture: A group with distinct, discernible, and consistent cultural traits existing within and participating in a larger cultural grouping.

Suspect-specific incident: An incident in which an officer lawfully attempts to detain, apprehend, or otherwise be on the lookout for one or more specific suspects identified or described, in part, by national or ethnic origin, gender, or race.

Synergy: The benefit produced by the collaboration of two or more systems in excess of their individual contributions. Cultural synergy occurs when cultural differences are taken into account and used by a multicultural group.

Terrorism: A violent act or an act dangerous to human life, in violation of the criminal laws of the United States or any segment to intimidate or coerce a government, the civilian population, or any segment thereof, in furtherance of political or social objectives (*Source*: U.S. Department of Justice, 1997).

Terrorist Attack Pre-Incidence Indicators (TAPIs): A term used by the intelligence community to describe actions and behaviors taken by terrorists before they carry out an attack (*Source*: Nance, M. W. (2003). *The Terrorist Recognition Handbook*. Guilford, CT: Lyons Press).

Transgender: The term "transgender" covers a range of people, including heterosexual cross-dressers, homosexual drag queens, and transsexuals who believe they were born in the wrong body. This term includes those who consider themselves to be both male and female, or intersexed, as well as those who take hormones to complete their gender identity without a sex change.

Weapons of Mass Destruction (WMD): Three types of weapons are most commonly categorized as WMD: (1) nuclear weapons, (2) biological weapons, and (3) chemical weapons. The subcategories of WMD include activities that may be labeled as "agro terrorism," which is to harm our food supply chain, and "cyber terrorism," which is to harm our telecommunication, Internet, and computerized processes and transactions.

White supremacist group: Any ongoing organization, association, or group of three or more persons, whether formal or informal, having as one of its primary activities the promotion of white supremacy through the commission of criminal acts.

White supremacy: Helan Page, an African American anthropologist, defines white supremacy in the United States as an "ideological, structural and historic stratification process by which the population of European descent . . . has been able to intentionally sustain, to its own best advantage, the dynamic mechanics of upward or downward mobility or fluid class status over the non-European populations (on a global scale), using skin color, gender, class or ethnicity as the main criteria" for allocating resources and making decisions [*Source*: Ross, L. (1995). "White Supremacy in the 1990s." The Public Eye. Sponsored by the Political Research Associates. (www.publiceye.org/eyes/whitsup.html) Somerville, MA, p. 6].

Youth gang: A self-formed association of peers having four characteristics: (1) three or more members, generally ages 12 to 24; (2) a name and some sense of identity, generally indicated by such symbols as style of clothing, graffiti, tattoos, and hand signs (3) some degree of permanence and organization (4) and an elevated level of involvement in delinquent or criminal activity (*Source*: NYGC, 2006).

INDEX

Note: The 'b' and 'e' following the locators refers to boxes and exhibits cited in the text.